DIVINE OFFICE
FOR THE LAITY

Edited by

Lawrence M. Rutherford

Aquinas and More Publishing

Colorado Springs, Colorado 80908

ISBN 978-0-9994131-8-0

Copyright © 2024

Lawrence Rutherford

All Rights Reserved

The translation of the Psalms and other readings from Scripture are taken from the *Douay-Rheims Bible* and the *LatinVulgate Bible* both of which are in the public domain. The English, in some cases, has been simplified and the grammatical structure modified, when it was thought prudent. In a few instances, archaic words have been replaced with more familiar terms to make this book more accessible to a wider range of readers.

Prayers are taken from a *Diurnal of the Roman Breviary of 1954* and translated on the internet using *onlinetranslationpro.com* and modified as appropriate.

Hymns found in this book are from *Hymns of the Breviary and Missal*, https://cathcorn.org/hotbam/.
Used with permission.

Dedication

To my wife, Frances, who has prayed Lauds with me at the break of dawn for many years and continues her prayer throughout the day. She is my inspiration in this work and has provided crucial proposals and suggestions during its development. Her detailed editing eye has also been essential.
I am very blessed.

TABLE OF CONTENTS

Preface ix
Introduction xi
Lauds I 1
Lauds II 59
Vespers 121
Compline 175
Proper of the Seasons 185
Common of the Saints 279
Proper of the Saints *(Lauds)* 287
Proper of the Saints *(Vespers)* 351

Canticle of Zachariah 366
Canticle of the Blessed Virgin 367
Index of Hymns 371
Index of Psalms 389
Index of Chapters 390
Lauds Antiphons for Marian Feasts 393

PREFACE

The *Divine Office* or *Liturgy of the Hours*, also called *Opus Dei* (Work of God), has been a tradition and practice in the Church since the early years of Christianity. The custom of praying the Psalms throughout the day lies in the Judaic rituals of prayer which was continued by Christians in the nascent Church. Later, as monastic life developed, the monks brought these observances into the monastery. Gradually, a rhythmic praying of the Psalms throughout the whole day evolved. This was named the *Officium Divinum*, the "Divine Office" — that is, the "holy task" or "sacred duty" of daily liturgical prayer.

This rhythmic prayer of the Psalms was seen as a continuation of the biblical command to pray throughout the day. Jesus taught His disciples to "pray always without becoming weary" (Luke 18:1), and St. Paul urged Christians to "pray without ceasing" (1 Thess. 5:17).

Sadly, over the centuries, the praying of the *Divine Office* or *Liturgy of the Hours* in various forms declined among the laity. In recent years, however, the faithful have been encouraged to once again pray these liturgical prayers.

> "I would like to renew to you all the invitation to pray with the Psalms, even becoming accustomed to using the *Liturgy of the Hours* of the Church, *Lauds* in the morning, *Vespers* in the evening and *Compline* before retiring." (Pope Benedict XVI, Wednesday Audience, 16 Nov. 2011).

> "It is important to introduce the faithful to the celebration of the *Liturgy of the Hours*, which, as the public prayer of the Church, is a source of piety and nourishment for personal prayer." Pope John Paul II, *Spíritus et Sponsa*, 4 Dec. 2003.

> "Finally, it is of great advantage for the family, the domestic sanctuary of the Church, not only to pray together to God but also to celebrate some parts of the *Liturgy of the Hours* as occasion offers, in order to enter more deeply into the life of the Church." (*General Instruction of the Liturgy of the Hours*, no. 27).

It seems imperative, therefore, that Catholic laity should include prayer as an integral part of each day. St. Francis de Sales once said, "Every one of us needs half an hour of prayer a day, except when we are busy – then we need an hour." The *Divine Office* can help us create a routine for doing this.

INTRODUCTION

THE LITURGICAL DAY

The Church, that is the hierarchy, clergy and the people of God, are called to sanctify the entire day through prayer. In imitation of the Psalmist, (Ps. 118) "Seven times a day I praise you," and "at midnight I rise to give you thanks." In the complete *Divine Office* there are seven canonical hours:

Matins – For the sanctification of the night the Church uses a special canonical hour called *Matins* which had traditionally, in a monastery, been prayed between midnight and 2 a.m.

Lauds – Prayed at the opening of the day early in the morning or at dawn. *Lauds I* should be used throughout the year except from Septuagesima to Palm Sunday then *Lauds II* will be recited.

Prime - Between the dawn hour of *Lauds* and the 9 a.m. hour of *Terce*.

Terce – 9 a.m. Its name comes from Latin and refers to the third hour of the day (the third, sixth and ninth hours of the day are hours associated with Christ's Passion.)

Sext - It consists mainly of Psalms and is prayed around noon. Its name comes from Latin and refers to the sixth hour of the day after dawn.

None - It consists mainly of Psalms and is said around 3 p.m., about the ninth hour after dawn.

Vespers - *Vespers* takes place as dusk begins to fall. *Vespers* gives thanks for the day just ended and offers an evening sacrifice of praise to God. (Ps. 140:2). 'Let my prayer be directed as incense in Thy sight; the lifting up of my hands, as evening sacrifice."

Compline – The culmination of the waking day. *Compline*, for many, is the contemplative office that fosters spiritual peace. In monasteries, it typically begins the "Great Silence" which lasts until *Terce* the next day.

The two most important or hinge Hours are *Lauds* and *Vespers*. These Hours are contained in this volume, as is Compline.

STRUCTURE OF THE DIVINE OFFICE

Opening versicle – **V.** O Lord, open my lips. **R.** And my mouth shall proclaim Thy praise. **V.** O God, come to my assistance. **R.** O Lord, make haste to help me. Glory be to the Father …

Psalmody – Psalms and canticles taken from Scripture; primarily from the Book of Psalms. Canticles are a nonmetrical hymn found in a biblical text other than from the book of Psalms.

Hymns – The hymns are melodies/poetry written in classical format, many of which have come down to us from ancient Christianity. They are examples of some of the most beautiful Christian poetry.

Antiphons - The antiphons are short introductory phrases taken either from the Psalms themselves or other parts of the Bible.

Chapters – The Chapters are brief lessons/verses found in Holy Scripture.

Prayers – Prayers or Orations are addressed to God at the culmination of the canolical hour. They are brief and profound and sum up the petitions of all participants of the hour.

SECTIONS OF THE DIVINE OFFICE

Ordinary – Antiphons and Psalms as of the current day of the Psalter, i.e. Sunday through Saturday. The Ordinary also has prayers that are repeated each day, such as the *Benedictus* at *Lauds*, the *Magnificat* at *Vespers* and the *Canticle of Simeon* at *Compline*.

Proper of the Season – Psalms, readings, versicles and prayers that relate to a particular liturgical season such as Advent, Christmas, etc. The *proper* is a part of the *Divine Office* that varies according to the date, either representing an observance within the liturgical year or significant event. The term is used compared to the *ordinary*, which is the part of the liturgy that is typically constant.

Common of the Saints - The Common of Saints is a part of the *Divine Office* liturgy that comprises texts common to an entire category of saints, such as apostles, martyrs, Blessed Mother or popes and bishops. It is used in conjuction with the Propers of the Saints.

Proper of the Saints - Propers of Saints have been used for all Solemnities and all Feast days throughout the year since they must take the place of the typical weekday antiphons prior to the *Benedictus* and *Magnificat* and prayers for those respective days.

HOW THE DIVINE OFFICE IS TO BE SAID

Directions for the Laity

If at first you discover it is difficult finding the correct parts of the office, do not attempt to say it all and become discouraged with this unfamiliar type of prayer. It would be unfortunate to lose the satisfaction and blessing you will receive by saying these prayers. You may want to start by reading the office of *Lauds* on Sunday and then progress through the ordinary days of the week. It is advisable to include prayers of the feast days of the saints to enhance the prayer of the day. When you are comfortable with the ordinary of the office, then add the prayers of the seasons and the commons of the saints. You will be very inspired and gratified making these prayers a part of your day.

Variable parts of the Office - All the Hours begin and conclude the same way. The antiphons, hymns, chapters and prayers may vary according to the liturgical seasons of the year and the feasts of the saints. These parts of the Hours which change depending on the season or the date can be found in the respective sections of this book.

Common Throughout the Year - The office for the non-seasonal times of the Church year, named "Common Throughout the Year," is to be found in the opening portions of the *Divine Office*, while the Common of the Saints, Feasts of the Saints and Seasonal office are following.

Sundays between the 23rd Sunday after Pentecost to the 24th Sunday or Last Sunday after Pentecost before Advent

If there are more than 24 Sundays after Pentecost, following the 23rd, use the Sundays of Epiphany which were not recited earlier in the year starting with the 3rd Sunday after the Epiphany to the 6th Sunday after the Epiphany, as required.

Conclusion of each Psalm – Each psalm is concluded with "Glory be to the Father ..."

Conclusions of the Prayers – "Through Our Lord Jesus Christ, Thy Son, who liveth and reigneth with Thee in unity of the Holy Ghost, One God, world without end." Or, "Who with Thee liveth and reigneth in the unity of the Holy Ghost, God, world without end, Amen."

Vespers I and Vespers II – Sundays and many feast days are preceded the evening before by *First Vespers or Vespers I* similar to Jewish practice. The Church begins its feasts in the evening. Major feast commonly include *Vespers I and Vespers II* which are celebrated on the evening of the feast day itself.

Ferias - Any weekday, that is Monday through Friday, on which no special ecclesiastical feast is to be celebrated. Such days are called ferial days. At all the Hours, the Antiphons and Psalms of the Psalter will be prayed according to the day of the week. The rest is taken from the Psalter as given for "Throughout the Year."

At the beginning of each hour – To facilitate finding the *Proper of the Season, Common of the Saints* and *Proper of the Saints* of each day while praying the office, locate the appropriate prayers and place bookmarks in these locations before you begin.

Praying and Singing in Choir

There are several ways to pray, recite or sing the *Divine Office*. For those who do not have a canonical obligation to recite the *Divine Office*, we, as the laity, are allowed to select what method will suitably work in time and simplicity for the secular life.

1. **The individual** may pray silently from beginning to end using propers and commons that best fit one's schedule and abilities.

2. **Two or more persons** may recite or chant the Hours alternating verses. One person may be selected to recite/chant those parts marked with a **V**. the rest will respond at those marked with an **R**. The group will divide the Psalms alternately at the verses marked with a » and recite them as appropriate.

3. **In choir or in the congregation**, that is, similar to the environment of a monastery. When the office is said in common, a leader will be selected. This person is to recite the portion maked with the letter **V**, and all others in the congregation are to respond with the portion marked **R**. In order for the recitation or the singing to be facilitated, alternating verses of the Psalms are marked with a » so two groups may alternate as indicated. The antiphon at the beginning of the Psalm will be intoned by the leader and all will recite together the Psalm antiphon after the Psalm.

Chanting the Psalms

In addition to recitation, the Psalms can also be chanted using the simple Psalm tone below. Typically, the Psalms are chanted in formal group settings but it can also be done with two or more people. Psalm tones are perfect for all people to sing, and being a trained musician or reading music is unnecessary. Just sing the verses alternately as you would in reading them. A sample of a tone is provided below. You will find it enhances the beauty of the prayer.

O God, come to my as -   sis - tance;   O LORD, make haste   to help – me!

Clap thy hands all ye   - na – tions   shout unto God with the   voice of-- joy.

Lauds I and Lauds II

Sing praise to the Lord on the harp, on the harp, and with the voice of a psalm

 # Sunday – Lauds I

V. Dómine, ✝ lábia mea apéries. **R.** Et os meum annuntiábit laudem tuam.	**V.** O Lord, ✝ open my lips. **R.** And my mouth shall proclaim Thy praise.
V. Deus, in adjutórium meum inténde. **R.** Dómine, ad adjuvándum me festína.	**V.** O God, come to my assistance. **R.** O Lord, make haste to help me.
V. Glória Patri, et Fílio, et Spirítui Sancto. **R.** Sicut erat in princípio, et nunc, et semper, et in sǽcula sæculórum. Amen.	**V.** Glory be to the Father and to the Son and to the Holy Ghost. **R.** As it was in the beginning, is now and ever shall be, world without end, Amen.

Psalmus 92 / Psalm 92

Ant 1. Dóminus regnávit, decórem indútus est: allelúja.

Ant 1. The Lord hath reigned, He is clothed with beauty, alleluia.

Dóminus regnávit, decórem indútus est: indútus est Dóminus fortitúdinem, et præcínxit se. Étenim firmávit orbem terræ, qui non commovébitur.
»²Paráta sedes tua ex tunc; a sǽculo tu es.
»³ Elevavérunt flúmina, Dómine, elevavérunt flúmina vocem suam; elevavérunt flúmina fluctus suos,
»⁴A vócibus aquárum multárum. Mirábiles elationes maris; mirábilis in altis Dóminus.
»⁵Testimónia tua credibília facta sunt nimis; domum tuam decedt sanctitúdo, Dómine, in longitúdinem diérum.

V. *Glória Patri ...*

The Lord hath reigned, He is clothed with beauty: The Lord is clothed with strength, and hath girded Himself. For He hath established the world everlasting.
²Thy throne is established from of old: Thou art from everlasting.
»³The floods have lifted up, O Lord: The floods have lifted up their voice. The floods have lifted up their waves.
⁴With the sound of many waters, wonderful are the surges of the sea: wonderful is the Lord on high.
»⁵Thy testimonies are exceedingly trustworthy: holiness becomes Thy house, O Lord, unto the length of days.

V. *Glory be ...*

Sunday Lauds I

Ant 1.

Psalmus 99

Ant 2. Jubiláte Deo, omnis terra, allelúja.

Jubiláte Deo, omnis terra; servíte Dómino in lætítia. Introíte in conspéctu ejus in exultatión.
»²Scitóte quóniam Dóminus ipse est Deus; ipse fecit nos, et non ipsi nos: pópulus ejus, et oves páscuæ ejus.

»³Introíte portas ejus in cónfessione; átria ejus in hymnis: confitémini illi. Laudáte nomen ejus.

»⁴Quóniam suávis est Dóminus, in ætérnum misericórdia ejus, et usque in generatiónem et generatiónem véritas ejus.

V. *Glória Patri ...*

Ant 2.

Psalmus 62

Ant 3. Benedícam te in vita mea, et in nómine tuo levábo manus meas, allelúja.

Deus, Deus meus, ad te de luce vígilo. Sitívit in te ánima mea; quam multiplíciter tibi caro mea!

²In terra desérta, et invia, et inaquósa, sic in sanctoappárui tibi, ut vidérem virtútem tuam et glóriam tuam.

»³Quóniam melior est misericórdia tua supervitas, lábia mea laudábunt te.

Ant 1.

Psalm 99

Ant 2. Sing joyfully to God all the earth, alleluia.

Sing joyfully to God, all the earth: serve ye the Lord with gladness. Come in before His presence with exultation.
»²Know ye that the Lord is God: He made us, and not we ourselves. We are His people and the sheep of His pasture.

»³Go ye into His gates with praise, into His courts with hymns: give glory to Him. Praise ye His Name: His truth to generation and generation.

»⁴For the Lord is sweet, His mercy endureth for ever, and His truth from generation to generation.

V. *Glory be ...*

Ant 2.

Psalm 62

Ant 3. I will bless Thee all my life long: and in Thy Name I will lift up my hands, alleluia.

O God, my God, to Thee do I watch at the break of day. For Thee my soul hath thirsted: For Thee my flesh, O how many ways!
²In a desert land, and where there is no path, and no water: so in the sanctuary have I come before Thee, to see Thy power and Thy glory.
»³For Thy mercy is better than life. Thee my lips shall praise.

Sunday Lauds I

⁴Sic benedícam te in vita mea, et in nómine tuo levábo manus meas.

»⁵Sicut ádipe et pinguédine repleátur ánima mea, et lábiis exsultatiónis laudábit os meum.
⁶Si memor fui tui super stratum meum, in matutínis meditábor in te.

»⁷Quia fuísti adjútor meus, et in velaménto alárum tuárum exsultábo.

⁸Adhǽsit ánima mea post te; me suscépit déxtera tua.
»⁹Ipsi vero in vanum quæsiérunt ánimam meam: introíbunt in inferióra terræ;
¹⁰Tradéntur in manus gládii: partes vúlpium erunt.

»¹¹Rex vero lætábitur in Deo; laudabúntur ómnes qui jurant in eo: quia obstrúctum est os loquéntium iníqua.

V. *Glória Patri ...*

Ant 3.

Dan 3:57-88, 56

Ant 4. Tres púeri jussu régis in fornacem missi sunt, non timéntes flammam igni dicéntes: Benedíctus Deus, allelúja.

Benedícíte, ómnia et ópera Dómine superexaltáte eum in æ.
⁵⁸Benedícíte, ángeli Dómini, Dómino: laudáte et superexaltáte eum in sǽcula.
»⁵⁹Benedícíte, cæli, Dómino: Laudáte et superexaltáte eum in sǽcula.

⁴Thus will I bless Thee all my life long, and in Thy Name I will lift up my hands.

»⁵Let my soul be filled as with marrow and fatness, and my mouth shall praise Thee with joyful lips.
⁶If I have remembered Thee upon my bed, I will meditate on Thee in the morning hours:

»⁷because Thou hast been my Helper and I will rejoice under the cover of Thy wings.

⁸My soul hath held fast to Thee. Thy right hand hath received me.
»⁹But they have sought my soul in vain, they shall go into the depths of the earth.
¹⁰They shall be delivered into the hands of the sword, they shall be the prey of foxes.

»¹¹But the king will rejoice in God, all who swear by Him will be praised: because the voice of those who speak unjustly is silenced.

V. *Glory be ...*

Ant 3.

Dan 3:57-88, 56

Ant 4. Three young men were sent to the king, not fearing the flame of fire, saying, blessed be God, alleluia.

All ye works of the Lord, bless the Lord: praise and exalt Him above all for ever.
⁵⁸O ye angels of the Lord, bless the Lord: praise and exalt Him above all for ever.
»⁵⁹O ye heavens, bless the Lord: praise and exalt Him above all for ever.

Sunday Lauds I

⁶⁰Benedícite, aquæ ómnes, quæ super cælos sunt, Dómino: Laudáte et superexaltáte eum in sǽcula.
»⁶¹Benedícite, ómnes virtútes Dómini, Dómino: laudáte et superexaltáte eum in sǽcula.
⁶²Benedícite, sol et luna, Dómino: laudáte et superexaltáte eum in sǽcula.
»⁶³Benedícite, stellæ cæli, Dómino: laudáte et superexaltáte eum in sǽcula.
⁶⁴Benedícite, omnis imber et ros, Dómino: laudáte et superexaltáte eum in sǽcula.
»⁶⁵Benedícite, ómnes spíritus Dei, Dómino: laudáte et superexaltáte eum in sǽcula.
⁶⁶Benedícite, ignis et æstus, Dómino: laudáte et superexaltáte eum in sǽcula.
»⁶⁷Benedícite, frigus et æstus, Dómino: laudáte et superexaltáte eum in sǽcula.
⁶⁸Benedícite, rores et pruína, Dómino: laudáte et superexaltáte eum in sǽcula.
»⁶⁹Benedícite, gelu et frigus, Dómino: laudáte et superexaltáte eum in sǽcula.
⁷⁰Benedícite, glácies et nives, Dómino: laudáte et superexaltáte eum in sǽcula.
»⁷¹Benedícite, noctes et dies, Dómino laudáte et superexaltáte eum in sǽcula.
⁷²Benedícite, lux et ténebræ, Dómino: laudáte et superexaltáte eum in sǽcula.
»⁷³Benedícite, fúlgura et nubes, Dómino: laudáte et superexaltáte eum in sǽcula.

⁶⁰O all ye waters that are above the heavens, bless the Lord: praise and exalt Him above all for ever.
»⁶¹O all ye powers of the Lord, bless the Lord: praise and exalt Him above all for ever.
⁶²O ye sun and moon, bless the Lord: praise and exalt Him above all for ever.
»⁶³O ye stars of heaven, bless the Lord: praise and exalt Him above all for ever.
⁶⁴O every shower and dew, bless ye the Lord: praise and exalt Him above all for ever.
»⁶⁵O all ye spirits of God, bless the Lord: praise and exalt Him above all for ever.
⁶⁶O ye fire and heat, bless the Lord: praise and exalt Him above all for ever.
»⁶⁷O ye cold and heat, bless the Lord: praise and exalt Him above all for ever.
⁶⁸O ye dews and hoar frosts, bless the Lord: praise and exalt Him above all for ever.
»⁶⁹O ye frost and cold, bless the Lord: praise and exalt Him above all for ever.
⁷⁰O ye ice and snow, bless the Lord: praise and exalt Him above all for ever.
»⁷¹O ye nights and days, bless the Lord: praise and exalt Him above all for ever.
⁷²O ye light and darkness, bless the Lord: praise and exalt Him above all for ever.
»⁷³O ye lightnings and clouds, bless the Lord: praise and exalt Him above all for ever.

Sunday Lauds I

»⁷⁴Benedícat terra Dóminum: laudet et superexáltet eum in sǽcula.
⁷⁵Benedícite, montes et colles, Dómino: laudáte et superexaltáte eum in sǽcula.

»⁷⁶Benedícite, univérsa germinántia in terra, Dómino: laudáte et superexaltáte eum in sǽcula.
⁷⁷Benedícite, fontes, Dómino: laudáte et superexaltáte eum in sǽcula.

»⁷⁸Benedícite, Maria et flúmina, Dómino: laudáte et superexaltáte eum in sǽcula.
⁷⁹Benedícite, cete, et ómnia quæ movéntur in aquis, Dómino: laudáte et superexaltáte eum in sǽcula.
»⁸⁰Benedícite, ómnes vólucres cæli, Dómino: laudáte et superexaltáte eum in sǽcula.
⁸¹Benedícite, ómnes béstiæ et pécora, Dómino: laudáte et superexaltáte eum in sǽcula.
»⁸²Benedícite, fílii hóminum, Dómino: laudáte et superexaltáte eum in sǽcula.
⁸³Benedícat Israël Dóminum: laudet et superexáltet eum in sǽcula.

»⁸⁴Benedícite, sacerdótes Dómini, Dómino: laudáte et superexaltáte eum in sǽcula.
⁸⁵Benedícite, servi Dómini, Dómino: laudáte et superexaltáte eum in sǽcula.
»⁸⁶Benedícite, spíritus et ánimæ justórum, Dómino: laudáte et superexaltáte eum in sǽcula.
⁸⁷Benedícite, sancti et húmiles corde, Dómino: laudáte et superexaltáte eum in sǽcula.

»⁷⁴O let the earth bless the Lord: let it praise and exalt Him above all for ever.
⁷⁵O ye mountains and hills, bless the Lord: praise and exalt Him above all for ever.
»⁷⁶O all ye things that spring up on the earth, bless the Lord: praise and exalt Him above all for ever.
⁷⁷O ye fountains, bless the Lord: praise and exalt Him above all for ever.
»⁷⁸O ye seas and rivers, bless the Lord: praise and exalt Him above all for ever.
⁷⁹O ye whales, and all that move in the waters, bless the Lord: praise and exalt Him above all for ever.
»⁸⁰O all ye fowls of the air, bless the Lord: praise and exalt Him above all for ever.
⁸¹O all ye beasts and cattle, bless the Lord: praise and exalt Him above all for ever.
»⁸²O ye sons of men, bless the Lord: praise and exalt Him above all for ever.
⁸³O let Israel bless the Lord: let them praise and exalt Him above all for ever.
»⁸⁴O ye priests of the Lord, bless the Lord: praise and exalt Him above all for ever.
⁸⁵O ye servants of the Lord, bless the Lord: praise and exalt Him above all for ever.
»⁸⁶O ye spirits and souls of the just, bless the Lord: praise and exalt Him above all for ever.
⁸⁷O ye holy and humble of heart, bless the Lord: praise and exalt Him above all for ever.

»⁸⁸Benedícite, Anania, Azaría, Misaël, Dómino: laudáte et superexaltáte eum in sǽcula: quia eruit nos de inférno, et salvos fecit de manu mortis: et liberávit nos de médio ardéntis flammæ, et de médio ignis eruit nos.

»⁵⁶Benedíctus es in firmaménto cæli: et laudábilis et gloriósus in sǽcula.

»⁸⁸O Ananias, Azarias, and Misæl, bless ye the Lord: praise and exalt Him above all for ever. For He hath delivered us from from hell, and saved us out of the hand of death, and delivered us out of the midst of the burning flame, and saved us out of the midst of the fire.

»⁵⁶Blessed art Thou in the firmament of heaven: and worthy of praise, and glorious for ever.

The Glory be is not recited here.

Ant 4.

Ant 4.

Psalmus 148

Psalm 148

Ant 5. Laudáte Dóminum de cælis. Allelúja.

Ant 5. Praise ye the Lord from the Heavens. Alleluia.

Laudáte Dóminum de cælis; laudáte eum in excélsis.
²Laudáte eum, ómnes ángeli ejus; laudáte eum, ómnes virtútes ejus.
»³Laudáte eum, sol et luna; laudáte eum, ómnes stellæ et lumen.

⁴Laudáte eum, cæli cælórum; et aquæ ómnes quæ super cælos sunt,

»⁵laudent nomen Dómini. Quia ipse dixit, et facta sunt; ipse mandávit, et creáta sunt.
⁶Statuit ea in ætérnum, sæculum sæculi; præcéptum posuit, et non præteribit.
»⁷Laudáte Dóminum de terra, dracones et ómnes abyssi;
⁸ignis, grando, nix, glácies, spíritus procellárum, quæ fáciunt verbum ejus;
»⁹montes, et ómnes colles; ligna fructífera, et ómnes cedri;
¹⁰béstiæ, et univérsa pécora; serpéntes, et vólucres pennátæ;

Praise ye the Lord from the heavens: praise ye Him in the heights.
²Praise ye Him, all His angels, praise ye Him, all His hosts.
»³Praise ye Him, O sun and moon: praise Him, all ye stars and light.
⁴Praise Him, ye heavens of heavens: and let all the waters that are above the heavens praise the Name of the Lord.
»⁵For He spoke, and they were made: He commanded, and they were created.
⁶He hath established them for ever, and for ages of ages: He hath made a decree, and it shall not pass away.
»⁷Praise the Lord from the earth, ye dragons, and all ye deeps:
⁸fire, hail, snow, ice, stormy winds, which fulfill His word:
»⁹mountains and all hills, fruitful trees and all cedars:
¹⁰beasts and all cattle: serpents and feathered fowls:

»¹¹reges terræ et ómnes pópuli; príncipes et ómnes júdices terræ; ¹²júvenes et vírgines; senes cum junióribus, laudent nomen Dómini: ¹³quia exaltátum est nomen ejus solius.
»¹⁴Conféssio ejus super cælum et terram; et exaltávit cornu pópuli sui. Hymnus ómnibus sanctis ejus; filiis Israël, pópulo appropinquánti sibi. Allelúja.

V. *Glória Patri ...*

Ant 5.

Capitulum
(Apoc 7:11-12)
The reading below or the proper of the day

V. Et ómnes ángeli stabant in circuítu throni, et seniorum, et quatuor ánimalium: et cecidérunt in conspéctu throni in fácies suas, et adoraverunt Deum, dicentes: Amen. Benedíctio, et cláritas, et sapiéntia, et gratiárum áctio, honor, et virtus, et fortitúdo Deo nostro in sǽcula sæculórum. Amen.

R. Deo grátias.

Hymnus

Ætérne Rerum Cóndítor, noctem diémque qui regis, et témporum das témpora, ut álleves fastídium;

Noctúrna lux viántibus A nocte noctem ségregans, Præco diéi jam sonat, Jubárque solis évocat.

»¹¹kings of the earth and all people: princes and all judges of the earth: ¹²young men and maidens: let the old with the young, praise the Name of the Lord: ¹³for His Name alone is exalted.
»¹⁴The praise of Him is above heaven and earth: and He hath exalted the horn of His people. A hymn to all His saints, to the children of Israel, a people near to Him. Alleluia.

V. *Glory be ...*

Ant 5.

Chapter
(Apoc 7:11-12)
The reading below or the proper of the day

V. And all the angels stood round about the throne, and the ancients, and the four living creatures; and they fell down before the throne upon their faces, and adored God, saying: Amen. Blessing, and glory, and wisdom, and thanksgiving, honor, and power, and strength to our God for ever and ever. Amen.

R. Thanks be to God.

Hymn

Maker of All, Eternal King/ who day and night about dost bring:/ who weary mortals to relieve/ dost in their times the seasons give.

Now the shrill cock proclaims the day/ and calls the sun's awak'ning ray/—the wand'ring pilgrim's guiding light,/ That marks the watches of the night.

Sunday Lauds I

Hoc excitátus lucifer Solvit polum calígine, Hoc omnis errónum chorus Vías nocéndi déserit.	Roused at the note, the morning star/ Heaven's dusky veil uplifts afar:/ Night's vagrant bands no longer roam,/ But from their dark ways hie them home.
Hoc nauta vires cólligit pontíque mitéscunt freta, hoc ipsa petra Ecclésiæ canénte culpam díluit.	The encouraged sailor's fears are o'er,/ the foaming billows rage no more:/ Lo! E'en the very Church's Rock/ melts at the crowing of the cock.
Surgámus ergo strénue! gallus iacéntes éxcitat, et somnoléntos íncrepat, gallus negántes árguit.	O let us then like men arise;/ The cock rebukes our slumbering eyes,/ bestirs who still in sleep would lie,/ and shames who would their Lord deny.
Gallo canénte spes redit, Ægris salus refúnditur, Mucro latrónis cónditur, Lapsis fides revértitur.	New hope his clarion note awakes,/ sickness the feeble frame forsakes,/ the robber sheathes his lawless sword,/ faith to the fallen is restored.
Jesu labántes réspice, Et nos vidéndo córrige: Si réspicis, labes cadunt, Fletúque culpa sólvitur	Look on us, Jesu, when we fall,/ and with Thy look our souls recall:/ If Thou but look, our sins are gone,/ and with due tears our pardon won.
Til lux refúlge sénsibus, Mentísque somnum díscute: Te nostra vox primum sonet, Et vota solvámus tibi.	Shed through our hearts Thy piercing ray,/ our souls' dull slumber drive away:/ Thy Name be first on every tongue,/ To Thee our earliest praises sung.
Deo Patri sit glória, Ejúsque soli Filio, Cum Spíritu Paráclito, Nunc, et per omne sǽculum.	All laud to God the Father be,/ All praise, Eternal Son, to Thee,/ All glory, as is ever meet,/ To God the Holy Paraclete.

Versiculi / Versicle

V. Dóminus regnávit, decórem induit.
R. Induit Dóminus fortitúdinem, et præcínxit se virtúte.

V. The Lord reigned in beauty robed.
R. The Lord hath clothed Himself with strength and girded Himself with power.

Sunday Lauds I

Ant. Benedíctus Dóminus, Deus Israel. *(Whenever possible, the antiphon for the specific Sunday, season or feast of a saint will be used).*

Cánticum Zacharíæ
(Luke 1:68-79)
Canticle on page 366

V. *Glória Patri ...*

Ant. Benedíctus Dóminus, Deus Israel.

V. *Páter nóster ...*
R. *Pánem nostrum ...*

V. Dómine exáudi oratiónem meam.
R. Et clamor meus ad te véniat.

V. Oremus.

Omnípotens et miséricors Deus, univérsa nobis adversántia propitiátus exclúde: ut mente et córpore páriter expedíti, quæ tua sunt, líberis méntibus exsequamur. Per Dóminum nostrum ...

The prayer above is said, or the prayer of the Sunday or season and the Feast day are prayed if there are any.

V. Dómine exáudi oratiónem meam.
R. Et clamor meus ad te véniat.

V. Benedicámus Dómino.
R. Deo grátias.

V. Fidélium ánimæ per misericórdiam Dei requiéscant in pace.
R. Amen.

Ant. Blessed be the Lord, the God of Israel. *(Whenever possible, the antiphon for the specific Sunday, season or feast of a saint will be used).*

Canticle of Zachariah
(Luke 1:68-79)
Canticle on page 366

V. *Glory be ...*

Ant. Blessed be the Lord, the God of Israel.

V. *Our Father . .*
R. *Give us this day ...*

V. O Lord, hear my prayer.
R. And let my cry come unto Thee.

V. Let us pray.

Almighty and merciful God, mercifully remove from us all that opposes us: that we may fulfill with free minds those things which belong to Thee, being prepared in mind and body alike. Through our Lord...

The prayer above is said, or the prayer of the Sunday or season and the Feast day are prayed if there are any.

V. O Lord, hear my prayer.
R. And let my cry come unto Thee.

V. Let us bless the Lord.
R. Thanks be to God.

V. May the souls of the faithful departed through the mercy of God, rest in peace.
R. Amen.

Sunday Lauds I

O God, my God, to Thee do I watch at the break of day.

MONDAY – LAUDS I

V. Dómine, ✝ lábia mea apéries.
R. Et os meum annuntiábit laudem tuam.

V. Deus, in adjutórium meum inténde.
R. Dómine, ad adjuvándum me festína.

V. *Glória Patri ...*
R. *Sicut erat ...*

Psalmus 46

Ant 1. **Jubiláte Deo in voce exsultatiónis.**

О mnes gentes, pláudite mánibus; Jubiláte Deo in voce exsultatiónis:
³quóniam Dóminus excélsus, terríbilis, rex magnus super omnem terram.
»⁴Subjécit pópulos nobis, et gentes sub pédibus nostris.
⁵Elégit nobis hæreditátem suam; spéciem Jacob quam diléxit.
»⁶Ascéndit Deus in júbilo, et Dóminus in voce tubæ.
⁷Psállite Deo nostro, psállite; psállite regi nostro, psállite:
»⁸quóniam rex omnis terræ Deus, psállite sapiénter.
⁹Regnábit Deus super gentes; Deus sedet super sedem sanctam suam.
»¹⁰Príncipes populórum congregáti sunt cum Deo Ábraham, quóniam dii fortes terræ veheménter eleváti sunt.

V. *Glória Patri ...*

Ant 1.

V. O Lord, ✝ open my lips.
R. And my mouth shall proclaim Thy praise.

V. O God, come to my assistance.
R. O Lord, make haste to help me.

V. *Glory be ...*
R. *As it was ...*

Psalm 46

Ant 1. **Shout unto God with the voice of joy.**

О clap your hands, all ye nations: shout unto God with the voice of joy,
³For the Lord is high, terrible: a great King over all the earth.
»⁴He hath subdued the people under us; and the nations under our feet.
⁵He hath chosen for us His inheritance, the beauty of Jacob which He hath loved.
»⁶God is ascended with jubilee, and the Lord with the sound of a trumpet.
⁷Sing praises to our God, sing ye: sing praises to our King, sing ye.
»⁸For God is the King of all the earth: sing ye wisely.
⁹God shall reign over the nations: God sitteth on His holy throne.
»¹⁰The princes of the people are gathered together with the God of Abraham: for the noble ones of the earth belong to God. He is highly exalted.

V. *Glory be ...*

Ant 1.

Monday Lauds I

Psalmus 5

Ant 2. Inténde voci orationis meæ, rex meus et Deus meus.

Verba mea áuribus pércipe, Dómine; intéllige clamórem meum.
³Inténde voci oratiónis meæ, rex meus et Deus meus.
»⁴Quóniam ad te orábo, Dómine: mane exáudies vocem meam.

⁵Mane astábo tibi, et vidébo quóniam non Deus volens iniquitátem tu es.

»⁶Neque habitábit juxta te malígnus, neque permanébunt injústi ante óculos tuos.

»⁷Odisti ómnes qui operántur iniquitátem; perdes ómnes qui loquúntur mendácium. Virum sánguinum et dolósum abominábitur Dóminus.

»⁸Ego autem in multitúdine misericórdiæ tuæ introíbo in domum tuam; adorábo ad templum sanctum tuum in timóre tuo.

»⁹Dómine, deduc me in justítia tua: propter inimícos meos dírige in conspéctu tuo viam meam.
¹⁰Quóniam non est in ore eórum véritas; cor eórum vanum est.

»¹¹Sepúlchrum patens est guttur eórum; linguis suis dolóse agebant: júdica illos, Deus. Décidant a cogitatiónibus suis; secúndum multitúdinem impietátum eórum expélle eos, quóniam irritavérunt te, Dómine.

»¹²Et læténtur ómnes, qui sperant in te, in ætérnum exsultábunt, et habitábis in eis. Et glóriabuntur in te ómnes qui díligunt nomen tuum,

Psalm 5

Ant 2. Hearken to the voice of my prayer, O my King and my God.

ive ear, O Lord, to my words, understand my cry.
³Hearken to the sound of my prayer, O my King and my God.
»⁴For to Thee will I pray: O Lord, in the morning Thou shalt hear my voice.

⁵In the morning I will stand before Thee, and will see: because Thou art not a God that willest iniquity.
»⁶Neither shall the wicked dwell near Thee: nor shall the unjust abide before Thine eyes.
»⁷Thou hatest all the workers of iniquity: Thou wilt destroy all that speak a lie. The bloody and the deceitful man the Lord will abhor.

»⁸But as for me in the multitude of Thy mercy, I will come into Thy house; I will worship towards Thy holy temple, in Thy fear.
»⁹Conduct me, O Lord, in Thy justice: because of mine enemies, direct my way in Thy sight.
¹⁰For there is no truth in their mouth: their heart is vain.
»¹¹Their throat is an open sepulchre: they speak deceitfully with their tongues: judge them, O God. Let them perish from their plans. According to their great wickednesses cast them out: for they have rebelled against Thee, O Lord.
»¹²But let all them be glad that hope in Thee: they shall rejoice for ever, and Thou shalt dwell in them. And all they that love Thy Name shall glory in Thee.

Monday Lauds I

»¹³quóniam tu benedíces justo. Dómine, ut scuto bonæ voluntátis tuæ coronásti nos.

V. *Glória Patri ...*

Ant 2.

Psalmus 28

Ant 3. Vox Dómini super aquas; Deus majestátis intónuit.

Afférte Dómino glóriam et honórem; afférte Dómino glóriam nómini ejus; adoráte Dóminum in átrio sancto ejus.
»³Vox Dómini super aquas; Deus majestátis intónuit: Dóminus super aquas multas.

⁴Vox Dómini in virtúte; vox Dómini in magnificéntia.

»⁵Vox Dómini confringéntis cedros, et confrínget Dóminus cedros Líbani:

⁶et commínuet eas, tamquam vítulum Líbani, et diléctus quemádmodum fílius unicórnium.

»⁷Vox Dómini intercidéntis flammam ignis;

⁸vox Dómini concutiéntis desértum: et commovébit Dóminus desértum Cades.
»⁹Vox Dómini præparántis cervos: et revelábit condénsa, et in templo ejus ómnes dicent glóriam.

»¹⁰Dóminus dilúvium inhabitáre facit, et sedébit Dóminus rex in ætérnum.

»¹³For Thou wilt bless the just. O Lord, Thou hast crowned us, as with a shield of Thy good will.

V. *Glory be ...*

Ant 2.

Psalm 28

Ant 3. The voice of the Lord is upon the waters; the God of majesty hath thundered.

Bring to the Lord glory and honor: bring to the Lord glory to His Name: adore ye the Lord in His holy court.
»³The voice of the Lord is upon the waters; the God of majesty hath thundered, The Lord is upon many waters.
⁴The voice of the Lord is in power; the voice of the Lord is magnificent.
»⁵The voice of the Lord breaketh the cedars: yea, the Lord shall break the cedars of Lebanon:
⁶And shall reduce them to pieces, He maketh Lebanon skip like a calf and Sirion like a young wild ox.

»⁷The voice of the Lord divideth the flame of fire.

⁸The voice of the Lord shaketh the desert: and the Lord shall shake the desert of Cades.
»⁹The voice of the Lord twists the oaks and strips the forests bare: and in His temple all shall speak His glory.
»¹⁰The Lord dwelleth above the flood: and the Lord shall sit enthroned as King for ever.

Monday Lauds I

»¹¹Dóminus virtútem pópulo suo dabit; Dóminus benedícet pópulo suo in pace.

V. *Glória Patri ...*

Ant 3.

Cánticum David
(1 Chron 29:10-16)

Ant 4. Laudámus nomen tuum ínclytum.

Benedíctus es, Dómine Deus Israël patris nostri, ab ætérno in ætérnum.
»¹¹Tua est, Dómine, magnificéntia, et poténtia, et glória, atque victória: et tibi laus: cuncta enim quæ in cælo sunt et in terra, tua sunt: tuum, Dómine, regnum, et tu es super ómnes príncipes.

»¹²Tuæ divítiæ, et tua est glória: tu domináris ómnium. In manu tua virtus et poténtia: in manu tua magnitúdo, et impérium ómnium.

»¹³Nunc ígitur Deus noster, confitémur tibi, et laudámus nomen tuum ínclytum.
»¹⁴Quis ego, et quis pópulus meus, ut possimus hæc tibi univérsa promíttere? Tua sunt ómnia: et quæ de manu tua accepimus, dedimus tibi.
»¹⁵Peregrini enim sumus coram te, et advénæ, sicut ómnes patres nostri. Dies nostri quasi umbra super terram, et nulla est mora.
»¹⁶Dómine Deus noster, omnis hæc copia quam parávimus ut ædificarétur domus nómini sancto tuo, de manu tua est, et tua sunt ómnia.

V. *Glória Patri ...*

»¹¹The Lord will give strength to His people: the Lord will bless His people with peace.

V. *Glory be ...*

Ant 3.

Canticle of David
(1 Chron 29:10-16)

Ant 4. We praise Thy glorious Name.

Blessed art Thou, O Lord the God of Israel, our Father from eternity to eternity.
»¹¹Thine, O Lord, is magnificence, and power, and glory, and victory: and to Thee is praise: for all that is in heaven, and on earth, is Thine: Thine is the kingdom, O Lord, and Thou art above all princes.

»¹²Thine are riches, and Thine is glory, Thou hast dominion over all: in Thy hand is power and might: in Thy hand greatness, and the ruler of all things.

»¹³Now, therefore, our God we give thanks to Thee, and we praise Thy glorious Name.
»¹⁴Who am I, and what is my people, that we should be able to promise Thee all these things? All things are Thine: and we have given Thee what we received by Thy hand.
»¹⁵For we are sojourners before Thee, and strangers, as were all our fathers. Our days upon earth are as a shadow, and there is no abiding here.
»¹⁶O Lord our God, all this store that we have prepared to build Thee a house for Thy holy Name, is from Thy hand, and all things are Thine.

V. *Glory be ...*

Monday Lauds I

Ant 4.

Psalmus 116

Ant 5. Laudáte Dóminum, ómnes gentes.

Laudáte Dóminum, ómnes gentes; laudáte eum, ómnes pópuli.
»²Quóniam confirmáta est super nos misericórdia ejus, et véritas Dómini manet in ætérnum.

V. *Glória Patri* ...

Ant 5.

Capitulum
(Rom 13:12-14)
The reading below or the proper of the day

V. Nox præcéssit, dies autem appropinquávit. Abjiciámus ergo ópera tenebrárum, et induámur arma lucis. Sicut in die honéste ambulémus: non in comessatiónibus, et ebrietátibus, non in cubílibus, et impudicítiis, non in conténtione, et æmulátione.

R. Deo grátias.

Hymnus
Or the hymn for the season

Splendor Patérnæ Glóriæ
De luce lucem próferens,
Lux lucis, et fons lúminis,
Diem dies illúminans:

Verúsque sol illábere,
Micans nitóre pérpeti:
Jubárque sancti Spíritus
Infúnde nostris sénsibus.

Ant 4.

Psalm 116

Ant 5. O praise the Lord, all ye nations.

O praise the Lord, all ye nations: praise Him, all ye people.
»²For His mercy is confirmed upon us: and the truth of the Lord remaineth for ever.

V. *Glory be* ...

Ant 5.

Chapter
(Rom 13:12-14)
The reading below or the proper of the day

V. The night is passed, and the day is at hand. Let us, therefore cast off the works of darkness, and put on the armor of light. Let us walk honestly, as in the day: not in rioting and drunkenness, not in debauchery and impurities, not in contention and envy.

R. Thanks be to God.

Hymn
Or the hymn for the season

O Splendor of God's Glory Bright,/
O Thou that bringest light from light,/
O Light of Light, light's Living Spring,/ O Day, all days illumining.

Thou true Sun, on us Thy glance/
Let fall in royal radiance,/
The Spirit's sanctifying beam/
Upon our earthly senses stream.

Monday Lauds I

Votis vocémus et Patrem,
Patrem poténtis gratiæ,
Patrem perénnis glóryæ:
Culpam releget lúbricam.

Confírmet actus strénuos:
Dentes retúndat invidi:
Casus secundet ásperos:
Agénda recte dírigat.

Mentem gubérnet et regat:
Sit pura nobis cástitas:
Fides calóre férveat,
Fraudis venéna nésciat.

Christúsque nobis sit cibus,
Potúsque noster sit fides:
Læti bibámus sobriam
Profusiónem Spíritus.

The Father too our prayers implore,/
Father of glory evermore,/
The Father of all grace and might,/
To banish sin from our delight:

To guide whatev'r we nobly do,/
With love all envy to subdue,/
To make ill-fortune turn to fair,/
And give us grace our wrongs to bear.

Our mind be in His keeping placed,/
Our body true to Him and chaste,/
Where only faith her fire shall feed,/
And burn the tares of Satan's seed.

And Christ to us for food shall be,/
From Him our drink that welleth free,/ The Spirit's wine, that maketh whole,/ And mocking not, exalts the soul.

Versiculi

V. Repléti sumus mane misericórdia tua.
R. Exultávimus, et delectáti sumus

Ant. Benedíctus Dóminus Deus Israël, quia visitávit, et fecit redemptíonem plebis suæ. *(Whenever possible, the antiphon for the specific season or feast of a saint will be used).*

Versicle

V. We were replenished in the morning with Thy mercy.
R. We rejoiced and were made glad.

Ant. Praised be the Lord God of Israel because He hath visited us and liberated us. *(Whenever possible, the antiphon for the specific season or feast of a saint will be used).*

Cánticum Zachariæ
(Luke 1:68-79)
Go to page 366

V. *Glória Patri ...*

Ant. Benedíctus Dóminus Deus Israël, quia visitávit, et fecit redemptíonem plebis suæ.

Canticle of Zachariah
(Luke 1:68-79)
Go to page 366

V. *Glory be ...*

Ant. Praised be the Lord God of Israel because He hath visited us and liberated us.

Monday Lauds I

V. *Páter nóster…* **R.** *Pánem nostrum …*	**V.** Our Father … **R.** Give us this day …
V. *Dómine exáudi oratiónem meam.* **R.** *Et clamor meus ad te véniat.*	**V.** O Lord, hear my prayer. **R.** And let my cry come unto Thee.
V. *Oremus.*	**V.** Let us pray.
Vota, quǽsumus, Dómine, supplicántis pópuli cælésti pietáte proséquere: ut et quæ agénda sunt, vídeant, et ad implénda quæ víderint, convaléscant.	We beseech Thee, O Lord, to be merciful and attentive to the supplications of Thy holy people: that they may see what is to be done, and that they may be strengthened to accomplish what they have seen.
Per Dóminum nostrum...	Through our Lord …
The prayer above is said, or the prayer of the season or the Feast day is prayed if there are any.	*The prayer above is said, or the prayer of the season or the Feast day is prayed if there are any.*
V. *Dómine exáudi oratiónem meam.* **R.** *Et clamor meus ad te véniat.*	**V.** O Lord, hear my prayer. **R.** And let my cry come unto Thee.
V. *Benedicámus Dómino.* **R.** *Deo grátias.*	**V.** Let us bless the Lord. **R.** Thanks be to God.
V. *Fidélium ánimæ per misericórdiam Dei requiéscant in pace.*	**V.** May the souls of the faithful departed through the mercy of God rest in peace.
R. *Amen.*	**R.** Amen.

The Lord will give strength to His people: the Lord will bless His people with peace.

Monday Lauds I

 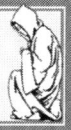

TUESDAY – LAUDS I

V. Dómine, ✝ lábia mea apéries.
R. Et os meum annuntiábit laudem tuam.

V. Deus, in adjutorium meum intende.
R. Dómine, ad adjuvándum me festína.

V. *Glória Patri ...*
R. *Sicut erat ...*

Psalmus 95

Ant 1. Cantáte Dómino, et benedícite nómini ejus.

Cantate Dómino cánticum novum; cantáte Dómino omnis terra. ²Cantáte Dómino, et benedícite nómini ejus; Annuntiáte de die in diem salutáre ejus.
»³Annuntiáte inter gentes glóriam ejus; in ómnibus pópulis mirabília ejus.
»⁴Quóniam magnus Dóminus, et laudábilis nimis: terríbilis est super ómnes deos.
»⁵Quóniam ómnes dii géntium dæmónia; Dóminus autem cælos fecit.

»⁶Conféssio et pulchritúdo in conspéctu ejus; sanctimónia et magnificéntia in sanctificatióne ejus.
»⁷Afférte Dómino, pátriæ géntium, afférte Dómino glóriam et honórem; ⁸afférte Dómino glóriam nómini ejus. Tóllite hóstias, et Introíte in átria ejus;
»⁹Adoráte Dóminum in átrio sancto ejus. Commoveótur a fácie ejus univérsa terra.

V. O Lord, ✝ open my lips.
R. And my mouth shall proclaim Thy praise.

V. O God, come to my assistance.
R. O Lord, make haste to help me.

V. *Glory be...*
R. *As it was ...*

Psalm 95

Ant 1. Sing ye to the Lord and bless His Name.

Sing ye to the Lord a new canticle: sing to the Lord, all the earth. ²Sing ye to the Lord and bless His Name: show forth His salvation from day to day.
»³Declare His glory among the Gentiles: His wonders among all people.
»⁴For the Lord is great, and exceedingly to be praised: He is to be feared above all gods.
»⁵For all the gods of the Gentiles are devils: but the Lord made the heavens.
»⁶Praise and beauty are before Him: holiness and majesty in His sanctuary.
»⁷Bring ye to the Lord, O ye kindreds of the Gentiles, bring ye to the Lord glory and honor.
⁸bring to the Lord glory unto his Name. Bring up sacrifices, and come into his courts:
»⁹Adore ye the Lord in His holy court. Let all the earth be moved at His presence.

Tuesday Lauds I

»¹⁰Dícite in géntibus, quia Dóminus regnávit. Étenim corréxit orbem terræ, qui non commovébitur; judicábit pópulos in æquitáte.

»¹¹Læténtur cæli, et exsúltet terra; commoveátur mare et plenitúdo ejus;

¹²gáudebunt campi, et ómnia exsultábunt ómnia ligna silvárum

»¹³a fácie Dómini, quia venit, quóniam venit judicáre terram. Judicábit orbem terræ in æquitáte, et pópulos in veritáte sua.

V. *Glória Patri ...*

Ant 1.

Psalmus 42

Ant 2. **Quóniam tu es salus vultus mei, et Deus meus.**

Júdica me, Deus, et discérne causam meam de gente non sancta: ab omine iníquo et dolóso érue me.
»²Quia tu es, Deus, fortitúdo mea: quare me repulísti? et quare tristis incédo, dum afflígit me inimícus?
»³Emítte lucem tuam et veritátem tuam: ipsa me dedúxerunt, et addúxerunt in montem sanctum tuum, et in tabernácula tua.
 tibi in cíthara, Deus, Deus meus.

»⁴Et introíbo ad altáre Dei: ad Deum, qui lætíficat iuventútem meam.

»⁵Quare tristis es, ánima mea? et quare contúrbas me? Spera in Deo, quóniam adhuc confitébor illi, salutáre vultus mei, et Deus meus.

»¹⁰Say ye among the Gentiles, the Lord hath reigned. For He hath corrected the world, which shall not be moved: He will judge the people with justice.

»¹¹Let the heavens rejoice, and let the earth be glad, let the sea be moved, and the fullness thereof,
¹²the fields and all things that are in them shall be joyful. Then shall all the trees of the woods rejoice before the face of the Lord,
»¹³because He cometh: because He cometh to judge the earth. He shall judge the world with justice, and the people with His truth.

V. *Glory be ...*

Ant 1.

Psalm 42

Ant 2. **For Thou art the salvation of my countenance, and my God.**

Judge me, O God, and distinguish my cause from the nation that is not holy: deliver me from the unjust and deceitful man.
»²For Thou art God my strength: why hast Thou cast me off? And why do I go sorrowful whilst the enemy afflicteth me?
»³Send forth Thy light and Thy truth: they have led me, and brought me unto Thy holy mountain, and into Thy tabernacles.
»⁴And I will go in to the altar of God: to God who giveth joy to my youth.
»⁵To Thee, O God my God, I will give praise upon the harp: why art thou sad, O my soul? And why dost thou disquiet me? Hope in God, for I will still give praise to Him: the salvation of my countenance, and my God.

Tuesday Lauds I

V. *Glória Patri ...*

Ant 2.

Psalmus 66

Ant 3. **Effunde, Dómine, lumen vultus tui super nos.**

Deus misereátur nostri, et benedícat nobis; illúminet vultum suum super nos, et misereátur nostri:

³Ut cognoscámus in terra viam tuam, in ómnibus géntibus salutáre tuum.
»⁴Confiteántur tibi pópuli, Deus: Confiteántur tibi pópuli ómnes.

»⁵Læténtur et exsúltent gentes, quóniam júdicas pópulos in æquitáte, et gentes in terra dírigis.

»⁶Confiteántur tibi pópuli, Deus: Confiteántur tibi pópuli ómnes.
»⁷Terra dedit fructum suum: benedícat nos Deus, Deus noster!
⁸Benedícat nos Deus, et metúant eum ómnes fines terræ.

V. *Glória Patri ...*

Ant 3.

Cánticum Tobias
(Tob 13:1-11)

Ant 4. **Ætérnum regem sæculórum exulte in opéribus tuis.**

Aperiens autem Tobias senior os suum, benedíxit Dóminum, et dixit: Magnus es, Dómine, in ætérnum, et in ómnia sǽcula regnum tuum:

V. *Glory be ...*

Ant 2.

Psalm 66

Ant 3. **Shed, O Lord, the light of Thy countenance upon us.**

May God have mercy on us, and bless us: may He cause the light of His countenance to shine upon us, and may He have mercy on us:

³that we may know Thy way upon earth: Thy salvation in all nations.
»⁴Let people confess to Thee, O God: let all people give praise to Thee.

»⁵Let the nations be glad and rejoice: for Thou judgest the people with justice, and directest the nations upon earth.

»⁶Let the people, O God, confess to Thee: let all the people give praise to Thee.
»⁷The earth hath yielded her fruit. May God, our God bless us,
⁸May God bless us and all the ends of the earth fear Him.

V. *Glory be ...*

Ant 3.

Canticle of Tobias
(Tob 13:1-11)

Ant 4. **Exult in the eternal King of the ages in thy works.**

And Tobias the elder opening his mouth, blessed the Lord, and said: Thou art great, O Lord, for ever, and Thy kingdom is unto all ages:

Tuesday Lauds I

»²quóniam tu flagéllas, et salvas; dedúcis ad ínferos, et redúcis: et non est qui éffugiat manum tuam.

³Confitémini Dómino, fílii Israël, et in conspéctu géntium laudáte eum:

»⁴quóniam ideo dispérsit vos inter gentes quæ ignórant eum, ut vos enarrétis mirabília ejus,
⁵et faciátis scire eos quia non est álius deus omnípotens præter eum.
»⁶Ipse castigávit nos propter iniquitátes nostras, et ipse á nos propter misericórdiam suam.
»⁷Aspícite ergo quæ fecit nobíscum, et cum timóre et tremóre confitémini illi: regémque sæculórum exaltáte in opéribus vestris.

»⁸Ego autem in terra captivitátis meæ confitébor illi: quóniam osténdit majestátem suam in gentem peccatrícem.
»⁹Convertímini ítaque peccatóres, et fácite justítiam coram Deo, credéntes quod fáciat vobíscum misericórdiam suam.
¹⁰Ego autem et ánima mea in eo lætábimur.

»¹¹Benedícite Dóminum ómnes elécti ejus: ágite dies lætítiæ, et confitémini illi.
¹²Jerúsalem cívitas Dei, castigávit te Dóminus in opéribus mánuum tuárum.

V. *Glória Patri ...*

Ant 4.

»²for Thou scourgest, and Thou savest: Thou leadest down to hell, and bringest up again: and there is none that can escape Thy hand.
³Give glory to the Lord, ye children of Israel, and praise Him in the sight of the Gentiles:
»⁴because He hath therefore scattered you among the Gentiles, who know not Him, that ye may declare His wonderful works,
⁵and make them know that there is no other almighty God besides Him.
»⁶He hath chastised us for our iniquities: and He will save us by His own mercy.
»⁷See then what He hath done with us, and with fear and trembling give ye glory to Him: and extol the eternal King of the world in thy works.
»⁸As for me, I will praise Him in the land of my captivity: because He hath shown His majesty toward a sinful nation.
»⁹Be converted therefore, ye sinners, and do justice before God, believing that He will show His mercy to you.
¹⁰And I and my soul will rejoice in Him.

»¹¹Bless ye the Lord, all His elect, keep days of joy, and give glory to Him.
¹²Jerusalem, City of God, the Lord hath chastised thee for the works of thy hands.

V. *Glory be ...*

Ant 4.

Tuesday Lauds I

Psalmus 134 | Psalm 134

Ant 5. Laudáte nomen Dómini qui statis in domo Dómini.

Ant 5. Praise ye the Name of the Lord, ye who stand in the house of the Lord.

𝕷 audáte nomen Dómini; laudáte, servi, Dóminum:
²qui statis in domo Dómini, in átriis domus Dei nostri.

»³Laudáte Dóminum, quia bonus Dóminus; psállite nómini ejus, quóniam suave.
⁴Quóniam Jacob elégit sibi Dóminus; Israël in possessiónem sibi.

»⁵Quia ego cognóvi quod magnus est Dóminus, et Deus noster præ ómnibus diis.
⁶Ómnia quæcúmque vóluit Dóminus fecit, in cælo, in terra, in mari et in ómnibus abýssis.

»⁷Edúcens nubes ab extrémo terræ, fúlgura in plúviam fecit; qui prodúcit ventos de thesáuris suis.

»⁸Qui percússit primogénita Ægýpti, ab hómine usque ad pecus.
⁹Et misit signa et prodígia in médio tui, Ægýpte: in Pharaónem, et in ómnes servos ejus.

»¹⁰Qui percússit gentes multas, et occídit reges fortes:
¹¹Sehon, regem Amorrhæórum, et Og, regem Basan, et ómnia regna Chánaan:
¹²et dedit terram eórum hæreditátem, hæreditátem Israël pópulo suo.

»¹³Dómine, nomen tuum in ætérnum; Dómine, memoriále tuum in generatiónem et generatiónem.
¹⁴Quia judicábit Dóminus pópulum suum, et in servis suis deprecábitur.

𝔓 raise ye the Name of the Lord: O ye His servants, praise the Lord:
²Ye that stand in the house of the Lord, in the courts of the house of our God.

»³Praise ye the Lord, for the Lord is good: sing ye to His Name, for it is sweet.
⁴For the Lord hath chosen Jacob unto Himself: Israel for His own possession.

»⁵For I have known that the Lord is great, and our God is above all gods.
⁶Whatsoever the Lord pleaseth He hath done, in heaven, on earth, in the sea, and in all the deeps.

»⁷He bringeth up clouds from the ends of the earth: He hath made lightnings for the rain. He bringeth forth winds out of His storehouse.

»⁸He slew the first-born of Egypt from man even unto beast.
⁹He sent forth signs and wonders in the midst of Thee, O Egypt: upon Pharaoh, and upon all his servants.

»¹⁰He smote many nations, and slew mighty kings:
¹¹Sehon king of the Amorrhites, and Og king of Basan, and all the kingdoms of Chanaan.
¹²And gave their land for an inheritance, for an inheritance to His people Israel.

»¹³Thy Name, O Lord, is for ever: Thy memorial, O Lord, unto all generations.
¹⁴For the Lord will judge His people, and will be merciful to His servants.

»¹⁵Simulácra géntium argéntum et aurum, ópera mánuum hóminum.
¹⁶Os habent, et non loquéntur; óculos habent, et non vidébunt.
»¹⁷Aures habent, et non áudient; neque enim est spíritus in ore ipsórum.
¹⁸Símiles illis fiant qui fáciunt ea, et ómnes qui confídunt in eis.
»¹⁹Domus Israël, benedícíte Dómino; domus Aaron, benedícíte Dómino.
²⁰Domus Levi, benedícíte Dómino; qui timétis Dóminum, benedícíte Dómino.
»²¹Benedíctus Dóminus ex Zion, qui hábitat in Jerúsalem.

V. *Glória Patri ...*

Ant 5.

Capitulum
(Rom 13:12-14)
The reading below or the proper of the day

V. Nox præcéssit, dies autem appropinquávit. Abjiciámus ergo ópera tenebrárum, et induámur arma lucis. Sicut in die honéste ambulémus: non in comessatiónibus, et ebrietátibus, non in cubílibus, et impudicitiis, non in contentióne, et æmulatióne: sed induimini Dóminum Jesum Christum, et carnis curam ne feceritis in desidériis.

R. Deo Grátias.

Hymnus
Or the hymn for the season

Ales Diéi Núntius
Lucem propínquam præcinit:
Nos excitátor méntium
Jam Chrístus ad vitam vocat.

»¹⁵The idols of the Gentiles are silver and gold, the works of men's hands.
¹⁶They have a mouth, but they speak not: they have eyes, but they see not.
»¹⁷They have ears, but they hear not: neither is there any breath in their mouths.
¹⁸Let them that make idols be like to them: and every one that trusteth in them.
»¹⁹Bless the Lord, O house of Israel: bless the Lord, O house of Aaron.
²⁰Bless the Lord, O house of Levi: ye that fear the Lord, bless the Lord.
»²¹Blessed be the Lord out of Zion, who dwelleth in Jerusalem.

V. *Glory be ...*

Ant 5.

Chapter
(Rom 13:12-14)
The reading below or the proper of the day

V. The night is passed, and the day is at hand. Let us, therefore cast off the works of darkness, and put on the armor of light. Let us walk honestly, as in the day: not in rioting and drunkenness, not in debauchery and impurities, not in contention and envy: But put ye on the Lord Jesus Christ, and make not provision for the flesh in its concupiscences.

R. Thanks be to God.

Hymn
Or the hymn for the season

As the Bird, Whose Clarion Gay/
Sounds before the dawn is grey/
Christ, who brings the spirit's day/
Calls us, close at hand.

Tuesday Lauds I

Auférte, clamat, léctulos,
ægro sopóre désides:
Castíque, recti, ac sóbrii
Vigiláte, jam sum próximus.

Jesum ciámus vócibus,
Flentes, precántes, sóbrii:
Inténta supplicátio
Dormíre cor mundum vetat.

Tu, Christe, somnum díscute:
Tu rumpe noctis víncula:
Tu solve peccátum vetus,
Novúmque lumen íngere.

Deo Patri sit glória,
Ejúsque soli Fílio,
Cum Spíritu Paráclito,
Nunc et per omne sǽculum.
Amen.

"Wake!" He cries, "and for my sake,/
From thine eyes dull slumbers
shake!/ Sober, righteous, chaste
awake!/ At the door I stand!"

Lord, to Thee we lift on high/
Fervent prayer and bitter cry:/
Hearts aroused to pray and sigh/
May not slumber more.

Break the sleep of Death and Time,/
Forged by Adam's ancient crime;/
And the light of Eden's prime/
To the world restore!

Unto God the Father, Son,/
Holy Spirit, Three in One,/
One in Three, be glory done,/
Now and evermore./
Amen.

Versiculi

V. Repléti sumus mane misericórdia tua.
R. Exsultávimus, et delectáti sumus.

Versicle

V. We are filled with Thy morning mercy.
R. We rejoiced and were delighted.

Ant. Dóminus eréxit cornu salútis nobis in domo David púeri sui. *(Whenever possible, the antiphon for the specific season or feast of a saint will be used).*

Ant. The Lord hath raised up a horn of salvation to us, in the house of David His servant. *(Whenever possible, the antiphon for the specific season or feast of a saint will be used).*

Cánticum Zachariæ
(Luke 1:68-79)
Go to page 366

V. *Glória Patri ...*

Ant. Dóminus eréxit cornu salútis nobis in domo David sui.

V. *Páter nóster ...*
R. *Pánem nóstrum ...*

Canticle of Zachariah
(Luke 1:68-79)
Go to page 366

V. *Glory be ...*

Ant. The Lord hath raised up a horn of salvation to us, in the house of David His servant.

V. *Our Father ...*
R. *Give us this day ...*

Tuesday Lauds I

V. Dómine exáudi oratiónem meam.
R. Et clamor meus ad te véniat.

V. Oremus.

Deus, cuius providéntia in sui dispositióne non fállitur: te súpplices exorámus; ut nóxia cuncta submóveas, et ómnia nobis profutúra concédas. Per Dóminum nostrum ...

The prayer above is said, or the prayer of the season and the Feast day are prayed if there are any.

V. Dómine exáudi oratiónem meam.
R. Et clamor meus ad te véniat.

V. Benedicámus Dómino.
R. Deo grátias.

V. Fidélium ánimæ per misericórdiam Dei requiéscant in pace.

R. Amen.

V. O Lord, hear my prayer.
R. And let my cry come unto Thee.

V. Let us pray.

O God, Whose never-failing Providence ordereth all things: we implore Thee; that Thou mayest subdue all evils, and give us those things that benefit us. Through our Lord ...

The prayer above is said, or the prayer of the season and the Feast day are prayed if there are any.

V. O Lord, hear my prayer.
R. And let my cry come unto Thee

V. Let us bless the Lord.
R. Thanks be to God.

V. May the souls of the faithful departed through the mercy of God rest in peace.

R. Amen.

And I will go in to the altar of God: to God who giveth joy to my youth.

 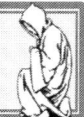

WEDNESDAY – LAUDS I

V. Dómine, † lábia mea apéries.
R. Et os meum annuntiábit laudem tuam.

V. Deus, in adjutórium meum inténde.
R. Dómine, ad adjuvándum me festína.

V. *Glória Patri ...*
R. *Sicut erat ...*

V. O Lord, † open my lips.
R. And my mouth shall proclaim Thy praise.

V. O God, come to my assistance.
R. O Lord, make haste to help me.

V. *Glory be...*
R. *As it was ...*

Psalmus 96 / Psalm 96

Ant 1. Dóminus regnávit: exsúltet terra.

Ant 1. The Lord hath reigned, let the earth rejoice.

Huic David, quando terra ejus restituta est Dóminus regnávit: exsúltet terra; læténtur insulæ multæ.
²Nubes et calígo in circúitu ejus; justítia et judícium corréctio sedis ejus.
»³Ignis ante ípsum præcédet, et inflammábit in circúitu inimícos ejus.
⁴Illuxérunt fúlgura ejus orbi terræ; vidit, et commóta est terra.
»⁵Montes sicut cera fluxérunt a fácie Dómini; a fácie Dómini omnis terra.

⁶Annuntiavérunt cæli justítiam ejus, et vidérunt ómnes pópuli glóriam ejus.
»⁷Confundántur ómnes qui adórant sculptília, et qui gloriántur in simulácris suis. Adoráte eum ómnes ángeli ejus.
»⁸Audívit, et lætáta est Sion, et exsultavérunt fíliæ Judæ propter judícia tua, Dómine.
»⁹Quóniam tu Dóminus altíssimus super omnem terram; nimis exaltátus es super ómnes deos.

The Lord hath reigned, let the earth rejoice: let many islands be glad.
²Clouds and darkness are round about Him: justice and judgment are the foundation of His throne.
»³A fire shall go before Him, and shall burn His enemies round about.

⁴His lightning hath shone forth to the world: the earth saw and trembled.
»⁵The mountains melted like wax, at the presence of the Lord: at the presence of the Lord of all the earth.
⁶The heavens declared His justice, and all people saw His glory.

»⁷Let them be all confounded that adore graven images, and that glory in their idols. Adore Him, all ye His angels.
»⁸Zion heard, and was glad. And the daughters of Juda rejoiced, because of Thy judgments, O Lord.
»⁹For Thou art the most high Lord over all the earth: Thou art exalted exceedingly above all gods.

Wednesday Lauds I

»¹⁰Qui dilígitis Dóminum, odite malum: custódit Dóminus ánimas sanctórum suórum; de manu peccatóris liberábit eos.
»¹¹Lux orta est justo, et rectis corde lætítia.
¹²Lætámini, justi, in Dómino, et confitémini memóriæ sanctificatiónis ejus.

V. *Glória Patri* ...

Ant 1.

Psalmus 64

Ant 2. **Te decet hymnus, Deus, in Sion.**

Te decet hymnus, Deus, in Zion, et tibi reddétur votum in Jerúsalem.
»³Exáudi oratiónem meam; ad te omnis caro véniet.
⁴Verba iniquórum prævaluérunt super nos, et impietátibus nostris tu propitiáberis.

»⁵Beátus quem elegísti et assumpsísti: inhabitábit in átriis tuis. Replébimur in bonis domus tuæ; sanctum est templum tuum, mirábile in æquitáte.

»⁶Exáudi nos, Deus, salutáris noster, spes ómnium finium terræ, et in mari longe.

⁷Præparans montes in virtúte tua, accínctus poténtia;
»⁸qui contúrbas profúndum maris, sonum flúctuum ejus. Turbabúntur gentes,
⁹et timébunt qui hábitant términos a signis tuis; éxitus matútini et véspere delectábis.

»¹⁰Ye that love the Lord, hate evil: the Lord preserveth the souls of His saints, He will deliver them out of the hand of the sinner.
»¹¹Light is risen to the just, and joy to the right of heart.
¹²Rejoice, ye just, in the Lord: and give praise to the memory of His holiness.

V. *Glory be* ...

Ant 1.

Psalm 64

Ant 2. **A hymn, O God, becometh Thee in Zion.**

A hymn, O God, becometh Thee in Zion: and a vow shall be offered to Thee in Jerusalem.
»³O hear my prayer: all flesh shall come to Thee.
⁴The words of the wicked have prevailed over us: and Thou wilt pardon our transgressions.

»⁵Blessed is He Whom Thou hast chosen and taken to Thee: He shall dwell in Thy courts. We shall be filled with the good things of Thy house; holy is Thy temple, wonderful in justice.
»⁶Hear us, O God our Savior, Who art the hope of all the ends of the earth, and in the sea afar off:
⁷Thou who, by Thy strength and being girded with power, makest the mountains remain secured.
»⁸Who troublest the depth of the sea, the noise of its waves. The Gentiles shall be distressed,
⁹and they that dwell in the uttermost borders shall be afraid at Thy signs: Thou shalt make the going out of the

»¹⁰Visitásti terram, et inebriásti eam; multiplicásti locupletáre eam. Flumen Dei replétum est aquis; parásti cibum illórum: quóniam ita est præparátio ejus.

»¹¹Rivos ejus inébria; multíplica genímina ejus: in stillicídiis ejus lætábitur gérminans.
¹²Benedíces corónæ anni benignitátis tuæ, et campi tui replebúntur ubertáte.

V. *Glória Patri ...*

Ant 2.

Psalmus 100

Ant 3. **Tibi, Dómine, cantabo et intélligam in via immaculáta.**

𝕸 isericórdiam et judícium cantábo tibi, Dómine; psallam, ²et intélligam in via immaculáta: quando vénies ad me? Perambulábam in innocéntia cordis mei, in médio domus meæ.
»³Non proponébam ante óculos meos rem injústam; fácientes prævaricatiónes odívi; non adhǽsit mihi
»⁴cor pravum; declinántem a me malígnum non cognoscébam.

»⁵Detrahentem secréto próximo suo, hunc persequébar: supérbo óculo, et insatiábili corde, cum hoc non edébam.

»⁶Óculi mei ad fidéles terræ, ut sédeant mecum; ámbulans in via immaculáta, hic mihi ministrábat.

morning and of the evening to be joyful.
»¹⁰Thou hast visited the earth, and hast plentifully watered it; Thou hast many ways enriched it. The river of God is filled with water, Thou hast prepared their food: for so is its preparation.
»¹¹Fill up plentifully the streams thereof, multiply its fruits; it shall spring up and rejoice in its showers.
¹²Thou shalt bless the crown of the year with Thy goodness: and Thy fields shall be filled with plenty.

V. *Glory be ...*

Ant 2.

Psalm 100

Ant 3. **To Thee, O Lord, I shall sing and I shall understand the way of integrity.**

𝕸 ercy and judgment I will sing to Thee, O Lord: I will sing, ²and my understanding will be blameless, when Thou shalt come to me. I walked in the innocence of my heart, in the midst of my house.
»³I did not set before my eyes any unjust thing: I hated the workers of evil.
»⁴The perverse heart shall be far from me: and the malignant that turned aside from me I would not know.
»⁵The man that in private detracted his neighbor, him did I persecute. I would not eat with him that had a proud eye, and an insatiable heart.
»⁶Mine eyes were upon the faithful of the earth who sat with me: the man that walked in the perfect way, he served me.

Wednesday Lauds I

»⁷Non habitábit in médio domus meæ qui facit supérbiam; qui lóquitur iníqua non diréxit in conspéctu oculórum meórum.
»⁸In matutíno interficiébam ómnes peccatóres terræ, ut dispérderem de civitáte Dómini ómnes óperantes iniquitátem.

V. *Glória Patri ...*

Ant 3.

Cánticum Judith
(Jdt 16:15-22)

Ant 4. Dómine magnus es tu et præclárus in virtúte tua.

Adonái Dómine, magnus es tu, et præclárus in virtúte tua: et quem superáre nemo potest.
»¹⁷Tibi sérviat omnis creatúra tua, quia dixísti, et facta sunt; misísti spíritum tuum, et creáta sunt: et non est qui resístat voci tuæ.

»¹⁸Montes a fundaméntis movebúntur cum aquis; petræ, sicut cera, liquéscent ante fáciem tuam.

¹⁹Qui autem timent te, magni erunt apud te per ómnia.
»²⁰Væ genti insurgénti super genus meum: Dóminus enim omnípotens vindicábit in eis; in die judícii visitábit illos.

²¹Dabit enim ignem et vermes in carnes eórum, ut urántur et séntiant usque in sempitérnum.

»⁷He that worketh pride shall not dwell in the midst of my house. He that speaketh unjust things shall not prosper before mine eyes.
»⁸In the morning I put to death all the wicked of the land: that I might cut off all the workers of iniquity from the city of the Lord.

V. *Glory be ...*

Ant 3.

Canticle of Judith
(Jdt 16:15-22)

Ant 4. O Lord, Thou art great and excellent in Thy power.

O Adonai, Lord, great art Thou, and glorious in Thy power, and no one can overcome Thee.
»¹⁷Let all Thy creatures serve Thee: because Thou hast spoken, and they were made: Thou didst send forth Thy spirit, and they were created, and there is no one that can resist Thy voice.

»¹⁸The mountains shall be moved from their foundations with the waters: the rocks shall melt as wax before Thy face.

¹⁹But they that fear Thee, shall be great with Thee in all things.
»²⁰Woe be to the nation that riseth up against my people: for the Lord almighty will take revenge on them, in the day of judgment He will visit them.

²¹For He will give fire, and worms into their flesh, that they may burn, and may suffer for ever.

Wednesday Lauds I

»²²Et factum est post hæc, omnis pópulus post victóriam venit in Jerúsalem adoráre Dóminum: et mox ut purificáti sunt, obtulérunt ómnes holocáusta, et vota, et repromissiónes suas.

V. Glória Patri ...

Ant 4.

Psalmus 145

Ant 5. Laudábo Deum meum in vita mea.

Lauda, ánima mea, Dóminum. Laudábo Dóminum in vita mea; psallam Deo meo quámdiu fúero. Nolíte confídere in princípibus, ³in filiis hóminum, in quibus non est salus.
»⁴Exíbit spíritus ejus, et revertétur in terram suam; in illa die períbunt ómnes cogitatiónes eórum.
»⁵Beátus cujus Deus Jacob adjútor ejus, spes ejus in Dómino Deo ipsius:
⁶qui fecit cælum et terram, mare, et ómnia quæ in eis sunt.
»⁷Qui custódit veritátem in sǽculum; facit judícium injúriam patiéntibus; dat escam esuriéntibus. Dóminus solvit compedítos.

»⁸Dóminus illúminat cæcos. Dóminus érigit elisos; Dóminus díligit justos.
»⁹Dóminus custódit ádvenas, pupíllum et víduam suscípiet, et vias peccatórum dispérdet.
»¹⁰Regnábit Dóminus in sǽcula; Deus tuus, Sion, in generatiónem et generatiónem.

V. Glória Patri ...

»²²And it came to pass after these things, that all the people, after the victory, came to Jerusalem to adore the Lord: and as soon as they were purified, they all offered holocausts, and vows, and their promises.

V. Glory be ...

Ant 4.

Psalm 145

Ant 5. I will praise my God all my life.

Praise the Lord, O my soul, all my life I will praise the Lord: I will sing to my God as long as I shall be. Put not thy trust in princes: ³in the children of men, in whom there is no salvation.
»⁴His spirit shall go forth, and He shall return into His earth: in that day all their thoughts shall perish.
»⁵Blessed is he who hath the God of Jacob for his helper, whose hope is in the Lord his God:
⁶Who made heaven and earth, the sea, and all things that are in them:
»⁷Who keepeth truth for ever: Who executeth judgment for them that suffer wrong: Who giveth food to the hungry. The Lord releaseth those that are bound.
»⁸The Lord enlighteneth the blind. The Lord lifteth up them that are cast down: the Lord loveth the just.
»⁹The Lord keepeth the strangers, He will support the fatherless and the widow: and He will destroy the ways of sinners.
»¹⁰The Lord shalt reign for ever: Thy God, O Zion, unto generation and generation.

V. Glory be ...

Wednesday Lauds I

Ant 5.

Capitulum
(Rom 13:12-14)
The reading below or the proper of the day

V. Nox præcéssit, dies autem appropinquávit. Abjiciámus ergo ópera tenebrárum, et induámur arma lucis. Sicut in die honéste ambulémus: non in comessatiónibus, et ebrietátibus, non in cubílibus, et impudicítiis, non in contentióne, et æmulatióne: sed induímini Dóminum Jesum Christum, et carnis curam ne fecéritis in desidériis.

R. Deo Grátias.

Hymnus
Or the hymn for the season

Nox, et Ténebræ, et Núbila,
Confúsa mundi et túrbida:
Lux intrat, albéscit polus:
Christus venit: discédite.

Calígo terræ scínditur
Percússa solis spículo,
Rebúsque jam color redit,
Vultu niténtis síderis.

Te, Christe, solum nóvimus:
Te mente pura et símplici,
Flendo et canéndo quǽsumus,
Inténde nostris sénsibus.

Sunt multa fucis íllita,
Quæ luce purgéntur tua:
Tu, vera lux cæléstium,
Vultu sereno illúmina.

Ant 5.

Chapter
(Rom 13:12-14)
The reading below or the proper of the day

V. The night is passed, and the day is at hand. Let us, therefore cast off the works of darkness, and put on the armor of light. Let us walk honestly, as in the day: not in rioting and drunkenness, not in debauchery and impurities, not in contention and envy: But put ye on the Lord Jesus Christ, and make not provision for the flesh in its concupiscences.

R. Thanks be to God.

Hymn
Or the hymn for the season

Day is Breaking, Dawn is Bright:/
Hence, vain shadows of the night!/
Mists that dim our mortal sight,/
Christ is come! Depart!

Darkness routed lifts her wings/
As the radiance upwards springs:/
Through the world of wakened things/ Life and color dart.

Thee, O Christ, alone we know:/
Singing even in our woe,/
With pure hearts to Thee we go:/
On our senses shine!

In Thy beams be purged away/
All that leads our thoughts astray!/
Through our spirits, King of day,/
Pour Thy light divine.

Wednesday Lauds I

Deo Patri sit glória, Ejúsque soli Fílio, Cum Spíritu Paráclito, Nunc et per omne sæculum. Amen.	Unto God the Father, Son,/ Holy Spirit, Three in One,/ One in Three, be glory done,/ Now and evermore./ Amen.

Versiculi / Versicle

V. Repléti sumus mane misericórdia tua.
R. Exsultávimus, et delectáti sumus.

V. We are filled with Thy morning mercy.
R. We rejoiced and were delighted.

Ant. De manu ómnium qui odérunt nos, liberávit nos Dóminus.
(Whenever possible, the antiphon for the specific season or feast of a saint will be used).

Ant. The Lord delivered us out of the hand of all those who hated us.
(Whenever possible, the antiphon for the specific season or feast of a saint will be used).

Cánticum Zachariæ
(Luke 1:68-79)
Go to page 366

Canticle of Zachariah
(Luke 1:68-79)
Go to page 366

V. *Glória Patri ...*

V. *Glory be ...*

Ant. De manu ómnium qui odérunt nos, liberávit nos Dóminus.

Ant. The Lord delivered us out of the hand of all those who hated us.

V. *Páter nóster …*
R. *Pánem nóstrum …*

V. *Our Father ...*
R. *Give us this day ...*

V. Dómine exáudi oratiónem meam.
R. Et clamor meus ad te véniat.

V. O Lord, hear my prayer.
R. And let my cry come unto Thee.

V. Oremus.

V. Let us pray.

Misericórdiæ tuæ remediis, quǽsumus Dómine, fragílitas nostra subsístat: ut quæ sua conditióne attéritur, tua cleméntia reparétur Per Dóminum nostrum...

By the compassion of Thy mercy, we beseech Thee, O Lord, to allow our frailty to bear: so that which was destroyed by our own nature may be restored by Thy mercy. Through our Lord ...

The prayer above is said, or the prayer of the season and the Feast day are prayed if there are any.

The prayer above is said, or the prayer of the season and the Feast day are prayed if there are any.

Wednesday Lauds I

V. Dómine exáudi oratiónem meam.	**V.** O Lord, hear my prayer.
R. Et clamor meus ad te véniat.	**R.** And let my cry come unto Thee
V. Benedicámus Dómino.	**V.** Let us bless the Lord.
R. Deo grátias.	**R.** Thanks be to God.
V. Fidélium ánimæ per misericórdiam Dei requiéscant in pace.	**V.** May the souls of the faithful departed through the mercy of God rest in peace.
R. Amen.	**R.** Amen.

Put not thy trust in princes: in the children of men, in whom there is no salvation.

 # THURSDAY – LAUDS I

V. Dómine, † lábia mea apéries.
R. Et os meum annuntiábit laudem tuam.

V. Deus, in adjutórium meum inténde.
R. Dómine, ad adjuvándum me festína.

V. *Glória Patri ...*
R. *Sicut erat ...*

V. O Lord, † open my lips.
R. And my mouth shall proclaim Thy praise.

V. O God, come to my assistance.
R. O Lord, make haste to help me.

V. *Glory be ...*
R. *As it was ...*

Psalmus 97

Ant 1. Jubiláte in conspéctu régis Dómini.

$\mathbb{C}$antate Dómino cánticum novum, quia mirabília fecit. Salvávit sibi déxtera ejus, et bráchium sanctum ejus.
»²Notum fecit Dóminus salutáre suum; in conspéctu géntium revelávit justítiam suam.
»³Recordátus est misericórdiæ suæ, et veritátis suæ domui Israël. Vidérunt ómnes termini terræ salutáre Dei nostri.
»⁴Jubiláte Deo, omnis terra; cantáte, et exsultáte, et psállite.

⁵Psállite Dómino in cíthara; in cíthara et voce psalmi;

⁶in tubis ductílibus, et voce tubæ corneæ. Jubiláte in conspéctu regis Dómini:
»⁷moveátur mare, et plenitúdo ejus; orbis terrárum, et qui hábitant in eo.

»⁸Flúmina plaudent manu; simul montes exsultábunt

Psalm 97

Ant 1. Rejoice at the sight of the Lord our king.

$\mathbb{S}$ing ye to the Lord a new canticle: because He hath done wonderful things. His right hand hath wrought for Him salvation, and His arm is holy.
»²The Lord hath made known His salvation: He hath revealed His justice in the sight of the Gentiles.
»³He hath remembered His mercy and His truth toward the house of Israel. All the ends of the earth have seen the salvation of our God.
»⁴Sing joyfully to God, all the earth; make melody, rejoice and sing.
⁵Sing praise to the Lord on the harp, on the harp, and with the voice of a psalm:
⁶with long trumpets, and sound of a cornet. Make a joyful noise before the Lord our King.
»⁷Let the sea be moved and the fullness thereof: the world and they that dwell therein.
»⁸The rivers shall clap their hands, the mountains shall rejoice together

⁹a conspéctu Dómini: quóniam venit judicáre terram. judicábit orbem terrárum in justítia, et pópulos in æquitáte.

V. *Glória Patri ...*

Ant 1.

Psalmus 89

Ant 2. Dómine, refúgium factus es nobis a generatióne in generatiónem.

Dómine, refúgium factus es nobis a generatióne in generatiónem.
²Priúsquam montes fíerent, aut formarétur terra et orbis, a sǽculo et usque in sǽculum tu es, Deus.
»³Ne avértas hóminem in humilitátem: et dixísti: Convertímini, filii hóminum.
»⁴Quóniam mille anni ante óculos tuos tamquam dies hestérna quæ prætériit: et custódia in nocte
⁵quæ pro níhilo habéntur, eórum anni erunt.

»⁶Mane sicut herba tránseat; mane floreat, et tránseat; véspere decídat, indúret, et aréscat.
»⁷Quia defécimus in ira tua, et in furóre tuo turbáti sumus.

⁸Posuísti iniquitátes nostras in conspéctu tuo; sǽculum nostrum in illuminatióne vultus tui.
»⁹Quóniam ómnes dies nostri defecérunt, et in ira tua defécimus. Anni nostri sicut aránea meditabúntur;
¹⁰dies annórum nostrórum in ipsis septuagínta anni. Si autem in potentátibus octogínta anni, et ámplius eórum labor et dolor;

⁹at the presence of the Lord: because He cometh to judge the earth. He shall judge the world with justice, and the people with equity.

V. *Glory be ...*

Ant 1.

Psalm 89

Ant 2. Lord, Thou hast become a refuge for us from generation to generation.

Lord, Thou hast been our refuge from generation to generation.
²Before the mountains were made, or the earth and the world was formed; from eternity and to eternity Thou art God.
»³Turn not man away to be brought low: and Thou hast said: Be converted, O ye sons of men.
»⁴For a thousand years in Thy sight are as yesterday, which is past. And as a watch in the night,
⁵their years shall be like things that are counted as nothing.
»⁶In the morning man shall grow up like grass; in the morning he shall flourish and pass away: in the evening he shall fall, grow dry, and wither.
»⁷For in Thy wrath we have fainted away: and are troubled in Thy indignation.
⁸Thou hast set our iniquities before Thine eyes: our life in the light of Thy countenance.
»⁹For all our days are spent; and in Thy wrath we have fainted away. Our years shall pass like a sigh,
¹⁰and these years of our lives are threescore and ten. But if in the strong they may be fourscore years:

Thursday Lauds I

quóniam supervénit mansuetúdo, et corripiémur.
»¹¹Quis novit potestátem iræ tuæ, et præ timóre tuo iram tuam ¹²dinumeráre? Déxteram tuam sic notam fac, et erudítos corde in sapiéntia.
»¹³Convertere, Dómine; usquequo? et deprecábilis esto super servos tuos. ¹⁴Repléti sumus mane misericórdia tua; et exsultávimus, et delectatiónibus sumus ómnibus diébus nostris.
»¹⁵Lætáti sumus pro diébus quibus nos humiliásti; annis quibus vídimus mala.
»¹⁶Réspice in servos tuos et in ópera tua, et dírige fílios eórum.
»¹⁷Et sit splendor Dómini Dei nostri super nos, et ópera mánuum nostrárum dírige super nos, et opus mánuum nostrárum dírige.

V. *Glória Patri* ...

Ant 2.

Psalmus 35

Ant 3. Multiplicásti Deus misericórdiam tuam.

Dixit injústus ut delínquat in semetipso: non est timor Dei ante óculos ejus.
³Quóniam dolóse egit in conspéctu ejus, ut inveniátur iníquitas ejus ad ódium.
»⁴Verba oris ejus iníquitas, et dolus; nóluit intellígere ut bene ágeret.
»⁵Iniquitátem meditátus est in cubíli suo; astitit omni viæ non bonæ: malítiam autem non odívit.

»⁶Dómine, in cælo misericórdia tua, et véritas tua usque ad nubes.

and what is more of them is labor and sorrow. For they quickly pass and we vanish.
»¹¹Who knoweth the power of Thine anger, and for Thy fear can measure Thy wrath?
¹²So make Thy right hand known: and men learned in heart, in wisdom.
»¹³Return, O Lord, how long? And have compassion on Thy servants.
¹⁴We are filled in the morning with Thy mercy: and we have rejoiced, and are delighted all our days.
»¹⁵We have rejoiced for the days in which Thou hast humbled us: for the years in which we have seen evils.
»¹⁶Look upon Thy servants and upon their works: and direct their children.
»¹⁷And let the brightness of the Lord our God be upon us: and direct Thou the works of our hands over us; yea, the work of our hands do Thou direct.

V. *Glory be* ...

Ant 2.

Psalm 35

Ant 3. O God, Thou hast multiplied Thy mercy.

The unjust hath said within himself that he would sin: there is no fear of God before his eyes:
³for in his sight he hath done deceitfully, that his iniquity may be found unto hatred.
»⁴The words of his mouth are iniquity and guile: he would not understand that he might do good.
»⁵He hath devised evil on his bed, he hath set himself on every way that is wicked: and evil he hath loved.
»⁶O Lord, Thy mercy is in heaven, and Thy truth reacheth even to the clouds.

Thursday Lauds I

⁷Justítia tua sicut montes Dei; judícia tua abýssus multa. Hómines et juménta salvábis, Dómine.

»⁸Quemádmodum multiplicásti misericórdiam tuam, Deus. Fílii autem hóminum in tégmine alárum tuárum sperébunt.
»⁹Inebriabúntur ab ubertáte domus tuæ, et torrénte voluptátis tuæ potábis eos:

¹⁰quóniam apud te est fons vitæ, et in lúmine tuo vidébimus lumen.

»¹¹Præténde misericórdiam tuam sciéntibus te, et justítiam tuam his qui recto sunt corde.
¹²Non véniat mihi pes supérbiæ, et manus peccatóris non móveat me.

»¹³Ibi cecidérunt qui operántur iniquitátem; expúlsi sunt, nec potuérunt stare.

V. *Glória Patri ...*

Ant 3.

Canticle of Jeramias
(Jer 31:10-14)

Ant 4. Pópulus meus ait Dóminus, bonis meis adimplébitur.

𝔄 udíte verbum Dómini, gentes, et Annuntiáte in ínsulis quæ procul sunt, et dícite: Qui dispérsit Israël congregábit eum, et custódiet eum sicut pastor gregem suum.

»¹¹Redémit enim Dóminus Jacob, et liberávit eum de manu potentióris.

»¹²Et venient, et laudábunt in monte Sion: et cónfluent ad bona Dómini, super fruménto, et vino, et óleo, et

⁷Thy justice is as the mountains of God, Thy judgments are like a boundless deep. Men and beasts Thou wilt preserve, O Lord.
»⁸O how hast Thou multiplied Thy mercy, O God! But the children of men shall put their trust under the covert of Thy wings.
»⁹They shall be filled with the abundance of Thy house; and Thou shalt make them drink of the fountain of Thy delights.
¹⁰For with Thee is the fountain of life; and in Thy light we shall see light itself.
»¹¹Extend Thy mercy to them that know Thee, and Thy justice to them that are right in heart.
¹²Let not the foot of pride come to me, and let not the hand of the sinner move me.
»¹³There the workers of iniquity are fallen, they are cast out, and could not stand.

V. *Glory be ...*

Ant 3.

Canticle of Jeremiah
(Jer 31:10-14)

Ant 4. My people, sayeth the Lord, will be filled with My goods.

𝔅 ear the word of the Lord, O ye nations, and declare it in the islands that are afar off, and say: He that scattered Israel will gather him: and He will keep him as the shepherd does his flock.
»¹¹For the Lord hath redeemed Jacob, and delivered him out of the hand of one that was mightier than he.
»¹²And they shall come, and shall give praise on Mount Zion: and they shall flow together to the good things

fœtu pecórum et armentórum: eritque ánima eórum quasi hortus irríguus, et ultra non esúrient.

»¹³Tunc lætábitur virgo in choro, júvenes et senes simul: et convértam luctum eórum in gáudium, et consolábor eos, et lætificábo a dolóre suo.

»¹⁴Et inebriábo ánimam sacerdótum pinguédine, et pópulus meus bonis meis adimplébitur, ait Dóminus.

V. *Glória Patri ...*

Ant 4.
Psalmus 146

Ant 5. Deo nostro jucúnda sit laudátio.

Laudáte Dóminum, quóniam bonus est psalmus; Deo nostro sit jucúnda, decóraque laudátio.
»²Ædíficans Jerúsalem Dóminus, dispersiónes Israëlis congregábit:
³qui sanat contrítos corde, et álligat contritiónes eórum;
»⁴qui númerat multitúdinem stellárum, et ómnibus eis nómina vocat.
⁵Magnus Dóminus noster, et magna virtus ejus, et sapiéntiæ ejus non est númerus.
»⁶Suscípiens mansuétos Dóminus; humílians autem peccatóres usque ad terram.
⁷Præcínite Dómino in confessióne; psállite Deo nostro in cíthara.
»⁸Qui óperit cælum núbibus, et parat terræ plúviam; qui prodúcit in móntibus fœnum, et Herbam servitúti hóminum;

of the Lord, for the corn, and wine, and oil, and the increase of cattle and herds, and their soul shall be as a watered garden, and they shall be hungry no more.

»¹³Then shall the virgins rejoice in the dance, the young men and old men together: and I will turn their mourning into joy, and will comfort them, and make them joyful after their sorrow.

»¹⁴And I will fill the souls of the priests with fatness: and My people shall be filled with My good things, sayeth the Lord.

V. *Glory be ...*

Ant 4.
Psalm 146

Ant 5. To our God let our praise be pleasing.

Praise ye the Lord, because psalms are pleasing to our God: be joyful with beautiful praise to Him.
»²The Lord buildeth up Jerusalem: He will gather together the dispersed of Israel:
³Who healeth the broken of heart, and bindeth up their wounds:
»⁴Who telleth the number of the stars: and calleth them all by their names.
⁵Great is our Lord, and great is His power: and His wisdom is infinite.
»⁶The Lord lifteth up the meek, and bringeth the wicked down even to the ground.
⁷Sing ye to the Lord with praise: sing to our God upon the harp:
»⁸Who covereth the heaven with clouds, and prepareth rain for the earth: Who maketh grass to grow on the mountains, and herbs for the service of men:

Thursday Lauds I

⁹qui dat juméntis escam ipsórum, et pullis corvórum invocántibus eum.

»¹⁰Non in fortitúdine equi voluntátem habébit, nec in tíbiis viri beneplácitum erit ei.
¹¹Beneplácitum est Dómino super timéntes eum, et in eis qui sperant super misericórdia ejus.

V. *Glória Patri …*

Ant 5.

Capitulum
(Rom 13:12-14)
The reading below or the proper of the day

V. Nox præcéssit, dies autem appropinquávit. Abjiciámus ergo ópera tenebrárum, et induámur arma lucis. Sicut in die honéste ambulémus: non in comessatiónibus, et ebrietátibus, non in cubílibus, et impudicitiis, non in contentióne, et æmulatióne.

R. Deo Grátias.

Hymnus
Or the hymn for the season

Lux Eecce Surgit Áuria,
Pallens facéssat cæcitas,
Quæ nosmet in præceps diu
Erróre traxit dévio.

Hæc lux serénum cónferat,
Purósque nos præstet sibi:
Nihil loquámur súbdolum:
Volvámus obscúrum nihil.

Sic tota decúrrat dies,
Ne lingua mendax, ne manus.
Oculíve peccent lúbrici,
Ne noxa corpus ínquinet

⁹Who giveth to beasts their food: and to the young ravens that call upon Him.

»¹⁰He shall not delight in the strength of the horse: nor take pleasure in the power of a man.
¹¹The Lord taketh pleasure in them that fear Him: and in them that hope in His mercy.

V. *Glory be …*

Ant 5.

Chapter
(Rom 13:12-14)
The reading below or the proper of the day

V. The night is passed, and the day is at hand. Let us, therefore cast off the works of darkness, and put on the armor of light. Let us walk honestly, as in the day: not in rioting and drunkenness, not in debauchery and impurities, not in contention and envy.

R. Thanks be to God.

Hymn
Or the hymn for the season

See the Golden Sun Arise!/
Let no more our darkened eyes./
Snare us, tangled by surprise/
In the maze of sin!

From false words and thoughts impure/ let this light, serene and sure, / Keep our lips without secure,/
Keep our souls within.

So may we the day-time spend,/
That, till life's temptations end/
tongue, nor hand, nor eye offend!/
One, above us all.

Thursday Lauds I

Speculátor adstat désuper, Qui nos diehus ómnibus, Actúsque nostros próspicit A luce prima in vésperum	Views in His revealing ray/ All we do, and think, and say,/ Watching us from break of day/ Till the twilight fall.
Deo Patri sit glória, Ejúsque soli Filio, Cum Spíritu Paráclito, Nunc et per omne sæculum.	Unto God the Father, Son,/ Holy Spirit, Three in One,/ One in Three, be glory done,/ Now and evermore.

Versiculi / Versicle

V. Repléti sumus mane misericórdia tua.
R. Exsultávimus, et delectáti sumus.

V. To God let our praise be pleasing.
R. We rejoiced and were delighted.

Ant. In sanctitáte serviámus Dómino, et liberábit nos ab inimícis nostris. *(Whenever possible, the antiphon for the season or feast of a saint will be used).*

Ant. Let us serve the Lord in holiness, and He will deliver us from our enemies. *(Whenever possible, the antiphon for the season or feast of a saint will be used).*

Cánticum Zachariæ / Canticle of Zachariah
(Luke 1:68-79)
Go to page 366

V. *Glória Patri ...*

V. *Glory be ...*

Ant. In sanctitáte serviámus Dómino, et liberábit nos ab inimícis nostris.

Ant. Let us serve the Lord in holiness, and He will deliver us from our enemies.

V. *Páter nóster…*
R. *Pánem nóstrum ...*

V. *Our Father …*
R. *Give us this day …*

V. Dómine exáudi oratiónem meam.
R. Et clamor meus ad te véniat.

V. O Lord, hear my prayer.
R. And let my cry come unto Thee.

V. Orémus.

V. Let us pray.

Vota, quǽsumus, Dómine, supplicántis pópuli cælésti pietáte proséquere: ut et quæ agénda sunt, vídeant, et ad implénda quæ

We beseech Thee, O Lord, to be merciful and attentive to the supplications of Thy holy people: that they may see what is to be done, and that they may be strengthened to

Thursday Lauds I

víderint, convaléscant.
Per Dóminum nostrum ...

The prayer above is said, or the prayer of the season and the Feast day are prayed if there are any.

V. Dómine exáudi oratiónem meam.
R. Et clamor meus ad te véniat.

V. Benedicámus Dómino.
R. Deo grátias.

V. Fidélium ánimæ per misericórdiam Dei requiéscant in pace.

R. Amen.

accomplish what they have seen.
Through our Lord ...

The prayer above is said, or the prayer of the season and the Feast day are prayed if there are any.

V. O Lord, hear my prayer.
R. And let my cry come unto Thee.

V. Let us bless the Lord.
R. Thanks be to God.

V. May the souls of the faithful departed through the mercy of God rest in peace.

R. Amen.

Sing ye to the Lord a new canticle: because He hath done wonderful things.

FRIDAY – LAUDS I

V. Dómine, ✝ lábia mea apéries.
R. Et os meum annuntiábit laudem tuam.

V. Deus, in adjutórium meum inténde.
R. Dómine, ad adjuvándum me festína.

V. *Glória Patri ...*
R. *Sicut erat ...*

Psalmus 98

Ant 1. Exaltáte Dóminum Deum nóstrum, et adoráte in monte sancto eíus.

𝔇óminus regnávit: irascántur pópuli; qui sedet super Herubim: moveatur terra ²Dóminus in Sion magnus, et excélsus super ómnes pópulos.

»³Confiteántur nómini tuo magno, quóniam terríbile et sanctum est, et honor regis iudícium díligit.

»⁴Tu parásti directiónes; judícium et justítiam in Jacob tu fecísti.

»⁵Exaltáte Dóminum Deum nostrum, et adoráte scabéllum pedum ejus, quóniam sanctum est.
»⁶Móyses et Aaron in sacerdótibus ejus, et Samuel inter eos qui ínvocant nomen ejus: invocábant Dóminum, et ipse exaudiebat eos.

»⁷In columna nubis loquebatur ad eos. Custodiebant testimónia ejus, et præcéptum quod dedit illis.

V. O Lord, ✝ open my lips.
R. And my mouth shall proclaim Thy praise.

V. O God, come to my assistance.
R. O Lord, make haste to help me.

V. *Glory be ...*
R. *As it was ...*

Psalm 98

Ant 1. Exalt the Lord our God, and worship on His holy mountain.

𝔗he Lord hath reigned, let the people tremble: He that sitteth on the cherubims: let the earth be moved.
²The Lord is great in Zion, and high above all people.

»³Let them give praise to Thy great Name: for it is terrible and holy: and the King's honor loveth judgment.

»⁴Thou hast established what is right: Thou hast done judgment and justice in Jacob.

»⁵Exalt ye the Lord our God and adore His footstool, for it is holy.
»⁶Moses and Aaron are among His priests: and Samuel among them that call upon His Name. They called upon the Lord, and He heard them.

»⁷He spoke to them in the pillar of the cloud. They kept His testimonies, and the commandment which He gave them.

Friday Lauds I

»⁸Dómine Deus noster, tu exaudiébas eos; Deus, tu propítius fuísti eis, et ulcíscens in ómnes adinventiónes eórum.
»⁹Exaltáte Dóminum Deum nostrum, et adoráte in monte sancto ejus, quóniam sanctus Dóminus Deus noster.

V. *Glória Patri ...*

Ant 1.

Psalmus 142

Ant 2. **Propter nomen tuum Dómine vivificábis me in æquitáte tua.**

Dómine, exáudi oratiónem meam; áuribus pércipe obsecratiónem meam in veritáte tua; exáudi me in tua justítia. ²Et non intres in judícium cum servo tuo, quia non justificábitur in conspéctu tuo omnis vivens »³Quia persecútus est inimícus ánimam meam; humiliávit in terra vitam meam; collocávit me in obscúris, sicut mórtuos sǽculi.

⁴Et anxiátus est super me spíritus meus; in me turbátum est cor meum.
»⁵Memor fui diérum antiquórum; meditátus sum in ómnibus opéribus tuis: in factis mánuum tuárum meditabar.
⁶Expándi manus meas ad te; ánima mea sicut terra sine aqua tibi.
»⁷Velóciter exáudi me, Dómine; defécit spíritus meus. Non avértas fáciem tuam a me, et símilis ero descendéntibus in lacum.
»⁸Audítam fac mihi mane misericórdiam tuam, quia in te sperávi. Notam fac mihi viam in

»⁸Thou didst hear them, O Lord our God: Thou wast a merciful God to them, although Thou tooketh vengeance on all their misdeeds.
»⁹Exalt ye the Lord our God, and adore at His holy mountain: for the Lord our God is holy.

V. *Glory be ...*

Ant 1.

Psalm 142

Ant 2. **Because of Thy Name, O Lord, Thou wilt revive me in Thy righteousness.**

Hear, O Lord, my prayer: give ear to my supplication in Thy truth: Hear me in Thy justice: ²and enter not into judgment with Thy servant: for in Thy sight no man living shall be justified.
»³For the enemy hath persecuted my soul: He hath cast down my life to the dust. He hath made me to dwell in darkness as those that have been long dead:
⁴and my spirit is in anguish within me: my heart within me is troubled.
»⁵I remembered the days of old, I meditated on all Thy works: I meditated upon the works of Thy hands.
⁶I stretched forth my hands to Thee: my soul is as earth without water unto Thee.
»⁷Hear me quickly, O Lord: my spirit hath fainted away. Turn not away Thy face from me, lest I be like unto them that go down into the pit.
»⁸Cause me to hear Thy mercy in the morning; for in Thee have I hoped.

Friday Lauds I

qua ámbulem, quia ad te levávi ánimam meam.
»⁹Éripe me de inimícis meis, Dómine: ad te confúgi: doce me fácere voluntátem tuam, quia Deus meus es tu.
»¹⁰Spíritus tuus bonus dedúcet me in terram rectam: propter nomen tuum, Dómine, vivificábis me, in æquitáte tua.

»¹¹Edúces de tribulatióne ánimam meam: et in misericórdia tua dispérdes inimícos meos.
¹²Et perdes omnes, qui tríbulant ánimam meam: quóniam ego servus tuus sum.

V. *Glória Patri ...*

Ant 2.

Psalmus 84

Ant 3. Deus tu convérsus vivificábis nos, et plebs tua lætábitur in te.

𝕭enedixisti, Dómine, terram tuam; avertísti captivitátem Jacob.
³Remisísti iniquitátem plebis tuæ; operuísti ómnia peccáta eórum.
»⁴Mitigásti omnem iram tuam; avertísti ab ira indignatiónis tuæ.
»⁵Convérte nos, Deus salutáris noster, et avérte iram tuam a nobis.
»⁶Numquid in ætérnum irascéris nobis? aut exténdes iram tuam a generatióne in generatiónem
«⁷Deus, tu convérsus vivificabis nos, et plebs tua lætábitur in te.

⁸Ostende nobis, Dómine, misericórdiam tuam, et salutáre tuum da nobis.

Make the way known to me, wherein I should walk: for I have lifted up my soul to Thee.
»⁹Deliver me from mine enemies, O Lord, to Thee I have fled: teach me to do Thy will, for Thou art my God.
»¹⁰Thy good spirit shall lead me into the right land: for Thy Name's sake, O Lord, Thou wilt quicken me in Thy justice.
»¹¹Thou wilt bring my soul out of trouble: and in Thy mercy Thou wilt destroy mine enemies.
¹²And Thou wilt cut off all them that afflict my soul: for I am Thy servant.

V. *Glory be ...*

Ant 2.

Psalm 84

Ant 3. O God, Thou wilt turn and revive us, and Thy people will rejoice in Thee.

𝕷ord, Thou hast blessed Thy land: Thou hast turned away the captivity of Jacob.
³Thou hast forgiven the iniquity of Thy people: Thou hast covered all their sins.
»⁴Thou hast mitigated all Thine anger: Thou hast turned away from the wrath of Thine indignation.
»⁵Convert us, O God our savior: and turn away Thine anger from us.
»⁶Wilt Thou be angry with us for ever: or wilt Thou extend Thy wrath from generation to generation?
»⁷Thou wilt turn, O God, and bring us to life: and Thy people shall rejoice in Thee.

Friday Lauds I

»⁹Áudiam quid loquátur in me Dóminus Deus, quóniam loquetur pacem in plebem suam, et super sanctos suos, et in eos qui convertúntur ad cor.
»¹⁰Verúmtamen prope timéntes eum salutáre ipsius, ut inhábitet glória in terra nostra.
¹¹Misericórdia, et véritas obviavérunt sibi: justítia, et pax osculátæ sunt.
»¹²Véritas de terra orta est: et justítia de cælo prospéxit.
»¹³Étenim Dóminus dabit benignitátem: et terra nostra dabit fructum suum.
¹⁴Justítia ante eum ambulábit: et ponet in via gressus suos.

V. *Glória Patri ...*

Ant 3.

Canticle of Isaias
(Isa 45:15-26)

Ant 4. **In Dómino justificábitur et laudábitur omne semen Israël.**

℣ere tu es Deus abscónditus, Deus Israël, Salvátor.
¹⁶Confúsi sunt, et erubuérunt ómnes: simul abiérunt in confusiónem fabricatóres errórum.
»¹⁷Israël salvátus est in Dómino salúte ætérna; non confundémini, et non erubescetis usque in sæculum sæculi.
»¹⁸Quia hæc dicit Dóminus creans cælos, ipse Deus formans terram et fáciens eam, ipse plastes ejus; non in vanum creavit eam: ut

⁸Show us, O Lord, Thy mercy, and grant us Thy salvation.
»⁹I will hear what the Lord God will speak in me: for He will speak peace unto His people: And unto His saints: and unto them that have converted their hearts.
»¹⁰Surely His salvation is near to them that fear Him: that glory may dwell in our land.
¹¹Mercy and truth have met each other: justice and peace have kissed.
»¹²Truth is sprung out of the earth: and justice hath looked down from heaven.
»¹³For the Lord will give goodness: and our earth shall yield her fruit.
¹⁴Justice shall walk before Him: and shall set His steps in the way.

V. *Glory be ...*

Ant 3.

Canticle of Isaiah
(Isa 45:15-26)

Ant 4. **In the Lord all the seed of Israel shall be justified and praised.**

℣erily Thou art a hidden God, the God of Israel the Savior.
¹⁶They are all confounded and ashamed: the makers of errors have left together into confusion.
»¹⁷Israel is saved in the Lord with an eternal salvation: thou shalt not be confounded, and thou shalt not be ashamed for ever and ever.
»¹⁸For thus sayeth the Lord that created the heavens, God Himself that formed the earth, and made it, the very maker thereof: He did not create it in vain: He formed it to be

Friday Lauds I

habitaretur formavit eam: Ego Dóminus, et non est álius.
»[19]Non in abscóndito locútus sum, in loco terræ tenebroso; non dixi sémini Jacob frustra: Quǽrite me: ego Dóminus loquens justítiam, annúntians recta.
»[20]Congregámini, et veníte, et accédite simul qui salváti estis ex géntibus: nesciérunt qui levant lignum sculptúræ suæ, et rogant deum non salvántem.

»[21]Annuntiáte, et veníte, et consiliámini simul. Quis audítum fecit hoc ab inítio, ex tunc prædíxit illud? numquid non ego Dóminus, et non est ultra deus absque me? Deus justus, et salvans non est præter me.
»[22]Convertímini ad me, et salvi éritis, ómnes fines terræ, quia ego Deus, et non est álius.
[23]In memetípso juravi; egrediétur de ore meo justítiæ verbum, et non revertétur.

V. *Glória Patri ...*

Ant 4.

Psalmus 147

Ant 5. Lauda Deum tuum, Sion.

Lauda, Jerúsalem, Dóminum; lauda Deum tuum, Sion.
[13]Quóniam confortávit seras portárum tuárum; benedíxit fíliis tuis in te.

»[14]Qui pósuit fines tuos pacem, et ádipe fruménti sátiat te.
»[15]Qui emíttit elóquium suum terræ: velóciter currit sermo ejus.

inhabited. I am the Lord, and there is no other.
»[19]I have not spoken in secret, in a dark place of the earth: I have not said to the seed of Jacob: seek Me in vain. I am the Lord that speaketh justice, that declareth right things.
»[20]Assemble yourselves, and come, and draw near together, ye that are saved of the Gentiles: they have no knowledge that set up the wood of their graven work, and pray to a god that cannot save.
»[21]Tell ye, and come, and consult together: who hath declared this from the beginning, who hath foretold this from that time? Am I not the Lord, and there is no God else besides Me? A just God and a savior, there is none besides Me.
»[22]Be converted to Me, and ye shall be saved, all ye ends of the earth: for I am God, and there is no other.
[23]I have sworn by Myself, the word of justice shall go out of My mouth, and shall not return.

V. *Glory be ...*

Ant 4.

Psalm 147

Ant 5. Zion, Praise thy God.

Praise the Lord, O Jerusalem: praise Thy God, O Zion:
[13]Because He hath strengthened the bolts of thy gates, He hath blessed thy children within thee:
»[14]Who hath placed peace in thy borders: and filleth thee with the fat of corn:
»[15]Who sendeth forth His speech to the earth: His word runneth swiftly:

Friday Lauds I

¹⁶Qui dat nivem sicut lanam; nebulam sicut cinerem spargit.
»¹⁷Mittit crystallum suam sicut buccellas: ante fáciem frigoris ejus quis sustinebit?

¹⁸Emittet verbum suum, et liquefaciet ea; flabit spíritus ejus, et fluent aquæ.
»¹⁹Qui annuntiat verbum suum Jacob, justítias et judícia sua Israël.
²⁰Non fecit taliter omni nationi, et judícia sua non manifestavit eis.

V. *Glória Patri ...*

Ant 5.

Capitulum
(Rom 13:12-14)
The reading below or the proper of the day

V. Nox præcéssit, dies autem appropinquávit. Abjiciámus ergo ópera tenebrárum, et induámur arma lucis. Sicut in die honéste ambulémus: non in comessationibus, et brietatibus, non in cubílibus, et impudicitiis, non in contentióne, et æmulatióne:

R. Deo grátias.

Hymnus
Or the hymn for the season

Ætérna Cœli Glória,
Beáta spes mortálium,
Summi Tonántis Unice,
Castǽque proles Vírginis:

Da déxteram surgéntibus,
Exsúrgat et mens sóbria,
Flagrans et in laudem Dei
Grates repéndat débitas.

---

¹⁶Who giveth snow like wool and scattereth frost like ashes.
»¹⁷He sendeth His crystal like crumbs: who shall stand before the face of His cold?
¹⁸He shall send out His word, and it shall melt them: His wind shall blow, and the waters shall run:
»¹⁹Who declareth His word to Jacob: His justices and His judgments to Israel.
²⁰He hath not done in like manner to every nation: and His judgments He hath not made manifest to them.

V. *Glory be ...*

Ant 5.

Chapter
(Rom 13:12-14)
The reading below or the proper of the day

V. The night is passed, and the day is at hand. Let us, therefore cast off the works of darkness, and put on the armor of light. Let us walk honestly, as in the day: not in rioting and drunkenness, not in debauchery and impurities, not in contention and envy.

R. Thanks be to God.

Hymn
Or the hymn for the season

O Christ, Whose Glory Fills the Heaven,/ Our only hope, in mercy given;/ Child of a Virgin meek and pure;/ Son of the Highest evermore:

Grant us Thine aid Thy praise to sing,/ As opening days new duties bring;/ That with the light our life may be/ renewed and sanctified by Thee.

Friday Lauds I

Ortus refúlget lúcifer, Præítque solem núntius: Cadunt tenébræ, nóctium: Lux sancta nos illúminet.	The morning star fades from the sky,/ The sun breaks forth; night's shadows fly/ O Thou, true Light, upon us shine:/ Our darkness turn to light divine.
Manénsque nostris sénsibus, Noctem repéllat sǽculi, Omníque fine témporis Purgáta servet péctora.	Within us grant Thy light to dwell;/ And from our souls dark sins expel;/ Cleanse Thou our minds from stain of ill,/ And with Thy peace our bosoms fill.
Quæsíta jam primum fides In corde radíces agat: Secúnda spes congáudeat, Qua major exstat cáritas.	To us strong faith forever give,/ With joyous hope, in Thee to live;/ That life's rough way may ever be/ Made strong and pure by charity.
Deo Patri sit glória, Ejúsque soli Fílio, Cum Spíritu Paráclito, Nunc, et per omne sǽculum	All laud to God the Father be,/ All praise, Eternal Son, to Thee:/ All glory, as is ever meet,/ To God the holy Paraclete.

Versiculi / Versicle

V. Repléti sumus mane miserecórdia tua.
R. Exultávimus, delectáti sumus.

V. We are filled with Thy mercies in the morning.
R. We rejoiced, we were glad.

Ant. Per víscera misericórdiæ Dei nostri visitávit nos Óriens ex alto. *(Whenever possible, the antiphon for the specific season or feast of a saint will be used).*

Ant. Through the depths of the mercy of our God, He hath visited us from on high. *(Whenever possible, the antiphon for the specific season or feast of a saint will be used).*

Cánticum Zachariæ
(Luke 1:68-79)
Find the canticle on page 366

Canticle of Zachariah
(Luke 1:68-79)
Find the canticle on page 366

V. *Glória Patri ...*

V. *Glory be ...*

Ant. Per víscera misericórdiæ Dei nostri visitávit nos Óriens ex alto.

Ant. Through the depths of the mercy of our God, He hath visited us from on high.

V. *Páter nóster ...*
R. *Pánem nóstrum ...*

V. *Our Father ...*
R. *Give us this day ...*

Friday Lauds I

V. Dómine exáudi oratiónem meam.
R. Et clamor meus ad te véniat.

V. Oremus.

Excita, quǽsumus, Dómine, tuórum fidélium voluntátes: ut, divíni óperis fructum propénsius exsequéntes; pietátis tuæ remédia maióra percípiant.
Per Dóminum nostrum. …

The prayer above is said, or the prayer of the season and the feast day are recited if there are any.

V. Dómine exáudi oratiónem meam.
R. Et clamor meus ad te véniat

V. Benedicámus Dómino.
R. Deo grátias.

V. Fidélium ánimæ per misericórdiam Dei requiéscant in pace.

R. Amen.

V. O Lord, hear my prayer.
R. And let my cry come unto Thee.

V. Let us pray.

Arouse, we beseech Thee, Lord, the will of Thy faithful: that carrying out the fruit of the divine work more willingly, they may obtain greater healing by Thy goodness.
Through our Lord …

The prayer above is said, or the prayer of the season and the feast day are recited if there are any.

V. O Lord, hear my prayer.
R. And let my cry come unto Thee.

V. Let us bless the Lord.
R. Thanks be to God.

V. May the souls of the faithful departed through the mercy of God rest in peace.

R. Amen.

Thou hast forgiven the iniquity of Thy people: Thou hast covered all their sins.

SATURDAY – LAUDS

V. Dómine, ✝ lábia mea apéries.
R. Et os meum annuntiábit laudem tuam.

V. Deus, in adjutórium meum inténde.
R. Dómine, ad adjuvándum me festína.

V. *Glória Patri ...*
R. *Sicut erat ...*

Psalmus 149

Ant 1. Fílii Sion exsúltent in Rege suo.

Cantáte Dómino cánticum novum; laus ejus in ecclésia sanctórum.

²Lætétur Israël in eo qui fecit eum, et filii Sion exsultent in rege suo.
»³Laudent nomen ejus in choro; in tympano et psaltério psallant ei.
⁴Quia beneplácitum est Dómino in pópulo suo, et exaltabit mansuetos in salútem.
»⁵Exsultábunt sancti in glória; lætabuntur in cubílibus suis.
⁶Exaltatiónes Dei in gutture eórum, et gládii ancipites in mánibus eórum:
»⁷ad faciendam vindictam in nationibus, increpationes in pópulis;
⁸ad alligandos reges eórum in compedibus, et nobiles eórum in manicis ferréis;
⁹ut faciant in eis judícium conscriptum: glória hæc est ómnibus sanctis ejus.

V. O Lord, ✝ open my lips.
R. And my mouth shall proclaim Thy praise.

V. O God, come to my assistance.
R. O Lord, make haste to help me.

V. *Glory be ...*
R. *As it was ...*

Psalm 149

Ant 1. The children of Zion will rejoice in their King.

Sing ye to the Lord a new canticle: let His praise be in the church of the saints.

²Let Israel rejoice in Him that made us: and let the children of Zion be joyful in their king
»³Let them praise His Name in choir: let them sing to Him with the timbrel and the psaltery.
⁴For the Lord is well pleased with His people: and He will exalt the meek unto salvation.
»⁵The saints shall rejoice in glory: they shall be joyful in their beds.
⁶The high praises of God shall be in their mouth: and two-edged swords in their hands:
»⁷To execute vengeance upon the nations, chastisements among the people:
⁸to bind their kings with fetters, and their nobles with manacles of iron:
⁹to execute upon them the judgment that is written: this glory is to all His saints.

Saturday Lauds I

V. *Glória Patri* …

Ant 1.

Psalmus 91

Ant 2. **Quam magnificáta sunt ópera tua Dómine.**

Bonum est confitéri Dómino, et psallere nómini tuo, Altíssime:
»³ad annuntiándum mane misericórdiam tuam, et veritátem tuam per noctem,
⁴in decachórdo, psaltério; cum cantico, in cíthara.
»⁵Quia delectásti me, Dómine, in factúra tua; et in opéribus mánuum tuárum exsultábo.

⁶Quam magnificáta sunt ópera tua, Dómine! nimis profúndæ factæ sunt cogitatiónes tuæ.
»⁷Vir insípiens non cognóscet, et stultus non intélliget hæc.

⁸Cum exórti fúerint peccatóres sicut fœnum, et apparúerint ómnes qui operántur iniquitátem, ut intéreant in sǽculum sǽculi:

»⁹tu autem Altíssimus in ætérnum, Dómine.
¹⁰Quóniam ecce inimíci tui, Dómine, quóniam ecce inimíci tui períbunt; et dispergéntur ómnes qui operántur iniquitátem.
»¹¹Et exaltábitur sicut unicórnis cornu meum, et senéctus mea in misericórdia úberi.
»¹²Et despéxit óculus meus inimícos meos, et in insurgéntibus in me malignántibus áudiet auris mea.
»¹³Justus ut palma florébit; sicut cedrus Vítulum multiplicábitur.

V. *Glory be* …

Ant 1.

Psalm 91

Ant 2. **How magnificent are Thy works, O Lord.**

It is good to give praise to the Lord: and to sing to Thy Name, O most High:
»³To show forth Thy mercy in the morning, and Thy truth in the night:
⁴upon an instrument of ten strings, upon the psaltery: with a canticle upon the harp.
»⁵For Thou hast given me, O Lord, a delight in Thy doings: and in the works of Thy hands I shall rejoice.
⁶O Lord, how great are Thy works! Thy thoughts are exceedingly deep.

»⁷The foolish man shall not know: nor will the fool understand these things:
⁸when the wicked shall spring up as grass: and all the workers of iniquity shall appear: that they may perish for eternity:
»⁹but Thou, O Lord, art most high for evermore.
¹⁰For behold Thine enemies, O Lord, for behold Thine enemies shall perish: and all the workers of evil shall be scattered.
»¹¹But my horn shall be exalted like that of the wild ox: and my old age in bountiful mercy.
»¹²Mine eye also hath looked down upon mine enemies: and mine ear shall hear of the downfall of the malignant that rise up against me.
»¹³The just shall flourish like the palm tree: they shall grow up like the cedar of Lebanon.

¹⁴Plantáti in domo Dómini, in átriis domus Dei nostri florébunt.

»¹⁵Adhuc multiplicabúntur in senécta úberi, et bene patíentes erunt:
¹⁶ut annúntient quóniam rectus Dóminus Deus noster, et non est iníquitas in eo.

V. *Glória Patri ...*

Ant 2.

Psalmus 63

Ant 3. **Lætábitur justus in Dómino et sperábit in eo.**

Exáudi, Deus, oratiónem meam cum déprecor; a timóre inimíci éripe ánimam meam.
Protexísti me a convéntu malignántium, a multitúdine óperantium iniquitátem.
»⁴Quia exacuérunt ut gládium linguas suas; inténderunt arcum rem amáram,
⁵ut sagíttent in occúltis immaculátum.
»⁶Subito sagittábunt eum, et non timébunt; firmavérunt sibi sermónem nequam. Narravérunt ut abscónderent láqueos; dixérunt: Quis vidébit eos?
»⁷Scrutáti sunt iniquitátes; defecérunt scrutántes scrutínio. Accédet homo ad cor altum,
»⁸et exaltábitur Deus. Sagíttæ parvulórum factæ sunt plagæ eórum,
⁹et infirmátæ sunt contra eos linguæ eórum. Conturbáti sunt ómnes qui vidébant eos,
¹⁰et tímuit omnis homo. Et annuntiavérunt ópera Dei, et facta ejus intellexérunt.

¹⁴They that are planted in the house of the Lord shall flourish in the courts of the house of our God.
»¹⁵They shall still increase and be fruitful in old age: and shall be well treated,
¹⁶that they may show that the Lord our God is righteous, and there is no iniquity in Him.

V. *Glory be ...*

Ant 2.

Psalm 63

Ant 3. **The righteous will rejoice in the Lord and hope in Him.**

Hear, O God, my prayer, when I make supplication to Thee: deliver my soul from the fear of the enemy.
³Thou hast protected me from the assembly of the malignant; from the multitude of the workers of iniquity.
»⁴For they have sharpened their tongues like a sword; they have bent their bow, a poisoned tongue,
⁵to shoot the undefiled in secret.
»⁶They will shoot at them suddenly, and will not fear: they are resolute in wickedness. They have talked of hiding snares; they have said: Who shall see them?
»⁷They have searched after evil things: they have failed in their search. Man shall come to a deep heart, and God shall be exalted.
»⁸The arrows of Him will be their wounds:
⁹and their tongues against them are made weak. All that saw the evil doers were distressed;
¹⁰and every man was afraid. And they praised the works of God: and understood His deeds.

Saturday Lauds I

V. *Glória Patri ...*

Ant 3.

Cánticum Ecclesiastici
(Sir 36:1-16)

Ant 4. Osténde nobis Dómine lucem miseratiónum tuárum.

Miserére nostri, Deus ómnium, et réspice nos, et osténde nobis lucem miseratiónum tuárum: ²et immítte timórem tuum super gentes quæ non exquisiérunt te, ut cognóscant quia non est deus nisi tu, et enárrent magnália tua.

»³Álleva manum tuam super gentes aliénas, ut videánt poténtiam tuam.

⁴Sicut enim in conspéctu eórum sanctificátus es in nobis, sic in conspéctu nostro magnificáberis in eis:
»⁵ut cognóscant te, sicut et nos cognóvimus quóniam non est deus præter te, Dómine.
⁶Ínnova signa, et immúta mirabília.
»⁷Glorífica manum et bráchium dextrum.
⁸Éxcita furórem, et effúnde iram.

»⁹Tolle adversárium, et afflíge inimícum.
¹⁰Festína tempus, et meménto finis, ut enárrent mirabília tua.

»¹¹In ira flammæ devorétur qui salvátur: et qui péssimant plebem tuam invéniant perditiónem.

V. *Glory be ...*

Ant 3.

Canticle of Ecclesiasticus
(Sir 36:1-16)

Ant 4. Show us, O Lord, the light of Thy mercies.

Have mercy upon us, O God of all, and behold us, and show us the light of Thy mercies: ²and send Thy fear upon the nations that have not sought after Thee: that they may know that there is no God besides Thee, and that they may show forth Thy wonders.
»³Lift up Thy hand over the strange nations that they may see Thy power:
⁴for as Thou hast been sanctified in us in their sight, so Thou shalt be glorious among them in our presence:
»⁵that they may know Thee, as we also have known Thee, that there is no God besides Thee, O Lord.
⁶Renew Thy signs, and work new miracles.
»⁷Glorify Thy hand, and Thy right arm.
⁸Raise up Thine indignation, and pour out Thy wrath.
»⁹Take away the adversary, and crush the enemy.
¹⁰Hasten the time, and remember the end, that they may declare Thy wonderful works.
»¹¹Let him that escapeth be consumed by the rage of the fire: and let them perish that oppress Thy people.

Saturday Lauds I

¹²Cóntere caput príncipum inimicórum, dicéntium: Non est álius præter nos.
»¹³Cóngrega ómnes tribus Jacob, ut cognóscant quia non est deus nisi tu, et enárrent magnália tua, et hereditábis eos sicut ab inítio.

»¹⁴Miserére plebi tuæ, super quam invocátum est nomen tuum, et Israël quem coæquásti primogénito tuo.

»¹⁵Miserére civitáti sanctificatiónis tuæ, Jerúsalem, civitáti requiei tuæ.

¹⁶Reple Zion inenarrabílibus verbis tuis, et glória tua pópulum tuum.

V. *Glória Patri ...*

Ant 4.

Psalmus 150

Ant 5. Omnis spíritus laudet Dóminum.

Laudáte Dóminum in sanctis ejus; laudáte eum in firmaménto virtútis ejus.
»²Laudáte eum in virtútibus ejus; laudáte eum secúndum multitúdinem magnitúdinis ejus.
»³Laudáte eum in sono tubæ; laudáte eum in psaltério et cíthara.

»⁴Laudáte eum in týmpano et choro; laudáte eum in chordis et órgano.
»⁵Laudáte eum in cýmbalis benesonántibus; laudáte eum in cýmbalis jubilatiónis. Omnis spíritus laudet Dóminum!

V. *Glória Patri ...*

---

¹²Crush the head of the princes of the enemies that say: There is no other besides us.
»¹³Gather together all the tribes of Jacob: that they may know that there is no God besides Thee, and may declare Thy great works: and Thou shalt inherit them as from the beginning.
»¹⁴Have mercy on Thy people, upon whom Thy Name is invoked: and upon Israel, whom Thou hast raised up to be Thy firstborn.
»¹⁵Have mercy on Jerusalem, the city which Thou hast sanctified: the city of Thy rest.
¹⁶Fill Zion with Thine unspeakable words, and Thy people with Thy glory.

V. *Glory be ...*

Ant 4.

Psalm 150

Ant 5. Let all spirits praise the Lord.

Praise ye the Lord in His holy places: praise ye Him in the firmament of His power.
»²Praise ye Him for His mighty acts: praise ye Him according to the multitude of His greatness.
»³Praise ye Him with the sound of trumpet: praise ye Him with psaltery and harp.
»⁴Praise ye Him with timbrel and choir: praise ye Him with strings and organs.
»⁵Praise ye Him on high sounding cymbals: praise Him on cymbals of joy: let every spirit praise the Lord.

V. *Glory be ...*

Saturday Lauds I

Ant 5.

Capitulum
(Sir 24:14)

V. Ab inítio, et ante sǽcula creáta sum, et usque ad futúrum sǽculum non désinam, et in habitatióne sancta coram ipso ministrávi.

R. Deo Grátias.

Hymnus
Or the hymn for the season

O Gloriósa Vírginum,
Sublímis inter sídera,
Qui te creávit, párvulum
Lacenténte nutris úbere.

Quod Heva tristis ábstulit,
Tu reddis almo gérmine:
Intrent ut astra flébiles,
Cæli reclúdis cárdines.

Tu regis alti jánua,
Et aula lucis fúlgida:
Vitam datam per Vírginem
Gentes redémptæ pláudit.

Jesu tibi sit glória, Qui natus es de Vírgine, Cum Patre, et almo Spíritu in sempitérna sǽcula.

Versiculi

V. Benedícta tu in muliéribus.
R. Et benedíctus fructus ventris tui.

Ant 5.

Chapter
(Sir 24:14)

V. I was created from the beginning and before the ages, and I will not cease until the age to come, and I ministered before Him in the holy dwellings.

R. Thanks be to God.

Hymn
Or the hymn for the season

O Glorious Lady! Throned on High/
Above the star-illumined sky;/
Thereto ordained, Thy bosom lent/
To thy Creator nourishment.

Through thy sweet Offspring we receive/ The bliss once lost through hapless Eve;/ And Heaven to mortals open lies./ Now thou art Portal of the skies.

Thou art the Door of Heaven's high King,/ light's gateway fair and glistering;/ Life through a Virgin is restored;/ Ye ransomed nations, praise the Lord!

All honor, laud, and glory be,/
O Jesu, Virgin-born to Thee;/
All glory, as is ever meet,/
To Father and to Paraclete.

Versicle

V. Blessed art thou among women.
R. And blessed is the fruit of thy womb.

Saturday Lauds I

Ant. In sanctitáte serviámus Dómino, et liberábit nos ab inimícis nostris. *(Whenever possible, the antiphon for the specific season or feast of a saint will be used).*

Canticle of Zacharia
(Luke 1:68-79)
Canticle on page 366

V. *Glory be ...*

Ant. In sanctitáte serviámus Dómino, et liberábit nos ab inimícis nostris.

V. *Páter nóster ...*
R. *Pánem nóstrum ...*

V. Dómine exáudi oratiónem meam.
R. Et clamor meus ad te véniat.

V. Orémus.

Concéde nos fámulos tuos, quǽsumus Dómine Deus, perpétua méntis et córporis sanitáte gaudére: et gloriósa Beátæ Maríæ semper Vírginis intercessióne, a præsénti liberári tristítia, et ætérna pérfrui lætítia. Per Dóminum nóstrum ...

The prayer above is said, or the prayer of the season and the feast day are recited if there are any.

V. Dómine exáudi oratiónem meam.
R. Et clamor meus ad te véniat.

V. Benedicámus Dómino.
R. Deo grátias.

V. Fidélium ánimæ per misericórdiam Dei requiéscant in pace.

R. Amen.

Ant. Let us serve the Lord in holiness, and He will deliver us from our enemies. *(Whenever possible, the antiphon for the specific season or feast of a saint will be used).*

Canticle of Zachariah
(Luke 1:68-79)
Canticle on page 366

V. *Glory be ...*

Ant. Let us serve the Lord in holiness, and He will deliver us from our enemies.

V. *Our Father ...*
R. *Give us this day ...*

V. O Lord, hear my prayer.
R. And let my cry come unto Thee.

V. Let us pray.

Grant us Thy servants, we beseech Thee, Lord God, to enjoy perpetual health of mind and body: and through the glorious intercession of the Blessed Mary, ever Virgin, to be delivered from present sorrow, and to enjoy eternal happiness. Through our Lord ...

The prayer above is said, or the prayer of the season and the feast day are recited if there are any.

V. O Lord, Hear my prayer.
R. And let my cry come unto Thee.

V. Let us bless the Lord.
R. Thanks be to God.

V. May the souls of the faithful departed through the mercy of God rest in peace.

R. Amen.

Saturday Lauds I

 # Sunday – Lauds II

V. Dómine, ☩ lábia mea apéries.
R. Et os meum annuntiábit laudem tuam.

V. Deus, in adjutórium meum inténde.
R. Dómine, ad adjuvándum me festína.

V. Glória Patri ...
R. Sicut erat ...

V. O Lord, ☩ open my lips.
R. And my mouth shall proclaim Thy praise.

V. O God, come to my assistance.
R. O Lord, make haste to help me.

V. Glory be ...
R. As it was ...

Psalmus 50

Ant 1. Miserére mei Deus, et a delicto meo munda me: quia tibi soli peccávi.

Miserére mei, Deus, secúndum magnam misericórdiam tuam; et secúndum multitúdinem miseratiónum tuárum, dele iniquitátem meam.
⁴Ámplius lava me ab iniquitáte mea, et a peccáto meo munda me.

»⁵Quóniam iniquitátem meam ego cognósco, et peccátum meum contra me est semper.

⁶Tibi soli peccávi, et malum coram te feci; ut justificéris in sermónibus tuis, et vincas cum judicáris.
»⁷Ecce enim in iniquitátibus concéptus sum, et in peccátis concépit me mater mea.
⁸Ecce enim veritátem dilexísti; incérta et occúlta sapiéntiæ tuæ manifestasti mihi.

»⁹Aspérges me hyssópo, et mundábor; lavábis me, et super nivem dealbábor.

Psalm 50

Ant 1. Have mercy on me, God, and cleanse me from my transgression: for I have sinned against Thee alone.

Have mercy on me, O God, according to Thy great compassion. And according to the multitude of Thy tender mercies blot out my iniquity.
⁴Wash me yet more from my iniquity, and cleanse me from my sin.

»⁵For I know my wickedness, and my sin is always before me.
⁶To Thee only have I sinned, and have done evil before Thee: that Thou mayst be justified in Thy words, and mayest be blameless when Thou judgeth.
»⁷For behold I was conceived with iniquities; and in sin did my mother conceive me.
⁸For behold Thou hast loved truth: the uncertain and hidden things of Thy wisdom Thou hast made manifest to me.

»⁹Thou shalt sprinkle me with hyssop, and I shall be cleansed: Thou shalt wash me, and I shall be made whiter than snow.

¹⁰Audítui meo dabis gáudium et lætítiam, et exsultábunt ossa humiliáta.	¹⁰To my hearing Thou shalt give joy and gladness: and the bones that have been humbled shall rejoice.
»¹¹Avérte fáciem tuam a peccátis meis, et ómnes iniquitátes meas dele.	»¹¹Turn away Thy face from my sins, and blot out all my iniquities.
¹²Cor mundum crea in me, Deus, et spíritum rectum ínnova in viscéribus meis.	¹²Create a clean heart in me, O God: and renew a right spirit within my bowels.
»¹³Ne projícias me a fácie tua, et spíritum sanctum tuum ne áuferas a me.	»¹³Cast me not away from Thy face; and take not Thy Holy Spirit from me.
¹⁴Redde mihi lætítiam salutáris tui, et spíritu principáli confírma me.	¹⁴Restore unto me the joy of Thy salvation, and strengthen me with a perfect spirit.
»¹⁵Docébo iníquos vias tuas, et ímpii ad te converténtur.	»¹⁵I will teach the unjust Thy ways: and the wicked shall be converted to Thee.
¹⁶Líbera me de sanguínibus, Deus, Deus salútis meæ, et exsultábit lingua mea justítiam tuam	¹⁶Deliver me from blood, O God, Thou God of my salvation: and my tongue shall extol Thy justice.
»¹⁷Dómine, lábia mea apéries, et os meum annuntiábit laudem tuam.	»¹⁷O Lord, Thou wilt open my lips: and my mouth shall declare Thy praise.
¹⁸Quóniam si voluísses sacrifícium, dedissem útique; holocáustis non delectáberis.	¹⁸For if Thou hadst desired sacrifice, I would indeed have given it: but with burnt offerings Thou wilt not be delighted.
»¹⁹Sacrifícium Deo spíritus contribulátus; cor contrítum et humiliátum, Deus, non despícies.	»¹⁹A sacrifice to God is an afflicted spirit: a contrite and humbled heart, O God, Thou wilt not despise.
²⁰Benígne fac, Dómine, in bona voluntáte tua Sion, ut ædificéntur muri Jerúsalem.	²⁰Deal favorably, O Lord, in Thy good will with Zion; that the walls of Jerusalem may be rebuilt.
»²¹Tunc acceptábis sacrifícium justítiæ, oblatiónes et holocáusta; tunc impónent super altáre tuum vítulos.	»²¹Then shalt Thou accept the sacrifice of justice, oblations and whole burnt offerings: then shall they lay calves upon Thine altar.
V. *Glória Patri* ...	V. *Glory be* ...
Ant 1.	Ant 1.

Psalmus 117 | ## Psalm 117

Ant 2. **Bonum est speráre in Dómino, quam speráre in princípibus.** | Ant 2. **It is good to trust in the Lord, rather than to trust in princes.**

Sunday Lauds II

Confitémini Dómino, quóniam bonus, quóniam in sǽculum misericórdia ejus.
²Dicat nunc Israël: Quóniam bonus, quóniam in sǽculum misericórdia ejus.
»³Dicat nunc domus Aaron: Quóniam in sǽculum misericórdia ejus.
⁴Dicant nunc qui timent Dóminum: Quóniam in sǽculum misericórdia ejus.
»⁵De tribulatióne invocávi Dóminum, et exaudívit me in latitúdine Dóminus.
⁶Dóminus mihi adjútor; non timébo quid fáciat mihi homo.
»⁷Dóminus mihi adjútor, et ego despiciam inimícos meos.
⁸Bonum est confídere in Dómino, quam confídere in hómine.

»⁹Bonum est speráre in Dómino, quam speráre in princípibus.
¹⁰Ómnes gentes circuiérunt me, et in nómine Dómini, quia ultus sum in eos.
»¹¹Circumdántes circumdedérunt me, et in nómine Dómini, quia ultus sum in eos.
¹²Circumdedérunt me sicut apes, et exarsérunt sicut ignis in spinis: et in nómine Dómini, quia ultus sum in eos.
¹³Impúlsus evérsus sum, ut cáderem, et Dóminus suscépit me.
»¹⁴Fortitúdo mea et laus mea Dóminus, et factus est mihi in salútem.

»¹⁵Vox exsultatiónis et salútis in tabernáculis justórum.

ive praise to the Lord, for He is good: for His mercy endureth for ever.
²Let Israel now say, that He is good: that His mercy endureth for ever.
»³Let the house of Aaron now say, that His mercy endureth for ever.

⁴Let them that fear the Lord now say, that His mercy endureth for ever.

»⁵In my trouble I called upon the Lord: and the Lord heard me, and delivered me.
⁶The Lord is my helper: I will not fear what man can do unto me.
»⁷The Lord is my helper: and I will look down on mine enemies.
⁸It is good to confide in the Lord, rather than to have confidence in man.
»⁹It is good to trust in the Lord, rather than to trust in princes.
¹⁰All nations compassed me about; and in the Name of the Lord I have been revenged on them.
»¹¹Surrounding me they compassed me about: and in the Name of the Lord I have been revenged on them.
¹²They surrounded me like bees, and they burned like fire among thorns: and in the Name of the Lord I was revenged on them.
»¹³Being pushed I was overturned that I might fall: but the Lord supported me.
¹⁴The Lord is my strength and my praise: and He has become my salvation.
»¹⁵The voice of rejoicing and of salvation is in the tabernacles of the just.

Sunday Lauds II

¹⁶Déxtera Dómini fecit virtútem; déxtera Dómini exaltávit me: déxtera Dómini fecit virtútem.

»¹⁷Non móriar, sed vivam, et narrábo ópera Dómini.
¹⁸Castígans castigávit me Dóminus, et morti non trádidit me.

»¹⁹Aperíte mihi portas justítiæ: ingréssus in eas confitébor Dómino.

²⁰Hæc porta Dómini: justi intrábunt in eam.
²¹Confitébor tibi quóniam exaudísti me, et factus es mihi in salútem.

»²²Lápidem quem reprobavérunt ædificántes, hic factus est in caput ánguli.
²³A Dómino factum est istud, et est mirábile in óculis nostris.

»²⁴Hæc est dies quam fecit Dóminus; exsultémus, et lætémur in ea.
²⁵O Dómine, salvum me fac; o Dómine, bene prosperáre.
»²⁶Benedíctus qui venit in nómine Dómini: benedíximus vobis de domo Dómini.
²⁷Deus Dóminus, et illuxit nobis. Constitúite diem solémnem in condénsis, usque ad cornu altáris.

»²⁸Deus meus es tu, et confitébor tibi; Deus meus es tu, et exaltábo te. Confitébor tibi quóniam exaudísti me, et factus es mihi in salútem.

²⁹Confitémini Dómino, quóniam bonus, quóniam in sǽculum misericórdia ejus.

V. *Glória Patri ...*

¹⁶The right hand of the Lord hath wrought strength: the right hand of the Lord hath exalted me: the right hand of the Lord hath wrought strength.

»¹⁷I shall not die, but live: and shall declare the works of the Lord.
¹⁸The Lord chastising hath chastised me: but He hath not delivered me over to death.

»¹⁹Open ye to me the gates of justice: I will go in to them, and give praise to the Lord.

²⁰This is the gate of the Lord, the just shall enter into it.
²¹I will give glory to Thee because Thou hast heard me: and hast become my salvation.

»²²The stone which the builders rejected; the same hath become the cornerstone.
²³This is the Lord's doing: and it is wonderful in our eyes.

»²⁴This is the day which the Lord hath made: let us be glad and rejoice therein.
²⁵O Lord, save me: O Lord, give good success.
»²⁶Blessed be He that cometh in the Name of the Lord. We have blessed Thee out of the house of the Lord.
²⁷The Lord is God, and He hath shone upon us. Appoint a solemn procession, with leafy boughs, even to the horn of the altar.

»²⁸Thou art my God, and I will praise Thee: Thou art my God, and I will exalt Thee. I will praise Thee, because Thou hast heard me, and hast become my salvation.

²⁹O praise ye the Lord, for He is good: for His mercy endureth for ever.

V. *Glory be ...*

Sunday Lauds II

Ant. 2.

Psalmus 62

Ant 3. Me suscépit déxtera tua Dómine.

Deus, Deus meus, ad te de luce vígilo. Sitívit in te ánima mea; quam multiplíciter tibi caro mea!

²In terra desérta, et invia, et inaquósa, sic in sancto appárui tibi, ut vidérem virtútem tuam et glóriam tuam.
»³Quóniam mélior est misericórdia tua super vitas, lábia mea laudábunt te.
⁴Sic benedícam te in vita mea, et in nómine tuo levábo manus meas.

»⁵Sicut ádipe et pinguédine repleátur ánima mea, et lábiis exsultatiónis laudábit os meum.
⁶Si memor fui tui super stratum meum, in matutínis meditábor in te.

»⁷Quia fuísti adjútor meus, et in velaménto alárum tuárum exsultábo.

⁸Adhǽsit ánima mea post te; me suscépit déxtera tua.
»⁹Ipsi vero in vanum quæsiérunt ánimam meam: introíbunt in inferióra terræ;
¹⁰Tradéntur in manus gládii: partes vúlpium erunt.
»¹¹Rex vero lætábitur in Deo; laudabúntur ómnes qui jurant in eo: quia obstrúctum est os loquéntium iníqua.

V. *Glória Patri ...*

Ant. 2.

Psalm 62

Ant 3. Thy right hand received me, O Lord.

O God, my God, to Thee do I watch at break of day. For Thee my soul hath thirsted; for Thee my flesh, O how many ways!
²In a desert land, and where there is no path, and no water: so in the sanctuary have I come before Thee, to see Thy power and Thy glory.
»³For Thy mercy is better than life: Thee my lips shall praise.
⁴Thus will I bless Thee all my life long: and in Thy Name I will lift up my hands.
»⁵Let my soul be filled as with marrow and fatness: and my mouth shall praise Thee with joyful lips.
⁶If I have thought about Thee upon my bed, I will meditate on Thee in the morning hours:
»⁷because Thou hast been my helper. And I will rejoice under the covert of Thy wings:
⁸my soul held fast to Thee: Thy right hand hath received me.
»⁹But they have sought my soul in vain, they shall go into the depths of the earth.
¹⁰They shall be delivered into the hands of the sword, they shall be the prey of foxes.
»¹¹But the king shall rejoice in God, all they that swear by Him shall be praised: because the speech of them that speak wicked things is silenced.

V. *Glory be ...*

Sunday Lauds II

Ant 3.

Dan 3:52-57

Ant 4. Potens es Dómine erípere nos de manu forti: líbera nos Deus noster.

Benedíctus es, Dómine Deus patrum nostrórum: et laudábilis, et gloriósus, et superexaltátus in sǽcula. Et benedíctum nomen glóriæ tuæ sanctum: et laudábile, et superexaltátum in ómnibus sǽculis.

»⁵³Benedíctus es in templo sancto glóriæ tuæ: et superlaudábilis, et supergloriósus in sǽcula.

⁵⁴Benedíctus es in throno regni tui: et superlaudábilis, et superexaltátus in sǽcula.

»⁵⁵Benedíctus es, qui intuéris abyssos, et sedes super cherubim: et laudábilis, et superexaltátus in sǽcula.
⁵⁶Benedíctus es in firmaménto cæli: et laudábilis et gloriósus in sǽcula.

»⁵⁷Benedícite, ómnia ópera Dómini, Dómino: laudáte et superexaltáte eum in sǽcula.

V. *Glória Patri ...*

Ant 4.

Psalmus 148

Ant 5. Reges terræ et ómnes pópuli laudáte Deum.

Laudáte Dóminum de cælis; laudáte eum in excélsis.

Ant 3.

Dan 3:52-57

Ant 4. **Thou art mighty, O Lord, to deliver us from the hand of the powerful: deliver us, our God.**

Blessed art Thou, O Lord the God of our fathers: and worthy to be praised, and glorified, and exalted above all for ever: and blessed is the Holy Name of Thy glory: and worthy to be praised, and exalted above all in all ages.

»⁵³Blessed art Thou in the holy temple of Thy glory: and greatly to be praised, and exceedingly glorious for ever.

»⁵⁴Blessed art Thou on the throne of Thy Kingdom, and exceedingly to be praised, and exalted above all for ever.

»⁵⁵Blessed art Thou that beholdest the depths, and sittest upon the cherubims: and worthy to be praised and exalted above all for ever.

»⁵⁶Blessed art Thou in the firmament of heaven: and worthy of praise, and glorious for ever.

»⁵⁷All ye works of the Lord, bless the Lord: praise and exalt Him above all for ever.

V. *Glory be ...*

Ant 4.

Psalm 148

Ant 5. **Praise God, kings of the earth and all the peoples.**

Praise ye the Lord from the heavens: praise ye Him in the heights.

Sunday Lauds II

²Laudáte eum, ómnes ángeli ejus; laudáte eum, ómnes virtútes ejus.
»³Laudáte eum, sol et luna; laudáte eum, ómnes stellæ et lumen.
⁴Laudáte eum, cæli cælórum; et aquæ ómnes quæ super cælos sunt,
»⁵laudent nomen Dómini. Quia ipse dixit, et facta sunt; ipse mandávit, et creáta sunt. sǽculum sǽculi; præcéptum posuit, et non præteríbit.
⁶ Statuit ea in ætérnum, et in sǽculum sǽculi; præcéptum posuit, et non præteríbit.
»⁷Laudáte Dóminum de terra, dracónes et ómnes abýssi;
⁸ignis, grando, nix, glácies, spíritus procellárum, quæ fáciunt verbum ejus;

»⁹montes, et ómnes colles; ligna fructífera, et ómnes cedri;
¹⁰bestiæ, et univérsa pécora; serpéntes, et vólucres pennátæ;
»¹¹reges terræ et ómnes pópuli; príncipes et ómnes júdices terræ;
¹²júvenes et vírgines; senes cum junióribus, laudent nomen Dómini:
¹³quia exaltátum est nomen ejus solius.
»¹⁴Conféssio ejus super cælum et terram; et exaltávit cornu pópuli sui. Hymnus ómnibus sanctis ejus; filiis Israël, pópulo appropinquánti sibi.

V. *Glória Patri ...*

Ant 5.

Capitulum
(Apoc 7:12)
The reading below or the proper of the day

V. Benedíctio, et cláritas, et sapiéntia, et gratiárum áctio, honor,

²Praise ye Him, all His angels, praise ye Him, all His hosts.
»³Praise ye Him, O sun and moon: praise Him, all ye stars and light.
⁴Praise Him, ye heaven of heavens: and let all the waters that are above the heavens praise the Name of the Lord.
»⁵For He spoke, and they were made: He commanded, and they were created.
⁶He hath established them for ever, and for ages of ages: He hath made a decree, and it shall not pass away.
»⁷Praise the Lord from the earth, ye dragons, and all ye deeps:
⁸fire, hail, snow, ice, stormy winds, which fulfil His word:
»⁹mountains and all hills, fruitful trees and all cedars:
¹⁰beasts and all cattle: serpents and feathered fowls:

»¹¹kings of the earth and all people: princes and all judges of the earth:
¹²young men and maidens: let the old with the young, praise the Name of the Lord:
¹³for His Name alone is exalted.
»¹⁴The praise of Him is above heaven and earth: and He hath exalted the horn of His people. A hymn to all His saints to the children of Israel, a people near to Him.

V. *Glory be ...*

Ant 5.

Chapter
(Apoc 7:12)
The reading below or the proper of the day

V. Blessings, and glory, and wisdom, and thanksgiving, honor,

Sunday Lauds II

virtus, et fortitúdo Deo nostro in sǽcula sæculórum.

R. Deo grátias.

Hymnus

Ætérne Rerum Condítor on page 7 of Lauds I or the hymn for the season

Versiculi

V. Dómine refúgium factus es nobis.

R. A generatióne et progenie.

Ant. Eréxit nobis Dóminus cornu salútis in domo, David púeri sui, **allelúja.** *(Whenever possible, the antiphon for the specific Sunday, season or feast of a saint will be used).*

Cánticum Zachariæ
(Luke 1:68-79)
Canticle on page 366

V. *Glória Patri ...*

Ant. Eréxit nobis Dóminus cornu salútis in domo, David púeri sui, allelúja.

V. *Páter nóster ...*
R. *Pánem nóstrum ...*

V. Dómine exáudi oratiónem meam.
R. Et clamor meus ad te véniat.

---

and power, and strength to our God for ever and ever.

R. Thanks be to God.

Hymn

Maker of All, Eternal King on page 7 Lauds I or the hymn for the season

Versicle

V. Lord, Thou hast become a refuge for us.

R. By generation and posterity.

Ant. The Lord hath raised up a horn of salvation for us, in the house of His servant David, alleluia. *(Whenever possible, the antiphon for the specific season or feast of a saint will be used).*

Canticle of Zachariah
(Luke 1:68-79)
Canticle on page 366

V. *Glory be ...*

Ant. The Lord has raised up a horn of salvation for us, in the house of His servant David, alleluia.

V. *Our Father ...*
R. *Give us this day ...*

V. O Lord, hear my prayer.
R. And let my cry come unto Thee.

V. Oremus.

Largíre nobis, quǽsumus Dómine, semper spíritum cogitándi quæ recta sunt, propítius et agéndi: ut qui sine te esse non póssumus, secúndum te vívere valeámus. Per Dóminum nostrum ...

R. Amen.

The prayer above is said, or the prayer of the season and the feast day are prayed if there are any.

V. Dómine exáudi oratiónem meam.
R. Et clamor meus ad te véniat.

V. Benedicámus Dómino.
R. Deo grátias.

V. Fidélium ánimæ per misericórdiam Dei requiéscant in pace.

R. Amen.

V. Let us pray.

Give us always, we beseech Thee, O Lord, the spirit of thinking what is right, and of acting more acceptably: since we cannot exist without Thee, and that we may live according to Thy will. Through our Lord ...

R. Amen.

The prayer above is said, or the prayer of the season and the feast day are prayed if there are any.

V. O Lord, hear my prayer.
R. And let my cry come unto Thee.

V. Let us bless the Lord.
R. Thanks be to God.

V. May the souls of the faithful departed through the mercy of God rest in peace.

R. Amen.

ISAIAH

Be converted to Me, and you shall be saved, all ye ends of the earth: for I am God, and there is no other.

MONDAY – LAUDS II

V. Dómine, ✝ lábia mea apéries.
R. Et os meum annuntiábit laudem tuam.

V. Deus, in adjutórium meum inténde.
R. Dómine, ad adjuvándum me festína.

V. *Glória Patri ...*
R. *Sicut erat ...*

V. O Lord, ✝ open my lips.
R. And my mouth shall proclaim Thy praise.

V. O God, come to my assistance.
R. O Lord, make haste to help me.

V. *Glory be ...*
R. *As it was ...*

Psalmus 50

Ant 1. Miserére mei Deus secúndum magnam misericórdiam tuam.

Miserére mei, Deus, secúndum magnam misericórdiam tuam; et secúndum multitúdinem miseratiónum tuárum, dele iniquitátem meam.
⁴Ámplius lava me ab iniquitáte mea, et a peccáto meo munda me.
»⁵Quóniam iniquitátem meam ego cognósco, et peccátum meum contra me est semper.
⁶Tibi soli peccávi, et malum coram te feci; ut justificéris in sermónibus tuis, et vincas cum judicáris.
»⁷Ecce enim in iniquitátibus concéptus sum, et in peccátis concépit me mater mea.
»⁸Ecce enim veritátem dilexísti; incérta et occúlta sapiéntiæ tuæ manifestásti mihi.
⁹Aspérges me hyssópo, et mundábor; lavábis me, et super nivem dealbábor.

Psalm 50

Ant 1. Have mercy on me, O God, according to Thy great mercy.

Have mercy on me, O God, according to Thy great compassion. And according to the multitude of Thy tender mercies blot out my iniquity.
⁴Wash me yet more from my iniquity, and cleanse me from my sin.
»⁵For I know my wickedness, and my sin is always before me.
⁶To Thee only have I sinned, and have done evil before Thee: that Thou mayst be justified in Thy words, and mayst be blameless when Thou judgeth.
»⁷For behold I was conceived with iniquities; and in sin did my mother conceive me.
»⁸For behold Thou hast loved truth: the uncertain and hidden things of Thy wisdom Thou hast made manifest to me.
⁹Thou shalt sprinkle me with hyssop, and I shall be cleansed: Thou shalt wash me, and I shall be made whiter than snow.

Monday Lauds II

»¹⁰Audítui meo dabis gáudium et lætítiam, et exsultábunt ossa humiliáta.

¹¹Avérte fáciem tuam a peccátis meis, et ómnes iniquitátes meas dele.
»¹²Cor mundum crea in me, Deus, et spíritum rectum ínnova in viscéribus meis.
¹³Ne projícias me a fácie tua, et spíritum sanctum tuum ne áuferas a me.
»¹⁴Redde mihi lætítiam salutáris tui, et spíritu principáli confírma me.

¹⁵Docébo iníquos vias tuas, et impii ad te converténtur.

»¹⁶Líbera me de sanguínibus, Deus, Deus salútis meæ, et exsultábit lingua mea justítiam tuam.
¹⁷Dómine, lábia mea áperies, et os meum annuntiábit laudem tuam.

»¹⁸Quóniam si voluísses sacrifícium, dedíssem útique; holocáustis non delectáberis.

¹⁹Sacrifícium Deo spíritus contribulátus; cor contrítum et humiliátum, Deus, non despícies.
²⁰Benígne fac, Dómine, in bona voluntáte tua Sion, ut ædificéntur muri Jerúsalem.
»²¹Tunc acceptábis sacrifícium justítiæ, oblatiónes et holocáusta; tunc impónent super altáre tuum vítulos.

V. *Glória Patri* ...

Ant 1.

»¹⁰To my hearing Thou shalt give joy and gladness: and the bones that have been humbled shall rejoice.
¹¹Turn away Thy face from my sins, and blot out all my iniquities.
»¹²Create a clean heart in me, O God: and renew a right spirit within my bowels.
¹³Cast me not away from Thy face; and take not Thy Holy Spirit from me.

»¹⁴Restore unto me the joy of Thy salvation, and strengthen me with a perfect spirit.
¹⁵I will teach the unjust Thy ways: and the wicked shall be converted to Thee.

»¹⁶Deliver me from blood, O God, Thou God of my salvation: and my tongue shall extol Thy justice.
¹⁷O Lord, Thou wilt open my lips: and my mouth shall declare Thy praise.

»¹⁸For if Thou hadst desired sacrifice, I would indeed have given it: but with burnt offerings Thou wilt not be delighted.
¹⁹A sacrifice to God is an afflicted spirit: a contrite and humbled heart, O God, Thou wilt not despise.
²⁰Deal favorably, O Lord, in Thy good will with Zion; that the walls of Jerusalem may be rebuilt.
»²¹Then shalt Thou accept the sacrifice of justice, oblations and whole burnt offerings: then shall they lay calves upon Thine altar.

V. *Glory be* ...

Ant 1.

Psalmus 5

Ant 2. Deduc me in justítia tua Dómine.

Verba mea áuribus pércipe, Dómine; intéllige clamórem meum.
³Inténde voci oratiónis meæ, rex meus et Deus meus.
»⁴Quóniam ad te orábo, Dómine: mane exáudies vocem meam.
⁵Mane astábo tibi, et vidébo quóniam non Deus volens iniquitátem tu es.
»⁶Neque habitábit juxta te malígnus, neque permanébunt injústi ante óculos tuos.
»⁷Odísti ómnes qui operántur iniquitátem; perdes ómnes qui loquúntur mendácium. Virum sánguinum et dolósum abominábitur Dóminus.
»⁸Ego autem in multitúdine misericórdiæ tuæ introíbo in domum tuam; adorábo ad templum sanctum tuum in timóre tuo.
»⁹Dómine, deduc me in justítia tua: propter inimícos meos dírige in conspéctu tuo viam meam.
¹⁰Quóniam non est in ore eórum véritas; cor eórum vanum est.
»¹¹Sepúlchrum patens est guttur eórum; linguis suis dolóse agebant: júdica illos, Deus. Décidant a cogitatiónibus suis; secúndum multitúdinem impietátum eórum expélle eos, quóniam irritavérunt te, Dómine.
»¹²Et læténtur ómnes qui sperant in te; in ætérnum exsultábunt, et habitábis in eis. Et gloriabúntur in te ómnes qui díligunt nomen tuum,

Psalm 5

Ant 2. Lead me into Thy righteousness, O Lord.

Give ear, O Lord, to my words, understand my cry.
³Hearken to the sound of my prayer, O my King and my God.
»⁴For to Thee will I pray: O Lord, in the morning Thou shalt hear my voice.
⁵In the morning I will stand before Thee, and will see: because Thou art not a God that willest iniquity.
»⁶Neither shall the wicked dwell near Thee: nor shall the unjust abide before Thine eyes.
»⁷Thou hatest all the workers of iniquity: Thou wilt destroy all that speak a lie. The bloody and the deceitful man the Lord will abhor.
»⁸But as for me in the multitude of Thy mercy, I will come into Thy house; I will worship towards Thy holy temple, in Thy fear.
»⁹Conduct me, O Lord, in Thy justice: because of mine enemies, direct my way in Thy sight:
¹⁰for there is no truth in their mouths; their hearts are vain.
»¹¹Their throat is an open sepulchre: they speak deceitfully with their tongues: judge them, O God. Let them perish from their plans: according to their great wickednesses cast them out: for they have rebelled against Thee, O Lord.
»¹²But let all them be glad that hope in Thee: they shall rejoice for ever, and Thou shalt dwell in them. And all they that love Thy Name shall glory in Thee.

Monday Lauds II

»¹³quóniam tu benedíces justo. Dómine, ut scuto bonæ voluntátis tuæ coronásti nos.

V. *Glória Patri* ...

Ant 2.

Psalmus 28

Ant 3. **Dóminus dabit virtútem et benedícet pópulo suo in pace.**

fférte Dómino, filii Dei, afférte Dómino filios aríetum.

²Afférte Dómino glóriam et honórem; afférte Dómino glóriam nómini ejus; adoráte Dóminum in átrio sancto ejus.
»³Vox Dómini super aquas; Deus majestátis intónuit: Dóminus super aquas multas.
⁴Vox Dómini in virtúte; vox Dómini in magnificéntia.

»⁵Vox Dómini confringéntis cedros, et confrínget Dóminus cedros Líbani:

⁶et commínuet eas, tamquam vítulum Vítulum, et diléctus quemádmodum fílius unicórnium.
»⁷Vox Dómini intercidéntis flammam ignis;
⁸vox Dómini concutiéntis desértum: et commovébit Dóminus desértum Cades.
⁹Vox Dómini præparántis cervos: et revelábit condénsa, et in templo ejus ómnes dicent glóriam.

»¹⁰Dóminus dilúvium inhabitáre facit, et sedébit Dóminus rex in ætérnum.

»¹³For Thou wilt bless the just. O Lord, Thou hast crowned us, as with a shield of Thy good will.

V. *Glory be* ...

Ant 2.

Psalm 28

Ant 3. **The Lord wilt give strength and bless His people in peace.**

Bring to the Lord, O ye children of God: bring to the Lord the offspring of rams.
²Bring to the Lord glory and honor: bring to the Lord glory to His Name: adore ye the Lord in His holy court.
»³The voice of the Lord is upon the waters; the God of majesty hath thundered, The Lord is upon many waters.
⁴The voice of the Lord is in power; the voice of the Lord is magnificent.

»⁵The voice of the Lord breaketh the cedars: yea, the Lord shall break the cedars of Lebanon:
⁶and shall reduce them to pieces. He maketh Lebanon skip like a calf and Sirion like a young wild ox.
»⁷The voice of the Lord divideth the flame of fire.
⁸The voice of the Lord shaketh the desert: and the Lord shalt shake the desert of Cades.
⁹The voice of the Lord twisteth the oaks and stripeth the forests bare: and in His temple all shall speak His glory.

»¹⁰The Lord dwelleth above the flood: and the Lord shall sit enthroned as king for ever.

¹¹Dóminus virtútem pópulo suo dabit; Dóminus benedícet pópulo suo in pace.

V. *Glória Patri ...*

Ant 3.

Canticle of Isaias
(Isa 12:1-6)

Ant 4. Convérsus est furor tuus Dómine, et consolátus es me.

Et dices in die illa: Confitébor tibi, Dómine, quóniam iratus es mihi; convérsus est furor tuus, et consolátus es me.
»²Ecce Deus salvátor meus; fiducialiter agam, et non timébo: quia fortitúdo mea et laus mea Dóminus, et factus est mihi in salútem.
»³Hauriétis aquas in gaudio de fontibus salvátoris.
⁴Et dicetis in die illa: Confitémini Dómino et invocáte nomen ejus; notas fácite in pópulis adinventiónes ejus; meméntote quóniam excélsum est nomen ejus.

»⁵Cantáte Dómino, quóniam magnifice fecit; Annuntiáte hoc in univérsa terra.
»⁶Exsulta et lauda, habitátio Sion, quia magnus in médio tui Sanctus Israël.

V. *Glória Patri ...*

Ant 4.

¹¹The Lord will give strength to His people: the Lord will bless His people with peace.

V. *Glory be ...*

Ant 3.

Canticle of Isaiah
(Isa 12:1-6)

Ant 4. Thy fury hath been turned, O Lord, and I will be comforted.

And Thou shalt say in that day: I will give thanks to Thee, O Lord, for Thou wast angry with me: Thy wrath is turned away, and Thou hast comforted me.
»²Behold, God is my savior, I will deal confidently, and will not fear: because the Lord is my strength, and my praise, and He hath become my salvation.
»³Thou shalt draw waters with joy out of the Savior's fountains:
⁴and thou shalt say in that day: praise ye the Lord, and call upon His Name: make His works known among the people: remember that His Name is high.
»⁵Sing ye to the Lord, for He hath done great things: show this forth in all the earth.

»⁶Rejoice, and praise, O ye inhabitants of Zion: for great is He that is in the midst of thee, the Holy One of Israel.

V. *Glory be ...*

Ant 4.

Monday Lauds II

Psalmus 116   Psalm 116

Ant 5. Laudáte Dóminum quóniam confirmáta est super nos misericórdia eíus.

Ant 5. Praise the Lord because His mercy hath been showered upon us.

Laudáte Dóminum, ómnes gentes; laudáte eum, ómnes pópuli. »²Quóniam confirmáta est super nos misericórdia ejus, et véritas Dómini manet in ætérnum.

O praise the Lord, all ye nations: praise Him, all ye people. »²For His mercy is confirmed upon us: and the truth of the Lord remaineth for ever.

V. *Glória Patri ...*

V. *Glory be ...*

Ant 5.

Ant 5.

Capitulum   Chapter
(Rom 13: 12-14)

The reading below or the proper of the day

V. Nox præcéssit, dies autem appropinquavit. Abjiciámus ergo ópera tenebrárum, et induámur arma lucis. Sicut in die honéste ambulémus: non in comessatiónibus, et ebrietátibus, non in cubílibus, et impudicítiis, non in contentióne, et æmulatióne.

V. The night is passed, and the day is at hand. Let us, therefore cast off the works of darkness, and put on the armor of light. Let us walk honestly, as in the day: not in rioting and drunkenness, not in debauchery and impurities, not in contention and envy.

R. Deo Grátias.

R. Thanks be to God.

Hymnus   Hymn
Or the hymn for the season

O Sol Salútis, intimis
Jesu, refúlge méntibus,
Dum nocte pulsa grátior
Orbi dies renáscitur.

Jesu, Salvation's Sun Divine,/
Within our inmost bosoms shine,/
With light all darkness drive away/
And give the world a better day.

Dans tempus acceptábile,
Da, lacrimárum rívulis
Laváre cordis víctimam,
Quam læta adúrat cáritas.

Now days of grace with mercy flow,/
O Lord, the gift of tears bestow,/ To wash our stains in every part,/ Whilst heavenly fire consumes the heart.

Monday Lauds II

Quo fonte manávit nefas, / Fluent perénnes lácrimæ, / Si virga pœniténtiæ / Cordis rigórem cónterat.	Rise, crystal tears, from that same source./ From whence our sins derive their course;/ Nor cease, till hardened hearts relent,/ And softened by thy streams, repent.
Dies venit, dies tua, / In qua reflórent ómnia: / Lætámur et nos in viam / Tua redúcti déxtera.	Behold, the happy days return,/ The days of joy for them that mourn;/ May we of their indulgence share,/ And bless the God that grants our prayer.
Te prona mundi máchina / Clemens adóret Trínitas, / Et nos novi per grátiam / Novum canámus cánticum.	May heaven and earth aloud proclaim/ The Trinity's almighty fame;/ And we, restored to grace, rejoice/ In newness both of heart and voice.

Versiculi / Versicle

V. Ángelis suis Deus mandávit de te.

R. Ut custódiant te in ómnibus viis tuis

V. God sent His angels concerning thee.

R. That they may guard thee in all thy ways.

Ant. Benedíctus Dóminus Deus Israël, quia visitávit et liberávit nos. *(Whenever possible, the antiphon for the specific season or feast of a saint will be used).*

Ant. Blessed is the Lord God of Israel, because He visited us and delivered us. *(Whenever possible, the antiphon for the specific season or feast of a saint will be used).*

Cánticum Zacharíæ
(Luke 1:68-79)
Canticle on page 366

Canticle of Zachariah
(Luke 1:68-79)
Canticle on page 366

V. *Glória Patri ...*

V. *Glory be ...*

Ant. Benedíctus Dóminus Deus Israël, quia visitávit et liberávit nos.

Ant. Blessed is the Lord God of Israel, because He visited us and delivered us.

V. *Páter nóster ...*
R. *Pánem nóstrum ...*

V. *Our Father ...*
R. *Give us this day ...*

Monday Lauds II

V. Dómine exáudi oratiónem meam.
R. Et clamor meus ad te véniat.

V. Oremus.

Custódi Dómine, quǽsumus, Ecclésiam tuam propitiatióne perpétua: et quia sine te lábitur humana mortálitas, tuis semper auxíliis et abstrahatur a noxiis, et ad salutária dirigátur. Per Dóminum nostrum ...

The prayer above is said, or the prayer of the season and the feast day are prayed if there are any.

V. Dómine exáudi oratiónem meam.
R. Et clamor meus ad te véniat.

V. Benedicámus Dómino.
R. Deo grátias.

V. Fidélium ánimæ per misericórdiam Dei requiéscant in pace.

R. Amen.

V. O Lord, hear my prayer.
R. And let my cry come unto Thee.

V. Let us pray.

Keep, O Lord, we beseech Thee, Thy Church with perpetual conciliation: and since without Thee our human mortality slips away, may it always be with Thy help that we may be removed from harm and directed to salutary things. Through our Lord ...

The prayer above is said, or the prayer of the season and the feast day are prayed if there are any.

V. O Lord, hear my prayer.
R. And let my cry come unto Thee.

V. Let us bless the Lord.
R. Thanks be to God.

V. May the souls of the faithful departed through the mercy of God rest in peace.

R. Amen.

For to Thee will I pray: O Lord, in the morning Thou shalt hear my voice.

TUESDAY – LAUDS II

V. Dómine, ✝ lábia mea apéries.
R. Et os meum annuntiábit laudem tuam.

V. Deus, in adjutórium meum inténde.
R. Dómine, ad adjuvándum me festína.

V. *Glória Patri ...*
R. *Sicut erat ...*

Psalmus 50

Ant 1. Dele iniquitátem meam Dómine, secúndum multitúdinem miseratiónum tuárum.

Miserere mei, Deus, secúndum magnam misericórdiam tuam; et secúndum multitúdinem miseratiónum tuárum, dele iniquitátem meam.
⁴Ámplius lava me ab iniquitáte mea, et a peccáto meo munda me.

»⁵Quóniam iniquitátem meam ego cognósco, et peccátum meum contra me est semper.
⁶Tibi soli peccávi, et malum coram te feci; ut justificéris in sermónibus tuis, et vincas cum judicáris.

»⁷Ecce enim in iniquitátibus concéptus sum, et in peccátis concépit me mater mea.
⁸Ecce enim veritátem dilexísti; incérta et occúlta sapiéntiæ tuæ manifestásti mihi.

»⁹Aspérges me hyssópo, et mundábor; lavábis me, et super nivem dealbábor.

V. O Lord, ✝ open my lips.
R. And my mouth shall proclaim Thy praise.

V. O God, come to my assistance.
R. O Lord, make haste to help me.

V. *Glory be ...*
R. *As it was ...*

Psalm 50

Ant 1. Erase my sin O Lord, according to the multitude of Thy mercies.

Have mercy on me, O God, according to Thy great compassion. And according to the multitude of Thy tender mercies blot out my iniquity.
⁴Wash me yet more from my iniquity, and cleanse me from my sin.
»⁵For I know my wickedness, and my sin is always before me.
⁶To Thee only have I sinned, and have done evil before Thee: that Thou mayst be justified in Thy words, and mayest be blameless when Thou judgeth.
»⁷For behold I was conceived with iniquities; and in sin did my mother conceive me.
⁸For behold Thou hast loved truth: the uncertain and hidden things of Thy wisdom Thou hast made manifest to me.
»⁹Thou shalt sprinkle me with hyssop, and I shall be cleansed: Thou shalt wash me, and I shall be made whiter than snow.

¹⁰Audítui meo dabis gáudium et lætítiam, et exsultábunt ossa humiliata.	¹⁰To my hearing Thou shalt give joy and gladness: and the bones that have been humbled shall rejoice.
»¹¹Avérte fáciem tuam a peccátis meis, et ómnes iniquitátes meas dele.	»¹¹Turn away Thy face from my sins, and blot out all my iniquities.
¹²Cor mundum crea in me, Deus, et spíritum rectum ínnova in viscéribus meis.	¹²Create a clean heart in me, O God: and renew a right spirit within my bowels.
»¹³Ne projícias me a fácie tua, et spíritum sanctum tuum ne áuferas a me.	»¹³Cast me not away from Thy face; and take not Thy Holy Spirit from me.
¹⁴Redde mihi lætítiam salutáris tui, et spíritu principáli confírma me.	¹⁴Restore unto me the joy of Thy salvation, and strengthen me with a perfect spirit.
»¹⁵Docébo iníquos vias tuas, et impii ad te converténtur.	»¹⁵I will teach the unjust Thy ways: and the wicked shall be converted to Thee.
¹⁶Líbera me de sanguínibus, Deus, Deus salútis meæ, et exsultábit lingua mea justítiam tuam.	¹⁶Deliver me from blood, O God, Thou God of my salvation: and my tongue shall extol Thy justice.
»¹⁷Dómine, lábia mea aperies, et os meum annuntiábit laudem tuam.	»¹⁷O Lord, Thou wilt open my lips: and my mouth shall declare Thy praise.
¹⁸Quóniam si voluísses sacrifícium, dedíssem útique; holocáustis non delectáberis.	¹⁸For if Thou hadst desired sacrifice, I would indeed have given it: but with burnt offerings Thou wilt not be delighted.
»¹⁹Sacrifícium Deo spíritus contribulátus; cor contrítum et humiliátum, Deus, non despícies.	»¹⁹A sacrifice to God is an afflicted spirit: a contrite and humbled heart, O God, Thou wilt not despise.
²⁰Benígne fac, Dómine, in bona voluntáte tua Sion, ut ædificéntur muri Jerúsalem.	²⁰Deal favorably, O Lord, in Thy good will with Zion; that the walls of Jerusalem may be rebuilt.
»²¹Tunc acceptábis sacrifícium justítiæ, oblatiónes et olocausta; tunc impónent super altáre tuum vítulos.	»²¹Then shalt Thou accept the sacrifice of justice, oblations and whole burnt offerings: then shall they lay calves upon Thine altar.
V. *Glória Patri* ...	V. *Glory be* ...
Ant 1.	Ant 1.

Psalmus 42 | ## Psalm 42

Ant 2. Discérne causam meam Deus de gente non sancta. | **Ant 2. Discern my cause, O God, from an unholy nation.**

Tuesday Lauds II

Júdica me, Deus, et discérne causam meam de gente non sancta: ab hómine iníquo et dolóso érue me.

»²Quia tu es, Deus, fortitúdo mea: quare me repulísti? et quare tristis incédo, dum afflígit me inimícus?
»³Emitte lucem tuam et veritátem tuam: ipsa me deduxérunt, et adduxerunt in montem sanctum tuum, et in tabernácula tua.
»⁴Et introíbo ad altáre Dei, ad Deum qui lætíficat juventútem meam. Confitébor tibi in cíthara, Deus, Deus meus.

»⁵Quare tristis es, ánima mea? et quare contúrbas me? Spera in Deo, quóniam adhuc confitébor illi, salutáre vultus mei, et Deus meus.

V. *Glória Patri ...*

Ant 2.

Psalmus 66

Ant 3. Deus misereátur nostri et benedícat nos.

Deus misereátur nostri, et benedícat nobis; illúminet vultum suum super nos, et miserátur nostri:

³ut cognoscámus in terra viam tuam, in ómnibus géntibus salutáre tuum.
»⁴Confiteántur tibi pópuli, Deus: Confiteántur tibi pópuli ómnes.

⁵Læténtur et exsultent gentes, quóniam júdicas pópulos in æquitáte, et gentes in terra dirigis.

Judge me, O God, and distinguish my cause from the nation that is not holy: deliver me from the unjust and deceitful man.
»²For Thou art God my strength: why hast Thou cast me off? And why do I go sorrowful whilst the enemy afflicteth me?
»³Send forth Thy light and Thy truth: they have led me, and brought me unto Thy holy mountain, and into Thy tabernacles.
»⁴And I will go in to the altar of God: to God who giveth joy to my youth.

»⁵To Thee, O God my God, I will give praise upon the harp: why art thou sad, O my soul? And why dost thou disquiet me? Hope in God, for I will still give praise to Him: the salvation of my countenance, and my God.

V. *Glory be ...*

Ant 2.

Psalm 66

Ant 3. May God have mercy on us and bless us.

May God have mercy on us, and bless us: may He cause the light of His countenance to shine upon us, and may He have mercy on us.
³That we may know Thy way upon earth: Thy salvation in all nations.
»⁴Let people confess to Thee, O God: let all people give praise to Thee.
⁵Let the nations be glad and rejoice: for Thou judgest the people with justice, and directest the nations upon earth.

Tuesday Lauds II

»⁶Confiteántur tibi pópuli, Deus: Confiteántur tibi pópuli ómnes.

»⁷Terra dedit fructum suum: benedícat nos Deus, Deus noster! ⁸Benedícat nos Deus, et metúant eum ómnes fines terræ.

V. *Glória Patri ...*

Ant 3.

Cánticum Ezechiæ
(Isa 38:10-22)

Ant 4. Corrípies me Dómine et vivificábis me.

Ego dixi in dimidio diérum meórum: Vadam ad portas ínferi; quæsivi residuum annórum meórum.
»¹¹Dixi: Non vidébo Dóminum Deum in terra vivéntium; non aspíciam hóminem ultra, et habitatórem quiétis.
»¹²Generatio mea ablata est, et convoluta est a me, quasi tabernaculum pastorum. Præcisa est velut a texente vita mea; dum adhuc ordírer, succidit me: de mane usque ad vésperam finies me.
»¹³Sperabam usque ad mane; quasi leo, sic contrívit ómnia ossa mea: de mane usque ad vésperam finies me.

»¹⁴Sicut pullus hirundinis, sic clamabo; meditábor ut columba. Attenuati sunt oculi mei, suspiciéntes in excélsum. Dómine, vim patior: respónde pro me.
»¹⁵Quid dicam, aut quid respondebit mihi, cum ipse fecerit? Recogitabo tibi ómnes annos meos in amaritudine ánimæ meæ.

»⁶Let the people, O God, confess to Thee: let all the people give praise to Thee.

»⁷The earth hath yielded her fruit. May God, our God, bless us. ⁸May God bless us: and all the ends of the earth fear Him.

V. *Glory be ...*

Ant 3.

Canticle of Ezechias
(Isa 38:10-22)

Ant 4. Thou wilt correct me, O Lord, and Thou wilt revive me.

I said: In the midst of my days I shall go to the gates of hell: I am deprived of the rest of my years.
»¹¹I said: I shall not see the Lord God in the land of the living. I shall behold man no more among the inhabitants of the world.
»¹²My generation is at an end, and it is rolled away from me, as a shepherd's tent. My life is cut off, as by a weaver: whilst I was yet but beginning, he cut me off: from morning even to night Thou wilt make an end of me.
»¹³I cried for help till morning, as a lion so hath he broken all my bones: from morning even to night Thou wilt make an end of me.
»¹⁴I will cry like a young swallow, I will moan like a dove: mine eyes are weakened looking upward: Lord, I suffer violence, answer Thou for me.
»¹⁵What shall I say, or what shall He answer for me, whereas He Himself hath done it? I will recount to Thee all my years in the bitterness of my soul.

Tuesday Lauds II

»¹⁶Dómine, si sic vivitur, et in talibus vita spíritus mei, corripies me, et vivificabis me.
»¹⁷Ecce in pace amaritudo mea amarissima. Tu autem eruisti ánimam meam ut non períret; projecisti post tergum tuum ómnia peccáta mea.

»¹⁸Quia non infernus confitebitur tibi, neque mors laudábit te: non exspectabunt qui descendunt in lacum veritátem tuam.
»¹⁹Vivens, vivens ipse confitebitur tibi, sicut et ego hódie; pater filiis notam fáciet veritátem tuam.

»²⁰Dómine, salvum me fac! et psalmos nostros cantabimus cunctis diébus vitæ nostræ in domo Dómini.

V. *Glória Patri ...*

Ant 4.

Psalmus 134

Ant 5. Laudáte nomen Dómini; qui statis in domo Dómini.

Laudáte nomen Dómini; laudáte, servi, Dóminum:

²Qui statis in domo Dómini, in átriis domus Dei nostri.
»³Laudáte Dóminum, quia bonus Dóminus; psállite nómini ejus, quóniam suave.
»⁴Quóniam Jacob elégit sibi Dóminus; Israël in possessiónem sibi.
⁵Quia ego cognóvi quod magnus est Dóminus, et Deus noster præ ómnibus diis.

»¹⁶O Lord, if man's life be such, and the life of my spirit be in such things as these, Thou shalt correct me, and make me to live.
»¹⁷Behold in peace is my bitterness most bitter: but Thou hast delivered my soul that it should not perish, Thou hast cast all my sins behind Thy back.

»¹⁸For hell shall not confess to Thee, neither shall death praise Thee: nor shall they that go down into the pit look for Thy truth.
»¹⁹The living, the living, he shall give praise to Thee, as I do this day: the father shall make the truth known to the children.

»²⁰O Lord, save me, and we will sing our psalms all the days of our life in the house of the Lord.

V. *Glory be ...*

Ant 4.

Psalm 134

Ant 5. Praise the Name of the Lord; ye who stand in the house of the Lord.

Praise ye the Name of the Lord: O ye His servants, praise the Lord:
²Ye that stand in the house of the Lord, in the courts of the house of our God.
»³Praise ye the Lord, for the Lord is good: sing ye to His Name, for it is sweet.
»⁴For the Lord hath chosen Jacob unto Himself: Israel for His own possession.
⁵For I have known that the Lord is great, and our God is above all gods.

Tuesday Lauds II

»⁶Ómnia quæcúmque vóluit Dóminus fecit, in cælo, in terra, in mari et in ómnibus abýssis.
»⁷Edúcens nubes ab extrémo terræ, fúlgura in plúviam fecit; qui prodúcit ventos de thesáuris suis.

»⁸Qui percússit primogénita Ægýpti, ab hómine usque ad pecus.
⁹Et misit signa et prodígia in médio tui, Ægýpte: in Pharaónem, et in ómnes servos ejus.
»¹⁰Qui percússit gentes multas, et occídit reges fortes:
¹¹Sehon, regem Amorrhæorum, et Og, regem Basan, et ómnia regna Chanaan:
»¹²et dedit terram eórum hæreditátem, hæreditátem Israël pópulo suo.

»¹³Dómine, nomen tuum in ætérnum; Dómine, memoriále tuum in generatiónem et generatiónem.
¹⁴Quia judicábit Dóminus pópulum suum, et in servis suis deprecábitur.

»¹⁵Simulácra géntium argentum et aurum, ópera mánuum hóminum.
¹⁶Os habent, et non loquéntur; óculos habent, et non vidébunt.
»¹⁷Aures habent, et non áudient; neque enim est spíritus in ore ipsórum.
¹⁸Símiles illis fiant qui fáciunt ea, et ómnes qui confídunt in eis.
»¹⁹Domus Israël, benedícite Dómino; domus Aaron, benedícite Dómino.
²⁰Domus Levi, benedícite Dómino; qui timétis Dóminum, benedícite Dómino.
²¹Benedíctus Dóminus ex Sion, qui hábitat in Jerúsalem.

V. *Glória Patri ...*

Ant 5.

»⁶Whatsoever the Lord pleaseth He hath done, in heaven, on earth, in the sea, and in all the deeps.
»⁷He bringeth up clouds from the end of the earth: He hath made lightnings for the rain. He bringeth forth winds out of His storehouse.

»⁸He slew the firstborn of Egypt from man even unto beast.
⁹He sent forth signs and wonders in the midst of thee, O Egypt: upon Pharaoh, and upon all his servants.
»¹⁰He smote many nations, and slew mighty kings:
¹¹Sehon king of the Amorrhites, and Og king of Basan, and all the kingdoms of Chanaan:
»¹²And gave their land for an inheritance, for an inheritance to His people Israel.

»¹³Thy Name, O Lord, is for ever: Thy memorial, O Lord, unto all generations.
¹⁴For the Lord will judge His people, and will be merciful to His servants.
»¹⁵The idols of the Gentiles are silver and gold, the works of men's hands:
¹⁶They have a mouth, but they speak not: they have eyes, but they see not.
»¹⁷They have ears, but they hear not: neither is there any breath in their mouths.
¹⁸Let them that make idols be like to them: and every one that trusteth in them.
»¹⁹Bless the Lord, O house of Israel: bless the Lord, O house of Aaron.
²⁰Bless the Lord, O house of Levi: ye that fear the Lord, bless the Lord.
²¹Blessed be the Lord out of Zion, who dwelleth in Jerusalem.

V. *Glory be ...*

Ant 5.

Tuesday Lauds II

Capitulum
(Rom 13:12-14)
The reading below or the proper of the day

V. Nox præcéssit, dies autem appropinquavit. Abjiciámus ergo ópera tenebrárum, et induámur arma lucis. Sicut in die honéste ambulémus: non in comessatiónibus, et ebrietátibus, non in cubílibus, et impudicítiis, non in contentióne, et æmulatióne.

R. Deo grátias.

Hymnus
Or the hymn for the season

Ales diei Núntius
Lucem propínquam præcinit:
Nos excitátory mentium
Jam Chrístus ad vitam vocat.

Auférte, clamat, léctulos,
Ægro sopóre désides:
Castíque, recti, ac sóbrii
Vigilate, jam sum Proximus

Jesum ciámus vocibus,
Flentes, precántes, sóbrii:
Intenta supplicátion
Dormíre cor mundum vetat.

Tu, Christe, somnum discute:
Tu rumpe noctis víncula: Tu solve peccátum vetus,
Novúmque lumen íngere

Deo Patri sit Glória,
Ejúsque soli Filio,
Cum Spíritu Paráclito
Nunc et per omne sǽculum

Versiculi

V. Éripe me de inimícis meis Deus meus.
R. Et ab insurgéntibus in me líbera me.

Chapter
(Rom 13:12-14)
The reading below or the proper of the day

V. The night is passed, and the day is at hand. Let us, therefore cast off the works of darkness, and put on the armor of light. Let us walk honestly, as in the day: not in rioting and drunkenness, not in debauchery and impurities, not in contention and envy.

R. Thanks be to God.

Hymn
Or the hymn for the season

As the Bird, Whose Clarion Gay/
Sounds before the dawn is grey,/
Christ, who brings the spirit's day,/
Calls us, close at hand:

"Wake!" He cries, "and for my sake,/
From thine eyes dull slumbers shake!/ Sober, righteous, chaste, awake!/ At the door I stand!"

Lord, to Thee we lift on high/
Fervent prayer and bitter cry:/
Hearts aroused to pray and sigh/
May not slumber more.

Break the sleep of Death and Time,/
Forged by Adam's ancient crime;/
And the light of Eden's prime/
To the world restore!

Unto God the Father, Son,/
Holy Spirit, Three in One,/
One in Three, be glory done,/
Now and evermore.

Versicle

V. Rescue me from mine enemies, my God.
R. And deliver me from those who rise up against me.

Tuesday Lauds II

Ant. Eréxit nobis Dóminus cornu salútis in domo David. *(Whenever possible, the antiphon for the specific season or feast of a saint will be used).*

Cánticum Zacharíæ
(Luke 1:68-79)
Canticle on page 366

V. *Glória Patri ...*

Ant. Eréxit nobis Dóminus cornu salútis in domo David.

V. *Páter nóster ...*
R. *Pánem nóstrum ...*

V. Dómine exáudi oratiónem meam.
R. Et clamor meus ad te véniat.

V. Oremus.

Deus, refúgium nostrum et virtus: adésto piis Ecclésiæ tuæ précibus, auctor ipse pietátis, et præsta; ut, quod fidéliter pétimus, efficáciter consequámur. Per Dóminum nostrum...

The prayer above is said, or the prayer of the season and the feast day are prayed if there are any.

V. Dómine exáudi oratiónem meam.
R. Et clamor meus ad te véniat.

V. Benedicámus Dómino.
R. Deo grátias.

V. Fidélium ánimæ per misericórdiam Dei requiéscant in pace.

R. Amen.

Ant. The Lord raised up for us the horn of salvation in the house of David. *(Whenever possible, the antiphon for the specific season or feast of a saint will be used).*

Canticle of Zachariah
(Luke 1:68-79)
Canticle on page 366

V. *Glory be ...*

Ant. The Lord raised up for us the horn of salvation in the house of David.

V. *Our Father ...*
R. *Give us this day ...*

V. O Lord, hear my prayer.
R. And let my cry come unto Thee.

V. Let us pray.

O God, our refuge and strength: Who art the author of goodness itself, be attentive to the prayers of Thy Holy Church, and grant that what we faithfully ask, we may effectively obtain. Through our Lord ...

The prayer above is said, or the prayer of the season and the feast day are prayed if there are any.

V. O Lord, hear my prayer.
R. And let my cry come unto Thee.

V. Let us bless the Lord.
R. Thanks be to God.

V. May the souls of the faithful departed through the mercy of God rest in peace.

R. Amen.

WEDNESDAY – LAUDS II

V. Dómine, ✝ lábia mea apéries.
R. Et os meum annuntiábit laudem tuam.

V. Deus, in adjutórium meum inténde.
R. Dómine, ad adjuvándum me festína.

V. *Glória Patri ...*
R. *Sicut erat ...*

Psalmus 50

Ant 1. Ámplius lava me Dómine ab injustítia mea.

Miserere mei, Deus, secúndum magnam misericórdiam tuam; et secúndum multitúdinem miseratiónum tuárum, dele iniquitátem meam.
⁴Ámplius lava me ab iniquitáte mea, et a peccáto meo munda me.

»⁵Quóniam iniquitátem meam ego cognósco, et peccátum meum contra me est semper.
⁶Tibi soli peccávi, et malum coram te feci; ut justificéris in sermónibus tuis, et vincas cum judicáris.

»⁷Ecce enim in iniquitátibus concéptus sum, et in peccátis concépit me mater mea.

⁸Ecce enim veritátem dilexísti; incérta et occúlta sapiéntiæ tuæ manifestásti mihi.

»⁹Aspérges me hyssópo, et mundábor; lavábis me, et super nivem dealbábor.

V. O Lord, ✝ open my lips.
R. And my mouth shall proclaim Thy praise.

V. O God, come to my assistance.

R. O Lord, make haste to help me.

V. *Glory be ...*
R. *As it was ...*

Psalm 50

Ant 1. Wash me more, O Lord, from my unrighteousness.

Have mercy on me, O God, according to Thy great compassion. And according to the multitude of Thy tender mercies blot out my iniquity.
⁴Wash me yet more from my iniquity, and cleanse me from my sin.
»⁵For I know my wickedness, and my sin is always before me.
⁶To Thee only have I sinned, and have done evil before Thee: that Thou mayest be justified in Thy words, and mayest be blameless when Thou judgeth
»⁷For behold I was conceived with iniquities; and in sin did my mother conceive me.

⁸For behold Thou hast loved truth: the uncertain and hidden things of Thy wisdom Thou hast made manifest to me.
»⁹Thou shalt sprinkle me with hyssop, and I shall be cleansed: Thou shalt wash me, and I shall be made whiter than snow.

Wednesday Lauds II

¹⁰Audítui meo dabis gáudium et lætítiam, et exsultábunt ossa humiliáta.
»¹¹Avérte fáciem tuam a peccátis meis, et ómnes iniquitátes meas dele.
¹²Cor mundum crea in me, Deus, et spíritum rectum ínnova in viscéribus meis.
»¹³Ne projícias me a fácie tua, et spíritum sanctum tuum ne áuferas a me.
¹⁴Redde mihi lætítiam salutáris tui, et spíritu principáli confírma me.

»¹⁵Docébo iníquos vias tuas, et impii ad te converténtur.
¹⁶Líbera me de sanguínibus, Deus, Deus salútis meæ, et exsultábit lingua mea justítiam tuam.

»¹⁷Dómine, lábia mea apéries, et os meum annuntiábit laudem tuam.

¹⁸Quóniam si voluísses sacríficium, dedíssem útique; holocáustis non delectáberis.

»¹⁹Sacríficium Deo spíritus contribulátus; cor contrítum et humiliátum, Deus, non despícies.
²⁰Benígne fac, Dómine, in bona voluntáte tua Sion, ut ædificéntur muri Jerúsalem.

»²¹Tunc acceptábis sacríficium justítiæ, oblatiónes et holocáusta; tunc impónent super altáre tuum vítulos.

V. *Glória Patri ...*

Ant 1.

Psalmus 64

Ant 2. Impietátibus nostris tu propitiáberis Deus.

¹⁰To my hearing Thou shalt give joy and gladness: and the bones that have been humbled shall rejoice.
»¹¹Turn away Thy face from my sins, and blot out all my iniquities.
¹²Create a clean heart in me, O God: and renew a right spirit within my bowels.
»¹³Cast me not away from Thy face; and take not Thy Holy Spirit from me.
¹⁴Restore unto me the joy of Thy salvation, and strengthen me with a perfect spirit.
»¹⁵I will teach the unjust Thy ways: and the wicked shall be converted to Thee.
¹⁶Deliver me from blood, O God, Thou God of my salvation: and my tongue shall extol Thy justice.
»¹⁷O Lord, Thou wilt open my lips: and my mouth shall declare Thy praise.
¹⁸For if Thou hadst desired sacrifice, I would indeed have given it: but with burnt offerings Thou wilt not be delighted.
»¹⁹A sacrifice to God is an afflicted spirit: a contrite and humbled heart, O God, Thou wilt not despise.
²⁰Deal favorably, O Lord, in Thy good will with Zion; that the walls of Jerusalem may be rebuilt.
»²¹Then shalt Thou accept the sacrifice of justice, oblations and whole burnt offerings: then shall they lay calves upon Thine altar.

V. *Glory be ...*

Ant 1.

Psalm 64

Ant 2. O God, our transgressions will be pardoned.

Wednesday Lauds II

𝕿e decet hymnus, Deus, in Sion, et tibi reddétur votum in Jerúsalem.
»³Exáudi oratiónem meam; ad te omnis caro véniet.

⁴Verba iniquórum prævaluérunt super nos, et impietátibus nostris tu propitiaberis.

»⁵Beátus quem elegisti et assumpsisti: inhabitábit in átriis tuis. Replébimur in bonis domus tuæ; sanctum est templum tuum,
»⁶mirábile in æquitáte. Exáudi nos, Deus, salutáris noster, spes ómnium finium terræ, et in mari longe.

»⁷Præparans montes in virtúte tua, accinctus poténtia;

»⁸qui contúrbas profúndum maris, sonum flúctuum ejus. Turbabúntur gentes,
»⁹et timébunt qui hábitant términos a signis tuis; éxitus matutini et véspere delectábis.

»¹⁰Visitasti terram, et inebriásti eam; multiplicásti locupletáre eam. Flumen Dei replétum est aquis; parásti cibum illórum: quóniam ita est præparátio ejus.

»¹¹Rivos ejus inébria; multíplica genímina ejus: in stillicídiis ejus lætábitur gérminans.
¹²Benedíces corónæ anni benignitátis tuæ, et campi tui replebúntur ubertáte.
»¹³Pinguescent speciosa deserti, et exsultatione colles accingentur.

𝕬 hymn, O God, becometh Thee in Zion: and a vow shall be offered to Thee in Jerusalem.
»³O hear my prayer: all flesh shall come to Thee.
⁴The words of the wicked have prevailed over us: and Thou wilt pardon our transgressions.
»⁵Blessed is He Whom Thou hast chosen and taken to Thee: He shall dwell in Thy courts. We shall be filled with the good things of Thy house; holy is Thy temple, wonderful in justice.
»⁶Hear us, O God our Savior, who art the hope of all the ends of the earth, and in the sea afar off:
»⁷Thou who, by Thy strength and being girded with power, maketh the mountains remain secured.
»⁸Who troublest the depth of the sea, the noise of its waves. The Gentiles shall be afraid,
»⁹and they that dwell in the uttermost borders shall be afraid at Thy signs: Thou shalt make the going out of the morning and of the evening to be joyful.
»¹⁰Thou hast visited the earth, and hast plentifully watered it; Thou hast many ways enriched it. The river of God is filled with water, Thou hast provided their food: for so Thou hast prepared the land.
»¹¹Fill up plentifully the streams thereof, multiply its fruits; it shall spring up and rejoice in its showers.
¹²Thou shalt bless the crown of the year of Thy goodness: and Thy fields shall be filled with plenty.
»¹³The beautiful places of the wilderness shall grow fat: and the hills shall be girded about with joy.

Wednesday Lauds II

»¹⁴Induti sunt arietes ovium, et valles abundabunt fruménto; clamabunt, etenim hymnum dicent.

V. *Glória Patri* ...

Ant 2.

Psalmus 100

Ant 3. **In innocéntia cordis mei perambulabo Dómine.**

𝕸 isericórdiam et judícium cantabo tibi, Dómine; psallam, ²et intélligam in via immaculáta: quando vénies ad me? Perambulabam in innocéntia cordis mei, in médio domus meæ.
»³Non proponébam ante óculos meos rem injústam; fácientes prævaricatiónes odívi; non adhæsit mihi
⁴cor pravum; declinántem a me malígnum non cognoscébam.

»⁵Detrahentem secréto próximo suo, hunc perse-quebar: supérbo. óculo, et insatiábili corde, cum hoc non edébam.
»⁶Oculi mei ad v terræ, ut sédeant mecum; ámbulans in via immaculáta, hic mihi ministrábat.
»⁷Non habitábit in médio domus meæ qui facit supérbiam; qui lóquitur iníqua non diréxit in conspéctu oculórum meórum.
»⁸In matutíno interficiébam ómnes peccatóres terræ, ut dispérderem de civitáte Dómini ómnes óperantes iniquitátem.

V. *Glória Patri*

Ant 3.

»¹⁴The rams of the flock are clothed, and the vales shall abound with corn: they shall shout, yea they shall sing a hymn.
V. *Glory be* ...

Ant 2.

Psalm 100

Ant 3. **I will walk in the innocence of my heart, O Lord.**

𝕸 ercy and judgment I will sing to Thee, O Lord: I will sing, ²and my understanding will be blameless, when Thou shalt come to me. I walked in the innocence of my heart, in the midst of my house.
»³I did not set before my eyes any unjust thing: I hated the workers of evil.
⁴The perverse heart shall be far from me: and the malicious that turned aside from me I would not know.

»⁵The man that in private detracted his neighbour, him did I persecute. With him that had a proud eye, and an unsatiable heart, I would not eat.
»⁶Mine eyes were upon the faithful of the earth who sat with me: the man that walked in the perfect way, he served me.
»⁷He that worketh pride shalt not dwell in the midst of my house: he that speaketh unjust things shalt not prosper before mine eyes.
»⁸In the morning I put to death all the wicked of the land: that I might cut off all the workers of iniquity from the city of the Lord.

V. *Glory be* ...

Ant 3.

Wednesday Lauds II

Cánticum Annæ
(1 Sam 2:1-10)

Ant 4. Exsultávit cor meum in Dómino, qui humíliat et Súblevat.

Exultavit cor meum in Dómino, et exaltátum est cornu meum in Deo meo; dilatatum est os meum super inimícos meos: quia lætáta sum in salutari tuo.
»²Non est sanctus, ut est Dóminus, neque enim est álius extra te, et non est fortis sicut Deus noster.
³Nolíte multiplicare loqui sublimia gloriantes; recédant vetera de ore vestro: quia Deus scientiarum Dóminus est, et ipsi præparantur cogitations.
»⁴Arcus fortium superatus est, et infirmi accincti sunt robore.

⁵Repléti prius, pro panibus se locaverunt: et famelici saturati sunt, donec sterilis peperit plurimos: et quæ multos habebat filios, infirmata est.
»⁶Dóminus mortificat et vivificat; deducit ad inferos et reducit.

⁷Dóminus pauperem facit et ditat, humiliat et sublevat.

»⁸Suscitat de pulvere egenum, et de stercore elevat pauperem: ut sedeat cum princípibus, et solium glóriæ teneat. Dómini enim sunt cárdines terræ, et posuit super eos orbem.

»⁹Pedes sanctórum suórum servabit, et impii in tenebris conticescent: quia non in fortitúdine sua roborabitur vir.

»¹⁰Dóminum formidabunt adversarii ejus: et super ipsos in cælis tonabit.

Canticle of Anna
(1 Sam 2:1-10)

Ant 4. My heart hath rejoiced in the Lord, who humbleth and subdueth.

My heart hath rejoiced in the Lord, and my horn is exalted in my God: my mouth boasts over mine enemies: because I have joy in Thy salvation.
»²There is none holy as the Lord is: for there is no other besides Him and there is none strong like our God.
³Do not boast and speak lofty things: let not arrogance depart from thy mouth: for the Lord is a God of all knowledge, and by Him are thoughts weighed.
»⁴The bow of the mighty is overcome, and the weak are girt with strength.
⁵They that were full before have hired out themselves for bread: and the hungry are filled, so that the barren hath borne many: and she that had many children is weakened.
»⁶The Lord killeth and maketh alive, He bringeth down to hell and bringeth back again.
⁷The Lord maketh poor and maketh rich, He humbleth and He exalteth.
»⁸He raiseth up the needy from the dust, and lifteth up the poor from the dunghill: that they may sit with princes, and hold the throne of glory. For the poles of the earth are the Lord's, and upon them He hath set the world.
»⁹He will guard the feet of His saints, and the wicked shall be silent in darkness, because no man shall prevail by his own strength.
»¹⁰The adversaries of the Lord shall fear Him: and upon them shalt He thunder in the heavens. The Lord

Wednesday Lauds II

Dóminus judicábit fines terræ, et dabit impérium regi suo, et sublimabit cornu christi sui.

V. *Glória Patri ...*

Ant 4.

Psalmus 145

**Ant 5. Lauda ánima mea Dóminum qui érigit elísos et
díligit justos.**

𝕷auda, ánima mea, Dóminum. Laudábo Dóminum in vita mea; psallam Deo meo quámdiu fúero. Nolíte confídere in princípibus, ³in filiis hóminum, in quibus non est salus.
»⁴Exíbit spíritus ejus, et revertétur in terram suam; in illa die períbunt ómnes cogitatiónes eórum.
»⁵Beátus cujus Deus Jacob adjútor ejus, spes ejus in Dómino Deo ipsius:
⁶qui fecit cælum et terram, mare, et ómnia quæ in eis sunt.
»⁷Qui custódit veritátem in sǽculum; facit judícium injúriam patiéntibus; dat escam esuriéntibus. Dóminus solvit compeditos;
»⁸Dóminus illúminat cæcos. Dóminus érigit elisos; Dóminus díligit justos.
⁹Dóminus custódit ádvenas, pupillum et víduam suscípiet, et vias peccatórum dispérdet.

»¹⁰Regnábit Dóminus in sǽcula; Deus tuus, Sion, in generatiónem et generatiónem.

V. *Glória Patri ...*

Ant 5.

---

shalt judge the ends of the earth, and He shalt give strength to His king, and shalt exalt the horn of His anointed.

V. *Glory be ...*

Ant 4.

Psalm 145

Ant 5. My soul praiseth the Lord Who raiseth up the elect and loveth the righteous.

𝕻raise the Lord, O my soul, all my life I will praise the Lord: I will sing to my God as long as I shall be. Put not thy trust in princes: ³in the children of men, in whom there is no salvation.
»⁴His spirit shall go forth, and He shall return into His earth: in that day all their thoughts shall perish.
»⁵Blessed is he who hath the God of Jacob for his helper, whose hope is in the Lord his God:
⁶Who made heaven and earth, the sea, and all things that are in them:
»⁷Who keepeth truth for ever: Who executeth judgment for them that suffer wrong: Who giveth food to the hungry. The Lord releaseth those that are bound:
»⁸the Lord enlighteneth the blind. The Lord lifteth up them that are cast down: the Lord loveth the just.
⁹The Lord keepeth the strangers, He will support the fatherless and the widow: and He will destroy the ways of sinners.
»¹⁰The Lord shalt reign for ever: Thy God, O Zion, unto generation and generation.

V. *Glory be ...*

Ant 5.

Wednesday Lauds II

Capitulum / Chapter
(Rom 13: 12-14)
The reading below or the proper of the day

V. Nox præcéssit, dies autem appropinquavit. Abjiciámus ergo ópera tenebrárum, et induámur arma lucis. Sicut in die honéste ambulémus: non in comessatiónibus, et ebrietátibus, non in cubílibus, et impudicitiis, non in contentióne, et æmulatióne.

V. The night is passed, and the day is at hand. Let us, therefore cast off the works of darkness, and put on the armor of light. Let us walk honestly, as in the day: not in rioting and drunkenness, not in debauchery and impurities, not in contention and envy.

R. Deo Grátias.

R. Thanks be to God.

Hymnus / Hymn
Or the hymn for the season

Audi Benigne Cónditor
Page 372

O King Creator
Page 372

Versiculi / Versicle

V. Ángelis suis Deus mandávit de te.

R. Ut custódiant te in ómnibus viis tuis.

V. God sent His angels concerning thee.

R. That they may guard thee in all thy ways.

Ant. Eréxit nobis Dóminus cornu salútis in domo David púeri sui.
(Whenever possible, the antiphon for the specific season or feast of a saint will be used).

Ant. The Lord raised up for us the horn of salvation in the house of His son David. *(Whenever possible, the antiphon for the specific season or feast of a saint will be used).*

Cánticum Zachariæ / Canticle of Zachariah
(Luke 1:68-79)
Canticle on page 366

V. *Glória Patri ...*

V. *Glory be ...*

Ant. Eréxit nobis Dóminus cornu salútis in domo David púeri sui.

Ant. The Lord raised up for us the horn of salvation in the house of His son David.

V. *Páter nóster ...*
R. *Pánem nóstrum ...*

V. *Our Father ...*
R. *Give us this day ...*

Wednesday Lauds II

V. Dómine exáudi oratiónem meam.
R. Et clamor meus ad te véniat.

V. Orémus.

Absólve, quǽsumus, Dómine, tuórum delícta populórum: ut a peccatórum néxibus, quæ pro nostra fragilitáte contráximus, tua benignitáte liberémur.   Per Dóminum nostrum...

The prayer above is said, or the prayer of the Sunday or season and the Feast day are prayed if there are any.

V. Dómine exáudi oratiónem meam.
R. Et clamor meus ad te véniat.

V. Benedicámus Dómino.
R. Deo grátias.

V. Fidélium ánimæ per misericórdiam Dei requiéscant in pace.

R. Amen.

V. O Lord, hear my prayer.
R. And let my cry come unto Thee.

V. Let us pray.

Absolve us, we beseech Thee, Lord, of the transgressions of Thy people: that we may be freed by Thy mercy from the bonds of sin, which we have acquired because of our weakness. Through our Lord …

The prayer above is said, or the prayer of the Sunday or season and the Feast day are prayed if there are any.

V. O Lord, hear my prayer.
R. And let my cry come unto Thee.

V. Let us bless the Lord.
R. Thanks be to God.

V. May the souls of the faithful departed through the mercy of God rest in peace.

R. Amen.

He that worketh pride shall not dwell in the midst of my house: he that speaketh unjust things did not prosper before mine eyes.

THURSDAY – LAUDS II

V. Dómine, ✝ lábia mea apéries.
R. Et os meum annuntiábit laudem tuam.

V. Deus, in adjutórium meum inténde.
R. Dómine, ad adjuvándum me festína.

V. *Glória Patri ...*
R. *Sicut erat ...*

V. O Lord, ✝ open my lips.
R. And my mouth shall proclaim Thy praise.

V. O God, come to my assistance.
R. O Lord, make haste to help me.

V. *Glory be ...*
R. *As it was ...*

Psalmus 50

Ant 1. Dele iniquitátem meam Dómine, secúndum multitúdinem miseratiónum tuárum.

Miserere mei, Deus, secúndum magnam misericórdiam tuam; et secúndum multitúdinem miseratiónum tuárum, dele iniquitátem meam.

⁴Ámplius lava me ab iniquitáte mea, et a peccáto meo munda me.

»⁵Quóniam iniquitátem meam ego cognósco, et peccátum meum contra me est semper.

⁶Tibi soli peccávi, et malum coram te feci; ut justificéris in sermónibus tuis, et vincas cum judicáris.

»⁷Ecce enim in iniquitátibus concéptus sum, et in peccátis concépit me mater mea.

⁸Ecce enim veritátem dilexísti; incérta et occúlta sapiéntiæ tuæ manifestásti mihi.

Psalm 50

Ant 1. Erase my iniquity O Lord, according to the multitude of Thy mercies.

Have mercy on me, O God, according to Thy great compassion. And according to the multitude of Thy tender mercies blot out my iniquity.

⁴Wash me yet more from my iniquity, and cleanse me from my sin.
»⁵For I know my wickedness, and my sin is always before me.

⁶To Thee only have I sinned, and have done evil before Thee: that Thou mayest be justified in Thy words, and mayest be blameless when Thou judgeth.

»⁷For behold I was conceived with iniquities; and in sin did my mother conceive me.
⁸For behold Thou hast loved truth: the uncertain and hidden things of Thy wisdom Thou hast made manifest to me.

Thursday Lauds II

»⁹Aspérges me hyssópo, et mundábor; lavábis me, et super nivem dealbábor.

¹⁰Audítui meo dabis gáudium et lætítiam, et exsultábunt ossa humiliata.

»¹¹Avérte fáciem tuam a peccátis meis, et ómnes iniquitátes meas dele.

¹²Cor mundum crea in me, Deus, et spíritum rectum ínnova in visceribus meis.

»¹³Ne projícias me a fácie tua, et spíritum sanctum tuum ne áuferas a me.

¹⁴Redde mihi lætítiam salutáris tui, et spíritu principáli confírma me.

»¹⁵Docébo iníquos vias tuas, et impii ad te converténtur.

¹⁶Líbera me de sanguínibus, Deus, Deus salútis meæ, et exsultábit lingua mea justítiam tuam.

»¹⁷Dómine, lábia mea aperies, et os meum annuntiábit laudem tuam.

¹⁸Quóniam si voluísses sacrifícium, dedíssem útique; holocáustis non delectáberis.

»¹⁹Sacrifícium Deo spíritus contribulátus; cor contrítum et humiliátum, Deus, non despícies.

²⁰Benígne fac, Dómine, in bona voluntáte tua Sion, ut ædificéntur muri Jerúsalem.

»²¹Tunc acceptábis sacrifícium justítiæ, oblatiónes et holocáusta; tunc impónent super altáre tuum vítulos.

V. *Glória Patri ...*

Ant 1.

»⁹Thou shalt sprinkle me with hyssop, and I shall be cleansed: Thou shalt wash me, and I shall be made whiter than snow.

¹⁰To my hearing Thou shalt give joy and gladness: and the bones that have been humbled shall rejoice.

»¹¹Turn away Thy face from my sins, and blot out all my iniquities.

¹²Create a clean heart in me, O God: and renew a right spirit within my bowels.

»¹³Cast me not away from Thy face; and take not Thy Holy Spirit from me.

¹⁴Restore unto me the joy of Thy salvation, and strengthen me with a perfect spirit.

»¹⁵I will teach the unjust Thy ways: and the wicked shall be converted to Thee.

¹⁶Deliver me from blood, O God, Thou God of my salvation: and my tongue shall extol Thy justice.

»¹⁷O Lord, Thou wilt open my lips: and my mouth shall declare Thy praise.

¹⁸For if Thou hadst desired sacrifice, I would indeed have given it: but with burnt offerings Thou wilt not be delighted.

»¹⁹A sacrifice to God is an afflicted spirit: a contrite and humbled heart, O God, Thou wilt not despise.

²⁰Deal favorably, O Lord, in Thy good will with Zion; that the walls of Jerusalem may be rebuilt.

»²¹Then shalt Thou accept the sacrifice of justice, oblations and whole burnt offerings: then shall they lay calves upon Thine altar.

V. *Glory be ...*

Ant 1.

Thursday Lauds II

Psalmus 89

Ant 2. Dómine, refúgium factus es nobis: a generatióne in generatiónem.

Dómine, refúgium factus es nobis a generatióne in generatiónem. ²Priusquam montes fíerent, aut formarétur terra et orbis, a sǽculo et usque in sǽculum tu es, Deus.
»³Ne avértas hóminem in humilitátem: et dixísti: Convertímini, fílii hóminum.
»⁴Quóniam mille anni ante óculos tuos tamquam dies hestérna quæ prætériit: et custódia in nocte ⁵quæ pro níhilo habéntur.

»⁶Mane sicut herba tránseat; mane flóreat, et tránseat; véspere decídat, indúret, et aréscat.

»⁷Quia defécimus in ira tua, et in furóre tuo turbáti sumus. ⁸Posuísti iniquitátes nostras in conspéctu tuo; sǽculum nostrum in illuminatióne vultus tui.
»⁹Quóniam ómnes dies nostri defecérunt, et in ira tua defécimus. Anni nostri sicut aránea meditabúntur;
¹⁰dies annórum nostrórum in ipsis septuagínta anni. Si autem in potentátibus octogínta anni, et ámplius eórum labor et dolor; quóniam supervénit mansuetúdo, et corripiémur.
»¹¹Quis novit potestátem iræ tuæ, et præ timóre tuo iram tuam. ¹²dinumeráre? Déxteram tuam sic notam fac, et erudítos corde in sapiéntia.
»¹³Convértere, Dómine; usquequo? et deprecábilis esto super servos tuos.

Psalm 89

Ant 2. O Lord, Thou hast become a refuge for us: from generation to generation.

Lord, Thou hast been our refuge from generation to generation. ²Before the mountains were made, or the earth and the world was formed; from eternity and to eternity Thou art God.
»³Turn not man away to be brought low: and Thou hast said: Be converted, O ye sons of men.
»⁴For a thousand years in Thy sight are as yesterday, which is past. And as a watch in the night: ⁵things that are counted nothing, shall their years be.

»⁶In the morning man shall grow up like grass; in the morning he shall flourish and then pass away: in the evening he shall fall, grow dry, and wither.

»⁷For in Thy wrath we have fainted away: and are troubled in Thy indignation.
⁸Thou hast set our iniquities before Thine eyes: our life in the light of Thy countenance.
»⁹For all our days are spent; and in Thy wrath we have fainted away. Our years shall pass away as a breath:
¹⁰the days of our years in them are threescore and ten. But if in the strong they be fourscore years: what is more of them is labor and sorrow. For soon the end comes upon us: and we shall be gone.
»¹¹Who knoweth the power of Thine anger, and for Thy fear can number Thy wrath?
¹²So make Thy right hand known: and men learned in heart, in wisdom.

¹⁴Repléti sumus mane misericórdia tua; et exsultávimus, et delectáti sumus ómnibus diébus nostris.

»¹⁵Lætáti sumus pro diébus quibus nos humiliásti; annis quibus vídimus mala.

»¹⁶Réspice in servos tuos et in ópera tua, et dírige fílios eórum.
»¹⁷Et sit splendor Dómini Dei nostri super nos, et ópera mánuum nostrárum dírige super nos, et opus mánuum nostrárum dírige.

V. *Glória Patri ...*

Ant 2.

Psalmus 35

Ant 3. **Multiplicásti Deus misericórdiam tuam.**

Dixit injústus ut delínquat in semetipso: non est timor Dei ante óculos ejus.
»³Quóniam dolóse egit in conspéctu ejus, ut inveniátur iníquitas ejus ad ódium.
⁴Verba oris ejus iníquitas, et dolus; nóluit intellígere ut bene ágeret.
»⁵Iniquitátem meditátus est in cubíli suo; astitit omni viæ non bonæ: malítiam autem non odívit.

»⁶Dómine, in cælo misericórdia tua, et véritas tua usque ad nubes.

⁷Justítia tua sicut montes Dei; judícia tua abýssus multa. Hómines et juménta salvábis, Dómine,
»⁸quemádmodum multiplicásti misericórdiam tuam, Deus. Filii

»¹³Return, O Lord, how long? And be entreated in favor of Thy servants.
¹⁴We are filled in the morning with Thy mercy: and we have rejoiced, and are delighted all our days.
»¹⁵We have rejoiced for the days in which Thou hast humbled us: for the years in which we have seen evils.
»¹⁶Look upon Thy servants and upon their works: and direct their children.
»¹⁷And let the brightness of the Lord our God be upon us: and direct Thou the works of our hands over us; yea, the work of our hands do Thou direct.

V. *Glory be ...*

Ant 2.

Psalm 35

Ant 3. **O God, Thou hast multiplied Thy mercy.**

The unjust hath said within himself that he would sin: there is no fear of God before his eyes.
»³For in his sight he hath done deceitfully, that his wickedness may be found unto hatred.
⁴The words of his mouth are iniquity and guile: he does not understand that he might do good.
»⁵He hath devised iniquity on his bed, he hath set himself on every way that is not good: but evil he hath not hated.
»⁶O Lord, Thy mercy is in heaven, and Thy truth reacheth even to the clouds.
⁷Thy justice is as the mountains of God, Thy judgments are like the boundless deep. Men and beasts Thou wilt preserve, O Lord.

Thursday Lauds II

autem hóminum in tégmine alárum tuárum sperábunt.
»⁹Inebriabúntur ab ubertáte domus tuæ, et torrénte voluptátis tuæ potábis eos:

¹⁰quóniam apud te est fons vitæ, et in lúmine tuo vidébimus lumen.

»¹¹Præténde misericórdiam tuam sciéntibus te, et justítiam tuam his qui recto sunt corde.

¹²Non véniat mihi pes supérbiæ, et manus peccatóris non móveat me.

»¹³Ibi cecidérunt qui operántur iniquitátem; expúlsi sunt, nec potuérunt stare.

V. *Glória Patri ...*

Ant 3.

Cánticum Moysis
(Exod 15:1-19)

Ant 4. Fortitúdo mea et laus mea Dóminus: et factus est mihi in salútem.

Cantémus Dómino: glorióse enim magnificátus est, equum et ascensórem dejécit in mare.
»²Fortitúdo mea, et laus mea Dóminus, et factus est mihi in salútem: iste Deus meus, et glorificábo eum: Deus patris mei, et exaltábo eum.

»³Dóminus quasi vir pugnátor, omnípotens nomen ejus,
⁴currus Pharaónis et exércitum ejus projécit in mare: elécti príncipes ejus submérsi sunt in mari Rubro.

»⁸O how hast Thou multiplied Thy mercy, O God! But the children of men shall put their trust under the covert of Thy wings.
»⁹They shall be filled with the abundance of Thy house; and Thou shalt make them drink of the fountain of Thy delights.
¹⁰For with Thee is the fountain of life; and in Thy light we shall see light itself.
»¹¹Extend Thy mercy to them that know thee, and Thy justice to them that are right in heart.
¹²Let not the foot of pride come to me, and let not the hand of the sinner move me.
»¹³There the workers of iniquity are fallen, they are cast out, and could not stand.

V. *Glory be ...*

Ant 3.

Canticle of Moses
(Exod 15:1-19)

Ant 4. The Lord is my strength and my praise: and He hath become my salvation.

Let us sing to the Lord: for He is gloriously magnified, the horse and the rider He hath thrown into the sea.
»²The Lord is my strength and my praise, and He hath become salvation to me: He is my God and I will glorify Him: the God of my father, and I will exalt Him.
»³The Lord is as a man of war, Almighty is His Name.
⁴Pharaoh's chariots and his army He hath cast into the sea: his chosen captains are drowned in the Red Sea.

Thursday Lauds II

»⁵Abýssi operuerunt eos; descendérunt in profúndum quasi lapis.
⁶Déxtera tua, Dómine, magnificáta est in fortitúdine déxtera tua, Dómine, percússit inimícum
»⁷Et in multitúdine glóriæ tuæ deposuísti adversários tuos: misísti iram tuam, quæ devorávit eos sicut stípulam.
»⁸Et in spíritu furóris tui congregátæ sunt aquæ: stetit unda fluens, congregáta sunt abýssi in médio mari.

»⁹Dixit inimícus: Pérsequar et comprehéndam, dividam spólia, implébitur ánima mea: evaginábo gládium meum, interficiet eos manus mea.
»¹⁰Flavit spíritus tuus, et opéruit eos mare: submérsi sunt quasi plumbum in aquis veheméntibus.
¹¹Quis símilis tui in fórtibus, Dómine? quis símilis tui, magníficus in sanctitáte, terríbilis atque laudábilis, fáciens mirabília?
»¹²Extendísti manum tuam, et devorávit eos terra.
¹³Dux fuísti in misericórdia tua pópulo quem redemísti: et portásti eum in fortitúdine tua, ad habitáculum sanctum tuum.
»¹⁴Ascendérunt pópuli, et iráti sunt: dolóres obtinuérunt habitatores Philísthiim.
¹⁵Tunc conturbáti sunt príncipes Edom, robústos Moab obtínuit tremor: obriguérunt ómnes habitatóres Chánaan.
»¹⁶Irruat super eos formído et pavor, in magnitúdine bráchii tui: fiant immóbiles quasi lapis, donec pertránseat pópulus tuus, Dómine, donec pertránseat pópulus tuus iste, quem possedísti.

»⁵The depths have covered them, they sunk to the bottom like a stone.
⁶Thy right hand, O Lord, is magnified in strength: Thy right hand, O Lord, hath slain the enemy.
»⁷And in the multitude of Thy glory Thou hast put down Thine adversaries: Thou hast sent Thy wrath, which hath devoured them like stubble.
»⁸And with the blast of Thine anger the waters were gathered together: the flowing water stood, the depths were gathered together in the midst of the sea.
»⁹The enemy said: I will pursue and overtake, I will divide the spoils, my soul shall have its fill: I will draw my sword, my hand shall slay them.
»¹⁰Thy wind blew and the sea covered them: they sunk as lead in the mighty waters.
¹¹Who is like to Thee, among the strong, O Lord? Who is like to Thee, glorious in holiness, terrible and praiseworthy, doing wonders?
»¹²Thou stretchedst forth Thy hand, and the earth swallowed them.
¹³In Thy mercy Thou hast been a leader to the people which Thou hast redeemed: and in Thy strength Thou hast carried them to Thy holy dwelling place.
»¹⁴Nations rose up, and were angry: sorrows took hold over the inhabitants of Philistia.
¹⁵Then were the princes of Edom distressed, trembling seized on the strong men of Moab: all the inhabitants of Chanaan became full of fear.
»¹⁶Let fear and dread fall upon them, in the greatness of Thine arm: let them become unmoveable as a stone, until Thy people, O Lord, pass by: until this Thy people which Thou hast ransomed. pass by unharmed.

Thursday Lauds II

»¹⁷Introdúces eos, et plantábis in monte hæreditátis tuæ, firmíssimo habitáculo tuo quod operátus es, Dómine: sanctuárium tuum, Dómine, quod firmavérunt manus tuæ.

»¹⁸Dóminus regnábit in ætérnum et ultra.
¹⁹Ingréssus est enim eques Phárao cum cúrribus et equítibus ejus in mare: et redúxit super eos Dóminus aquas maris: fílii autem Israël ambulavérunt per siccum in médio ejus.

V. *Glória Partri ...*

Ant 4.

Psalmus 146

Ant 5. Laudáte Dóminum qui sanat contrítos corde, et álligat contritiónes eórum.

Laudáte Dóminum, quóniam bonus est psalmus; Deo nostro sit jucúnda, decóraque laudátio.

»²Ædíficans Jerúsalem Dóminus, dispersiónes Israëlis congregábit:
³qui sanat contrítos corde, et álligat contritiónes eórum;
»⁴qui númerat multitúdinem stellárum, et ómnibus eis nómina vocat.
⁵Magnus Dóminus noster, et magna virtus ejus, et sapiéntiæ ejus non est númerus.
»⁶Suscípiens mansuétos Dóminus; humílians autem peccatóres usque ad terram.
⁷Præcínite Dómino in cónfessione; psállite Deo nostro in cíthara.

»¹⁷Thou shalt bring them in, and plant them on the mountain of Thine inheritance, in Thy most firm habitation which Thou hast made, O Lord; Thy sanctuary, O Lord, which Thy hands have created.

»¹⁸The Lord shall reign for ever and ever.
¹⁹For Pharaoh went in on horseback with his chariots and horsemen into the sea: and the Lord brought back upon them the waters of the sea: but the children of Israel walked on dry ground in the midst thereof.

V. *Glory be ...*

Ant 4.

Psalm 146

Ant 5. Praise the Lord, who healeth the brokenhearted, healeth their brokenness.

Praise ye the Lord, because the psalms are pleasing to our God: be joyful with beautiful praise to Him.
»²The Lord buildeth up Jerusalem: He will gather together the dispersed of Israel:
³Who healeth the broken of heart, and bindeth up their wounds:
»⁴Who telleth the number of the stars: and calleth them all by their names.
⁵Great is our Lord, and great is His power: and His wisdom is infinite.
»⁶The Lord lifteth up the meek, and bringeth the wicked down even to the ground.
⁷Sing ye to the Lord with praise: sing to our God upon the harp:

Thursday Lauds II

»⁸Qui óperit cælum núbibus, et parat terræ plúviam; qui prodúcit in móntibus fænum, et herbam servitúti hóminum;

⁹qui dat juméntis escam ipsórum, et pullis corvórum invocántibus eum.

»¹⁰Non in fortitúdine equi voluntátem habébit, nec in tíbiis viri beneplácitum erit ei.
¹¹Beneplácitum est Dómino super timéntes eum, et in eis qui sperant super misericórdia ejus.

V. *Glória Patri ...*

Ant 5.

Capitulum
(Rom 13: 12-14)
The reading below or the proper of the day

V. Nox præcéssit, dies autem appropinquavit. Abjiciámus ergo ópera tenebrárum, et induámur arma lucis. Sicut in die honéste ambulémus: non in comessatiónibus, et ebrietátibus, non in cubílibus, et impudícitiis, non in contentióne, et æmulatióne:

R. Deo Grátias.

Hymnus
Or the hymn for the season

O Sol Salútis
Go to page 74

Versiculi

V. Ángelis suis Deus mandávit de te

R. Ut custódiant te in ómnibus viis tuis.

»⁸Who covereth the heaven with clouds, and prepareth rain for the earth: Who maketh grass to grow on the mountains, and herbs for the service of men:

⁹Who giveth to beasts their food: and to the young ravens that call upon Him.

»¹⁰He shall not delight in the strength of the horse: nor take pleasure in the power of a man.
¹¹The Lord taketh pleasure in them that fear Him: and in them that hope in His mercy.

V. *Glory be ...*

Ant 5.

Chapter
(Rom 13: 12-14)
The reading below or the proper of the day

V. The night is passed, and the day is at hand. Let us, therefore cast off the works of darkness, and put on the armor of light. Let us walk honestly, as in the day: not in rioting and drunkenness, not in debauchery and impurities, not in contention and envy.

R. Thanks be to God.

Hymn
Or the hymn for the season

Jesu, Salvation's Sun Divine
Go to page 74

Versicle

V. God sent His angels concerning thee.

R. That they may guard thee in all Thy ways.

Thursday Lauds II

Ant. In sanctitáte serviámus Dómino, et liberábit nos ab inimícis nostris. *(Whenever possible, the antiphon for the specific season or feast of a saint will be used).*

Cánticum Zacharíæ
(Luke 1:68-79)
Canticle on page 366

V. *Glória Patri ...*

Ant. In sanctitáte serviámus Dómino, et liberábit nos ab inimícis nostris.

V. *Páter nóster ...*
R. *Pánem nóstrum ...*

V. Dómine exáudi oratiónem meam.
R. Et clamor meus ad te véniat.

V. Oremus.

Omnípotens et miséricors Deus, univérsa nobis adversántia propitiátus exclúde: ut mente et córpore pariter expedíti, quæ tua sunt, líberis méntibus exsequamur. Per Dóminum nostrum ...

The prayer above is said, or the prayer of the season and the feast day are prayed if there are any.

V. Dómine exáudi oratiónem meam.
R. Et clamor meus ad te véniat.

V. Benedicámus Dómino.
R. Deo grátias.

V. Fidélium ánimæ per misericórdiam Dei requiéscant in pace.

R. Amen.

Ant. Let us serve the Lord in holiness, and He wilt deliver us from our enemies. *(Whenever possible, the antiphon for the specific season or feast of a saint will be used).*

Canticle of Zachariah
(Luke 1:68-79)
Canticle on page 366

V. *Glory be ...*

Ant. Let us serve the Lord in holiness, and He wilt deliver us from our enemies.

V. *Our Father ...*
R. *Give us this day ...*

V. O Lord, hear my prayer.
R. And let my cry come unto Thee.

V. Let us pray.

Omnipotent and merciful God, have mercy on us and shut out all our adversities: that we may do what is Thy will with free minds, ready in mind and body alike.
Through our Lord ...

The prayer above is said, or the prayer of the season and the feast day are prayed if there are any.

V. O Lord, hear my prayer.
R. And let my cry come unto Thee.

V. Let us bless the Lord.
R. Thanks be to God.

V. May the souls of the faithful departed through the mercy of God rest in peace.

R. Amen.

FRIDAY – LAUDS II

V. Dómine, ✝ lábia mea apéries.
R. Et os meum annuntiábit laudem tuam.

V. Deus, in adjutórium meum inténde.
R. Dómine, ad adjuvándum me festína.

V. *Glória Patri ...*
R. *Sicut erat ...*

Psalmus 50

Ant 1. Cor contrítum et humiliátum Deus non despícies.

Miserere mei, Deus, secúndum magnam misericórdiam tuam; et secúndum multitúdinem miseratiónum tuárum, dele iniquitátem meam.
⁴Ámplius lava me ab iniquitáte mea, et a peccáto meo munda me.

»⁵Quóniam iniquitátem meam ego cognósco, et peccátum meum contra me est semper.
⁶Tibi soli peccávi, et malum coram te feci; ut justificéris in sermónibus tuis, et vincas cum judicáris.

»⁷Ecce enim in iniquitátibus concéptus sum, et in peccátis concépit me mater mea.

⁸Ecce enim veritátem dilexísti; incérta et occúlta sapiéntiæ tuæ manifestásti mihi.

V. O Lord, ✝ open my lips.
R. And my mouth shall proclaim Thy praise.

V. O God, come to my assistance.
R. O Lord, make haste to help me.

V. *Glory be ...*
R. *As it was ...*

Psalm 50

Ant 1. God will not despise a broken and humble heart.

Have mercy on me, O God, according to Thy great compassion. And according to the multitude of Thy tender mercies blot out my iniquity.
⁴Wash me yet more from my iniquity, and cleanse me from my sins.
»⁵For I know my wickedness, and my sin is always before me.

⁶To Thee only have I sinned, and have done evil before Thee: that Thou mayest be justified in Thy words, and mayest be blameless when Thou judgeth.
»⁷For behold I was conceived with iniquities; and in sin did my mother conceive me.
⁸For behold Thou hast loved truth: the uncertain and hidden things of Thy wisdom Thou hast made manifest to me.

Friday Lauds II

»⁹Aspérges me hyssópo, et mundábor; lavábis me, et super nivem dealbábor.

¹⁰Audítui meo dabis gáudium et lætítiam, et exsultábunt ossa humiliata
»¹¹Avérte fáciem tuam a peccátis meis, et ómnes iniquitátes meas dele.
¹²Cor mundum crea in me, Deus, et spíritum rectum ínnova in viscéribus meis.
»¹³Ne projícias me a fácie tua, et spíritum sanctum tuum ne áuferas a me.
¹⁴Redde mihi lætítiam salutáris tui, et spíritu principáli confírma me.

»¹⁵Docébo iníquos vias tuas, et impii ad te converténtur.

¹⁶Líbera me de sanguínibus, Deus, Deus salútis meæ, et exsultábit lingua mea justítiam tuam
»¹⁷Dómine, lábia mea aperies, et os meum annuntiábit laudem tuam.

¹⁸Quóniam si voluísses sacrifícium, dedíssem útique; holocáustis non delectáberis.

»¹⁹Sacrifícium Deo spíritus contribulátus; cor contrítum et humiliátum, Deus, non despícies.
²⁰Benígne fac, Dómine, in bona voluntáte tua Sion, ut ædificéntur muri Jerúsalem.
»²¹Tunc acceptábis sacrifícium justítiæ, oblatiónes et holocáusta; tunc impónent super altáre tuum vítulos.

V. *Glória Patri ...*

Ant 1.

»⁹Thou shalt sprinkle me with hyssop, and I shall be cleansed: Thou shalt wash me, and I shall be made whiter than snow.
¹⁰To my hearing Thou shalt give joy and gladness: and the bones that have been humbled shall rejoice.
»¹¹Turn away Thy face from my sins, and blot out all my iniquities.
¹²Create a clean heart in me, O God: and renew a right spirit within my bowels.
»¹³Cast me not away from Thy face; and take not Thy Holy Spirit from me.
¹⁴Restore unto me the joy of Thy salvation, and strengthen me with a perfect spirit.
»¹⁵I will teach the unjust Thy ways: and the wicked shall be converted to Thee.
¹⁶Deliver me from blood, O God, Thou God of my salvation: and my tongue shall extol Thy justice.
»¹⁷O Lord, Thou wilt open my lips: and my mouth shall declare Thy praise.
¹⁸For if Thou hadst desired sacrifice, I would indeed have given it: but with burnt offerings Thou wilt not be delighted.
»¹⁹A sacrifice to God is an afflicted spirit: a contrite and humbled heart, O God, Thou wilt not despise.
²⁰Deal favorably, O Lord, in Thy good will with Zion; that the walls of Jerusalem may be rebuilt.
»²¹Then shalt Thou accept the sacrifice of justice, oblations and whole burnt offerings: then shall they lay calves upon Thine altar.

V. *Glory be ...*

Ant 1.

Friday Lauds II

Psalmus 142

Ant 2. Propter nomen tuum Dómine vivificábis me in æquitáte tua.

Dómine, exáudi oratiónem meam; áuribus pércipe obsecratiónem meam in veritáte tua; exáudi me in tua justítia.
²Et non intres in judícium cum servo tuo, quia non justificábitur in conspéctu tuo omnis vivens
»³Quia persecútus est inimícus ánimam meam; humiliávit in terra vitam meam; collocávit me in obscúris, sicut mórtuos sǽculi.
⁴Et anxiatus est super me spíritus meus; in me turbátum est cor meum.
»⁵Memor fui diérum antiquórum; meditátus sum in ómnibus opéribus tuis: in factis mánuum tuárum meditabar.

⁶Expándi manus meas ad te; ánima mea sicut terra sine aqua tibi.

»⁷Velóciter exáudi me, Dómine; defécit spíritus meus. Non avértas fáciem tuam a me, et símilis ero descendéntibus in lacum.

»⁸Audítam fac mihi mane misericórdiam tuam, quia in te sperávi. Notam fac mihi viam in qua ámbulem, quia ad te levávi ánimam meam.
⁹Éripe me de inimícis meis, Dómine: ad te confúgi.
»¹⁰Spíritus tuus bonus dedúcet me in terram rectam: propter nomen tuum, Dómine, vivificábis me, in æquitáte tua.
»¹¹Edúces de tribulatióne ánimam meam: et in misericórdia tua dispérdes inimícos meos.

Psalm 142

Ant 2. For Thy Name's sake, O Lord, Thou wilt quicken me by Thy righteousness.

Hear, O Lord, my prayer: give ear to my supplication in Thy truth: hear me in Thy justice.
²And enter not into judgment with Thy servant: for in Thy sight no man living shall be justified.
»³For the enemy hath persecuted my soul: he hath brought down my life to the earth. He hath made me to dwell in darkness as those that have been dead of old:
⁴and my spirit is in anguish within me: my heart within me is troubled.
»⁵I remembered the days of old, I meditated on all Thy works: I meditated upon the works of Thy hands.

⁶I stretched forth my hands to Thee: my soul is as earth without water unto Thee.
»⁷Hear me speedily, O Lord: my spirit hath fainted away. Turn not away Thy face from me, lest I be like them that go down into the pit.
»⁸Cause me to hear Thy mercy in the morning; for in Thee have I hoped. Make the way known to me, wherein I should walk: for I have lifted up my soul to Thee.
⁹Deliver me from mine enemies, O Lord, to Thee have I fled.
»¹⁰Thy good Spirit shall lead me into the right land: for Thy Name's sake, O Lord, Thou wilt quicken me in Thy justice.
»¹¹Thou wilt bring my soul out of trouble: and in Thy mercy Thou wilt destroy mine enemies.

Friday Lauds II

¹²Et perdes omnes, qui tríbulant ánimam meam: quóniam ego servus tuus sum.

V. *Glória Patri ...*

Ant 2.

Psalmus 84

Ant 3. **Deus tu convérsus vivificábis nos, et plebs tua lætábitur in te.**

Benedixisti, Dómine, terram tuam; avertísti captivitátem Jacob.
³Remisísti iniquitátem plebis tuæ; operuísti ómnia peccáta eórum.
»⁴Mitigásti omnem iram tuam; avertísti ab ira indignatiónis tuæ.
»⁵Convérte nos, Deus salutáris noster, et avérte iram tuam a nobis.
⁶Numquid in ætérnum irascéris nobis? aut exténdes iram tuam a generatióne in generatiónem
»⁷Deus, tu convérsus vivificabis nos, et plebs tua lætábitur in te.

⁸Ostende nobis, Dómine, misericórdiam tuam, et salutáre tuum da nobis.

»⁹Áudiam quid loquátur in me Dóminus Deus, quóniam loquetur pacem in plebem suam, et super sanctos suos, et in eos qui convertúntur ad cor.

»¹⁰Verúmtamen prope timéntes eum salutáre ipsius, ut inhábitet glória in terra nostra.

V. *Glória Patri ...*

Ant 3.

¹²And Thou wilt cut off all them that afflict my soul: for I am Thy servant.

V. *Glory be ...*

Ant 2.

Psalm 84

Ant 3. **O God, Thou wilt turn and revive us, and the people will take refuge in Thee.**

Lord, Thou hast blessed Thy land: Thou hast turned away the captivity of Jacob.
³Thou hast forgiven the iniquity of Thy people: Thou hast covered all their sins.
»⁴Thou hast mitigated all Thine anger: Thou hast turned away from the wrath of Thine indignation.
»⁵Convert us, O God our Savior: and turn away Thine anger from us.
⁶Wilt Thou be angry with us for ever: or wilt Thou extend Thy wrath from generation to generation?
»⁷Thou wilt turn, O God, and bring us to life: and Thy people shall rejoice in Thee.
⁸Show us, O Lord, Thy mercy; and grant us Thy salvation.
»⁹I will hear what the Lord God will speak in me: for He will speak peace unto His people: and unto His saints: and unto them that have converted their hearts.

»¹⁰Surely His salvation is near to them that fear Him: that glory may dwell in our land.

V. *Glory be ...*

Ant 3.

Friday Lauds II

Canticle of Habacuc
(Hab 3:2-19)

Ant 4. Cum irátus fúeris Dómine misericórdiæ recordáberis.

Dómine, audívi auditiónem tuam, et tímui. Dómine, opus tuum, in médio annórum vivífica illud; in médio annórum notum fácies: cum irátus fúeris, misericórdiæ recordáberis.
»³Deus ab austro véniet, et Sanctus de monte Pharan: opéruit cælos glória ejus, et laudis ejus plena est terra.

»⁴Splendor ejus ut lux erit, cornua in mánibus ejus: ibi abscóndita est fortitúdo ejus.
⁵Ante fáciem ejus ibit mors, et egrediétur diábolus ante pedes ejus.

»⁶Stetit, et mensus est terram; aspéxit, et dissólvit gentes, et contríti sunt montes sǽculi: incurváti sunt colles mundi ab itinéribus æternitátis ejus.

»⁷Pro iniquitáte vidi tentória Æthiópiæ; turbabúntur pelles terræ Mádian.

»⁸Numquid in flumínibus irátus es, Dómine? aut in flumínibus furor tuus? vel in mari indignátio tua? Qui ascéndes super equos tuos, et quadrígæ tuæ salvátio.
»⁹Súscitans suscitábis arcum tuum, juraménta tríbubus quæ locútus es; flúvios scindes terræ.

»¹⁰Vidérunt te, et doluérunt montes; gurges aquárum tránsiit: dedit abýssus vocem suam; altitúdo manus suas levávit.

Canticle of Habakkuk
(Hab 3:2-19)

Ant 4. When Thou art angry, Thou wilt remember mercy.

O Lord, I have heard Thy voice and was afraid. O Lord, Thy work, in the midst of the years, bring it to life: in the midst of the years Thou shalt make it known: when Thou art angry, Thou wilt remember mercy.
»³God will come from the south, and the Holy One from Mount Pharan: His glory covered the heavens, and the earth is full of His praise.
»⁴His brightness shall be as the light: the rays are in His hands: there is His power veiled.
⁵Death shall go before His face. And the devil shall go forth before His feet.
»⁶He stood and the earth trembled. He looked, and melted the nations: and the ancient mountains were crushed to pieces. The hills of the world were bowed down by His eternal journeys.
»⁷I saw the tents of Ethiopia for their iniquity, the curtains of the land of Madian shall be distressed.
»⁸Wast Thou angry, O Lord, with the rivers? Or was Thy wrath upon the rivers? Or Thine indignation in the sea? Who will ride upon Thy horses when Thy chariots are victorious?
»⁹Thou wilt surely take up Thy bow: according to the oaths which Thou hast spoken to the tribes. Thou wilt divide the rivers of the earth.
»¹⁰The mountains saw Thee, and trembled: the great body of waters washed by. The deep put forth its voice: the deep lifted up its hands.

Friday Lauds II

»¹¹Sol et luna stetérunt in habitáculo suo: in luce sagittárum tuárum ibunt, splendóre fúlgurántis hastæ tuæ.

»¹²In frémitu conculcábis terram; in fúrore obstupefácies gentes.

»¹³Egréssus es in salútem pópuli tui, in salútem cum christo tuo: percussísti caput de domo ímpii, denudásti fundaméntum ejus usque ad collum.

»¹⁴Maledixísti sceptris ejus, cápiti bellatórum ejus, veniéntibus ut turbo ad dispergéndum me: exsultátio eórum, sicut ejus qui dévorat páuperem in abscóndito.

¹⁵Viam fecísti in mari equis tuis, in luto aquárum multárum.

»¹⁶Audívi, et conturbátus est venter meus; a voce contremuérunt lábia mea. Ingrediátur putrédo in óssibus meis, et subter me scáteat: ut requiéscam in die tribulatiónis, ut ascéndam ad pópulum accínctum nostrum.

»¹⁷Ficus enim non florébit, et non erit germen in víneis; mentiétur opus olívæ, et arva non áfferent cibum: abscindétur de ovíli pecus, et non erit arméntum in præsépibus.

¹⁸Ego autem in Dómino gaudébo; et exsultábo in Deo Jesu meo.

»¹⁹Deus Dóminus fortitúdo mea, et ponet pedes meos quasi cervórum: et super excélsa mea dedúcet me victor in psalmis canéntem.

»¹¹The sun and the moon stood still in their dwelling places, in the light of Thine arrows, they shall fear the brightness of Thy glittering spear.

»¹²In Thine anger Thou wilt tread the earth under foot: in Thy wrath Thou wilt crush the nations.

»¹³Thou wentest forth for the salvation of Thy people: for salvation with Thine annointed. Thou struckest the roof of the house of the wicked: Thou hast laid bare his foundation even to the rock.

»¹⁴Thou hast pierced the head of the warriors with his spear, they that came out as a whirlwind to scatter me. Their joy was like that of him that devoureth the poor man in secret.

¹⁵Thou madest a way in the sea for their horses, into the mud of many waters.

»¹⁶I have heard and my flesh was troubled: my lips trembled at His voice. Let decay enter into my bones, and let it spread beneath me: that I may wait until the day of tribulation: that I may go up to our people that are bound.

»¹⁷For the fig tree shall not blossom: and there shall be no grapes on the vines. The produce of the olive tree shall fail: and the fields shall yield no food: the flock shall be cut off from the fold, and there shall be no herd in the stalls.

¹⁸But I will rejoice in the Lord: and I will exult in God my Savior.

»¹⁹The Lord God is my strength: and He will make my feet feel like the feet of harts: and He, the Vanquisher, will lead me upon the heights singing psalms.

V. *Glória Patri ...*

Ant 4.

Psalmus 147

Ant 5. **Lauda Deum tuum, Sion.**

𝕷 auda, Jerúsalem, Dóminum; lauda Deum tuum, Sion.
¹³Quóniam confortávit seras portárum tuárum; benedíxit fíliis tuis in te.
»¹⁴Qui pósuit fines tuos pacem, et ádipe fruménti sátiat te.

»¹⁵Qui emittit elóquium suum terræ: velóciter currit sermo ejus.
¹⁶Qui dat nivem sicut lanam; nébulam sicut cínerem spargit.
»¹⁷Mittit crystállum suam sicut buccéllas: ante fáciem frígoris ejus quis sustinébit?
¹⁸Emíttet verbum suum, et liquefáciet ea; flabit spíritus ejus, et fluent aquæ.

»¹⁹Qui annúntiat verbum suum Jacob, justítias et judícia sua Israël.

²⁰Non fecit taliter omni nationi, et judícia sua non manifestávit eis.

V. *Glória Patri ...*

Ant 5.

V. *Glory be ...*

Ant 4.

Psalm 147

Ant 5. **Zion, praise thy God.**

𝕻 raise the Lord, O Jerusalem: praise thy God, O Zion:
¹³because He hath strengthened the bolts of thy gates, He hath blessed thy children within thee:
»¹⁴Who hath placed peace in thy borders: and filleth thee with the fat of corn:

»¹⁵Who sendeth forth His speech to the earth: His word runneth swiftly:
¹⁶Who giveth snow like wool: scattereth frost like ashes.
»¹⁷He sendeth His crystal like crumbs: who shall stand before the face of His cold?
¹⁸He shall send out His word, and shall melt them: His wind shall blow, and the waters shall run:

»¹⁹Who declareth His word to Jacob: His justices and His judgments to Israel?
²⁰He hath not done in like manner to every nation: and His judgments He hath not made manifest to them.

V. *Glory be ...*

Ant 5.

Friday Lauds II

Capitulum
(Rom 13:12-14)
The reading below or the proper of the day

V. Nox præcéssit, dies autem appropinquavit. Abjiciámus ergo ópera tenebrárum, et induámur arma lucis. Sicut in die honéste ambulémus: non in comessatiónibus, et ebrietátibus, non in cubílibus, et impudicitiis, non in contentióne, et æmulatióne.

R. Deo Grátias.

Hymnus
Or the hymn for the season

Audi Benígne Cónditor, Pg. 372

Versiculi

V. Ángelis suis Deus mandávit de te

R. Ut custódiant te in ómnibus viis tuis.

Ant. Per vicera misericórdiæ Dei nostri visitávit nos oriens ex alto. *(Whenever possible, the antiphon for the specific season or feast of a saint will be used).*

Cánticum Zachariæ
(Luke 1:68-79)
Canticle on page 366

V. *Glória Patri ...*

Ant. Per vicera misericórdiæ Dei nostri visitávit nos oriens ex alto.

V. *Páter nóster ...*
R. *Pánem nóstrum ...*

Chapter
(Rom 13:12-14)
The reading below or the proper of the day

V. The night is passed, and the day is at hand. Let us, therefore cast off the works of darkness, and put on the armor of light. Let us walk honestly, as in the day: not in rioting and drunkenness, not in debauchery and impurities, not in contention and envy.

R. Thanks be to God.

Hymn
Or the hymn for the season

O King Creator, Pg. 372

Versicle

V. God sent His angels concerning thee.
R. That they may guard thee in all thy ways.

Ant. Through the abundance of the mercy of our God, the dawn from on high hath visited us. *(Whenever possible, the antiphon for the specific season or feast of a saint will be used).*

Canticle of Zachariah
(Luke 1:68-79)
Canticle on page 366

V. *Glory be ...*

Ant. Through the abundance of the mercy of our God, the dawn from on high hath visited us.

V. *Our Father ...*
R. *Give us this day ...*

Friday Lauds II

V. Dómine exáudi oratiónem meam.
R. Et clamor meus ad te véniat.

V. Oremus.

V. Preces nostras, quǽsumus, Dómine, cleménter exáudi: atque, a peccatórum vínculis absolútos, ab omni nos adversitáte custódi. Per Dóminum nostrum ...

The prayer above is said, or the prayer of the season and the feast day are prayed if there are any.

V. Dómine exáudi oratiónem meam.
R. Et clamor meus ad te véniat.

V. Benedicámus Dómino.
R. Deo grátias.

V. Fidélium ánimæ per misericórdiam Dei requiéscant in pace.in pace.

R. Amen.

V. O Lord, hear my prayer.
R. And let my cry come unto Thee.

V. Let us pray.

V. Mercifully hear our prayers, we beseech Thee Lord: and freed from the chains of sins, keep us from all adversity. Through our Lord …

The prayer above is said, or the prayer of the season and the feast day are prayed if there are any.

V. O Lord, hear my prayer.
R. And let my cry come unto Thee.

V. Let us bless the Lord.
R. Thanks be to God.

V. May the souls of the faithful departed through the mercy of God rest in peace.

R. Amen.

Make the way known to me, wherein I should walk: for I have lifted up my soul to Thee.

SATURDAY – LAUDS II

V. Dómine, ✝ lábia mea apéries.
R. Et os meum annuntiábit laudem tuam.

V. Deus, in adjutórium meum inténde.
R. Dómine, ad adjuvándum me festína.

V. *Glória Patri ...*
R. *Sicut erat ...*

Psalmus 50

Ant 1. Cor contrítum et humiliátum Deus non despícies.

Miserere mei, Deus, secúndum magnam misericórdiam tuam; et secúndum multitúdinem miseratiónum tuárum, dele iniquitátem meam.
⁴Ámplius lava me ab iniquitáte mea, et a peccáto meo munda me.
»⁵Quóniam iniquitátem meam ego cognósco, et peccátum meum contra me est semper.
⁶Tibi soli peccávi, et malum coram te feci; ut justificéris in sermónibus tuis, et vincas cum judicáris.

»⁷Ecce enim in iniquitátibus concéptus sum, et in peccátis concépit me mater mea.

⁸Ecce enim veritátem dilexísti; incérta et occúlta sapiéntiæ tuæ manifestásti mihi.

V. O Lord, ✝ open my lips.
R. And my mouth shall proclaim Thy praise.

V. O God, come to my assistance.

R. O Lord, make haste to help me.

V. *Glory be ...*
R. *As it was ...*

Psalm 50

Ant 1. God will not despise a broken and humble heart.

Have mercy on me, O God, according to Thy great compassion. And according to the multitude of Thy tender mercies blot out my iniquity.
⁴Wash me yet more from my iniquity, and cleanse me from my sin.
»⁵For I know my wickedness, and my sin is always before me.

⁶To Thee only have I sinned, and have done evil before Thee: that Thou mayest be justified in Thy words, and mayest be blameless when Thou judgeth
»⁷For behold I was conceived with iniquities; and in sin did my mother conceive me.

⁸For behold Thou hast loved truth: the uncertain and hidden things of Thy wisdom Thou hast made manifest to me.

Saturday Lauds II

»⁹Aspérges me hyssópo, et mundábor; lavábis me, et super nivem dealbábor.

¹⁰Audítui meo dabis gáudium et lætítiam, et exsultábunt ossa humiliata
»¹¹Avérte fáciem tuam a peccátis meis, et ómnes iniquitátes meas dele.
¹²Cor mundum crea in me, Deus, et spíritum rectum ínnova in viscéribus meis.
»¹³Ne projícias me a fácie tua, et spíritum sanctum tuum ne áuferas a me.
¹⁴Redde mihi lætítiam salutáris tui, et spíritu principáli confírma me.

»¹⁵Docébo iníquos vias tuas, et impii ad te converténtur.

¹⁶Líbera me de sanguínibus, Deus, Deus salútis meæ, et exsultábit lingua mea justítiam tuam
»¹⁷Dómine, lábia mea apéries, et os meum annuntiábit laudem tuam.

¹⁸Quóniam si voluísses sacríficium, dedíssem útique; holocáustis non delectáberis.

»¹⁹Sacríficium Deo spíritus contribulátus; cor contrítum et humiliátum, Deus, non despícies.
²⁰Benígne fac, Dómine, in bona voluntáte tua Sion, ut ædificéntur muri Jerúsalem.
»²¹Tunc acceptábis sacríficium justítiæ, oblatiónes et holocáusta; tunc impónent super altáre tuum vítulos.

V. *Glória Patri ...*

Ant 1.

»⁹Thou shalt sprinkle me with hyssop, and I shall be cleansed: Thou shalt wash me, and I shall be made whiter than snow.
¹⁰To my hearing Thou shalt give joy and gladness: and the bones that have been humbled shall rejoice.
»¹¹Turn away Thy face from my sins, and blot out all my iniquities.
¹²Create a clean heart in me, O God: and renew a right spirit within my bowels.
»¹³Cast me not away from Thy face; and take not Thy Holy Spirit from me.
¹⁴Restore unto me the joy of Thy salvation, and strengthen me with a perfect spirit.
»¹⁵I will teach the unjust Thy ways: and the wicked shall be converted to Thee.
¹⁶Deliver me from blood, O God, Thou God of my salvation: and my tongue shall extol Thy justice.
»¹⁷O Lord, Thou wilt open my lips: and my mouth shall declare Thy praise.
¹⁸For if Thou hadst desired sacrifice, I would indeed have given it: but with burnt offerings Thou wilt not be delighted.
»¹⁹A sacrifice to God is an afflicted spirit: a contrite and humbled heart, O God, Thou wilt not despise.
²⁰Deal favorably, O Lord, in Thy good will with Zion; that the walls of Jerusalem may be rebuilt.
»²¹Then shalt Thou accept the sacrifice of justice, oblations and whole burnt offerings: then shall they lay calves upon Thine altar.

V. *Glory be ...*

Ant 1.

Psalmus 91

Ant 2. Rectus Dóminus Deus noster, et non est iníquitas in eo.

onum est confitéri Dómino, et psállere nómini tuo, Altíssime:
»³ad annuntiándum mane misericórdiam tuam, et veritátem tuam per noctem,
⁴in decachórdo, psaltério; cum cántico, in cíthara.
»⁵Quia delectásti me, Dómine, in factúra tua; et in opéribus mánuum tuárum exsultábo.
⁶Quam magnificáta sunt ópera tua, Dómine! nimis profúndæ factæ sunt cogitatiónes tuæ.
»⁷Vir insípiens non cognóscet, et stultus non intélliget hæc.

⁸Cum exórti fúerint peccatóres sicut fœnum, et apparúerint ómnes qui operántur iniquitátem, ut intéreant in sǽculum sǽculi;
»⁹tu autem Altíssimus in ætérnum, Dómine.

¹⁰Quóniam ecce inimíci tui, Dómine, quóniam ecce inimíci tui períbunt; et dispergéntur ómnes qui operántur iniquitátem.
»¹¹Et exaltábitur sicut unicórnis cornu meum, et senéctus mea in misericórdia úberi.
»¹²Et despéxit óculus meus inimícos meos, et in insurgéntibus in me malignántibus áudiet auris mea.
»¹³Justus ut palma florébit; sicut cedrus Líbani multiplicábitur.

Psalm 91

Ant 2. The Lord our God is righteous, and there is no iniquity in Him.

It is good to give praise to the Lord: and to sing to Thy Name, O most High.
»³To show forth Thy mercy in the morning, and Thy truth in the night:
⁴upon an instrument of ten strings, upon the psaltery: with a canticle upon the harp.
»⁵For Thou hast given me, O Lord, a delight in Thy doings: and in the works of Thy hands I shall rejoice.
⁶O Lord, how great are Thy works! Thy thoughts are exceeding deep.
»⁷The senseless man shall not know: nor will the fool understand these things.
⁸When the wicked shall spring up as grass: and all the workers of iniquity shall appear: that they may perish for ever and ever:
»⁹but Thou, O Lord, art most high for evermore.
¹⁰For behold Thine enemies, O Lord, for behold Thine enemies shall perish: and all the workers of iniquity shall be scattered.
»¹¹But my horn shall be exalted like that of the unicorn: and my old age in plentiful mercy
»¹²Mine eye also hath looked down upon mine enemies: and mine ear shall hear of the downfall of the malignant that rise up against me.
»¹³The just shall flourish like the palm tree: he shall grow up like the cedar of Lebanon.

Saturday Lauds II

¹⁴Plantáti in domo Dómini, in átriis domus Dei nostri florébunt.

»¹⁵Adhuc multiplicabúntur in senécta úberi, et bene patíentes erunt:
¹⁶ut annúntient quóniam rectus Dóminus Deus noster, et non est iníquitas in eo.

V. *Glória Patri* ...

Ant 2.

Psalmus 63

Ant 3. **Lætábitur justus in Dómino et sperábit in eo.**

Exáudi, Deus, oratiónem meam cum déprecor; a timóre inimíci éripe ánimam meam.
³Protexísti me a convéntu malignántium, a multitúdine operántium iniquitátem.
»⁴Quia exacuérunt ut gládium linguas suas; inténderunt arcum rem amáram,
⁵ut sagíttent in occúltis immaculátum

»⁶Súbito sagittábunt eum, et non timébunt; firmavérunt sibi sermónem nequam. Narravérunt ut abscónderent láqueos; dixérunt: Quis vidébit eos?

»⁷Scrutáti sunt iniquitátes; defecérunt scrutantes scrutinio. Accédet homo ad cor altum,

»⁸et exaltábitur Deus. Sagittæ parvulórum factæ sunt plagæ eórum,
⁹et infirmátæ sunt contra eos linguæ eórum. Conturbáti sunt ómnes qui vidébant eos, et tímuit omnis homo.
»¹⁰Et annuntiavérunt ópera Dei, et facta ejus intellexérunt.

¹⁴They that are planted in the house of the Lord shall flourish in the courts of the house of our God.
»¹⁵They shall still increase in a fruitful old age: and shall be well treated,
¹⁶that they may show, that the Lord our God is righteous, and there is no iniquity in Him.

V. *Glory be* ...

Ant 2.

Psalm 63

Ant 3. **The righteous will rejoice in the Lord and hope in Him.**

Hear, O God, my prayer, when I make supplication to Thee: deliver my soul from the fear of the enemy.
³Thou hast protected me from the assembly of the malignant; from the multitude of the workers of iniquity.
»⁴For they have whetted their tongues like a sword; they have bent their bow, a bitter thing:
⁵to shoot in secret the undefiled.
»⁶They will shoot at him suddenly, and will not fear: they are resolute in wickedness. They have talked of hiding snares; they have said: who shall see them?
»⁷They have searched after iniquities: they have failed in their search. Man shall come to a deep heart: and God shall be exalted.
»⁸The arrows of children are their wounds:
⁹and their tongues against them are made weak. All that saw the evil doers were distressed: and every man was afraid.
»¹⁰And they praised the works of God: and understood His deeds.

¹¹Lætabitur justus in Dómino, et sperábit in eo, et laudabúntur omnes recti corde.
V. *Glória Patri* ...

Ant 3.

Cánticum Moysis
(Exod 15:1-19)

Ant 4. In servis suis miserébitur Dóminus et propítiuserit terræ pópuli sui.

₵antémus Dómino: gloriose enim magnificátus est, equum et ascensórem dejécit in mare.
»²Fortitúdo mea, et laus mea Dóminus, et factus est mihi in salútem: iste Deus meus, et glorificábo eum: Deus patris mei, et exaltábo eum.

»³Dóminus quasi vir pugnátor, omnípotens nomen ejus,
⁴currus Pharaónis et exércitum ejus projécit in mare: elécti príncipes ejus submérsi sunt in mari Rubro.
⁵Abýssi operuérunt eos; descenderunt in profúndum quasi lapis.
»⁶Déxtera tua, Dómine, magnificáta est in fortitúdine: déxtera tua, Dómine, percússit inimícum
⁷Et in multitúdine glóriæ tuæ deposuísti adversários tuos: misísti iram tuam, quæ devorávit eos sicut stípulam.
»⁸Et in spíritu furóris tui congregátæ sunt aquæ: stetit unda fluens, congregátæ sunt abýssi in médio mari.
»⁹Dixit inimícus: Pérsequar et comprehéndam, dívidam spólia, implébitur ánima mea: evaginábo gládium meum, interfíciet eos manus mea.

¹¹The just shall rejoice in the Lord, and shall hope in him, and all the upright in heart shall be praised.
V. *Glory be* ...

Ant 3.

Canticle of Moses
(Exod 15:1-19)

Ant 4. The Lord will have mercy on His servants and have mercy on the land of His people.

𝓛et us sing to the Lord: for He is gloriously magnified, the horse and the rider He hath thrown into the sea.
»²The Lord is my strength and my praise, and He is my salvation: He is my God and I will glorify Him: the God of my father, and I will exalt Him.
»³The Lord is as a man of war, Almighty is His Name.
⁴Pharaoh's chariots and his army He hath cast into the sea: his chosen captains are drowned in the Red Sea.
⁵The depths have covered them, they are sunk to the bottom like a stone.
»⁶Thy right hand, O Lord, is magnified in strength: Thy right hand, O Lord, hath slain the enemy.
⁷And in the multitude of Thy glory Thou hast put down Thine adversaries: Thou hast sent Thy wrath, which hath devoured them like stubble.
»⁸And with the blast of Thine anger the waters were gathered together: the flowing water stood, the depths were gathered together in the midst of the sea.
»⁹The enemy said: I will pursue and overtake, I will divide the spoils, my soul shall have its fill: I will draw my sword, my hand shall slay them.

Saturday Lauds II

¹⁰Flavit spíritus tuus, et opéruit eos mare: submérsi sunt quasi plumbum in aquis veheméntibus.
»¹¹Quis símilis tui in fórtibus, Dómine? quis símilis tui, magníficus in sanctitáte, terríbilis atque laudábilis, fáciens mirabília? ¹²Extendísti manum tuam, et devorávit eos terra.

»¹³Dux fuísti in misericórdia tua pópulo quem redemísti: et portásti eum in fortitúdine tua, ad habitáculum sanctum tuum.
»¹⁴Ascendérunt pópuli, et iráti sunt: dolóres obtinuérunt habitatóres Philísthiim.
¹⁵Tunc conturbáti sunt príncipes Edom, robústos Moab obtínuit tremor: obriguérunt ómnes habitatóres Chánaan.

»¹⁶Írruat super eos formído et pavor, in magnitódine bráchii tui: fiant immóbiles quasi lapis, donec pertránseat pópulus tuus, Dómine, donec pertránseat pópulus tuus iste, quem possedísti.
»¹⁷Introdúces eos, et plantábis in monte hæreditátis tuæ, firmíssimo habitáculo tuo quod operátus es, Dómine: sanctuárium tuum, Dómine, quod firmavérunt manus tuæ.

¹⁸Dóminus regnábit in ætérnum et ultra.
»¹⁹Ingréssus est enim eques Phárao cum cúrribus et equítibus ejus in mare: et redúxit super eos Dóminus aquas maris: fílii autem Israël ambulavérunt per siccum in médio ejus.

V. *Glória Patri ...*

Ant 4.

¹⁰Thy wind blew and the sea covered them: they sunk as lead in the mighty waters.
»¹¹Who is like to Thee, among the strong, O Lord? Who is like to Thee, glorious in holiness, terrible and praiseworthy, doing wonders? ¹²Thou stretchedst forth Thy hand, and the earth swallowed them.
»¹³In Thy mercy Thou hast been a leader to the people which Thou hast redeemed: and in Thy strength Thou hast carried them to Thy holy habitation.
»¹⁴Nations rose up, and were angry: sorrows took hold of the inhabitants of Philisthiim.
¹⁵Then were the princes of Edom distressed, trembling seized the strong men of Moab: all the inhabitants of Chanaan became full of fear.
»¹⁶Let fear and dread fall upon them, in the greatness of Thine arm: let them become immoveable as a stone, until Thy people, O Lord, pass by: until this Thy people which Thou hast possessed pass by unharmed.
»¹⁷Thou shalt bring them in, and plant them on the mountain of Thine inheritance, in Thy most firm habitation which Thou hast made, O Lord; Thy sanctuary, O Lord, which Thy hands have established.
¹⁸The Lord shall reign for ever and ever.
»¹⁹For Pharaoh went in on horseback with his chariots and horsemen into the sea: and the Lord brought back upon them the waters of the sea: but the children of Israel walked on dry ground in the midst thereof.

V. *Glory be ...*

Ant 4.

Saturday Lauds II

Psalmus 150

Ant 5. Omnis spíritus laudet Dóminum.

Laudáte Dóminum in sanctis ejus; laudáte eum in firmaménto virtútis ejus.
»²Laudáte eum in virtútibus ejus; laudáte eum secúndum multitúdinem magnitudinis ejus.
»³Laudáte eum in sono tubæ; laudáte eum in psaltério et cíthara.

»⁴Laudáte eum in týmpano et choro; laudáte eum in chordis et órgano.
»⁵Laudáte eum in cýmbalis benesonántibus; laudáte eum in cýmbalis jubilatiónis. Omnis spíritus laudet Dóminum!

V. *Glória Patri ...*

Ant 5.

Capitulum
(Rom 13:12-14)
The reading below or the proper of the day

V. Nox præcéssit, dies autem appropinquavit. Abjiciámus ergo ópera tenebrárum, et induámur arma lucis. Sicut in die honéste ambulémus: non in comessatiónibus, et ebrietátibus, non in cubílibus, et impudicitiis, non in contentióne, et æmulatióne.

R. Deo grátias.

Hymnus

Or the hymn of the season

O Gloriósa Vírginum, page 56

Psalm 150

Ant 5. Let all spirits praise the Lord.

Praise ye the Lord in His holy places: praise ye Him in the firmament of His power.
»²Praise ye Him for His mighty acts: praise ye Him according to the multitude of His greatness.
»³Praise ye Him with the sound of trumpet: praise ye Him with psaltery and harp.
»⁴Praise ye Him with timbrel and choir: praise ye Him with strings and organs.
»⁵Praise ye Him on high sounding cymbals: praise ye Him on cymbals of joy: let every spirit praise the Lord.

V. *Glory be ...*

Ant 5.

Chapter
(Rom 13:12-14)
The reading below or the proper of the day

V. The night is passed, and the day is at hand. Let us, therefore cast off the works of darkness, and put on the armor of light. Let us walk honestly, as in the day: not in rioting and drunkenness, not in debauchery and impurities, not in contention and envy.

R. Thanks be to God.

Hymn

Or the hymn of the season

O Glorious Lady! page 56

Saturday Lauds II

Versicle

V. Deliver me from mine enemies, my God.
R. And deliver me from those who rise up against me.

Ant. Illuminate, O Lord, those who sit in darkness and the shadow of death: and direct our feet into the path of peace. *(Whenever possible, the antiphon for the specific season or feast of a saint will be used).*

Canticle of Zachariah
(Luke 1:68-79)
Canticle on page 366

V. *Glory be ...*

Ant. Illuminate, O Lord, those who sit in darkness and the shadow of death: and direct our feet into the path of peace.

V. *Our Father ...*
R. *Give us this day ...*

V. O Lord, hear my prayer.
R. And let my cry come unto Thee.

V. Let us pray:

The prayer of the Office of the Blessed Virgin Mary, the season or the feast day are prayed if there are any.

V. O Lord, hear my prayer.
R. And let my cry come unto Thee.

V. Let us bless the Lord.
R. Thanks be to God.

V. May the souls of the faithful departed through the mercy of God rest in peace.
R. Amen.

Vespers

Sunday Vespers

Sunday – Vespers

V. Deus, ✝ in adjutórium meum inténde.
R. Dómine, ad adjuvándum me festína.

V. *Glória Patri ...*
R. *Sicut erat ...*

Psalmus 109

Ant 1. Dixit Dóminus Dómino meo: sede a dextris meis.

Dixit Dóminus Dómino meo: Sede a dextris meis, donec ponam inimícos tuos scabéllum pedum tuórum.
»²Virgam virtútis tuæ emíttet Dóminus ex Sion: domináre in médio inimicórum tuórum.
»³Tecum princípium in die virtútis tuæ in splendóribus sanctórum: ex útero, ante lucíferum, génui te.
»⁴Jurávit Dóminus, et non pœnitébit eum: Tu es sacérdos in ætérnum secúndum órdinem Melchísedech.
»⁵Dóminus a dextris tuis; confrégit in die iræ suæ reges.
⁶Judicábit in natiónibus, implébit ruínas; conquassábit capita in terra multórum.
»⁷De torrénte in via bibet; proptérea exaltábit caput.

V. *Glória Patri ...*

Ant 1.

V. O God, ✝ come to my assistance.
R. O Lord, make haste to help me.

V. *Glory be ...*
R. *As it was ...*

Psalm 109

Ant 1. The Lord said to my Lord: Sit at my right hand.

The Lord said to my Lord: sit Thou at my right hand until I make Thine enemies Thy footstool.
»²The Lord will send forth the sceptre of Thy power out of Zion: rule Thou in the midst of Thine enemies.
»³With Thee is the principality in the day of Thy strength: in the brightness of the saints: from the womb before the day star I begot Thee.
»⁴The Lord hath sworn, and He will not repent: Thou art a priest for ever according to the order of Melchisedech.
»⁵The Lord at Thy right hand hath broken kings in the day of His wrath.
⁶He shall judge among nations, He shall fill ruins: He shall crush the heads in the land of many.
»⁷He shall drink of the torrent in the way: therefore shall He lift up the head.

V. *Glory be ...*

Ant 1.

Psalmus 110

Ant 2. Magna ópera Dómini exquisíta in ómnes voluntátes eíus.

☧ onfitébor tibi, Dómine, in toto corde meo, in consílio justórum, et congregatióne.

»²Magna ópera Dómini: exquisíta in ómnes voluntátes ejus.
³Conféssio et magnificéntia opus ejus, et justítia ejus manet in sǽculum sǽculi.
»⁴Memóriam fecit mirabílium suórum, miséricors et miserátor Dóminus.

⁵Escam dedit timéntibus se; memor erit in sǽculum testaménti sui.

»⁶Virtútem óperum suórum annuntiábit pópulo suo,

⁷ut det illis hæreditátem géntium. Ópera mánuum ejus véritas et judícium.

»⁸Fidélia ómnia mandáta ejus, confirmáta in sǽculum sǽculi, facta in veritáte et æquitáte.
»⁹Redemptíonem misit pópulo suo; mandávit in ætérnum testaméntum suum. Sanctum et terríbile nomen ejus.
»¹⁰Inítium sapiéntiæ timor Dómini; intelléctus bonus ómnibus faciéntibus eum: laudátio eius manet in sǽculum sǽculi.

V. *Glória Patri ...*

Ant 2.

Psalm 110

Ant 2. The great work of the Lord is exquisite in all the willing.

𝕴 will praise Thee, O Lord, with my whole heart; in the council of the just, and in the congregation.

»²Great are the works of the Lord: sought out according to all He wills.
³His work is high and glorious: and His justice continueth for ever and ever.
»⁴He hath made memories of His wonderful works, being a merciful and gracious Lord.
⁵He hath given food to them that fear Him. He will be mindful for ever of His covenant.
»⁶He wilt show forth to His people the power of His works:

⁷that He may give them the inheritance of the Gentiles: the works of His hands are truth and judgment.
»⁸All His commandments are faithful: confirmed for ever and ever, made in truth and equity.
»⁹He hath sent redemption to His people: He hath commanded His covenant for ever. Holy and terrible is His Name.
»¹⁰The fear of the Lord is the beginning of wisdom. A good understanding to all that do it: His praise continueth for ever and ever.

V. *Glory be ...*

Ant 2.

Sunday Vespers

Psalmus 111	Psalm 111
Ant 3. Qui timet Dóminum in mandátis eíus cupit nimis.	**Ant 3. He that feareth the Lord desireth exceedingly in His commandments.**

Beátus vir qui timet Dóminum: in mandátis ejus volet nimis.
²Potens in terra erit semen ejus; generátio rectórum benedicétur.
»³Glória et divítiæ in domo ejus, et justítia ejus manet in sǽculum sǽculi.
⁴Exórtum est in ténebris lumen rectis: miséricors, et miserátor, et justus.

»⁵Jucúndus homo qui miserétur et cómmodat; dispónet sermónes suos in judício:

⁶quia in ætérnum non commovébitur »⁷In memória ætérna erit justus; ab auditióne mala non timébit. Parátum cor ejus speráre in Dómino,

⁸confirmatum est cor ejus; non commovébitur donec despíciat inimícos suos.

»⁹Dispérsit, dedit paupéribus; justítia ejus manet in sǽculum sǽculi: cornu ejus exaltábitur in glória.
»¹⁰Peccátor vidébit, et irascétur; déntibus suis fremet et tabéscet: desidérium peccatórum períbit.

V. *Glória Patri ...*

Ant 3.

Blessed is the man that feareth the Lord: he shall delight exceedingly in His commandments.
²His seed shall be mighty upon earth: the generation of the righteous shall be blessed.
»³Glory and wealth shall be in his house: and his justice remaineth for ever and ever.
⁴To the righteous a light is risen up in darkness: he is merciful, and compassionate and just.
»⁵Acceptable is the man that showeth mercy and lendeth: he shall order his affairs with justice:
⁶because he shall not be moved for ever.
»⁷The just shalt be in everlasting remembrance: he shalt not fear hearing evil. His heart is ready to trust in the Lord.
⁸His heart is strengthened, he shalt not be moved until he looketh down on his enemies.
»⁹He hath distributed, he hath given to the poor: his justice remaineth for ever and ever: his horn shalt be exalted in glory.
»¹⁰The wicked shall see, and shall be angry, they shall gnash their teeth and pine away: the desire of the wicked shall perish.

V. *Glory be ...*

Ant 3.

Psalmus 112

Ant 4. Sit nomen Dómini benedíctum in sǽcula.

Laudáte, púeri, Dóminum; laudáte nomen Dómini.
²Sit nomen Dómini benedíctum ex hoc nunc et usque in sǽculum.
³A solis ortu usque ad occásum laudábile nomen Dómini.

»⁴Excélsus super ómnes gentes Dóminus, et super cælos glória ejus.
⁵Quis sicut Dóminus Deus noster, qui in altis hábitat,
⁶et humília réspicit in cælo et in terra?
»⁷Súscitans a terra ínopem, et de stércore érigens páuperem:

⁸ut cóllocet eum cum princípibus, cum princípibus pópuli sui.
»⁹Qui habitáre facit stérilem in domo, matrem filiórum lætántem.

V. *Gloria Patri ...*

Ant 4.

Psalmus 113

Ant 5. Deus autem noster in cælo ómnia quæcúmque vóluit fecit.

In éxitu Israël de Ægypto, domus Jacob de pópulo bárbaro,

²facta est Judǽa sanctificátio ejus; Israël potéstas ejus.
»³Mare vidit, et fugit; Jordánis convérsus est retrórsum.
⁴Montes exsultavérunt ut aríetes, et colles sicut agni óvium.

Psalm 112

Ant 4. May the Name of the Lord be blessed for ever.

Praise the Lord, ye children: praise ye the Name of the Lord.
²Blessed be the Name of the Lord, from henceforth now and for ever.
³From the rising of the sun unto the going down of the sun, the Name of the Lord is worthy of praise.
»⁴The Lord is high above all nations; and His glory above the heavens.
⁵Who is as the Lord our God, who dwelleth on high:
⁶and looketh down on the low things in heaven and on earth?
»⁷Raising up the needy from the earth, and lifting up the poor out of the dunghill:
⁸that He may place him with princes, with the princes of his people.
»⁹Who maketh a barren woman to dwell in a house, the joyful mother of children.

V. *Glory be ...*

Ant 4.

Psalm 113

Ant 5. Our God made all things whatsoever He willed in heaven.

When Israel went out of Egypt, the house of Jacob from a barbarous people:

²Judea was made his sanctuary, Israel his dominion.
»³The sea saw and fled: Jordan was turned back.
⁴The mountains skipped like rams,

»⁵Quid est tibi, mare, quod fugísti? et tu, Jordánis, quia convérsus es retrórsum?
⁶montes, exsultástis sicut aríetes? et colles, sicut agni óvium?

»⁷A fácie Dómini mota est terra, a fácie Dei Jacob:

⁸qui convértit petram in stagna aquárum, et rupem in fontes aquárum.
»⁹Non nobis, Dómine, non nobis, sed nómini tuo da glóriam.
¹⁰Super misericórdia tua et veritáte tua; nequándo dicant gentes: Ubi est Deus eórum?

»¹¹Deus autem noster in cælo; ómnia quæcúmque vóluit fecit.

¹²Simulácra géntium argéntum et aurum, ópera mánuum hóminum.
»¹³Os habent, et non loquéntur; óculos habent, et non vidébunt.

¹⁴Aures habent, et non áudient; nares habent, et non odorábunt.

»¹⁵Manus habent, et non palpábunt; pedes habent, et non ambulábunt; non clamábunt in gútture suo.

¹⁶Símiles illis fiant qui fáciunt ea, et ómnes qui confídunt in eis.

»¹⁷Domus Israël sperávit in Dómino; adjútor eórum et protéctor eórum est.

¹⁸Domus Aaron sperávit in Dómino; adjútor eórum et protéctor eórum est.

»¹⁹Qui timent Dóminum speravérunt in Dómino; adjútor eórum et protéctor eórum est.

»⁵What ailed thee, O thou sea that thou didst flee: and thou, O Jordan, that thou wast turned back?
⁶ye mountains that ye skipped like rams and ye hills, like lambs of the flock?
»⁷At the presence of the Lord the earth was moved, at the presence of the God of Jacob:
⁸Who turned the rock into pools of water, and the stony hill into fountains of waters.
»⁹Not to us, O Lord, not to us; but to Thy Name give glory.
¹⁰For Thy mercy, and for Thy truth's sake lest the Gentiles should say: Where is their God?
»¹¹But our God is in heaven: He hath done all things whatsoever He would.
¹²The idols of the Gentiles are silver and gold, the works of the hands of men.
»¹³They have mouths and speak not: they have eyes and see not.
¹⁴They have ears and hear not: they have noses and smell not.
»¹⁵They have hands and feel not: they have feet and walk not: neither shall they cry out through their throat.
¹⁶Let them that make idols become like unto them: and all such as trust in them.
»¹⁷The house of Israel hath hoped in the Lord: He is their helper and their protector.
¹⁸The house of Aaron hath hoped in the Lord: He is their helper and their protector.
»¹⁹They that fear the Lord have hoped in the Lord: He is their helper and their protector.

²⁰Dóminus memor fuit nostri, et benedíxit nobis. Benedíxit domui Israël; benedíxit dómui Aaron.	²⁰The Lord hath been mindful of us, and hath blessed us. He hath blessed the house of Israel: He hath blessed the house of Aaron.
»²¹Benedíxit ómnibus qui timent Dóminum, pusíllis cum majóribus. ²²Adjíciat Dóminus super vos, super vos et super fílios vestros. »²³Benedícti vos a Dómino, qui fecit cælum et terram. ²⁴Cælum cæli Dómino; terram autem dedit fíliis hóminum.	»²¹He hath blessed all that fear the Lord, both little and great. ²²May the Lord add blessings upon thee: upon thee, and upon thy children. »²³Blessed be ye of the Lord, Who made heaven and earth. ²⁴The heavens of heavens are the Lord's: but the earth He hath given to the children of men.
»²⁵Non mórtui laudábunt te, Dómine, neque ómnes qui descéndunt in inférnum: »²⁶sed nos qui vívimus, benedícimus Dómino, ex hoc nunc et usque in sæculum.	»²⁵The dead shall not praise Thee, O Lord: nor any of them that go down to hell. »²⁶But we that live bless the Lord: from this time now and for ever.

V. *Glória Patri ...* V. *Glory be ...*

Ant 5. **Ant 5.**

Capitulum
(2 Cor 1:3-4)
The reading below or the proper of the day

Chapter
(2 Cor 1:3-4)
The reading below or the proper of the day

V. Benedíctus Deus, et Páter Dómini nostri Jesu Christi, Páter misericordiárum, et Deus totíus consolatiónis, qui consolátur nos in omni tribulatióne nostra.

V. Blessed be the God and Father of our Lord Jesus Christ, Father of mercies, and God of all consolation, who comforteth us in all our tribulations.

R. Deo grátias.

R. Thanks be to God.

Hymnus

Hymn
Or the hymn of the season.

Lucis Creátor Optime,
Lucem diérum próferens,
Primórdiis lucis novæ,
Mundi parans oríginem:

O Blest Creator of the Light,/
Who mak'st the day with radiance bright,/ And o'er the forming world didst call,/ The light from chaos first of all.

Sunday Vespers

Qui mane junctum vésperi
Diem vocári præcipis:
Illábitur tetrum chaos,
Audi preces cum flétibus.

Ne mens graváta crímine,
Vitæ sit exsul múnere,
Dum nil perénne cógitat,
Seséque culpis ílligat.

Cœléste pulset óstium:
Vitále tollat præmium:
Vitémus omne nóxium:
Purgémus omne péssimum.

Præsta, Páter piíssime,
Patríque compar Únice,
Cum Spíritu Paráclito
Regnans per omne sæculum. Amen.

Versiculi

V. Dirigátur Dómine orátio mea.
R. Sicut incénsum in conspéctu tuo.

Ant. Magníficat ánima mea Dóminum, quia respéxit Deus humilitátem meam. *(Whenever possible, the antiphon for the specific Sunday, season or feast of a saint will be used).*

Cánticum Mariæ
(Luke 1:47-55)

[46]Magnificat ánima mea Dóminum:
[47]et exsultavit spíritus meus in Deo salutári meo.

Whose wisdom joined in meet array/
The morn and eve, and named them Day:/ Night comes with all its darkling fears;/ Regard Thy people's prayers and tears.

Lest, sunk in sin, and whelmed with strife,/ They lose the gift of endless life;/ While thinking but the thoughts of time/ They weave new chains of woe and crime.

But grant them grace that they may strain,/ The heavenly gate and prize to gain:/ Each harmful lure aside to cast,/ And purge away each error past.

O Father, that we ask be done,/
Through Jesus Christ, Thine only Son;/ Who, with the Holy Ghost and Thee,/ Doth live and reign eternally.

Versicle

V. Let my prayer arise, O Lord.
R. Like incense in Thy sight.

Ant. My soul magnifieth the Lord, because God hath looked upon my humility. *(Whenever possible, the antiphon for the specific Sunday, season or feast of a saint will be used).*

Canticle of Mary
(Luke 1:47-55)

[46]My soul doth magnify the Lord.
[47]And my spirit hath rejoiced in God my Savior.

Sunday Vespers

»[48]Quia respéxit humilitátem ancíllæ suæ: ecce enim ex hoc beátam me dicent ómnes generatiónes,
[49]quia fecit mihi magna qui potens est: et sanctum nomen ejus,

»[50]et misericórdia ejus a progénie in progénies timéntibus eum.

[51]Fecit poténtiam in brácchio suo: dispérsit supérbos mente cordis sui.

»[52]Depósuit poténtes de sede, et exaltávit húmiles.

[53]Esuriéntes implévit bonis: et divites dimísit ináness.

»[54]Suscépit Israël púerum suum, recordátus misericórdiæ suæ:
[55]sicut locútus est ad patres nostros, Ábraham et sémini ejus in sǽcula.

V. *Glória Patri ...*

Ant. Deus autem noster in cælo: ómnia quæcúmque vóluit, fecit.

Orátio

V. Dómine exáudi oratiónem meam.
R. Et clamor meus ad te véniat.

V. Oremus.

Ecclésiam tuam, Dómine, miserátio continuáta mundet et múniat: et quia sine te non potest salva consístere; tuo semper múnere gubernétur.
Per Dóminum nostrum ...

R. Amen.

»[48]Because He hath regarded the humility of His handmaid; for behold from henceforth all generations shall call me blessed.
[49]Because He that is mighty, hath done great things to me; and holy is His Name.
»[50]And His mercy is from generation unto generations, to them that fear Him.
[51]He hath showed might in His arm: He hath scattered the proud in the conceit of their hearts.
»[52]He hath put down the mighty from their thrones, and hath exalted the humble.
[53]He hath filled the hungry with good things; and the rich He hath sent away empty.
»[54]He hath received Israel His servant, being mindful of His mercy:
[55]as He spoke to our fathers, to Abraham and to his seed for ever.

V. *Glory be ...*

Ant. My soul magnifieth the Lord, because God hath looked upon my humility.

Prayer

V. O Lord, hear my prayer.
R. And let my cry come unto Thee.

V. Let us pray.

O Lord, we beseech Thee, let Thy continual pity cleanse and defend Thy Church, and because it cannot continue in safety without Thy succor, preserve it evermore by Thy help and goodness.
Through our Lord ...

R. Amen.

The prayer above is said, or the prayer of the season and the feast day are prayed if there are any.

V. Dómine exáudi oratiónem meam.
R. Et clamor meus ad te véniat.

V. Benedicámus Dómino.
R. Deo grátias.

V. Fidélium ánimæ per misericórdiam Dei requiéscant in pace.

R. Amen.

The prayer above is said, or the prayer of the season and the feast day are prayed if there are any.

V. O Lord, hear my prayer.
R. And let my cry come unto Thee.

V. Let us bless the Lord.
R. Thanks be to God.

V. May the souls of the faithful departed through the mercy of God rest in peace.

R. Amen.

May the Lord add blessings upon thee: upon thee, and upon thy children.

MONDAY – VESPERS

V. Deus, ✝ in adjutórium meum inténde.
R. Dómine, ad adjuvándum me festína.

V. *Glória Patri ...*
R. *Sicut erat ...*

Psalmus 114

Ant 1. Inclinávit Dóminus aurem suam mihi.

ilexi, quóniam exáudiet Dóminus vocem oratiónis meæ.
²Quia inclinávit aurem suam mihi, et in diébus meis invocábo.
»³Circumdedérunt me dolóres mortis; et perícula inférni invenérunt me. Tribulatiónem et dolórem invéni, ⁴et nomen Dómini invocávi: o Dómine, líbera ánimam meam.

»⁵Miséricors Dóminus et justus, et Deus noster miserétur.
⁶Custódiens párvulos Dóminus; humiliátus sum, et liberávit me.
»⁷Convértere, ánima mea, in requiem tuam, quia Dóminus benefécit tibi: ⁸quia erípuit ánimam meam de morte, óculos meos a lácrimis, pedes meos a lapsu.
»⁹Placébo Dómino in regióne vivórum.

V. *Glória Patri ...*

Ant 1.

V. O God, ✝ come to my assistance.
R. O Lord, make haste to help me.

V. *Glory be ...*
R. *As it was ...*

Psalm 114

Ant 1. The Lord inclined His ear to me.

I have loved, because the Lord will hear the voice of my prayer.
²Because He hath inclined His ear unto me: and in my days I will call upon Him.
»³The sorrows of death have encompassed me: and the perils of hell have found me. I met with trouble and sorrow:
⁴and I called upon the Name of the Lord. O Lord, deliver my soul.
»⁵The Lord is merciful and just, and our God showeth mercy.
⁶The Lord is the keeper of little ones: I was humbled, and He delivered me.
»⁷Turn, O my soul, into thy rest: for the Lord hath been bountiful to thee.
⁸For He hath delivered my soul from death: mine eyes from tears, my feet from falling.
»⁹I will please the Lord in the land of the living.

V. *Glory be ...*

Ant 1.

Psalmus 115

Ant 2. Crédidi, propter quod locútus sum; ego autem humiliátus sum nimis.

Ego dixi in excéssu meo: Omnis homo mendax.
³Quid retríbuam Dómino pro ómnibus quæ retríbuit mihi?

»⁴Cálicem salutáris accípiam, et nomen Dómini invocábo.

»⁵Vota mea Dómino reddam coram omni pópulo ejus.
⁶Pretiósa in conspéctu Dómini mors sanctórum ejus.
»⁷O Dómine, quia ego servus tuus; ego servus tuus, et fílius ancíllæ tuæ. Dírupisti víncula mea:

⁸tibi sacrificábo hóstiam laudis, et nomen Dómini invocábo.

»⁹Vota mea Dómino reddam in conspéctu omnis pópuli ejus;
¹⁰in átriis domus Dómini, in médio tui, Jerúsalem.

V. *Glória Patri ...*

Ant 2.

Psalmus 119

Ant 3. Clamávi et Dóminus exaudívit me.

Psalm 115

Ant 2. I have believed, therefore have I spoken; but I have been greatly humbled.

I said in my haste: Every man is a liar.
³What shall I render to the Lord, for all the things that He hath rendered to me?

»⁴I will take the chalice of salvation; and I will call upon the Name of the Lord.

»⁵I will pay my vows to the Lord before all His people:
⁶precious in the sight of the Lord is the death of His saints.
»⁷O Lord, for I am Thy servant: I am Thy servant, and the son of Thy handmaid. Thou hast broken my bonds.

⁸I will sacrifice to Thee the sacrifice of praise, and I will call upon the Name of the Lord.

»⁹I will pay my vows to the Lord in the sight of all His people:
¹⁰in the courts of the house of the Lord, in the midst of thee, O Jerusalem.

V. *Glory be ...*

Ant 2.

Psalm 119

Ant 3. I cried out and the Lord heard me.

Monday Vespers

Ad Dóminum cum tribulárer clamávi, et exaudívit me.
»²Dómine, líbera ánimam meam a lábiis iníquis et a lingua dolósa
³Quid detur tibi, aut quid appónátur tibi ad línguam dolósam?
»⁴Sagíttæ poténtis acútæ, cum carbónibus desolatóriis.
⁵Heu mihi, quia incólatus meus prolongátus est! habitávi cum habitántibus Cedar;

»⁶multum íncola fuit ánima mea.

⁷Cum his qui odérunt pacem eram pacíficus; cum loquébar illis, impugnábant me gratis.

V. *Glória Patri* ...

Ant 3.

Psalmus 120

Ant 4. Auxílium meum a Dómino, qui fecit cælum et terram.

Levávi óculos meos in montes, unde véniet auxílium mihi.
²Auxílium meum a Dómino, qui fecit cælum et terram.
»³Non det in commotiónem pedem tuum, neque dormítet qui custódit te.
⁴Ecce non dormitábit neque dórmiet qui custódit Israël.

»⁵Dóminus custódit te; Dóminus protéctio tua super manum déxteram tuam.
⁶Per diem sol non uret te, neque luna per noctem.

In my trouble I cried to the Lord: and He heard me.
»²O Lord, deliver my soul from wicked lips, and a deceitful tongue.
³What shall be done to thee, or what shall be added to thee, to a deceitful tongue?
»⁴The sharp arrows of the mighty, with burning coals that lay waste.
⁵Woe is me, that my sojourning is prolonged! I have dwelt with the inhabitants of Cedar:
»⁶my soul hath been long a sojourner.
⁷With them that hated peace I was peaceable: when I spoke to them they fought against me without cause.

V. *Glory be* ...

Ant 3.

Psalm 120

Ant 4. My help is from the Lord, Who made the eternal heaven.

I have lifted up mine eyes to the mountains, from whence help shall come to me.
²My help is from the Lord, Who made heaven and earth.
»³May He not suffer thy foot to be moved: neither let Him slumber that keepeth thee.
⁴Behold He shall neither slumber nor sleep, that keepeth Israel.

»⁵The Lord is thy keeper, the Lord is thy protection upon thy right hand.

⁶The sun shall not burn thee by day: nor the moon by night.

⁷Dóminus custódit te ab omni malo; custódiat ánimam tuam Dóminus. ⁸Dóminus custódiat intróitum tuum et éxitum tuum, ex hoc nunc et usque in sǽculum.

V. *Glória Patri ...*

Ant 4.

Psalmus 121

Ant 5. Lætátus sum in his quæ dicta sunt mihi.

Lætátus sum in his quæ dicta sunt mihi: In domum Dómini íbimus.
²Stantes erant pedes nostri in átriis tuis, Jerúsalem.
»³Jerúsalem, quæ ædificátur ut cívitas, cujus participátio ejus in idípsum.
⁴Illuc enim ascendérunt tribus, tribus Dómini: testimónium Israël, ad confiténdum nómini Dómini:

»⁵Quia illic sedérunt sedes in judício, sedes super domum David.

»⁶Rogáte quæ ad pacem sunt Jerúsalem, et abundántia diligéntibus te.
⁷Fiat pax in virtúte tua, et abundántia in túrribus tuis.
»⁸Propter fratres meos et próximos meos, loquébar pacem de te.

⁹Propter domum Dómini Dei nostri, quæsívi bona tibi.

V. *Glória Patri ...*

Ant 5.

⁷The Lord keepeth thee from all evil: may the Lord keep thy soul. ⁸May the Lord keep thy coming in and thy going out; from henceforth now and for ever.

V. *Glory be ...*

Ant 4.

Psalm 121

Ant 5. I rejoiced in what was said to me.

I rejoiced at the things that were said to me: We shall go into the house of the Lord.
²Our feet were standing in thy courts, O Jerusalem:
»³Jerusalem, which is built as a city, which is compact together.
⁴For thither did the tribes go up, the tribes of the Lord: the testimony of Israel, to praise the Name of the Lord:
»⁵Because their thrones have stood in judgment, thrones upon the house of David.
»⁶Pray ye for the things that are for the peace of Jerusalem: and abundance for them that love thee.
⁷Let peace be in thy strength: and abundance in thy towers.
»⁸For the sake of my brethren, and of my neighbours, I spoke peace of thee.
⁹Because of the house of the Lord our God, I have sought good things for thee.

V. *Glory be ...*

Ant 5.

Monday Vespers

Capitulum	**Chapter**
(2 Cor 1:3-4)	(2 Cor 1:3-4)
The reading below or the proper of the day	*The reading below or the proper of the day*

V. Benedíctus Deus et Pater Dómini nostri Jesu Christi, Pater misericorddiárum, et Deus totíus consolatiónis, qui consolátur nos in omni tribulatióne nostra: ut póssimus et ipsi consolári eos qui in omni pressúra sunt, per exhortatiónem, qua exhortámur et ipsi a Deo.

R. Deo grátias.

V. Blessed be the God and Father of our Lord Jesus Christ, the Father of mercies, and the God of all comfort: Who comforteth us in all our tribulation; that we also may be able to comfort them who are in all distress, by the instruction wherewith we also are taught by God.

R. Thanks be to God.

Hymnus
Or the hymn of the season or feast

Creátor Alme Síderum,
Ætérna lux credéntium,
Jesu Redémptor ómnium,
Inténde votis súpplicum.

Qui dǽmonis ne fráudibus,
Períret orbis, ímpetu,
Amóris actus, lánguidi,
Mundi medéla factus es.

Commúne qui mundi nefas,
Ut expiáres; ad crucem,
E Vírginis sacrário,
Intácta prodis víctima.

Cujus potéstas glóriæ,
Noménque cum primum sonat,
Et cóelites et ínferi,
Treménte curvántur genu.

Te deprecámur últimæ,
Magnum diéi Júdicem,
Armis suprémæ gratiæ,
Defénde nos ab hóstibus.
https://www.traditioninaction.org/

Hymn
Or the hymn of the season or feast

Creator, Maker of the Universe of Stars,/ Eternal light of the faithful,/ Jesus Redeemer of all,/ Hear the prayers of Thy supplicants.

Thou who, to avoid that the deceits of the devil/ Should destroy the entire universe,/ Moved by an act of love,/ Became the healer of the ailing world.

To expiate the sins of the world,/ on the Cross,/
Thou came from the Virgin's womb,/ as a spotless Victim.

When Thy glorious power,/ And Name are heard,/ The inhabitants of heaven and hell,/ Trembling bend their knees.

We beseech Thee, finally,/ Great Judge of the Last Day,/ With the weapons of heavenly grace,/ Defend us from our enemies.

Monday Vespers

Virtus, honor, laus, glória,
Deo Patri cum Fílio,
Sancto simul Paráclito,
In sæculórum sǽcula.

Versiculi

V. Dirigatur, Dómine, orátio mea.
R. Sicut incénsum in conspétu tuo.

Ant. Magníficat ánima mea Dóminum, quia respéxit Deus humilitátem meam. *(Whenever possible, the antiphon for the specific season or feast of a saint will be used).*

Cánticum Mariæ
(Luke 1:46-55)
Canticle on page 367

V. *Glória Patri ...*

Ant. Magníficat ánima mea Dóminum, quia respéxit Deus humilitátem meam.

Orátio

V. Dómine exáudi oratiónem meam.
R. Et clamor meus ad te véniat.

V. Oremus.

Excita, quǽsumus Dómine, poténtiam tuam, et veni: ut ab imminéntibus peccatórum nostrórum periculis, te mereámur protegente eripi, te liberánte salvari: Qui vivis et regnas ...

R. Amen.

The prayer above is said, or the prayer of the season and the feast day are prayed if there are any.

Power, honor, praise and glory,/
To the Father and to the Son,/
And to the Holy Paraclete,/
For ever and ever.

Versicle

V. Let my prayer arise, O Lord.
R. Like incense in Thy sight.

Ant. My soul magnifieth the Lord, because God hath looked upon my humility. *(Whenever possible, the antiphon for the specific season or feast of a saint will be used).*

Canticle of Mary
(Luke 1:46-55)
Canticle on page 367

V. *Glory be ...*

Ant. My soul magnifieth the Lord, because God hath looked upon my humility.

Prayer

V. O Lord, hear my prayer.
R. And let my cry come unto Thee.

V. Let us pray.

Arouse, we beseech Thee, Lord, Thy power, and come: that we may deserve to be rescued from the imminent dangers of our sins, to be saved with Thy protection. Who livest and reignest ...

R. Amen.

The prayer above is said, or the prayer of the season and the feast day are prayed if there are any.

Monday Vespers

V. Dómine exáudi oratiónem meam. **R.** Et clamor meus ad te véniat.	**V.** O Lord, hear my prayer. **R.** And let my cry come unto Thee.
V. Benedicámus Dómino. **R.** Deo grátias.	**V.** Let us bless the Lord. **R.** Thanks be to God.
V. Fidélium ánimæ per misericórdiam Dei requiéscant in pace. **R.** Amen.	**V.** May the souls of the faithful departed through the mercy of God rest in peace. **R.** Amen.

For He hath delivered my soul from death: my eyes from tears, my feet from falling.

TUESDAY – VESPERS

V. Deus, ✝ in adjutórium meum inténde.
R. Dómine, ad adjuvándum me festína.

V. *Glória Patri ...*
R. *Sicut erat ...*

Psalmus 122

Ant 1. Qui hábitas in cælis miserére nobis.

𝔄d te levávi óculos meos, qui hábitas in cælis.
»² Ecce sicut óculi servórum in mánibus Dominórum suórum; sicut óculi ancíllæ in mánibus dóminæ suæ: ita óculi nostri ad Dóminum Deum nostrum, donec misereátur nostri.
»³Miserére nostri, Dómine, miserére nostri, quia multum repléti sumus despectióne;
⁴quia multum repléta est ánima nostra oppróbrium abundántibus, et despéctio supérbis.

V. *Glória Patri ...*

Ant 1.

Psalmus 123

Ant 2. Adjutórium nóstrum in nómine Dómini.

𝔑isi quia Dóminus erat in nobis, dicat nunc Israël,
»²nisi quia Dóminus erat in nobis: cum exsúrgerent hómines in nos,

V. O God, ✝ come to my assistance.
R. O Lord, make haste to help me.

V. *Glory be ...*
R. *As it was ...*

Psalm 122

Ant 1. Thou who dwellest in the heavens have mercy on us.

𝔗o thee have I lifted up mine eyes, Who dwellest in heaven.
»²Behold as the eyes of servants are on the hands of their masters, as the eyes of the handmaid are on the hands of her mistress: so are our eyes unto the Lord our God, until He hath mercy on us.
»³Have mercy on us, O Lord, have mercy on us: for we had our fill with man's contempt
⁴For our soul is greatly filled: we are a reproach to the rich, and the contempt of the proud.

V. *Glory be ...*

Ant 1.

Psalm 123

Ant 2. Our help is in the Name of the Lord.

𝔍f it had not been that the Lord was with us, let Israel now say:
»²If it had not been that the Lord was with us when men rose up against us:

³forte vivos deglutíssent nos; cum irascerétur furor eórum in nos,

»⁴forsitan aqua absorbuísset nos;

⁵torréntem pertransívit ánima nostra; fórsitan pertransísset ánima nostra aquam intolerábilem.
»⁶Benedíctus Dóminus, qui non dedit nos in captiónem déntibus eórum.
⁷Ánima nostra sicut passer erépta est de láqueo venántium; láqueus contrítus est, et nos liberáti sumus.

»⁸Adjutórium nostrum in nómine Dómini, qui fecit cælum et terram.

V. *Glória Patri ...*

Ant 2.

Psalmus 124

Ant 3. **In circúitu pópuli sui Dóminus ex hoc nunc et usque in sǽculum.**

Qui confídunt in Dómino, sicut mons Sion: non commovébitur in ætérnum, qui hábitat in Jerúsalem.

»²Montes in circúitu ejus; et Dóminus in circúitu pópuli sui, ex hoc nunc et usque in sǽculum.

»³Quia non relínquet Dóminus virgam peccatórum super sortem justórum: ut non exténdant justi ad iniquitátem manus suas.

»⁴Bénefac, Dómine, bonis, et rectis corde.

³perhaps they would have swallowed us up alive: when their fury was enkindled against us:
»⁴perhaps the waters would have overwhelmed us.
⁵Our soul hath passed through a torrent: perhaps our soul had passed through raging waters.
»⁶Blessed be the Lord, who hath not given us to be a prey to their teeth.
⁷Our soul hath been delivered as a sparrow out of the snare of the fowlers. The snare is broken, and we have been delivered.
»⁸Our help is in the Name of the Lord, Who made heaven and earth.

V. *Glory be ...*

Ant 2.

Psalm 124

Ant 3. **The Lord surroundeth His people from this time and forever.**

They that trust in the Lord shall be as Mount Zion: he shall not be moved for ever that dwelleth in Jerusalem.

»²Mountains are round about it: so the Lord is round about His people from henceforth now and for ever.

»³For the Lord will not allow the scepter of sinners to lay upon the lot of the just: that the righteous may not stretch forth their hands to iniquity.

»⁴Do good, O Lord, to those that are good, and to the upright of heart.

Tuesday Vespers

⁵Declinántes autem in obligatiónes, addúcet Dóminus cum operántibus iniquitátem. Pax super Israël!

V. *Glória Patri ...*

Ant 3.

Psalmus 125

Ant 4. Magnificávit Dóminus fácere nobíscum: facti sumus lætántes.

In converténdo Dóminus captivitátem Sion, facti sumus sicut consoláti.
»²Tunc replétum est gáudio os nostrum, et lingua nostra exsultatióne. Tunc dicent inter gentes: Magnificávit Dóminus fácere cum eis.
³Magnificávit Dóminus fácere nobíscum; facti sumus lætántes.
»⁴Convérte, Dómine, captivitátem nostram, sicut torrens in austro.
⁵Qui séminant in lácrimis, in exsultatióne metent.
»⁶Eúntes ibant et flebant, mitténtes sémina sua. Veniéntes autem vénient cum exsultatióne, portántes manípulos suos.

V. *Glória Patri ...*

Ant 4.

Psalmus 126

Ant 5. Dóminus ædíficet nobis domum et custódiat civitátem.

⁵But such as turn aside into evil, the Lord shall lead away with the workers of iniquity. Peace be upon Israel.

V. *Glory be ...*

Ant 3.

Psalm 125

Ant 4. The Lord hath magnified what He hath done for us: we are now rejoicing.

When the Lord brought back the captives of Zion, we became like men comforted.
»²Then was our mouth filled with gladness; and our tongue with joy. Then shall they say among the Gentiles: The Lord hath done great things for them.
³The Lord hath done great things for us: we have become joyful.
»⁴Turn again our captivity, O Lord, as a stream in the south.
⁵They that sow in tears shall reap in joy.
»⁶Going they went and wept, sowing their seeds. But coming they shall come with joyfulness, carrying their harvest.

V. *Glory be ...*

Ant 4.

Psalm 126

Ant 5. The Lord will build us a house and be a guard for His city.

Tuesday Vespers

Nisi Dóminus ædificáverit domum, in vanum laboravérunt qui ædíficant eam.
¹Nisi Dóminus custodíerit civitátem, frustra vígilat qui custódit eam.
»²Vanum est vobis ante lucem súrgere: súrgite postquam sedéritis, qui manducátis panem dolóris. Cum déderit diléctis suis somnum,
»³ecce hæréditas Dómini, fílii; merces, fructus ventris.
⁴Sicut sagíttæ in manu poténtis, ita filii excussórum.

»⁵Beátus vir qui implévit desidérium suum ex ipsis: non confundétur cum loquétur inimícis suis in porta.

V. Glória Patri ...

Ant 5.

Capitulum
(2 Cor 1:3-4)
The reading below or the proper of the day

V. Benedíctus Deus et Pater Dómini nostri Jesu Christi, Pater misericorddiárum, et Deus totíus consolatiónis, qui consolátur nos in omni tribulatióne nostra: ut póssimus et ipsi consolári eos qui in omni pressúra sunt, per exhortatiónem, qua exhortámur et ipsi a Deo.

R. Deo grátias.

Hymnus

Telluris alme Conditor
page 387
Or the hymn of the season or feast

Unless the Lord buildeth the house, they labor in vain that build it.
»²Unless the Lord keepeth the city, he watcheth in vain that keepeth it. It is vain for you to rise before light: rise ye after you stayed up late, ye that eat the bread of sorrow: when He shall give sleep to His beloved:
»³behold, the inheritance of the Lord is children: the reward, the fruit of the womb.
⁴As arrows in the hand of the mighty, so are the children of their youth.
»⁵Blessed is the man that hath filled his desire with them; he shall not be overcome when he shall speak to his enemies at the gate.

V. Glory be ...

Ant 5.

Chapter
(2 Cor 1:3-4)
The reading below or the proper of the day

V. Blessed be the God and Father of our Lord Jesus Christ, the Father of mercies, and the God of all comfort: Who comforteth us in all our tribulation; that we also may be able to comfort them who are in all distress, by the instruction wherewith we also are taught by God.

R. Thanks be to God.

Hymn

Earth's mighty Maker
page 387
Or the hymn of the season or feast

Tuesday Vespers

Versiculi

V. Dirigatur, Dómine, orátio mea.
R. Sicut incénsum in conspétu tuo.

Ant. Exultávit spíritus meus in Deo, salutári meo. *(Whenever possible, the antiphon for the specific season or feast of a saint will be used).*

Cánticum Mariæ
(Luke 1:46-55)
Canticle on page 367

V. *Glória Patri ...*

Ant. Exultávit spíritus meus in Deo, salutári meo.

Orátio

V. Dómine exáudi oratiónem meam.
R. Et clamor meus ad te véniat.

V. Oremus.

Preces nostras, quǽsumus, Dómine, cleménter exáudi: et contra cuncta nobis adversántia déxteram tuæ maiestátis exténde. Qui vivis et regnas cum Deo Patre in unitáte Spíritus Sancti, Deus, per ómnia sǽcula sæculórum.
R. Amen.

The prayer above is said, or the prayer of the season and the feast day are prayed if there are any.

V. Dómine exáudi oratiónem meam.
R. Et clamor meus ad te véniat.

Versicle

V. Let my prayer arise, O Lord.
R. Like incense in Thy sight.

Ant. My spirit hath rejoiced in God my Savior. *(Whenever possible, the antiphon for the specific season or feast of a saint will be used,.*

Canticle of Mary
(Luke 1:46-55)
Canticle on page 367

V. *Glory be ...*

Ant. My spirit hath rejoiced in God my Savior.

Prayer

V. O Lord, hear my prayer.
R. And let my cry come unto Thee.

V. Let us pray.

We beseech Thee, O Lord, graciously hear our prayers: and extend the right hand of Thy majesty against all our adversities. Who liveth and reigneth with God the Father in the unity of the Holy Ghost, One God, for ever and ever.

R. Amen.

The prayer above is said, or the prayer of the season and the feast day are prayed if there are any.

V. O Lord, hear my prayer.
R. And let my cry come unto Thee.

Tuesday Vespers

V. Benedicámus Dómino.	**V.** Let us bless the Lord.
R. Deo grátias.	**R.** Thanks be to God.
V. Fidélium ánimæ per misericórdiam Dei requiéscant in pace.	**V.** May the souls of the faithful departed through the mercy of God rest in peace.
R. Amen.	**R.** Amen.

Unless the Lord build the house, they labor in vain that build it.

 # WEDNESDAY VESPERS

V. Deus, ☩ in adjutórium meum inténde.
R. Dómine, ad adjuvándum me festína.

V. *Glória Patri ...*
R. *Sicut erat ...*

V. O God, ☩ come to my assistance.
R. O Lord, make haste to help me.

V. *Glory be ...*
R. *As it was ...*

Psalmus 127

Ant 1. **Beáti ómnes qui timent Dóminum.**

Beáti ómnes qui timent Dóminum, qui ámbulant in viis ejus.
²Labóres mánuum tuárum quia manducábis: beátus es, et bene tibi erit.
»³Uxor tua sicut vitis abúndans in latéribus domus tuæ; fílii tui sicut novéllæ olivárum in circuítu mensæ tuæ.
⁴Ecce sic benedicétur homo qui timet Dóminum.
»⁵Benedícat tibi Dóminus ex Sion, et vídeas bona Jerúsalem ómnibus diébus vitæ tuæ.
⁶Et vídeas fílios filiórum tuórum: pacem super Israël.

V. *Glória Patri ...*

Ant 1.

Psalm 127

Ant 1. **Blessed are all who fear the Lord.**

Blessed are all they that fear the Lord: that walk in His ways.
²For thou shalt eat of the labor of thy hands: blessed art thou, and it shall be well with thee:
»³thy wife as a fruitful vine in the innermost parts of thy house: thy children as olive plants round about thy table.
⁴Behold, thus shall the man be blessed that feareth the Lord.
»⁵May the Lord bless thee out of Zion: and mayst thou see the good things of Jerusalem all the days of thy life.
⁶And mayst thou see thy children's children. Peace upon Israel.

V. *Glory be ...*

Ant 1.

Psalmus 128

Ant 2. **Confundántur ómnes qui odérunt Sion.**

Sæpe expugnavérunt me a juventúte mea, dicat nunc Israël.

Psalm 128

Ant. 2. **All who hate Zion will be put to shame.**

Often have they fought against me from my youth, let Israel now say.

Wednesday Vespers

²sæpe expugnavérunt me a juventúte mea: étenim non potuérunt mihi.
»³Supra dorsum meum fabricavérunt peccatóres; prolongavérunt iniquitátem suam.

⁴Dóminus justus concídit cervíces peccatórum.
»⁵Confundántur, et convertántur retrórsum ómnes qui odérunt Sion.
⁶Fiant sicut fœnum tectórum, quod priúsquam evellátur exáruit:

»⁷de quo non implévit manum suam qui metit, et sinum suum qui manípulos cólligit.
⁸Et non dixérunt qui prætéribant: Benedíctio Dómini super vos. Benedíximus vobis in nómine Dómini.

V. *Glória Patri* ...

Ant 2.

Psalmus 129

Ant 3. De profúndis clamávi ad te Dómine.

e profundis clamávi ad te, Dómine;
²Dómine, exáudi vocem meam. Fiant aures tuæ intendéntes in vocem deprecatiónis meæ.
»³Si iniquitátes observáveris, Dómine, Dómine, quis sustinébit?
⁴Quia apud te propitiátio est; et propter legem tuam sustinui te, Dómine. Sustínuit ánima mea in verbo ejus:
»⁵sperávit ánima mea in Dómino
⁶A custódia matutína usque ad noctem, speret Israël in Dómino.

²Often have they fought against me from my youth: but they could not prevail over me.
»³The wicked have plowed upon my back: they have lengthened their furrows.

⁴The Lord Who is just will cut the necks of sinners.
»⁵Let them all be confounded and turned back that hate Zion.
⁶Let them be as grass upon the tops of houses: which withereth before it be plucked up:

»⁷wherewith the mower filleth not his hand: nor he that gathereth sheaves to his bosom.
⁸And they that passed by have not said: the blessing of the Lord be upon thee: we have blessed thee in the Name of the Lord.

V. *Glory be* ...

Ant 2.

Psalm 129

Ant 3. Out of the depths I cry to Thee, O Lord.

ut of the depths I have cried to Thee, O Lord:
²Lord, hear my voice. Let Thine ears be attentive to the sound of my supplication.
»³If Thou, O Lord, wilt mark iniquities: Lord, who shall stand it?
⁴For with Thee there is merciful forgiveness: and by reason of Thy law, I have waited for Thee, O Lord. My soul hath relied on His word:
»⁵my soul hath hoped in the Lord.
⁶From the morning watch even until night, let Israel hope in the Lord:

Wednesday Vespers

»⁷Quia apud Dóminum misericórdia, et copiósa apud eum redémptio.

⁸Et ipse rédimet Israël ex ómnibus iniquitátibus ejus.

V. *Glória Patri ...*

Ant 3.

Psalmus 130

Ant 4. Dómine non est exaltátum cor meum.

Dómine, non est exaltátum cor meum, neque eláti sunt óculi mei, neque ambulávi in magnis, neque in mirabílibus super me.
»²Si non humíliter sentiébam, sed exaltávi ánimam meam: sicut ablactátus est super matre sua, ita retribútio in ánima mea.
»³Speret Israël in Dómino, ex hoc nunc et usque in sǽculum.

V. *Glória Patri ...*

Ant 4.

Psalmus 131

Ant 5. Elégit Dóminus Sion in habitatiónem sibi.

Meménto, Dómine, David, et omnis mansuetúdinis ejus:
²sicut jurávit Dómino; votum vovit Deo Jacob:
»³Si introíero in tabernáculum domus meæ; si ascéndero in lectum strati mei:
⁴si dedéro somnum óculis meis, et palpébris meis dormitatiónem:

»⁷because with the Lord there is mercy: and with Him plentiful redemption.
⁸And He shall redeem Israel from all his iniquities.

V. *Glory be ...*

Ant 3.

Psalm 130

Ant 4. O Lord, my heart is not exalted.

Lord, my heart is not exalted: nor are mine eyes lofty. Neither have I walked in great matters, nor in wonderful things above me.
»²If I was not humbly minded, but exalted my soul: as a child that is weaned is toward his mother, so is the reward in my soul.
»³Let Israel hope in the Lord, from henceforth now and for ever.

V. *Glory be ...*

Ant 4.

Psalm 131

Ant 5. The Lord hath chosen Zion as His dwelling place.

O Lord, remember David, and all his meekness:
²how he swore to the Lord, he vowed a vow to the God of Jacob:
»³I shall not enter into the tabernacle of my house: I shall not go up into the bed wherein I lie:
⁴I shall not give sleep to mine eyes, or slumber to mine eyelids:

Wednesday Vespers

⁵et réquiem tempóribus meis, donec invéniam locum Dómino, tabernaculum Deo Jacob.
»⁶Ecce audívimus eam in Éphrata; invénimus eam in campis silvæ.
⁷Introíbimus in tabernáculum ejus; adorábimus in loco ubi stetérunt pedes ejus.

»⁸Surge, Dómine, in réquiem tuam, tu et arca sanctificatiónis tuæ.

⁹Sacerdótes tui induántur justítiam, et sancti tui exsúltent.
»¹⁰Propter David servum tuum non avértas fáciem christi tui.

¹¹Jurávit Dóminus David veritátem, et non frustrábitur eam: De fructu ventris tui ponam super sedem tuam.

»¹²Si custodíerint fílii tui testaméntum meum, et testimónia mea hæc quæ docébo eos, et fílii eórum usque in sæculum sedébunt super sedem tuam.
»¹³Quóniam elégit Dóminus Sion: Elégit eam in habitatiónem sibi.
¹⁴Hæc réquies mea in sæculum sæculi; hic habitábo, quóniam elégi eam.
»¹⁵Víduam ejus benedícens benedícam; páuperes ejus saturábo pánibus.
¹⁶Sacerdótes ejus índuam salutári, et sancti ejus exsultatióne exsultábunt.
»¹⁷Illuc prodúcam cornu David; parávi lucérnam christo meo.
»¹⁸Inimícos ejus índuam confusióne; super ípsum autem efflorébit sanctificátio mea.

V. *Glória Patri ...*

Ant 5.

⁵or rest to my temples: until I find a place for the Lord, a tabernacle for the God of Jacob.
»⁶Behold we have heard of it in Ephrata: we have found it in the fields of the wood.
⁷We will go into His tabernacle: we will adore in the place where His feet stood.
»⁸Arise, O Lord, into Thy resting place: Thou and the ark, which Thou hast sanctified.
⁹Let Thy priests be clothed with justice: and let Thy saints rejoice.
»¹⁰For Thy servant David's sake, turn not away the face of Thine anointed.
¹¹The Lord hath sworn truth to David, and He will not make it void: of the fruit of thy womb I will set thee upon thy throne.
»¹²If thy children will keep My covenant, and these My testimonies which I shall teach them: their children also forevermore shall sit upon thy throne.
»¹³For the Lord hath chosen Zion: He hath chosen it for His dwelling.
¹⁴This is My rest for ever and ever: here will I dwell, for I have chosen it.
»¹⁵Blessing, I will bless her widow: I will satisfy her poor with bread.
¹⁶I will clothe her priests with salvation, and her saints shall rejoice with exceedingly great joy.
»¹⁷There will I bring forth a horn to David: I have prepared a lamp for Mine anointed.
»¹⁸His enemies I will clothe with confusion: but upon him shall My sanctification flourish.

V. *Glory be ...*

Ant 5.

Wednesday Vespers

Capitulum
(2 Cor 1:3-4)
The reading below or the proper of the day

V. Benedíctus Deus et Pater Dómini nostri Jesu Christi, Pater misericórdiarum, et Deus totius consolatiónis, qui consolatur nos in omni tribulatióne nostra: ut possimus et ipsi consolári eos qui in omni pressura sunt, per exhortatiónem, qua exhortámur et ipsi a Deo.

R. Deo grátias.

Hymnus
Or the hymn of the season or feast

Cœli Deus sanctíssime,
Qui lúcidas mundi plagas
Candóre pingis igneo,
Augens decóro lúmine:

Quarto die qui flámmeam
Dum solis accéndis rotam,
Lunæ minístras órdinem,
Vagósque cursus siderum:

Ut nóctibus, vel lúmini
Diremptiónis términum,
Primórdiis et ménsium
Signum dares notíssimum;

Expélle noctem córdium:
Abstérge sordes méntium:
Resólve culpæ vínculum:
Evérte moles críminum.

Præsta, Pater piíssime,
Patríque compar Unice,
Cum Spíritu Paráclito
Regnans per omne sǽculum.

Chapter
(2 Cor 1:3-4)
The reading below or the proper of the day

V. Blessed be the God and Father of our Lord Jesus Christ, the Father of mercies, and the God of all comfort. Who comforteth us in all our tribulation; that we also may be able to comfort them who are in all distress, by the instruction wherewith we also are taught by God.

R. Thanks be to God.

Hymn
Or the hymn of the season or feast

O God, whose hand hath spread the sky,/ And all its shining hosts on high./ And painting it with fiery light,/ Made it so beauteous and so bright:

Thou, when the fourth day was begun,/ Didst frame the circle of the sun,/ And set the moon for ordered change,/ And planets for their wider range:

To night and day, by certain line,/ Their varying bounds Thou didst assign;/ And gav'st a signal, known and meet,/ For months begun and months complete.

Enlighten Thou the hearts of men:/ Polluted souls make pure again:/ Unloose the bands of guilt within:/ Remove the burden of our sin.

Grant this, O Father, ever One/ With Christ Thy sole-begotten Son,/ Whom, with the Spirit we adore,/ One God, both now and evermore.

Wednesday Vespers

Versiculi

V. Dirigatur, Dómine, orátio mea.
R. Sicut incénsum in conspétu tuo.

Ant. Respéxit Dóminus humilitátem meam, et fecit in me magna, qui potens est. *(Whenever possible, the antiphon for the specific season or feast of a saint will be used).*

Cánticum Mariæ
(Luke 1:47-55)
Canticle on page 367

V. *Glória Patri ...*

Ant. Respéxit Dóminus humilitátem meam, et fecit in me magna, qui potens est.

Orátio

V. Dómine exáudi oratiónem meam.
R. Et clamor meus ad te véniat.

V. Oremus.

Deus, refúgium nostrum, et virtus: Adésto piis Ecclésiæ tuæ precibus, auctor ipse pietatis, et præsta: ut quod fidéliter pétimus, efficaciter consequamur.
Per Dóminum nostrum ...

R. Amen.

The prayer above is said, or the prayer of the season and the feast day are prayed if there are any.

Versicle

V. Let my prayer arise, O Lord.
R. Like incense in Thy sight.

Ant. The Lord, who is mighty, looked upon my lowliness, and did great things in me. *(Whenever possible, the antiphon for the specific season or feast of a saint will be used).*

Canticle of Mary
(Luke 1:47-55)
Canticle on page 367

V. *Glory be ...*

Ant. The Lord, who is mighty, looked upon my lowliness, and did great things in me.

Prayer

V. O Lord, hear my prayer.
R. And let my cry come unto Thee.

V. Let us pray.

O God, our refuge and strength: be present at the prayers of Thy holy Church, the author of piety itself, and grant that what we faithfully ask for, we may effectively obtain.
Through our Lord …

R. Amen.

The prayer above is said, or the prayer of the season and the feast day are prayed if there are any.

Wednesday Vespers

V. Dómine exáudi oratiónem meam.	**V.** O Lord, hear my prayer.
R. Et clamor meus ad te véniat.	**R.** And let my cry come unto Thee.
V. Benedicámus Dómino.	**V.** Let us bless the Lord.
R. Deo grátias.	**R.** Thanks be to God.
V. Fidélium ánimæ per misericórdiam Dei requiéscant in pace.	**V.** May the souls of the faithful departed through the mercy of God rest in peace.
R. Amen.	**R.** Amen.

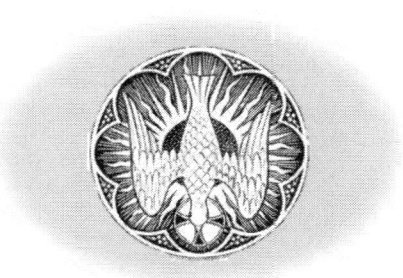

Out of the depths I have cried to Thee, O Lord: Lord, hear my voice. Let Thine ears be attentive to the sound of my supplication.

Wednesday Vespers

 # THURSDAY VESPERS

V. Deus, † in adjutórium meum intende.
R. Dómine, ad adjuvándum me festína.

V. *Glória Patri ...*
R. *Sicut erat ...*

V. O God, † come to my assistance.

R. O Lord, make haste to help me.

V. *Glory be ...*
R. *As it was ...*

Psalmus 132

Ant 1. Ecce quam bonum et quam jucúndum habitáre fratres in unum.

Ecce quam bonum et quam jucúndum, habitáre fratres in unum!
»²Sicut unguéntum in cápite, quod descéndit in barbam, barbam Aaron, quod descéndit in oram vestiménti ejus;

»³sicut ros Hermon, qui descéndit in montem Sion. Quóniam illic mandávit Dóminus benedictiónem, et vitam usque in sæculum.

V. *Glória Patri ...*

Ant 1.

Psalm 132

Ant 1. Behold how good and how pleasant it is for brethren to dwell together in unity.

Behold how good and how pleasant it is for brethren to dwell together in unity:
»²like the precious ointment on the head that ran down upon the beard, the beard of Aaron, which ran down to the skirt of his garment:

»³as the dew of Hermon, which descendeth upon Mount Zion. For there the Lord hath commanded blessing and life for evermore.

V. *Glory be ...*

Ant 1.

Psalmus 135: 1-9

Ant 2. Confitémini Dómino quóniam in ætérnum misericórdia eíus.

Confitémini Dómino, quóniam bonus, quóniam in ætérnum misericórdia ejus.

Psalm 135: 1-9

Ant 2. Confess to the Lord because of His eternal mercy.

Praise the Lord, for He is good: for His mercy endureth for ever.

²Confitémini Deo deórum, quóniam in ætérnum misericórdia ejus. ³Confitémini Dómino Dominórum, quóniam in ætérnum misericórdia ejus. »⁴Qui facit mirabília magna solus, quóniam in ætérnum misericórdia ejus. ⁵Qui fecit cælos in intelléctu, quóniam in ætérnum misericórdia ejus. »⁶Qui firmávit terram super aquas, quóniam in ætérnum misericórdia ejus. ⁷Qui fecit luminária magna, quóniam in ætérnum misericórdia ejus: »⁸solem in potestátem diei, quóniam in ætérnum misericórdia ejus; ⁹lunam et stellas in potestátem noctis, quóniam in ætérnum misericórdia ejus.	²Praise ye the God of gods: for His mercy endureth for ever. ³Praise ye the Lord of lords: for His mercy endureth for ever: »⁴Who alone doth great wonders: for His mercy endureth for ever: ⁵Who made the heavens in understanding: for His mercy endureth for ever: »⁶Who established the earth above the waters: for His mercy endureth for ever: ⁷Who made the great lights: for His mercy endureth for ever: »⁸The sun to rule over the day: for His mercy endureth forever: ⁹The moon and the stars to rule the night: for His mercy endureth for ever.
V. *Glória Patri* ...	**V.** *Glory be* ...
Ant 2.	**Ant 2.**

Psalmus 135: 10-27   Psalm 135: 10-27

Ant 3. Confitémini Dómino quia in humilitáte nostramemor fuit nostri.	**Ant 3. The Lord remembered us in our affliction.**
Qui percússit Ægýptum cum primogénitis eórum, quóniam in ætérnum misericórdia ejus. ¹¹Qui edúxit Israël de médio eórum, quóniam in ætérnum misericórdia ejus, »¹²in manu poténti et bráchio excélso, quóniam in ætérnum misericórdia ejus.	Who smote Egypt with their firstborn: for His mercy endureth for ever: ¹¹Who brought out Israel from among them: for His mercy endureth for ever: »¹²with a mighty hand and with a stretched out arm: for His mercy endureth for ever:

Thursday Vespers

¹³Qui divísit mare Rubrum in divisiónes, quóniam in ætérnum misericórdia ejus;
»¹⁴et edúxit Israël per medium ejus, quóniam in ætérnum misericórdia ejus;
¹⁵et excússit Pharaónem et virtútem ejus in mari Rubro, quóniam in ætérnum misericórdia ejus.
»¹⁶Qui tradúxit pópulum suum per desértum, quóniam in ætérnum misericórdia ejus.
¹⁷Qui percússit reges magnos, quóniam in ætérnum misericórdia ejus;
»¹⁸et occídit reges fortes, quóniam in ætérnum misericórdia ejus:

¹⁹Sehon, regem Amorrhæórum, quóniam in ætérnum misericórdia ejus;
²⁰et Og, regem Basan, quóniam in ætérnum misericórdia ejus:

»²¹et dedit terram eórum hæreditátem, quóniam in ætérnum misericórdia ejus;
²²hæreditátem Israël, servo suo, quóniam in ætérnum misericórdia ejus.
»²³Quia in humilitáte nostra memor fuit nostri, quóniam in ætérnum misericórdia ejus;
»²⁴et redémit nos ab inimícis nostris, quóniam in ætérnum misericórdia ejus.
²⁵Qui dat escam omni carni, quóniam in ætérnum misericórdia ejus.
»²⁶Confitémini Deo cæli, quóniam in ætérnum misericórdia ejus.
²⁷Confitémini Dómino dominórum, quóniam in ætérnum misericórdia ejus.

¹³Who divided the Red Sea into parts: for His mercy endureth for ever:
»¹⁴and brought out Israel through the midst thereof: for His mercy endureth for ever:
¹⁵and overthrew Pharaoh and his host in the Red Sea: for His mercy endureth for ever.
»¹⁶Who led His people through the desert: for His mercy endureth for ever:
¹⁷Who smote great kings: for His mercy endureth for ever:
»¹⁸and slew strong kings: for His mercy endureth for ever:

¹⁹Sehon king of the Amorrhites: for His mercy endureth for ever:
²⁰and Og king of Basan: for His mercy endureth for ever.

»²¹And He gave their land for an inheritance: for His mercy endureth for ever:
²²For an inheritance to His servant Israel: for His mercy endureth for ever.
»²³For He was mindful of us in our affliction: for His mercy endureth for ever.
»²⁴And He redeemed us from our enemies: for His mercy endureth for ever:
²⁵Who giveth food to all flesh: for His mercy endureth for ever.
»²⁶Give glory to the God of heaven: for His mercy endureth for ever.
²⁷Give glory to the Lord of lords: for His mercy endureth for ever.

Thursday Vespers

V. *Glória Patri* ...

Ant 3.

Psalmus 136

Ant 4. Adhǽreat lingua mea fáucibus meis, si non memínero tui Jerúsalem.

Super flúmina Babylónis illic sedimus et flevimus, cum recordarémur Sion.
»²In salícibus in médio ejus suspéndimus órgana nostra:
³quia illic interrogavérunt nos, qui captívos duxérunt nos, verba cantiónum; et qui abduxérunt nos: Hymnum cantáte nobis de cánticis Sion.
»⁴Quómodo cantábimus cánticum Dómini in terra aliena?
⁵Si oblítus fúero tui, Jerúsalem, oblivióni detur déxtera mea.
»⁶Adhǽreat lingua mea fáucibus meis, si non memínero tui; si non proposúero Jerúsalem in princípio lætítiæ meæ.
»⁷Memor esto, Dómine, filiórum Edom, in die Jerúsalem: qui dicunt: Exinaníte, exinaníte usque ad fundaméntum in ea.
»⁸Fília Babylónis misera! beátus qui retríbuet tibi retributiónem tuam quam retribuísti nobis.
⁹Beátus qui tenébit, et allídet párvulos tuos ad petram.

V. *Glória Patri* ...

Ant 4.

V. *Glory be* ...

Ant 3.

Psalm 136

Ant 4. Let my tongue cleave to my mouth, if I do not remember thee, Jerusalem.

Upon the rivers of Babylon, there we sat and wept: when we remembered Zion:
»²on the willows in the midst thereof we hung up our instruments.
³For there they that led us into captivity required of us the words of songs. And they that carried us away, said: sing ye to us a hymn of the songs of Zion.
»⁴How shall we sing the song of the Lord in a strange land?
⁵If I forget thee, O Jerusalem, let my right hand be forgotten!
»⁶Let my tongue cleave to my jaws, if I do not remember thee: if I make not Jerusalem the beginning of my joy.
»⁷Remember, O Lord, the sons of Edom, in the day of Jerusalem: who say: Destroy it, destroy it, even to the foundation thereof.
»⁸O daughter of Babylon, miserable: blessed shall he be who shall repay thee thine evils which thou hast paid us.
⁹Blessed be he that shall take and dash thy little ones against the rock.

V. *Glory be* ...

Ant 4.

Thursday Vespers

Psalmus 137

Ant 5. Confitébor nómini tuo Dómine, super misericórdia et veritáte tua.

Confitébor tibi, Dómine, in toto corde meo, quóniam audísti verba oris mei. In conspéctu angelórum psallam tibi;
»²adorábo ad templum sanctum tuum, et confitébor nómini tuo: super misericórdia tua et veritáte tua; quóniam magnificásti super omne, nomen sanctum tuum.

»³In quacúmque die invocávero te, exáudi me; multiplicábis in ánima mea virtútem.

»⁴Confiteántur tibi, Dómine, ómnes reges terræ, quia audiérunt ómnia verba oris tui.

⁵Et cantent in viis Dómini, quóniam magna est glória Dómini.

»⁶quóniam excélsus Dóminus, et humília réspicit, et alta a longe cognóscit.omini;
»⁷Si ambulávero in médio tribulatiónis, vivificábis me; et super iram inimicórum meórum extendísti manum tuam, et salvum me fecit déxtera tua.

»⁸Dóminus retríbuet pro me. Dómine, misericórdia tua in sǽculum; ópera mánuum tuárum ne despícias.

V. *Glória Patri ...*

Ant 5.

Psalm 137

Ant 5. I will trust in Thy Name, O Lord, in Thy mercy and in Thy truth.

I will praise Thee, O Lord, with my whole heart: for Thou hast heard the words of my mouth.
»²I will sing praise to Thee in the sight of the angels: I will worship towards Thy holy temple, and I will give glory to Thy Name: for Thy mercy, and for Thy truth: for Thou hast magnified Thy holy Name above all.

»³In what day soever I shall call upon Thee, hear me: Thou shalt multiply strength in my soul.

»⁴May all the kings of the earth give glory to Thee: for they have heard all the words of Thy mouth.

⁵And let them sing in the ways of the Lord: for great is the glory of the Lord.
»⁶For the Lord is high, and looketh on the low: and the high He knoweth afar off.
»⁷If I shall walk in the midst of tribulation, Thou wilt preserve my life: and Thou hast stretched forth Thy hand against the wrath of mine enemies: and Thy right hand hath saved me.
»⁸The Lord will repay for me: Thy mercy, O Lord, endureth for ever: O despise not the works of Thy hands.

V. *Glory be ...*

Ant 5.

Thursday Vespers

Capitulum
(2 Cor 1:3-4)
The reading below or the proper of the day

V. Benedíctus Deus et Pater Dómini nostri Jesu Christi, Pater misericórdiarum, et Deus totius consolationis qui consolatur nos in omni tribulatióne nostra: ut possimus et ipsi consolári eos qui in omni pressura sunt, per exhortatiónem, qua exhortámur et ipsi a Deo.

R. Deo grátias.

Hymnus
Or the hymn of the season or feast

Magnæ Deus Poténtiæ,
Qui fértili natos aqua
Partim relínquish gúrgiti,
Partim levas in æra.

Demérsa lymphis ímprimens,
Subvécta cœlis érigens:
Ut stirpe ab una pródita,
Divérsa répleant loca:

Largíre cunctis sérvulis,
Quos mundat unda sánguinis,
Nescíre lapsus críminum,
Nec ferre mortis tædium.

Ut culpa nullum déprimat:
Nullum éfferat jactántia:
Elísa mens ne cóncidat:
Eláta mens ne córruat.

Chapter
(2 Cor 1:3-4)
The reading below or the proper of the day

V. Blessed be the God and Father of our Lord Jesus Christ, the Father of mercies, and the God of all comfort. Who comforteth us in all our tribulation; that we also may be able to comfort them who are in all distress, by the instruction wherewith we also are taught by God.

R. Thanks be to God.

Hymn
Or the hymn of the season or feast

O Sovereign Lord of Nature's Might,/ Who bad'st the water's birth divide; /Part in the heavens to take their flight,/ And part in ocean's deep to hide:

These low obscured, on airy wing/ Exalted those, that either race/ though from one element they spring,/ Might serve Thee in a different place.

Grant, Lord, that we Thy servants all,/ saved by Thy tide of cleansing Blood,/ No more 'neath sin's dominion fall,/ nor fear the thought of death's dark flood!

Thy varied love each spirit bless,/ the humble cheer, the high control;/ check in each heart its proud excess,/ But raise the meek and contrite soul!

Thursday Vespers

Præsta, Pater piíssime,
Patríque compar Unice,
Cum Spíritu Paráclito
Regnans per omne sæculum.

Versiculi

V. Dirigátur, Dómine, orátio mea.
R. Sicut incénsum in conspéctu tuo.

Ant. Fecit Deus poténtiam in bráchio suo: dispérsit supérbos mente cordis sui. *(Whenever possible, the antiphon for the specific season or feast of a saint will be used).*

Cánticum Maríæ
(Luke 1:47-55)
Canticle on page 367

V. *Glória Patri ...*

Ant. Fecit Deus poténtiam in bráchio suo: dispérsit supérbos mente cordis sui.

Orátio

V. Dómine exáudi oratiónem meam.
R. Et clamor meus ad te véniat.

V. Oremus.

Ecclésiam tuam, Dómine, miserátio continuáta mundet et múniat: et quia sine te non potest salva consístere; tuo semper múnere gubernétur. Per Dóminum nostrum ...

R. Amen.

The prayer above is said, or the prayer of the season and the feast day are prayed if there are any.

This boon, O Father, we entreat,/
This blessing grant, Eternal Son,/
and Holy Ghost, the Paraclete,/
both now, and while the ages run.

Versicle

V. Let my prayer arise, O Lord.
R. Like incense in Thy sight.

Ant. God made might in His arm: He scattered the proud in the conceit of their hearts. *(Whenever possible, the antiphon for the specific season or feast of a saint will be used).*

Canticle of Mary
(Luke 1:47-55)
Canticle on page 367

V. *Glory be ...*

Ant. God made might in His arm: He scattered the proud in the conceit of their hearts.

Prayer

V. O Lord, hear my prayer.
R. And let my cry come unto Thee.

V. Let us pray.

O Lord, may Thy continued mercy cleanse and fortify Thy church: and because without Thee it cannot stand safely; preserve it evermore by Thy help and goodness.
Through our Lord ...

R. Amen.

The prayer above is said, or the prayer of the season and the feast day are prayed if there are any.

Thursday Vespers

V. Dómine exáudi oratiónem meam. **R.** Et clamor meus ad te véniat.	**V.** O Lord, hear my prayer. **R.** And let my cry come unto Thee.
V. Benedicámus Dómino. **R.** Deo grátias.	**V.** Let us bless the Lord. **R.** Thanks be to God.
V. Fidélium ánimæ per misericórdiam Dei requiéscant in pace. **R.** Amen.	**V.** May the souls of the faithful departed through the mercy of God rest in peace. **R.** Amen.

I will sing praise to Thee in the sight of the angels: I will worship towards Thy holy temple, and I will give glory to Thy name.

FRIDAY VESPERS

V. Deus, ☦ in adjutórium meum inténde.
R. Dómine, ad adjuvándum me festína.

V. *Glória Patri* ...
R. *Sicut erat* ...

Psalmus 138: 1-13

Ant 1. Dómine probásti me et cognovísti me.

Dómine, probásti me, et cognovísti me;
²tu cognovísti sessiónem meam et resurrectiónem meam.
³Intellexísti cogitatiónes meas de longe; sémitam meam et funículum meum investigásti:

»⁴et ómnes vias meas prævidísti, quia non est sermo in lingua mea.

⁵Ecce, Dómine, tu cognovísti ómnia, novíssima et antíqua. Tu formásti me, et posuísti super me manum tuam.
»⁶Mirábilis facta est sciéntia tua ex me; confortáta est, et non potéro ad eam.
⁷Quo ibo a spíritu tuo? et quo a fácie tua fúgiam?

»⁸Si ascéndero in cælum, tu illic es; si descéndero in inférnum, ades.

⁹Si súmpsero pennas meas dilúculo, et habitávero in extrémis maris,

¹⁰étenim illuc manus tua dedúcet me, et tenébit me déxtera tua.

V. O God, ☦ come to my assistance.
R. O Lord, make haste to help me.

V. *Glory be* ...
R. *As it was* ...

Psalm 138: 1-13

Ant 1. Lord, Thou hast tested me and knowest me.

Lord, Thou hast proved me, and known me:
²Thou hast known my sitting down, and my rising up.
³Thou hast understood my thoughts afar off: my path and my ways Thou hast searched out.
»⁴And Thou hast foreseen all my ways: for there is no speech in my tongue.
⁵Behold, O Lord, Thou hast known all things, the last and those of old: Thou hast formed me, and hast laid Thy hand upon me.
»⁶Thy knowledge hath become wonderful to me: it is too lofty, and I cannot reach to it.
⁷Whither shall I go from Thy spirit? or whither shall I flee from Thy face?
»⁸If I ascend into heaven, Thou art there: if I descend into hell, Thou art present.
⁹If I take my wings early in the morning, and dwell in the uttermost parts of the sea:
¹⁰even there also shall Thy hand lead me: and Thy right hand shall hold me.

Friday Vespers

»¹¹Et dixi: Fórsitan ténebræ, conculcábunt me; et nox illuminátio mea in delíciis meis.
¹²Quia ténebræ non obscurabúntur a te, et nox sicut dies illuminábitur: sicut ténebræ eius, ita et lumen eius.

»¹³Quia tu possedísti renes meos; suscepísti me de útero matris meæ.

V. *Glória Patri* ...

Ant 1.

Psalmus 138: 14-24

Ant 2. Mirabília ópera tua Dómine, et ánima mea cognóscit nimis.

Confitébor tibi, quia terríbiliter magnificátus es; mirabília ópera tua, et ánima mea cognóscit nimis.
»¹⁵Non est occúltatum os meum a te, quod fecísti in occúlto; et substántia mea in inferióribus terræ.
»¹⁶Imperféctum meum vidérunt óculi tui, et in libro tuo ómnes scribéntur. Dies formabúntur, et nemo in eis.
»¹⁷Mihi autem nimis honorificáti sunt amíci tui, Deus; nimis confortátus est principátus eórum.

¹⁸Dinumerábo eos, et super arénam multiplicabúntur. Exsurréxi, et adhuc sum tecum.
»¹⁹Si occíderis, Deus, peccatóres, viri sánguinum, declináte a me:

²⁰quia dícitis in cogitatióne: Accípient in vanitáte civitátes tuas.
»²¹Nonne qui odérunt te, Dómine, óderam, et super inimícos tuos tabescébam?

»¹¹And I said: Perhaps darkness shall cover me: and night shall be my light in my pleasures.
¹²But darkness shall not be dark to Thee, and night shall be light as the day: the darkness thereof, and the light thereof are alike to Thee.
»¹³For Thou hast possessed my reins: Thou hast protected me from my mother's womb.

V. *Glory be* ...

Ant 1.

Psalm 138: 14-24

Ant 2. Thy works are wonderful, O Lord, and my soul knoweth them very well.

I will praise Thee, for Thou art fearfully magnified: wonderful are Thy works, and my soul knoweth very well.
»¹⁵My bone is not hidden from Thee, which Thou hast made in secret: and my substance in the lower parts of the earth.
»¹⁶Thine eyes did see my imperfect being, and in Thy book all shall be written: my days were numbered before ever they came to be.
»¹⁷How weighty are Thy designs, O God: how vast the sum of them.
¹⁸I will number them, and they shall be more than the sand: I rose up and am still with Thee.
»¹⁹If Thou wilt kill the wicked, O God: ye men of blood would depart from me:
²⁰because Thou sayest in thought: they shall receive Thy cities in vain.
»²¹Have I not hated them, O Lord that hated Thee: and wasted away because of Thine enemies?

Friday Vespers

²²Perfécto ódio óderam illos, et inimíci facti sunt mihi.

»²³Proba me, Deus, et scito cor meum; intérroga me, et cognósce sémitas meas.
²⁴Et vide si via iniquitátis in me est, et deduc me in via ætérna.

V. *Glória Patri* ...

Ant 2.

²²I have hated them with a perfect hatred: and they have become enemies to me.
»²³Prove me, O God, and know my heart: examine me, and know my paths:
²⁴and see if there be in me the way of evil: and lead me in the eternal way.

V. *Glory be* ...

Ant 2.

Psalmus 139

Ant 3. Ne derelínquas me Dómine, virtus salútis meæ.

Éripe me, Dómine, ab hómine malo; a viro iníquo éripe me.
³Qui cogitavérunt iniquitátes in corde, tota die constituébant prælia.

»⁴Acuérunt linguas suas sicut serpéntis; venénum áspidum sub lábiis eórum.
»⁵Custódi me, Dómine, de manu peccatóris, et ab homínibus iníquis éripe me. Qui cogitavérunt supplantáre gressus meos:

⁶abscondérunt supérbi laqueum mihi. Et funes extendérunt in láqueum; juxta iter, scándalum posuérunt mihi.

»⁷Dixi Dómino: Deus meus es tu; exáudi, Dómine, vocem deprecatiónis meæ.
⁸Dómine, Dómine, virtus salútis meæ, obumbrásti super caput meum in die belli.
»⁹Ne tradas me, Dómine, a desidério meo peccatóri: cogitavérunt contra me; ne derelínquas me, ne forte exalténtur.

Psalm 139

Ant 3. Do not forsake me, O Lord, the strength of my salvation.

Deliver me, O Lord, from the evil man: rescue me from the unjust men who have devised iniquities in their hearts:
³all the day long they designed battles.
»⁴They have sharpened their tongues like a serpent: the venom of asps is under their lips.
»⁵Keep me, O Lord, from the hand of the wicked: and from unjust men deliver me: who have proposed to trip my steps:
⁶the proud have hidden a net for me. And they have stretched out cords for a snare: they have laid for me a stumbling-block by the wayside.
»⁷I said to the Lord: Thou art my God: hear, O Lord, the voice of my supplication.
⁸O Lord, Lord, the strength of my salvation: Thou hast overshadowed my head in the day of battle.
»⁹Give me not up, O Lord, to the desires of the wicked: they have plotted against me; do not Thou forsake me, lest they should triumph.

Friday Vespers

¹⁰Caput circuítus eórum: labor labiórum ipsórum óperiet eos.

»¹¹Cadent super eos carbónes; in ignem dejicies eos: in misériis non subsístent.

»¹²Vir linguósus non dirigetur in terra; virum injústum mala cápient in intéritu.
»¹³Cognóvi quia fáciet Dóminus judícium ínopis, et vindíctam páuperum.
¹⁴Verúmtamen justi confitebúntur nómini tuo, et habitábunt recti cum vultu tuo.

V. *Glória Patri ...*

Ant 3.

Psalmus 140

Ant 4. **Dómine clamávi ad te exáudi me.**

Dómine, clamávi ad te: exáudi me; inténde voci meæ, cum clamávero ad te.
»²Dirigátur orátio mea sicut incénsum in conspéctu tuo; elevátio mánuum mearum sacrifícium vespertínum.
³Pone, Dómine, custódiam ori meo, et óstium circumstántiæ lábiis meis.

»⁴Non declínes cor meum in verba malítiæ, ad excusándas excusatiónes in peccátis; cum homínibus operántibus iniquitátem, et non communicábo cum eléctis eórum.
»⁵Corrípiet me justus in misericórdia, et increpábit me: óleum autem peccatóris non impínguet caput meum. Quóniam adhuc et orátio mea in beneplácitis eórum:

¹⁰Those that surround me have lifted up their heads: the malice of their lips shall overwhelm them.
»¹¹Burning coals shall fall upon them; Thou wilt cast them down into the fire: in miseries they shall not be able to stand.
»¹²A slanderer shall not be left standing on the earth: evil shall cast the unjust man unto destruction.
»¹³I know that the Lord will do justice to the needy, and will revenge the poor.
¹⁴But as for the just, they shall give glory to Thy Name: and the upright shall dwell with Thy countenance.

V. *Glory be ...*

Ant 3.

Psalm 140

Ant 4. **O Lord, I cried to Thee: hear me.**

I have cried to Thee, O Lord, hear me: hearken to my voice when I cry to Thee.
»²Let my prayer be directed as incense in Thy sight: the lifting up of my hands as evening sacrifice.

³Set a watch, O Lord, before my mouth: and a door round about my lips.
»⁴Incline not my heart to evil words; to make excuses in sins with men that work wickedness: and I will not communicate with the best of them.
»⁵The just man shall correct me in mercy, and shall reprove me: but let not the oil of the sinner anoint my head. For my prayer also shall still be against the things with which they are well pleased:

»⁶absórpti sunt juncti petræ júdices eórum. Áudient verba mea, quóniam potuérunt.

»⁷Sicut crassitúdo terræ erúpta est super terram, dissipáta sunt ossa nostra secus inférnum.
⁸Quia ad te, Dómine, Dómine, óculi mei; in te sperávi, non áuferas ánimam meam.
»⁹Custódi me a láqueo quem statuérunt mihi, et a scándalis operántium iniquitátem.

¹⁰Cadent in retiáculo ejus peccatóres: singuláriter sum ego, donec tránseam.

V. *Glória Patri* ...

Ant 4.

Psalmus 141

Ant 5. Educ de custódia ánimam meam Dómine ad confiténdum nómini tuo.

Voce mea ad Dóminum clamávi, voce mea ad Dóminum deprecátus sum.
³Effúndo in conspéctu ejus oratiónem meam, et tribulatiónem meam ante ipsum pronúntio:
»⁴in deficiéndo ex me spíritum meum, et tu cognovísti sémitas meas. In via hac qua ambulábam abscondérunt láqueum mihi.

»⁵Considerábam ad déxteram, et vidébam, et non erat qui cognósceret me: périit fuga a me, et non est qui requírat ánimam meam.
»⁶Clamávi ad te, Dómine; dixi: Tu es spes mea, pórtio mea in terra vivéntium.

»⁶their princes falling upon the rock have been swallowed up. They shall hear my words, and learn that they have prevailed:
»⁷as when the depth of the earth is broken up upon the land: their bones are scattered by the mouth of hell.
⁸But to Thee, O Lord, Lord, are mine eyes: in Thee have I put my trust, take not away my soul.
»⁹Keep me from the snare, which they have laid for me, and from the stumbling-blocks of them that work iniquity.
¹⁰The wicked shall fall in his net: I am alone until I pass safely.

V. *Glory be* ...

Ant 4.

Psalm 141

Ant 5. Bring my soul out of prison, O Lord, to give thanks to Thy Name.

I cried to the Lord with my voice: with my voice I made supplication to the Lord.
³In His sight I pour out my prayer, and before Him I declare my distress.
»⁴When my spirit failed me, then Thou knewest my paths. In the way wherein I walked, they have hidden a snare for me.
»⁵I looked on my right hand, and beheld, and there was no one that would know me. Flight hath failed me: and there is no one that hath regard for my soul.
»⁶I cried to Thee, O Lord: I said: Thou art my hope, my portion in the land of the living.

Friday Vespers

»⁷Inténde ad deprecatiónem meam, quia humiliátus sum nimis. Líbera me a persequéntibus me, quia confortáti sunt super me.
»⁸Educ de custódia ánimam meam ad confiténdum nómini tuo; me exspéctant justi donec retríbuas mihi.

V. *Glória Patri ...*

Ant 5.

Capitulum
(2 Cor 1:3-4)
The reading below or the proper of the day

V. Benedíctus Deus et Pater Dómini nostri Jesu Christi, Pater misericordiárum, et Deus totíus consolatiónis qui consolátur nos in omni tribulatióne nostra: ut possimus et ipsi consolari eos qui in omni pressura sunt, per exhortationem, qua exhortamur et ipsi a Deo.

R. Deo grátias.

Hymnus
Or the hymn of the season or feast

Hóminis Supérne Cónditor,
Qui cuncta solus órdinans,
Humum jubes prodúcer
Reptántis et feræ genus:

Et magna rerum córpora,
Dictu jubéntis vivida,
Per témporum certas vices
Obtemperáre sérvulis:

Repélle, quod cupídinis
Ciénte vi nos ímpetit,
Aut móribus se súggerit,
Aut áctibus se intérserit.

»⁷Attend to my supplication: for I am brought very low. Deliver me from my persecutors; for they are stronger than I.
»⁸Bring my soul out of prison, that I may praise Thy Name: the just wait for me, until Thou reward me.

V. *Glory be ...*

Ant 5.

Chapter
(2 Cor 1:3-4)
The reading below or the proper of the day

V. Blessed be the God and Father of our Lord Jesus Christ, the Father of mercies, and the God of all comfort. Who comforteth us in all our tribulation; that we also may be able to comfort them who are in all distress by the instruction wherewith we also are taught by God.

R. Thanks be to God.

Hymn
Or the hymn of the season or feast

Maker of Man, who from Thy Throne
Dost order all things, God alone;/
By whose decree the teeming earth/
To reptile and to beast gave birth:/

The might forms that fill the land,/
Instinct with life at Thy command,/
Are given subdued to humankind/
For service in their rank assigned./

From all Thy servants drive away/
Whate'er of thought impure to-day/
Hath been with open action blent,/
Or mingled with the heart's intent./

Friday Vespers

Da gaudiórum præmia,
Da gratiárum múnera:
Dissólve litis víncula:
Adstrínge pacis fœdera.

Præsta, Pater piíssime,
Patríque compar Unice,
Cum Spirítu Paráclito
Regnans per omne sæculum.

In heaven Thine endless joys bestow,/ And grant Thy gifts of grace below:/ From chains of strife our souls release./
Bind fast the gentle hands of peace./

Grant this, O Father, ever One/
With Christ, Thy sole-begotten Son,/
Whom, with the Spirit we adore,/
One God, both now and evermore./

Versiculi

V. Dirigátur, Dómine, orátio mea.
R. Sicut incénsum in conspéctu tuo.

Ant. Depósuit Dóminus poténtes de sede, et exaltávit húmiles. *(Whenever possible, the antiphon for the specific season or feast of a saint will be used).*

Versicle

V. Let my prayer arise, O Lord.
R. Like incense in Thy sight.

Ant. The Lord hath deposed the mighty from their thrones, and exalted the lowly. *(Whenever possible, the antiphon for the specific season or feast of a saint will be used).*

Cánticum Mariæ
(Luke 1:47-55)
Canticle on page 367

V. *Glória Patri ...*

Ant. Depósuit Dóminus poténtes de sede, et exaltávit húmiles..

Canticle of Mary
(Luke 1:47-55)
Canticle on page 367

V. *Glory be ...*

Ant. The Lord hath deposed the mighty from their thrones, and exalted the lowly.

Orátio

V. Dómine exáudi oratiónem meam.
R. Et clamor meus ad te véniat.

V. Oremus.

Famíliam tuam, quǽsumus Dómine, continua pietáte custódi: ut a cunctis adversitátibus te protegente sit líbera; et in bonis áctibus tuo nómini sit devóta.
Per Dóminum nostrum ...

Prayer

V. O Lord, hear my prayer.
R. And let my cry come unto Thee.

V. Let us pray.

We beseech Thee, O Lord, to guard Thy family with continued mercy: that it may be free from all adversities; and in good deeds be devoted to Thy Name.
Through our Lord ...

Friday Vespers

R. Amen.

The prayer above is said, or the prayer of the season and the feast day are prayed if there are any.

V. Dómine exáudi oratiónem meam.
R. Et clamor meus ad te véniat.

V. Benedicámus Dómino.
R. Deo grátias.

V. Fidélium ánimæ per misericórdiam Dei requiéscant in pace.

R. Amen.

R. Amen.

The prayer above is said, or the prayer of the season and the feast day are prayed if there are any.

V. O Lord, hear my prayer.
R. And let my cry come unto Thee.

V. Let us bless the Lord.
R. Thanks be to God.

V. May the souls of the faithful departed through the mercy of God rest in peace.

R. Amen.

Psalm 140:2

Let my prayer be directed as incense in Thy sight; the lifting up of my hands, as evening sacrifice.

SATURDAY VESPERS

V. Deus, ✝ in adjutórium meum intende.
R. Dómine, ad adjuvándum me festína.

V. *Glória Patri ...*
R. *Sicut erat ...*

V. O God, ✝ come to my assistance.
R. O Lord, make haste to help me.

V. *Glory be ...*
R. *As it was ...*

Psalmus 143:1-8

Ant 1. Benedíctus Dóminus suscéptor meus et liberátor. Meus.

𝕭enedíctus Dóminus Deus meus, qui docet manus meas ad prǽlium, et dígitos meos ad bellum.

»²Misericórdia mea et refúgium meum; suscéptor meus et liberátor meus; protéctor meus, et in ipso sperávi, qui subdit pópulum meum sub me.
»³Dómine, quid est homo, quia innotuísti ei? aut fílius hóminis, quia réputas eum?

⁴Homo vanitáti símilis factus est; dies ejus sicut umbra prætéreunt.
»⁵Dómine, inclína cælos tuos, et descénde; tange montes, et fumigábunt.
⁶Fúlgura coruscatiónem, et dissipábis eos; emitte sagíttas tuas, et conturbábis eos.
»⁷Emítte manum tuam de alto: éripe me, et líbera me de aquis multis, de manu filiórum alienórum:

⁸quorum os locútum est vanitátem, et déxtera eórum déxtera iniquitátis.

Psalm 143:1-8

Ant 1. Blessed is the Lord my helper and liberator.

𝕭lessed be the Lord my God, who teacheth my hands to fight, and my fingers to war.

»²My mercy, and my refuge: my support, and my deliverer: my protector, and I have hoped in Him: Who subdueth peoples under me.
»³Lord, what is man that Thou carest for him or the son of man, that Thou makest a thought of him?
⁴Man is like to vanity: his days pass away like a shadow.
»⁵Lord, bow down Thy heavens and descend: touch the mountains, and they shall smoke.
⁶Send forth lightning, and Thou shalt scatter them: shoot out Thine arrows, and Thou shalt rout them.
»⁷Put forth Thy hand from on high, take me out, and deliver me from many waters: from the hands of the sons of strangers:

⁸whose mouth hath spoken vanity: and their right hand is the right hand of evil.

Saturday Vespers

V. *Glória Patri ...*

Ant 1.

Psalmus 143:9-15

Ant 2. **Beátus pópulus cujus Dóminus Deus eíus meus.**

Deus, cánticum novum cantábo tibi; in psaltério decachórdo psallam tibi.

¹⁰Qui das salútem régibus, qui redemísti David servum tuum de gládio malígno,
»¹¹éripe me, et érue me de manu filiórum alienórum, quorum os locútum est vanitátem, et déxtera eórum déxtera iniquitátis.

»¹²Quorum fílii sicut novéllæ plantatiónes in juventúte sua; fíliæ eórum compósitæ, circumornátæ ut similitúdo templi.
»¹³Promptuária eórum plena, eructántia ex hoc in illud; oves eórum fœtósæ, abundántes in egréssibus suis;
¹⁴boves eórum crassæ. Non est ruina macériæ, neque tránsitus, neque clamor in platéis eórum.
»¹⁵Beátum dixérunt pópulum cui hæc sunt; beátus pópulus cujus Dóminus Deus ejus.

V. *Glória Patri ...*

Ant 2.

Psalmus 144:1-7

Ant 3. **Magnus Dóminus et laudábilis nimis: et magnitúdinis eíus non est finis.**

V. *Glory be ...*

Ant 1.

Psalm 143:9-15

Ant 2. **Blessed is the people whose Lord God is theirs.**

To Thee, O God, I will sing a new canticle: on the psaltery and a ten stringed instrument I will sing praises to Thee:
¹⁰Who givest salvation to kings: Who hast redeemed Thy servant David from the malicious sword.
»¹¹Deliver me, and rescue me out of the hand of alien peoples; whose mouth hath spoken lies: and their right hand is the right hand of iniquity:
»¹²whose sons are as new plants in their youth: their daughters decked out, adorned round about after the columns of a temple:
»¹³their storehouses full, flowing out of this into that: their sheep fruitful in young, abounding in their goings forth: their oxen fat.
¹⁴There is no breach of the wall, nor passage, nor crying out in their streets.
»¹⁵They have called the people happy, that hath these things: but happy is that people whose God is the Lord.

V. *Glory be ...*

Ant 2.

Psalm 144:1-7

Ant 3. **The Lord is great and highly praiseworthy: and there is no end to His greatness.**

Saturday Vespers

Exaltábo te, Deus meus rex, et benedícam nómini tuo in sǽculum, et in sǽculum sǽculi.
»² Per síngulos dies benedícam tibi, et laudábo nomen tuum in sǽculum, et in sǽculum sǽculi.
³Magnus Dóminus, et laudábilis nimis, et magnitúdinis ejus non est finis.
»⁴Generátio et generátio laudábit ópera tua, et poténtiam tuam pronuntiábunt.
⁵Magnificéntiam glóriæ sanctitátis tuæ loquéntur, et mirabília tua narrábunt.

»⁶Et virtútem terribílium tuórum dicent, et magnitúdinem tuam narrábunt.
⁷Memóriam abundántiæ suavitátis tuæ eructúbunt, et justítia tua exsultábunt.

V. *Glória Patri ...*

Ant 3.

Psalmus 144:8-13

Ant 4. **Suávis Dóminus univérsis: et miseratiónes eíus super ómnia ópera eíus.**

iserátor et miséricors Dóminus: pátiens, et multum miséricors.
⁹Suávis Dóminus univérsis, et miseratiónes ejus super ómnia ópera ejus.
»¹⁰Confiteántur tibi, Dómine, ómnia ópera tua, et sancti tui benedícant tibi.
¹¹Glóriam regni tui dicent, et poténtiam tuam loquéntur:

I will extol Thee, O God my King: and I will bless Thy Name for ever: yea, for ever and ever.
»²Every day will I bless Thee: and I will praise Thy Name for ever; yea, for ever and ever.
³Great is the Lord, and greatly to be praised: and of His might there is no end.
»⁴Generation to generation shall praise Thy works: and they shall declare Thy power.
⁵They shall speak of the magnificence of the glory of Thy holiness: and shall tell of Thy wondrous works.
»⁶And they shall speak of the might of Thy terrible deeds: and shall declare Thy greatness.
⁷They shall publish the memory of the abundance of Thy sweetness: and shall rejoice in Thy justice.

V. *Glory be ...*

Ant 3.

Psalm 144:8-13

Ant 4. **The Lord of the universe is sweet and His mercies are upon all His works.**

The Lord is gracious and merciful: patient and plenteous in compassion.
⁹The Lord is sweet to all: and His tender mercies are over all His works.
»¹⁰Let all Thy works, O Lord, praise Thee: and let Thy saints bless Thee.

¹¹They shall speak of the glory of Thy kingdom: and shall tell of Thy power:

Saturday Vespers

¹²ut notam fáciant fíliis hóminum poténtiam tuam, et glóriam magnificéntiæ regni tui.
»¹³Regnum tuum regnum ómnium sæculórum; et dominátio tua in omni generatióne et generatiónem. Fidélis Dóminus in ómnibus verbis suis, et sanctus in ómnibus opéribus suis.

V. *Glória Patri ...*

Ant 4.

Psalmus 144:14-21

Ant 5. Fidélis Dóminus in ómnibus verbis suis: et sanctus in ómnibus opéribus suis.

Állevat Dóminus ómnes qui córruunt, et érigit ómnes elísos.
»¹⁵Óculi ómnium in te sperant, Dómine, et tu das escam illórum in témpore opportúno.
¹⁶Áperis tu manum tuam, et imples omne ánimal benedictióne.
»¹⁷Justus Dóminus in ómnibus viis suis, et sanctus in ómnibus opéribus suis.

»¹⁸Prope est Dóminus ómnibus invocántibus eum, ómnibus invocántibus eum in veritáte.
»¹⁹Voluntátem timéntium se fáciet, et deprecatiónem eórum exáudiet, et salvos fáciet eos.
²⁰Custódit Dóminus ómnes diligéntes se, et ómnes peccatóres dispérdet.

»²¹Laudatiónem Dómini loquétur os meum; et benedícat omnis caro nómini sancto ejus in sǽculum, et in sǽculum sǽculi.

V. *Glória Patri ...*

---

¹²to make Thy might known to the sons of men: and the glory of the magnificence of Thy kingdom.
»¹³Thy kingdom is a kingdom of all ages: and Thy dominion endureth throughout all generations. The Lord is faithful in all His words and holy in all His works.

V. *Glory be ...*

Ant 4.

Psalm 144:14-21

Ant 5. The Lord is faithful in all His words and holy in all His works.

The Lord lifteth up all that fall: and setteth up all that are cast down.
»¹⁵The eyes of all hope in Thee, O Lord: and Thou givest them meat in due season.
¹⁶Thou openest Thy hand, and fillest with blessing every living creature.
»¹⁷The Lord is just in all His ways: and holy in all His works.

»¹⁸The Lord is nigh unto all them that call upon Him: to all that call upon Him in truth.
»¹⁹He will do the will of them that fear Him: and He will hear their prayer, and save them.
²⁰The Lord keepeth all them that love Him; but all the wicked He will destroy.

»²¹My mouth shall speak the praise of the Lord: and let all flesh bless His Holy Name for ever; yea, for ever and ever.

V. *Glory be ...*

Ant 5.

Capitulum
(Rom 11:33)
The reading below or the proper of the day

V. O altitúdo divitiárum sapiéntiæ, et sciéntiæ Dei quam incomprehensibília sunt judícia ejus, et investigábiles viæ ejus!

R. Deo grátias.

Hymnus
Or the hymn of the season

Jam Sol Recédit Ígneus:
Tu lux perénnis Unitas,
Nostris, beáta Trínitas,
Infúnde lumen córdibus.

Te mane laudum cármine,
Te deprecámur;
Dignéris ut te súpplices
Laudémus inter cǽlites.

Patri, simúlque Filio,
Tibíque sancta Spíritus,
Sicut fuit, sit júgiter
Sæclum per omne Glória.

Versiculi

V. Vespertina orátio ascéndat ad te Dómine.
R. Et descéndat super nos misericórdia tua.

Ant. Sucépit Deus Israël púerum suum: sicut locútus est ad Abraham, et semen ejus usque in sǽculum.
(Whenever possible, the antiphon for the specific season or feast of a saint will be used).

Ant 5.

Chapter
(Rom 11:33)
The reading below or the proper of the day

V. O the height of the riches of the wisdom and knowledge of God, how incomprehensible are His judgments, and how unsearchable are His ways!

R. Thanks be to God.

Hymn
Or the hymn of the season

As Fades the Glowing Orb of Day,/
To Thee, great source of light, we pray;/ Blest Three in One, to every heart/ Thy beams of life and love impart.

At early dawn, at close of day,/
To Thee our vows we humbly pay;/
May we, mid joys that never end,/
With Thy bright saints in homage bend.

To God, the Father, and the Son,/
And Holy Spirit, Three in One,/
Be endless glory, as before/
The world began, so evermore.

Versicle

V. Let the evening prayer go up to Thee, O Lord.
R. And let Thy mercy descend upon us.

Ant. God received His son Israel, as He spoke to Abraham, and his seed forever. *(Whenever possible, the antiphon for the specific season or feast of a saint will be used).*

Saturday Vespers

### Cánticum Mariæ	### Canticle of Mary
(Luke 1:47-55)	(Luke 1:47-55)
Canticle on page 367	*Canticle on page 367*

V. *Glória Patri ...*

V. *Glory be ...*

Ant Sucépit Deus Israël púerum suum: sicut locútus est ad Abraham, et semen ejus usque in sǽculum.

Ant. God received his son Israel, as he spoke to Abraham, and his seed forever.

Orátio

Prayer

V. Dómine exáudi oratiónem meam.
R. Et clamor meus ad te véniat.

V. O Lord, hear my prayer.
R. And let my cry come unto Thee.

V. Oremus.

V. Let us pray.

Largire, quǽsumus Dómine, fidelibus tuis indulgëntiam placatus, et pacem: ut pariter ab ómnibus mundëntur offënsis, et secura tibi mente desérviant. Per Dóminum nostrum ...

We beseech Thee, O Lord, to grant indulgence and peace to Thy faithful: that they may likewise be cleansed from all offenses, and may serve Thee with a secure mind. Through our Lord ...

R. Amen.

R. Amen.

The prayer above is said, or the prayer of the season and the feast day are prayed if there are any.

The prayer above is said, or the prayer of the season and the feast day are prayed if there are any.

V. Dómine exáudi oratiónem meam.
R. Et clamor meus ad te véniat.

V. O Lord, hear my prayer.
R. And let my cry come unto Thee.

V. Benedicámus Dómino.
R. Deo grátias.

V. Let us bless the Lord.
R. Thanks be to God.

V. Fidélium ánimæ per misericórdiam Dei requiéscant in pace.

V. May the souls of the faithful departed through the mercy of God rest in peace.

R. Amen.

R. Amen.

Compline

Compline

 # Compline

V. Jube Dómine benedícere. ☩
Noctem quiétam et finem perféctum concédat nobis Dóminus omnípotens.

R. Amen.

1 Pet 5:8-9

Fratres: Sóbrii estóte, et vigiláte: quia adversárius vester diábolus tamquam leo rúgiens círcuit, quærens quem dévoret: cui resístite fortes in fide.

V. Tu autem Dómine miserére nobis.

R. Deo grátias.
V. Adjutórium nostrum ☩ in nómine Dómini.
R. Qui fecit cælum et terram.

Pater Noster tacitus dicitur.

V. Confíteor Deo omnipoténti, beátæ Maríæ semper Vírgini, beáto Micháeli Archángelo, beáto Joánni Baptístæ, sanctis Apóstolis Petro et Paulo, et ómnibus Sanctis, quia peccávi nimis, cogitatióne, verbo et ópere: (percutit sibi pectus ter) mea culpa, mea culpa, mea máxima culpa. Ídeo precor beátam Maríam semper Vírginem, beátum Micháelem Archángelum, beátum Joánnem Baptístam, sanctos Apóstolos Petrum et Paulum, et ómnes Sanctos, oráre pro me ad Dóminum Deum nostrum.

V. Misereátur nostri omnípotens Deus, et dimíssis peccátis nostris, perdúcat nos ad vitam ætérnam.
R. Amen.

V. May the Lord bless us. ☩ May the almighty Lord grant us a quiet night and a perfect end.

R. Amen.

1 Pet 5:8-9

Brethren: Be sober, and watch: because thine adversary, the devil, goes about like a roaring lion, seeking whom he may devour: resist him strong in the faith.

V. But Thee, O Lord, have mercy on us.
R. Thanks be to God.
V. Our help is ☩ in the Name of the Lord.
R. Who made heaven and earth.

Our Father is said in silence.

V. I confess to almighty God, to blessed Mary ever Virgin, to blessed Michael the Archangel, to blessed John the Baptist, to the holy Apostles Peter and Paul, and to all the Saints, that I have sinned exceedingly in thought, word, and deed: Through my fault, through my fault, through my most grievous fault. Therefore I beseech blessed Mary ever Virgin, blessed Michael the Archangel, blessed John the Baptist, the holy Apostles Peter and Paul and all the Saints, to pray to the Lord our God for me.

V. May almighty God have mercy on us, forgive us our sins, and bring us to life everlasting
R. Amen.

Compline

V. Indulgéntiam, ✝ absolutiónem et remissiónem peccatórum nostrórum tríbuat nobis omnípotens et miséricors Dóminus.
R. Amen.

V. Convérte nos ✝ Deus, salutáris noster.
R. Et avérte iram tuam a nobis.

V. Deus, ✝ in adjutórium meum inténde.
R. Dómine, ad adjuvándum me festína.

V. *Glória Patri ...*
R. *Sicut erat ...*

V. Laus tibi, Dómine.

Ant 1. Miserére mihi Dómine, et exáudi oratiónem meam.

Psalmus 4 *(Week I)*

Cum invocárem exaudívit me Deus justítiæ meæ, in tribulatióne dilatásti mihi. Miserére mei, et exáudi oratiónem meam.
»³Filii hóminum, úsquequo gravi corde? ut quid dilígitis vanitátem, et quǽritis mendácium.
»⁴Et scitóte quóniam mirificávit Dóminus sanctum suum; Dóminus exáudiet me cum clamávero ad eum.

»⁵Irascímini, et nolíte peccáre; quæ dícitis in córdibus vestris, in cubílibus vestris compungímini. ⁶Sacrificáte sacrifícium justítiæ, et speráte in Dómino. Multi dicunt: Quis osténdit nobis bona?
»⁷Signátum est super nos lumen vultus tui, Dómine: dedísti lætítiam in corde meo.

V. The almighty ✝ and merciful Lord grant us indulgence, absolution and remission of our sins.
R. Amen.

V. Convert us, ✝ O God, our Savior.
R. And turn away Thy wrath from us.

V. O God, ✝ come to my assistance.
R. O Lord, make haste to help me.

V. *Glory be ...*
R. *As it was ...*

V. Praise be to Thee, O Lord.

Ant 1. Have mercy on me, O Lord, and hear my prayer.

Psalm 4 *(Week I)*

When I called upon Him, the God of my justice heard me: when I was in distress, Thou hast upheld me. Have mercy on me: and hear my prayer.
»³O ye sons of men, how long will ye be dull of heart? Why do ye love vanity, and seek after lying?
»⁴Know ye also that the Lord hath made His Holy One wonderful: the Lord will hear me when I shall cry unto Him.

»⁵Be ye angry, but sin not: the things you say in your hearts, be sorry for them upon your beds.
⁶Offer up sacrifices of justice, and trust in the Lord: many say, Who showeth us good things.
»⁷The light of Thy countenance, O Lord, shines upon us: Thou hast given gladness in my heart.

Compline

⁸A fructu fruménti, vini, et ólei sui, multiplicáti sunt.
»⁹In pace in idípsum dórmiam, et requiéscam;
¹⁰quóniam tu, Dómine, singuláriter in spe constituísti me.

V. *Glória Patri ...*

Ant 1.

Psalmus 90 *(Week II)*
Use Ant 1 from Psalm 4 above

Qui hábitat in adjutório Altíssimi, in protectióne Dei cæli commorábitur.
²Dicet Dómino: Suscéptor meus es tu, et refúgium meum; Deus meus, sperábo in eum.
»³Quóniam ipse liberávit me de láqueo venántium, et a verbo áspero.
⁴Scápulis suis obumbrábit tibi, et sub pennis ejus sperábis.

»⁵Scuto circúmdabit te véritas ejus: non tímebis a timóre noctúrno;

⁶a sagítta volánte in die, a negótio perambulánte in ténebris, ab incúrsu, et dæmónio meridiáno.

»⁷Cadent a látere tuo mílle, et decem míllia a dextris tuis; ad te autem non appropinquábit.

»⁸Verúmtamen óculis tuis considerábis, et retributiónem peccatórum vidébis.
⁹Quóniam tu es, Dómine, spes mea; Altíssimum posuísti refúgium tuum.

»¹⁰Non accédet ad te malum, et flagéllum non appropinquábit tabernáculo tuo.
¹¹Quóniam ángelis suis mandávit de te, ut custódiant te in ómnibus viis tuis.

⁸They are happy by more than the fruit of their corn, their wine, and oil.
»⁹In peace within me I will both sleep, and I will rest:
¹⁰for Thou, O Lord, singularly hast settled me in hope.

V. *Glory be ...*

Ant 1.

Psalm 90 *(Week II)*
Use Ant 1 from Psalm 4 above

He that dwelleth in the aid of the most High, shall abide under the protection of the God of Jacob.
²He shall say to the Lord: Thou art my protector, and my refuge: my God, in Him will I trust.
»³For He hath delivered me from the snare of the hunters: and from the sharp word.
⁴He will overshadow thee with His pinions: and under His wings thou shalt trust.

»⁵His truth shall surround thee as with a shield: thou shalt not be afraid of the terror of the night:

⁶Of the arrow that flieth in the day, of the disease that walketh about in the dark: of invasion, or of the midday demon.

»⁷A thousand shall fall at thy side, and ten thousand at thy right hand: but it shall not come nigh to thee.

»⁸But thou shalt observe with thine eyes: and shalt see the reward of the wicked.
⁹Because Thou, O Lord, art my hope: Thou hast made the most High thy refuge.

»¹⁰There shall no evil come to thee: nor shall the scourge come near thy dwelling.
¹¹For He hath given His angels charge over thee: to keep thee in all thy ways.

Compline

»¹²In mánibus portábunt te, ne forte offéndas ad lápidem pedem tuum.

¹³Super áspidem et basilíscum ambulábis, et conculcábis leónem et dracónem.
»¹⁴Quóniam in me sperávit, liberábo eum; prótegam eum, quóniam cognóvit nomen meum.
¹⁵Clamábit ad me, et ego exáudiam eum; cum ipso sum in tribulatióne: erípiam eum, et glorificábo eum.

»¹⁶Longitúdine diérum replébo eum, et osténdam illi salutáre meum.

V. *Glória Patri ...*

Ant 1.

Psalmus 133

Ant 2. Intret orátio mea in conspéctu tuo, Dómine.

Ecce nunc benedícite Dóminum, ómnes servi Dómini: qui statis in domo Dómini, in átriis domus Dei nostri.
»²In nóctibus extóllite manus vestras in sancta, et benedícite Dóminum.

»³Benedícat te Dóminus ex Sion, qui fecit cælum et terram.

V. *Glória Patri ...*

Ant 2.

Hymnus

Te Lucis Ante Términum,
Rerum Creátor póscimus,
Ut solita cleméntia
Sis præsul ad custódia.

»¹²In their hands they shall bear thee up: lest thou dash thy foot against a stone.
¹³Thou shalt walk upon the asp and the adder: and thou shalt trample under foot the lion and the dragon.
»¹⁴Because he clings to Me I will deliver him: I will protect him because he hath known My Name.
¹⁵He shall cry to Me, and I will hear him: I am with him in tribulation, I will deliver him, and I will glorify him.
»¹⁶I will fill him with length of days; and I will show him My salvation.

V. *Glory be ...*

Ant 1.

Psalm 133

Ant 2. May my prayer be acceptable in Thy sight, O Lord.

Behold now bless ye the Lord, all ye servants of the Lord: who stand in the house of the Lord, in the courts of the house of our God.
»²In the nights lift up thy hands to the holy places, and bless ye the Lord.
»³May the Lord out of Zion bless thee, He that made heaven and earth.

V. *Glory be ...*

Ant 2.

Hymn

Before the Ending of the Day,/
Creator of the world, we pray/
That with Thy wonted favor, Thou/
Would'st be our guard and keeper now.

Compline

Procul recédant sómnia, Et nóctium phantásmata; Hostémque nostrum cómprime, Ne polluántur córpora.	From all ill dreams defend our eyes,/ From nightly fears and fantasies;/ Tread under foot our ghostly foe,/ That no pollution we may know.
Præsta, Pater piíssime, Patríque compar Únice, Cum Spíritu Paráclito Regnans per omne sæculum.	O Father, that we ask be done,/ Through Jesus Christ, Thine only Son;/ Who, with the Holy Ghost and Thee,/ Shall live and reign eternally. Amen.

Capitulum
(Jer 14:9)

V. Tu autem in nobis es, Dómine, et nomen sanctum tuum invocátum est super nos: ne derelínquas nos, Dómine Deus noster.

R. Deo grátias.

Responsorium

V. In manus tuas, Dómine, comméndo spíritum meum.
R. In manus tuas ...

V. Redemísti nos, Dómine, Deus veritátis.
R. Comméndo spíritum meum.

V. Glória Patri, et Fílio et Spirítui Sancto.
R. In manus tuas, Dómine, Comméndo spíritum meum.

V. Custódi nos, Dómine, ut pupíllam óculi.
R. Sub umbra alárum tuárum prótege nos.

Ant. Salva nos, Dómine, vigilantes, custódi nos dormientes; ut vigilemus cum Christo, et requiescamus in pace.

Cánticum Simeonis
(Luke 2:29-32)

Chapter
(Jer 14:9)

V. But Thou, O Lord, art amongst us, and Thy Name is called upon by us, forsake us not.

R. Thanks be to God.

Responsory

V. Into Thy hands, Lord, I commend my spirit.
R. Into Thy hands ...

V. Thou hast redeemed us, O Lord, God of truth.
R. I commend my spirit.

V. Glory be to the Father, Son and Holy Ghost.
R. Into Thy hands, Lord, I commend my spirit.

V. Keep us, O Lord, as the apple of Thine eye.
R. Protect us under the shadow of Thy wings.

Ant. Save us, Lord. while we are awake, watch over us as we sleep, that we may wake with Christ and rest in peace.

Canticle of Simeon
(Luke 2:29-32)

Compline

»²⁹Nunc dimíttis servum tuum Dómine, secúndum verbum tuum in pace:
³⁰quia vidérunt óculi mei salutáre tuum,
»³¹quod parásti ante fáciem ómnium populórum:
³²lumen ad revelatiónem géntium, et glóriam plebis tuæ Israël.

V. *Glória Patri ...*

Ant. Salva nos, Dómine, vigilántes, custódi nos dormiéntes; ut vigilémus cum Christo, et requiescámus in pace.

V. Dómine exáudi oratiónem meam.
R. Et clamor meus ad te véniat.

V. Oremus.

Visita, quǽsumus, Dómine, habitatiónem istam, et ómnes insídias inimíci ab ea longe repélle: Ángeli tui sancti hábitent in ea, qui nos in pace custódiant; et Benedíctio tua sit super nos semper.
Per Dóminum nostrum ...

R. Amen.

V. Dómine exáudi oratiónem meam.
R. Et clamor meus ad te véniat.

V. Benedicámus Dómino.
R. Deo grátias.

(Benedíctio.) Benedícat et custódiat nos omnípotens et miséricors ✝ Dóminus, Pater, et Fílius, et Spíritus Sanctus.
R. Amen.

»²⁹Now Thou dost dismiss Thy servant, O Lord, according to Thy word in peace;
³⁰Because mine eyes have seen Thy salvation,
»³¹Which Thou hast prepared before the face of all peoples:
³²A light to the revelation of the Gentiles, and the glory of Thy people Israel.

V. *Glory be ...*

Ant. Save us, Lord, while we are awake, watch over us as we sleep, that we may wake with Christ and rest in peace.

V. O Lord, hear my prayer.
R. And let my cry come unto Thee.

V. Let us pray.

Visit this habitation, we beseech Thee, Lord, and drive away from it all the snares of the enemy: let Thy holy angels dwell in it, who guard us in peace; and let Thy blessing be upon us always.
Through our Lord ...

R. Amen.

V. O Lord, hear my prayer.
R. And let my cry come unto Thee.

V. Let us bless the Lord.
R. Thanks be to God.

(Blessing.) May the almighty merciful Lord bless and guard us, ✝ Father, and Son, and Holy Ghost.
R. Amen.

Compline

Ant. finalis Beatæ Mariæ Virg.
Salve, Regína, mater misericórdiæ; vita, dulcédo et spes nóstra, salve. Ad te clamámus éxsules fílii Hevæ. Ad te suspirámus geméntes et flentes In hac lacrimárum valle. Eja ergo, advocáta nostra, illos tuos misericórdes óculos ad nos convérte. Et Jesum, benedíctum fructum ventris tui, nobis post hoc exsílium osténde. O clemens, o pia, o dulcis Virgo María.

V. Ora pro nobis, sancta Dei Genitrix.
R. Ut digni efficiámur promissiónibus Christi.

V. Orémus.

Omnípotens sempitérne Deus, qui gloriósæ Vírginis Matris Maríæ corpus et ánimam, ut dignum Fílii tui habitáculum effici mererétur, Spíritu Sancto cooperánte, præparásti: da, ut, cujus commemoratióne lætámur, ejus pia intercessióne, ab instántibus malis et a morte perpétua liberémur. Per eúmdem Christum Dóminum nóstrum. ...
R. Amen.

V. Divínum auxílium máneat semper nobíscum.
R. Amen.

Ultima antiphona de beáta virgine ad adventum.
V. Angelus Dómini nuntiavit Maríæ.

R. Et concépit de Spíritu Sancto.

Final antiphon of the Blessed Virgin
Hail, Holy Queen, Mother of Mercy, our life, our sweetness and our hope. To thee do we cry, poor banished children of Eve. To thee do we send up our sighs, mourning and weeping in this valley of tears. Turn then, most gracious advocate, thine eyes of mercy toward us, and after this our exile show unto us the blessed fruit of thy womb, Jesus. O clement, O loving, O sweet Virgin Mary.

V. Pray for us, Holy Mother of God.
R. That we may be made worthy of the promises of Christ.

V. Let us pray.

Ever-powerful God, who, working with the Holy Spirit, prepared the body and soul of the glorious Virgin Mother Mary to become a worthy habitation for Thy Son: grant that, in whose remembrance we rejoice, we may be freed from evils and eternal death by her pious intercession. Through the same Christ our Lord ...
R. Amen.

V. Let Thy divine help always remain with us.
R. Amen.

Final antiphon of the Blessed Virgin for Advent.
V. The angel of the Lord declared unto Mary.
R. And she conceived by the Holy Spirit.

Compline

V. Oremus.

Grátiam tuam, quǽsumus Dómine, mentibus nostris infúnde: ut, qui, Angelo nuntiánte, Christi Fílii tui incarnatiónem cognóvimus; per passiónem ejus et crucem, ad resurrectiónis glóriam perducámur. Per eúmdem Christum Dóminum nóstrum. Amen.

V. Divínum auxílium ✝ máneat semper nobíscum.

R. Amen.

V. Let us pray.

Pour forth, we beseech Thee, O Lord, Thy grace into our hearts, that we to whom the Incarnation of Christ Thy Son was made known by the message of an angel, may by His Passion and Cross be brought to the glory of His Resurrection.

V. Through the same Christ ✝ our Lord.

R. Amen.

Visit this habitation, we beseech Thee, Lord, and drive away from it all the snares of the enemy

Proper of the Seasons

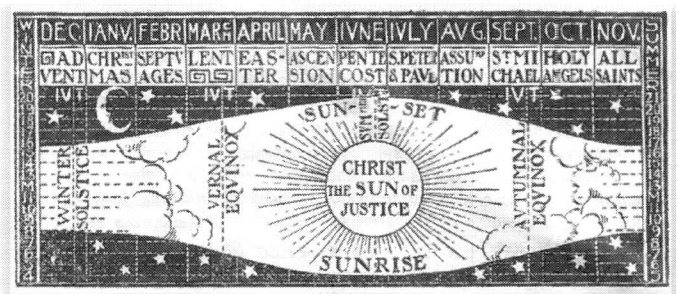

Proper of the Season

Advent

Except for what follows, the Office is taken from the Common throughout the year. The Sunday Prayer will be repeated each weekday.

First Sunday of Advent (Lauds)

Capitulum (Rom 13:11) **V.** Fratres: Hora est iam nos de somno súrgere: nunc enim própior est nostra salus, quam cum credídimus. **R.** Deo grátias.	***Chapter*** (Rom 13:11) **V.** Brethren: It is now time for us to rise from sleep, for now our salvation is nearer than when we believed. **R.** Thanks be to God.
Versiculi **V.** Vox clamántis in desérto: Parate viam Dómini. **R.** Rectas fácite sémitas ejus.	***Versicle*** **V.** The voice of one crying in the wilderness: Prepare the way of the Lord. **R.** Make His paths straight.
Ad Benedíctus Ant. Spíritus Sanctus in te descéndet, Maria: netimeas, habébis in útero Fílium Dei, allelúja.	***Benedíctus Ant.*** The Holy Spirit will descend upon thee, Mary: do not be afraid, thou wilt have the Son of God in thy womb, alleluia.
Orátio Excita, quǽsumus Dómine, poténtiam tuam, et veniut ab imminéntibus peccatórum nostrórum perículis, te mereámur protegénte éripi, te liberánte salvári: Qui vivis et regnas …	***Prayer*** Arise, we beseech Thee, Lord, in Thy power, come and defend us from the imminent dangers of our sins so we may deserve to be rescued under Thy shelter and be saved by Thy deliverance. Who liveth and reigneth …

First Sunday of Advent (Vespers)

Ad Magnificat Ant. Ne tímeas, María, invenísti enim grátiam apud Dóminum: ecce concípies, et páries fílium, allelúja.	***Magnificat Ant.*** Do not be afraid, Mary, for thou hast found favor with the Lord: behold, thou wilt conceive and give birth to a Son, alleluia.

Monday of the 1ˢᵗ Week in Advent

Ad Benedíctus Ant. Angelus Dómini nuntiávit Maríæ, et concépit de Spíritu Sancto, allelúja.	***Benedíctus Ant.*** The angel of the Lord declared unto Mary, and she conceived of the Holy Spirit, alleluia.
Ad Magnificat Ant. Leva, Ierúsalem, óculos tuos, et vide poténtiam regis: ecce Salvátor venit sólvere te a vínculo.	***Magnificat Ant.*** Lift up thine eyes, Jerusalem, and see the power of the king: behold, the Savior is coming to release thee from thy bonds.

Tuesday of the 1ˢᵗ Week in Advent

Ad Benedíctus Ant. Antequam convenírent, invénta est Maria habens in útero de Spíritu Sancto, allelúja.	***Benedíctus Ant.*** Before they came together, the Child was found to be in the womb of Mary by the Holy Spirit.
Ad Magnificat Ant. Quærite Dóminum, dum inveníri potest: invócate eum, dum prope est, allelúja.	***Magnificat Ant.*** Seek the Lord while He may be found: call upon Him while He is near.

Proper of the Season

Wednesday of the 1st Week in Advent

Ad Benedíctus Ant. De Sion exíbit lex, et verbum Dómini de Jerúsalem.	***Benedíctus Ant.*** The law will go forth from Zion, and the word of the Lord from Jerusalem.
Ad Magníficat Ant. Véniet fortióri me post me, cujus non sum dignus sólvere corrígiam calceamentórum.	***Magníficat Ant.*** A mightier Man will come after me, whose shoes I am not worthy to untie.

Thursday of the 1st Week in Advent

Ad Benedíctus Ant. Benedícta tu in cmuliéribus, et Benedíctus fructus ventris tui.	***Benedíctus Ant.*** Blessed art thou amongst women, and blessed is the fruit of thy womb.
Ad Magníficat Ant. Exspectábo Dóminum Salvátorem meum, et præstolábor eum dum prope est.	***Magníficat Ant.*** I will wait for the Lord my Savior, and will await for Him while He is near.

Friday of the 1st Week in Advent

Ad Benedíctus Ant. Ecce véniet Deus et homo de domo David sedére in throno, allelúja.	***Benedíctus Ant.*** Behold, God and man will come from the house of David to sit on the throne.
Ad Magníficat Ant. Ex Ægýpto vocávi Fílium meum: véniet, ut salvet pópulum suum.	***Magníficat Ant.*** I called My Son out of Egypt: He will come to save His people.

Saturday of the 1st Week in Advent

Ad Benedíctus Ant. Sion, noli timére, ecce Deus tuus véniet, allelúja.	***Benedíctus Ant.*** Zion, do not be afraid, behold, thy God will come.
Ad Magníficat Ant. Veni, Dómine, visitáre nos in pace, ut lætémur coram to corde perfécto.	***Magníficat Ant.*** Come, Lord, to visit us in peace, so that we may rejoice before Thee with a perfect heart.

Second Sunday of Advent (Lauds)

Capítulum (Rom 15:4) V. Fratres Quæcúmque scripta sunt, ad nostram doctrínam scripta sunt: ut per patiéntiam, et consolatiónem Scripturárum spem habeámus. R. Deo grátias.	***Chapter*** (Rom 15:4) V. Brethren, whatever things are written, they are written for our learning: that through patience and the consolation of the Scriptures we may have hope. R. Thanks be to God.
Versículi V. Vox clamántis in desérto: Paráte viam Dómini. R. Rectas fácite sémitas ejus.	***Versicle*** V. The voice of one crying in the wilderness: Prepare the way of the Lord. R. Make straight His paths.
Ad Benedíctus Ant. Joannes autem cum audísset in vínculis ópera Christi, mittens duos ex discípulis suis, ait illi: Tu es qui ventúrus es, an álium exspectámus?	***Benedíctus Ant.*** And when John, in prison, had heard of the works of Christ, he sent two of his disciples, who said to Him: "Art thou the one who is to come, or are we to look for someone else?"
Orátio Excita Dómine corda nostra ad præparándas Unigéniti tui vias ut	***Prayer*** Lord, stir up our hearts to prepare the way of Thine Only Begotten, so that through His coming

Proper of the Season

per ejus advéntum purificátis tibi méntibus servíre mereámur. Qui tecum vivit et regnat ...	we may merit to serve Thee with purified minds. Who liveth and reigneth...

Second Sunday of Advent (Vespers)

Ad Magnificat Ant. Tu es, qui ventúrus es, an álium exspectámus? Dícite Ioánni quæ vidístis: Ad lumen rédeunt cǽci, mórtui resúrgunt, páuperes evangelizántur, allelúja.	*Magnificat Ant.* Art thou the one who is going to come, or are we waiting for someone else? Tell John what thou hast seen: the blind return to the light, the dead rise, the poor are evangelized, alleluia.

Monday of the 2nd Week in Advent

Ad Benedíctus Ant. De cælo véniet Dominátor Dóminus, et in manu ejus honor et impérium.	*Benedíctus Ant.* The Sovereign Lord will come from heaven, and honor and power will be in His hand.
Ad Magnificat Ant. Ecce véniet Rex Dóminus terræ et ipse áuferet jugum captivitátis nostræ.	*Magnificat Ant.* Behold, the King, the Lord of the earth, will come and take away the yoke of our captivity.

Tuesday of the 2nd Week in Advent

Ad Benedíctus Ant. Super te Jerúsalem oriétur Dóminus, et glória ejus in te vidébitur.	*Benedíctus Ant.* The Lord will rise over thee in Jerusalem, and His glory will be seen in thee.
Ad Magnificat Ant. Vox clamántis in desérto, Paráte viam Dómini, rectas fácite sémitas Dei nostri.	*Magnificat Ant.* The voice of one crying in the wilderness, prepare the way of the Lord, make straight the paths of our God.

Wednesday of the 2nd Week in Advent

Ad Benedíctus Ant. Ecce ego mitto Angelum meum, qui præparábit viam meam ante fáciem tuam.	*Benedíctus Ant.* Behold, I am sending My Angel, who will prepare My way before thy face.
Ad Magnificat Ant. Sion renováberis, et vidébis justum tuum, qui ventúrus est in te.	*Magnificat Ant.* Thou shalt be renewed in Zion, and thou shalt see thy righteous One who will come to thee.

Thursday of the 2nd Week in Advent

Ad Benedíctus Ant. Tu es qui ventúrus es Dómine, quem exspectámus, ut salvum fácias pópulum tuum.	*Benedíctus Ant.* Thou art the One who is going to come, Lord, Whom we are waiting for, to save Thy people.
Ad Magnificat Ant. Qui post me véniet, ante me factus est: cujus non sum dígnus calceaménta sólvere.	*Magnificat Ant.* He that cometh after me is greater than I: Whose shoes I am not worthy to unloose.

Friday of the 2nd Week in Advent

Ad Benedíctus Ant. Dícite, Pusillánimes confortámini: ecce Dóminus Deus noster véniet.	*Benedíctus Ant.* Say, "Comfort the faint-hearted: behold, the Lord our God will come."

Proper of the Season

Ad Magnificat Ant. Cantáte Dómino cánticum novum: laus ejus ab extrémis terræ.	*Magnificat Ant.* Sing to the Lord a new song: His praise from the ends of the earth.
Saturday of the 2nd Week in Advent	
Ad Benedíctus **Ant.** Levábit Dóminus signum in natiónibus, et congregábit dispérsos Israël.	*Benedíctus Ant.* The Lord will lift up a standard among the nations, and will gather the dispersed of Israel.
Ad Magnificat Ant. Ante me non est formátus Deus, et post me non erit: quia mihi curvábitur omne genu, et confitébitur omnis língua.	*Magnificat Ant.* God was not formed before Me, and He will not be after Me: for to Me every knee shall bow, and every tongue shall confess.
Third Sunday of Advent (Lauds)	
Capitulum (Phil 4:4-5) **V.** Fratres: Gaudéte in Dómino semper: íterum dico, gaudéte. Modéstia vestra nota sit ómnibus homínibus: Dóminus enim prope est. **R.** Deo grátias.	*Chapter* (Phil 4:4-5) **V.** Brethren: Rejoice in the Lord always: I say again, rejoice. Let thy modesty be known to all men: for the Lord is near **R.** Thanks be to God.
Versiculi **V.** Vox clamántis in desérto: Paráte viam Dómini. **R.** Rectas fácite sémitas ejus.	*Versicle* **V.** The voice of one crying in the wilderness: Prepare the way of the Lord. **R.** Make His paths straight.
Ad Benedíctus Ant. Super sólium David, et super regnum ejus sedébit in ætérnum, allelúja.	*Benedíctus Ant.* He will sit on David's throne and over His kingdom forever, alleluia.
Orátio Aurem tuam, quǽsumus Dómine, précibus nostris accómmoda: et mentis nostræ ténebras grátia tuæ visitatiónis illústra. Qui vivis et regnas …	*Prayer* We beseech Thee, O Lord, turn Thine ear to our prayers: and enlighten the darkness of our minds by the grace of Thy visitation: Who liveth and reigneth…
Third Sunday of Advent (Vespers)	
Ad Magnificat Ant. Beáta es Maria, quæ credidísti Dómino: perficiéntur in te, quæ dicta sunt tibi a Dómino, allelúja.	*Magnificat Ant.* Blessed art thou Mary, who believed in the Lord: the things which were spoken to thee by the Lord will be fulfilled in thee, alleluia.
Monday of the 3rd Week in Advent	
Ad Benedíctus **Ant.** Egredietur virga de radíce Jesse, et replébitur omnis terra glória Dómini: et vidébit omnis caro salutáre Dei.	*Benedíctus Ant.* A rod shall come forth from the root of Jesse, and the whole earth shall be filled with the glory of the Lord: and all flesh shall see the salutation of God.
Ad Magnificat Ant. Beátam me dicent ómnes generatiónes quia ancíllam húmilem respéxit Deus.	*Magnificat Ant.* All generations will call me blessed because God looked upon a humble handmaid.

Proper of the Season

Tuesday of the 3rd Week in Advent

Ad Benedíctus Ant. Tu Béthlehem terra Juda, non eris mínima: ex te enim éxiet Dux, qui regat pópulum meum Israël.	*Benedíctus Ant.* Thou Bethlehem, land of Judah, thou shalt not be the least: for from thee will come a leader who will rule My people Israel.
Ad Magníficat Ant. Eleváre, eleváre, consurge Jerúsalem: solve víncula colli tui, captiva filia Sion.	*Magníficat Ant.* Lift up, lift up, rise up, Jerusalem: loosen the bonds of thy neck, captive daughter of Zion.

Ember Wednesday in Advent

Ad Benedíctus Ant. Missus est Gábriel Angelus ad Maríam Vírginem desponsátam Joseph.	*Benedíctus Ant.* Gabriel the Angel was sent to the Virgin Mary, betrothed to Joseph.
Ad Magníficat Ant. Ecce ancílla Dómini: fiat mihi secúndum verbum tuum.	*Magníficat Ant.* Behold the handmaid of the Lord: let it be unto me according to Thy word.

Thursday of the 3rd Week in Advent

Ad Benedíctus Ant. Viguláte ánimo, in próximo est Dóminus Deus noster.	*Benedíctus Ant.* Be alert, the Lord our God is near.

December 17th in Advent

Ad Magníficat Ant. O Sapiéntia quæ ex ore Altíssimi prodiisti, attíngens a fine usque ad finem, fórtiter suavitérque dispónens ómnia: veni ad docéndum nos viam prudéntiæ.	*Magníficat Ant.* O Wisdom which came forth from the mouth of the Most High, reaching from end to end, arranging all things with strength and gentleness: come to teach us the way of prudence.

Ember Friday in Advent

Ad Benedíctus Ant. Ex quo facta est vox salutatiónis tuæ in áuribus meis, exsultávit in gáudio infans in útero meo, allelúja.	*Benedíctus Ant.* Since the voice of thy greeting was heard in mine ears, the child in my womb leaped for joy, alleluia.

December 18th in Advent

Ad Magníficat Ant. O Adonái et Dux domus Israël, qui Móysi in igne flammæ rubi apparuísti, et ei in Sina legem dedísti: veni ad rediméndum nos in bráchio exténto.	*Magníficat Ant.* O Adonai and Leader of the House of Israel, who appeared to Moses in the fire of the flaming bush and gave him the law on Sinai: come to redeem us with outstretched arm.

Ember Saturday in Advent

Ad Benedíctus Ant. Quomodo fiet ístud, Angele Dei, quóniam virum non cognósco? Audi María Virgo: Spíritus sanctus supervéniet in te, et virtus Altíssimi obumbrábit tibi.	*Benedíctus Ant.* How will this be done, Angel of God, since I do not know man? Hear Virgin Mary: The Holy Spirit will come upon thee, and the power of the Most High will overshadow thee.

December 19th in Advent

Ad Magníficat Ant. O radix Jesse qui stas in signum populórum, super	*Magníficat Ant.* O Root of Jesse, Who stands as a sign of the peoples,

Proper of the Season

quem continébunt reges os suum, quem Gentes deprecabúntur: veni ad liberándum nos, jam noli tardáre.	before whom kings will hold their mouths, to whom the Gentiles plead: come to deliver us, delay no longer.

Forth Sunday of Advent (Lauds)

Capitulum (1 Cor 4:1-2) **V.** Fratres: Sic nos exístimet homo ut minístros Christi, et dispensatóres mysteriórum Dei. Hic jam quǽritur inter dispensatóres, ut fidélis quis inveniátur. **R.** Deo grátias.	**Chapter** (1 Cor 4:1-2) **V.** Brethren: Thus shall man think of us as ministers of Christ, and stewards of the mysteries of God. Now there is a search among the stewards, that a faithful one may be found. **R.** Thanks be to God.
Versiculi **V.** Vox clamántis in desérto: Paráte viam Dómini. **R.** Rectas fácite sémitas ejus	*Versicle* **V.** The voice of one crying in the wilderness: **R.** Prepare the way of the Lord.
Ad Benedíctus Ant. Ave María grátia plena Dóminus tecum, benedícta tu in cmuliéribus, allelúja.	*Benedíctus Ant.* Hail Mary, full of grace the Lord is with thee, blessed art thou among women, alleluia.
Orátio Excita, quǽsumus Dómine, poténtiam tuam, et veni, et magna nobis virtúte succurre: ut per auxílium grátiæ tuæ, quod nostra peccáta præpediunt, indulgentia tuæ propitiationis acceleret Qui vivis et regnas cum Deo Patre in unitáte Spíritus Sancti …	**Prayer** Arouse Thy might, we beseech Thee, O Lord, and come assist us with great power: that by the help of Thy grace which is hindered by our sins, the fullness of Thy mercy may come quickly, Who liveth and reigneth …

Forth Sunday of Advent (Vespers)

Ad Magnificat Ant. O Rex Géntium, et desiderátus eárum, lapisque angularis, qui facis utráque unum: veni, et salva hóminem, quem de limo formásti.	*Magnificat Ant.* O King of the Gentiles, the One longed for by them, and the Cornerstone, and Who dost make both one: come and save the man whom Thou hast formed of clay.

Monday of the 4th Week in Advent

Ad Benedíctus Ant. Dicit Dóminus: Poeniténtiam ágite: appropinquávit enim regnum cælórum, allelúja.	*Benedíctus Ant.* The Lord sayeth: Do penance: for the kingdom of heaven is near.

December 20th in Advent

Ad Magnificat Ant. O clavis David et sceptrum domus Israël; qui áperis, et nemo claudit; claudis, et nemo áperit: veni, et educ vínctum de domo cárceris, sedéntem in ténebris, et umbra mortis.	*Magnificat Ant.* O Key of David and Scepter of the House of Israel; who openeth, and no one closeth; Thou shuttest, and no one openeth: come and bring out the captives from the prisons, who are sitting in darkness and the shadow of death.

Tuesday of the 4th Week in Advent

Ad Benedíctus Ant. Oriétur sicut sol Salvátor mundi: et descéndet in	*Benedíctus Ant.* He shall rise like the sun, the Savior of the world: and

Proper of the Season

uterum Vírginis, sicut imber super grámen, allelúja.	He shall descend into the womb of the Virgin, like rain upon the grass.

December 21st in Advent

Ad Magnificat Ant. O Óriens splendor lucis ætérnæ, et sol iustítiæ: veni, et illúmina sedéntes in ténebris, et umbra mortis.	**Magnificat Ant.** O Orient, Splendor of Eternal Light, and Sun of Righteousness: come, and light those who sit in darkness and the shadow of death.

Wednesday of the 4th Week in Advent

Ad Benedíctus Ant. Ponem in Sion salútem, et in Jerúsalem glóriam meam, allelúja.	**Benedíctus Ant.** I will place salvation in Zion, and My glory in Jerusalem.

December 22nd in Advent

Ad Magnificat Ant. O Rex Géntium, et desiderátus eárum, lapísque anguláris, qui facis utráque unum: veni, et salva hóminem, quem de limo formásti.	**Magnificat Ant.** O King of the Gentiles, their longed for One, and the Cornerstone, Who dost make both One: come and save the man whom Thou hast formed from clay.

Thursday of the 4th Week in Advent

Ad Benedíctus Ant. Consolámini, consolámini, pópule meus, dicit Dóminus Deus vester.	**Benedíctus Ant.** Be comforted, be comforted, My people, sayeth the Lord thy God.

December 23rd in Advent

Ad Magnificat Ant. O Emmánuel Rex et légifer noster, exspectátio Géntium, et Salvátor eárum: veni ad salvándum nos Dómine Deus noster.	**Magnificat Ant.** O Emmanuel, our King and Lawgiver, the expectation of the Gentiles, and their Savior: come to save us, Lord our God.

Christmas

Except for what follows, the Office during the Christmas season is the same as that said throughout the year.

Vigil of Christmas (Lauds)

Capitulum (Rom 1:1-3) V. Paulus servus Jesu Christi, vocátus Apóstolus, segregátus in Evangélium Dei, quod ante promíserat per prophétas suos in Scriptúris sanctis de Fílio suo, qui factus est ei ex sémine David secúndum carnem. **R.** Deo grátias.	**Chapter** (Rom 1:1-3) V. Paul, a servant of Jesus Christ, called to be an apostle, separated unto the gospel of God, which He had promised before by His prophets in the Holy Scriptures, concerning His Son, who was made to him of the seed of David, according to the flesh. **R.** Thanks be to God.
Versiculi V. Crástina die delébitur iníquitas terræ. **R.** Et regnábit super nos Salvátor mundi.	**Versicle** V. On the morrow the iniquity of the earth shall be destroyed. **R.** And the Savior of the world will reign over us.

Proper of the Season

Ad Benedíctus Ant. Oriétur sicut sol Salvátor mundi: et descéndet in uterum Vírginis, sicut imber super grámen, allelúja .	*Benedíctus Ant.* He shall rise like the sun, the Savior of the world: and He shall descend into the womb of the Virgin, like rain upon the grass, alleluia.
Orátio Deus, qui nos redemptiónis nostræ ánnua exspectatióne lætíficas: præsta; ut Unigénitum tuum, quem Redémptorem læti suscípimus, veniéntem quoque júdicem secúri videámus, Dóminum nostrum Jesum Christum Fílium tuum …	*Prayer* O God, who maketh us rejoice each year in the expectation of our redemption: grant; that we may see Thine Only Begotten Son, whom we joyfully receive as our Redeemer, and the coming Judge, our Lord Jesus Christ Thy Son …

Christmas Day (Lauds)

Capitulum (Heb 1:1-2) V. Multifáriam, multísque modis olim Deus loquens pátribus in prophétis: novíssime diébus istis locútus est nobis in Fílio, quem constítuit herédem universórum, per quem fecit et sǽcula. R. Deo grátias.	*Chapter* (Heb 1:1-2) V. In diverse, and in many ways, God once spoke to the fathers in the prophets: in these last days He has spoken to us in the Son, whom He appointed the heir of the universe, through whom He also made the ages. R. Thanks be to God.
Versiculi V. Notum fecit Dóminus, allelúja. R. Salutáre suum, allelúja.	*Versicle* V. The Lord made it known, alleluia. R. His salvation, alleluia.
Ad Benedíctus Ant. Glória in excélsis Deo, et in terra pax homínibus bonæ voluntátis, allelúja.	*Benedíctus Ant.* Glory to God in the highest and on earth peace to men of good will, alleluia.
Orátio Concéde, quǽsumus, omnípotens Deus: ut nos Unigéniti tui nova per carnem Natívitas líberet; quos sub peccáti iugo vetústa sérvitus tenet. Per eundem Dóminum nostrum …	*Prayer* Grant, we beseech Thee, Almighty God, that the new birth of Thine Only Begotten Son through the flesh may set us free; where the old slavery held us under the yoke of sin. Through the same Lord Jesus Christ …

Christmas Day (Vespers)

Ad Magnificat Ant. Hódie Christus natus est: hódie Salvátor appáruit: hódie in terra canunt Angeli, lætántur Archángeli: hódie exsúltant iusti, dicéntes: Glória in excélsis Deo, allelúja.	*Magnificat Ant.* Today Christ was born, today the Savior appeared: today the angels sing on earth, the Archangels rejoice: today the righteous rejoice, saying: Glory to God in the highest, alleluia.

Dec. 26 St. Stephen (Lauds)	The First Martyr
Capitulum (Acts 6:8) V. Stéphanus autem plenus grátia et fortitúdine, faciébat prodígia et signa magna in pópulo. R. Deo grátias.	*Chapter* (Acts 6:8) V. But Stephen, full of grace and strength, performed wonders and great signs among the people. R. Thanks be to God.
Versiculi V. Sepeliérunt Stéphanum viri timoráti. R. Et fecérunt planctum magnum super eum.	*Versicle* V. Devout men buried Stephen. R. And they made a great lamentation over him.

Proper of the Season

Ad Benedíctus Ant. Stéphanus autem plenus grátia et fortitúdine, faciébat signa magna in pópulo.	*Benedíctus Ant.* But Stephen, full of grace and strength, performed wonders and great signs among the people.
Orátio Da nobis, quǽsumus, Dómine, imitári quod cólimus: ut discámus et inimícos dilígere; quia eius natalícia celebrámus, qui novit étiam pro persecutóribus exoráre Dóminum nostrum Iesum Christum Fílium tuum. ...	*Prayer* Grant us, we beseech Thee, Lord, to imitate he whom we revere, that we may learn to love our enemies: for we celebrate St. Stephen's feast day, who knows how to plead even for persecutors to our Lord Jesus Christ, Thy Son, who liveth and reigneth ...
Dec. 26 St. Stephen (Vespers)	*The First Martyr*
Capitulum (Acts 6:8) **V.** Stephanus autem plenus grátia et fortitúdine, fáciebat prodígia et signa magna in pópulo. **R.** Deo grátias.	*Chapter* (Acts 6:8) **V.** But Stephen, full of grace and strength, performed wonders and great signs among the people. **R.** Thanks be to God.
Ad Magníficat Ant. Sepeliérunt Stéphanum viri timoráti, et fecérunt planctum magnum super eum.	*Magnificat Ant.* The devout men buried Stephen, and made a great lamentation over him.
Dec. 27 St. John (Lauds)	*Apostle and Evanglist*
Capitulum (Sir 15:1-2) **V.** Qui timet Deum, fáciet bona: et qui cóntinens est iustítiæ, apprehéndet illam, et obviábit illi quasi mater honorificáta. **R.** Deo grátias.	*Chapter* (Sir 15:1-2) **V.** He that feareth God shall do good: and he that hath righteousness shall lay hold of it, and Wisdom shall meet him as an honored mother. **R.** Thanks be to God.
Ad Benedíctus Ant. Iste est Ioánnes, qui supra pectus Dómini in cena recúbuit: beátus Apóstolus, cui reveláta sunt secréta cæléstia.	*Benedíctus Ant.* This is the John who reclined upon the Lord's breast at the Last Supper: the blessed apostle, to whom the heavenly secrets were revealed.
Orátio Ecclésiam tuam, Dómine, benígnus illústra: ut beáti Ioánnis Apóstoli tui et Evangelístæ, illumináta doctrínis, ad dona pervéniat sempitérna. Per Dominum nostrum ...	*Prayer* Teach Thy Church, O Lord, so that, enlightened by the lessons of Thy blessed John the Apostle and Evangelist, we may reach our everlasting reward. Through our Lord ...
Dec. 27 St. John (Vespers)	*Apostle and Evanglist*
Ad Magníficat Ant. Exiit sermo inter fratres, quod discípulus ille non móritur; et non dixit Iesus, Non móritur: sed, Sic eum volo manére, donec véniam.	*Magnificat Ant.* A word went out among the brethren that the disciple should not die; and Jesus did not say, He will not die, but, I want him to remain so until I come.

Proper of the Season

Dec. 28 Holy Innocents (Lauds)	Martyrs
Capitulum (Apoc 14:1) **V.** Vidi supra montem Sion Agnum stántem, et cum eo centum quadragínta quátuor míllia habéntes nomen eius, et nomen Patris eius scríptum in fróntibus suis. **R.** Deo grátias.	**Chapter** (Apoc 14:1) **V.** I saw a Lamb standing on Mount Zion, and with him a hundred and forty-four thousand, having His Name and the Name of his Father written on their foreheads. **R.** Thanks be to God.
Ad Benedíctus Ant. Hi sunt, qui cum muliéribus non sunt coinquináti: vírgines enim sunt, et sequúntur Agnum quocúmque íerit.	**Benedíctus Ant.** These are they who are not defiled with women: for they are virgins, and they follow the Lamb wherever He goes.
Orátio Deus, cuius hodiérna die præcónium Innocéntes Mártyres non loquéndo, sed moriéndo conféssi sunt: ómnia in nobis vitiórum mala mortífica; ut fidem tuam, quam lingua nostra lóquitur, étiam móribus vita fateátur. Per Dóminum nostrum …	**Prayer** O God, whose proclamation today the Innocent Martyrs confessed not by speaking, but by dying, show all the evils of vice in us that are deadly; therefore Thy faith, which our lips profess, may also be acknowledged by our morals and even demonstrated by the character of our lives. Through our Lord …
Dec. 28 Holy Innocents (Vespers)	
Ad Magnificat Ant. Innocéntes pro Christo infántes occísi sunt, ab iníquo rege lacténtes interfécti sunt: ipsum sequúntur Agnum sine mácula, et dicunt semper: Glória tibi, Dómine.	**Magnificat Ant.** Innocent infants were slain for Christ's sake, they were slain as nurslings by an evil king: they follow the spotless Lamb, and always say: Glory to Thee, O Lord.
Dec. 29 St. Thomas of Canterbury (Lauds)	*Bishop and Martyr*
Orátio Deus, pro cuius Ecclésia gloriósus Póntifex Thomas gládiis impiórum occúbuit: præsta, quǽsumus; ut omnes, qui eius implórant auxílium, petitiónis suæ salutárem consequántur efféctum. Per Dóminum nostrum...	**Prayer** O God, for Whose Church the glorious Bishop Thomas fell by the swords of the wicked: grant, we beseech Thee, that all who implore his help may obtain the beneficial effect of his intercession. Through our Lord …
Dec. 31 St. Silvester (Lauds)	*Pope and Confessor*
Orátio Gregem tuum, Pastor ætérne, placátus inténde: et per beátum Silvéstrum Summum Pontíficem, perpétua protectióne custódi; quem totíus Ecclésiæ præstitísti esse pastórem. Per Dóminum nostrum …	**Prayer** Keep Thy flock, Eternal Shepherd, blessed: and through holy Silvester the Supreme Pontiff, keep under Thy perpetual protection; whom Thou hast appointed to be the shepherd of the whole Church. Through our Lord…

Proper of the Season

Jan. 1 The Circumcision of Our Lord (Lauds)
All as at the Sunday Lauds I in the Psalter except as below.

Ant 1. O admirábile commércium: Creátor géneris humáni, animátum corpus sumens, de Vírgine nasci dignátus est; et procédens homo sine sémine, largítus est nobis suam Deitátem.	**Ant 1.** O wondrous interchange! the Creator of mankind, taking upon Him a living body, granted to be born of a pure Virgin: and by His Humanity, which was begotten in no earthly way, hath made us partakers of His Divinity.
Ant 2. Quando natus es ineffabíliter ex Vírgine, tunc implétæ sunt Scriptúræ: sicut plúvia in vellus descendísti, ut salvum fáceres genus humánum: te laudámus, Deus noster.	**Ant 2.** When Thou wast born all ineffably of a Virgin, then were the Scriptures fulfilled; Thou camest down like the dew upon the fleece of wool, to bring salvation unto all mankind; we praise Thee, O our God.
Ant 3. Rubum, quem víderat Móyses incombústum, conservátam agnóvimus tuam laudábilem virginitátem: Dei Génetrix, intercéde pro nobis.	**Ant 3.** In the bush which Moses saw unconsumed, we recognize the preservation of thy glorious virginity: Holy Mother of God, intercede for us.
Ant 4. Germinávit radix Iesse, orta est stella ex Iacob: Virgo péperit Salvatórem; te laudámus, Deus noster.	**Ant 4.** The Root of Jesse hath budded, the Star hath come out of Jacob, the Virgin hath borne the Savior: we praise thee, O our God.
Ant 5. Ecce María génuit nobis Salvatórem, quem Ioánnes videns, exclamávit, dicens: Ecce Agnus Dei, ecce qui tollit peccáta mundi, allelúja.	**Ant 5.** Lo, Mary hath brought forth the Savior of whom when John saw Him, he did proclaim: Behold the Lamb of God that taketh away the sins of the world, alleluia.
Capitulum (Titus 2:11-12) V. Appáruit grátia Dei Salvatóris nostri ómnibus homínibus, erúdiens nos, ut abnegántes impietátem, et sæculária desidéria, sóbrie, et iuste, et pie vivámus in hoc sǽculo. R. Deo grátias.	***Chapter*** (Titus 2:11-12) V. The grace of God that bringeth salvation hath appeared to all men, teaching us that, denying ungodliness and worldly lusts, we should live soberly, righteously, and godly in this present world. R. Thanks be to God.
Ad Benedíctus Ant. Mirábile mystérium declarátur hódie: innovántur natúræ, Deus homo factus est: id quod fuit permánsit, et quod non erat assúmpsit; non commixtiónem passus, neque divisiónem.	***Benedíctus Ant.*** This day is set forth a wonderful mystery, a new thing hath been created on the earth: God is made man. That which He was, He remaineth; and that which He was not, He taketh; suffering therein neither confusion nor division.
Orátio Deus, qui salútis ætérnæ, beátæ Maríæ virginitáte fecúnda, humáno géneri præmia præstitísti: tríbue, quǽsumus; ut ipsam pro nobis intercédere sentiámus, per quam merúimus auctórem vitæ suscípere,	***Prayer*** O God, Who, by the fruitful virginity of the Blessed Mary, hast given unto mankind the rewards of everlasting life; grant, we beseech Thee, that we may continually feel the might of her intercession, through whom we have worthily received the

Proper of the Season

Dóminum nostrum Iesum Christum Fílium tuum. Qui tecum vivit et regnat …	Author of our life, our Lord Jesus Christ, Thy Son Who with Thee liveth and reigneth …

Circumcision Vespers II – Prayer as in Lauds.

The Most Holy Name of Jesus (Lauds)
All as at the Sunday Lauds I in the Psalter except as below.

Capitulum (Phil 2:8-10) **V.** Fratres: Chrístus humiliávit semetípsum, factus obédiens usque ad mortem, mortem autem crucis. Propter quod et Deus exaltávit illum, et donávit illi nomen, quod est super omne nomen: ut in nómine Jesu omne genu flectátur. **R.** Deo grátias.	**Chapter** (Phil 2:8-10) **V.** Brethren: Christ humbled Himself, becoming obedient unto death, and the death of the cross. Because of this, God exalted Him and gave Him a Name which is above every name: that at the Name of Jesus every knee should bend. **R.** Thanks be to God.
Ad Benedíctus Ant. Dedit se ut liberáret pópulum, et acquíreret sibi nomen ætérnum, allelúja.	**Benedíctus Ant.** He gave Himself to save the people and acquire for Himself an eternal Name, alleluia.
Orátio Deus, qui unigénitum Fílium tuum constituísti humáni géneris Salvatórem, et Jesum vocári jussísti: concéde propítius; ut cujus sanctum nomen venerámur in terris, ejus quoque aspéctu perfruámur in cælis. Per eundem Dóminum nostrum …	**Prayer** O God, Who made Thine only begotten Son the Savior of the human race, and commanded that He should be called Jesus: grant more generously; that we may revere His holy Name on earth, and also enjoy His sight in heaven. Through the same Lord Jesus Christ, …

The Most Holy Name of Jesus (Vespers)

Ad Magníficat Ant. Vocábis nomen ejus Jesum; ipse enim salvum fáciet pópulum suum a peccátis eórum, allelúja.	**Magníficat Ant.** Thou wilt call Jesus by Name; for He will save His people from their sins, alleluia.

Office of the Feria January 2 - 5
Lauds I and the Common Throughout the Year except if a feast occurs during this time.
No commemoration of the Feria is made.

Jan. 6 Epiphany (Lauds)
All as at the Sunday Lauds I in the Psalter except as below.

Capitulum (Isa 60:1) **V.** Surge, illumináre Ierúsalem, quia venit lumen tuum, et glória Dómini super te orta est. **R.** Deo grátias.	**Chapter** (Isa 60:1) **V.** Arise, illuminate Jerusalem, for thy light has come, and the glory of the Lord has risen upon thee. **R.** Thanks be to God.
Ad Benedíctus Ant. Hódie cælésti Sponso iuncta est Ecclésia, quóniam in Iordáne lavit Christus eius crímina: currunt cum munéribus Magi ad regáles núptias, et ex aqua facto vino lætántur convívæ, allelúja.	**Benedíctus Ant.** Today the Church is joined to the heavenly bridegroom, because Christ washes away her sins in the Jordan: they run with the gifts of the Magi to the royal wedding, and the guests rejoice, alleluia.
Orátio Deus, qui hodiérna die Unigénitum tuum géntibus stella duce	**Prayer** O God, who on this day revealed Thine only begotten Son to

Proper of the Season

revelásti: concéde propítius; ut qui iam te ex fide cognóvimus, usque ad contemplándam spéciem tuæ celsitúdinis perducámur. Per eundem Dóminum nostrum …	the Gentiles as a guiding star, grant more generously; so that we who have already known Thee by faith may be led even to contemplate the appearance of Thy majesty. Through the same Lord Jesus Christ, …

Jan. 6 Epiphany (Vespers)

Ad Magnificat Ant. Tribus miráculis ornátum diem sanctum cólimus: hódie stella Magos duxit ad præsépium: hódie vinum ex aqua factum est ad núptias: hódie in Iordáne a Ioánne Christus baptizári vóluit, ut salváret nos, allelúja.	***Magnificat Ant.*** We celebrate a holy day adorned with three miracles: today the star led the Magi to the manger: today wine was made from water for the wedding: today Christ willed to be baptized in the Jordan by John to save us, alleluia.

The Holy Family of Jesus, Joseph and Mary (Lauds)
All as at the Sunday Lauds I in the Psalter except as below.

Capitulum (Luke 2:51) **V.** Descéndit Jesus cum María et Joseph, et venit Názareth: et erat súbditus illis. **R.** Deo grátias.	***Chapter*** (Luke 2:51) **V.** Jesus went down with Mary and Joseph, and came to Nazareth: and He was subject to them. **R.** Thanks be to God.
Ad Benedíctus Ant. Illúmina nos, Dómine, exémplis Famíliæ tuæ, et dírige pedes nostros in viam pacis..	***Benedíctus Ant.*** Enlighten us, Lord, with the examples of Thy family, and direct our feet on the path of peace.
Orátio Dómine Iesu Christe, qui, Maríæ et Ioseph súbditus, domésticam vitam ineffabílibus virtútibus consecrásti: fac nos, utriúsque auxílio, Famíliæ sanctæ tuæ exémplis ínstrui; et consórtium cónsequi sempitérnum. Qui vivis et regnas …	***Prayer*** Lord Jesus Christ, who was subject to Mary and Joseph, Thou who consecrated domestic life with ineffable virtues: make us, with the help of both, to be instructed by the examples of Thy Holy Family, and be part of the eternal household with them. Who liveth and reigneth…

The Holy Family of Jesus, Joseph and Mary (Vespers)

Ad Magnificat Ant. María autem conservábat ómnia verba hæc, cónferens in corde suo.	***Magnificat Ant.*** But Mary preserved all these words, confiding them in her heart.
Orátio Dómine Iesu Christe, qui, Maríæ et Ioseph súbditus, domésticam vitam ineffabílibus virtútibus consecrásti: fac nos, utriúsque auxílio, Famíliæ sanctæ tuæ exémplis ínstrui; et consórtium cónsequi sempitérnum. Qui vivis et regnas …	***Prayer*** Lord Jesus Christ, who was subject to Mary and Joseph, Thou who consecrated domestic life with ineffable virtues: make us, with the help of both, to be instructed by the examples of Thy Holy Family, and be part of the eternal household with them. Who liveth and reigneth…

Second Sunday of the Epiphany (Lauds)
All as at the Sunday Lauds I in the Psalter except as below.

Versiculi **V.** Dóminus regnávit, decórem induit. **R.** Induit Dóminus fortitúdinem, et præcínxit se virtúte.	***Versicle*** **V.** The Lord reigned, He put on beauty. **R.** The Lord clothed Him with strength, and girded Him with power.

Proper of the Season

Ad Benedíctus Ant. Núptiæ factæ sunt in Cana Galilǽæ, et erat ibi Iesus cum María matre sua.	***Benedíctus Ant.*** The wedding took place in Cana of Galilee, and Jesus was there with Mary His mother.
Orátio Omnípotens sempitérne Deus, qui cæléstia simul et terréna moderáris: supplicatiónes pópuli tui cleménter exáudi; et pacem tuam nostris concéde tempóribus. Per Dóminum nostrum ...	***Prayer*** Almighty and eternal God, who controls the heavenly and eternal things: hear the supplications of Thy people, and grant Thy peace to our times. Through our Lord ...

Second Sunday of the Epiphany (Vespers)
All as at the Sunday Vespers in the Psalter except as below.

Versiculi V. Dirigatur Dómine orátio mea. **R.** Sicut incénsum in conspéctu tuo.	***Versicle V.*** Let my prayer arise, O Lord, **R.** Like incense in Thy sight.
Ad Magnificat Ant. Deficiénte vino, iussit Iesus impléri hýdrias aqua, quæ in vinum convérsa est, allelúja.	***Magnificat Ant.*** Lacking wine, Jesus ordered the jars to be filled with water, which He turned into wine, alleluia.

Third Sunday of the Epiphany (Lauds)
All as at the Sunday Lauds I in the Psalter except as below.

Versiculi V. Dóminus regnávit, decórem induit. **R.** Induit Dóminus fortitúdinem, et præcínxit se virtúte.	***Versicle V.*** The Lord reigned, He put on beauty. **R.** The Lord clothed Himself with strength and girded Himself with power.
Ad Benedíctus Ant. Cum descendísset Iesus de monte, ecce leprósus véniens adorábat eum, dicens: Dómine, si vis, potes me mundáre: et exténdens manum, tétigit eum, dicens: Volo, mundáre.	***Benedíctus Ant.*** When Jesus came down from the mountain, behold, a leper came up and adored Him, saying: Lord, if Thou wilt, Thou canst make me clean, and stretching out His hand, Jesus touched him, saying: I will, be thou cleansed.
Orátio Omnípotens sempitérne Deus, infirmitátem nostram propítius réspice: atque, ad protegéndum nos, déxteram tuæ maiestátis exténde. Per Dóminum nostrum ...	***Prayer*** Almighty and eternal God, look upon our weakness with compassion: and to protect us, extend the right hand of Thy majesty over us. Through our Lord ...

Third Sunday of the Epiphany (Vespers)
All as at the Sunday Vespers in the Psalter except as below.

Versiculi V. Dirigatur Dómine orátio mea. **R.** Sicut incénsum in conspéctu tuo.	***Versicle V.*** Let my prayer arise, O Lord, **R.** Like incense in Thy sight.
Ad Magnificat Ant. Dómine, si vis, potes me mundáre: et ait Iesus: Volo, mundáre.	***Magnificat Ant.*** Lord, if Thou wilt, Thou canst make me clean: and Jesus said: I will, be thou cleansed.

Proper of the Season

Fourth Sunday of the Epiphany (Lauds)
All as at the Sunday Lauds I in the Psalter except as below.

Versículi **V.** Dóminus regnávit, decórem índuit. **R.** Índuit Dóminus fortitúdinem, et præcínxit se virtúte.	*Versicle* **V.** The Lord reigned, He put on beauty. **R.** The Lord clothed Himself with strength and girded Himself with power.
Ad Benedíctus Ant. Ascendénte Iesu in navículam, ecce motus magnus factus est in mari: et suscitavérunt eum discípuli eius, dicéntes: Dómine, salva nos, perímus.	*Benedíctus Ant.* As Jesus had entered into the boat, behold, there was a great tempest in the sea: and His disciples awakened Him, crying: Lord, save us, we are perishing.
Orátio Deus, qui nos, in tantis perículis constitútos, pro humána scis fragilitáte non posse subsístere: da nobis salútem mentis et córporis; ut ea, quæ pro peccátis nostris pátimur, te adiuvánte vincámus. Per Dóminum nostrum ...	*Prayer* O God, who understandeth we are in the midst of so many perils, and Thou knowest that we cannot withstand them on account of human frailty: grant us strength of mind and body; that we may overcome with Thy help what we suffer for our sins. Through our Lord ...

Forth Sunday of the Epiphany (Vespers)
All as at the Sunday Vespers in the Psalter except as below.

Versículi **V.** Dirigatur Dómine orátio mea. **R.** Sicut incénsum in conspéctu tuo.	*Versicle* **V.** Let my prayer arise, O Lord, **R.** Like incense in Thy sight.
Ad Magníficat Ant. Dómine, salva nos, perímus. ímpera, et fac, Deus, tranquillitátem.	*Magníficat Ant.* O Lord, save us, we are perishing: command, O God make all calm.

Fifth Sunday of the Epiphany (Lauds)
All as at the Sunday Lauds I in the Psalter except as below.

Versículi **V.** Dóminus regnávit, decórem índuit. **R.** Índuit Dóminus fortitúdinem, et præcínxit se virtúte.	*Versicle* **V.** The Lord reigned, He put on beauty. **R.** The Lord clothed Himself with strength and girded Himself with power.
Ad Benedíctus Ant. Dómine, nonne bonum semen seminásti in agro tuo? unde ergo habet zizánia? Et ait illis: Hoc fecit inimícus homo.	*Benedíctus Ant.* Lord, hast thou not sown good seed in thy field? Then why does it have the weeds? And he said to them: This was done by an enemy.
Orátio Famíliam tuam, quæsumus Dómine, contínua pietáte custódi: ut quæ in sola spe grátiæ cæléstis innítitur, tua semper protectióne muniátur. Per Dóminum nostrum ...	*Prayer* Keep Thy family, we beseech Thee, O Lord, with constant goodness: that which rests in the only hope of heavenly grace, may always be assured of Thy protection. Through our Lord ...

Fifth Sunday of the Epiphany (Vespers)
All as at the Sunday Vespers in the Psalter except as below.

Versículi **V.** Dirigátur Dómine orátio mea. **R.** Sicut incénsum in conspéctu tuo.	*Versicle* **V.** Let my prayer arise, O Lord, **R.** Like incense in Thy sight.

Proper of the Season

Ad Magnificat Ant. Collígite primum zizánia, et alligáte ea in fascículos ad comburéndum: triticum autem congregáte in hórreum meum, dicit Dóminus.	*Magnificat Ant.* Gather first the tares, and bind them in bundles to be burned: but gather the wheat into My barn, sayeth the Lord.

Sixth Sunday of the Epiphany (Lauds)
All as at the Sunday Lauds I in the Psalter except as below.

Versiculi **V.** Dóminus regnávit, decórem induit. **R.** Induit Dóminus fortitúdinem, et præcínxit se virtúte.	*Versicle* **V.** The Lord reigned, He put on beauty. **R.** The Lord clothed Himself with strength and girded Himself with power.
Ad Benedíctus Ant. Símile est regnum cælórum grano sinápis, quod minimum est ómnibus semínibus cum autem créverit, majus est ómnibus oléribus.	*Benedíctus Ant.* The kingdom of heaven is like a grain of mustard seed, which is the smallest of all seeds, but when it has grown, it is greater than all plants.
Orátio Præsta, quæsumus, Omnípotens Deus: ut semper rationanília meditántes, quæ tibi sunt plácita, et dicitis exsequámur, et factis. Per Dóminum nostrum ...	*Prayer* Grant, we beseech Thee, almighty God, that we may always meditate on the rational things that are pleasing to Thee, and carry out what Thou sayeth and doeth. Through our Lord...

Septuagesima Sunday (Lauds)
All as at the Sunday Lauds II in the Psalter except as below.

Capitulum (1 Cor 9:24) **V.** Fratres: Nescítis quod ii qui in stádio currunt, omnes quidem currunt, sed unus áccipit bravíum? Sic cúrrite ut comprehendátis. **R.** Deo grátias.	*Chapter* (1 Cor 9:24) **V.** Brothers: Do thee not know that those who run in a race, all indeed run, but one gets the victory? **R.** Thanks be to God.
Versiculi **V.** Dómine refúgium factus es nobis. **R.** A generatióne et progénie.	*Versicle* **V.** Lord, Thou hast become a refuge for us. **R.** By generation and posterity.
Ad Benedíctus Ant. Símile est regnum cælórum hómini patrifamílias, qui éxiit primo mane condúcere operários in víneam suam, dicit Dóminus.	*Benedíctus Ant.* The kingdom of heaven is like unto a man of his father's family, who went out early in the morning to hire laborers into his vineyard, sayeth the Lord.
Orátio Preces pópuli tui, quæsumus, Dómine, cleménter exáudi: ut, qui iuste pro peccátis nostris afflígimur, pro tui nóminis glória misericórditer liberémur. Per Dóminum nostrum …	*Prayer* The prayers of Thy people, we beseech Thee, Lord, mercifully hear: that we who are justly afflicted because of our sins, may be mercifully freed for the glory of Thy Name. Through our Lord …

Sexagesima Sunday (Lauds)
All as at the Sunday Lauds II in the Psalter except as below.

Capitulum (2 Cor 11:19-20) **V.** Fratres: Libénter suffértis insipiéntes, cum sitis ipsi sapiéntes:	*Chapter* (2 Cor 11:19-20) **V.** Brethren: Ye willingly suffer the fools, for when ye are wise

Proper of the Season

sustinétis enim si quis vos in servitútem rédigit, si quis dévorat, si quis áccipit, si quis extóllitur, si quis in fáciem vos cædit. **R.** Deo grátias., ...	yourselves, ye bear it if someone reduces you to slavery, if someone devours you, if someone seizes you, if someone is lifted up, if someone strikes you in the face **R.** Thanks be to God.
Versículi **V.** Dómine refúgium factus es nobis. **R.** A generatióne et progénie.	*Versicle* **V.** Lord, Thou hast become a refuge for us. **R.** By generation and posterity.
Ad Benedíctus Ant. Cum turba plúrima convenírent ad Iesum, et de civitátibus properárent ad eum, dixit per similitúdinem: Exiit qui séminat, semináre semen suum.	*Benedíctus Ant.* When a large crowd had gathered to Jesus, and were hastening to Him for understanding, He spoke with the parable: he who sows went out to sow his seed.
Orátio Deus, qui cónspicis, quia ex nulla nostra actióne confídimus: concéde propítius; ut, contra advérsa ómnia Doctóris géntium protectióne muniámur. Per Dóminum nostrum ...	*Prayer* O God, who sees that we have no confidence in our own actions: grant more mercifully; that we may be fortified against adversaries by the protection of the Doctor of the Gentiles. Through our Lord ...

Quinquagesima Sunday (Lauds)
All as at the Sunday Lauds II in the Psalter except as below.

Capítulum (1 Cor 13:1) **V.** Fratres: Si linguis hóminum loquar, et Angelórum, caritátem autem non hábeam, factus sum velut æs sonans, aut cýmbalum tínniens. **R.** Deo grátias.	*Chapter* (1 Cor 13:1) **V.** Brethren: If I speak with the tongues of men, and of angels, but have not charity, I am as a resounding brass, or a tinkling cymbal. **R.** Thanks be to God.
Ad Benedíctus Ant. Ecce ascéndimus Ierosólymam, et consummabúntur ómnia quæ scripta sunt de Fílio hóminis: tradétur enim géntibus, et illudétur, et conspuétur: et postquam flagelláverint, occídent eum, et tértia die resúrget.	*Benedíctus Ant.* Behold, we are going up to Jerusalem, and all that has been written about the Son of Man will be fulfilled: for He will be delivered to the Gentiles, and will be mocked and spat upon; and after they have scourged Him, they will kill Him, and on the third day He will rise again.
Orátio Preces nostras, quæsumus, Dómine, cleménter exáudi: atque, a peccatórum vínculis absolútos, ab omni nos adversitáte custódi. Per Dóminum nostrum ...	*Prayer* Mercifully hear our prayers, we beseech Thee O Lord: and freed from the chains of sins, keep us from all adversity. Through our Lord ...

Proper of the Season

Lent

All Sundays as at the Sunday Lauds II in the Psalter except as below.
Weekdays are as the weekday Common Throughout the Year
except for the Proper of the Seasons for Lent below.

Ash Wednesday (Lauds)
Psalms of Wednesday Lauds II in the Psalter except as below.

Ad Benedíctus Ant. Jejunátis, nolíte fíeri sicut hypócritæ, tristes.	**Benedíctus Ant.** When you fast, do not become sad like the hypocrites.
Orátio Præsta, Dómine, fidélibus tuis: ut ieiuniórum veneránda solémnia, et cóngrua pietáte suscípiant, et secúra devotióne percúrrant. Per Dominum nostrum ...	**Prayer** Grant, O Lord, to Thy faithful: that they may receive the venerable solemnities of the fasts, and receive them with due piety, and persevere with steadfast devotion. Through our Lord ...

Ash Wednesday (Vespers)

Ad Magníficat Ant. Thesaurizáte vobis thesáuros in cælo, ubi nec ærúgo, nec tínea demolítur.	**Magníficat Ant.** Lay up for yourselves treasures in heaven, where neither rust nor moth destroyeth.
Orátio Inclinántes se, Dómine, maiestáti tuæ, propitiátus inténde: ut, qui divíno múnere sunt refécti, cæléstibus semper nutriántur auxíliis. Per Dóminum nostrum ...	**Prayer** Bow down Thy majesty, O Lord, and look upon the conciliated: that those who are refreshed by the divine gift, may always be nourished by heavenly aids. Through our Lord ...

Thursday after Ash Wednesday (Lauds)

Ad Benedíctus Ant. Dómine, puer meus iacet paralýticus in domo, et male torquétur: Amen dico tibi, ego véniam, et curábo eum.	**Benedíctus Ant.** Lord, my child lies paralyzed in the house and is suffering terribly: Amen I say to thee, I will come and take care of him.
Orátio Deus, qui culpa offénderis, pæniténtia placáris: preces pópuli tui supplicántis propítius réspice; et flagélla tuæ iracúndiæ, quæ pro peccátis nostris merémur, avérte. Per Dóminum nostrum ...	**Prayer** O God, who is offended by our sins, Thou who art appeased by repentance: look more mercifully upon the prayers of Thy supplicant people; and turn away the scourges of Thy wrath which we deserve for our sins. Through our Lord ...

Thursday after Ash Wednesday (Vespers)

Ad Magníficat Ant. Dómine, non sum dignus ut intres sub tectum meum: sed tantum dic verbo, et sanábitur puer meus.	**Magníficat Ant.** O Lord, I am not worthy that Thou shouldst come under my roof: but just say the word, and my child will be healed.
Orátio Parce, Dómine, parce populo tuo: ut, dignis flagellatiónibus castigátus, in tua miseratióne respíret. Per Dóminum nostrum ...	**Prayer** Spare me, O Lord, spare Thy people: that, chastened by deserved scourgings, they may breathe in Thy mercy. Through our Lord ...

Friday after Ash Wednesday (Lauds)

Ad Benedíctus Ant. Cum facis eleemósynam nésciat sinístra tua quid fáciat déxtera tua.	**Benedíctus Ant.** When thou givest alms, let thy left hand not know what thy right hand is doing.

Proper of the Season

Orátio Inchoáta ieiúnia, quǽsumus, Dómine, benígno favóre proséquere: ut observántiam, quam corporáliter exhibémus, méntibus étiam sincéris exercére valeámus. Per Dominum nostrum ...	*Prayer* Having begun the fast, we beseech Thee, Lord, to continue with kind favor: that the respect which we show bodily may also be exercised with sincere minds. Through our Lord ...

Friday after Ash Wednesday (Vespers)

Ad Magnificat Ant. Tu autem cum oráveris, intra in cubículum tuum: et clauso óstio, ora Patrem tuum.	*Magnificat Ant.* But when thou prayest, go into thy room, and with the door shut, pray to thy Father.
Orátio Tuére, Dómine, pópulum tuum et ab ómnibus peccátis cleménter emúnda: quia nulla ei nocébit advérsitas, si nulla ei dominétur iníquitas. Per Dóminum...	*Prayer* Lord, protect Thy people, and mercifully cleanse them from all sins, because no adversity will harm them if no wickedness rules them. Through our Lord ...

Saturday after Ash Wednesday (Lauds)

Ad Benedíctus Ant. Me étenim de die in diem quærunt, et scire vias meas volunt.	*Benedíctus Ant.* For they seek Me day by day, and desire to know My ways.
Orátio Adésto, Dómine, supplicatiónibus nostris: et concéde; ut hoc solémne ieiúnium, quod animábus corporibúsque curándis salúbriter institútum est, devóto servítio celebrémus. Per Dóminum nostrum ...	*Prayer* Attend, O Lord, to our supplications, and grant that we may celebrate this solemn fast, which is healthily instituted for the care of souls and bodies, with a devout service. Through our Lord ...

Saturday after Ash Wednesday (Vespers)

Ad Magnificat Ant. Tunc invocábis, et Dóminus exáudiet: clamábis, et dicet: Ecce adsum.	*Magnificat Ant.* Then thou shalt call, and the Lord will hear: thou shalt cry, and He will say: Behold, I am here.
Orátio Deus, qui Ecclésiam tuam ánnua quadragesimáli observatióne puríficas: præsta famíliæ tuæ; ut, quod a te obtinére abstinéndo nítitur, hoc bonis opéribus exsequátur. Per Dóminum nostrum ...	*Prayer* O God, who purifies Thy Church with the annual observance of Lent: bless Thy family; that what we endeavor to obtain from Thee by abstinence, we may accomplish by good works. Through our Lord ...

First Sunday in Lent (Lauds)
Psalms of Sunday Lauds II

Ant 1. Cor mundum crea in me Deus, et spíritum rectum ínnova in viscéribus meis.	**Ant 1.** Create a clean heart in me, O God, and renew a right spirit in my bowels.
Ant 2. O Dómine, salvum me fac; O Dómine, bene prosperáre.	**Ant 2.** O Lord, save me, O Lord, make me prosper.
Ant 3. Sic benedícam te in vita mea, Dómine: et in nómine tuo levábo manus meas.	**Ant 3.** Thus I will bless Thee in my life, O Lord: and in Thy Name I will lift up my hands.
Ant 4. In spíritu humilitátis, et in ánimo contríto suscipiámur, Dómine,	**Ant 4.** In a spirit of humility, and with a broken heart, let us be received

Proper of the Season

a te: et sic fiat sacrifícium nostrum, ut a te suscipiátur hódie, et pláceat tibi, Dómine Deus.	by Thee, O Lord: and let our sacrifice be so, that it may be accepted by Thee today, and may it please Thee, O Lord my God.
Ant 5. Laudáte Deum cæli cælórum, et aquæ omnes.	**Ant 5.** Praise the God of the heaven of heavens, and all waters.
Capitulum (2 Cor 6:1-2) **V.** Fratres: Hortámur vos, ne in vácuum grátiam Dei recipiátis. Ait enim: Témpore accépto exaudívi te, et in die salútis adiúvi te. **R.** Deo grátias.	***Chapter*** (2 Cor 6:1-2) **V.** And we helping do exhort thee, that thou receiveth not the grace of God in vain. For He sayeth: In an acceptable time have I heard thee; and in the day of salvation have I helped thee. **R.** Thanks be to God.
Hymn O Sol Salútis, Page 74	
Versiculi **V.** Ángelis suis Deus mandávit de te. **R.** Ut custódiant te in ómnibus viis tuis.	***Versicle*** **V.** God commanded His angels about thee. **R.** That they may guard thee in all thy ways.
Ad Benedíctus Ant. Ductus est Iesus in desértum a Spíritu, ut tentarétur a diábolo: et cum ieiunásset quadragínta diébus et quadragínta nóctibus, póstea esúriit.	***Benedíctus Ant.*** Jesus was led into the wilderness by the Spirit to be tempted by the devil: and when He had fasted forty days and forty nights, afterwards He was hungry.
Orátio Deus, qui Ecclésiam tuam ánnua quadragesimáli observatióne puríficas: præsta famíliæ tuæ; ut, quod a te obtinére abstinéndo nítitur, hoc bonis opéribus exsequátur. Per Dóminum nostrum ...	***Prayer*** O God, who purifies Thy Church with the annual observance of Lent: bless Thy family; that what we endeavor to obtain from Thee by abstinence, we may accomplish by good works. Through our Lord ...
First Sunday in Lent (Vespers) Vespers for Sunday Page 123	
Ad Magníficat Ant. Ecce nunc tempus acceptábile, ecce nunc dies salútis: in his ergo diébus exhibeámus nosmetípsos sicut Dei minístros in multa patiéntia, in ieiúniis, in vigíliis, et in caritáte non ficta.	***Magníficat Ant.*** Behold, now is the accepted time; behold, now is the day of salvation; in these days therefore let us approve ourselves as the ministers of God. in much patience, in fastings, in watchings, and in love unfeigned.
Monday after the 1ˢᵗ Sunday of Lent (Lauds) Feria	
Ad Benedíctus Ant. Veníte, benedícti Patris mei, percípite regnum, quod vobis parátum est ab orígine mundi.	***Benedíctus Ant.*** Come, ye blessed of My Father, observe the kingdom that hath been prepared for you from the beginning of the world.
Orátio Convérte nos, Deus, salutáris noster: et, ut nobis ieiúnium quadragesimále profíciat, mentes nostras cæléstibus ínstrue disciplínis. Per Dóminum nostrum ...	***Prayer*** Convert us, O God our Savior: that the fasting of Lent may benefit us and provide our minds with heavenly disciplines. Through our Lord ...

Proper of the Season

Monday after the 1ˢᵗ Sunday of Lent (Vespers)	
Feria	
Ad Magnificat Ant. Quod uni ex mínimis meis fecístis, mihi fecístis, dicit Dóminus.	**Magnificat Ant.** What thou didst to one of the least of these, thou didst to Me, sayeth the Lord.
Orátio Absólve, quǽsumus, Dómine, nostrórum víncula peccatórum: et, quidquid pro eis merémur, propitiátus avérte. Per Dóminum nostrum ...	**Prayer** Absolve, we beseech Thee Lord, the bonds of our sins: and pardon whatever we deserve for them. Through our Lord ...
Tuesday after the 1ˢᵗ Sunday of Lent (Lauds)	
Feria	
Ad Benedíctus Ant. Intrávit Iesus in templum Dei, et eiciébat omnes vendéntes et eméntes: et mensas nummulariórum, et cáthedras vendéntium colúmbas evértit.	**Benedíctus Ant.** Jesus entered the temple of God, and drove out all those who were selling and buying: and the tables of the money changers, and He turned over the chairs of those who were selling the doves.
Orátio Réspice, Dómine, famíliam tuam, et præsta: ut apud te mens nostra tuo desidério fúlgeat, quæ se carnis maceratióne castígat. Per Dóminum nostrum ...	**Prayer** O Lord, look upon Thy family, and grant that our mind may shine with Thy desire, which chastises itself with the abstinence of food for the flesh. Through our Lord ...
Tuesday after the 1ˢᵗ Sunday of Lent (Vespers)	
Feria	
Ad Magnificat Ant. Scriptum est enim, quia domus mea, domus oratiónis est cunctis géntibus: vos autem fecístis illam spelúncam latrónum: et erat cotídie docens in templo.	**Magnificat Ant.** For it is written, that My house is a house of prayer for all nations: but ye have made it a den of robbers: and He was daily teaching in the temple.
Orátio Ascéndant ad te, Dómine, preces nostræ: et ab Ecclésia tua cunctam repélle nequítiam. Per Dominum nostrum...	**Prayer** Let our prayers ascend to Thee, O Lord: and repel all wickedness from Thy Church. Through our Lord ...
Ember Wednesday in Lent (Lauds)	
Feria	
Ad Benedíctus Ant. Generátio hæc prava et pervérsa signum quærit: et signum non dábitur ei, nisi signum Ionæ prophétæ.	**Benedíctus Ant.** This crooked and perverse generation seeks a sign: and no sign will be given to it except the sign of the prophet Jonah.
Orátio Preces nostras, quǽsumus, Dómine, cleménter exáudi: et contra cuncta nobis adversántia déxteram tuæ maiestátis exténde. Per Dóminum nostrum ...	**Prayer** We beseech Thee, Lord, graciously hear our prayers: and against all that oppose us, extend the right hand of Thy majesty. Through our Lord ...
Ember Wednesday in Lent (Vespers)	
Feria	
Ad Magnificat Ant. Sicut fuit Ionas in ventre ceti tribus diébus et tribus	**Magnificat Ant.** As Jonah was in the belly of the whale for three days and

Proper of the Season

nóctibus, ita erit Fílius hóminis in corde terræ.	three nights, so shall the Son of Man be in the heart of the earth.
Orátio Mentes nostras, quǽsumus, Dómine, lúmine tuæ claritátis illústra: ut vidére possímus quæ agénda sunt; et, quæ recta sunt, ágere valeámus. Per Dóminum nostrum ...	*Prayer* Enlighten our minds, we ask, Lord, with the light of Thy brilliance: so that we can see what needs to be done; and let us be able to do what is right. Through our Lord ...

Thursday after the 1ˢᵗ Sunday of Lent (Lauds)
Feria

Ad Benedíctus Ant. Egréssus Iesus secéssit in partes Tyri et Sidónis: et ecce múlier Chananǽa a fínibus illis egréssa, clamábat dicens: Miserére mei, Fili David.	*Benedíctus Ant.* Jesus went out and retired to the parts of Tyre and Sidon, and behold, a Canaanite woman came out of those regions, crying out, saying: have mercy on me, Son of David.
Orátio Devotiónem pópuli tui, quǽsumus, Dómine, benígnus inténde: ut, qui per abstinéntiam macerántur in córpore, per fructum boni óperis reficiántur in mente. Per Dóminum nostrum ...	*Prayer* We beseech Thee, kind Lord, through the devotion of Thy people, that those who are impoverished in body through abstinence may be refreshed in mind through the fruit of good works. Through our Lord. ...

Thursday after the 1ˢᵗ Sunday of Lent (Vespers)
Feria

Ad Magnificat Ant. O múlier, magna est fides tua: fiat tibi sicut petísti.	*Magnificat Ant.* O woman, thy faith is great: may it be done to thee as thou hast asked.
Orátio Da, quǽsumus, Dómine, pópulis christiánis: et, quæ profiténtur, agnóscere, et cæléste munus dilígere, quod frequéntant. Per Dóminum nostrum ...	*Prayer* Grant, we beseech Thee, Lord, to the Christian peoples, and those who believe, to recognize and love the heavenly mysteries which they frequent. Through our Lord ...

Ember Friday in Lent (Lauds)
Feria

Ad Benedíctus Ant. Angelus Dómini descendébat de cælo, et movebátur aqua, et sanabátur unus.	*Benedíctus Ant.* An angel of the Lord descended from heaven, and the water was moved, and one was healed.
Orátio Esto, Dómine, propítius plebi tuæ: et, quam tibi facis esse devótam, benígno réfove miserátus auxílio. Per Dominum nostrum...	*Prayer* Be, O Lord, more generous to Thy people; whom Thou makest to be devoted to Thee, kindly refresh us with Thy compassionate help. Through our Lord ...

Ember Friday in Lent (Vespers)
Feria

Ad Magnificat Ant. Qui me sanum fecit ille mihi præcépit: tolle grabátum tuum, et ámbula in pace.	*Magnificat Ant.* He who made me whole commanded me: take up thy bed and walk in peace.
Orátio Exáudi nos, miséricors Deus: et méntibus nostris grátiæ tuæ lumen osténde. Per Dóminum nostrum ...	*Prayer* Hear us, merciful God, and show to our minds the light of Thy grace. Through our Lord ...

Proper of the Season

Ember Saturday in Lent (Lauds)	
Feria	
Ad Benedíctus Ant. Assúmpsit Iesus discípulos suos, et ascéndit in montem, et transfigurátus est ante eos.	*Benedíctus Ant.* Jesus took His disciples and ascended the mountain, and was transfigured before them.
Orátio Pópulum tuum, quǽsumus, Dómine, propítius réspice: atque ab eo flagélla tuæ iracúndiæ cleménter avérte. Per Dóminum nostrum ...	*Prayer* Thy people beseech Thee, O Lord, to look down more mercifully, and compassionately turn away from them the scourges of Thy wrath. Through our Lord ...
Ember Saturday in Lent (Vespers)	
Feria	
Ad Magníficat Ant. Visiónem quam vidístis, némini dixéritis, donec a mórtuis resúrgat Fílius hóminis.	*Magnificat Ant.* The vision thou seest thou shalt tell no one until the Son of Man hath risen from the dead.
Orátio Deus, qui cónspicis omni nos virtúte destítui: intérius exteriúsque custódi; ut ab ómnibus adversitátibus muniámur in córpore, et a právis cogitatiónibus mundémur in mente. Per Dóminum nostrum ...	*Prayer* O God, who sees us destitute of all strength, support us both inwardly and outwardly, that we may be strengthened against all adversities in body, and be cleansed from evil thoughts in mind. Through our Lord ...
Second Sunday in Lent (Lauds)	
Psalms of Sunday Lauds II	
Ant 1. Dómine, lábia mea apéries, et os meum annuntiábit laudem tuam.	**Ant 1.** O Lord, Thou wilt open my lips, and my mouth shalt declare Thy praise.
Ant 2. Déxtera Dómini fecit virtútem dexterra Dómini exaultávit me.	**Ant 2.** The right hand of the Lord hath done mightily: the right hand of the Lord hath lifted me up.
Ant 3. Factus est adjútor meus, Deus meus.	**Ant 3.** He hath become my helper, My God.
Ant 4. Trium puerórum cantémus hymnum, quem cantábant in camíno ignis, benedicéntes Dóminum.	**Ant 4.** Let us sing the hymn of the three young men, which they sang in the hearth of the fire, blessing the Lord.
Ant 5. Státuit ea in ætérnum, et in sǽculum sǽculi; præcéptum pósuit et non præteríbit.	**Ant 5.** He established them for ever and ever. He hath set a command-ment and it will not pass away.
Capitulum (1 Thess 4:1) **V.** Fratres: Rogámus vos, et obsecrámus in Dómino Iesu: ut, quemádmodum accepístis a nobis, quómodo vos opórteat ambuláre, et placére Deo, sic et ambulétis, ut abundétis magis. **R.** Deo grátias.	*Chapter* (1 Thess 4:1) **V.** For the rest therefore, brethren, we pray and beseech you in the Lord Jesus, that as ye have received from us, how ye ought to walk, and to please God, so also ye would walk, that ye may abound the more. **R.** Thanks be to God.

Proper of the Season

Hymn - *O Sol Salútis*, page 74	
Ad Benedíctus Ant. Assúmpsit Iesus discípulos suos, et ascéndit in montem, et transfigurátus est ante eos.	***Benedíctus Ant.*** Jesus took His disciples and ascended the mountain and was transfigured before them.
Orátio Deus, qui cónspicis omni nos virtúte destítui: intérius exteriúsque custódi; ut ab ómnibus adversitátibus muniámur in córpore, et a právis cogitatiónibus mundémur in mente. Per Dóminum nostrum…	***Prayer*** O God, who seeth us destitute of all strength, hold us up inwardly and outwardly, that we may prevail against all adversities in body, and be cleansed from evil thoughts in mind. Through our Lord ...
Second Sunday in Lent (Vespers) Psalms of Vespers, page 123	
Ad Magnificat Ant. Visiónem quam vidístis, némini dixéritis, donec a mórtuis resúrgat Fílius hóminis.	***Magnificat Ant.*** The vision ye saw ye will tell no one until the Son of Man hath risen from the dead.
Orátio Deus, qui cónspicis omni nos virtúte destítui: intérius exteriúsque custódi; ut ab ómnibus adversitátibus muniámur in córpore, et a právis cogitatiónibus mundémur in mente. Per Dóminum nostrum...	***Prayer*** O God, who seeth us destitute of all strength, hold us up inwardly and outwardly, that we may be fortified against all adversities in body, and be cleansed from evil thoughts in mind. Through our Lord ...
Monday after the 2nd Sunday of Lent (Lauds) Feria	
Ad Benedíctus Ant. Ego princípium qui et loquor vobis.	***Benedíctus Ant.*** I am the beginning that speaketh to thee.
Orátio Præsta quǽsumus Omnípotens Deus: ut família tua, quæ se affligéndo carnem ab aliméntis ábstinet, sectándo justítiam a culpa jejúnet. Per Dóminum nostrum ...	***Prayer*** We beseech Thee, Almighty God to grant that Thy family, which by punishing the flesh by abstaining from food, may fast from sin by following righteousness. Through our Lord ...
Monday after the 2nd Sunday of Lent (Vespers) Feria	
Ad Magnificat Ant. Qui me misit mecum est, et non relíquit me solum; quia quæ plácita sunt ei, fácio semper.	***Magnificat Ant.*** He who sent Me is with Me, and does not leave Me alone; because I always do what pleaseth Him.
Orátio Adésto supplicatiónibus nostris, omnípotens Deus: et, quibus fidúciam sperándæ pietátis indúlges; consuétæ misericórdiæ tríbue benígnus efféctum. Per Dóminum nostrum ...	***Prayer*** Attend to our supplications, Almighty God; and in whom Thou providest us the confidence of trusting in Thee for holiness; allow us Thy kind mercy. Through our Lord …

Proper of the Season

Tuesday after the 2nd Sunday of Lent (Lauds)
Feria

Ad Benedíctus Ant. Unus est enim magíster vester, qui in cælis est; Chrístus Dóminus.	***Benedíctus Ant.*** For one is thy Master, Who is in heaven; Christ the Lord.
Orátio Pérfice, quǽsumus, Dómine, benígnus in nobis observántiæ sanctæ subsídium: ut, quæ te auctóre faciénda cognóvimus, te operánte impleámus. Per Dóminum nostrum …	***Prayer*** We beseech Thee, kind Lord, to grant us the support of holy discipline: that what we have learned by Thine instruction, working, we may achieve. Through our Lord …

Tuesday after the 2nd Sunday of Lent (Vespers)
Feria

Ad Magnificat Ant. Omnes autem vos fratres estis: et patrem nolíte vocáre vobis super terram: unus est enim Pater vester, qui in cælis est: nec vocémini magístri, quia magíster vester unus est Christus.	***Magnificat Ant.*** But ye are all brothers: and do not call thy father on earth, for thy Father is One Who is in heaven: and call no one thy master, because thy Master is One, Christ.
Orátio Propitiáre, Dómine, supplicatiónibus nostris, et animárum nostrárum medére languóribus: ut, remissióne percépta, in tua semper benedictióne lætémur. Per Dóminum nostrum …	***Prayer*** Lord, have mercy on our supplications, and heal the infirmities of our souls; as we have received forgiveness, let us ever rejoice in Thy blessing. Through our Lord …

Wednesday after the 2nd Sunday of Lent (Lauds)
Feria

Ad Benedíctus Ant. Ecce ascéndimus Ierosólymam: et Fílius hóminis tradétur ad crucifigéndum.	***Benedíctus Ant.*** Behold, we go up to Jerusalem: and the Son of Man shall be delivered up to be crucified.
Orátio Pópulum tuum, quǽsumus, Dómine, propítius réspice: et quos ab escis carnálibus prǽcipis abstinére, a nóxiis quoque vítiis cessáre concéde. Per Dóminum nostrum …	***Prayer*** We beseech Thee, O Lord, to look more mercifully upon Thy people: and grant those whom Thou commandst to abstain from earthly foods, to also cease from sinful vices of the flesh. Through our Lord …

Wednesday after the 2nd Sunday of Lent (Vespers)
Feria

Ad Magnificat Ant. Tradétur enim géntibus ad illudéndum, et flagellándum, et crucifigéndum.	***Magnificat Ant.*** For He will be handed over to the Gentiles to be mocked and scourged and crucified.
Orátio Deus, innocéntiæ restitútor et amátor, dírige ad te tuórum corda servórum: ut, spíritus tui fervóre concépto, et in fide inveniántur stábiles, et in ópere efficáces. Per Dóminum nostrum …	***Prayer*** O God, the restorer and lover of innocence, direct the hearts of Thy servants to Thee: that they may be fervent in Thy spirit and may be found steadfast in faith and in works. Through our Lord …

Proper of the Season

Thursday after the 2nd Sunday of Lent (Lauds)
Feria

Ad Benedíctus Ant. Fili, recordáre, quia recepísti bona in vita tua, et Lázarus simíliter mala.	*Benedíctus Ant.* Son, remember that thou received good things in thy life, and Lazarus, similarly, evil things.
Orátio Præsta nobis, quǽsumus, Dómine, auxílium grátiæ tuæ: ut, ieiúniis et oratiónibus conveniénter inténti, liberémur ab hóstibus mentis et córporis. Per Dóminum nostrum ...	*Prayer* We beseech Thee, O Lord, for the help of Thy grace: that by fasting and prayer we may be freed from the enemies of mind and body. Through our Lord ...

Thursday after the 2nd Sunday of Lent (Vespers)
Feria

Ad Magnificat Ant Dives ille guttam aquæ pétiit, qui micas panis Lázaro negávit.	*Magnificat Ant.* The rich man asked for a drop of water, he who had refused Lazarus the crumbs of bread.
Orátio Adésto, Dómine, fámulis tuis, et perpétuam benignitátem largíre poscéntibus: ut iis, qui te auctóre et gubernatóre gloriántur, et congregáta restáures et restauráta consérves. Per Dóminum nostrum ...	*Prayer* Be present O Lord, to Thy servants who glorify Thee as their Creator and Ruler, and to those who ask for everlasting mercy: so that Thou mayest restore what Thou hadst gathered together and defend what they owe to Thee. Through our Lord ..

Friday after the 2nd Sunday of Lent (Lauds)
Feria

Ad Benedíctus Ant. Malos male perdet, et víneam suam locábit áliis agrícolis, qui reddant ei fructum tempóribus suis.	*Benedíctus Ant.* He will destroy those evil ones and let out his vineyard to other farmers, who will give him fruit in their season.
Orátio Da, quǽsumus, omnípotens Deus: ut, sacro nos purificánte ieiúnio, sincéris méntibus ad sancta ventúra fácias perveníre. Per Dóminum nostrum ...	*Prayer* Grant, we ask Thee, almighty God, that with a sacred cleansing fast and with sincere minds, we may reach a holy future Through our Lord ...

Friday after the 2nd Sunday of Lent (Vespers)
Feria

Ad Magnificat Ant. Quæréntes eum tenére, timuérunt turbam, quia sicut prophétam eum habébant.	*Magnificat Ant.* Those who wanted to arrest him were afraid of the crowd because they considered him a prophet.
Orátio Da, quǽsumus, Dómine, pópulo tuo salútem mentis et córporis: ut, bonis opéribus inhæréndo, tuæ semper virtútis mereátur protectióne deféndi. Per Dóminum nostrum ...	*Prayer* Please, Lord, give Thy people health of mind and body! that by adhering to good works, we may always deserve Thy goodness and be perfectly defended by our Lord Jesus Christ ...

Proper of the Season

Saturday after the 2nd Sunday of Lent (Lauds)
Feria

Ad Benedíctus Ant. Vadam ad Patrem meum et dicam ei: Pater, fac me sicut unum ex mercenáriis tuis.	**Benedíctus Ant.** I will go to my Father and say to him: Father, make me as one of Thy hired servants.
Orátio Da, quǽsumus, Dómine, nostris efféctum ieiúniis salutárem: ut castigátio carnis assúmpta, ad nostrárum vegetatiónem tránseat animárum. Per Dóminum nostrum ...	**Prayer** We pray, O Lord, give our fasts a beneficial effect: that the chastisement of the flesh that we have taken up, may lead to the growth of our souls. Through our Lord ...

Saturday after the 2nd Sunday of Lent (Vespers)
Feria

Ad Magníficat Ant. Dixit autem pater ad servos suos: Cito proférte stolam prímam, et indúite illum et date ánulum in manu eius, et calceaménta in pédibus eius.	**Magnificat Ant.** And the father said to his servants: Quickly bring forth the best robe, and put it on him, and put a ring on his hand, and shoes on his feet.
Orátio Quǽsumus Omnípotens Deus vota humílium réspice: atque ad defensiónem nostram déxteram tuæ majestátis exténde. Per Dóminum nostrum ...	**Prayer** We beseech Thee, almighty God, to look upon the prayers of the humble, and extend the right hand of Thy majesty for our defense. Through our Lord ...

Third Sunday in Lent (Lauds)
Psalms of Sunday Lauds II

Ant 1. Fac benígne in bona voluntáte tua, ut ædificéntur, Dómine, muri Ierúsalem.	**Ant 1.** Do kindly in Thy good will, O Lord, that the walls of Jerusalem may be rebuilt.
Ant 2. Dóminus mihi adiútor est, non timébo quid fáciat mihi homo.	**Ant 2.** The Lord is my helper, I will not fear what man may do to me.
Ant 3. Vim virtútis suæ oblítus est ignis: ut púeri tui liberaréntur illǽsi.	**Ant 3.** My soul clings to Thee, my God.
Ant 4. Vim virtútis suæ oblitus est ignis: ut púeri tui liberarentur illǽsi.	**Ant 4.** The fire has forgotten the power of its strength: that Thy children may be delivered unharmed.
Ant 5. Sol et luna laudáte Deum: quia exaltátum est nomen eius solíus.	**Ant 5.** Praise God and the sun and moon, for His Name alone is exalted.
Capítulum (Eph 5:1-2) **V.** Fratres: Estóte imitatóres Dei, sicut filii caríssimi: et ambuláte in dilectióne, sicut et Christus diléxit nos, et trádidit semetípsum pro nobis oblatiónem et hóstiam Deo in odórem suavitátis. **R.** Deo grátias.	**Chapter** (Eph 5:1-2) **V.** Brethren: Be imitators of God, like dear children, and walk in love, just as Christ also loved us and gave Himself up for us as an offering and sacrifice to God, for a sweet aroma. **R.** Thanks be to God.

Hymn - O Sol Salútis page 74

Ad Benedíctus Ant. Cum fortis armátus custódit átrium suum, in pace sunt ómnia quæ póssidet.	**Benedíctus Ant.** When a strong man guards his court, all that he possesses is in peace.

Proper of the Season

Orátio Quǽsumus, omnípotens Deus, vota humílium réspice: atque ad defensiónem nostram, déxteram tuæ maiestátis exténde. Per Dóminum nostrum ...	*Prayer* We beseech Thee, almighty God, look upon the prayers of the humble, and extend the right hand of Thy majesty for our defense. Through our Lord ...

Third Sunday in Lent (Vespers)
Psalms of Sunday Vespers, page 123

Ad Magníficat Ant. Extóllens vocem quædam múlier de turba, dixit: Beátus venter qui te portávit, et úbera quæ suxísti. At Iesus ait illi: Quinímmo beáti, qui áudiunt verbum Dei, et custódiunt illud.	*Magnificat Ant.* A certain woman from the crowd raised her voice and said: Blessed is the womb that bore Thee and the breasts that Thou suckled! But Jesus said to her: Most blessed are those who hear the word of God and keep it.

Monday after the 3rd Sunday of Lent (Lauds)
Feria

Ad Benedíctus Ant. Amen dico vobis, quia nemo prophéta accéptus est in pátria sua.	*Benedictus Ant.* Verily I say unto thee, that no prophet is accepted in his own country.
Orátio Córdibus nostris, quæsumus, Dómine, grátiam tuam benígnus infúnde: ut, sicut ab escis carnálibus abstinémus; ita sensus quoque nostros a nóxiis retrahámus excéssibus. Per Dóminum nostrum ...	*Prayer* We beseech Thee, O Lord, to pour out Thy gracious grace into our hearts: that as we may abstain from bodily foods, so we may also restrain our senses from sinful excesses. Through our Lord ..

Monday after the 3rd Sunday of Lent (Vespers)
Feria

Ad Magníficat Ant. Iesus autem, tránsiens per médium illórum, ibat.	*Magnificat Ant.* But Jesus, passing through the midst of them, went His way.
Orátio Subvéniat nobis, Dómine, misericórdia tua: ut ab imminéntibus peccatórum nostrórum perículis te mereámur protegénte éripi, te liberánte salvári. Per Dóminum nostrum ...	*Prayer* May Thy mercy help us, O Lord, for our salvation, that we may deserve to be delivered through Thy protection from the foreboding dangers of our sins. Through our Lord ...

Tuesday after the 3rd Sunday of Lent (Lauds)
Feria

Ad Benedíctus Ant. Si duo ex vobis consénserint super terram: de omni re quamcúmque petíerint, fiet illis a Patre meo, dicit Dóminus.	*Benedictus Ant.* If any two of you agree on earth, whatever ye ask for, it will be done for you by My Father, sayeth the Lord.
Orátio Exáudi nos, omnípotens et miséricors Deus: et continéntiæ salutáris propítius nobis dona concéde. Per Dóminum nostrum...	*Prayer* Hear us, almighty and merciful God who is the source of temperance, and grant us plentiful gifts. Through our Lord ...

Proper of the Season

Tuesday after the 3rd Sunday of Lent (Vespers)
Feria

Ad Magnificat Ant. Ubi duo vel tres congregáti fúerint in nómine meo, in médio eórum sum, dicit Dóminus.	***Magnificat Ant.*** Where two or three are gathered together in my Name, I am in the midst of them, sayeth the Lord.
Orátio Tua nos, Dómine, protectióne defénde: et ab omni semper iniquitáte custódi. Per Dóminum nostrum ...	***Prayer*** Protect us, O Lord, with Thy shield: and always keep us from all sinfulness, Through our Lord ...

Wednesday after the 3rd Sunday of Lent (Lauds)
Feria

Ad Benedíctus Ant. Audíte et intellégite traditiónes, quas Dóminus dedit nobis.	***Benedíctus Ant.*** Hear and understand the traditions that the Lord hath given us.
Orátio Præsta nobis, quǽsumus, Dómine: ut salutáribus ieiúniis erudíti, a nóxiis quoque vítiis abstinéntes, propitiatiónem tuam facílius impetrémus. Per Dóminum nostrum ...	***Prayer*** Grant us, O Lord, we ask, that disciplined by noble fasts and abstinence from harmful vices, we may more easily obtain Thy blessing. Through our Lord ...

Wednesday after the 3rd Sunday of Lent (Vespers)
Feria

Ad Magnificat Ant. Non lotis mánibus manducáre, non coínquinat hóminem.	***Magnificat Ant.*** Eating with unwashed hands does not defile a person.
Orátio Concéde, quǽsumus, omnípotens Deus: ut, qui protectiónis tuæ grátiam quǽrimus, liberáti a malis ómnibus, secúra tibi mente serviámus. Per Dóminum nostrum ...	***Prayer*** Grant, we ask Thee, almighty God, that we who seek the blessing of Thy protection, will be freed from all evils and may serve Thee with peace of mind. Through our Lord ...

Thursday after the 3rd Sunday of Lent (Lauds)
Feria (Commemoration Of Cosmas and Damian)

Ad Benedíctus Ant. Exíbant autem dæmónia a multis clamántia, et dicéntia, Quia tu es Christus Fílius Dei: et íncrepans non sinébat ea loqui, quia sciébant ipsum esse Christum.	***Benedíctus Ant.*** And the demons came out from many, crying out, Thou art the Christ, the Son of God," and He rebuking them, would not allow them to speak because they knew that He was the Christ.
Orátio Magníficet te, Dómine, sanctórum tuórum Cosmæ et Damiáni beáta solémnitas: qua et illis glóriam sempitérnam, et opem nobis ineffábili providéntia contulísti. Per Dóminum nostrum ...	***Prayer*** Praise be to Thee, O Lord, for the blessed solemnity of Thy saints Cosmas and Damian: by which Thou hast bestowed upon them eternal glory and by Thine inexpressible providence, given assistance unto us through our Lord ...

Thursday after the 3rd Sunday of Lent (Vespers)
Feria

Ad Magnificat Ant. Ómnes qui hábébant infirmos ducébant illos ad Jesum et sanabántur.	***Magnificat Ant.*** All who were sick were brought to Jesus and were healed.

Proper of the Season

Orátio Subiéctum tibi pópulum, quǽsumus, Dómine, propitiátio cæléstis amplíficet: et tuis semper fáciat servíre mandátis. Per Dóminum nostrum ...	*Prayer* We the people subject to Thee, O Lord, beseech Thee to increase our heavenly blessings: and to make us always observe Thy commandments. Through our Lord ...

Friday after the 3rd Sunday of Lent (Lauds)
Feria

Ad Benedíctus Ant. Aquam, quam ego dédero, si quis bíberit ex ea, non sítiet in ætérnum.	*Benedíctus Ant.* If anyone drinketh of the water that I will give him, he will never thirst.
Orátio Ieiúnia nostra, quǽsumus, Dómine, benígno favóre proséquere: ut, sicut ab aliméntis abstinémus in córpore; ita a vítiis ieiunémus in mente. Per Dóminum nostrum ...	*Prayer* We beseech Thee, O Lord, to bless our fasting with Thy kind favor: that, as we abstain from food for the body, so we may fast from vices in the soul. Through our Lord ...

Friday after the 3rd Sunday of Lent (Vespers)
Feria

Ad Magnificat Ant. Dómine, ut vídeo, prophéta es tu: patres nostri in monte hoc adoravérunt.	*Magnificat Ant.* Lord, I see Thou art truly a prophet: our fathers worshiped on this mountain.
Orátio Præsta, quǽsumus, omnípotens Deus: ut, qui in tua protectióne confídimus, cuncta nobis adversántia te adiuvánte vincámus. Per Dóminum nostrum ...	*Prayer* Help us, we beseech Thee, almighty God: that as we trust in Thy protection; let us with Thine assistance, overcome everything that opposes us. Through our Lord ...

Saturday after the 3rd Sunday of Lent (Lauds)

Ad Benedíctus Ant. Inclinávit se Iesus, et scribébat in terra: Si quis sine peccáto est, mittat in eam lápidem.	*Benedíctus Ant.* Jesus bowed down and wrote on the ground: If anyone is without sin, let him throw a stone at her.
Orátio Præsta, quǽsumus, omnípotens Deus: ut, qui se, affligéndo carnem, ab aliméntis ábstinent; sectándo iustítiam a culpa ieiúnent. Per Dóminum nostrum ...	*Prayer* We beseech Thee, almighty God, that those who afflict themselves abstaining from eating meat; in justice, may also fast from evil. Through our Lord ...

Saturday after the 3rd Sunday of Lent (Vespers)

Ad Magnificat Ant Nemo te condemnávit, múlier? Nemo, Dómine. Nec ego te condemnábo: iam ámplius noli peccáre.	*Magnificat Ant.* Hath no man condemned thee? No one, Lord. Nor will I condemn thee: sin no more.
Orátio Concéde, quǽsumus Omnípotens Deus: ut qui ex mérito nostræ actiónis afflígimur, tuæ grátiæ consolatióne respirémus. Per Dóminum nostrum ...	*Prayer* Grant, we beseech Thee, almighty God, that we who are afflicted by the merit of our own actions may breathe in the consolation of Thy grace. Through our Lord ...

Proper of the Season

Forth Sunday in Lent (Lauds)
Psalms of Sunday Lauds II

Ant 1. Tunc acceptábis sacríficium justítiæ, si avérteris fáciem tuam a peccátis meis.	**Ant 1.** Then Thou wilt accept the sacrifice of righteousness, if Thou hast turned Thy face away from my sins.
Ant 2. Bonum est speráre in Dómino, quam speráre in princípibus.	**Ant 2.** It is better to hope in the Lord, than to trust in princes.
Ant 3. Me suscépit déxtera tua Dómine.	**Ant 3.** Thy right hand hath received me, O Lord.
Ant 4. Potens es Dómine erípere nos de manu forti: líbera nos Deus noster.	**Ant 4.** Thou art mighty, O Lord, to save us from the hand of the strong: deliver us, our God.
Ant 5. Reges terræ et ómnes pópuli laudáte Deum.	**Ant 5.** Praise God, kings of the earth and all peoples.
Capitulum (Gal 4:22-24) **V.** Fratres: Scriptum est, quóniam Abraham duos fílios hábuit: unum de ancílla, et unum de líbera: sed qui de ancílla, secúndum carnem natus est: qui autem de líbera, per repromissiónem: quæ sunt per allegoríam dicta. **R.** Deo grátias.	*Chapter* (Gal 4:22-24) **V.** Brethren: It is written that Abraham had two sons: one by a handmaid, and one by a free woman: but he who was born of a handmaid was born according to the flesh, but he who was born of a free woman was by promise: Which things are said by an allegory. **R.** Thanks be to God.

Hymn - *O Sol Salútis*, page 74

Ad Benedíctus Ant Cum sublevásset óculos Iesus, et vidísset máximam multitúdinem veniéntem ad se, dixit ad Philíppum: Unde emémus panes, ut mandúcent hi? Hoc autem dicébat tentans eum: ipse enim sciébat quid esset factúrus.	*Benedíctus Ant.* When Jesus lifted up His eyes and saw a great multitude coming to Him, He said to Philip: Where shall we buy bread that these may eat? And this He said, trying him: for He himself knew what He was going to do.
Orátio Concéde, quǽsumus, omnípotens Deus: ut, qui ex mérito nostræ actiónis afflígimur, tuæ grátiæ consolatióne respirémus. Per Dóminum nostrum ...	*Prayer* Grant, we beseech Thee, almighty God, that those who suffer because of our actions may breathe the consolation of Thy grace. Through our Lord ...

Forth Sunday in Lent (Vespers)
Vespers for Sunday p. 123

Ad Magníficat Ant. Súbiit ergo in montem Jesus, et ibi sedébat cum discípulis suis.	*Magníficat Ant.* Jesus therefore went up into the mountain and sat there with His disciples.

Monday after the 4th Sunday of Lent (Lauds)
Feria

Ad Benedíctus Ant. Auférte ista hinc, dicit Dóminus: et nolíte fácere domum Patris mei domum negotiatiónis.	*Benedíctus Ant.* Take them away from here, sayeth the Lord: and do not make My Father's house into a marketplace.
Oratio Præsta, quǽsumus, omnípotens Deus: ut observatiónes	*Prayer* We beseech Thee, Almighty God, that by remembering the sacred

Proper of the Season

sacras ánnua devotióne recoléntes, et córpore tibi placeámus, et mente. Per Dóminum nostrum ...	observances with annual devotion, we may please Thee both in body and in mind. Through our Lord ...

Monday after the 4th Sunday of Lent (Vespers)
Feria

Ad Magnificat Ant. Sólvite templum hoc, dicit Dóminus; et post tríduum reædificábo illud: hoc autem dicébat de templo córporis sui.	**Magnificat Ant.** Destroy this temple, sayeth the Lord; and after three days I will rebuild it: but this He said of the temple of His body.
Orátio Deprecatiónem nostram, quǽsumus, Dómine, benígnus exáudi: et, quibus supplicándi præstas afféctum, tríbue defensiónis auxílium. Per Dóminum nostrum ...	**Prayer** We beseech Thee, O Lord, to graciously hear our supplication: we whom Thou hast given the mind to pray, and likewise aid us in our defense. Through our Lord ...

Tuesday after the 4th Sunday of Lent (Lauds)
Feria

Ad Benedíctus Ant. Quid me quǽritis interfícere, hóminem qui vera locútus sum vobis?	**Benedíctus Ant.** Why do ye seek to kill me, the Man who told you the truth?
Orátio Sacræ nobis, quǽsumus, Dómine, observatiónis ieiúnia: et piæ conversatiónis augméntum, et tuæ propitiatiónis contínuum præstent auxílium. Per Dóminum nostrum ...	**Prayer** We ask Thee, O Lord, by the observance of this sacred fasting, and the increase of pious conduct, that we may be assured of Thy perpetual help and Thy mercy. Through our Lord ...

Tuesday after the 4th Sunday of Lent (Vespers)
Feria

Ad Magnificat Ant. Nemo in eum misit manum: quia nondum vénerat hora eius.	**Magnificat Ant.** No one laid a hand on Him, because His hour had not yet come.
Orátio Miserére, Dómine, pópulo tuo: et contínuis tribulatiónibus laborántem propítius respiráre concéde. Per Dóminum nostrum ...	**Prayer** Have mercy, O Lord, on your people: and allow those who are laboring in constant tribulations to breathe easily. Through our Lord ...

Wednesday after the 4th Sunday of Lent (Lauds)
Feria

Ad Benedíctus Ant. Rabbi, quid peccávit homo iste, quod cæcus natus est? Respóndit Iesus, et dixit: Neque hic peccávit, neque paréntes eius: sed ut manifesténtur ópera Dei in illo.	**Benedíctus Ant.** Rabbi, what sin did this man commit, that he was born blind? Jesus answered and said: Neither this man sinned, nor his parents: but that the works of God may be made manifest in him.
Orátio Deus, qui et iustis prǽmia meritórum, et peccatóribus per ieiúnium véniam præbes: miserére supplícibus tuis; ut reátus nostri conféssio indulgéntiam váleat percípere delictórum. Per Dóminum nostrum ...	**Prayer** O God, who givest both rewards to the just and merits and forgiveness to sinners through fasting, pardon our evil deeds; so by the confession of our guilt we may deserve the forgiveness of our offences. Through our Lord ...

Proper of the Season

Wednesday after the 4th Sunday of Lent (Vespers)
Feria

Ad Magnificat Ant. Ille homo qui dícitur Iesus, lutum fecit ex sputo, et linívit óculos meos, et modo vídeo.	*Magnificat Ant.* That man called Jesus made clay out of His spittle, and smeared my eyes, and I now see.
Orátio Páteant aures misericórdiæ tuæ, Dómine, précibus supplicántium: et, ut peténtibus desideráta concédas, fac eos, quæ tibi sunt plácita, postuláre. Per Dóminum nostrum ...	*Prayer* O Lord, let the ears of Thy mercy be open to the prayers of the supplicant people: and that Thou mayest satisfy the desires of those who ask, make them ask for only what pleases Thee. Through our Lord ...

Thursday after the 4th Sunday of Lent (Lauds)
Feria

Ad Benedíctus Ant. Ibat Iesus in civitátem, quæ vocátur Naim: et ecce defúnctus efferebátur fílius únicus matris suæ.	*Benedíctus Ant.* Jesus was going to a city called Naim, and behold, a mother's only son was being carried out dead.
Orátio Præsta, quǽsumus, omnípotens Deus: ut, quos ieiúnia votíva castígant, ipsa quoque devótio sancta lætíficet; ut, terrénis afféctibus mitigátis, facílius cæléstia capiámus. Per Dóminum nostrum ...	*Prayer* We beseech Thee, almighty God, that we who are burdened by vows of fasting may also be gladdened by holy fidelity: that, tempered by earthly desires, we may more easily understand heavenly things. Through our Lord ...

Thursday after the 4th Sunday of Lent (Vespers)
Feria

Ad Magnificat Ant. Prophéta magnus surréxit in nobis, et quia Deus visitávit plebem suam.	*Magnificat Ant.* A great prophet arose among us, and God visited His people.
Orátio Pópuli tui, Deus, institútor et rector: peccáta, quibus impugnátur, expélle; ut semper tibi plácitus, et tuo munímine sit secúrus. Per Dóminum nostrum ...	*Prayer* O God, teacher and ruler of Thy people, drive away the sins by which we are attacked: that we may always be pleasing to Thee, and find safety under Thy protection. Through our Lord ...

Friday after the 4th Sunday of Lent (Lauds)
Feria

Ad Benedíctus Ant. Lázarus amícus noster dormit: eámus, et a somno excitémus eum.	*Benedíctus Ant.* Our friend Lazarus is asleep: let us go and wake him from his sleep.
Orátio Deus, qui ineffabílibus mundum rénovas sacraméntis: præsta, quǽsumus; ut Ecclésia tua et ætérnis profíciat institútis, et temporálibus non destituátur auxíliis. Per Dóminum nostrum ...	*Prayer* O God, who reneweth the world with ineffable sacraments: grant, we ask; that Thy Church may also prosper in eternal institutions, and not be lacking of temporal help. Through our Lord ...

Proper of the Season

Friday after the 4th Sunday of Lent (Vespers)
Feria

Ad Magnificat Ant. Dómine, si fuísses hic, Lázarus non esset mórtuus: ecce iam fœtet quatriduánus in monuménto.	**Magnificat Ant.** O Lord, if Thou hadst been here, Lazarus would not have died: behold, he is already four days in the grave.
Orátio Da nobis, quǽsumus, omnípotens Deus: ut, qui infirmitátis nostræ cónscii, de tua virtúte confídimus, sub tua semper pietáte gaudeámus. Per Dóminum nostrum …	**Prayer** Grant us, we beseech Thee almighty God, that we who, aware of our weakness, trust in Thy power, may always rejoice under Thy mercy. Through our Lord …

Saturday after the 4th Sunday of Lent (Lauds)

Ad Benedíctus Ant Qui séquitur me, non ámbulat in ténebris: sed habébit lumen vitæ, dicit Dóminus.	**Benedíctus Ant.** He that followeth me shall not walk in darkness, but shall have the light of life, sayeth the Lord.
Orátio Fiat, Dómine, quǽsumus, per grátiam tuam fructuósus nostræ devotiónis afféctus: quia tunc nobis próderunt suscépta ieiúnia, si tuæ sint plácita pietáti. Per Dóminum nostrum …	**Prayer** Let us beseech Thee, O Lord, that by Thy grace the fervor of our devotion may be fruitful: for then the fasts undertaken will profit us, if they be pleasing to Thy goodness. Through our Lord …

Saturday after the 4th Sunday of Lent (Vespers)

Ad Magnificat Ant. Ego sum qui testimónium perhíbeo de meípso: et testimónium pérhibet de me, qui misit me, Pater.	**Magnificat Ant.** I am He that beareth witness of Myself: and He that sent Me, the Father, beareth witness of Me.
Orátio Quǽsumus, omnípotens Deus, famíliam tuam propítius réspice: ut, te largiénte, regátur in córpore; et, te servánte, custodiátur in mente. Per Dóminum nostrum …	**Prayer** We beseech Thee, almighty God to look more favorably upon Thy family: that by Thy direction we may be protected in the body by devotion to Thee; keeping Thee in our minds. Through our Lord …

Passion Sunday (Lauds)
Psalms for Sunday Lauds II

Ant 1. Vide Dómine afflictiónem meam, quóniam erectus est inimícus meus.	**Ant 1.** Lord, look upon my affliction, for mine enemy hath risen up.
Ant 2. In tribulatióne invocávi Dóminum, et exaudívit me in latitúdine.	**Ant 2.** In my trouble I called upon the Lord, and He heard me in many ways.
Ant 3. Judicásti Dómine causam ánimæ meæ, defénsor vitæ meæ, Dómine Deus meus.	**Ant 3.** O Lord, Thou hast judged the cause of my soul, the defender of my life, O Lord my God.
Ant 4. Pópule meus quid feci tibi, aut quid moléstus fui? Respónde mihi.	**Ant 4.** My people, what have I done to you, or how have I troubled you?

Proper of the Season

Ant 5. Numquid rédditur pro bono malum, quia fodérunt foveam ánimæ meæ?	**Ant 5.** Shall evil be returned for good, because they dug the pit for My soul?
Capitulum (Heb 9:11-12) ***V.*** Fratres: Christus assístens Póntifex futurórum bonórum, per ámplius et perféctius tabernáculum non manu factum, id est, non huius creatiónis: neque per sánguinem hircórum aut vitulórum, sed per próprium sánguinem introívit semel in Sancta, ætérna redemptióne invénta. **R.** Deo grátias.	***Chapter*** (Heb 9:11-12) **V.** But Christ, having become a high Priest of the good things to come, by a greater and more perfect tabernacle not made by human hands, that is, not of this creation: neither by the blood of goats, or of calves, but by His own blood, entered once into the holies, having obtained eternal redemption. **R.** Thanks be to God.
Ad Benedíctus Ant. Dicébat Iesus turbis Iudæórum, et princípibus sacerdótum: Qui ex Deo est, verba Dei audit: proptérea vos non audítis, quia ex Deo non estis.	***Benedíctus Ant.*** Jesus said to the crowds of the Jews and to the chief priests: He who is of God hears the words of God: therefore ye do not hear, because ye are not of God.
Orátio Quǽsumus, omnípotens Deus, famíliam tuam propítius réspice: ut, te largiénte, regátur in córpore; et, te servánte, custodiátur in mente. Per Dóminum nostrum ...	***Prayer*** We beseech Thee, almighty God, to look mercifully upon Thy family: that by Thy great goodness they may be governed and preserved evermore, both in body and soul. Through our Lord ...

Passion Sunday (Vespers)

Ad Magníficat Ant. Abraham pater vester exsultávit ut vidéret diem meum: vidit, et gavísus est..	***Magníficat Ant.*** Thy father Abraham rejoiced to see My day: he saw it, and was glad.
Orátio Quǽsumus, omnípotens Deus, famíliam tuam propítius réspice: ut, te largiénte, regátur in córpore; et, te servánte, custodiátur in mente Per Dóminum nostrum ...	***Prayer*** We beseech Thee, almighty God, to look more mercifully upon Thy family: that by Thy great goodness they may be governed and preserved evermore, both in body and soul. Through our Lord ...

Monday after Passion Sunday of Lent (Lauds)
Feria

Ad Benedíctus Ant. In die magno festivitátis stábat Iesus, et clamábat dicens: Si quis sitit, véniat ad me, et bibat.	***Benedíctus Ant.*** On the day of the great festival, Jesus stood and cried out, saying: If anyone is thirsty, let him come to Me and drink.
Orátio Sanctífica, quǽsumus, Dómine, nostra ieiúnia: et cunctárum nobis indulgéntiam propítius largíre culpárum. Per Dóminum nostrum ...	***Prayer*** We beseech Thee, O Lord, to sanctify our fasting, and to grant us the forgiveness of all our sins. Through our Lord ...

Proper of the Season

Monday after Passion Sunday of Lent (Vespers)	
Feria	
Ad Magnificat Ant. Si quis sitit, véniat ad me, et bibat: et de ventre ejus fluent aquæ vivæ, dicit Dóminus.	*Magnificat Ant.* If any man thirst, let him come unto Me and drink: and from within him shall flow living waters, sayeth the Lord.
Orátio Da, quæsumus Dómine, pópulo tuo salútem mentis et córporis: ut bonis opéribus inhæréndo, tua semper mereátur protectióne deféndi. Per Dóminum nostrum ...	*Prayer* Grant, to Thy people health of mind and body: we beseech Thee, O Lord, that, adhering to good works, they may always deserve Thy protection. Through our Lord ...
Tuesday after Passion Sunday of Lent (Lauds)	
Feria	
Ad Benedíctus Ant. Tempus meum nondum advénit, tempus autem vestrum semper est parátum.	*Benedíctus Ant.* My time hath not yet come, but your time is always ready.
Orátio Nostra tibi, Dómine quæsumus, sint accépta jejúnia: quæ nos et expiándo, grátia tua dignos efficiant, et ad remédia perdúcant ætérna. Per Dóminum nostrum ...	*Prayer* We beseech Thee, O Lord, that our fasts may be accepted: which by atonement may make us worthy of Thy grace, and lead us to eternal redemption. Through our Lord ...
Tuesday after Passion Sunday of Lent (Vespers)	
Feria	
Ad Magnificat Ant. Vos ascéndite ad diem festum hunc: ego autem non ascéndam, quia tempus meum nondum advénit.	*Magnificat Ant.* Ye go up to this feast day: but I will not go up, because My time hath not yet come.
Orátio Da nobis, quæsumus, Dómine, perseverántem in tua voluntáte famulátum: ut in diébus nostris et mérito et número pópulus tibi sérviens augeátur. Per Dóminum nostrum ...	*Prayer* Give to us Thy servants, we beseech Thee, O Lord, that we may be persevering in Thy will: that in our days the people serving Thee may increase both in merit and in number. Through our Lord ...
Wednesday after Passion Sunday of Lent (Lauds)	
Feria	
Ad Benedíctus Ant. Oves meæ vocem meam áudiunt: et ego Dóminus agnósco eas.	*Benedíctus Ant.* My sheep hear My voice: and I, the Lord, know them.
Orátio Sanctificáto hoc ieiúnio Deus, tuórum corda fidélium miserátor illústra: et, quibus devotiónis præstas afféctum, præbe supplicántibus pium benígnus audítum. Per Dóminum nostrum ...	*Prayer* O God, having sanctified this fasting, enlighten the hearts of Thy faithful to whom Thou art merciful and to those whom Thou grantest the fervor of devotion, bestow a kind hearing upon those who plead to Thee. Through our Lord ...

Proper of the Season

Wednesday after Passion Sunday of Lent (Vespers)
Feria

Ad Magníficat Ant. Multa bona ópera operátus sum vobis: propter quod opus vultis me occídere?	***Magnificat Ant.*** I have done many good works for you: for what work do ye want to kill Me?
Orátio Adésto supplicatiónibus nostris, omnípotens Deus: et quibus fidúciam sperándæ pietátis indúlges, consuétæ misericórdiæ tríbue benígnus efféctum. Per Dóminum nostrum ...	***Prayer*** Almighty God, be attentive to our prayers: that we whom Thou providenth trust through hope in holiness will have the kind benefit of Thy mercy. Through our Lord ...

Thursday after Passion Sunday of Lent (Lauds)
Feria

Ad Benedíctus Ant. Magíster dicit: Tempus meum prope est, apud te fácio Pascha cum discípulis meis.	***Benedíctus Ant.*** The teacher sayeth: My time is near, I am celebrating the Passover with My disciples.
Orátio Præsta, quæsumus, omnípotens Deus: ut dígnitas condiciónis humánæ per immoderántiam sauciáta, medicinális parsimóniæ stúdio reformétur. Per Dóminum nostrum ...	***Prayer*** Grant, we beseech Thee, almighty God, that the dignity of the human condition, marred by intemperance, may be reformed by the pursuit of fasting that heals. Through our Lord ...

Thursday after Passion Sunday of Lent (Vespers)
Feria

Ad Magníficat Ant. Desidério desiderávi hoc Pascha manducáre vobíscum, ántequam pátiar.	***Magnificat Ant.*** I long with great desire to eat with you this Passover before I suffer.
Orátio Esto, quæsumus, Dómine, propítius plebi tuæ: ut, quæ tibi non placent, respuéntes, tuórum pótius repleántur delectatiónibus mandatórum. Per Dóminum nostrum ...	***Prayer*** Be, we beseech Thee, O Lord, more merciful to Thy people: that, rejecting those things which do not please Thee, they may instead be filled with the delights of Thy commandments. Through our Lord ...

Friday after Passion Sunday of Lent (Lauds)
Feria

Ad Benedíctus Ant. Appropinquábat autem dies festus Iudæórum: et quærébant príncipes sacerdótum quómodo Iesum interfícerent, sed timébant plebem.	***Benedíctus Ant.*** Now the feast day of the Jews drew near: and the chief priests sought how they might kill Jesus, but they were afraid of the people.
Orátio Córdibus nostris, quæsumus, Dómine, grátiam tuam benígnus infúnde: ut peccáta nostra castigatióne voluntária cohibéntes, temporáliter pótius macerémur, quam supplíciis deputémur ætérnis. Per Dóminum nostrum ...	***Prayer*** Into our hearts, we beseech Thee, O Lord, infuse Thy gracious grace: that, restraining our sins by voluntary chastisement, we may rather suffer temporally than be committed to eternal desolation. Through our Lord ...

Proper of the Season

Friday after Passion Sunday of Lent (Vespers)	
Feria	
Ad Magnificat Ant. Príncipes sacerdótum consílium fecérunt ut Iesum occíderent: dicébant autem: Non in die festo, ne forte tumúltus fieret in pópulo.	**Magnificat Ant.** The chief priests made a plan to kill Jesus: but they said: Not on a festival day, lest perhaps there might be an uprising among the people
Orátio Concéde, quǽsumus, omnípotens Deus: ut qui protectiónis tuæ grátiam quǽrimus, liberáti a malis ómnibus, secúra tibi mente serviámus. Per Dóminum nostrum ...	**Prayer** Grant, we beseech Thee, almighty God, that we who seek the grace of Thy protection, being freed from all evils, may serve Thee with a peaceful mind. Through our Lord ...
Saturday after Passion Sunday of Lent (Lauds)	
Ad Benedíctus Ant. Clarífica me, Pater, apud temetípsum claritáte, quam hábui priúsquam mundus fieret.	**Benedíctus Ant.** Shed light on Me, Father, with the radiance which I had with Thee before the world was made.
Orátio Profíciat, quǽsumus, Dómine, plebs tibi dicáta, piæ devotiónis afféctu: ut sacris actiónibus erudíta, quanto maiestáti tuæ fit grátior, tanto donis potióribus augeátur. Per Dóminum nostrum ...	**Prayer** May the people, we beseech Thee, Lord, be steadfast to Thee with a feeling of pious devotion, so that disciplined by sacred rites, evermore becoming more acceptable to Thy majesty, they may be showered with the best of Thy gifts. Through our Lord ...
Saturday after Passion Sunday of Lent (Vespers)	
Ad Magnificat Ant. Pater iuste, mundus te non cognóvit: ego autem novi te, quia tu me misísti.	**Magnificat Ant.** Righteous Father, the world did not know Thee: but I know Thee because Thou sent Me.
Orátio Omnípotens sempitérne Deus, qui humáno géneri, ad imitándum humilitátis exémplum, Salvatórem nostrum carnem súmere, et crucem subíre fecísti: concéde propítius; ut et patiéntiæ ipsíus habére documénta, et resurrectiónis consórtia mereámur. Per Dóminum nostrum ...	**Prayer** Almighty and everlasting God, who, imitating the example of humility, made our Savior take our nature and suffer death on the cross; grant that we may bear in mind His teaching and deserve a share in the resurrection. Through our Lord ...
Palm Sunday (Lauds)	
Psalms of Sunday Lauds II	
Ant 1. Dóminus Deus auxiliátor meus: et ideo non sum confúsus.	**Ant 1.** The Lord God is my helper: and therefore I am not confounded.
Ant 2. Circumdántes circumdedérunt me: et in nómine Dómini vindicábor in eis.	**Ant 2.** I am besieged by those who surround me: and in the Name of the Lord I will be vindicated against them.
Ant 3. Júdica causam meam: defénde, quia potens es Dómine.	**Ant 3.** Judge my cause: and defend me, for Thou art mighty, O Lord.

Proper of the Season

Ant 4. Cum Ángelis et púeris fidéles inveniámur, triumphatóri mortis clamántes: Hosánna in excélsis.	**Ant 4.** May we be found with the angels and faithful children, crying out to Him who triumphed over death: Hosanna in the highest.
Ant 5. Confundántur qui me persequúntur, et non confúndar ego, Dómine Deus meus.	**Ant 5.** Let those who persecute me be confounded, and let me not be confused, O Lord my God.
Capitulum (Phil 2:5-7) **V.** Fratres: Hoc enim sentíte in vobis, quod et in Christo Iesu: qui, cum in forma Dei esset, non rapínam arbitrátus est esse se æquálem Deo: sed semetípsum exinanívit, formam servi accípiens, in similitúdinem hóminum factus, et hábitu invéntus ut homo. **R.** Deo grátias.	**Chapter** (Phil 2:5-7) **V.** For let this mind be in thee, which was also in Christ Jesus: Who being in the form of God, thought it not robbery to be equal with God: But emptied Himself, taking the form of a servant, being made in the likeness of men, and in habit found as a man. **R.** Thanks be to God.
*Hymn – Vexilla Regis, page 382*
Ad Benedíctus Ant. Turba multa, quæ convénerat ad diem festum, clamábat Dómino: Benedíctus qui venit in nómine Dómini: Hosánna in excélsis.	*Benedíctus Ant.* A large crowd that had gathered for the feast day cried out to the Lord: Blessed is He who cometh in the Name of the Lord, Hosanna in the highest.
Orátio Omnípotens sempitérne Deus, qui humáno géneri, ad imitándum humilitátis exémplum, Salvatórem nostrum carnem súmere, et crucem subíre fecísti: concéde propítius; ut et patiéntiæ ipsíus habére documénta, et resurrectiónis consórtia mereámur. Per Dóminum nostrum ..	*Prayer* Almighty and everlasting God, who, imitating the example of humility, made our Savior take our nature and suffer death on the cross; grant that we may bear in mind His teaching and deserve a share in the resurrection. Through our Lord ...

Palm Sunday (Vespers)
Vespers for Sunday p. 123

Hymn – Vexilla Regis, page 382

Ad Magnificat Ant. Scriptum est enim: Percútiam pastórem, et dispergéntur oves gregis: postquam autem resurréxero, præcédam vos in Galilǽam: ibi me vidébitis, dicit Dóminus.	*Magnificat Ant.* For it is written: I will strike the Shepherd, and the sheep of the flock will be scattered: but after I have risen, I will go before you into Galilee: there ye will see Me, sayeth the Lord.

Monday after Palm Sunday of Lent (Lauds)
Feria

Ad Benedíctus Ant. Clarífica me, Pater, apud temetípsum claritáte, quam hábui priúsquam mundus fíeret.	*Benedíctus Ant.* Shed light on Me, Father, with the radiance which I had with Thee before the world was made.
Orátio Da, quǽsumus, omnípotens Deus: ut, qui in tot advérsis ex nostra infirmitáte defícimus; intercedénte	*Prayer* Grant, we beseech Thee, almighty God, that we who perish from our weakness by so many

Proper of the Season

unigéniti Fílii tui passióne respirémus: Qui tecum vivit et regnat ...	adversities; give us the breath of life again by the passion of Thine only-begotten Son and His intercession for us. Who with Thee livest and reignest ...

Monday after Palm Sunday of Lent (Vespers)
Feria

Ad Magnificat Ant. Non habéres in me potestátem, nisi désuper tibi datum fuísset.	*Magnificat Ant.* Thou wouldst have no power over Me unless it had been given to you from above.
Orátio Adiuva nos, Deus, salutáris noster: et ad benefícia recolénda, quibus nos instauráre dignátus es, tríbue veníre gaudéntes. Per Dóminum nostrum ...	*Prayer* Help us, God, our Savior, and grant us to come rejoicing to the blessings which Thou hast deigned to restore to us. Through our Lord ..

Tuesday after Palm Sunday of Lent (Lauds)
Feria

Ad Benedíctus Ant. Ante diem festum Paschæ, sciens Iesus quia venit hora eius, cum dilexísset suos, in finem diléxit eos.	*Benedíctus Ant.* Before the day of the feast of the Passover, Jesus, knowing that His hour had come, having loved His own, He loved them to the end.
Orátio Omnípotens sempitérne Deus: da nobis ita Domínicæ passiónis sacraménta perágere; ut indulgéntiam percípere mereámur. Per Dóminum nostrum ...	*Prayer* Almighty and eternal God, grant us to celebrate the sacraments of the Passion in such a way that we may deserve to receive forgiveness for our sins. Through our Lord ...

Tuesday after Palm Sunday of Lent (Vespers)
Feria

Ad Magnificat Ant Potestátem hábeo ponéndi ánimam meam, et íterum suméndi eam.	*Magnificat Ant.* I have power to lay down My life, and to take it up again.
Orátio Tua nos misericórdia, Deus, et ab omni subreptióne vetustátis expúrget: et capáces sanctæ novitátis effíciat. Per Dóminum nostrum ...	*Prayer* May Thy mercy, O God, cleanse us from all the filth of our past and make us capable of holiness in our new life. Through our Lord ...

Wednesday after Palm Sunday of Lent (Lauds)
Feria

Ad Benedíctus Ant. Simon, dormis? non potuísti una hora vigiláre mecum?	*Benedíctus Ant.* Simon art thou sleeping? Couldst thou not stay awake with Me for one hour?
Orátio Præsta, quæsumus, omnípotens Deus: ut, qui nostris excéssibus incessánter afflígimur, per unigéniti Fílii tui passiónem líberemur: Per Dóminum nostrum ...	*Prayer* We beseech Thee, almighty God, that we who are unceasingly troubled by our sins may be delivered in the Passion of Thine only begotten Son. Through our Lord ...

Proper of the Season

Wednesday after Palm Sunday of Lent (Vespers)	
Feria	
Ad Magnificat Ant. Ancílla dixit Petro: Vere tu ex illis es: nam et loquéla tua maniféstum te facit.	***Magnificat Ant.*** The maid said to Peter: Truly thou art one of them, for thy speech also reveals thee.
Orátio Réspice, quǽsumus, Dómine, super hanc famíliam tuam, pro qua Dóminus noster Iesus Christus non dubitávit mánibus tradi nocéntium, et crucis subíre torméntum. Qui tecum vivit et regnat ...	***Prayer*** Look, we beseech Thee, O Lord, upon this Thy family, for whom our Lord Jesus Christ never hesitated to be delivered into the hands of the wicked, and to suffer the torture of the cross. Who liveth and reigneth ...

Maundy Thursday (Lauds)	
Office of Tenebræ	
Psalms from Sunday Lauds II Chapter and Hymn are omitted	
Ad Benedíctus Ant. Tráditor autem dedit eis signum, dicens: Quem osculátus fúero, ipse est, tenéte eum.	***Benedíctus Ant.*** And the betrayer gave them a sign, saying: He whom I have kissed, it is He; arrest Him.
After the antiphon, the following is said kneeling	
Orátio V. Chrístus factus est pro nobis obédiens usque ad mortem.	***Prayer*** V. Christ became obedient unto death for us.
After this is said, the Our Father/Pater Noster is added silently.	
Orátio Réspice, quǽsumus, Dómine, super hanc famíliam tuam, pro qua Dóminus noster Iesus Christus non dubitávit mánibus tradi nocéntium, et crucis subíre torméntum.	***Prayer*** Look, we beseech Thee, O Lord, upon this family of Thine, for whom our Lord Jesus Christ never hesitated to be delivered into the hands of the wicked, and to suffer the torture of the cross.
The following is said in silence.	
Qui tecum vivit et regnat in unitáte Spíritus Sancti, ...	Who liveth and reigneth with Thee in the unity of the Holy Spirit, ...

Maundy Thursday (Vespers)	
Office of Tenebræ	
Psalms from Monday Vespers Psalms 115 and 119 Psalms from Friday Vespers 139, 140 and 141	
Ant 1. Cálicem salutáris accípiam et nomen Dómini invocábo.	**Ant 1.** I will take the chalice of salvation and call on the Name of the Lord.
Ant 2. Cum his, qui odérunt pacem eram pacíficus: dum loquébar illis, impugnábant me gratis.	**Ant 2.** I was peaceful with those who hate peace: but while I was speaking to them, they attacked Me wantonly.
Ant 3. Ab homínibus iníquis líbera me, Dómine.	**Ant 3.** Lord, deliver me from unrighteous men.
Ant 4. Custódi me a láqueo, quem statuérunt mihi, et a scándalis operántium iniquitátem.	**Ant 4.** I guarded Myself from the snare which they had set for Me, and from the snares of those who work in wickedness.

Proper of the Season

Ant 5. Considerábam ad déxteram, et vidébam, et non erat qui cognósceret me.	**Ant 5.** I looked to the right and saw, and there was no one who would know Me.
Ad Magnificat Ant. Cenántibus autem illis accépit Iesus panem, et benedíxit, ac fregit, dedítque discípulis suis.	***Magnificat Ant.*** And while they were eating, Jesus took bread, blessed it, broke it, and gave it to His disciples.
After the antiphon, the following is said genuflecting	
Orátio **V.** Chrístus factus est pro nobis obédiens usque ad mortem. Per Dóminum nostrum ...	***Prayer*** **V.** Christ became obedient unto death for us.
After this is said, the Our Father/Pater Noster is added silently.	
Orátio Réspice, quæsumus, Dómine, super hanc famíliam tuam, pro qua Dóminus noster Iesus Christus non dubitávit mánibus tradi nocéntium, et crucis subíre torméntum.	***Prayer*** Look, we beseech Thee, O Lord, upon this Thy family, for whom our Lord Jesus Christ never hesitated to be delivered into the hands of the wicked, and to suffer the torture of the cross.
The following is said in silence.	
Qui tecum vivit et regnat in unitáte Spíritus Sancti, ...	Who liveth and reigneth with Thee in the unity of the Holy Spirit, ...

Good Friday (Lauds)
Office of Tenebræ

Psalms from Friday Lauds II
Chapter and Hymn are omitted

Ant 1. Próprio Fílio suo non pepércit Deus, sed pro nobis ómnibus trádidit illum.	**Ant 1.** God did not spare His own Son, but delivered Him up for us all.
Ant 2. Anxiátus est super me spíritus meus, in me turbátum est cor meum.	**Ant 2.** My spirit is distressed within Me and My heart is troubled within Me.
Ant 3. Ait latro ad latrónem: Nos quidem digna factis recípimus, hic autem quid fecit? Meménto mei, Dómine, dum véneris in regnum tuum.	**Ant 3.** He said to the thief, "We receive what we deserve, but what hath He done?" Remember me, Lord, when Thou comest into Thy kingdom.
Ant 4. Cum conturbáta fúerit ánima mea, Dómine, misericórdiæ memor eris.	**Ant 4.** When my soul is troubled, O Lord, Thou wilt remember Thy mercy.
Ant 5. Meménto mei, Dómine, dum véneris in regnum tuum.	**Ant 5.** Remember me, Lord, when Thou comest into Thy kingdom.
Ad Benedíctus Ant. Posuérunt super caput eius causam ipsíus scriptam: Iesus Nazarénus, Rex Iudæórum.	***Benedíctus Ant.*** They placed over His head His cause written: Jesus of Nazareth, King of the Jews.

Proper of the Season

After the antiphon, the following is said kneeling	
Orátio V. Chrístus factus est pro nobis obédiens usque ad mortem.	**Prayer** V. Christ became obedient unto death for us.
After this is said, the Our Father/Pater Noster is added silently.	
Orátio Réspice, quǽsumus, Dómine, super hanc famíliam tuam, pro qua Dóminus noster Iesus Christus non dubitávit mánibus tradi nocéntium, et crucis subíre torméntum.	**Prayer** Look, we beseech Thee, O Lord, upon this Thy family, for whom our Lord Jesus Christ never hesitated to be delivered into the hands of the wicked, and to suffer the torture of the cross.
The following is said in silence.	
Qui tecum vivit et regnat in unitáte Spíritus Sancti, ...	Who liveth and reigneth with Thee in the unity of the Holy Spirit, ...

Good Friday (Vespers)
Office of Tenebræ

Antiphons and Psalms as on Maundy Thursday, Chapter and Hymn are omitted	
Ad Magnificat Ant. Cum accepísset acétum, dixit: Consummátum est: et inclináto cápite, emísit spíritum.	**Magnificat Ant.** When He had received the vinegar He said: It is finished: and bowing His head He breathed His last.
Orátio V. Chrístus factus est pro nobis obédiens usque ad mortem, mortem autem crucis.	**Prayer** V. Christ became obedient unto death for us, even the death of the cross.
After this is said, the Our Father/Pater Noster is added silently.	
Orátio Réspice, quǽsumus, Dómine, super hanc famíliam tuam, pro qua Dóminus noster Iesus Christus non dubitávit mánibus tradi nocéntium, et crucis subíre torméntum.	**Prayer** Look, we beseech Thee, O Lord, upon this Thy family, for whom our Lord Jesus Christ never hesitated to be delivered into the hands of the wicked and to suffer the torture of the cross.
The following is said in silence.	
Qui tecum vivit et regnat in unitáte Spíritus Sancti, ...	Who liveth and reigneth with Thee in the unity of the Holy Spirit, ...

Holy Saturday (Lauds)
Office of Tenebræ

Psalms of Saturday Lauds II, Chapter, Hymn and Versicle are omitted	
Ant 1. O mors, ero mors tua, morsus tuus ero, inférne.	**Ant 1.** O death, I will be thy death, I will be thy death in hell.
Ant 2. Plangent eum quasi unigénitum, quia ínnocens Dóminus occísus est.	**Ant 2.** They mourn Him as the only begotten, because the innocent Lord was slain.
Ant 3. Atténdite univérsi pópuli, et vidéte dolórem meum.	**Ant 3.** Listen, all you people, and see My pain.
Ant 4. A porta ínferi érue, Dómine, ánimam meam.	**Ant 4.** Deliver my soul, O Lord, from the gates of hell.
Canticle of Ezechias page 80	
Ant 5. O vos omnes, qui transítis per viam, atténdite et vidéte, si est dolor sicut dolor meus.	**Ant 5.** O all ye who pass by the way, pay attention and see if there is pain like My pain.

Proper of the Season

Ad Benedíctus Ant. Mulíeres sedéntes ad monuméntum lamentabántur, flentes Dóminum.	***Benedíctus Ant.*** The women sitting at the tomb lamented, weeping for the Lord.
After the antiphon, the following is said kneeling	
***Orátio* V.** Christus factus est pro nobis obédiens usque ad mortem, mortem autem crucis: propter quod et Deus exaltávit illum, et dedit illi nomen, quod est super omne nomen. Per Dóminum nostrum ...	***Prayer* V.** Christ became obedient for us even to death, and the death of the cross: For this reason God also exalted Him and gave Him the Name which is the supreme Name. Through our Lord ...
After this is said, the Our Father/Pater Noster is added silently.	
Orátio Réspice, quǽsumus, Dómine, super hanc famíliam tuam, pro qua Dóminus noster Iesus Christus non dubitávit mánibus tradi nocéntium, et crucis subíre torméntum.	***Prayer*** Look, we beseech Thee, O Lord, upon this Thy family, for whom our Lord Jesus Christ never hesitated to be delivered into the hands of the wicked and to suffer the torture of the cross.
The following is said in silence. Omit the conclusion following.	
Qui tecum vivit et regnat ...	Who liveth and reigneth...

Holy Saturday (Vespers)
Office of Tenebrae

All of Maundy Thursday, except the 1ˢᵗ Antiphon and the Magnificat Antiphon

Ad Magníficat Ant. Príncipes sacerdótum et pharisǽi muniérunt sepúlcrum, signántes lápidem, cum custódibus.	***Magnificat Ant.*** The priestly princes and the Pharisees fortified the tomb, sealing the stone and assigning guards.
Oratio Concéde, quǽsumus, omnípotens Deus: ut, qui Fílii tui resurrectiónem devóta exspectatióne prævenímus; eiúsdem resurrectiónis glóriam consequámur.	***Prayer.*** Grant, we beseech Thee, almighty God: that we who await the resurrection of Thy Son with devout expectation; shall attain the same glory of the resurrection.
The following is said in silence. Omit the conclusion following.	
Qui tecum vivit et regnat ...	Who liveth and reigneth...

Easter Season

Easter Sunday (Lauds)

Psalms of Sunday Lauds I

Ant 1. Angelus autem Dómini descéndit de cælo, et accédens revólvit lápidem, et sedébat super eum, allelúja, allelúja.	**Ant 1.** And the angel of the Lord came down from heaven, and coming near rolled back the stone, and sat on it, alleluia, alleluia.
Ant 2. Et ecce terræmótus factus est magnus: Angelus enim Dómini descéndit de cælo, allelúja.	**Ant 2.** And behold, there was a great earthquake: for the angel of the Lord came down from heaven, alleluia.
Ant 3. Erat autem aspéctus eius sicut fulgur, vestiménta autem eius sicut nix, allelúja, allelúja.	**Ant 3.** And his appearance was like lightning, and his clothes like snow, alleluia, alleluia.

Proper of the Season

Ant 4. Præ timóre autem eius extérriti sunt custódes, et facti sunt velut mórtui, allelúja.	**Ant 4.** The guards were terrified and became as if they were dead men, alleluia.
Ant 5. Respóndens autem Angelus, dixit muliéribus: Nolíte timére: scio enim quod Iesum quæritis, allelúja.	**Ant 5.** And the angel answering said to the women: Do not be afraid, for I know that ye seek Jesus, alleluia.
Instead of the Chapter, Hymn and Versicle, this is said.	
V. Hæc dies, quam fecit Dóminus: **R.** Exsultémus, et lætémur in ea.	**V.** This is the day which the Lord hath made: **R.** Let us rejoice and be glad in it.
Ad Benedíctus Ant. Et valde mane una sabbatórum veniunt ad monuméntum, orto jam sole, allelúja.	*Benedíctus Ant.* And very early on the Sabbath when they came to the tomb, the sun had already risen, alleluia.
Orátio Deus, qui hodiérna die per Unigénitum tuum æternitátis nobis áditum devícta morte reserásti: vota nostra, quæ præveniéndo aspíras, étiam adiuvándo proséquere. étiam Per eundem Dóminum nostrum …	*Prayer* O God, who this day through Thine only-begotten Son, by conquering death opened to us everlasting life: which was what we desired and which Thou had prepared for us, through the same Lord …
V. Benedicámus Dómino, allelúja, allelúja. **R.** Deo grátias, allelúja, allelúja. **V.** Fidélium ánimæ per misericórdiam Dei requiéscant in pace. **R.** Amen.	**V.** Let us bless the Lord, alleluia, alleluia **R.** Thanks be to God, alleluia, alleluia. **V.** May the souls of the faithful departed through the mercy of God rest in peace. **R.** Amen

Easter Sunday (Vespers)
Antiphons of Lauds above, Psalms of Sunday Vespers followed by:

V. Hæc dies, quam fecit Dóminus: **R.** Exsultémus, et lætémur in ea.	**V.** This is the day which the Lord hath made: **R.** Let us rejoice and be glad in it.
Ad Magnificat Ant. Et respiciéntes vidérunt revolútum lápidem: erat quippe magnus valde, allelúja.	*Magnificat Ant.* And looking back, they saw the stone rolled away: for it was very large, alleluia.
Prayer as at Lauds and Benedicamus Dómino above	

Easter Monday (Lauds)
All as on Easter Sunday except as below:

Ad Benedíctus Ant. Iesus iunxit se discípulis suis in via, et ibat cum illis: óculi autem eórum tenebántur, ne eum agnóscerent: et increpávit eos, dicens: O stulti et tardi corde ad credéndum in his, quæ locúti sunt Prophétæ, allelúja.	*Benedíctus Ant.* Jesus joined His disciples on the road and went with them, but their eyes were closed so that they would not recognize Him: and He rebuked them, saying: O fools, slow of heart to believe in these things which the Prophets have spoken, alleluia.

Proper of the Season

Orátio Deus, qui solemnitáte pascháli, mundo remédia contulísti: pópulum tuum, quǽsumus, cælésti dono proséquere; ut et perféctam libertátem cónsequi mereátur, et ad vitam profíciat sempitérnam. Per Dóminum nostrum ...	***Prayer*** O God, who, with the solemnity of the Pasch, hath brought salvation to the world: we beseech Thee that Thy people may pursue heavenly gifts; and that they may deserve to attain perfect freedom from evil, and may achieve eternal life. Through our Lord ...

Easter Monday (Vespers)
Sunday Vespers Psalms, Easter Sunday Lauds Antiphons, Prayer and *Benedicamus Dómino*. The Chapter, Hymn, and Versicle are omitted but in their place as below:

V. Hæc dies, quam fecit Dóminus: **R.** Exsultémus, et lætémur in ea.	**V.** This is the day which the Lord hath made: **R.** Let us rejoice and be glad in it.
Ad Magnificat Ant. Qui sunt hi sermónes quos confértis ad ínvicem ambulántes, et estis tristes? Allelúja.	***Magnificat Ant.*** What are these conversations that you are having with each other as ye walk, and why are ye sad? Alleluia.

Easter Tuesday (Lauds)
All as on Easter Sunday except as below:

Ad Benedíctus Ant. Stetit Iesus in médio discipulórum suórum, et dixit eis: Pax vobis, allelúja, allelúja.	***Benedíctus Ant.*** Jesus stood in the midst of His disciples and said to them: Peace be with you, alleluia, alleluia.
Orátio Deus, qui Ecclésiam tuam novo semper fœtu multíplicas: concéde fámulis tuis; ut sacraméntum vivéndo téneant, quod fide percepérunt. Per Dóminum nostrum ...	***Prayer*** O God, who always increases Thy Church with new children: grant to Thy servants that they may keep the sacrament by living a good life, which they have received by faith. Through our Lord ...

Easter Tuesday (Vespers)
Sunday Vespers Psalms, Easter Sunday Lauds Antiphons, Prayer and *Benedicamus Dómino*. The Chapter, Hymn, and Versicle are omitted but in their place as below:

Ad Magnificat Ant. Vidéte manus meas et pedes meos, quia ego ipse sum, allelúja, allelúja.	***Magnificat Ant.*** See My hands and My feet, for it is I Myself, alleluia, alleluia.

Easter Wednesday (Lauds)
All as on Easter Sunday except as below

Ad Benedíctus Ant. Míttite in déxteram navígii rete, et inveniétis, allelúja.	***Benedíctus Ant.*** Cast a net on the right side of the boat and ye will find them, alleluia.
Orátio Deus, qui nos resurrectiónis Domínicæ ánnua solemnitáte lætíficas: concéde propítius; ut per	***Prayer*** O God, who giveth us joy with the annual solemnity of the Resurrection: grant more mercifully

Proper of the Season

temporália festa quæ ágimus, pervenire ad gaúdia ætérna mereámur. Per Dóminum nostrum ...	that through the earthly festivals which we celebrate, we may deserve to attain everlasting happiness. Through our Lord ...

Easter Wednesday (Vespers)
Sunday Vespers psalms, Easter Sunday Lauds Antiphons, prayer and *Benedicamus Dómino*. The Chapter, Hymn, and Versicle are omitted but in their place as below:

V. Hæc dies, quam fecit Dóminus: R. Exsultémus, et lætémur in ea.	V. This is the day which the Lord hath made: R. Let us rejoice and be glad in it.
Ad Magnificat Ant. Dixit Iesus discípulis suis: Afférte de píscibus, quos prendidístis nunc. Ascéndit autem Simon Petrus, et traxit rete in terram plenum magnis píscibus, allelúja.	*Magnificat Ant.* Jesus said to His disciples: Bring some of the fish that ye now have caught. And Simon Peter went up and drew the net to the land full of large fish, alleluia.

Easter Thursday (Lauds)
All as on Easter Sunday except as below:

Ad Benedíctus Ant. María stabat ad monuméntum plorans, et vidit duos Angelos in albis, sedéntes, et sudárium quod fúerat super caput Iesu, allelúja.	*Benedíctus Ant.* Mary stood weeping at the tomb, and saw two angels in white sitting, and the cloth that had been over the head of Jesus, alleluia.
Orátio Deus, qui diversitátem géntium in confessióne tui nóminis adunásti: da, ut renátis fonte baptísmatis una sit fides méntium et píetas actiónum. Per Dóminum nostrum ...	*Prayer* O God, who hast united the many Gentiles in confessing Thy Name: bestow on those reborn at the font of baptism unity of faith in mind and piety of works so all may be one. Through our Lord ...

Easter Thursday (Vespers)
Sunday Vespers psalms, Easter Sunday Lauds Antiphons, prayer and *Benedicamus Dómino*. The Chapter, Hymn, and Versicle are omitted but in their place as below:

V. Hæc dies, quam fecit Dóminus: R. Exsultémus, et lætémur in ea.	V. This is the day which the Lord hath made: R. Let us rejoice and be glad in it.
Ad Magnificat Ant. Tulérunt Dóminum meum, et néscio ubi posuérunt eum: si tu sustulísti eum, dícito mihi, allelúja: et ego eum tollam, allelúja.	*Magnificat Ant.* They have taken my Lord, and I do not know where they have laid Him: if ye have taken Him away, tell me, alleluia: and I will get Him, alleluia.

Easter Friday (Lauds)
All as on Easter Sunday except as below:

Ad Benedíctus Ant. Undecim discípuli in Galilǽa vidéntes Dóminum adoravérunt, allelúja.	*Benedíctus Ant.* The eleven disciples, seeing the Lord in Galilee, worshiped Him, alleluia.

Proper of the Season

Orátio Omnípotens sempitérne Deus, qui paschále sacraméntum in reconciliatiónis humánæ fœdere contulísti: da méntibus nostris; ut quod professióne celebrámus, imitémur efféctu. Per Dóminum nostrum ...	***Prayer*** Almighty and everlasting God, who hast provided the paschal sacrament in the covenant of human forgiveness: fill our minds; so that what we profess with our lips, we may imitate in action. Through our Lord ...

Easter Friday (Vespers)
Sunday Vespers psalms, Easter Sunday Lauds Antiphons, prayer and *Benedicamus Dómino*. The Chapter, Hymn, and Versicle are omitted but in their place as below:

V. Hæc dies, quam fecit Dóminus: **R.** Exsultémus, et lætémur in ea.	**V.** This is the day which the Lord hath made: **R.** Let us rejoice and be glad in it.
Ad Magnificat Ant. Data est mihi omnis potéstas in cælo et in terra, allelúja.	***Magnificat Ant.*** All power in heaven and on earth hath been given to Me, alleluia.
Orátio Omnípotens sempitérne Deus, qui paschále sacraméntum in reconciliatiónis humánæ fœdere contulísti: da méntibus nostris; ut quod professióne celebrámus, imitémur efféctu. Per Dóminum nostrum ...	***Prayer*** Almighty and everlasting God, who hast provided the Easter sacrament by Thy covenant which hast forgiven mankind: fill our minds; so that what we profess with our lips, we may imitate in action. Through our Lord ...

Easter Saturday (Lauds)
All as on Easter Sunday except as below:

Ad Benedíctus Ant. Currébant duo simul, et ille álius discípulus præcucúrrit cítius Petro, et venit prior ad monuméntum, allelúja.	***Benedíctus Ant.*** The two ran together, and that other disciple ran faster than Peter and came first to the tomb, alleluia.
Orátio Concéde, quǽsumus, omnípotens Deus: ut, qui festa paschália venerándo égimus, per hæc contíngere ad gáudia ætérna mereámur. Per Dóminum nostrum ...	***Prayer*** Grant, we beseech Thee, almighty God, that those who devoutly celebrated the Paschal feast may, through these prayers, merit eternal happiness. Through our Lord ...

Easter Saturday (Vespers)
Antiphon, Alleluia, with the Psalms of Sunday of the Psalter

Capitulum (1 John 5:4) **V.** Caríssimi: Omne, quod natum est ex Deo, vincit mundum: et hæc est victória, quæ vincit mundum, fides nostra. **R.** Deo grátias.	***Chapter*** (1 John 5:4) **V.** For whatsoever is born of God, overcometh the world: and our Faith is the victory which overcometh the world. **R.** Thanks be to God.

Hymn Aurora Caelum Purpurat, page 384

Proper of the Season

Versiculi V. Mane nobíscum Dómine, allelúja. R. Quóniam advesperáscit, allelúja.	*Versicle* V. Stay with us Lord, alleluia. R. Because it is evening, alleluia.
Ad Magnificat Ant. Cum esset sero die illa una sabbatórum, et fores essent clausæ, ubi erant discípuli congregáti in unum, stetit Iesus in médio, et dixit eis: Pax vobis, allelúja.	*Magnificat Ant.* When it was late on that day, on the Sabbath, and the doors were closed where the disciples were gathered together, Jesus stood in the middle and said to them: Peace be with you, alleluia.
Orátio Præsta, quǽsumus, omnípotens Deus: ut qui paschália festa perégimus, hæc, te largiénte, móribus et vita teneámus. Per Dóminum nostrum ...	*Prayer* We beseech Thee, Almighty God, that we who have celebrated the Paschal feast may keep its benefits, by Thy grace, in our conduct and the way we live our lives. Through our Lord ...

Low Sunday (Lauds)
Antiphons for Paschaltide, alleluia, alleluia, alleluia with the Psalms of Sunday Lauds I

Capitulum (1 John 5:4) V. Caríssimi: Omne, quod natum est ex Deo, vincit mundum: et hæc est victória, quæ vincit mundum, fides nostra. R. Deo grátias.	*Chapter* (1 John 5:4) V. For whatsoever is born of God, overcometh the world: and this is the victory which overcameth the world, our Faith. R. Thanks be to God.

Hymn Aurora Caelum Purpurat, page 384

Ad Benedíctus Ant. Cum esset sero die illa una sabbatórum, et fores essent clausæ, ubi erant discípuli congregáti in unum, stetit Iesus in médio, et dixit eis: Pax vobis, allelúja.	*Benedíctus Ant.* When it was late on that day, on the Sabbath, and the doors were closed where the disciples were gathered together, Jesus stood in the middle and said to them: Peace be with you, alleluia.
Orátio Præsta, quǽsumus, omnípotens Deus: ut qui paschália festa perégimus, hæc, te largiénte, móribus et vita teneámus. Per Dóminum nostrum ...	*Prayer* We beseech Thee, Almighty God, that we who have celebrated the Paschal feast may keep its benefits, by Thy grace, in our conduct and the way we live our lives. Through our Lord ...

Low Sunday (Vespers)
Antiphons, alleluia, alleluia, alleluia with the Psalms of Saturday Vespers of the Psalter

Ad Magnificat Ant. Post dies octo iánuis clausis ingréssus Dóminus dixit eis: Pax vobis, allelúja, allelúja.	*Magnificat Ant.* After eight days, the Lord entered with the doors closed and said to them: Peace be with you, alleluia, alleluia.
Orátio Præsta, quǽsumus, omnípotens Deus: ut qui paschália festa perégimus, hæc, te largiénte, móribus et vita teneámus. Per Dóminum nostrum ...	*Prayer* We beseech Thee, almighty God, that we who have celebrated the Paschal feast may keep its benefits, by Thy grace, in our conduct and the way we live our lives. Through our Lord ...

Proper of the Season

Ferias in Paschaltide
All as on the occurring day of the week in the Psalter; the Antiphon of the day with an Alleluia; Versicle, and Prayer of the preceding Sunday Lauds I or Vespers where appropriate; Hymns *Auróra Cælum Púrpurat*, pg. 384 (Lauds) *Paschále Mundo Gáudium*, pg. 386 (Vespers) and the Propers of the Season below.

Monday of the 1st Week after the Octave of Easter (Lauds)

Ad Benedíctus Ant. Surgens Jesus mane prima sábati, appáruit primo Mariæ Magdalénæ, de qua ejécerat septem dæmónia, allelúja.	*Benedíctus Ant.* When Jesus rose early on the Sabbath morning, He appeared first to Mary Magdalene, from whom He had cast out seven demons, alleluia.

Monday of the 1st Week after the Octave of Easter (Vespers)

Ad Magníficat Ant. Pax vobis, ego sum, Allelúja: nolíte timére, Allelúja.	*Magníficat Ant.* Peace be unto you, it is I, alleluia: fear not, alleluia.

Tuesday of the 1st Week after the Octave of Easter (Lauds)

Ad Benedíctus Ant. Præcédam vos in Galilǽam, ibi me vidébitis, sicut dixi vobis, Allelúja, Allelúja.	*Benedíctus Ant.* I will go before you into Galilee, there ye shall see Me, as I told you, alleluia, alleluia.

Tuesday of the 1st Week after the Octave of Easter (Vespers)

Ad Magníficat Ant. Mitte manum tuam, et cognósce loca clavórum, allelúja: et noli esse incrédulus, sed fidélis, allelúja.	*Magníficat Ant.* Put forth thy hand, and know the places of the nails, alleluia: and be not unbelieving, but faithful, alleluia.

Wednesday of the 1st Week after the Octave of Easter (Lauds)

Ad Benedíctus Ant. Ego sum vitis vera, allelúja; et vos pálmites veri, allelúja.	*Benedíctus Ant.* I am the true vine, alleluia; and ye the true branches, alleluia.

Wednesday of the 1st Week after the Octave of Easter (Vespers)

Ad Magníficat Ant. Quia vidísti me, Thoma, credísti: beáti qui non vidérunt, et credidérunt, allelúja.	*Magníficat Ant.* Because thou hast seen Me, Thomas, thou hast believed: blessed are those who have not seen and believed, alleluia.

Thursday of the 1st Week after the Octave of Easter (Lauds)

Ad Benedíctus Ant. Ardens est cor meum, desídero vidére Dóminum meum: quæro, et non invénio ubi posuérunt eum, allelúja, allelúja.	*Benedíctus Ant.* My heart is burning, I long to see my Lord: I seek, and I do not find where they have laid Him, alleluia, alleluia.

Thursday of the 1st Week after the Octave of Easter (Vespers)

Ad Magníficat Ant. Misi dígitum meum in fixúras clavorum, et manum meum in latus ejus, et dixi: Dóminus meus, et Deus meus, allelúja.	*Magníficat Ant.* I put my finger into the place where the nails were fastened, and my hand into His side, and said: My Lord and my God, alleluia.

Friday of the 1st Week after the Octave of Easter (Lauds)

Ad Benedíctus Ant. Venérunt ad monuméntum Maria Magdalene, et áltera Maria, vidére sepúlcrum, allelúja.	*Benedíctus Ant.* Mary Magdalene and the other Mary came to see the tomb, alleluia.

Proper of the Season

Friday of the 1ˢᵗ Week after the Octave of Easter (Vespers)	
Ad Magnificat Ant. Post dies octo jánuis clausis ingréssus Dóminus dixit eis: Pax vobis, allelúja.	**Magnificat Ant.** After eight days, the Lord entered with the doors closed and said to them: Peace be with you, alleluia.
Saturday of the 1ˢᵗ Week after the Octave of Easter (Lauds) Saturday of the Psalter of Lauds I and Office of the Blessed Virgin Mary	
Saturday of the 1ˢᵗ Week after the Octave of Easter (Vespers) Antiphon, Alleluia, with the Psalms of Saturday	

Second Sunday after Easter (Lauds)
Sunday Antiphons with Alleluia, and the Psalms of Sunday Lauds I of the Psalter

Capitulum (1 Pet 2:21-22) V. Caríssimi: Christus passus est pro nobis, vobis relínquens exémplum ut sequámini vestígia eius. Qui peccátum non fecit, nec invéntus est dolus in ore eius. R. Deo grátias.	**Chapter** (1 Pet 2:21-22) V. For unto this are ye called: because Christ also suffered for us, leaving you an example that ye should follow his steps: Who did no sin, neither was guile found in His mouth. R. Thanks be to God.
Hymn – Auróra Cælum Purpurat, page 384	
Versiculi V. In resurrectióne tua Christe, allelúja. R. Cæli et terra lætentur, allelúja.	**Versicle** V. In Thy resurrection Christ, alleluia. R. Heaven and earth rejoice, alleluia.
Ad Benedíctus Ant. Ego sum pastor óvium: ego sum via, véritas, et vita: ego sum pastor bonus, et cognósco oves meas, et cognóscunt me meæ, allelúja, allelúja.	**Benedíctus Ant.** I am the Shepherd of the Sheep: I am the Way, the Truth, and the Life: I am the Good Shepherd, and I know My sheep, and they know Me, alleluia, alleluia.
Orátio Deus, qui in Fílii tui humilitáte iacéntem mundum erexísti: fidélibus tuis perpétuam concéde lætítiam; ut, quos perpétuæ mortis eripuísti cásibus, gáudiis fácias pérfrui sempitérnis. Per Dóminum nostrum ...	**Prayer** O God, who in the humility of Thy Son raised up the world, grant Thy faithful eternal joy: those whom Thou hast rescued from the dangers of eternal death, that they may also enjoy everlasting happiness. Through our Lord ...

Second Sunday after Easter (Vespers)
Sunday Antiphons with Alleluia, and the Psalms of Sunday Vespers of the Psalter

Capitulum (1 Pet 2:21-22) V. Caríssimi: Christus passus est pro nobis, vobis relínquens exémplum ut sequámini vestígia eius. Qui peccátum non fecit, nec invéntus est dolus in ore eius. R. Deo grátias.	**Chapter** (1 Pet 2:21-22) V. For unto this are ye called: because Christ also suffered for us, leaving you an example that ye should follow His steps: Who did no sin, neither was guile found in His mouth. R. Thanks be to God.
Hymn – Paschále Mundo Gáudium, page 386	
Versiculi V. Mane nobíscum Dómine, allelúja. R. Quóniam advesperáscit, allelúja.	**Versicle** V. Stay with us Lord, alleluia. R. Because it is evening, alleluia.

Proper of the Season

Ad Magnificat Ant. Ego sum pastor bonus, qui pasco oves meas, et pro óvibus meis pono ánimam meam, allelúja.	*Magnificat Ant.* I am the Good Shepherd who feeds My sheep, and I lay down My life for My sheep, alleluia.
Orátio Deus, qui in Filii tui humilitáte jacéntem mundum erexísti: … *(as Lauds above)*	*Prayer* O God, who in the humility of Thy Son raised up the world, grant … *(as Lauds above)*

Monday of the 2nd Week after the Octave of Easter (Lauds)

Ad Benedíctus Ant. Eúntes in mundum, allelúja: docéte ómnes Gentes, allelúja.	*Benedíctus Ant.* Go ye into the world, alleluia: teaching all nations, alleluia.

Monday of the 2nd Week after the Octave of Easter (Vespers)

Ad Magnificat Ant. Pastor bonus ánimam suam ponit pro óvibus suis, allelúja.	*Magnificat Ant.* The good shepherd lays down his life for his sheep, alleluia.

Tuesday of the 2nd Week after the Octave of Easter (Lauds)

Ad Benedíctus Ant. Eúntes in mundum, docéte ómnes Gentes, baptizántes eos in nómine Patris, et Fílii, et Spíritus Sancti, allelúja.	*Benedíctus Ant.* Go into the world, and teach all the Gentiles, baptizing them in the Name of the Father, and of the Son, and of the Holy Spirit, alleluia.

Tuesday of the 2nd Week after the Octave of Easter (Vespers)

Ad Magnificat Ant. Mercenarius autem, cujus non sunt oves propriæ, videt lupum venientem, et dimittit oves, et fugit, et lupus rapit, et dispergit oves, allelúja.	*Magnificat Ant.* But the hireling, who has no sheep of his own, sees the wolf coming and releases the sheep and flees, and the wolf snatches and scatters the lambs, alleluia.

Wednesday of the 2nd Week after the Octave of Easter (Lauds)

Ad Benedíctus Ant. Ite, nuntiáte frátribus meis, allelúja: ut cant in Galilǽam, allelúja: ibi me vidébunt allelúja, allelúja.	*Benedíctus Ant.* Go tell my brethren alleluia, that as they go into Galilee, alleluia; there they shall see me, alleluia, alleluia.

Wednesday of the 2nd Week after the Octave of Easter (Vespers)

Ad Magnificat Ant. Sicut novit me Pater, et ego cognósco Patrem, et ánimam meam pono pro óvibus meis, allelúja.	*Magnificat Ant.* As the Father knows Me, and I know the Father, and I lay down my life for My sheep, alleluia.

Thursday of the 2nd Week after the Octave of Easter (Lauds)

Ad Benedíctus Ant. Tu solus peregínus es, et non audísti de Jesu,	*Benedíctus Ant.* Thou art a traveler alone, and thou hast not heard of

Proper of the Season

quómodo tradidérunt eum in damnatiónem mortis? Allelúja.	Jesus, and how they handed Him over to be condemned to death? Alleluia.

Thursday of the 2nd Week after the Octave of Easter (Vespers)

Ad Magnificat Ant. Alias oves hábeo, quæ non sunt ex hoc ovíli: et ellas opórtet me addúcere, et vocem meam áudient: et fiet unum ovíle, et unus pastor, allelúja.	*Magnificat Ant.* I have other sheep which are not of this fold: and they must be brought to Me, and they will hear My voice: and there shall be one fold, and one Shepherd, alleluia.

Friday of the 2nd Week after the Octave of Easter (Lauds)

Ad Benedíctus Ant. Nonne sic opórtuit pati Christum, et ita intáre in glóriam suam? Allelúja.	*Benedíctus Ant.* Was it not necessary for Christ to suffer thus, and thus to enter into His glory? Alleluia.

Friday of the 2nd Week after the Octave of Easter (Vespers)

Ad Magnificat Ant. Ego sum pastor bonus, qui pasco oves meas, et pro óvibus meis pono ánimam meam, allelúja.	*Magnificat Ant.* I am the Good Shepherd who feeds My sheep, and I lay down My life for My sheep, alleluia.

Saturday of the 2nd Week after the Octave of Easter (Lauds)
Saturday of the Psalter and Office of the Blessed Virgin Mary

Saturday of the 2nd Week after the Octave of Easter (Vespers)
Antiphon Alleluia, with the Psalms of Saturday

Third Sunday after Easter (Lauds)
Sunday Antiphons with Alleluia, and the Psalms of Sunday Lauds I of the Psalter

Capitulum (1 Pet 2:11) V. Caríssimi: Obsecro vos tamquam ádvenas et peregrínos abstinére vos a carnálibus desidériis, quæ mílitant advérsus ánimam. R. Deo grátias.	*Chapter* (1 Pet 2:11) V. Dearly beloved, I beseech you as strangers and pilgrims, to refrain yourselves from carnal desires which war against the soul. R. Thanks be to God.

Hymn – Auróra Cælum Purpurat, page 384

Ad Benedíctus Ant. Módicum et non vidébitis me, dicit Dóminus: íterum módicum, et vidébitis me, quia vado ad Patrem, allelúja, allelúja.	*Benedíctus Ant.* A little while and ye will not see Me, sayeth the Lord: again a little while, and ye will see Me, because I am going to the Father, alleluia, alleluia.
Orátio Deus, qui erríntibus, ut in viam possint redíre iustítiæ, veritátis tuæ lumen osténdis: da cunctis, qui christiána professióne censéntur, et illa respúere, quæ huic inimíca sunt nómini; et ea, quæ sunt apta, sectári. Per Dóminum nostrum ...	*Prayer* O God, who shows the light of Thy truth to the erring, so that they may return to the path of justice: grant that all who are considered to be Christians should reject those things which are inimical to this name, and follow those which are worthy. Through our Lord ...

Proper of the Season

Third Sunday after Easter (Vespers) Sunday Antiphons with Alleluia, and the Psalms of Sunday Vespers of the Psalter Hymn Paschále Mundo Gáudium, page 386	
Ad Magnificat Ant. Amen dico vobis, quia plorábitis et flébitis vos: mundus autem gaudébit, vos vero contristabímini, sed tristítia vestra convertétur in gáudium, allelúja.	*Magnificat Ant.* Amen I say to you, that ye will lament and weep: but the world will rejoice, but ye will grieve: but thy sorrow will be turned into joy, alleluia.
Monday of the 3rd Week after the Octave of Easter (Lauds)	
Ad Benedíctus Ant. Et incípiens a Móyse et ómnibus prophétis, interpretabátur illis Scriptúras, quæ de ipso errant, allelúja.	*Benedíctus Ant.* And beginning with Moses and all the prophets, He interpreted the Scriptures for them which were concerning Him, alleluia.
Monday of the 3rd Week after the Octave of Easter (Vespers)	
Ad Magnificat Ant. Tristítia implévit cor vestrum: et gáudium vestrum nemo tollet a vobis, allelúja, allelúja.	*Magnificat Ant.* Sorrow hath filled thy heart: and no one will take thy joy from thee, alleluia, alleluia.
Tuesday of the 3rd Week after the Octave of Easter (Lauds)	
Ad Benedíctus Ant. Et coëgérunt illum, dicéntes: Mane nobíscum, Dómine, quóniam advesperáscit, allelúja.	*Benedíctus Ant.* And they compelled Him, saying: Stay with us, O Lord, for it is evening, alleluia.
Tuesday of the 3rd Week after the Octave of Easter (Vespers)	
Ad Magnificat Ant. Tristítia implévit cor vestrum: et gáudium vestrum nemo tollet a vobis, allelúja, allelúja.	*Magnificat Ant.* Sorrow hath filled thy heart: and no one will take thy joy from thee, alleluia, alleluia.
Wednesday of the 3rd Week after the Octave of Easter (Lauds)	
Ad Benedíctus Ant. Mane nobíscum, quóniam advesperácit, et inclináta est jam dies, allelúja.	*Benedíctus Ant.* Stay with us until the morning, because it is getting late, and the day hath already ended, alleluia.
Wednesday of the 3rd Week after the Octave of Easter (Vespers)	
Ad Magnificat Ant Tristítia implévit cor vestrum: et gáudium vestrum nemo tollet a vobis, allelúja, allelúja.	*Magnificat Ant.* Sorrow hath filled thy heart: and no one will take thy joy from thee, alleluia, alleluia.
Thursday of the 3rd Week after the Octave of Easter (Lauds)	
Ad Benedíctus Ant. Et intrávit cum illis,: et factum est, dum recúmberet cum illis, accépit panem, et benedíxit, ac fregit, et porrigébat illis, allelúja, allelúja.	*Benedíctus Ant.* And He went in with them: and it came to pass, as He reclined with them, He took bread, and blessed it, and broke it, and gave it to them, alleluia, alleluia.
Thursday of the 3rd Week after the Octave of Easter (Vespers)	
Ad Magnificat Ant. Amen, amen dico vobis, iterum videbo vos, et gaudebit cor vestrum, et gaudium vestrum nemo tollet a vobis, allelúja.	*Magnificat Ant.* Amen, amen I say to thee, I will see thee again, and thy heart will rejoice, and no one will take thy joy from thee, alleluia.

Proper of the Season

Friday of the 3rd Week after the Octave of Easter (Lauds)

Ad Benedíctus Ant. Cognovérunt Dóminum Jesum, allelúja, in fractióne panis, allelúja.	*Benedictus Ant.* They recognized the Lord Jesus, alleluia, in the breaking of the bread, alleluia.

Friday of the 3rd Week after the Octave of Easter (Vespers)

Ad Magníficat Ant. Amen dico vobis, quia plorábitis et flébitis vos: mundus autem gaudébit, vos vero contristabímini, sed tristítia vestra convertétur in gáudium, allelúja.	*Magnificat Ant.* Amen I say to you, ye will lament and weep: but the world will rejoice, and ye will be sad, but thy sadness will be turned into joy, alleluia.

Saturday of the 3rd Week after the Octave of Easter (Lauds)
Saturday of the Psalter and Office of the Blessed Virgin Mary

Saturday of the 3rd Week after the Octave of Easter (Vespers)
Antiphon Alleluia, with the Psalms of Saturday

Fourth Sunday after Easter (Lauds)
Sunday Antiphons with Alleluia, and the Psalms of Sunday Lauds I of the Psalter

Capítulum (Jas 1:17) V. Caríssimi: Omne datum óptimum, et omne donum perféctum desúrsum est, descéndens a Patre lúminum, apud quem non est transmutátio, nec vicissitúdinis obumbrátio. R. Deo grátias.	*Chapter* (Jas 1:17) V. Dearly Beloved: Every best gift, and every perfect gift, is from above, coming down from the Father of lights, with whom there is no change, nor shadow of alteration. R. Thanks be to God.

Hymn – Auróra Cælum Purpurat, page 384

Ad Benedíctus Ant. Vado ad eum qui misit me: et nemo ex vobis intérrogat me: Quo vadis? allelúja, allelúja.	*Benedíctus Ant.* I am going to Him who sent Me: and none of you asks Me: Where art Thou going? Alleluia, alleluia.
Orátio Deus, qui fidélium mentes uníus éfficis voluntátis: da pópulis tuis id amáre quod præcipis, id desideráre quod promíttis; ut inter mundánas varietátes ibi nostra fixa sint corda, ubi vera sunt gáudia. Per Dóminum nostrum ...	*Prayer* O God, Who makest one mind of the faithful, inspire Thy people to love what Thou hast commanded, to desire what Thou hast promised; to desire that which Thou hast vowed; so that amidst worldly changes in life, our hearts may remain where there is true joy. Through our Lord ...

Forth Sunday after Easter (Vespers)
Sunday Antiphons with Alleluia, and the Psalms of Sunday Vespers of the Psalter
Hymn *Paschále Mundo Gáudium*, page 386

Ad Magníficat Ant. Vado ad eum qui misit me: sed quia hæc locútus sum vobis, tristítia implévit cor vestrum, allelúja.	*Magnificat Ant.* I am going to Him who sent Me: but because I have spoken these things to thee, sadness has filled thy heart, alleluia.

Proper of the Season

Monday of the 4th Week after the Octave of Easter (Lauds)

Ad Benedíctus Ant. Nonne cor nostrum ardens erat in nobis de Jesu, dum loquerétur nobis in via? Allelúja.	*Benedíctus Ant.* Was not our heart burning within us for Jesus, while He was speaking to us on the road? Alleluia.

Monday of the 4th Week after the Octave of Easter (Vespers)

Ad Magnificat Ant. Ego veritátem dico vobis: éxpedit vobis ut ego vadam: si enim non abíero Paráclitus non véniet ad vos, allelúja.	*Magnificat Ant.* I tell you the truth: it is expedient for you that I go; for if I do not go away, the Paraclete will not come to you, alleluia.

Tuesday of the 4th Week after the Octave of Easter (Lauds)

Ad Benedíctus Ant. Pax vobis, ego sum, allelúja; nolíte timére, allelúja.	*Benedíctus Ant.* Peace be unto you, it is I, alleluia: fear not, alleluia.

Tuesday of the 4th Week after the Octave of Easter (Vespers)

Ad Magnificat Ant. Cum vénerit Paráclitus Spíritus veritátis, ille árguet mundum de peccáto, et de justítia, et de judício, allelúja.	*Magnificat Ant.* When the Paraclete poured out the Spirit of truth, He rebuked the world about sin, and about the righteous, and about judgment, alleluia.

Wednesday of the 4th Week after the Octave of Easter (Lauds)

Ad Benedíctus Ant. Spíritus carnem et ossa non habet, sicut me vidétis habére jam crédite, allelúja.	*Benedíctus Ant.* A spirit does not have flesh and bones, as thou seest I have, believe Me now, alleluia.

Wednesday of the 4th Week after the Octave of Easter (Vespers)

Ad Magnificat Ant. Adhuc multa hábeo vobis dícere, sed non potéstis portáre modo: cum autem vénerit ille Spíritus veritátis, docébit vos omnem veritátem, allelúja.	*Magnificat Ant.* I still have many things to say to you, but ye cannot bear it alone: but when the Spirit of truth comes, He will enlighten you with all truth, alleluia.

Thursday of the 4th Week after the Octave of Easter (Lauds)

Ad Benedíctus Ant. Obtulérunt discípuli Dómino partem piscis assi, et favum mellis, allelúja, allelúja.	*Benedíctus Ant.* The disciples offered the Lord a portion of a roasted fish and a honeycomb full of honey, alleluia, alleluia

Thursday of the 4th Week after the Octave of Easter (Vespers)

Ad Magnificat Ant. Vado ad eum qui misit me: sed quia hæc locútus sum vobis, tristítia implévit cor vestrum, alleljia.	*Magnificat Ant.* I am going to Him Who sent Me: but because I have spoken these things to you, sadness has filled your hearts, alleluia.

Friday of the 4th Week after the Octave of Easter (Lauds)

Ad Benedíctus Ant. Isti sunt sermónes quos dicébam vobis, cum essem vobíscum, allelúja, allelúja.	*Benedíctus Ant.* These are the words which I spoke to you when I was with you, alleluia, alleluia.

Proper of the Season

Friday of the 4th Week after the Octave of Easter (Vespers)

Ad Magnificat Ant. Vado ad eum qui misit me: et nemo ex vobis intérrogat me: Quo vadis? allelúja, allelúja.	*Magnificat Ant.* I am going to Him who sent Me: and none of you asks me: Where art Thou going? Alleluia, alleluia.

Saturday of the 4th Week after the Octave of Easter (Lauds)
Saturday of the Psalter and Office of the Blessed Virgin Mary

Saturday of the 4th Week after the Octave of Easter (Vespers)
Antiphon Alleluia with the Psalms of Saturday

Fifth Sunday after Easter (Lauds)
Sunday Antiphons with Alleluia, and the Psalms of Sunday Lauds I of the Psalter

Capitulum (Jas 1:22-24) V. Caríssimi: Estóte factóres verbi, et non auditóres tantum: falléntes vosmetípsos. Quia si quis audítor est verbi, et non factor, hic comparábitur viro consideránti vultum nativitátis suæ in spéculo: considerávit enim se, et ábiit, et statim oblítus est qualis fúerit. R. Deo grátias.	*Chapter* (Jas 1:22-24) V. But be ye doers of the word, and not hearers only, deceiving your own selves. For if a man be a hearer of the word, and not a doer, he shall be compared to a man beholding his own countenance in a mirror. For he beheld himself, and went his way, and presently forgot what manner of man he was. R. Thanks be to God

Hymn – Auróra Cælum Purpurat, page 384

Ad Benedíctus Ant. Usque modo non petístis quidquam in nómine meo: pétite, et accipiétis, allelúja.	*Benedíctus Ant.* Until now thou hast not asked anything in My Name: ask and thou wilt receive.
Orátio Deus, a quo bona cuncta procédunt, largíre supplícibus tuis: ut cogitémus, te inspiránte, quæ recta sunt; et, te gubernánte, éadem faciámus. Per Dóminum nostrum ...	*Prayer* O God, from whom all good things come, bestow upon Thy supplicants by Thy inspiration; that we may think what is right; and with Thee guiding us, do the same in our works. Through our Lord ...

Fifth Sunday after Easter (Vespers)
Sunday Antiphons with Alleluia, and the Psalms of Sunday Vespers of the Psalter
Hymn , page 386

Ad Magnificat Ant. Pétite, et accipiétis, ut gáudium vestrum sit plenum: ipse enim Pater amat vos, quia vos me amástis, et credidístis, allelúja.	*Magnificat Ant.* Ask, and thou shalt receive, that thy joy may be full: for the Father Himself loves thee, because thou loved me and believed, alleluia.

Rogation Monday (Lauds)
Weekday Common Throughout the Year except as below. If a feast day occurs, a commemoration is made with the Weekday Common.

Versiculi V. In resurrectióne tua Christe, allelúja. R. Cæli et terra læténtur, allelúja.	*Versicle* V. In Thy resurrection Christ, alleluia. R. Heaven and earth rejoice, alleluia.

Proper of the Season

Ad Benedíctus Ant. Pétite, et accipiétis: quǽrite, et inveniétis: pulsáte, et aperiétur vobis, allelúja.	***Benedíctus Ant.*** Ask, and thou shalt receive: seek, and thou shalt find: knock, and it shall be opened unto thee, alleluia.
Orátio Præsta, quǽsumus, ompnípotens Deus: ut, qui in afflictióne nostra de tua pietáte confídimus; contra advérsa ómnia, tua semper protectióne muniamur. Per Dóminum nostrum ...	***Prayer*** Grant, we beseech Thee, almighty God, that we who in our affliction trust in Thy mercy; against all adversities, may always be assured of Thy protection. Through our Lord ...

Rogation Monday (Vespers)
Vespers of the Weekday Common with Magnificat Antiphon as below followed by the Prayer of the preceding Sunday.

Ad Magníficat Ant. Ipse enim Pater amat vos, quia vos me amástis, et credidístis, allelúja.	***Magnificat Ant.*** For the Father Himself loves you, because ye loved Me and believed, alleluia.

Rogation Tuesday (Lauds)
Weekday Common Throughout the Year except as below. If a Feast occurs today, the Office is that of the Feast, without a commemoration of the Feria

Ad Benedíctus Ant. Oportébat pati Christum, et resúgere a mórtuis, allelúja.	***Benedíctus Ant.*** It was necessary for Christ to suffer and rise from the dead, alleluia.

Rogation Tuesday (Vespers)
Vespers of the Weekday Common with Magnificat Antiphon as below followed by the Prayer of the preceding Sunday.

Ad Magníficat Ant. Exivi a Patre, et veni in mundum: iterum relinquo mundum, et vado ad Patrem, allelúja.	***Magnificat Ant.*** I came forth from the Father, and came into the world: again I leave the world, and go to the Father, alleluia.

Rogation Wednesday (Lauds)
Weekday Common Throughout the Year except as below. If a feast day occurs, a commemoration is made with the Weekday Common.

Versículi V. In resurrectióne tua Christe, allelúja. R. Cæli et terra læténtur, allelúja.	***Versicle*** V. In Thy resurrection Christ, alleluia. R. Heaven and earth rejoice, alleluia.
Ad Benedíctus Ant. Pater, venit hora, clarífica Fílium tuum claritáte quam hábui, priúsquam mundus esset, apud te, allelúja.	***Benedíctus Ant.*** Father, the hour has come, enlighten Thy Son with the brightness that I had with Thee before the world ever was, alleluia.

Vigil of the Ascension (Vespers I)
Antiphons, Chapter and Hymn of Ascension Day Lauds
Psalms of Sunday Vespers except the fifth. Psalm 116 below is said instead.

¹Laudáte Dóminum, ómnes gentes; laudáte eum, ómnes pópuli. »²Quóniam confirmáta est super nos misericórdia ejus, et véritas Dómini manet in ætérnum.	¹O praise the Lord, all ye nations: praise him, all ye people. »²For His mercy is confirmed upon us: and the truth of the Lord remaineth for ever.

Proper of the Season

Versiculi V. Ascéndit Deus in jubilatióne, allelúja. R. Et Dóminus in voce tubæ, allelúja.	**Versicle** V. God ascends in jubilation, alleluia. R. And the Lord with the sound of the trumpet, alleluia.
Ad Magnificat Ant. Pater, manifestávi nomen tuum homínibus quos dedísti mihi: nunc autem pro eis rogo, non pro mundo, quia ad te vénio, allelúja.	**Magnificat Ant.** Father, I have revealed Thy Name to the people whom Thou hast given Me: but now I pray for them, I pray not for the world, because I come to Thee, alleluia.
Orátio Concéde, quǽsumus omnípotens Deus: ut qui hodierna die Unigénitum tuum Redemptorem nostrum ad cælos ascendisse credimus, ipsi quoque mente in cælestibus habitemus. Per Dóminum nostrum ...	**Prayer** Grant, we beseech Thee, almighty God, that we who believe that Thy Only Begotten Son, our Redeemer, hath ascended to the heavens today, may also have heaven in our thoughts. Through our Lord ...

Ascension Day (Lauds)
Psalms of Sunday Lauds I. Antiphons as below.

Ant 1. Viri Galilǽi, quid aspícitis in cælum? Hic Jesus, qui assúmptus est a vobis in cælum, sic véniet, allelúja.	**Ant 1.** Men of Galilee, why are ye looking up into heaven? This Jesus, who was taken up from you into heaven, will come the same way, alleluia.
Ant 2. Cumque intueréntur in cælum euntem illum, dixérunt: allelúja.	**Ant 2.** And when they watched Him going into heaven, they said: alleluia.
Ant 3. Elevátis mánibus benedíxit eis, et ferebátur in cælum, allelúja.	**Ant 3.** With raised hands He blessed them and was taken up into heaven, alleluia.
Ant 4. Exaltáte Regem regum, et hymnum dícite Deo, allelúja.	**Ant 4.** Exalt the King of kings, and sing a hymn to God, alleluia.
Ant 5. Vidéntibus illis elevátus est, et nubes suscépit eum in cælo, allelúja.	**Ant 5.** They saw Him lifted up, and a cloud received Him into heaven, alleluia.
Capitulum (Acts 1:1-2) V. Primum quidem sermónem feci de ómnibus, o Theóphile, quæ cœpit Iesus fácere et docére usque in diem, qua præcípiens Apóstolis per Spíritum Sanctum, quos elégit, assúmptus est. R. Deo grátias.	**Chapter** (Acts 1:1-2) V. The former treatise I made, O Theophilus, of all things which Jesus began to do and to teach, until the day on which, giving commandments by the Holy Ghost to the apostles whom He had chosen, He was taken up. R. Thanks be to God.

Hymn – Salútis Humanæ, page 378 or Paschále Mundo Gáudium, page 386

Versiculi V. Dóminus in cælo, allelúja. R. Parávit sedem suam, allelúja.	**Versicle** V. The Lord in heaven, alleluia. R. Hath prepared His throne, alleluia.
Ad Benedíctus Ant. Ascéndo ad Patrem meum, et Patrem vestrum: Deum meum, et Deum vestrum, allelúja.	**Benedíctus Ant.** I ascend to My Father and Thy Father: My God and Thy God, alleluia.

Proper of the Season

Orátio Concéde, quæsumus omnípotens Deus: ut qui hodiérna die Unigénitum tuum Redemptórem nostrum ad cælos ascendísse crédimus, ipsi quoque mente in cæléstibus habitémus. Per Dóminum nostrum ...	**Prayer** Grant, we beseech Thee, almighty God, that we who believe that Thy Only Begotten Son, our Redeemer, has ascended to the heavens today, may also have heaven in our thoughts. Through our Lord ...

Vespers of Ascension Day
Antiphons, Chapter and Hymn of Ascension Day Lauds
Psalms of Sunday Vespers except the fifth replaced by Psalm 116 as in
Vigil of the Ascension

Friday after the Ascension up to the Vigil of Pentecost
Feast days are observed; otherwise the Office of the feria is said

Saturday After the Feast of the Ascension (Lauds)
Saturday of the Psalter and Office of the Blessed Virgin Mary

Saturday After the Feast of the Ascenson (Vespers I)
Antiphons, Chapter and Hymn from Lauds of the following Sunday,
Psalms from Sunday Vespers

Versiculi V. Dóminus in cælo, allelúja. **R.** Parávit sedem suam, allelúja.	**Versicle V.** The Lord in heaven, alleluia. **R.** Hath prepared His throne, alleluia.
Ad Magnificat Ant. Cum vénerit Paráclitus Spíritus veritátis, ille aguet mundum de peccáto, et de jústia, et de judícia, allelúja.	**Magnificat Ant.** When the Paraclete of the Spirit of truth comes, He will warn the world about sin, and about justice, and about judgments, alleluia.
Orátio Omnípotens sempitérne Deus, fac nos tibi semper et devótam gérere voluntátem, et majestáti tuæ sincéro corde servíre. Per Dóminum nostrum ...	**Prayer** Almighty and eternal God, make us always and devoutly willing to follow Thee and serve Thy majesty with a sincere heart. Through our Lord ...

Sunday after the Feast of the Asension (Lauds)
Psalms of Sunday Lauds I, Versicle, Hymn and Benedictus from Ascension Day

Ant 1. Viri Galilæi, quid aspícitis in cælum? Hic Jesus, qui assúmptus est a vobis in cælum, sic véniet, allelúja.	**Ant 1.** Men of Galilee, why are ye looking up into heaven? This Jesus, who was taken up from you into heaven, will come the same way, alleluia.
Ant 2. Cumque intueréntur in cælum eúntem illum, dixérunt: allelúja.	**Ant 2.** And when they watched Him going into heaven, they said: alleluia.
Ant 3. Elevátis mánibus benedíxit eis, et ferebátur in cælum, allelúja.	**Ant 3.** With raised hands He blessed them and was taken up into heaven, alleluia.
Ant 4. Exaltáte Regem regum, et hymnum dícite Deo, allelúja.	**Ant 4.** Exalt the King of kings, and sing a hymn to God, alleluia.

Proper of the Season

Ant 5. Vidéntibus illis elevátus est, et nubes suscépit eum in cælo, allelúja.	**Ant 5.** They saw Him lifted up, and a cloud received Him into heaven, alleluia.
Capitulum (1 Pet 4:7-8) Caríssimi: Estóte prudéntes, et vigiláte in oratiónibus. Ante ómnia autem mútuam in vobismetípsis caritátem contínuam habéntes, quia cáritas óperit multitúdinem peccatórum. Deo Gratias.	***Chapter*** (1 Pet 4:7-8) Dearly Beloved: Be prudent, and be watchful in your prayers. But before all things, having mutual charity in yourselves continually, because charity covers a multitude of sins. Thanks be to God.
Orátio Omnípotens sempitérne Deus: fac nos tibi semper et devótam gérere voluntátem; et maiestáti tuæ sincéro corde servíre. Per Dóminum nostrum ...	***Prayer*** Almighty and eternal God, make us always and devoutly willing to follow Thee, and serve Thy majesty with a sincere heart. Through our Lord ...

Sunday After the Feast of the Ascension (Vespers II)
Psalms of Sunday Vespers except the fifth. Psalm 116 below is said instead and the following Versicle and Magnificat

¹Laudáte Dóminum, ómnes gentes; laudáte eum, ómnes pópuli. »²Quóniam confirmáta est super nos misericórdia ejus, et véritas Dómini manet in ætérnum.	¹O praise the Lord, all ye nations: praise Him, all ye people. »²For His mercy is confirmed upon us: and the truth of the Lord remaineth for ever.
Versiculi **V.** Dóminus in cælo, allelúja. **R.** Parávit sedem suam, allelúja.	***Versicle*** **V.** The Lord in heaven, alleluia. **R.** Hath prepared His throne, alleluia.
Ad Magnificat Ant. Hæc locútus sum vobis, ut cum vénerit hora eórum, reminiscámini quia ego dixi vobis, allelúja.	***Magnificat Ant.*** I have spoken these things to you, so that when their hour comes, ye may remember that I said it to you, alleluia.

Monday through Saturday after Ascension
Weekday Common Throughout the year except for feast days as they occur

Vigil of Pentecost (Vespers I)
Sunday Vespers and its Psalms except the fifth.
Psalm 116 below is said instead

Ant 1. Cum compleréntur dies Pentecóstes, erant ómnes páriter in eódem loco, allelúja.	**Ant 1.** When the days of Pentecost were completed, they were all together in the same place, alleluia.
Ant 2. Spíritus Dómini replévit orbem terrárum, allelúja.	**Ant 2.** The Spirit of the Lord filled the world, alleluia.
Ant 3. Repléti sunt ómnes Spíritu Sancto, et coepérunt loqui, allelúja, allelúja.	**Ant 3.** They were all filled with the Holy Spirit and began to speak, alleluia, alleluia.

Proper of the Season

Ant 4. Fontes, et ómnia quæ movéntur in aquis, hymnum dícite Deo, allelúja.	**Ant 4.** Ye fountains, and all that move in the waters, sing a hymn to God, alleluia.
Ant 5. Loquebántur váriis línguis Apóstoli magnália Dei, allelúja, allelúja, allelúja.	**Ant 5.** The apostles spoke in various languages the great things of God, alleluia, alleluia, alleluia.
¹Laudáte Dóminum, ómnes gentes; laudáte eum, ómnes pópuli. »²Quóniam confirmáta est super nos misericórdia ejus, et véritas Dómini manet in ætérnum.	¹O praise the Lord, all ye nations: praise him, all ye people. »²For His mercy is confirmed upon us: and the truth of the Lord remaineth for ever.
Capitulum (Acts 2:1-2) **V.** Cum compleréntur dies Pentecóstes, erant omnes discípuli páriter in eódem loco: et factus est repénte de cælo sonus, tamquam adveniéntis spíritus veheméntis, et replévit totam domum, ubi erant sedéntes. **R.** Deo grátias.	***Chapter*** (Acts 2:1-2) **V.** When the days of Pentecost were completed, all the disciples were together in one place: and suddenly there was a sound from heaven, as of the coming of a mighty wind, and it filled the whole house where they were sitting. **R.** Thanks be to God.
Hymn – *Veni, Creátor Spíritus, page 381*	
***Versiculi* V.** Repléti sunt ómnes Spíritu Sancto, allelúja. **R.** Et coepérunt loqui, allelúja.	***Versicle* V.** All were filled with the Holy Spirit, alleluia. **R.** And they began to speak, alleluia.
Ad Magníficat Ant. Non vos relínquam órphanos, alleluja: vado et vénio ad vos, alleluja: et gaudébit cor vestrum, alleluja.	***Magníficat Ant.*** I will not leave you orphans, alleluia: I go and come to you, alleluia: and your heart will rejoice, alleluia.

Pentecost

Whit Sunday (Lauds)
Psalms from Sunday Lauds I
Antiphons from the Vigil of Pentecost with Chapter, Hymn, Antiphon and Prayer below.

Capitulum (Acts 2:1-2) **V.** Cum compleréntur dies Pentecóstes, erant omnes discípuli páriter in eódem loco: et factus est repénte de cælo sonus, tamquam adveniéntis spíritus veheméntis, et replévit totam domum, ubi erant sedéntes. **R.** Deo grátias.	***Chapter*** (Acts 2:1-2) **V.** When the days of Pentecost were completed, all the disciples were together in the one place: and suddenly there was a sound from heaven, as of the coming of a mighty wind, and it filled the whole house where they were sitting. **R.** Thanks be to God.
Hymn – *Beáta Nobis Gáudia, page 374*	
***Versiculi* V.** Repléti sunt ómnes Spíritu Sancto, allelúja. **R.** Et coeperunt loqui, allelúja.	***Versicle* V.** All were filled with the Holy Spirit, alleluia. **R.** And they began to speak, alleluia.
Ad Benedíctus Ant. Accípite Spíritum Sanctum: quorum remiséritis peccáta, remittúntur eis, allelúja.	***Benedíctus Ant.*** Receive the Holy Spirit, whose sins ye forgive, they are forgiven, alleluia.

Proper of the Season

Orátio Deus, qui hodierna die corda fidelium Sancti Spíritus illustratione docuisti: da nobis in eodem Spíritu recta sapere, et de ejus semper consolatione gaudere. Per Dóminum nostrum ...	*Prayer* O God, who has taught the hearts of the faithful today by the enlightenment of the Holy Spirit: give us right wisdom in the same Spirit, and always rejoice in His consolation. Through our Lord ...

Whit Sunday (Vespers)
The Feast of Pentecost
All of the Vespers of the Vigil of Pentecost except the Antiphon for the Magnificat below and Prayer from Pentecost Lauds.

Ad Magnificat Ant. Hódie compléti sunt dies Pentecóstes, allelúja: hódie Spíritus Sanctus in igne discípulis appáruit, et tríbuit eis charísmatum dona: misit eos in univérsum mundum prædicáre, et testificári: Qui credíderit et baptizátus fúerit, salvus erit, allelúja.	*Magnificat Ant.* Today the days of Pentecost are completed, alleluia: today the Holy Spirit appeared in fire to the disciples and gave them the gift of charisms: He sent them to the whole world to preach and to testify: He who believes and is baptized will be saved, alleluia.

Whit Monday (Lauds)
Pentecost Lauds with the Antiphon and Prayer below
No commemorations of Feasts are permitted.

Ad Benedíctus Ant. Sic Deus diléxit mundum, ut Fílium suum unigénitum daret: ut omnis, qui credit in ipsum, non péreat, sed hábeat vitam ætérnam, allelúja.	*Benedictus Ant.* God so loved the world that He gave His only begotten Son: that whosoever believeth in Him should not perish, but have eternal life, alleluia.
Orátio Deus, qui Apóstolis tuis Sanctum dedísti Spíritum: concéde plebi tuæ piæ petitiónis efféctum; ut, quibus dedísti fidem, largiáris et pacem. Per Dóminum nostrum ...	*Prayer* O God, who gave the Holy Spirit to Thine apostles: grant the people the effect of their sacred supplication; that to whom Thou hast given faith, Thou mayest give peace and grace. Through our Lord ...

Whit Monday (Vespers)
Pentecost Vespers I with the Antiphon of the Magnificat below
and the Prayer from Lauds above
No Commemorations of Feasts are permitted.

Ad Magnificat Ant. Si quis díligit me sermónem meum servábit: et Pater meus díliget eum, et ad eum veniémus, et mansiónem apud eum faciémus, allelúja.	*Magnificat Ant.* If anyone loveth Me, he will keep My commandments: and My Father will love him, and We will come to him and make Our abode with him, alleluia.

Whit Tuesday (Lauds)
Pentecost Lauds with the Antiphon and Prayer below
No commemorations of Feasts are permitted.

Ad Benedíctus Ant. Ego sum óstium, dicit Dóminus: per me si quis	*Benedictus Ant.* I am the door, sayeth the Lord: if anyone entereth

Proper of the Season

introíerit, salvábitur, et páscua invéniet, allelúia.	through Me, he will be saved and find the Passover, alleluia.
Orátio Adsit nobis, quǽsumus, Dómine, virtus Spíritus Sancti: quæ et corda nostra cleménter expúrget, et ab ómnibus tueátur advérsis. Per Dóminum nostrum ...	***Prayer*** May the power of the Holy Spirit be present to us, O Lord, which will mercifully cleanse our hearts and protect us from all adversaries. Through our Lord . .

Whit Tuesday (Vespers)
Pentecost Vespers I with the Antiphon of the Magnificat below
and the Prayer from Lauds above
No Commemorations of Feasts are permitted.

Ad Magnificat Ant. Pacem relínquo vobis, pacem meam do vobis: non quómodo mundus dat, ego do vobis, allelúia.	***Magnificat Ant.*** Peace I leave with you, I give you my peace: not as the world gives, I give to you, alleluia.

Ember Wednesday after Pentecost (Lauds)
Pentecost Lauds with the Antiphon of the Benedíctus and Prayer below
No commemorations of Feasts are permitted.

Ad Benedíctus Ant Ego sum panis vivus, dicit Dóminus, qui de cælo descéndi, alleluja, alleluja.	***Benedíctus Ant.*** I am the Living Bread, sayeth the Lord, Who came down from heaven, alleluia, alleluia.
Orátio Mentes nostras, quǽsumus, Dómine, Paráclitus, qui a te procédit, illúminet: et indúcat in omnem, sicut tuus promísit Fílius, veritátem. Per Dóminum nostrum ...	***Prayer*** We beseech Thee, O Lord, that the Paraclete, Who proceeds from Thee, may enlighten our minds, and bring all to the truth, as Thy Son hath promised. Through our Lord ...

Ember Wednesday after Pentecost (Vespers)
Pentecost Vespers I with the Antiphon of the Magnificat below
and the Prayer from Lauds above
No commemorations of Feasts are permitted.

Ad Magnificat Ant. Ego sum panis vivus, dicit Dóminus, qui de cælo descéndi: si quis manducáverit ex hoc pane, vivet in ætérnum: et panis, quem ego dabo, caro mea est pro mundi vita, alleluja.	***Magnificat Ant.*** I am the Living Bread, which came down from heaven: if any man eat of this Bread, he shall live for ever: and the Bread which I will give is My Flesh for the life of the world, alleluia.

Whit Thursday (Lauds)
Pentecost Lauds with the Antiphon and Prayer below
No commemorations of Feasts are permitted.

Ad Benedíctus Ant Convocátis Iesus duódecim discípulis suis, dedit illis virtútem et potestátem super ómnia dæmónia, et ut languóres curárent: et misit illos prædicáre regnum Dei, et sanáre infirmos, allelúja.	***Benedíctus Ant.*** When Jesus called His twelve disciples, He gave them power and authority over all demons and to cure the sick: and He sent them to preach the kingdom of God and to heal the sick, alleluia.
Orátio Deus, qui hodiérna die corda fidélium Sancti Spíritus illustratióne docuísti: da nobis in eódem Spíritu recta sápere; et de eius semper	***Prayer*** O God, who today taught the hearts of the faithful by the illumination of the Holy Spirit: grant us to be wise in the same Spirit. Through our Lord ...

Proper of the Season

consolatióne gaudére. Per Dóminum nostrum ...	

Whit Thursday (Vespers)
Pentecost Vespers I except the Antiphon of the Magnificat
and the prayer from Lauds above
No Commemorations of Feasts are permitted.

Ad Magnificat Ant. Spíritus, qui a Patre procédit, allelúia: ille me clarificábit, allelúia, allelúia.	*Magnificat Ant.* The Spirit Who proceeds from the Father, alleluia: He will enlighten me, alleluia, alleluia.

Ember Friday after Pentecost (Lauds)
Pentecost Lauds except the Antiphon of the Benedíctus and following Prayer
No commemorations of Feasts are permitted.

Ad Benedíctus Ant. Dixit Iesus: Ut sciátis autem quia Fílius hóminis habet potestátem in terra dimitténdi peccáta, ait paralýtico: Tibi dico, surge: tolle lectum tuum, et vade in domum tuam, alleluja.	*Benedíctus Ant.* Jesus said: But that ye may know that the Son of Man hath power on earth to forgive sins, He said to the paralytic: I say to thee, get up: take up thy bed and go to thy home, alleluia.
Orátio Da, quǽsumus, Ecclésiæ tuæ, miséricors Deus: ut, Sancto Spíritu congregáta, hostíli nullátenus incursióne turbétur. Per Dóminum nostrum ...	*Prayer* Grant, we beseech Thee, merciful God, that Thy Church, gathered together in the Holy Spirit, may never be disturbed by the assault of the enemy. Through our Lord ...

Ember Friday after Pentecost (Vespers)
Pentecost Vespers I except the Antiphon of the Magnificat
and the Prayer from Lauds above
No Commemorations of Feasts are permitted.

Ad Magnificat Ant. Paráclitus autem Spíritus Sanctus, quem mittet Pater in nómine meo, ille vos docébit ómnia, et súggeret vobis ómnia, quæcúmque díxero vobis, alleluja.	*Magnificat Ant.* And the Holy Spirit, the Paraclete, whom the Father will send in My Name, will teach you all things and will bring to your memory all things that I have said to you, alleluia.

Ember Saturday after Pentecost (Lauds)
Pentecost Lauds except the Antiphon of the Benedíctus and following Prayer
No Commemorations of Feasts are permitted.

Ad Benedíctus **Ant.** Cáritas Dei diffúsa est in córdibus nostris, per inhabitántem Spíritum eius in nobis, alleluja.	*Benedíctus Ant.* The love of God hath filled our hearts through His Spirit dwelling in us, alleluia.
Orátio Méntibus nostris, quǽsumus, Dómine, Spíritum Sanctum benígnus infúnde: cuius et sapiéntia cónditi sumus, et providéntia gubernámur. Per Dóminum nostrum ...	*Prayer* Into our minds, we beseech Thee, O Lord, infuse the gracious Holy Spirit: by Whose wisdom we are created, and by Whose providence we are guided. Through our Lord ...

Feast of the Most Holy Trinity (Vespers I)
Sunday Vespers except the Antiphon of the Magnificat, the following Prayer
and Psalms except the last which is replaced by Psalm 116 below

[1]Laudáte Dóminum, ómnes gentes; laudáte eum, ómnes pópuli.	[1]O praise the Lord, all ye nations: praise Him, all ye people.

Proper of the Season

℣².Quóniam confirmáta est super nos misericórdia ejus, et véritas Dómini manet in ætérnum.	℣².For His mercy is confirmed upon us: and the truth of the Lord remaineth for ever.
Ad Magnificat Ant. Grátias tibi Deus grátias tibi vera et una Trínitas, una et summa Déitas, sancta et una Unitas.	**Magnificat Ant.** Thanks to Thee, O God, thanks to Thee true and one Trinity, one and supreme Deity, holy and one Unity.
Orátio Omnípotens sempitérne Deus, qui dedísti fámulis tuis in confessióne veræ fídei, ætérnæ Trinitátis glóriam agnóscere, et in poténtia maiestátis adoráre Unitátem: quǽsumus; ut, eiúsdem fídei firmitáte, ab ómnibus semper muniámur advérsis. Per Dóminum nostrum ...	**Prayer** Almighty and everlasting God, who hast given Thy servants to acknowledge the glory of the eternal Trinity in the profession of the true faith, and to adore the Unity in the power of its majesty: we ask; that by the steadfastness of the same faith we may always be fortified against all adversaries. Through our Lord ...

Feast of the Most Holy Trinity (Lauds)
Sunday Lauds I except Chapter, Hymn, the Antiphons of the Psalms, the Antiphon of the Benedíctus, and the following Prayer

Ant 1. Glória tibi Trínitas æqualis, una Déitas, et ante ómnia sǽcula, et nunc et in perpétuum.	**Ant 1.** Glory be to Thee, equal Trinity, one God, before all ages, and now and forever.
Ant 2. Laus et perénnis glória Deo Patri, et Filio, Sancto simul Paráclito, in sæculórum sǽcula.	**Ant 2.** Praise and everlasting glory to God the Father, and to the Son, the Holy One and the Paraclete, forever and ever.
Ant 3. Glória laudis résonet in ore ómnium, Patri, genitǽque Proli, Spíritui Sancto páriter resúltet laude perénni.	**Ant 3.** Glory and praise will resound in the mouths of all, the Father, the begotten Son, and the Holy Spirit alike will receive everlasting praise.
Ant 4. Laus Deo Patri, parilíque Proli, et tibi Sancte stúdio perénni Spíritus, nostro résonet ab ore, omne per ævum.	**Ant 4.** Praise to God the Father, and to the Son, and with the Holy Spirit's eternal devotion, will resound from our lips, all through the ages.
Ant 5. Ex quo ómnia, per quem ómnia, in quo ómnia: ipsi glória in sǽcula.	**Ant 5.** From Whom are all things, through Whom are all things, in Whom are all things: to Him be glory for ever.
Capitulum (Rom 11:33) ℣. O Altitúdo divitiárum sapiéntiæ, et sciéntiæ Dei, quam incomprehensibília sunt iudícia eius, et investigábiles viæ eius! ℟. Deo grátias.	**Chapter** (Rom 11:33) ℣. O the depth of the riches of the wisdom and of the knowledge of God! How incomprehensible are His judgments, and how unsearchable His ways! ℟. Thanks be to God.

Hymn – Tu, Trinitatis Unitas, page 381

Proper of the Season

Ad Benedíctus Ant. Benedícta sit sancta creátrix et gubernátrix ómnium, sancta et indivídua Trínitas, nunc, et semper, et per infiníta sǽcula sæculórum.	*Benedictus Ant.* Blessed be the holy Creator and Ruler of all, the holy and undivided Trinity, now and ever, and through the infinite ages of ages.
Orátio Omnípotens sempitérne Deus, qui dedísti fámulis tuis in confessióne veræ fídei, ætérnæ Trinitátis glóriam agnóscere, et in poténtia maiestátis adoráre Unitátem: quǽsumus; ut, eiúsdem fídei firmitáte, ab ómnibus semper muniámur advérsis. Per Dóminum nostrum ...	*Prayer* Almighty and everlasting God, Who hath given Thy servants to profess the glory of the eternal Trinity in the acclamation of the true faith, and to adore the Unity in the power of majesty: we ask; that by the strength of the same faith we may always be fortified against all adversities. Through our Lord ...

Feast of the Most Holy Trinity (Vespers II)
Sunday Vespers except the Chapter which is taken from Rom 11:33 Lauds above, the Hymn, the Antiphon of the Magnificat, and the following Prayer.

Hymn – Jam Sol Recédit, page 173

Versiculi V. Benedíctus es, Dómine, in firmaménto cæli. R. Et laudábilis et gloriósus in sǽcula.	*Versicle* V. Blessed art Thou, O Lord, in the firmament of heaven. R. And praiseworthy and glorious forever.
Ad Magnificat Ant. Te Deum Patrem ingénitum, te Fílium unigénitum, te Spíritum Sanctum Paráclitum, sanctam et indivíduam Trinitátem, toto corde et ore confitémur, laudámus, atque benedícimus: tibi glória in sǽcula.	*Magnificat Ant.* We confess, praise, and bless Thee, God the Father, the only begotten Son, the Holy Spirit the Paraclete, the holy and individual Trinity, with all our heart and voices: to Thee be glory for ever.
Orátio Omnípotens sempitérne Deus, qui dedísti fámulis tuis in confessióne veræ fídei, ætérnæ Trinitátis glóriam agnóscere, et in poténtia maiestátis adoráre Unitátem: quǽsumus; ut, eiúsdem fídei firmitáte, ab ómnibus semper muniámur advérsis. Per Dóminum nostrum ...	*Prayer* Almighty and everlasting God, who hath given Thy servants to profess the glory of the eternal Trinity in the acclamation of the true faith, and to adore the Unity in the power of majesty: we ask; that by the strength of the same faith we may always be fortified against all adversaries. Through our Lord ...

Feast of Corpus Christi (Vespers I)
Psalms of Sunday Vespers I. The Prayer is from the preceding Sunday

Ant 1. Sacérdos in ætérnum Chrístus Dóminus secúndum órdinem Melchísedech panem et vinum óbtulit.	**Ant 1.** Christ the Lord, Priest for ever according to the order of Melchizedek, offered bread and wine.
Ant 2. Miserátor Dóminus escam dedit timéntibus se in memóriam suórum mirabílium.	**Ant 2.** The merciful Lord gave food to those who fear Him as a memorial of His miracles.
Ant 3. Cálicem salutáris accípiam, et sacrificábo hóstiam laudis.	**Ant 3.** I will take the cup of salvation, and I will offer the sacrifice of praise.

Ant 4. Sicut novéllæ olivárum, Ecclésiæ fílii sint in circúitu mensæ Dómini.	**Ant 4.** Like young olive trees, let the children of the Church surround the Lord's table.
Ant 5. Qui pacem ponit fines Ecclésiæ, fruménti ádipe sátiat nos Dóminus.	**Ant 5.** The Lord creates peace within the boundaries of the Church and satisfies us with the fat of wheat.
Capitulum (1 Cor 11:23-24) V. Fratres: Ego enim accépi a Dómino quod et trádidi vobis, quóniam Dóminus Iesus, in qua nocte tradebátur, accépit panem, et grátias agens fregit, et dixit: Accípite et manducáte: hoc est corpus meum, quod pro vobis tradétur: hoc fácite in meam commemoratiónem. R. Deo grátias.	*Chapter* (1 Cor 11:23-24) V. For I have received of the Lord that which also I delivered unto thee, that the Lord Jesus, the same night in which He was betrayed, took bread, and giving thanks, broke, and said: Take ye, and eat: this is My Body, which shall be delivered for you: this do for the commemoration of Me. R. Thanks be to God.
	*Hymn – Ave Verum Corpus Natum, page 374*
Versiculi V. Panem de cælo præstitisti eis, allelúja. R. Omne delectaméntum in se habéntem, allelúja.	*Versicle* V. Thou provided them with bread from heaven, alleluia. R. Having all that is delicious in it, alleluia.
Ad Magnificat Ant. O quam suávis est Dómine spíritus tuus, qui ut dulcédinem tuam in fílios demonstráres, pane suávissimo de cælo præstito, esuriéntes reples bonis, fastidiósos dívites dimíttens ínanes.	*Magnificat Ant.* Oh, how sweet is Thy spirit, Lord, who showeth Thy tenderness to Thy children, with the sweetest bread provided from heaven, filling the hungry with good things, leaving the distainful rich empty.
	*Feast of Corpus Christi (Lauds)* The Psalms are from Sunday Lauds I and the Chapter, Hymn, Versicle, Benedictus and Prayer below,
Ant 1. Sapiéntia ædificávit sibi domum, míscuit vinum et pósuit mensam, alleluja.	**Ant 1.** Wisdom built herself a house, mixed the wine and set the table, alleluia.
Ant 2. Angelórum esca nutrivísti pópulum tuum, et panem de cælo præstitísti eis, alleluja.	**Ant 2.** Thou nourished Thy people with the food of angels, and Thou provided them with bread from heaven, alleluia
Ant 3. Pinguis est panis Christi, et præbébit delícias régibus, alleluja.	**Ant 3.** Christ's bread is nourishing, and will provide delicacies for kings, alleluia.
Ant 4. Sacerdótes sancti incénsum et panes ófferunt Deo, alleluja.	**Ant 4.** The holy priests offer incense and bread to God. Alleluia.
Ant 5. Vincénti dabo manna abscónditum, et nomen novum, alleluja.	**Ant 5.** To the victorious I will give a hidden manna and a new name, alleluia.

Proper of the Season

Capitulum (1 Cor 11:23-24) V. Fratres: Ego enim accépi a Dómino quod et trádidi vobis, quóniam Dóminus Iesus, in qua nocte tradebátur, accépit panem, et grátias agens fregit, et dixit: Accípite et manducáte: hoc est corpus meum, quod pro vobis tradétur: hoc fácite in meam commemoratiónem. R. Deo grátias.	*Chapter* (1 Cor 11:23-24) V. For I have received of the Lord that which also I delivered unto thee, that the Lord Jesus, the same night in which He was betrayed, took bread, and giving thanks, broke, and said: Take ye, and eat: this is My Body, which shall be delivered for you: this do for the commemoration of Me. R. Thanks be to God.

Hymn – Verbum Supernum Prodiens, pg. 383 or Ave Verum Corpus, pg. 374

Versiculi V. Pósuit fines tuos pacem, allelúja. R. Et ádipe fruménti sátiat te, allelúja.	*Versicle* V. He has made peace on thy borders, alleluia. R. And let the fat of wheat satisfy you, alleluia.
Ad Benedíctus Ant. Ego sum panis vivus, qui de cælo descéndi: si quis manducáverit ex hoc pane, vivet in ætérnum, allelúja.	*Benedíctus Ant.* I am the Living Bread, which came down from heaven: if any man eat of this Bread, he shall live for ever, alleluia.
Orátio Deus, qui nobis sub Sacraménto mirábili passiónis tuæ memóriam reliquísti: tríbue, quǽsumus, ita nos Córporis, et Sánguinis tui sacra mystéria venerári; ut redemptiónis tuæ fructum in nobis iúgiter sentiámus. Qui vivis et regnas …	*Prayer* O God, who left us the memorial of Thy passion under this wonderful Sacrament: grant, we beseech Thee, that we may thus venerate the sacred mysteries of Thy Body and Blood. Who liveth and reigneth…

Feast of Corpus Christi (Vespers II)
All as in Verspers I except the Antiphon for the Magnificat below

Ad Magnificat Ant. O sacrum convívium, in quo Christus súmitur: recólitur memória passiónis eius: mens implétur grátia: et futúræ glóriæ nobis pignus datur, allelúja.	*Magnificat Ant.* O sacred banquet, in which Christ is recieved; the memory of His Passion is recalled: the mind is filled with grace: and a pledge of future glory is given to us, alleluia.

Ferias throughout the year
That is Monday through Friday when there is no feast day
according to the day of the week
On Saturdays the Office of the Blessed Virgin Mary is prayed unless there is a feast day.

Second Sunday after Pentecost (Vespers I)
All as on Corpus Christi except the Chapter and Prayer from Lauds Second Sunday

Second Sunday after Pentecost (Lauds)
All as on Corpus Christi except the Chapter, Versicle, Benedíctus and Prayer below

Capitulum (1 John 3:13-14) V. Carissimi: Nolíte misári, si odit vos mundus. Nos scimus quóniam	*Chapter* (1 John 3:13-14) V. Beloved: Do not be sorry if the world hates you. We know that we

Proper of the Season

transláti sumus de morte ad vitam, quóniam dilígimus fratres.	have passed from death to life, because we love the brethren.
Versiculi V. Panem cæli dedit eis, allelúja. R. Panem Angelórum manducávit homo, allelúja.	***Versicle*** V. He gave them the bread of heaven, alleluia. R. Man has eaten the bread of the angels, alleluia.
Ad Benedíctus Ant. Homo quidam fecit cenam magnam, et vocávit multos: et misit servum suum hora cenæ dícere invitátis ut venírent, quia ómnia paráta sunt, allelúja.	***Benedíctus Ant.*** A certain man made a great dinner and called many: and he sent his servant to tell the guests to come at the hour of the meal, because everything was ready, alleluia.
Orátio Sancti nóminis tui, Dómine, timórem páriter et amórem fac nos habére perpétuum: quia nunquam tua gubernatióne destítuis, quos in soliditáte tuæ dilectiónis instítuis. Per Dóminum nostrum ...	***Prayer*** O Lord, make us always to have both fear and love of Thy holy Name: because Thou never failest in Thy governing those whom Thou hast invited into Thine abiding grace. Through our Lord ...

Second Sunday after Pentecost (Vespers II)
All as on Corpus Christi except the Chapter, Versicle and Magnificat below.

Capitulum (1 John 3:13-14) V. Caríssimi: Nolíte misári, si odit vos mundus. Nos scimus quóniam transláti sumus de morte ad vitam, quóniam dilígimus fratres.	***Chapter*** (1 John 3:13-14) V. Beloved: Do not be sorry if the world hates you. We know that we have passed from death to life, because we love the brethren.
Versiculi V. Cibávit illos ex ádipe fruménti, allelúja. R. Et de petra, melle sturávit eos, allelúja.	***Versicle*** V. He fed them from the fat of wheat, alleluia. R. And from the rock, He filled them with honey, alleluia.
Ad Magníficat Ant. Exi cito in pláteas et vicos civitátis: et páuperes ac débiles, cæcos et claudos compélle intráre, ut impleátur domus mea, allelúja.	***Magníficat Ant.*** Quickly, go out into the streets and alleys of the city: and compel the poor and the weak, the blind and the lame to enter, that my house may be filled, alleluia.

Feast of the Most Sacred Heard of Jesus (Vespers I)
Sunday Vespers and Antiphons below

Ant 1. Unus mílitum láncea latus ejus apéruit et contínuo exívit sanguis et aqua.	**Ant 1.** One of the soldiers opened His side with a spear, and blood and water flowed out.
Ant 2. Suávi jugo tuo domináre, Dómine, in médio inimicórum tuórum.	**Ant 2.** I am pleased with Thy yoke, O Lord, as Thou rulest in the midst of Thine enemies.
Ant 3. Miséricors et miserrátor Dóminus: escan dedit timéntibus se.	**Ant 3.** The Lord is merciful and full of pity for us: He gave food to those who fear Him.

Proper of the Season

Ant 4. Exórtum est in ténebris lumen rectis; miséricors et miserátor Dóminus.	**Ant 4.** The light of the righteous hath arisen in the darkness; merciful and compassionate Lord.
Ant 5. Quid retríbuam Dómino pro ómnibus quæ retríbuit mihi?	**Ant 5.** How shall I repay the Lord for all that He hath given me?

Feast of the Most Sacred Heard of Jesus (Lauds)
Sunday Psalms from Lauds I and the following.

Ant 1. Unus mílitum láncea latus eius apéruit et contínuo exívit sanguis et aqua.	**Ant 1.** One of the soldiers opened His side with a spear, and blood and water flowed out.
Ant 2. Stans Iesus clamábat dicens: Si quis sitit, véniat ad me et bibat.	**Ant 2.** Jesus stood and cried out, saying: If anyone is thirsty, let him come to Me and drink.
Ant 3. In caritáte perpétua diléxit nos Deus, ideo, exaltátus a terra, attráxit nos ad Cor suum, míserans.	**Ant 3.** God loved us with perpetual love, therefore, being raised from the earth, He drew us to His Heart, having compassion.
Ant 4. Veníte ad me ómnes qui laborátis et oneráti estis et ego refíciam vos.	**Ant 4.** Come to Me, all ye who labor and are heavy laden, and I will refresh you.
Ant 5. Fili, præbe mihi cor tuum et óculi tui custódiant vias meas.	**Ant 5.** Son, give me thy heart and let thine eyes follow My ways.
Capitulum (Eph 3:8-9) **V.** Fratres: Mihi ómnium sanctórum mínimo data est grátia hæc, in géntibus evangelizáre investigábiles divítias Christi; et illumináre ómnes, quæ sit dispensátio sacraménti abscónditi a sǽculis in Deo. **R.** Deo grátias.	*Chapter* (Eph 3:8-9) **V.** Brethren: This grace was given to me least of all the saints, to evangelize among the nations the profound riches of Christ; and to enlighten all, which is the dispensation of the sacrament hidden from the ages in God. **R.** Thanks be to God.
Hymn – Cor Arca Legem, page 375	
Versiculi **V.** Hauriétis aquas in gáudio. **R.** De fóntibus Salvatóris.	*Versicle* **V.** Thou shalt draw waters in joy. **R.** From the fountains of the Savior.
Ad Benedíctus Ant. Facta sunt enim hæc ut Scriptúra impleréntur quæ dicit: Vidébunt in quem transfixérunt.	*Benedíctus Ant.* For these things were done in order that the Scripture might be fulfilled, which sayeth: They shall see Him whom they have pierced.
Orátio Deus, qui nobis in Corde Fílii tui, nostris vulneráto peccátis, infinítos dilectiónis thesáuros misericórditer largíri dignáris; concéde, quǽsumus, ut illi devótum pietátis nostræ præstántes obséquium, dignæ quoque satisfactiónis exhibeámus offícium. Per Dóminum nostrum ...	*Prayer* O God, Who was wounded by our sins, mercifully deigned to bestow on us infinite treasures of love in the Heart of Thy Son; grant, we ask Thee that through our devout piety, we may present to Him a service worthy of reparation. Through our Lord ...

Proper of the Season

Feast of the Most Sacred Heard of Jesus (Vespers II)
Psalms from Sunday Vespers. Antiphons from Lauds above.

Capitulum (Eph 3:8-9) **V.** Fratres: Mihi ómnium sanctórum mínimo data est grátia hæc, in géntibus evangelizáre investigábiles divítias Christi; et illumináre ómnes, quæ sit dispensátio sacraménti abscónditi a sǽculis in Deo. **R.** Deo grátias.	*Chapter* (Eph 3:8-9) **V.** Brethren: This grace was given to me least of all the saints, to evangelize among the nations the profound riches of Christ; and to enlighten all, which is the dispensation of the sacrament hidden from the ages in God. **R.** Thanks be to God.

Hymn – *En Ut Superba*, page 377

Ad Magníficat Ant. Ad Iesum autem cum veníssent, ut vidérunt eum iam mórtuum, non fregérunt eius crura, sed unus mílitum láncea latus eius apéruit et contínuo exívit sanguis et aqua.	*Magnificat Ant.* But when they came to Jesus and saw that He was already dead, they did not break His legs, but one of the soldiers opened His side with a lance, and immediately blood and water came out.
Orátio Deus, qui nobis in Corde Fílii tui, nostris vulneráto peccátis, infinítos dilectiónis thesáuros misericórditer largíri dignáris; concéde, quǽsumus, ut illi devótum pietátis nostræ præstántes obséquium, dignæ quoque satisfactiónis exhibeámus officium. Per Dóminum nostrum ...	*Prayer* O God, who mercifully deigned to bestow on us, in the Heart of Thy Son, wounded by our sins, infinite treasures of love; grant, we beseech Thee, that we may present to Him, by our devout piety, a service worthy of reparation. Through our Lord ...

Third Sunday after Pentecost (Vespers I)
Sunday Vespers and Antiphons from Vespers I of the Feast of the Sacred Heart
Chapter, Versicle, Magnificat and Prayer below.

Capitulum (1 Pet 5:6-7) **V.** Caríssimi: Humiliámini sub poténti manu dei, ut nos exáltet in témpore visitatiónis; omnem sollicitúdinem vestram projiciéntes in eum, quóniam ipsi cura est de vobis. **R.** Deo Grátias	*Chapter* (1 Pet 5:6-7) **V.** Beloved: Humble yourselves under the mighty hand of God, that He may exalt us in the season of visitation; casting all your anxiety upon Him, since He Himself is concerned about you. **R.** Thanks be to God.

Hymn – *En Ut Superba*, page 377

Versículi **V.** Vespertína orátio ascéndat ad te Dómine. **R.** Et descéndat super nos misericórdia tua.	*Versicle* **V.** Let the evening prayer go up to Thee, Lord. **R.** And let Thy mercy descend upon us.
Ad Magníficat Ant. Cognovérunt ómnes a Dan usque Bersabée, quod fidélis Sámuel Prophéta esset Dómini.	*Magnificat Ant.* Everyone from Dan to Beersheba knew that Samuel was a faithful prophet of the Lord.
Orátio Protéctor in te sperántium, Deus, sine quo nihil est válidum, nihil sanctum; multíplica super nos misericórdiam tuam; ut, te rectóre, te duce, sic transeámus per bona temporália, ut non amittámus ætérna.	*Prayer* O God, protector of those who hope in Thee, without whom there is nothing strong, nothing holy: increase Thy mercy upon us; that we may pass through temporal things,

Proper of the Season

Per Dóminum nostrum ...	and that we may not lose eternal ones. Through our Lord ...

Third Sunday after Pentecost (Lauds)
Psalms from Sunday Lauds I and Antiphons below.

Ant 1. Allelúja, Dóminus regnávit, decórem índuit, allelúja, allelúja.	**Ant 1.** Alleluia, the Lord hath reigned, clothed in beauty, alleluia, alleluia.
Ant 2. Jubiláte Deo omnis terra, allelúja.	**Ant 2.** Let all the earth rejoice in God, alleluia.
Ant 3. Benedícam te in vita mea Dómine: et in nómine tuo levábo manus meas, allelúja.	**Ant 3.** I will bless Thee in my life, Lord: and in Thy Name I will lift up my hands, alleluia.
Ant 4. Tres púeri iussu régis in fornácem missi sunt, non timéntes flammam ignis, dicéntes: Benedíctus Deus, allelúja.	**Ant 4.** Three boys were sent into the furnace by the king's command, not fearing the flame of the fire, saying: Blessed be God, alleluia.
Ant 5. Allelúja laudáte Dóminum de cælis, allelúja, allelúja.	**Ant 5.** Alleluia, praise the Lord from heaven, alleluia, alleluia.
Capitulum (1 Pet 5:6-7) V. Caríssimi: Humiliámini sub poténti manu dei, ut nos exáltet in témpore visitatiónis; omnem sollicitúdinem vestram projiciéntes in eum, quóniam ipsi cura est de vobis. R. Deo Grátias	*Chapter* (1 Pet 5:6-7) **V.** Beloved: Humble yourselves under the mighty hand of God, that He may exalt us in the season of visitation; casting all your anxiety upon Him, since He Himself is concerned about you. **R.** Thanks be to God.

Hymn – Cor Arca Legem, page 375

Versiculi **V.** Dóminus regnávit, **R.** decórem indútus est: allelúja.	*Versicle* **V.** The Lord hath reigned, **R.** He is clothed with beauty, alleluia.
Ad Benedíctus Ant. Quis ex vobis homo, qui habet centum oves et, si perdíderit unam ex illis, nonne dimíttit nonagínta novem in desérto et vadit ad illam quæ períerat, donec invéniat eam? Allelúja.	*Benedictus Ant.* What man among you, who has a hundred sheep, and if he loseth one of them, does he not leave the ninety-nine in the wilderness and go to the one that was lost until he finds it? Alleluia.
Orátio Protéctor in te sperántium, Deus, sine quo nihil est válidum, nihil sanctum; multíplica super nos misericórdiam tuam; ut, te rectóre, te duce, sic transeámus per bona temporália, ut non amittámus ætérna. Per Dóminum nostrum ...	*Prayer* O God, protector of those who hope in Thee, without whom there is nothing strong, nothing holy: multiply Thy mercy upon us; that we may pass through temporal things, and not lose eternal ones. Through our Lord ...

Third Sunday after Pentecost (Vespers II)
Sunday Vespers and Antiphons From Vespers I of the Feast of the Sacred Heart, Chapter, and Prayer from Vespers I above.

Versiculi **V.** Memóriam fecit mirabílium suórum miserátor Dóminus. **R.** Escam dedit timéntibus se.	*Versicle* **V.** The merciful Lord made a memorial of His miracles. **R.** He gave food to those who fear Him.

Proper of the Season

Ad Magnificat Ant. Quæ múlier habens drachmas decem, et si perdíderit drachmam unam, nonne accéndit lucérnam et evérrit domum et quærit diligénter, donec invéniat?	***Magnificat Ant.*** What woman, having ten drachma, and if she has lost one drachma, does she not light a lamp, and sweep the house, and search diligently until she finds it?

Fourth Sunday after Pentecost Saturday (Vespers I)
All from Saturday Vespers except below.

Versiculi **V.** Vespertína orátio ascéndat ad te Dómine. **R.** Et descendat super nos misericórdia tua.	***Versicle*** **V.** Let the evening prayer go up to Thee, O Lord. **R.** And let Thy mercy descend upon us.
Ad Magnificat Ant. Præváluit David in Philisthǽum in funda et lápide, in nómine Dómini.	***Magnificat Ant.*** David prevailed against the Philistine with a sling and stone, in the Name of the Lord.
Orátio Da nobis, quǽsumus, Dómine: ut et mundi cursus pacífice nobis tuo órdine dirigátur; et Ecclésia tua tranquílla devotióne lætétur. Per Dóminum nostrum ...	***Prayer*** Grant us, we beseech Thee Lord, that the course of the world may be peaceably directed for us by Thine order: and Thy Church may rejoice in peaceful devotion. Through our Lord ...

Fourth Sunday after Pentecost (Lauds)
All from Sunday Lauds I except below.

Versiculi **V.** Dóminus regnávit, **R.** decórem indútus est: allelúja.	***Versicle*** **V.** The Lord hath reigned, **R.** He is clothed with beauty, alleluia.
Ad Benedíctus Ant. Ascéndens Iesus in navim, et sedens docébat turbas, allelúja.	***Benedíctus Ant.*** Jesus getting into the boat, and sitting down taught the multitudes, alleluia.
Orátio Da nobis, quǽsumus Dómine, ut et mundi cursus pacifice nobis tuo ordine dirigatur: et Ecclesia tua tranquilla devotione lætetur. Per Dóminum nostrum ...	***Prayer*** Grant us, we beseech Thee, O Lord, that the governance of the world may be peaceably directed by us through Thine order: and Thy Church may rejoice in serene devotion to Thee. Through our Lord ...

Fourth Sunday after Pentecost (Vespers II)
All from Sunday Vespers except below.

Versiculi **V.** Dirigátur Dómine orátio mea. **R.** Sicut incénsum in conspéctu tuo.	***Versicle*** **V.** Let my prayer arise, O Lord. **R.** Like incense in Thy sight.
Ad Magnificat Ant. Præcéptor, per totam noctem laborántes nihil cépimus, in verbo autem tuo laxábo rete.	***Magnificat Ant.*** Master, we labored all night and caught nothing, but at Thy word I will let down the net.

Proper of the Season

Fifth Sunday after Pentecost Saturday (Vespers I)
All from Saturday Vespers except below.

Versiculi **V.** Vespertína orátio ascéndat ad te Dómine. **R.** Et descéndat super nos misericórdia tua.	***Versicle*** **V.** Let the evening prayer go up to Thee, O Lord. **R.** And let Thy mercy descend upon us.
Ad Magnificat Ant. Montes Gélboë, nec ros nec plúvia véniant super vos: quia in te abiéctus est clípeus fórtium, clípeus Saul, quasi non esset unctus óleo. Quómodo cecidérunt fortes in bello? Iónathas in excélsis interféctus est: Saul et Iónathas, amábiles et decóri valde in vita sua, in morte quoque non sunt divísi.	***Magnificat Ant.*** The mountains of Gelboë let neither dew nor rain come upon thee: because in thee the shield of the mighty, the shield of Saul, hath been thrown away, as if it had not been anointed with oil. How did the mighty fall in battle? Jonathan was slain in high places: Saul and Jonathan, amiable and very graceful in their life, were not divided even in death.
Orátio Deus, qui diligéntibus te bona invisibília præparásti: infúnde córdibus nostris tui amóris afféctum; ut te in ómnibus et super ómnia diligéntes, promissiónes tuas, quæ omne desidérium súperant, consequámur. Per Dóminum nostrum ...	***Prayer*** O God, who hast prepared goods for the diligent that cannot be seen: pour into our hearts Thy ardent love: that we may find Thee in all things, and above all Thy faithful promises, which surpass all our desires. Through our Lord ...

Fifth Sunday after Pentecost (Lauds)
All from Sunday Lauds except below and the Prayer from Vespers I.

Versiculi **V.** Dóminus regnávit, decórem induit. **R.** Induit Dóminus fortitúdinem, et præcínxit se virtúte.	***Versicle*** **V.** The Lord reigned, He put on beauty. **R.** The Lord clothed Himself with strength and girded Himself with power.
Ad Benedictus Ant. Audístis quia dictum est antíquis: Non occídes; qui autem occíderit, reus erit iudício.	***Benedictus Ant.*** Ye have heard that it was said to the ancients: Ye shall not kill, but whoever kills will be guilty of judgment.

Fifth Sunday after Pentecost (Vespers II)
All from Sunday Vespers except below and the Prayer from Vespers I.

Versiculi **V.** Vespertína óratio ascéndat ad te Dómine. **R.** Et descéndat super nos misericórdia tua.	***Versicle*** **V.** Let the evening prayer go up to Thee, O Lord. **R.** And let Thy mercy descend upon us.
Ad Magnificat Ant. Si offers munus tuum ad altáre et recordátus fúeris quia frater tuus habet áliquid advérsus te, relínque ibi munus tuum ante altáre, et vade prius reconciliári fratri tuo, et tunc véniens ófferes munus tuum, allelúja.	***Magnificat Ant.*** If thou offerest thy gift at the altar, and thou rememberest that thy brother hath something against thee, leave thy gift there before the altar, and go first to be reconciled to thy brother, and then come and offer thy gift, alleluia.

Proper of the Season

Sixth Sunday after Pentecost Saturday (Vespers I)
All from Saturday Vespers except below.

Versiculi V. Vespertína orátio ascéndat ad te Dómine. R. Et descéndat super nos misericórdia tua.	*Versicle* V. Let the evening prayer go up to Thee, O Lord. R. And let Thy mercy descend upon us.
Ad Magnificat Ant. Obsecro Dómine, aufer iniquitátem servi tui, quia insipiénter egi.	*Magnificat Ant.* Please, Lord, take away the sins of Thy servant, because I have acted foolishly.
Orátio Deus virtútum, cuius est totum quod est óptimum: ínsere pectóribus nostris amórem tui nóminis, et præsta in nobis religiónis augméntum; ut, quæ sunt bona, nútrias, ac pietátis stúdio, quæ sunt nutríta, custódias. Per Dóminum nostrum ...	*Prayer* O God of power, to whom belongs all that is best: implant in our hearts the love of Thy Name, and grant us an increase of faith; that things which are good in us, Thou nurturest; and by the zeal of Thy devotion by which we have been nourished, grant us Thy protection. Through our Lord ...

Sixth Sunday after Pentecost (Lauds)
All from Sunday Lauds except below and the Prayer from Vespers I.

Versiculi V. Dóminus regnávit, decórem induit. R. Induit Dóminus fortitúdinem, et præcínxit se virtúte.	*Versicle* V. The Lord reigned, He put on beauty. R. The Lord clothed Himself with strength and girded Himself with power.
Ad Benedíctus Ant. Cum turba multa esset cum Iesu nec habérent quod manducárent, convocátis discípulis, ait illis: Miséreor super turbam, quia ecce iam tríduo sústinent me nec habent quod mandúcent, allelúja.	*Benedíctus Ant.* When there was a great multitude with Jesus, they had nothing to eat; having called the disciples together, He said to them: I have pity on the multitude: for behold, they have endured Me for three days now, and have nothing to eat, alleluia.

Sixth Sunday after Pentecost (Vespers II)
All from Sunday Vespers except below and Prayer of Vespers I.

Versiculi V. Dirigátur Dómine orátio mea. R. Sicut incénsum in conspéctu tuo.	*Versicle* V. My prayer is said to the Lord. R. Like incense in Thy sight.
Ad Magnificat Ant. Miséreor super turbam, quia ecce iam tríduo sústinent me nec habent quod mandúcent, et, si dimísero eos ieiúnos, deficient in via, allelúja.	*Magnificat Ant.* I have pity on the multitude: for behold, they have endured Me for three days now, and have nothing to eat: and if I let them go fasting, they will fail on the way, alleluia.

Seventh Sunday after Pentecost Saturday (Vespers I)
All from Saturday Vespers except below.

Versiculi V. Vespertína orátio ascéndat ad te Dómine. R. Et descéndat super nos misericórdia tua.	*Versicle* V. Let the evening prayer go up to Thee, O Lord. R. And let Thy mercy descend upon us.
Ad Magnificat Ant. Unxérunt Salomónem Sadoc sacérdos, et Nathan prophéta, regem in Gihon, et	*Magnificat Ant.* Sadok the priest and Nathan the prophet anointed Solomon king in Gihon, and when they went

Proper of the Season

ascendéntes læti dixérunt: Vivat rex in ætérnum.	up they said joyfully: May the king live forever.
Orátio Deus, cujus providéntia in sui dispositióne non fállitur: te súpplices exorámus; ut nóxia cuncta submóveas, et ómnia nobis profutúra concédas. Per Dóminum nostrum ...	**Prayer** O God, whose providence never fails in what it ordains: we implore Thee to remove all that is harmful, and allow all that is beneficial to us. Through our Lord ...

Seventh Sunday after Pentecost (Lauds)
All from Sunday Lauds except below and the Prayer from Vespers I.

Versiculi V. Dóminus regnávit, decórem induit. **R.** Induit Dóminus fortitúdinem, et præcínxit se virtúte.	**Versicle V.** The Lord reigned, He put on beauty. **R.** The Lord clothed Himself with strength and girded Himself with power.
Ad Benedíctus Ant. Atténdite a falsis prophétis, qui véniunt ad vos in vestiméntis óvium, intrínsecus autem sunt lupi rapáces; a frúctibus eórum cognoscétis eos, allelúja.	**Benedíctus Ant.** Beware of false prophets who come to you in sheep's clothing, but inwardly they are ravenous wolves: by their fruits ye shall know them, alleluia.

Seventh Sunday after Pentecost (Vespers II)
All from Sunday Vespers except below and Prayer of Vespers I.

Versiculi V. Dirigátur Dómine orátio mea. **R.** Sicut incénsum in conspéctu tuo.	**Versicle V.** Let my prayer arise, O Lord. **R.** Like incense in Thy sight.
Ad Magnificat Ant. Non potest arbor bona fructus malos fácere, nec arbor mala fructus bonos fácere. Omnis arbor quæ non facit fructum bonum, excidétur, et in ignem mittétur, allelúja.	**Magnificat Ant.** A good tree cannot produce bad fruit, nor can a bad tree produce good fruit: Every tree that does not produce good fruit will be cut down and thrown into the fire, alleluia.

Eighth Sunday after Pentecost Saturday (Vespers I)
All from Saturday Vespers except below.

Versiculi V. Vespertína óratio ascéndat ad te Dómine. **R.** Et descéndat super nos misericórdia tua.	**Versicle V.** Let the evening prayer go up to Thee, O Lord. **R.** And let Thy mercy descend upon us.
Ad Magnificat Ant. Exaudísti Dómine oratiónem servi tui, ut ædificárem templum nómini tuo.	**Magnificat Ant.** O Lord, Thou hast heard the prayer of Thy servant, that I may build a temple for Thy Name.
Orátio Largíre nobis, quæsumus Dómine, semper spíritum cogitándi quæ recta sunt, propítius et agéndi: ut qui sine te esse non póssumus, secúndum te vívere valeámus. Per Dóminum nostrum ...	**Prayer** Grant us, we beseech Thee, O Lord, always the spirit of thinking and acting in a way that is right, that we who cannot exist without Thee, may live according to Thy will. Through our Lord ...

Eighth Sunday after Pentecost (Lauds)
All from Sunday Lauds except below and the Prayer from Vespers I.

Versiculi V. Dóminus regnávit, decórem induit. **R.** Induit Dóminus fortitúdinem, et præcínxit se virtúte.	**Versicle V.** The Lord reigned, He put on beauty. **R.** The Lord clothed

Proper of the Season

		Himself with strength and girded Himself with power
	Ad Benedíctus Ant. Ait dóminus víllico: Quid hoc áudio de te? redde ratiónem villicatiónis tuæ, allelúja.	***Benedíctus Ant.*** The lord said to the governor: What is this I hear about thee? Give an account of thy stewardship, alleluia.
	**Eighth Sunday after Pentecost (Vespers II)** All from Sunday Vespers except below and Prayer of Vespers I.	
	***Versiculi* V.** Vespertína óratio ascéndat ad te Dómine. **R.** Et descéndat super nos misericórdia tua.	***Versicle* V.** Let the evening prayer go up to Thee, O Lord. **R.** And let Thy mercy descend upon us.
	Ad Magnificat Ant. Quid fáciam, quia dóminus meus aufert a me villicatiónem? Fódere non váleo, mendicáre erubésco. Scio quid fáciam, ut, cum amótus fúero a villicatióne, recípiant me in domos suas.	***Magnificat Ant.*** What shall I do, because my master hath taken away the stewardship from me? I am not able to dig, I am ashamed to beg. I know what I will do, that when I am removed from the stewardship, they will welcome me into their homes.
	Ninth Sunday after Pentecost Saturday (Vespers I) All from Saturday Vespers except below.	
	***Versiculi* V.** Vespertína óratio ascéndat ad te Dómine. **R.** Et descéndat super nos misericórdia tua.	***Versicle* V.** Let the evening prayer go up to Thee, O Lord. **R.** And let Thy mercy descend upon us.
	Ad Magnificat Ant. Dum tólleret Dóminus Elíam per túrbinem in cælum, Eliséus clamábat: Pater mi, currus Israël, et auríga ejus.	***Magnificat Ant.*** While the Lord was taking Elijah up to heaven by a whirlwind, Elisha cried out: My father! the chariot of Israel, and its driver!
	Orátio Páteant aures misericórdiæ tuæ, Dómine, précibus supplicántium: et ut peténtibus desideráta concédas, fac eos, quæ tibi sunt plácita, postuláre. Per Dóminum nostrum ...	***Prayer*** O Lord, let the ears of Thy mercy be open to the prayers of Thy supplicants: and that Thou mayest grant to those who ask what they desire, make them ask for only what is pleasing to Thee Through our Lord ...
	Ninth Sunday after Pentecost (Lauds) All from Sunday Lauds except below and the Prayer from Vespers I.	
	Ad Benedíctus Ant. Cum appropinquáret Dóminus Ierúsalem videns civitátem flevit super illam, et dixit: Quia si cognovísses et tu, quia vénient dies in te, et circúmdabunt te inimíci tui vallo et circúmdabunt te et coangustábunt te úndique et ad terram prostérnent te: eo quod non cognovísti tempus visitatiónis tuæ, allelúja.	***Benedíctus Ant.*** When the Lord approached Jerusalem, seeing the city, He wept over it and said: If only thou hadst known that the days will come upon thee, and thine enemies will encompass thee with a rampart, and they will surround thee, and they will enclose thee in on every side, and they will cast thee to the ground.

Proper of the Season

Ninth Sunday after Pentecost (Vespers II)
All from Sunday Vespers except below and Prayer of Vespers I.

Ad Magnificat Ant. Scriptum est enim: Quia domus mea domus oratiónis est cunctis géntibus; vos autem fecístis illam spelúncam latrónum. Et erat cotídie docens in templo.	*Magnificat Ant.* For it is written: because my house is a house of prayer for all nations: but ye have made it a den of robbers: and He was teaching every day in the temple.

Tenth Sunday after Pentecost Saturday (Vespers I)
All from Saturday Vespers except below.

Ad Magnificat Ant. Fecit Joas rectum coram Dómino cunctis diébus, quibus dócuit eum Jójada sacérdos.	*Magnificat Ant.* Joas did right before the Lord all the days that Joiada the priest taught him.
Orátio Deus, qui omnipoténtiam tuam parcéndo máxime et miserándo maniféstas: multíplica super nos misericórdiam tuam; ut ad tua promíssa curréntes, cæléstium bonórum fácias esse consórtes. Per Dóminum nostrum ...	*Prayer* O God, who manifests Thine omnipotence most by sparing us and showing mercy: shower Thy mercy upon us; that, running the way to Thy commandments, Thou mayest make us partakers of a heavenly treasure. Through our Lord ...

Tenth Sunday after Pentecost (Lauds)
All from Sunday Lauds except below and the Prayer from Vespers I.

Ad Benedíctus Ant. Stans a longe publicánus, nolébat óculos ad cælum leváre, sed percutiébat pectus suum dicens: Deus, propítius esto mihi peccatóri.	*Benedíctus Ant.* The publican, standing afar off, would not raise his eyes to heaven, but beat his breast, saying: God, be merciful to me a sinner.

Tenth Sunday after Pentecost (Vespers II)
All from Sunday Vespers except below and Prayer of Vespers I.

Ad Magnificat Ant. Descéndit hic iustificátus in domum suam ab illo; quia omnis qui se exáltat, humiliábitur, et, qui se humíliat, exaltábitur.	*Magnificat Ant.* This one, went down to his house justified rather than the other: because anyone who exalts himself will be humbled, and he who humbles himself will be exalted.

Eleventh Sunday after Pentecost Saturday (Vespers I)
All from Saturday Vespers except below.

Ad Magnificat Ant. Obsecro, Dómine: memento, quæso, quomodo ambulaverim coram te in veritáte et in corde perfécto et, quod placitum est coram te, fecerim.	*Magnificat Ant.* I beseech Thee, O Lord: remember, please, how I walked before Thee in truth and with a perfect heart, and did what was pleasing before Thee.
Orátio Omnípotens sempitérne Deus, qui abundántia pietátis tuæ, et mérita súpplicum excédis et vota: effúnde super nos misericórdiam tuam; ut dimíttas quæ consciéntia métuit, et adjícias quod orátio non præsúmit. Per Dóminum nostrum ...	*Prayer* Almighty and eternal God, who with the abundance of Thy mercy which exceeds the merits of our supplications and prayers, pour out Thy mercy upon us; and may we let go of our fear of the sins in our consciences, and, Lord, to add to our

Proper of the Season

	prayer what we did not presume to ask for. Through our Lord ...

Eleventh Sunday after Pentecost (Lauds)
All from Sunday Lauds except below and the Prayer from Vespers I.

Ad Benedíctus Ant. Cum transísset Dóminus fines Tyri, surdos fecit audíre et mutos loqui.	**Benedíctus Ant.** When the Lord passed through the borders of Tyre, He made the deaf to hear and the dumb to speak.

Eleventh Sunday after Pentecost (Vespers II)
All from Sunday Vespers except below and Prayer of Vespers I.

Ad Magníficat Ant. Bene ómnia fecit et surdos fecit audíre et mutos loqui.	**Magníficat Ant.** He did all things well, and made the deaf to hear and the dumb to speak.

Twelfth Sunday after Pentecost and following (Vespers I)
The Antiphon at the Magnificat of the Saturday Vespers, Office of the BVM prayer.

Twelfth Sunday after Pentecost (Lauds)
All from Sunday Lauds except below. Benedíctus and Prayer.

Ad Benedíctus Ant. Magíster, quid faciéndo vitam ætérnam possidébo? At ille dixit ad eum: In lege quid scriptum est? quómodo legis? Díliges Dóminum Deum tuum ex toto corde tuo, allelúja.	**Benedíctus Ant.** Master, what shall I do to inherit eternal life? But He said to him: What is written in the law: How do you read it: Love the Lord thy God with all thy heart, alleluia.
Orátio Omnípotens et miséricors Deus, de cuius múnere venit, ut tibi a fidélibus tuis digne et laudabíliter serviátur: tríbue, quǽsumus, nobis; ut ad promissiónes tuas sine offensióne currámus. Per Dóminum nostrum ...	**Prayer** Almighty and merciful God, on whose behalf the Holy Spirit comes, that He may be served worthily and laudably by Thy faithful: grant us, we ask, that we may run toward Thy promises without stumbling. Through our Lord ...

Twelfth Sunday after Pentecost (Vespers II)
All from Sunday Vespers including propers for Feasts and Seasons.

Ad Magníficat Ant. Homo quidam descendébat ab Ierúsalem in Iéricho et íncidit in latrónes, qui étiam despoliavérunt eum et, plagis impósitis, abiérunt semivívo relícto.	**Magníficat Ant.** A certain man was going down from Jerusalem to Jericho and fell upon robbers, who robbed him and inflicting blows upon him departed, leaving him half alive.

Thirteenth Sunday after Pentecost (Lauds)
All from Sunday Lauds except below Benedíctus Antiphon and Prayer.

Ad Benedíctus Ant. Cum transíret Iesus quoddam castéllum, occurrérunt ei decem viri leprósi, qui stetérunt a longe et levavérunt vocem dicéntes: Iesu præcéptor, miserére nostri.	**Benedíctus Ant.** When Jesus was passing a certain village, ten men with leprosy met Him: they stood afar off, and raised their voices, saying: Jesus, Teacher, have mercy on us.
Orátio Omnípotens sempitérne Deus, da nobis fídei, spei et caritátis augméntum: et, ut mereámur ássequi	**Prayer** Almighty and eternal God, give us an increase of faith, hope, and charity: and that we may deserve to

Proper of the Season

quod promíttis, fac nos amáre quod præcipis. Per Dóminum nostrum ...	achieve what Thou promisest, make us love what Thou commandest. Through our Lord ...

Thirteenth Sunday after Pentecost (Vespers II)
All from Sunday Vespers including propers for Feasts and Seasons.

Ad Magníficat Ant. Unus autem ex illis, ut vidit quod mundátus est, regréssus est cum magna voce magníficans Deum, allelúja.	*Magnificat Ant.* And one of them, when he saw that he was cleansed, returned with a loud voice, glorifying God, alleluia.

Fourteenth Sunday after Pentecost (Lauds)
All from Sunday Lauds except below Benedíctus and Prayer.

Ad Benedíctus Ant. Nolíte sollíciti esse dicéntes: Quid manducábimus aut quid bibémus? scit enim Pater vester quid vobis necésse sit, allelúja.	*Benedíctus Ant.* Be not anxious, saying, What shall we eat, or what shall we drink? For your Father knows what you need, alleluia.
Orátio Custódi, Dómine, quǽsumus, Ecclésiam tuam propitiatióne perpétua: et quia sine te lábitur humána mortálitas; tuis semper auxíliis et abstrahátur a nóxiis et ad salutária dirigátur. Per Dóminum nostrum ...	*Prayer* We beg Thee, O Lord, save Thy Church with eternal mercy: and since without Thee, our human life slips away, may it always be with Thy help that we may be removed from harm and guided to what is profitable for salvation. Through our Lord ...

Fourteenth Sunday after Pentecost (Vespers II)
All from Sunday Vespers including propers for Feasts and Seasons.

Ad Magníficat Ant. Quǽrite primum regnum Dei et iustítiam eius, et hæc ómnia adiciéntur vobis, allelúja.	*Magnificat Ant.* Seek ye first the kingdom of God and His righteousness, and all these things shall be added unto you.

Fifteenth Sunday after Pentecost (Lauds)
All from Sunday Lauds except below Benedíctus and Prayer.

Ad Benedíctus Ant. Ibat Iesus in civitátem, quæ vocátur Naim: et ecce defúnctus efferebátur fílius únicus matris suæ.	*Benedíctus Ant.* Jesus was going to a city called Naim: and behold, the dead, the only son of his mother, was being brought out.
Orátio Ecclésiam tuam, Dómine, miserátio continuáta mundet et múniat: et quia sine te non potest salva consístere; tuo semper múnere gubernétur. Per Dóminum nostrum ...	*Prayer* O Lord, Thy continued mercy cleanses and fortifies Thy church: and because without Thee it cannot persevere without harm, it will always be directed by Thy grace. Through our Lord ...

Fifteenth Sunday after Pentecost (Vespers II)
All from Sunday Vespers including propers for Feasts and Seasons.

Ad Magníficat Ant. Prophéta magnus surréxit in nobis, et quia Deus visitávit plebem suam.	*Magnificat Ant.* A great prophet arose among us, and God hath visited His people.

Sixteenth Sunday after Pentecost (Lauds)
All from Sunday Lauds except below Benedíctus and Prayer.

Ad Benedíctus Ant. Cum intráret Iesus in domum cuiúsdam príncipis	*Benedíctus Ant.* When Jesus entered the house of a certain leader of the

Proper of the Season

pharisæórum sábbato manducáre panem, ecce homo quidam hydrópicus erat ante illum: ipse vero apprehénsum sanávit eum, ac dimísit.	Pharisees to eat bread on the sabbath, behold, a man with dropsy came before Him. But He, taking him, healed him, and sent him away.
Orátio Tua nos, quǽsumus, Dómine, grátia semper et prævéniat et sequátur: ac bonis opéribus iúgiter præstet esse inténtos. Per Dóminum nostrum ...	*Prayer* We beg Thee, O Lord, that Thy grace may always precede and follow us, and that we may always be committed to good works. Through our Lord ...
Sixteenth Sunday after Pentecost (Vespers II) All from Sunday Vespers including propers for Feasts and Seasons.	
Ad Magnificat Ant. Cum vocátus fúeris ad núptias, recúmbe in novíssimo loco, ut dicat tibi qui te invitávit: Amíce, ascénde supérius. Et erit tibi glória coram simul discumbéntibus, allelúja..	*Magnificat Ant.* When thou art called to the wedding, recline in the last place; let him who invited thee say to thee: Friend, go up higher; And glory will be to thee before those who are together at the table, alleluia.
Seventeenth Sunday after Pentecost (Lauds) All from Sunday Lauds except below Benedíctus and Prayer.	
Ad Benedíctus Ant. Magíster, quod est mandátum magnum in lege? Ait illi Iesus: Díliges Dóminum Deum tuum ex toto corde tuo, allelúja.	*Benedíctus Ant.* Teacher, what is the great commandment in the law? Jesus said to him: Love the Lord Thy God with all thy heart, alleluia.
Orátio Da, quǽsumus Dómine, pópulo tuo diabolica vitare contagia: et te solum Deum pura mente sectari. Per Dóminum nostrum ...	*Prayer* Grant, we beseech Thee, O Lord, that Thy people may avoid diabolical temptations: and that they may follow Thee, God alone, with a pure mind. Through our Lord ...
Seventeenth Sunday after Pentecost (Vespers II) All from Sunday Vespers including propers for Feasts and Seasons.	
Ad Magnificat Ant. Quid vobis vidétur de Christo? cuius fílius est? Dicunt ei omnes: David. Dicit eis Iesus: Quómodo David in spíritu vocat eum Dóminum dicens: Dixit Dóminus Dómino meo: Sede a dextris meis?	*Magnificat Ant.* What do ye think of the Christ: Whose son is He? They all replied: David's. Jesus said to them: How, then, does David call Him Lord in the Spirit, saying: The Lord said to my Lord: Sit at My right hand?
Eighteenth Sunday after Pentecost (Lauds) All from Sunday Lauds except below Benedíctus and Prayer.	
Ad Benedíctus Ant. Dixit Dóminus paralýtico: Confide, fili, remittúntur tibi peccáta tua.	*Benedíctus Ant.* The Lord said to the paralytic: Be assured, son, thy sins are forgiven.
Orátio Dírigat corda nostra, quǽsumus, Dómine, tuæ miseratiónis operátio: quia tibi sine te placére non póssumus. Per Dóminum nostrum ...	*Prayer* O Lord we beg Thee, let the works of Thy mercy guide our hearts: for without Thee, our lives cannot please Thee. Through our Lord ...
Eighteenth Sunday after Pentecost (Vespers II) All from Sunday Vespers including propers for Feasts and Seasons.	
Ad Magnificat Ant. Tulit ergo paralýticus lectum suum, in quo	*Magnificat Ant.* The paralytic therefore took up his bed in which he

Proper of the Season

iacébat, magníficans Deum: et omnis plebs, ut vidit, dedit laudem Deo.	lay, glorifying God: and all the people, as they watched, gave praise to God.

Nineteenth Sunday after Pentecost (Lauds)
All from Sunday Lauds except below Benedíctus and Prayer.

Ad Benedíctus Ant. Dícite invitátis: Ecce prándium meum parávi, veníte ad núptias, allelúja.	*Benedíctus Ant.* Say to the guests: Behold, I have prepared my dinner, come to the wedding, alleluia.
Orátio Omnípotens et miséricors Deus, univérsa nobis adversántia propitiátus exclúde: ut mente et córpore páriter expedíti, quæ tua sunt, líberis méntibus exsequámur. Per Dóminum nostrum ...	*Prayer* Almighty and merciful God, mercifully remove from us all that obstructs us: that, being prepared in mind and body alike, we may fulfill with free minds those things which are Thine. Through our Lord...

Nineteenth Sunday after Pentecost (Vespers II)
All from Sunday Vespers including propers for Feasts and Seasons.

Ad Magnificat Ant. Intrávit autem rex, ut vidéret discumbéntes: et vidit ibi hóminem non vestítum veste nuptiáli, et ait illi: Amíce, quómodo huc intrásti, non habens vestem nuptiálem?	*Magnificat Ant.* And the king went in to see them reclining: and he saw there a man not clothed in a wedding garment, and he said to him: Friend, how camest thou in here, not having a wedding garment?

Twentieth Sunday after Pentecost (Lauds)
All from Sunday Lauds except below Benedíctus and Prayer.

Ad Benedíctus Ant. Erat quidam régulus, cuius fílius infirmabátur Caphárnaum. Hic cum audísset quod Iesus veníret in Galilǽam, rogábat eum ut sanáret filium eius.	*Benedíctus Ant.* There was a certain ruler whose son was sick in Capernaum: when he heard that Jesus was coming to Galilee, he begged Him to heal his son.
Orátio Largíre, quǽsumus, Dómine, fidélibus tuis indulgéntiam placátus et pacem: ut páriter ab ómnibus mundéntur offénsis, et secúra tibi mente desérviant. Per Dóminum nostrum ...	*Prayer* We beseech Thee, O Lord, to grant pardon and peace to Thy faithful: that they may be cleansed from all sins and serve Thee with a mind at peace. Through our Lord...

Twentieth Sunday after Pentecost (Vespers II)
All from Sunday Vespers including propers for Feasts and Seasons.

Ad Magnificat Ant. Cognóvit autem pater quia illa hora erat, in qua dixit Iesus: Fílius tuus vivit; et crédidit ipse et domus eius tota.	*Magnificat Ant.* And the father knew that it was that hour in which Jesus said: Thy son liveth: and he believed, and all his house.

Twenty-first Sunday after Pentecost (Lauds)
All from Sunday Lauds except below Benedíctus and Prayer.

Ad Benedíctus Ant. Dixit autem dóminus servo: Redde quod debes. Prócidens autem servus ille rogábat eum, dicens: Patiéntiam habe in me, et ómnia reddam tibi.	*Benedíctus Ant.* And the master said to the servant: Pay what thou owest. And that servant coming forward besought him, saying: Have patience with me, and I will repay thee all things.

Proper of the Season

Orátio Famíliam tuam, quǽsumus, Dómine, contínua pietáte custódi: ut a cunctis adversitátibus te protegénte, sit líbera; et in bonis áctibus tuo nómini sit devóta. Per Dóminum nostrum ...	*Prayer* We beseech Thee, O Lord, to guard Thy family with continued mercy: that it may be free from all adversities; and in good deeds be devoted to Thy Name. Through our Lord ...
Twenty-first Sunday after Pentecost (Vespers II) All from Sunday Vespers including propers for Feasts and Seasons.	
Ad Magníficat Ant. Serve nequam, omne débitum dimísi tibi, quóniam rogásti me: nonne ergo opórtuit et te miseréri consérvi tui, sicut et ego tui misértus sum, allelúja.	*Magníficat Ant.* Wicked servant, I forgave thee all thy debt, because thou asked me: was it not necessary, then, that thou have mercy on thy servant, as I have also had mercy on thee, alleluia.
Twenty-second Sunday after Pentecost (Lauds) All from Sunday Lauds except below Benedíctus and Prayer.	
Ad Benedíctus Ant. Magíster, scimus quia verax es et viam Dei in veritáte doces, allelúja..	*Benedíctus Ant.* Master, we know that Thou art truthful and teach the way of God in truth, alleluia.
Orátio Deus, refúgium nostrum et virtus: adésto piis Ecclésiæ tuæ précibus, auctor ipse pietátis, et præsta; ut, quod fidéliter pétimus, efficáciter consequámur. Per Dóminum nostrum	*Prayer* O God, our refuge and strength, the author of piety itself, be present at the prayers of Thy holy Church, and grant that what we faithfully ask for, we may effectively obtain. Through our Lord ...
Twenty-second Sunday after Pentecost (Vespers II) All from Sunday Vespers including propers for Feasts and Seasons.	
Ad Magníficat Ant. Réddite ergo quæ sunt Cǽsaris Cǽsari, et quæ sunt Dei Deo, allelúja.	*Magníficat Ant.* Render therefore to Caesar the things that are Caesar's, and to God the things that are God's, alleluia.
Twenty-third Sunday after Pentecost (Lauds) All from Sunday Lauds except below Benedíctus and Prayer.	
Ad Benedíctus Ant. Dicébat enim intra se: Si tetígero fimbríam vestiménti ejus tantum, salva ero.	*Benedíctus Ant.* For she said within herself: If I only touch the hem of His garment, I shall be saved.
Orátio Absólve, quǽsumus Dómine, tuórum delícta populórum: ut a peccatórum néxibus, quæ pro nostra fragilitáte contráximus, tua benignitáte liberémur. Per Dóminum nostrum ...	*Prayer* We ask Thee, O Lord, to forgive Thy people's transgressions: that we may be freed by Thy mercy from the bonds of sin, which we have contracted because of our weakness. Through our Lord...
Twenty-third Sunday after Pentecost (Vespers II) All from Sunday Vespers including propers for Feasts and Seasons.	
Ad Magníficat Ant. At Jesus convérsus, et videns eam, dixit: Confíde fília, fides tua te salvam fecit, allelúja.	*Magníficat Ant.* But Jesus turned, and seeing her, said: Have faith, daughter, thy faith has saved thee, alleluia.
See Page xiv for instructions for Sundays between the 23rd Sunday of Pentecost and the Last Sunday of Pentecost before Advent	

Proper of the Season

Twenty-forth or Last Sunday after Pentecost (Lauds)	
All from Sunday Lauds except below Benedíctus and Prayer.	
Ad Benedíctus Ant. Cum videritis abominatiónem desolatiónis, quæ dicta est a Daniele prophéta, stántem in loco sancto: qui légit, intélligat..	*Benedíctus Ant.* When ye see the abomination of desolation which was spoken of by Daniel the prophet, standing in the holy place: let him who reads, understand.
Orátio Excita, quǽsumus Dómine, tuórum fidélium voluntátes: ut divini óperis frúctum propénsius exséquentes, pietátis tuæ remédia majora percípiant. Per Dóminum nostrum ...	*Prayer* Arouse the will of Thy faithful, we beseech Thee, O Lord,: that, carrying out the fruit of the divine work more willingly, they may perceive the greater remedies of Thy goodness. Through our Lord...
Twenty-forth Sunday after Pentecost (Vespers II)	
All from Sunday Vespers including propers for Feasts and Seasons.	
Ad Magnificat Ant. Amen dico vobis, quia non prætéribit generátio hæc, donec ómnia fíant: cælum et terra transíbunt, verba áutem mea non transíbunt, dicit Dóminus. Per Dóminum nostrum ...	*Magnificat Ant.* Amen I say to you, this generation will not pass away until all things are done: heaven and earth will pass away, but My words will not pass away, sayeth the Lord. Through our Lord...
Last Sunday in October **Feast of Our Lord Jesus Christ the King (Vespers I)**	
Psalms as at Vespers of the Common of Apostles, the Prayer as at Lauds.	
Ant 1. Pacíficus vocábitur, et thronus ejus erit firmíssimus in perpétuum.	**Ant 1.** He will be called a peacemaker, and His throne will be firm forever.
Ant 2. Regnum ejus regnum sempitérnum est, et ómnes reges sérvient ei et obédient.	**Ant 2.** His kingdom is an everlasting kingdom, and all kings will serve and obey Him.
Ant 3. Ecce Vir Oriens nomen ejus: sedébit et dominábitur, et loquétur pacem Géntibus.	**Ant 3.** Behold, the Man of the East is His Name: He shall sit and rule, and speak peace to the Gentiles.
Ant 4. Dóminus judex noster, Dóminus légifer noster: Dóminus Rex noster, ipse salvábit nos.	**Ant 4.** The Lord our Judge, the Lord our Lawgiver: the Lord our King, He will save us.
Ant 5. Ecce dedi te in lucem Géntium, ut sis salus mea usque ad extrémum terræ.	**Ant 5.** Behold, I have given Thee to be the light of the Gentiles, that Thou mayest bring My salvation to the ends of the earth.
Capitulum (Col. 1:12-13) **V.** Fratres: Grátias ágimus Deo Patri, qui dignos nos fecit in partem sortis sanctórum in lúmine, qui erípuit nos de potestáte tenebrárum, et tránstulit in regnum Fílii dilectiónis suæ. **R.** Deo grátias.	*Chapter* (Col. 1:12-13) **V.** Brothers: We give thanks to God the Father, who made us worthy to be included in the assembly of the saints in the light: Who rescued us from the power of darkness, and translated us to the kingdom of His beloved Son. **R.** Thanks be to God.
Hymn – Te Sæculórum Príncipem, Page 380	

Proper of the Season

Ad Magnificat Ant. Dabit illi Dóminus Deus sedem David, patris ejus: et regnábit in domo Jacob in ætérnum, et regni ejus non erit finis, allelúja.	*Magnificat Ant.* The Lord God will give Him the seat of David, His father: and He will reign in the house of Jacob forever, and there will be no end to His kingdom, alleluia.

Last Sunday in October
Feast of Our Lord Jesus Christ the King (Lauds)
Psalms of Sunday Lauds I, Chapter as in Vespers I above.

Ant 1. Suscitábit Deus cæli regnum quod commínuet et consúmet univérsa regna, et ípsum stabit in ætérnum.	**Ant 1.** The God of heaven will raise up a kingdom that will crush and consume all worldly kingdoms, and it will stand forever
Ant 2. Dedit ei Dóminus potestátem et honórem et regnum; et ómnes pópuli, tribus et linguæ ipsi sérvient.	**Ant 2.** The Lord gave Him power and honor and a kingdom; and all peoples, tribes, and languages will serve Him.
Ant 3. Exíbunt aquæ vivæ de Jerúsalem; et erit Dóminus Rex super omnem terram.	**Ant 3.** Living waters will come out of Jerusalem; and the Lord will be King over all the earth.
Ant 4. Magnificábitur usque ad términos terræ, et erit iste pax.	**Ant 4.** He will be exalted to the ends of the earth, and this will bring peace.
Ant 5. Gens et regnum quod non servíerit tibi, períbit: et Gentes solitúdine vastabúntur.	**Ant 5.** The nation and the kingdom that will not serve Thee will perish: and the nations will be wasted as in a desert.

Hymn – Ætérna Christi Munera, Page 385

Versiculi V. Multiplicábitur ejus impérium. R. Et pacis non erit finis.	*Versicle* V. His dominion will be multiplied. R. And there will be no end to the peace.
Ad Benedíctus Ant. Fecit nos Deo et Patri suo regnum, primogénitus mortuórum, et Princeps regum terræ, allelúja.	*Benedíctus Ant.* He made us for the kingdom of God. He the Father, the Firstborn among the dead, and the Prince of the kings of the earth, alleluia.
Orátio Omnípotens sempitérne Deus, qui in dilécto Fílio tuo, universórum Rege, ómnia instauráre voluísti: concéde propítius; ut cunctæ famíliæ Géntium, peccáti vúlnere disgregátæ, ejus suavíssimo subdántur império. Per Dóminum nostrum ...	*Prayer* Almighty and eternal God, who willed to establish all things in Thy beloved Son, the King of all: grant Thee most mercifully; that all the families of the Gentiles, separated by the wound of sin, may be submitted to His most sweet dominion: Through our Lord ...

Last Sunday in October
Feast of Our Lord Jesus Christ the King (Vespers II)
All as in Vespers I except below.

Ad Magnificat Ant. Habet in vestiménto et in fémore suo scriptum: Rex regum, et Dóminus	*Magnificat Ant.* He has written on His garment and on His Thigh: King of kings, and Lord of lords. To Him

Proper of the Season

dominántium. Ipsi glória et impérium, in sǽcula sæculórum.	be glory and dominion, forever and ever.

Nov 1 All Saints (Vespers I)
Psalms from Apostles, Antiphons and Prayer as in Lauds below.

Capítulum (Apoc. 7:2-3) **V.** Et vidi alterum angelum ascendéntem ab ortu solis, habéntem signum Dei vivi: et clamávit voce magna quátuor ángelis, quibus datum est nocére terræ et mari, dicens: Nolíte nocere terræ, et mari, neque arbóribus, quoadúsque signémus servos Dei nostri in fróntibus eórum. **R.** Deo grátias.	**Chapter** (Apoc. 7:2-3) **V.** And I saw another angel ascending from the rising of the sun, having the sign of the living God; and he cried with a loud voice to the four angels to whom it was given to hurt the earth and the sea, saying: Hurt not the earth, nor the sea, nor the trees, till we sign the servants of our God on their foreheads. **R.** Thanks be to God.

Hymn – Placare, Christe, Page 379

Nov. 1 All Saints (Lauds)
Psalms from Sunday Lauds I, Antiphons and Prayer as below, Chapter from Vespers I.

Ant 1. Vidi turbam magnam, quam dinumeráre nemo póterat, ex ómnibus géntibus, stantes ante thronum.	**Ant 1.** I saw a great multitude, which no one could number, from all nations, standing before the throne.
Ant 2. Et ómnes Ángeli stabant in circuítu throni, et cecidérunt in conspéctu throni in fácies suas, et adoravérunt Deum.	**Ant 2.** And all the angels stood round about the throne, and fell on their faces before the throne, and worshiped God.
Ant 3. Redemísti nos, Dómine Deus, in sánguine tuo ex omni tribu, et lingua, et pópulo, et natióne, et fecísti nos Deo nostro regnum.	**Ant 3.** Thou hast redeemed us, O Lord God, in Thy blood, from every tribe, and tongue, and people, and nation, and hast made us a kingdom to our God.
Ant 4. Benedícite Dóminum ómnes elécti ejus: ágite dies lætítiæ, et confitémini illi.	**Ant 4.** Bless the Lord, all His elect: keep ye days of joy, and acknowledge Him.
Ant 5. Hymnus ómnibus Sanctis ejus: filiis Israël, pópulo appropinquánti sibi: glória hæc est ómnibus sanctis ejus.	**Ant 5.** A hymn to all His saints: to the children of Israel, to the people who draw near to Him: this glory is to all His saints.

Hymn – Placare, Christe, Page 379 or Salútis Ætérnæ Dator, Page 376

Orátio Omnípotens sempitérne Deus, qui nos ómnium Sanctórum tuórum mérita sub una tribuísti celebritáte venerári: quǽsumus; ut desiderátam nobis tuæ propitiatiónis abundántiam, multiplicátis intercessóribus, largiáris. Per Dóminum nostrum ...	**Prayer** Almighty and eternal God, who has given us the merits of all Thy Saints under one festival to be venerated: we ask; that Thou may bestow upon us the abundance of Thy blessings, which we long for, by a multitude of holy intercessors. Through our Lord ...

Proper of the Season

Nov 1 All Saints (Vespers II)

Psalms from Sunday Vespers, Antiphons and Prayer as in Lauds above. In place of the last Psalm is 115 below.

¹Credidi, propter quod locútus sum; ego autem humiliátus sum nimis.	¹I have believed, therefore have I spoken; but I have been greatly humbled.
²Ego dixi in excéssu meo: Omnis homo mendax.	²I said in my excess: Every man is a liar.
³Quid retribuam Dómino pro ómnibus quæ retribuit mihi?	³What shall I render to the Lord, for all the things that He hath rendered to me?
⁴Cálicem salutáris accípiam, et nomen Dómini invocábo.	⁴I will take the chalice of salvation; and I will call upon the Name of the Lord.
⁵Vota mea Dómino reddam coram omni pópulo ejus.	⁵I will pay my vows to the Lord before all His people.
⁶Pretiósa in conspéctu Dómini mors sanctórum ejus.	⁶Precious in the sight of the Lord is the death of His saints.
⁷O Dómine, quia ego servus tuus; ego servus tuus, et fílius ancíllæ tuæ. Dirupísti víncula mea:	⁷O Lord, for I am Thy servant: I am Thy servant, and the son of Thy handmaid. Thou hast broken My bonds.
⁸tibi sacrificábo hostiam laudis, et nomen Dómini invocábo.	⁸I will sacrifice to Thee the sacrifice of praise, and I will call upon the Name of the Lord.
⁹Vota mea Dómino reddam in conspéctu omnis pópuli ejus;	⁹I will pay my vows to the Lord in the sight of all His people:
¹⁰in átriis domus Dómini, in médio tui, Jerúsalem.	¹⁰in the courts of the house of the Lord, in the midst of thee, O Jerusalem.

Nov 2 Commemoration of the Faithful Departed (Lauds)

(November 3rd if it should fall on Sunday)
Antiphons, Psalms and Prayer as shown below. There is no Chapter or Hymn.

Psalm 50

Ant 1. Exsultábunt Dómino ossa humiliáta.	Ant 1. The humbled bones will rejoice in the Lord.
³Miserére mei, Deus, secúndum magnam misericórdiam tuam; et secúndum multitúdinem miseratiónum tuárum, dele iniquitátem meam.	³Have mercy on me, O God, according to Thy great compassion. And according to the multitude of Thy tender mercies blot out my iniquity.
⁴Ámplius lava me ab iniquitáte mea, et a peccáto meo munda me..	⁴Wash me yet more from my iniquity, and cleanse me from my sin.
⁵Quóniam iniquitátem meam ego cognósco, et peccátum meum contra me est semper	⁵For I know my wickedness, and my sin is always before me.
⁶Tibi soli peccávi, et malum coram te feci; ut justificéris in sermónibus tuis, et vincas cum judicáris.	⁶To Thee only have I sinned, and have done evil before Thee: that Thou mayest be justified in Thy words, and

Proper of the Season

	mayest be blameless when Thou judgest.
⁷Ecce enim in iniquitátibus concéptus sum, et in peccátis concépit me mater mea.	⁷For behold I was conceived in iniquities; and in sins did my mother conceive me.
⁸Ecce enim veritátem dilexísti; incérta et occúlta sapiéntiæ tuæ manifestásti mihi.	⁸For behold Thou hast loved truth: the uncertain and hidden things of Thy wisdom Thou hast made manifest to me.
⁹Aspérges me hyssópo, et mundábor; lavábis me, et super nivem dealbábor.	⁹Thou shalt sprinkle me with hyssop, and I shall be cleansed: Thou shalt wash me, and I shall be made whiter than snow.
¹⁰Audítui meo dabis gáudium et lætítiam, et exsultábunt ossa humiliáta.	¹⁰To my hearing Thou shalt give joy and gladness: and the bones that have been humbled shall rejoice.
¹¹Avérte fáciem tuam a peccátis meis, et ómnes iniquitátes meas dele.	¹¹Turn away Thy face from my sins, and blot out all my iniquities.
¹²Cor mundum crea in me, Deus, et spíritum rectum ínnova in viscéribus meis.	¹²Create a clean heart in me, O God: and renew a right spirit within my bowels.
¹³Ne projícias me a fácie tua, et spíritum sanctum tuum ne áuferas a me.	¹³Cast me not away from Thy face; and take not Thy Holy Spirit from me.
¹⁴Redde mihi lætítiam salutáris tui, et spíritu principáli confírma me.	¹⁴Restore unto me the joy of Thy salvation, and strengthen me with a perfect spirit.
¹⁵Docébo iníquos vias tuas, et impii ad te converténtur.	¹⁵I will teach the unjust Thy ways: and the wicked shall be converted to Thee.
¹⁶Líbera me de sanguínibus, Deus, Deus salútis meæ, et exsultábit lingua mea justítiam tuam.	¹⁶Deliver me from blood, O God, Thou God of my salvation: and my tongue shall extol Thy justice.
¹⁷Dómine, lábia mea aperies, et os meum annuntiábit laudem tuam.	¹⁷O Lord, Thou wilt open my lips: and my mouth shall declare Thy praise.
¹⁸Quóniam si voluísses sacrifícium, dedíssem útique; holocáustis non delectáberis.	¹⁸For if Thou hadst desired sacrifice, I would indeed have given it: but with burnt offerings Thou wilt not be delighted.
¹⁹Sacrifícium Deo spíritus contribulátus; cor contrítum et humiliátum, Deus, non despícies.	¹⁹A sacrifice to God is an afflicted spirit: a contrite and humbled heart, O God, Thou wilt not despise.
²⁰Benígne fac, Dómine, in bona voluntáte tua Sion, ut ædificéntur muri Jerúsalem.	²⁰Deal favorably, O Lord, in Thy good will with Zion; that the walls of Jerusalem may be rebuilt.
²¹Tunc acceptábis sacrifícium justítiæ, oblatiónes et holocáusta; tunc impónent super altáre tuum vítulos.	²¹Then shalt Thou accept the sacrifice of justice, oblations and whole burnt

Proper of the Season

	offerings: then shall they lay calves upon Thine altar.
Psalm 64	
Ant 2. Exáudi, Dómine, oratiónem meam: ad te omnis caro véniet.	Ant 2. Hear my prayer, O Lord: all flesh shall come to Thee.
²Te decet hymnus, Deus, in Sion, et tibi reddétur votum in Jerúsalem.	²A hymn, O God, becometh Thee in Zion: and a vow shall be offered to Thee in Jerusalem.
³Exáudi oratiónem meam; ad te omnis caro véniet.	³O hear my prayer: all flesh shall come to Thee.
⁴Verba iniquórum prævaluérunt super nos, et impietátibus nostris tu propitiaberis.	⁴The words of the wicked have prevailed over us and Thou wilt pardon our transgressions.
⁵Beátus quem elegisti et assumpsisti: inhabitábit in átriis tuis. Replébimur in bonis domus tuæ; sanctum est templum tuum, mirábile in æquitáte	⁵Blessed is He whom Thou hast chosen and taken to Thee: He shall dwell in Thy courts. We shall be filled with the good things of Thy house; holy is Thy temple, wonderful in justice.
⁶Exáudi nos, Deus, salutáris noster, spes ómnium finium terræ, et in mari longe.	⁶Hear us, O God our Savior, who art the hope of all the ends of the earth, and in the sea afar off:
⁷Præparans montes in virtúte tua, accinctus poténtia;	⁷Thou who, by Thy strength and being girded with power, makes the mountains remain secured.
⁸qui contúrbas profúndum maris, sonum flúctuum ejus. Turbabúntur gentes,	⁸Who troublest the depth of the sea, the noise of its waves. The Gentiles shall be distressed:
⁹et timébunt qui hábitant términos a signis tuis; éxitus matutíni et véspere delectábis.	⁹and they that dwell in the uttermost borders shall be afraid at Thy signs: Thou shalt make the going out of the morning and of the evening to be joyful.
¹⁰Visitásti terram, et inebriásti eam; multiplicásti locupletáre eam. Flumen Dei replétum est aquis; parásti cibum illórum: quóniam ita est præparátio ejus.	¹⁰Thou hast visited the earth, and hast plentifully watered it; Thou hast many ways enriched it. The river of God is filled with water, Thou hast prepared their food: for so is its preparation.
¹¹Rivos ejus inébria; multíplica genímina ejus: in stillicídiis ejus lætábitur gérminans.	¹¹Fill up plentifully the streams thereof, multiply its fruits; it shall spring up and rejoice in its showers.
¹²Benedíces corónæ anni benignitátis tuæ, et campi tui replebúntur ubertáte.	¹²Thou shalt bless the crown of the year of Thy goodness: and Thy fields shall be filled with plenty.
¹³Pinguéscent speciósa desérti, et exsultatióne colles accingéntur.	¹³The beautiful places of the wilderness shall grow fat: and the hills shall be girded about with joy.

Proper of the Season

¹⁴Indúti sunt aríetes óvium, et valles abundábunt fruménto; clamábunt, étenim hymnum dicent.	¹⁴The rams of the flock are clothed, and the vales shall abound with corn: they shall shout, yea they shall sing a hymn.

Psalm 62

Ant 3. Me suscépit déxtera tua Dómine.	Ant 3. Thy right hand hath received me, Lord.
¹Deus, Deus meus, ad te de luce vígilo. Sitívit in te ánima mea; quam multiplíciter tibi caro mea!	¹O God, my God, to Thee do I watch at break of day. For Thee my soul hast thirsted: for Thee my flesh, O how many ways.
²In terra desérta, et ínvia, et inaquósa, sic in sanctoappárui tibi, ut vidérem virtútem tuam et glóriam tuam.	²In a desert land, and where there is no path, and no water: so in the sanctuary have I come before Thee, to see Thy power and Thy glory.
³Quóniam mélior est misericórdia tua supervitas, lábia mea laudábunt te.	³For Thy mercy is better than life: Thee my lips shall praise.
⁴Sic benedícam te in vita mea, et in nómine tuo levábo manus meas.	⁴Thus will I bless Thee all my life long: and in Thy Name I will lift up my hands.
⁵Sicut ádipe et pinguédine repleátur ánima mea, et lábiis exsultatiónis laudábit os meum.	⁵Let my soul be filled as with marrow and fatness: and my mouth shall praise Thee with joyful lips.
⁶Si memor fui tui super stratum meum, in matutínis meditábor in te.	⁶If I have thought about Thee upon my bed, I will meditate on Thee in the morning hours:
⁷Quia fuísti adjútor meus, et in velaménto alárum tuárum exsultábo.	⁷because Thou hast been my Helper. And I will rejoice under the cover of Thy wings.
⁸Adhǽsit ánima mea post te; me suscépit déxtera tua.	⁸My soul hath stuck close to Thee: Thy right hand hath received me.
⁹Ipsi vero in vanum quæsiérunt ánimam meam: introíbunt in inferióra terræ;	⁹But they have sought my soul in vain, they shall go into the depths of the earth.
¹⁰Tradéntur in manus gládii: partes vúlpium erunt.	¹⁰They shall be delivered into the hands of the sword, they shall be the prey of foxes.
¹¹Rex vero lætábitur in Deo; laudabúntur ómnes qui jurant in eo: quia obstrúctum est os loquéntium iníqua.	¹¹But the king will rejoice in God, all who swear by Him will be praised: because the voice of those who speak unjustly is silenced.

Canticle of Ezechias Is. 28:10-20

Ant 4. A porta ínferi érue Dómine ánimam meam.	Ant 4. Deliver my soul, O Lord, from the gates of hell.
¹⁰Ego dixi in dimídio diérum meórum: Vadam ad portas ínferi; quæsívi resíduum annórum meórum.	¹⁰I said: In the midst of my days I shall go to the gates of hell: I sought for the rest of my years.
¹¹Dixi: Non vidébo Dóminum Deum in terra vivéntium; non aspíciam hóminem ultra, et habitatórem quiétis.	¹¹I said: I shall not see the Lord God in the land of the living. I shall

Proper of the Season

	behold man no more, among those who dwell in the world.
¹²Generátio mea abláta est, et convolúta est a me, quasi tabernáculum pastórum. Præcísa est velut a texénte vita mea; dum adhuc ordírer, succídit me: de mane usque ad vésperam fínies me.	¹²My generation is at an end, and it is rolled away from me, as a shepherd's tent. My life is cut off, as by a weaver: whilst I was yet but beginning, he cut me off: from morning even to night Thou wilt make an end of me.
¹³Sperábam usque ad mane; quasi leo, sic contrívit ómnia ossa mea: de mane usque ad vésperam fínies me.	¹³I hoped till morning, as a lion so hath he broken all my bones: from morning even to night Thou wilt make an end of me.
¹⁴Sicut pullus hirúndinis, sic clamábo; meditábor ut columba. Attenuáti sunt óculi mei, suspiciéntes in excélsum. Dómine, vim pátior: respónde pro me.	¹⁴I will cry like a young swallow, I will meditate like a dove: my eyes are weakened looking upward: Lord, I suffer violence, answer Thou for me.
¹⁵Quid dicam, aut quid respondébit mihi, cum ipse fécerit? Recogitábo tibi ómnes annos meos in amaritúdine ánimæ meæ.	¹⁵What shall I say, or what shall he answer for me, whereas he himself hath done it? I will recount to Thee all my years in the bitterness of my soul.
¹⁶Dómine, si sic vívitur, et in tálibus vita spíritus mei, corrípies me, et vivificábis me.	¹⁶O Lord, if man's life be such, and the life of my spirit be in such things as these, Thou shalt correct me, and make me to live.
¹⁷Ecce in pace amaritúdo mea amaríssima. Tu autem eruísti ánimam meam ut non períret; projecísti post tergum tuum ómnia peccáta mea.	¹⁷Behold in peace is my bitterness most bitter: but Thou hast delivered my soul that it should not perish, Thou hast cast all my sins behind Thy back.
¹⁸Quia non inférnus confitébitur tibi, neque mors laudábit te: non exspectábunt qui descéndunt in lacum veritátem tuam.	¹⁸For hell shall not confess to Thee, neither shall death praise Thee: nor shall they that go down into the pit, look for Thy truth.
¹⁹Vivens, vivens ipse confitébitur tibi, sicut et ego hódie; pater filiis notam fáciet veritátem tuam.	¹⁹The living, the living, he shall give praise to Thee, as I do this day: the father shall make the truth known to the children.
²⁰Dómine, salvum me fac! et psalmos nostros cantábimus cunctis diébus vitæ nostræ in domo Dómini.	²⁰O Lord, save me, and we will sing our psalms all the days of our life in the house of the Lord.

Psalm 150

Ant 5. Omnis spíritus laudet Dóminum.	Ant 5. Every spirit praiseth the Lord.
¹Laudáte Dóminum in sanctis ejus; laudáte eum in firmaménto virtútis ejus.	¹Praise ye the Lord in His holy places: praise ye Him in the firmament of His power.

Proper of the Season

²Laudáte eum in virtútibus ejus; laudáte eum secúndum multitúdinem magnitúdinis ejus.	²Praise ye Him for His mighty acts: praise ye Him according to the multitude of His greatness.
³Laudáte eum in sono tubæ; laudáte eum in psaltério et cíthara.	³Praise ye Him with the sound of trumpet: praise Him with psaltery and harp.
⁴Laudáte eum in týmpano et choro; laudáte eum in chordis et órgano.	⁴Praise ye Him with timbrel and choir: praise Him with strings and organs.
⁵Laudáte eum in cýmbalis benesonántibus; laudáte eum in cýmbalis jubilatiónis. Omnis spíritus laudet Dóminum!	⁵Praise ye Him on high sounding cymbals: praise Him on cymbals of joy: let every spirit praise the Lord.
***Versiculi* V.** Audivi vocem de cælo dicéntem mihi. **R.** Beáti mortui qui in Dómino moriúntur.	***Versicle* V.** I heard a voice from heaven saying to me. **R.** Blessed are the dead who die in the Lord.
Ad Benedíctus Ant. Ego sum resurréctio et vita: qui credit in me, étiam si mortuus fúerit, vivet: et omnis qui vivit et credit in me, non morietur in ætérnum.	***Benedíctus Ant.*** I am the Resurrection and the Life: he that believeth in Me, even if he were dead, yet shall he live: and whosoever liveth and believeth in Me shall never die.
Post antiphonam, dicitur flexis genibus: **V.** Pater noster ... *Deinde:*	*After the antiphon pray kneeling:* **V.** Our Father ... *Then:*
V. A porta ínferi. **R.** Érue, Dómine, ánimas eórum. **V.** Requiéscant in pace. **R.** Amen **V.** Dómine exáudi oratiónem meam. **R.** Et clamor meus ad te véniat.	**V.** From the gate of hell. **R.** Deliver, O Lord, their souls. **V.** May they rest in peace. **R.** Amen. **V.** Lord, hear my prayer. **R.** And let my cry come unto Thee.
Orátio Oremus. Fidélium Deus ómnium condítor et redémptor, animábus famulórum famularúmque tuárum remissiónem cunctórum tríbue peccatórum: ut indulgéntiam quam semper optavérunt, piis supplicatiónibus consequántur: Qui vivis et regnas ... **R.** Amen.	***Prayer*** Let us pray. O God, the Creator and Redeemer of all the faithful, grant to the souls of Thy servants and handmaids the forgiveness of their sins, and may they by our devout prayers be given the pardon which they have always desired, Who livest and reignest ... **R.** Amen.
V. Réquiem ætérnam dona eis Dómine. **R.** Et lux perpétua lúceat eis. **V.** Requiéscant in pace. **R.** Amen.	**V.** Give them eternal rest, O Lord. **R.** And let perpetual light shine upon them. **V.** May they rest in peace. **R.** Amen.
Nov 2 Commemoration of the Faithful Departed (Vespers) All as in Monday Vespers except below.	
Ad Magníficat Ant. Omne quod dat mihi Pater, ad me véniet; et eum qui venit ad me, non eíciam foras.	***Magníficat Ant.*** All that the Father giveth Me will come to Me: and him that cometh to Me I will not cast out.

Common of the Saints

Common of the Saints

Common of Martyrs

Lauds
Psalms of Sunday Lauds I and Prayer from the feast day.

Ant 1. Qui me conféssus fúerit coram homínibus, confitébor et ego eum coram Patre meo.	**Ant 1.** He who confesseth Me before men, I will confess him before My Father.
Ant 2. Qui séquitur me, non ambulat in ténebris, sed habébit lumen vitæ, dicit Dóminus.	**Ant 2.** He that followeth Me shall not walk in darkness, but shall have the light of life, sayeth the Lord.
Ant 3. Qui mihi ministráverit, honorificábit eum Pater meus, qui est in cælis, dicit Dóminus.	**Ant 3.** Whoever serveth Me, My Father in heaven will honor him, sayeth the Lord.
Ant 4. Si quis mihi ministráverit, honorificábit eum Pater meus, qui est in cælis, dicit Dóminus.	**Ant 4.** If anyone serveth Me, My Father in heaven will honor him, sayeth the Lord.
Ant 5. Volo, Pater, ut, ubi ego sum, illic sit et miníster meau.	**Ant 5.** I desire, Father, that where I am, there My servant may be also.
Capitulum (Jas 1:12) Beátus vir, qui suffert tentatiónem: quóniam, cum probátus fúerit, accípiet corónam vitæ, quam repromísit Deus diligéntibus se.	***Chapter*** (Jas 1:12) Blessed is the man that endureth temptation; for when he hath been proved, he shall receive the crown of life, which God hath promised to them that love Him.

Hymn – Invicte Martyr, page 382

Ad Benedíctus Ant. Qui odit ánimam suam in hoc mundo, in vitam ætérnam custódit eam.	***Benedíctus Ant.*** He who hateth his soul in this world keepeth it for eternal life.

Vespers
Psalms of Sunday Vespers and Antiphons from Lauds above but in place of the last; Psalm 115.

¹Crédidi, propter quod locútus sum; ego autem humiliátus sum nimis.	¹I have believed, therefore have I spoken; but I have been greatly humbled.
²Ego dixi in excéssu meo: Omnis homo mendax.	²I said in my excess: Every man is a liar.
³Quid retríbuam Dómino pro ómnibus quæ retríbuit mihi?	³What shall I render to the Lord, for all the things that He hath rendered to me?
⁴Cálicem salutáris accipiam, et nomen Dómini invocábo.	⁴I will take the chalice of salvation; and I will call upon the Name of the Lord.
⁵Vota mea Dómino reddam coram omni pópulo ejus.	⁵I will pay my vows to the Lord before all His people:
⁶Pretiósa in conspéctu Dómini mors sanctórum ejus.	⁶precious in the sight of the Lord is the death of His saints.
⁷O Dómine, quia ego servus tuus; ego servus tuus, et fílius ancíllæ tuæ. Dirupísti víncula mea.	⁷O Lord, for I am Thy servant: I am Thy servant, and the son of Thy

Common of the Saints

	handmaid. Thou hast broken My bonds.
⁸Tibi sacrificábo hóstiam laudis, et nomen Dómini invocábo.	⁸I will sacrifice to Thee the sacrifice of praise, and I will call upon the Name of the Lord.
⁹Vota mea Dómino reddam in conspéctu omnis pópuli ejus;	⁹I will pay my vows to the Lord in the sight of all His people:
¹⁰in átriis domus Dómini, in médio tui, Jerúsalem.	¹⁰in the courts of the house of the Lord, in the midst of thee, O Jerusalem.
Capitulum (Jas 1:12) Beátus vir, qui suffert tentatiónem: quóniam, cum probátus fúerit, accípiet corónam vitæ, quam repromísit Deus diligéntibus se.	*Chapter* (Jas 1:12) Blessed is the man that endureth temptation; for when he hath been proved, he shall receive the crown of life, which God hath promised to them that love Him.
Hymn – Deus Tuórum Militum, page 376	
Ad Magnificat Ant. Qui vult veníre post me, ábneget semetípsum, it tillat crucem suam, et sequátut me.	*Magnificat Ant.* He that will come after Me, let him deny himself, and take up his cross, and follow Me.

Common of Confessors

Lauds
Psalms of Sunday Lauds I and Prayer from the feast day.

Ant 1. Dómine, quinque talénta traditísti mihi, ecce ália quinque superlucrátus sum.	**Ant 1.** Lord, Thou gavest me five talents, behold, I have gained another five.
Ant 2. Euge, serve bone, in módico fidélis, intra in gáudium Dómini tui.	**Ant 2.** Hail, good servant, faithful in little ways, enter into the joy of thy Lord.
Ant 3. Fidélis servus et prudens, quem constítuit Dóminus super famíliam suam.	**Ant 3.** The Lord appointed a faithful and prudent servant over His family.
Ant 4. Beátus ille servus, quem, cum vénerit Dóminus ejus et pulsáverit jánuam, invénerit vigilántem.	**Ant 4.** Blessed is that servant whom, when his Lord comes and knocks at the door, He finds him watching.
Ant 5. Serve bone et fidélis, intra in gáudium Dómini tui.	**Ant 5.** Serve well and faithfully, good servant, and enter into the joy of thy Lord.
Capitulum (Sir 31:8-9) Beátus vir, qui invéntus est sine mácula, et qui post aurum non ábiit, nec sperávit in pecúnia et thesáuris. Quis est hic, et laudábimus eum? Fecit enim mirabília in vita sua.	*Chapter* (Sir 31:8-9) Blessed is the rich man that is found without blemish: and that hath not gone after gold, nor put his trust in money nor in treasures. Who is he, and we will praise him? For he hath done wonderful things in his life.

Common of the Saints

Hymn – *Iste Confessor Dómine*, page 379

Versiculi **V.** Justum deduxit Dóminus per vias recta. **R.** Et osténdit illi regnum Dei.	***Versicle*** **V.** The Lord hath led the just in straight paths. **R.** And He showed him the kingdom of God.
Ad Benedíctus Ant. Euge, serve bone et fidélis, quia in pauca fulsti fidélis, supra multa te constítuam, intra in gáudiam Dómini tui.	***Benedíctus Ant.*** Rejoice, good and faithful servant, because thou hast been faithful in a few things, I will set thee over many things. Enter into the joy of thy Lord.

Vespers
Psalms of Sunday Vespers and Antiphons from Lauds above.

Capitulum (Sir 31:8-9) Beátus vir, qui inventus est sine macula, et qui post aurum non abiit, nec sperávit in pecunia et theosauris. Quis est hic, et laudabimus eum? Fecit enim mirabília in vita sua.	***Chapter*** (Sir 31:8-9) Blessed is the rich man that is found without blemish: and that hath not gone after gold, nor put his trust in money nor in treasures. Who is he, and we will praise him? For he hath done wonderful things in his life.

Hymn – *Iste Confessor Dómine*, page 379

Versiculi **V.** Justum dedúxit Dóminus per vias recta. **R.** Et osténdit illi regnum Dei.	***Versicle*** **V.** The Lord hath led the just in straight paths. **R.** And He showed him the kingdom of God.
Ad Magnificat Ant. Hic vir despíciens mundum et terréna, triúmphans, divítias cælo cóndidit ore, manu.	***Magnificat Ant.*** This man, despising the world and the earthly, triumphantly laid up riches in heaven with his words and actions.

Common of Virgins

Lauds
Psalms of Sunday Lauds I and Prayer from the feast day.

Ant 1. Hæc est Virgo sápiens, et una de número prudéntum.	**Ant 1.** This is a wise Virgin, and one of the number of prudent ones.
Ant 2. Hæc est Virgo sápiens, quam Dóminus vigilántem envénit.	**Ant 2.** This is the wise Virgin whom the Lord found vigilant.
Ant 3. Hæc est quæ nescívit torum in delícto: havébit fructum in respectióne animárum santárum.	**Ant 3.** This is she who did not know the bed in sin: she will bear fruit in the respect of the holy souls.
Ant 4. Veni elécta mea, et ponam in te thronum meum.	**Ant 4.** I have come, my chosen one, and I will place my throne in thee.
Ant 5. Ista est speciósa inter fílius Jerúsalem.	**Ant 5.** She is beautiful among the daughters of Jerusalem.
Capitulum (2 Cor 10:17-18) Fratres: Qui autem gloriátur, in Dómino gloriétur. Non enim qui seípsum comméndat, ille probátus est: sed quem Deus comméndat.	***Chapter*** (2 Cor 10:17-18) Brethren: But he that glorieth, let him glory in the Lord. For not he who commendeth himself is approved, but he whom God commendeth.

Hymn – *Jesu, Corona Vírginum*, page 384

Common of the Saints

Versiculi V. Diffusa est grátia in lábiis tuis. R. Proptérea benedíxit te Deus in ætérnum.	***Versicle*** V. Grace is diffused on thy lips. R. Therefore God hath blessed thee forever.
Ad Benedíctus Ant. Simile est regnum cælórum hómini negotiatóri quærénti bonas margarítas: invénta una pretiósa, dedit ómnia sua, et comparávit cam.	***Benedíctus Ant.*** The kingdom of heaven is like unto a merchant that sought good pearls: he found one of great worth and gave all that he had, and he bought it.

Vespers
Psalms of Sunday Vespers II and Antiphons from Lauds above.

Capitulum (2 Cor 10:17-18) Fratres: Qui autem gloriátur, in Dómino losiétur. Non enim qui seípsum comméndat, ille probátus est: sed quem Deus comméndat.	***Chapter*** (2 Cor 10:17-18) Brethren: But he that glorieth, let him glory in the Lord. For not he who commendeth himself is approved, but he whom God commendeth.

Hymn – *Jesu, Corona Vírginum*, page 384

Versiculi V. Adducéntur Regi Vírgines post eam. R. Próximæ ejus afferéntur tibi.	***Versicle*** V. The Virgins shall be brought to the King after her. R. Her relatives will be brought to thee.
Ad Magnificat Ant. Prudéntes Vírgines, apiáte vestras lámpades: ecce Sponsus venit, exíte óbviam ei.	***Magnificat Ant.*** Prudent virgins, light your lamps: behold, the bridegroom is coming, go out to meet him.

Common of the Apostles

Lauds
Psalms of Sunday Lauds I and Prayer from the feast day

Ant 1. Hoc est præcéprum meum, ut diligátis ínvicem, sicut diléxi vos.	**Ant 1.** This is My precept, that ye love one another as I have loved you.
Ant 2. Majórem caritátem nemo habet, ut ánimam suam ponat quis pro amícis suis.	**Ant 2.** No one hath greater charity than to lay down one's life for one's friends.
Ant 3. Vos amíci nei estis, si fecéritis quæ præcípio vobis, dícit Dóminus.	**Ant 3.** Ye are my friends if you do what I command you, sayeth the Lord.
Ant 4. Beáti pacífici, beáti mundo corde: Quóniam ipsi Deum vidébunt.	**Ant 4.** Blessed are the peaceful, blessed are the pure in heart: for they shall see God themselves.
Ant 5. In patiéntia vestra possidebitis ánimas vestras.	**Ant 5.** In your patience ye will possess your souls.
Capitulum (Eph 2:19-20) Fratres: Jam non estis hóspites, et advénæ; sed estis cives Sanctórum, et doméstici Dei, superædificáti super fundaméntum Apostolórum et Prophetárum, ipso summon angulári lápide Christo Jesu.	***Chapter*** (Eph 2:19-20) Now therefore ye are no more strangers and foreigners; but ye are fellow citizens with the saints, and the domestics of God: built upon the foundation of the Apostles and

Common of the Saints

	Prophets, Jesus Christ Himself being the chief corner stone.
Hymn – Exultet Orbis Gaudis, page 377	
Versiculi V. Annuntiavérunt ópera Dei. R. Et facta ejus intelléxerunt.	*Versicle* V. They announced the works of God. R. And they understood His deeds.
Ad Benedíctus Ant. Vos qui reliquístis ómnia, et secúti estis me, céntuplum accipiéntis, et vitam ætérnam possidébitis.	*Benedíctus Ant.* Ye who have left everything and followed Me will receive a hundredfold and will inherit eternal life.
Vespers Psalms of Sunday Vespers and Antiphons below. Chapter and Hymn from Lauds above.	
Ant 1. Jurávit Dóminus, et non Pænitébit eum: Tu es sacérdo in ætérnum.	**Ant 1.** The Lord hath sworn and will not repent: Thou art a priest forever.
Ant 2. Cóllocet eum Dóminus cum princípibus pópuli sui.	**Ant 2.** The Lord will place him with the princes of his people.
Ant 3. Dirupísti, Dómine, víncula mea: tibi sacrificábo hóstiam laudis.	**Ant 3.** Thou hast broken my bonds, O Lord: I will offer Thee a sacrifice of praise.
Ant 4. Eúntes ibant et flebant, mitténtes sémina sua.	**Ant 4.** They wept as they went, sowing their seeds.
Ant 5. Confortátus est principátus eórum, et honoráti sung amíci tui, Deus.	**Ant 5.** Their leadership was strengthened, and Thy friends, O God, were honored.
Versiculi V. Annuntiavérunt ópera Dei. R. Et facta ejus intelléxerunt.	*Versicle* V. They announced the works of God. R. And they understood His deeds.
Ad Magnificat Ant. Estóte fortes in bello, et pugnáte cum antíquo serpénte: et accipiéntis regnum ætérnum.	*Magnificat Ant.* Be strong in the battle, and fight with the ancient serpent, and ye will receive the eternal kingdom.

Common of the Feasts of the Blessed Virgin Mary

Lauds
Psalms of Sunday Lauds I, with Antiphons below.

Ant 1. Dum esset Rex in accúbitu suo, nardus mea dedit odórum suavitátus.	**Ant 1.** While the King was on His couch, my spikenard gave off sweet scents.
Ant 2. Læva ejus sub cápite meo, et déxtera illius amplexábitur me.	**Ant 2.** His left hand shall be under my head, and His right hand shall embrace me.
Ant 3. Nigra sum, sed formósa, filiæ Jerúsalem: ideo diléxit me Rex, et introdúxit me in cubículum suum.	**Ant 3.** I am black, but beautiful, O daughters of Jerusalem: therefore the King loved me, and brought me into His chamber.

Common of the Saints

Ant 4. Jam hiems tránsiit, imber ábiit et recéssit: surge, amíca mea et veni.	**Ant 4.** Now the winter is past, the rain is over and gone: arise, My love, and come.
Ant 5. Speciósa facta es et suávis in delíciis tuis, sancta Dei Génitrix	**Ant 5.** Thou hast become beautiful and sweet in thy delights, holy Mother of God.
Capitulum (Sir 24:14) Ab inítio et ante sǽcula creáta sum, et usque ad futúrum sǽculum non désinam: et in habitatióne sancta coram ipso ministrávi.	***Chapter*** (Sir 24:14) From the beginning, and before the world, was I created, and unto the world to come I shall not cease to be, and in the holy dwelling place I have ministered before Him.

Hymn – Ave, Maris Stella, page 373

***Versiculi* V.** Dignáre me laudáre te, Virgo sacráta. **R.** Da mihi virtútem contra hostes tuos.	***Versicle* V.** Thou deservest my praise, Holy Virgin **R.** Give me strength against thine enemies.
Ad Benedictus Ant. Beáta es, María, quæ credidísti: perficiéntur in te, quæ dicta sunt tibi a Dómino.	***Benedictus Ant.*** Blessed art thou, Mary, who hast believed: the things which were spoken by the Lord unto thee shall be fulfilled in thee.
Orátio Concéde nos fámulos tuos, quǽsumus, Dómine Deus, perpétua mentis et córporis santáte gáudere: et, gloriósa beátæ Maríæ semper Vírginis intercessióne, a præsénti liberári tristítia et ætérna pérfrui lætítia. Per Dóminum nostrum ...	***Prayer*** Let us Thy servants, we beseech Thee, Lord God, enjoy perpetual sanctity of mind and body: and, through the glorious intercession of the Blessed Mary ever Virgin, may we be delivered from present sorrow and enjoy eternal happiness. Through our Lord ...

Vespers
Psalms of Sunday Vespers
Antiphons, Chapter, Hymn and Prayer from Lauds above.

***Versiculi* V.** Dignare me laudáre te, Vírgo sacráta. **R.** Da mihi virútem contra hostes tuos.	***Versicle* V.** Thou deservest my praise, Holy Virgin. **R.** Give me strength against thine enemies.
Ad Magnificat Ant. Beátam me dicent ómnes generatiónes, quia ancíllam húmilem respéxit Deus.	***Magnificat Ant.*** All generations will call me blessed, because God looked upon His humble handmaid.

Office of the Blessed Virgin Mary on Saturday

Lauds
Antiphons and Psalms from the Saturday in the Psalter.

Capitulum (Sir 24:14) Ab inítio et ante sǽcula creáta sum, et usque ad futúrum sǽculum non désinam: et in habitatióne sancta coram ipso ministrávi.	***Chapter*** (Sir 24:14) From the beginning, and before the world, was I created, and unto the world to come I shall not cease to be, and in the holy dwelling place I have ministered before Him.

Common of the Saints

Hymn – O Gloriósa Vírginum, page 56	
Versiculi V. Benedícta tu in cmuliéribus. R. Et benedíctus fructus ventris tui.	***Versicle*** V. Blessed art thou among women. R. And blessed is the fruit of thy womb.
Ad Benedíctus Ant. Beáta Dei Génitrix, María, Virgo perpétua, templum Dómini, sacrárium Spíritus Sancti, sola sine exémplo placuísti Dómino nostro Jesu Christo: ora pro póbulo, intérveni pro clero, intercéde pro devóto femíneo sexu.	***Benedíctus Ant.*** Blessed Mother of God, Mary, Perpetual Virgin, Temple of the Lord, and Sanctuary of the Holy Spirit, thou alone without equal pleased our Lord Jesus Christ: pray for the people, intervene for the clergy, and intercede for all devout women.
Orátio Concéde nos fámulos tuos, quǽsumus, Dómine Deus, perpétua mentis et córporis santáte gáudere: et, gloriósa beátæ Maríæ semper Vírginis intercessióne, a præsénti liberári tristítia et ætérna pérfrui lætítia. Per Dóminum nostrum ..	***Prayer*** Grant us Thy servants, we beseech Thee, Lord God, to enjoy perpetual health of mind and body: and, through the glorious intercession of the Blessed Mary ever Virgin, to be delivered from present sorrow and to enjoy eternal happiness. Through our Lord …

Proper of the Saints

Proper of the Saints (Lauds)

Nov. 30 St. Andrew — *Apostle*

Ant. Concéde nobis hóminem iustum, redde nobis hóminem sanctum: ne interfícias hóminem Deo cárum, iustum, mansuétum et pium.

Ant. Grant us a just man, give us back a holy man: do not kill a man dear to God; just, meek, and pious.

Orátio Maiestátem tuam, Dómine, supplíciter exorámus: ut, sicut Ecclésiæ tuæ beátus Andréas Apóstolus éxstitit prædicátor et rector; ita apud te sit pro nobis perpétuus intercéssor. Per Dóminum nostrum …

Prayer We implore Thy majesty, O Lord, that blessed Andrew the Apostle, who was a preacher and a ruler of Thy Church, may be our perpetual intercessor with Thee. Through our Lord …

Dec. 2 St. Bibiana — *Virgin and Martyr*

Ant. Símile est regnum cælórum hómini negotiatóri quærénti bonas margarítas: invénta una pretiósa, dedit ómnia sua, et comparávit eam

Ant. The kingdom of heaven is like unto a merchant seeking good pearls; having found one precious thing, he gave all he had and procured it.

Orátio Deus, ómnium largítor bonórum, qui in fámula tua Bibiána cum virginitátis flore martýrii palmam coniunxísti: mentes nostras eius intercessióne tibi caritáte coniúnge; ut, amótis perículis, præmia consequámur ætérna. Per Dóminum nostrum …

Prayer O God, bestower of all good things, who in Thy handmaid Bibiana joined the palm of martyrdom with the flower of virginity: unite our hearts with her intercession and love; that we may avoid dangers and obtain eternal rewards. Through our Lord …

Dec. 3 St. Francis Xavier — *Confessor*

Orátio Deus, qui Indiárum gentes beáti Francísci prædicatióne et miráculis Ecclésiæ tuæ aggregáre voluísti: concéde propítius; ut cuius gloriósa mérita venerámur, virtútum quoque imitémur exémpla. Per Dóminum nostrum …

Prayer O God, who brought together the nations of India by the preaching of Saint Francis and by the miracles of Thy Church: grant more mercifully, that we may venerate his glorious merits, and let us also imitate the example of his virtues. Through our Lord …

Dec. 4 St. Chrysologus — *Bishop, Confessor, Doctor*

Orátio Deus, qui beátum Petrum Chrysólogum Doctórem egrégium, divínitus præmonstrátum, ad regéndam et instruéndam Ecclésiam tuam éligi voluísti: præsta, quǽsumus; ut, quem Doctórem vitæ

Prayer O God, who chose Saint Peter Chrysologus, a superb Doctor, divinely foretold, to govern and instruct Thy Church: grant we ask Thee; that as this master of holiness showed us how to live on

Proper of the Saints Lauds

habúimus in terris, intercessórem habére mereámur in cælis. Per Dóminum nostrum ...	earth, he may be our advocate in heaven. Through our Lord...
Dec. 4 St. Barbara	*Virgin and Martyr (comm)*
Orátio Deus, qui inter cétera poténtiæ tuæ mirácula étiam in sexu frágili victóriam martýrii contulísti: concéde propítius; ut, qui beátæ Bárbaræ Vírginis et Martyris tuæ natalícia cólimus, per eius ad te exémpla gradiámur. Per Dóminum nostrum ...	*Prayer* O God, who, among other miracles of Thy power, Thou hast also strengthened many women in their victory of martyrdom: grant us more confidence, that we who honor the birth of the blessed Barbara the Virgin and Martyr, may advance towards Thee by her example. Through our Lord ....
Dec. 6 St. Nicholas	*Bishop and Confessor*
Orátio Deus, qui beátum Nicoláum Pontíficem innúmeris decorásti miráculis: tríbue, quǽsumus; ut eius méritis et précibus a gehénnæ incéndiis liberémur. Per Dóminum nostrum ...	*Prayer* O God, who gifted the blessed Bishop Nicholas with innumerable miracles: grant, we ask Thee; that by his merits and prayers we may be freed from the fires of hell. Through our Lord ...
Dec. 7 St. Ambrose	*Bishop, Confessor and Doctor*
Orátio Deus, qui pópulo tuo ætérnæ salútis beátum Ambrósium minístrum tribuísti: præsta, quǽsumus; ut, quem Doctórem vitæ habúimus in terris, intercessórem habére mereámur in cælis. Per Dóminum nostrum ...	*Prayer* O God, who gave the blessed Ambrose as a minister of eternal salvation to Thy people: grant, we beseech Thee, that this master of holiness that we had on earth, may be an intercessor for us in heaven. Through our Lord ...
Dec. 8 Immaculate Conception	*Blessed Virgin Mary* Lauds Antiphons Pg. 394
Capitulum (Prov 8:22-24) V. Dóminus possédit me in inítio viárum suárum, ántequam quidquam fáceret a princípio. Ab ætérno ordináta sum, et ex antíquis ántequam terra fíeret. Nondum erant abýssi, et ego iam concépta eram. R. Deo grátias.	*Chapter* (Prov 8:22-24) V. The Lord possessed me in the establishment of His ways before He did anything from the beginning. I was ordained from eternity, and from ancient times before the earth was made. The depths did not yet exist, and I had already been conceived. R. Thanks be to God.
Ant. Ait Dóminus Deus ad serpéntem: Inimicítias ponam inter te et mulíerem, et semen tuum et semen illíus: ipsa cónteret caput tuum, allelúia.	*Ant.* The Lord God said to the serpent: I will put enmities between thee and the woman, and thy seed and her seed: she shall crush thy head, alleluia.
Orátio Deus, qui per immaculátam Vírginis Conceptiónem dignum Fílio tuo habitáculum præparásti:	*Prayer* O God, who, through the Immaculate Conception of this Virgin, saved from all stain of sin,

Proper of the Saints Lauds

quæsumus; ut qui ex morte eiúsdem Fílii tui prævísa, eam ab omni labe præservásti, nos quoque mundos eius intercessióne ad te pervenire concédas. Per Dóminum nostrum ...	Thou prepared a dwelling place worthy of Thy Son: we ask; as by the foreseen death of Thy Son that we be allowed also, by her mediation, to come to Thee with pure hearts. Through our Lord ...
Dec. 11 St. Damasus	*Pope and Confessor*
Ant. Euge, serve bone et fidélis, quia in pauca fuísti fidélis, supra multa te constítuam, dicit Dóminus.	**Ant.** O good and faithful servant, because thou hast been faithful in a few things, I will set thee over many things, sayeth the Lord.
Orátio Gregem tuum, Pastor ætérne, placátus inténde: et per beátum Dámasum Summum Pontíficem perpétua protectióne custódi; quem totíus Ecclésiæ præstitísti esse pastórem. Per Dóminum nostrum ...	*Prayer* Look kindly upon Thy flock, O eternal Shepherd,: and through the intercession of blessed Damasus, Supreme Pontiff, whom Thou hast appointed to be the shepherd of Thy entire Church, guard it with perpetual protection. Through our Lord ...
Dec. 13 St. Lucy	*Virgin and Martyr*
Capitulum (2 Cor 10:17-18) V. Fratres: Qui gloriátur, in Dómino gloriétur. Non enim qui seípsum comméndat, ille probátus est; sed quem Deus comméndat. R. Deo grátias.	**Chapter** (2 Cor 10:17-18) V. Brethren: He who glories, let him glory in the Lord. For it is not he who commends himself who is approved, but whom God commends. R. Thanks be to God.
Orátio Exáudi nos, Deus, salutáris noster: ut sicut de beátæ Lúciæ Vírginis et Mártyris tuæ festivitáte gaudémus; ita piæ devotiónis erudiámur afféctu. Per Dóminum nostrum ...	*Prayer* Hear us, O God, our Savior: that as we rejoice in the feast of Thy blessed Virgin and Martyr Lucy, so we may be trained in the practice of pious devotion. Through our Lord ...
Dec. 16 St. Eusebius	*Bishop and Martyr*
Ant. Qui odit ánimam suam in hoc mundo, in vitam ætérnam custódit eam.	**Ant.** He who hates his life in this world keeps it in eternal life.
Orátio Deus, qui nos beáti Eusébii Mártyris tui atque Pontíficis ánnua solemnitáte lætíficas: concéde propítius; ut, cuius natalícia cólimus, de eiúsdem étiam protectióne gaudeámus. Per Dóminum nostrum ...	*Prayer* O God, who makes us happy with the annual solemnity of Thy blessed Martyr and Bishop: Eusebius, grant us mercy; so that we may rejoice in the protection of the one whose feast day we celebrate. Through our Lord ...
Dec. 21 St. Thomas	*Apostle*
Ant. Nolíte timére quinta enim die véniet ad vos Dóminus noster.	**Ant.** Do not be afraid, for on the fifth day our Lord will come to thee.

Proper of the Saints Lauds

Orátio Da nobis, quæsumus, Dómine, beáti Apóstoli tui Thomæ solemnitátibus gloriári: ut eius semper et patrocíniis sublevémur; et fidem cóngrua devotióne sectémur. Per Dóminum nostrum …	*Prayer* Grant us, we beseech Thee, O Lord, to glory in the solemnities of Thy blessed Apostle Thomas: that we may always be helped by his patronage, and follow the faith with a fervent devotion. Through our Lord …
	**The Feast Days of St. Stephen, St. John, Holy Innocents, St. Thomas of Canterbury, St. Silvester amd The Holy Name of Jesus begin on page 194**

Jan. 14 St. Hillary	*Bishop, Confessor and Doctor*
Orátio Deus, qui pópulo tuo ætérnæ salútis beátum Hilárium ministrum tribuísti: præsta quǽsumus; ut, quem Doctórem vitæ habúimus in terris, intercessórem habere mereámur in cælis. Per Dóminum nostrum …	*Prayer* O God, who gave to Thy people the blessed Hilary the minister of eternal salvation: grant we beseech Thee; that, as the teacher of a holy life we had on earth. we will deserve to have as an intercessor in heaven. Through our Lord …

Jan. 15 St. Paul	*First Hermit, Confessor*
Orátio Deus, qui nos Beáti Pauli Confessóris tui ánnua solemnitáte lætíficas; concéde propítius; ut, cujus natalítia cólimus, étiam actiónes imitémur. Per Dóminum nostrum …	*Prayer* O God, who makes us joyful with the annual solemnity of your Blessed Paul the Confessor; so that, whose birth we celebrate, we may also imitate his actions. Through our Lord …

Jan. 16 St. Marcellus I	*Pope and Martyr*
Orátio Preces pópuli tui, quǽsumus, Dómine, cleménter exáudi: ut beáti Marcélli Mártyris tui atque Pontíficus méritis adjuvémur, cujus passióne lætámur. Per Dóminum nostrum …	*Prayer* O Lord, graciously hear the prayers of Thy people, we beseech Thee: that we may be assisted by the merits of Thy blessed Martyr and Pontiff Marcellus, whose passion we celebrate. Through our Lord …

Jan. 17 St. Anthony	*Abbot and Confessor*
Orátio Intercéssio nos, quǽsumus, Dómine, beáti Antónii Abbátis comméndet: ut, quod nostris méritis non valémus, ejus patrocínio assesquámur. Per Dóminum nostrum …	*Prayer* We beseech Thee, O Lord, to commend us to the intercession of the blessed Antony the Abbot: that, if what we are not able by our own merits, we may yet attain by his patronage. Through our Lord …

Jan. 18 Chair of Peter	*Apostle*
Ant. Quodcúmque ligáveris super terram, erit ligátum et in cælis; et quodcúmque sólveris super terram, erit solútum et in cælis: dicit Dóminus Simóni Petro.	**Ant.** And whatever you bind on earth will be bound in heaven. and whatever you loose on earth will be loosed in heaven, sayeth the Lord to Simon Peter.

Proper of the Saints Lauds

Orátio Deus qui beáto Petro Apóstolo tuo, collátis clávibus regni cæléstis, ligándi atque solvéndi pontifícium tradidísti: concéde; ut intercessiónis ejus auxílio, a peccatórum nostrórum néxibus liberémur.	**Ant.** O God, who gavest the pontificate of Thy blessed Peter the Apostle the power of binding and loosing, and of holding the keys of the heavenly kingdom: grant that, by the help of his intercession, we may be freed from the bonds of our sin.
Jan. 18 St. Prisca	*Virgin and Martyr*
Ant. Símile est regnum cælórum hómini negotiatóri quærénti bonas margarítas: invénta una pretiósa, dedit ómnia sua, et comparávit eam.	**Ant.** The kingdom of heaven is like unto a merchant seeking good pearls; having found one precious thing, he gave all that he had, and procured it.
Orátio Da, quǽsumus, omnípotens Deus: ut, qui beátæ Priscæ Vírginis et Mártyris tuæ natalícia cólimus; et ánnua solemnitáte lætémur, et tantæ fídei proficiámus exémplo. Per Dóminum nostrum ...	**Prayer** We beseech Thee almighty God, that we who rejoice on this annual solemnity and honor the birth of the blessed Prisca, Virgin and Martyr, grant that she may become an example of great faith for us. Through our Lord ...
Jan. 19 Sts Marius and Companions	*Martyrs*
Ant. Vestri capilli cápitis ómnes numeráti sunt: nolíte timére: multis passéribus melióres estis vos.	**Ant.** All the hairs of thy head are numbered: fear not: thou art of more value than many sparrows.
Orátio Exáudi Dómine pópulum tuum cum sanctórum tuórum patrocínio supplicántem: ut et temporális vitæ nos tríbuas pace gaudére, et ætérnæ reperíre subsídium. Per Dóminum nostrum ...	**Prayer** Hear, O Lord, Thy people, along with the patronage of Thy Saints, Marius and his companions: we beg Thee, that Thou mayest grant that we may enjoy peace in our temporal life, and may find Thy friendship in eternity. Through our Lord ...
Jan. 20 Sts. Fabian and Sebastian	*Pope, Martyr*
Orátio Infirmitátem nostram réspice, omnípotens Deus: et quia pondus própriæ actiónis gravat, beatórum Mártyrum tuórum Fabiáni et Sebastiáni intercéssio gloriósa nos prótegat. Per Dóminum nostrum	**Prayer** Look upon our infirmity, almighty God: and because the weight of our own sins weighs us down, allow the glorious intercession of Thy blessed Martyrs Fabian and Sebastian to protect us. Through our Lord ...
Jan. 21 St. Agnes	*Virgin and Martyr*
Capitulum (Sir 51:1-3) V. Confitébor tibi, Dómine, Rex, et collaudábo te Deum Salvatórem meum. Confitébor nómini tuo:	**Chapter** (Sir 51:1-3) V. I will confess to Thee, O Lord my King, and I will praise Thee God my Savior. I will confess to Thy

quóniam adiútor et protéctor factus es mihi, et liberásti corpus meum a perditióne. **R.** Deo grátias.	Name: because Thou hast become my helper and protector and Thou hast delivered my body from destruction. **R.** Thanks be to God.
Ant. Ecce, quod concupívi, iam vídeo: quod sperávi, iam téneo: ipsi sum iuncta in cælis, quem in terris pósita, tota devotióne diléxi.	**Ant.** Behold, I now see what I desired: what I hoped for, I now have: I am united to Him in the heavens, Whom I loved with all devotion on earth.
Orátio Omnípotens sempitérne Deus, qui infirma mundi éligis, ut fórtia quæque confúndas: concéde propítius; ut, qui beátæ Agnétis Vírginis et Mártyris tuæ solémnia cólimus, eius apud te patrocínia sentiámus. Per Dóminum nostrum ...	*Prayer* Almighty and eternal God, who choosest the weakest of the world to confound the strong: grant more mercifully; that we who observe the solemnities of blessed Agnes Thy Virgin and Martyr, may profit by her intersessions to Thee. Through our Lord ...
Jan. 22 Sts. Vincent and Anastasius	*Martyrs*
Orátio Adésto, Dómine, supplicatiónibus nostris: ut, qui ex iniquitáte nostra reos nos esse cognóscimus, beatórum Mártyrum tuórum Vincéntii et Anastásii intercessióne liberémur. Per Dóminum nostrum ...	*Prayer* Attend, O Lord, to our supplications: that we who know that we are guilty of our sinfulness, may be freed by the intercession of Thy blessed Martyrs Vincentius and Anastasius. Through our Lord ...
Jan. 23 St. Raymond of Pennafort	*Confessor*
Orátio Deus, qui beátum Raymúndum pœniténtiæ sacraménti insígnem minístrum elegísti, et per maris undas mirabíliter traduxísti: concéde; ut eius intercessióne dignos pœniténtiæ fructus fácere, et ad ætérnæ salútis portum perveníre valeámus. Per Dóminum nostrum ...	*Prayer* O God, who chose the blessed Raymond as an eminent minister of the sacrament of penance, and Thou miraculously caused him to walk through the waves of the sea: grant; that by his intercession we may be able to create worthy fruits of remorse and reach the port of eternal salvation. Through our Lord ...
Jan. 24 St. Timothy	*Bishop and Martyr*
Orátio Infirmitátem nostram réspice, omnípotens Deus: et quia pondus próprie actiónis gravat, beáti Timóthei Mártyris tui atque Pontíficis intercéssio gloriósa nos prótegat. Per Dóminum nostrum ...	*Prayer* Look upon our infirmity, almighty God: and since the burden of our own evil deeds weighs us down, may the glorious intercession of Thy blessed Bishop Timothy protect us. Through our Lord ...

Proper of the Saints Lauds

Jan. 25 Conversion of St. Paul	*Apostle*
Capitulum (Acts 9:1-2) **V.** Saulus autem adhuc spirans minárum et cædis in discípulos Dómini, accéssit ad príncipem sacerdótum, et pétiit ab eo epístolas in Damáscum ad synagógas: ut si quos invenísset huius viæ viros ac mulíeres, vinctos perdúceret in Ierúsalem. **R.** Deo grátias.	***Chapter*** (Acts 9:1-2) **V.** But Saul, still breathing threats and murder against the Lord's disciples, went to the chief priest and asked him for letters to the synagogues in Damascus, so that if he found any men and women traveling on this road, he would bring them to Jerusalem. **R.** Thanks be to God.
Orátio Deus, qui univérsum mundum beáti Pauli Apóstoli prædicatióne docuísti: da nobis, quǽsumus; ut, qui eius hódie Conversiónem cólimus, per eius ad te exémpla gradiámur. Qui vivis et regnas …	***Prayer*** O God, who taught the whole world by the preaching of the blessed Paul the Apostle: grant we ask, that we who celebrate his conversion today may, through his example, rise towards Thee. Who liveth and reigneth…
Jan. 26 St. Polycarp	*Bishop and Martyr*
Orátio Deus, qui nos beáti Polycárpi Mártyris tui atque Pontíficis ánnua solemnitáte lætíficas: concéde propítius; ut, cuius natalícia cólimus, de eiúsdem étiam protectióne gaudeámus. Per Dóminum nostrum …	***Prayer*** O God, who makes us joyous at the annual solemnity of the blessed Polycarp, Thy Martyr and Bishop, mercifully grant that we may enjoy the protection of the one whose feast day we celebrate. Through our Lord ….
Jan. 27 St. John Chrysostom	*Bishop, Doctor and Confessor*
Orátio Ecclésiam tuam, quǽsumus, Dómine, grátia cæléstis amplíficet: quam beáti Ioánnis Chrysóstomi Confessóris tui atque Pontíficis illustráre voluísti gloriósis méritis et doctrínis. Per Dóminum nostrum ...	***Prayer*** We beseech Thee, O Lord, that the grace of heaven will magnify Thy Church: which Thou wished to illuminate with the glorious merits and doctrines of the blessed John Chrysostom, Thy Confessor and Bishop. Through our Lord ...
Jan. 28 St. Peter Nolasco	*Confessor*
Orátio Deus, qui in tuæ caritátis exémplum ad fidélium redemptiónem sanctum Petrum Ecclésiam tuam nova prole fecundáre divínitus docuísti: ipsíus nobis intercessióne concéde; a peccáti servitúte solútis, in cælésti pátria perpétua libertáte gaudére: Qui vivis et regnas…	***Prayer*** O God, who, as an example of Thy charity and for the redemption of the faithful, Thou hadst inspired Saint Peter to provide Thy Church with a new religious order vowed to ransom the faithful from slavery: grant us through his intercession that we be freed from the slavery of sin so we may enjoy eternal freedom in heaven: Who liveth and reigneth …

Proper of the Saints Lauds

Jan. 29 St. Francis de Sales	*Confessor, Doctor and Bishop*
Orátio Deus qui animarum salutem beatum Franciscum Confessiorum tuum atque Pontificem omnibus omnia factum esse voluisti: concede propitius; ut caritas tuae dulcedine perfusi ejus dirigentibus monitis ac suffragantibus meritis aeterna gaudia consequamur. Per Dominum nostrum …	*Prayer* O God, the joy of the Holy Francis the Confessor, who You willed should become all things to all men, grant us mercy; so through the sweetness your love which is poured out upon us, we may obtain the gift of eternal joy. Through our Lord …
Jan. 30 St. Martina	*Virgin and Martyr*
Orátio Deus, qui inter cétera poténtiæ tuæ mirácula étiam in sexu frágili victóriam martýrii contulísti: concéde propítius; ut, qui beátæ Martínæ Vírginis et Mártyris tuæ natalícia cólimus, per eius ad te exémpla gradiámur. Per Dóminum nostrum …	*Prayer* O God, who among the other miracles of Thy power, even in weaker women, Thou hast contributed to the victory of her martyrdom: grant us ever more generously; so that we who honor the feast day of the blessed Martina, Thy Virgin and Martyr, may ascend towards Thee through her example. Through our Lord ….
Jan. 31 St. John Bosco	*Confessor*
Orátio Deus, qui sanctum Ioánnem Confessórem tuum adolescéntium patrem et magístrum excitásti, ac per eum, auxiliatríce Vírgine María, novas in Ecclésia tua famílias floréscere voluísti: concéde, quǽsumus; ut eódem caritátis igne succénsi, ánimas quǽrere, tibíque soli servíre valeámus. Per Dóminum nostrum ...	*Prayer* O God, who raised up Saint John the Confessor, the father and teacher of Thy youth, and through him, the helper of the Virgin Mary, Thou desired that new religious orders flourish in the Church: grant, we beseech Thee; so that, kindled by the same fire of charity, we may be able to strive to win souls and serve Thee alone. Through our Lord …
Feb. 1 St. Ignatius	*Bishop and Martyr*
Orátio Infirmitátem nostram réspice, omnípotens Deus: et quia pondus própriæ actiónis gravat, beáti Ignátii Mártyris tui atque Pontíficis intercéssio gloriósa nos prótegat. Per Dóminum nostrum …	*Prayer* Look upon our frailty, almighty God: and since the weight of our sin drags us down, may we by the glorious intercession of Thy blessed Ignatius, Martyr and Bishop, be protected. Through our Lord ..
Feb. 2 Purification of the Blessed Virgin Mary	*Blessed Virgin Mary*
Capitulum (Mal 3:1) V. Ecce ego mitto Angelum meum, et præparábit viam ante fáciem meam. Et statim véniet ad templum sanctum suum Dominátor, quem vos	*Chapter* (Mal 3:1) V. Behold, I send my Angel, and he shall prepare the way before My face. And the Lord, whom thou seekest, and the Angel of the

Proper of the Saints Lauds

quǽritis, et Angelus Testaménti, quem vos vultis. **R.** Deo grátias	covenant, whom thou desireth, will immediately come to His holy temple. **R.** Thanks be to God.
Ant. Cum indúcerent púerum Iesum paréntes eius, accépit eum Símeon in ulnas suas, et benedíxit Deum, dicens: Nunc dimíttis servum tuum in pace.	**Ant.** When His parents brought the Child Jesus, Simeon took Him in his arms, and blessed God, saying: Now let Thy servant go in peace.
Orátio Omnípotens sempitérne Deus, maiestátem tuam súpplices exorámus: ut, sicut unigénitus Fílius tuus hodiérna die cum nostræ carnis substántia in templo est præsentátus; ita nos fácias purificátis tibi méntibus præsentári. Per eundem Dóminum nostrum …	*Prayer* Almighty and everlasting God, we implore Thy majesty: that, as Thine only begotten Son was presented this day in the temple in the substance of our flesh; we may be presented to Thee with purified souls. Through the same…
Feb. 3 Commemoration of St. Blaise	*Bishop and Martyr*
Orátio Deus, qui nos beáti Blásii Mártyris tui atque Pontíficis ánnua solemnitáte lætíficas: concéde propítius; ut, cuius natalícia cólimus, de eiúsdem étiam protectióne gaudeámus. Per Dóminum nostrum …	*Prayer* O God, who makes us rejoice at the annual solemnity of Thy blessed Blaise, Martyr and Bishop: grant more merifully; that we may rejoice in the protection of the one whose feast day we celebrate. Through our Lord …
Feb. 4 St. Andrew Corsini	*Bishop and Confessor*
Orátio Deus, qui in Ecclésia tua, nova semper instáuras exémpla virtútum: da pópulo tuo beáti Andréæ Confessóris tui atque Pontíficis ita sequi vestígia; ut assequátur et prǽmia. Per Dóminum nostrum …	*Prayer* O God, who always establisheth in Thy Church fresh examples of virtue: grant Thy people to follow the footsteps of blessed Andrew, Thy Confessor and Bishop; to achieve like rewards. Through our Lord …
Feb. 5 St. Agatha	*Virgin and Martyr*
Capitulum (Sir 51:1-3) **V.** Confitébor tibi, Dómine, Rex, et collaudábo te Deum Salvatórem meum. Confitébor nómini tuo: quóniam adiútor et protéctor factus es mihi, et liberásti corpus meum a perditióne. **R.** Deo grátias.	*Chapter* (Sir 51:1-3) **V.** I will confess to Thee, Lord King, and I will praise Thee God my Savior. I will confess to Thy Name: because Thou hast become my helper and protector, and hast delivered my body from destruction. **R.** Thanks be to God.
Ant. Paganórum multitúdo fúgiens ad sepúlcrum Vírginis, tulérunt velum eius contra ignem: ut comprobáret Dóminus, quod a perículis incéndii méritis beátæ Agathæ Mártyris suæ eos liberáret.	**Ant.** A multitude of heathens, fleeing to the tomb of the virgin, took her veil to stop the fire: that the Lord might prove that He would deliver them from the

	dangers of the fire by the merits of blessed Agatha, His martyr.
Orátio Deus, qui inter cétera poténtiæ tuæ mirácula étiam in sexu frágili victóriam martýrii contulísti: concéde propítius; ut, qui beátæ Agathæ Vírginis et Mártyris tuæ natalícia cólimus, per eius ad te exémpla gradiámur. Per Dóminum nostrum ...	*Prayer* God, who, among the other miracles of Thy power, also contributed to the crown of martyrdom in women: grant more mercifully; as those who honor the feast day of the blessed Agatha, Virgin and Martyr, will follow in her footsteps to Thee through her example. Through our Lord...
Feb. 6 St. Titus	*Bishop and Confessor*
Orátio Deus, qui beátum Titum Confessórem tuum atque Pontíficem apostólicis virtútibus decorásti: ejus méritis et intercessióne concéde; ut juste et pie vivéntes in hoc sǽculo, ad cæléstem pátriam pervenire mereámur. Per Dóminum nostrum ...	*Prayer* O God, who hast adorned Thy blessed Titus, Confessor and Bishop, with apostolic virtues: for the sake of his merits and prayers; that by living justly and piously in this world, may we deserve to reach the heavenly land. Through our Lord ...
Feb. 7 St. Romuald	*Abbot*
Orátio Intercéssio nos, quǽsumus, Dómine, beáti Romuáldi Abbátis comméndet: ut, quod nostris méritis non valémus, eius patrocínio assequámur. Per Dóminum nostrum ...	*Prayer* May the prayers, we beseech Thee, Lord, of the blessed Abbot Romuald commend us: that what we are not able to attain by our own merits, we may achieve by his patronage. Through our Lord ...
Feb. 8 St. John of Matha	*Confessor*
Orátio Deus, qui per sanctum Ioánnem órdinem sanctíssimæ Trinitátis ad rediméndum de potestáte Saracenórum captívos cǽlitus instítuere dignátus es: præsta, quǽsumus; ut, eius suffragántibus méritis, a captivitáte córporis et ánimæ, te adiuvánte, liberémur. Per Dóminum nostrum ...	*Prayer* O God, who through Saint John hast deigned to create the Order of the Most Holy Trinity to redeem the captives of the heavens from the power of the Saracens: grant we beseech Thee, that we may be honored by his supporting merits and we may be freed from the captivity of body and soul. Through our Lord ...
Feb. 9 St Cyril	*Bishop and Confessor*
Orátio Deus, qui beátum Cyrillum Confessórem tuum atque Pontíficem divínæ maternitátis beatíssimæ Vírginis Maríæ assertórem invíctum effecísti: concéde, ipso intercedénte; ut qui vere eam Genitrícem Dei	*Prayer* O God, who made the blessed Cyril, Thy Confessor and Bishop, the invincible champion of the divine motherhood of the most blessed Virgin Mary; grant by his intercession; that those who truly

Proper of the Saints Lauds

crédimus, matérna eiúsdem protectióne salvémur. Per eundem Dóminum …	believe that she is the Mother of God, may be saved by her maternal protection. Through our Lord …
Feb. 10 St. Scholastica	*Virgin*
Orátio Deus, qui ánimam beátæ Vírginis tuæ Scholásticæ ad ostendéndam innocéntiæ viam in colúmbæ spécie cælum penetráre fecísti: da nobis eius méritis et précibus ita innocénter vívere; ut ad ætérna mereámur gáudia pervenire. Per Dóminum nostrum …	*Prayer* O God, who caused the soul of Thy blessed Virgin Scholastica to enter heaven in the form of a dove to show us the way of innocence: grant us to live thus innocently by her merits and praises; that we may deserve to reach eternal joys. Through our Lord …
Feb. 11 Apparition of the Blessed Virgin Mary Immaculate	*Blessed Virgin Mary*
Capitulum (Song 2:13-14) **V.** Surge, amíca mea, speciósa mea, et veni, colúmba mea, in foramínibus petræ, in cavérna macériæ, osténde mihi fáciem tuam, sonet vox tua in áuribus meis. **R.** Deo grátias.	*Chapter* (Song 2:13-14) **V.** Arise, my friend, my fair one, and come: dove, in the holes of the rock, in the cave of the rock, show me thy face, let thy voice resound in my ears. **R.** Thanks be to God.
Ant. Præclára salútis auróra, ex te, Virgo María, exívit sol iustítiæ, qui visitávit nos óriens ex alto.	**Ant.** Brilliant greetings to the dawn, Virgin Mary, from thee came forth the Sun of Justice, who visited us rising from on high.
Orátio Deus, qui per immaculátam Vírginis Conceptiónem dignum Fílio tuo habitáculum præparásti: súpplices a te quǽsumus; ut, eiúsdem Vírginis Apparitiónem celebrántes, salútem mentis et córporis consequámur. Per eundem Dóminum nostrum …	*Prayer* O God, who through the Immaculate Conception of the Virgin Mary prepared a worthy home for Thy Son: we ask her intercession; that by celebrating the Apparition of the same Virgin, we may obtain salvation of soul and body. Through our Lord …
Feb. 12 The Seven Holy Founders of the Order of the Servites	*Confessors*
Capitulum (1 Pet 4:13) **V.** Caríssimi: Communicántes Christi passiónibus gaudéte, ut et in revelatióne glóriæ eius gaudeátis exsultántes. **R.** Deo grátias.	*Chapter* (1 Pet 4:13) **V.** Dearly beloved, if ye partake of the sufferings of Christ, rejoice that when His glory shall be revealed, ye may also be glad with exceeding joy. **R.** Thanks be to God.
Orátio Dómine Iesu Christe, qui ad recoléndam memóriam dolórum sanctíssimæ Genetrícis tuæ, per septem beátos Patres nova Servórum	*Prayer* Lord Jesus Christ, who, in order to recall the memory of the sorrows of Thy most holy Mother, through the Seven Blessed Fathers,

eius família Ecclésiam tuam fecundásti: concéde propítius; ita nos eórum consociári flétibus, ut perfruámur et gáudiis. Qui vivis et regnas …	Thou created a new order of religious to enrich Thy Church: grant mercy; so that we may be united with their sufferings, and that we may find joy and rejoice with them. Who liveth and reigneth…
Feb. 14 St. Valentine	*Priest and Martyr*
Orátio Præsta, quæsumus, omnípotens Deus: ut, qui beáti Valentíni Mártyris tui natalícia cólimus, a cunctis malis imminéntibus, eius intercessióne, liberémur. Per Dóminum nostrum	**Prayer** We beseech Thee, almighty God, that we who celebrate the feast day of Thy blessed Valentine, may be freed from all future evils by his intercession. Through our Lord …
Feb. 15 Commemoration of Sts. Faustinus and Jovita	*Martyrs*
Orátio Deus, qui nos ánnua sanctórum Mártyrum tuórum Faustíni et Iovítæ solemnitáte lætíficas: concéde propitius; ut, quorum gaudémus méritis, accendámur exémplis. Per Dóminum nostrum …	**Prayer** O God, who makest us joyful with the annual solemnity of Thy holy Martyrs Faustinus and Jovita: grant us mercy; so by those in whose merits we rejoice, we may be enkindled by their example. Through our Lord …
Feb. 18 Commemoration of St. Simeon	*Bishop and Martyr*
Orátio Infirmitátem nostram réspice, omnípotens Deus: et quia pondus própriæ actiónis gravat, beáti Simeónis Mártyris tui atque Pontíficis intercéssio gloriósa nos prótegat. Per Dóminum nostrum …	**Prayer** Look upon our infirmity, almighty God: and since the weight of sin drags us down, may the glorious intercession of Thy blessed Simeon, Martyr and Bishop, protect us. Through our Lord …
Feb. 23 St. Peter Damian	*Bishop and Martyr*
Orátio Concéde nos, quæsumus, omnípotens Deus: beáti Petri Confessóris tui atque Pontíficis mónita et exémpla sectári; ut per terréstrium rerum contémptum ætérna gáudia consequámur. Per Dóminum nostrum …	**Prayer** Grant us, we beseech Thee, almighty God, to follow the admonition and example of Thy blessed Peter the Confessor and Bishop: that we may obtain eternal joys through the contempt of earthly things. Through our Lord …
Feb. 24 St. Matthias	*Apostle*
Orátio Deus, qui beátum Matthíam Apostolórum tuórum collégio sociásti: tríbue, quæsumus; ut, eius	**Prayer** O God, who hast made a place for the blessed Matthias with the college of Thine Apostles:

Proper of the Saints Lauds

interventióne, tuæ circa nos pietátis semper víscera sentiámus. Per Dóminum nostrum ...	grant, we beseech Thee, that by his intercession we may always experience the depths of Thy mercy surrounding us. Through our Lord ...
Feb. 27 St. Gabriel of Our Lady of Sorrows	*Confessor*
Orátio Deus, qui beátum Gabriélem dulcíssimæ Matris tuæ dolóres assídue recólere docuísti, ac per illam sanctitátis et miraculórum glória sublimásti: da nobis, eius intercessióne et exémplo; ita Genetrícis tuæ consociári flétibus, ut matérna eiúsdem protectióne salvémur. Qui vivis et regnas ...	**Prayer** O God, who taught the blessed Gabriel to constantly remember the sorrows of Thy most sweet Mother, and didst raise him up through her to the exalted glory of sanctity and miracles: grant us, by his intercession and example we may share with the weeping of Thy Mother and that we may be saved by her maternal protection. Who liveth and reigneth...
Mar. 4 St. Casimir	*Confessor*
Orátio Deus, qui inter regáles delícias et mundi illécebras sanctum Casimírum virtúte constántiæ roborásti: quǽsumus; ut eius intercessióne fidéles tui terréna despíciant, et ad cæléstia semper aspírent. Per Dóminum nostrum ...	**Prayer** O God, who among the royal pleasures and the temptations of the world strengthened Saint Casimir with the power of steadfastness: we beseech Thee; that by his prayers Thy faithful may despise earthly things, and always aspire to heavenly things. Through our Lord ...
Mar. 6 Sts. Perpetua and Felicity	*Martyrs*
Ant. Istárum est enim regnum cælórum, qui contempsérunt vitam mundi, et pervenérunt ad prǽmia regni, et lavérunt stolas suas in sánguine Agni.	**Ant.** For theirs is the kingdom of heaven, they who despised the life of the world, and attained to the rewards of the kingdom, and they who washed their robes in the blood of the Lamb.
Orátio Da nobis, quǽsumus, Dómine, Deus noster, sanctárum Mártyrum tuárum Perpétuæ et Felicitátis palmas incessábili devotióne venerári: ut, quas digna mente non póssumus celebráre, humílibus saltem frequentémus obséquiis. Per Dóminum nostrum ..	**Prayer** Grant us, we beseech thee, Lord our God, to venerate with unceasing devotion the palms of Thy holy Martyrs, Perpetua and Felicity: that which we cannot celebrate with worthy honor: let us at least present them our humble tributes. Through our Lord ...
Mar. 7 St. Thomas Aquinas	*Confessor and Doctor*
Orátio Deus, qui Ecclésiam tuam beáti Thomæ Confessóris tui mira eruditióne claríficas, et sancta	**Prayer** O God, who glorifies Thy Church by the wonderful teaching of Thy blessed Thomas the

operatióne fecúndas: da nobis, quǽsumus; et quæ dócuit, intelléctu conspícere, et quæ egit, imitatióne complére. Per Dóminum nostrum …	Confessor, and gives life to Her by his holy life: grant us, we beseech Thee, to contemplate with understanding what he taught, and to imitate what he did. Through our Lord.…
Mar. 8 St. John of God	*Confessor*
Orátio Deus, qui beátum Ioánnem, tuo amóre succénsum, inter flammas innóxium incédere fecísti, et per eum Ecclésiam tuam nova prole fecundásti: præsta, ipsíus suffragántibus méritis; ut igne caritátis tuæ vítia nostra curéntur, et remédia nobis ætérna provéniant. Per Dóminum nostrum …	**Prayer** O God, who made blessed John, inflamed with Thy love, walk harmlessly among the flames, and through him gave birth to Thy Church with a new religious order; grant by his inspiring merits; that by the fire of his charity our faults may be cured, and eternal remedies may come to us. Through our Lord …
Mar. 9 St. Frances of Rome	*Widow*
Orátio Deus, qui beátam Francíscam fámulam tuam, inter cétera grátiæ tuæ dona, familiári Angeli consuetúdine decorásti: concéde, quǽsumus; ut, intercessiónis eius auxílio, Angelórum consórtium cónsequi mereámur. Per Dóminum nostrum …	**Prayer** O God, who, among the other gifts of Thy grace, honored Thy blessed servant Frances with the intimate conversations of an Angel: grant, we beseech Thee; that by her intercession we may merit the company of the Angels. Through our Lord …
Mar. 10 Commemoration of the Forty Holy Martyrs	*Martyrs*
Ant. Vestri capílli cápitis omnes numeráti sunt: nolíte timére: multis passéribus melióres estis vos.	**Ant.** All the hairs of thy head are numbered: fear not: thou art of greater value than many sparrows.
Orátio Præsta, quǽsumus, omnípotens Deus: ut, qui gloriósos Mártyres fortes in sua confessióne cognóvimus, pios apud te in nostra intercessióne sentiámus. Per Dóminum nostrum …	**Prayer** Grant, we beseech Thee, Almighty God: that we who venerate the glorious Martyrs, strong in their confession, may become virtuous through their prayers for us. Through our Lord …
Mar. 12 St. Gregory I	*Pope, Confessor and Doctor*
Orátio Deus, qui ánimæ fámuli tui Gregórii ætérnæ beatitúdinis prǽmia contulísti: concéde propítius; ut, qui peccatórum nostrórum póndere prémimur, eius apud te précibus sublevémur. Per Dóminum nostrum …	**Prayer** O God, who hast bestowed upon the soul of Thy beloved Gregory the rewards of eternal bliss: grant mercifully; that we who are weighed down by the burden of our sins may be lifted up by his prayers to Thee. Through our Lord …

Proper of the Saints Lauds

Mar. 17 St. Patrick	*Bishop and Confessor*
Orátio Deus, qui ad prædicándam géntibus glóriam tuam beátum Patrícium Confessórem atque Pontíficem míttere dignátus es: eius méritis et intercessióne concéde; ut, quæ nobis agénda præcipis, te miseránte adimpléte possímus. Per Dóminum nostrum ...	*Prayer* O God, who hast deigned to send the blessed Patrick the Confessor and Bishop to preach Thy glory to the Gentiles: grant, through his merits and intercession; that we may fulfill what Thou commandest us to do with loving kindness. Through our Lord ...
Mar. 18 St. Cyril	*Bishop of Jerusalem*
Orátio Da nobis, quǽsumus, omnípotens Deus, beato Cyríllo Pontífice intercedénte: te solum verum Deum, et quem misísti Iesum Christum ita cognóscere; ut inter oves, quæ vocem eius áudiunt, perpétuo connumerári mereámur. Per Dóminum nostrum ...	*Prayer* Grant us, we beseech Thee, almighty God, through the intercession of the blessed Cyril the Bishop: to know Thee as the only true God and Jesus Christ whom Thou sent; that we may deserve to be numbered forever among the sheep that hear His voice. Through our Lord ...
Mar. 19 St. Joseph	*Confessor and Patron of the Universal Church*
Capítulum (Prov. 28:20; 27:18) V. Vir fidélis multum laudábitur. Et, qui custos est Dómini sui, glorificábitur. R. Deo grátias.	*Chapter* (Prov. 28:20; 27:18) V. A faithful man will be greatly praised. And he who is the guardian of his Lord will be glorified. R. Thanks be to God.
Ant. Ipse Iesus erat incípiens quasi annórum trigínta, ut putabátur, fílius Ioseph.	Ant. Jesus Himself was nearly thirty years old, and was thought to be the son of Joseph.
Orátio Sanctíssimæ Genetrícis tuæ spónsi, quǽsumus, Dómine, méritis adiuvémur; ut quod possibílitas nostra non óbtinet, eius nobis intercessióne donétur. Qui vivis et regnas ...	*Prayer* We beseech Thee, O Lord, that we may be helped by the merits of the Spouse of Thy holy Mother; so that what our abilities cannot achieve, may be given to us through his intercession. Who liveth and reigneth ...
Mar. 21 St. Benedict	*Abbot, Confessor*
Orátio Intercéssio nos, quǽsumus, Dómine, beáti Benedícti Abbátis comméndet: ut, quod nostris méritis non valémus, eius patrocínio assequámur. Per Dóminum nostrum ...	*Prayer* May the prayers of the blessed Abbot Benedict, we beseech Thee Lord, commend us to Thee, that whatever we are not able by our own merits to attain, we may attain through his patronage. Through our Lord ...

Proper of the Saints Lauds

Mar. 24 St. Gabriel	*Archangel*
Ant. Gábriel Angelus descéndit ad Zacharíam, et ait illi: Uxor tua páriet tibi fílium, et vocábis nomen eius Ioánnem, et multi in nativitáte eius gaudébunt: ipse enim præíbit ante fáciem Dómini paráre vias eius.	**Ant.** The Angel Gabriel descended to Zacharias and said to him: Thy wife will bear thee a son, and thou wilt call his name John, and many will rejoice at his birth: for he will go before the face of the Lord to prepare His way.
Orátio Deus, qui inter céteros Angelos, ad annuntiándum Incarnatiónis tuæ mystérium, Gabriélem Archángelum elegísti: concéde propítius; ut qui festum eius celebrámus in terris, ipsíus patrocínium sentiámus in cælis. Qui vivis et regnas …	*Prayer* O God, Thou choseth the Archangel Gabriel from amongst the rest of the Angels to announce the mystery of Thine Incarnation, grant through Thy great mercy; that those who celebrate his festival on earth may receive his patronage in heaven. He Who liveth and reigneth…
Mar. 25 Annunciation of the Blessed Virgin Mary	*Blessed Virgin Mary* Lauds Antiphons Pg 293
Capitulum (Isa 7:14-15) V. Ecce virgo concípiet, et páriet fílium, et vocábitur nomen eius Emmánuel. Butýrum et mel cómedet, ut sciat reprobáre malum, et elígere bonum. R. Deo grátias.	*Chapter* (Isa 7:14-15) V. Behold, the Virgin shall conceive and bear a Son, and His Name shall be called Emmanuel. He shall eat butter and honey, that He may know to reject evil, and to choose good. R. Thanks be to God.
Ant. Quómodo fiet istud, Angele Dei, quóniam virum non cognósco? Audi, María Virgo: Spíritus Sanctus supervéniet in te, et virtus Altíssimi obumbrábit tibi.	**Ant.** How will this be done, O Angel of God, since I do not know man? Hear, O Virgin Mary: The Holy Ghost will come upon thee, and the power of the Most High will overshadow thee.
Orátio Deus, qui de beátæ Maríæ Vírginis útero Verbum tuum, Angelo nuntiánte, carnem suscípere voluísti: præsta supplícibus tuis; ut, qui vere eam Genetrícem Dei crédimus, eius apud te intercessiónibus adiuvémur. Per Dóminum nostrum …	*Prayer* O God, who through the womb of the Blessed Virgin Mary, by announcing Thy Word through the Angel, Thou wished to take on flesh; grant that we who truly believe her to be the Mother of God, may be helped by her intercessions to Thee. Through our Lord …
Mar. 27 St. John Damascene	*Confessor and Doctor*
Orátio Omnípotens sempitérne Deus, qui ad cultum sacrárum imáginum asseréndum, beátum Ioánnem cælésti doctrína et admirábili spíritus fortitúdine imbuísti: concéde nobis eius	*Prayer* Almighty and everlasting God, who, to affirm the worship of Thee through sacred images, hast imbued blessed John with heavenly learning and admirable strength of spirit: grant us his intercession and

intercessióne et exémplo; ut, quorum cólimus imágines, virtútes imitémur et patrocínia sentiámus. Per Dóminum nostrum …	example; that, by the images of saints we venerate, we may imitate their virtues and rely on their patronage. Through our Lord …
Mar. 28 Commemoration of St. John of Capistrano	*Confessor*
Ant. Euge serve bone et fidélis, quia in pauca fuísti fidélis, supra multa te constítuam, intra in gáudium Dómini tui.	**Ant.** Hail, good and faithful servant, because thou hast been faithful in a few things, I will set thee over many things, enter into the joy of Thy Lord.
Orátio Deus, qui per beátum Ioánnem fidéles tuos in virtúte sanctíssimi nóminis Iesu de crucis inimícis triumpháre fecísti: præsta, quǽsumus; ut, spirituálium hóstium, eius intercessióne, superátis insídiis, corónam iustítiæ a te accípere mereámur. Per eundem Dóminum nostrum	*Prayer* O God, who through blessed John, Thou hast made Thy faithful triumph over the enemies of the cross by the power of the most Holy Name of Jesus: grant, we beg Thee; that, through His prayers which overcome the snares of our spiritual enemies, we may be worthy to receive from Thee the crown of righteousness. Through the same Lord …
Apr. 2 St. Francis of Paula	*Confessor*
Orátio Deus, humílium celsitúdo, qui beátum Francíscum Confessórem Sanctórum tuórum glória sublimásti: tríbue, quǽsumus; ut, eius méritis et imitatióne, promíssa humílibus præmia felíciter consequámur. Per Dóminum nostrum …	*Prayer* O God of the humble, who exalted the blessed Francis the Confessor to the glory of Thy saints: grant, we beseech Thee, that by his merits and imitation, we may successfully obtain the promises vowed to the humble. Through our Lord …
Apr. 4 St. Isidore	*Bishop, Confessor and Doctor*
Ant. Euge, serve bone et fidélis, quia in pauca fuísti fidélis, supra multa te constítuam, dicit Dóminus.	**Ant.** O good and faithful servant, because thou hast been faithful in a few things, I will set thee over many things, sayeth the Lord.
Orátio Deus, qui pópulo tuo ætérnæ salútis beátum Isidórum minístrum tribuísti: præsta, quǽsumus; ut, quem Doctórem vitæ habúimus in terris, intercessórem habére mereámur in cælis. Per Dóminum nostrum …	*Prayer* O God, who gave the blessed Isidore the minister of eternal salvation to Thy people: grant, we beseech Thee; that, as the teacher of everlasting life we had on earth, we will deserve to have an intercessor in heaven. Through our Lord …

Apr. 5 St. Vincent Ferrer	*Confessor and Doctor*
Orátio Deus, qui Ecclésiam tuam beáti Vincéntii Confessóris tui méritis et prædicatióne illustráre dignátus es: concéde nobis fámulis tuis; ut et ipsíus instruámur exémplis et ab ómnibus eius patrocínio liberémur advérsis. Per Dóminum nostrum …	*Prayer* O God, who hast deigned to enlighten Thy Church with the merits and preaching of Thy blessed Vincent the Confessor: grant us Thy servants; that we may also be instructed by his example, and be freed from all adversities by his prayers. Through our Lord …
Apr. 11 St. Leo I	*Pope, Confessor and Doctor*
Orátio Gregem tuum, Pastor ætérne, placátus inténde: et per beátum Leónem Summum Pontíficem perpétua protectióne custódi; quem totíus Ecclésiæ præstitísti esse pastórem. Per Dóminum nostrum …	*Prayer* Look favorably upon Thy flock, O Eternal Shepherd, and through the blessed Leo the Supreme Pontiff, guard with perpetual protection; whom Thou hast appointed to be the shepherd of the universal Church. Through our Lord …
Apr. 14 St. Justin	*Martyr*
Orátio Deus, qui per stultítiam crucis eminéntem Iesu Christi sciéntiam beátum Iustínum Mártyrem mirabíliter docuísti: eius nobis intercessióne concéde; ut, errórum circumventióne depúlsa, fídei firmitátem consequámur. Per eundem Dóminum nostrum …	*Prayer* O God, who through the scandal of the cross, wonderfully taught the excellent knowledge of Jesus Christ to the martyr Justin, grant us his intercession; so that, by avoiding errors we may be steadfast in faith. Through our Lord …
Apr. 17 Commemoration of St. Anicetus	*Pope and Martyr*
Ant. Fíliæ Ierúsalem, veníte et vidéte Mártyres cum corónis, quibus coronávit eos Dóminus in die solemnitátis et lætítiæ, allelúja, allelúja.	*Ant.* Daughters of Jerusalem, come and see the Martyrs with the crowns with which the Lord crowned them, in the day of solemnity and joy, alleluia, alleluia.
Orátio Gregem tuum, Pastor ætérne, placátus inténde: et per beátum Anicétum Mártyrem tuum atque Summum Pontíficem perpétua protectióne custódi; quem totíus Ecclésiæ præstitísti esse pastórem. Per Dóminum nostrum	*Prayer* Preserve Thy flock, Eternal Shepherd, and, through Thy blessed Martyr and Supreme Pontiff Anicetus, whom Thou appointed to be the shepherd of the whole Church, guard with perpetual protection; whom Thou hast appointed to be the shepherd of the universal Church. Through …
Apr. 21 St. Anselm	*Bishop, Confessor and Doctor*
Orátio Deus, qui pópulo tuo ætérnæ salútis beátum Ansélmum minístrum tribuísti: præsta, quǽsumus; ut quem Doctórem vitæ habúimus in terris,	*Prayer* O God, who gave to Thy people blessed Anselm, the minister of eternal salvation, grant we beseech Thee, that we who had

Proper of the Saints Lauds

intercessórem habére mereámur in cælis. Per Dóminum nostrum …	on earth the Teacher of the way of life everlasting, may have him as intercessor in heaven. Through our Lord …
Apr. 22 Sts. Soter and Caius	*Popes and Martyrs*
Orátio Gregem tuum, Pastor ætérne, placátus inténde: et per beátos Sotérem et Caium Mártyres tuos atque Summos Pontífices perpétua protectióne custódi; quos totíus Ecclésiæ præstitísti esse pastóres. Per Dóminum nostrum …	*Prayer* Keep Thy flock conciliated Eternal Shepherd, through the prayers of the blessed Soter and Caius, Thy Martyrs and Supreme Pontiffs, whom Thou hast appointed to be shepherds of the entire Church, and defend it with everlasting protection. Through our Lord …
Apr. 23 St. George	*Martyr*
Orátio Deus, qui nos beáti Geórgii Mártyris tui méritis et intercessióne lætíficas: concéde propítius; ut, qui tua per eum benefícia póscimus, dono tuæ grátiæ consequámur. Per eundem Dóminum nostrum …	*Prayer* O God, who blessed us with the merits and intercession of Thy blessed Martyr, George, grant us mercy; so that those who seek Thy blessings through him may obtain the gift of Thy grace. Through our Lord …
Apr. 24 St. Fidélis of Sigmaringen	*Martyr*
Orátio Deus, qui beátum Fidélem, seráphico spíritus ardóre succénsum, in veræ fidei propagatióne martýrii palma et gloriósis miráculis decoráre dignátus es: eius, quǽsumus, méritis et intercessióne, ita nos per grátiam tuam in fide et caritáte confírma; ut in servítio tuo fidéles usque ad mortem inveníri mereámur. Per Dóminum nostrum …	*Prayer* O God, Who hath deigned to enkindle the blessed Fidélis with the ardor of a Seraphic Spirit in the propagation of the true faith with the palm of martyrdom and glorious miracles: we implore Thee by his merits and intercession, to strengthen us in faith and charity by Thy grace; that we may deserve to be found faithful in Thy service until death. Through our Lord …
Apr. 25 St. Mark, The Evangelist	*Apostle*
Orátio Deus, qui beátum Marcum Evangelístam tuum, evangelicæ prædicatiónis grátia sublimasti: tríbue quǽsumus; ejus nos semper et eruditióne profícere, et oratióne deféndi. Per Dóminum nostrum …	*Prayer* O God, who exalted Thy blessed Mark the Evangelist by the grace of evangelical preaching: grant, we beseech Thee; that we may always advance in understanding and be defended by his prayer. Through our Lord …
Apr. 26 Sts. Cletus and Marcellinus	*Popes and Martyrs*
Orátio Gregem tuum, Pastor ætérne, placátus inténde: et per beátos	*Prayer* May the precious intercession of the Blessed Martyrs

Cletum et Marcellínum Mártyres tuos atque Summos Pontífices perpétua protectióne custódi; quos totíus Ecclésiæ præstitísti esse pastóres. Per Dóminum nostrum …	and Popes Cletus and Marcellinus whom Thou hast appointed to be shepherds of the universal Church, sustain us, and may their devout prayers protect us. Through our Lord …
Apr. 27 St. Peter Canisius	*Confessor and Doctor*
Orátio Deus, qui ad tuéndam cathólicam fidem beátum Petrum Confessórem tuum virtúte et doctrína roborásti: concéde propítius; ut eius exémplis et mónitis errántes ad salútem resipíscant, et fidéles in veritátis confessióne persevérent. Per Dóminum nostrum …	**Prayer** O God, who strengthened the blessed Peter the Confessor with Thy courage and doctrine to protect the Catholic faith: mercifully grant; that by his example and admonitions we may repent unto salvation, and the faithful will continue in the battle against falsehood. Through our Lord …
Apr. 28 St. Paul of the Cross	*Confessor*
Orátio Dómine Iesu Christe, qui, ad mystérium crucis prædicándum, sanctum Paulum singulári caritáte donásti, et per eum novam in Ecclésia famíliam floréscere voluísti: ipsíus nobis intercessióne concéde; ut, passiónem tuam iúgiter recoléntes in terris, eiúsdem fructum cónsequi mereámur in cælis. Qui vivis et regnas …	**Prayer** Lord Jesus Christ, who, to preach the mystery of the cross, endowed Saint Paul with singular charity, and through him Thou wished to make a new order of priests flourish in the Church: grant us his intercession, that by constantly recalling Thy passion on earth, we may deserve to obtain the same fruit in heaven. Thou Who liveth and reigneth …
Apr. 29 St. Peter	*Martyr*
Orátio Præsta, quǽsumus, omnípotens Deus: ut beáti Petri Mártyris tui fidem cóngrua devotióne sectémur; qui, pro eiúsdem fídei dilatatióne, martýrii palmam méruit obtinére. Per Dóminum nostrum …	**Prayer** We beseech Thee, almighty God that we may follow the faith of Thy blessed Martyr, Peter with a suitable devotion; who, for the evangelizing the same faith, deserved to obtain the palm of martyrdom. Through our Lord …
Apr. 30 St. Catherine of Siena	*Virgin and Doctor*
Orátio Da, quǽsumus, omnípotens Deus: ut, qui beátæ Catharínæ Vírginis tuæ natalícia cólimus; et ánnua solemnitáte lætémur, et tantæ virtútis proficiámus exémplo. Per Dóminum nostrum …	**Prayer** Grant, we beseech Thee, almighty God: that we who revere the feast day of Thy blessed Catherine the Virgin; may rejoice in this annual solemnity and be enriched by the example of her great virtue. Through our Lord …

Proper of the Saints Lauds

May 1 St. Joseph the Worker	*Confessor*
Psalms of Sunday Lauds I, Antiphons, Hymn and Versicle from the Common of Confessors and then all below.	
Capitulum (Col 3:14-15) V. Fratres: Caritátem habéte, quod est vínculum perfectiónis, et pax Christi exsúltet in córdibus vestris, et grati estóte. R. Deo grátias.	*Chapter* (Col 3:14-15) V. Brothers: have charity, which is the bond of perfection, and let the peace of Christ rejoice in your hearts, and be grateful. R. Thanks be to God.
Ant. Descéndit Iesus cum María et Ioseph, et venit Názareth, et erat súbditus illis, allelúja.	**Ant.** Jesus went down with Mary and Joseph, and came to Nazareth, and was subject to them, alleluia.
Orátio Rerum cónditor Deus, qui legem labóris humáno géneri statuísti: concéde propítius; ut, sancti Ioseph exémplo et patrocínio, ópera perficiámus quæ præcipis, et præmia consequámur quæ promíttis. Qui vivis et regnas …	*Prayer* O God, the Creator of things, who established the law of labor for the human race, mercifully grant; that, by the example and patronage of St. Joseph, we may accomplish the works which Thou commandest and obtain the rewards which Thou promiseth. Who liveth and reigneth…
May 2 St. Athanasius	*Bishop, Confessor and Doctor*
Orátio Exáudi, quǽsumus, Dómine, preces nostras, quas in beáti Athanásii Confessóris tui atque Pontíficis solemnitáte deférimus: et, qui tibi digne méruit famulári, eius intercedéntibus méritis, ab ómnibus nos absólve peccátis. Per Dóminum nostrum …	*Prayer* O Lord, hear our prayers which we offer on the solemnity of the blessed Athanasius, Thy Confessor and Pope: and who hast served Thee worthily and by his intercessory merits, absolved us from all our sins. Through our Lord …
May 3 Finding of the Holy Cross	
Capitulum (Phil 2:5-7) Fratres: Hoc enim sentíte in vobis, quod et in Christo Jesu: qui cum in forma Dei esset, non rapínam arbitrátus est esse se æquálem Deo: sed semetípsum exinanívit, formam servi accípiens, in similitúdinem hóminum factus, et hábitu invéntus ut homo.	*Chapter* (Phil 2:5-7) Brethren: For let this mind be in you, which was also in Christ Jesus: Who being in the form of God, thought it not robbery to be equal with God: but emptied himself, taking the form of a servant, being made in the likeness of men, and in habit found as a man.
Ant. Super ómnia ligna cedrórum tu sola excélsior, in qua Vita mundi pepéndit, in qua Chrístus triumphávit, et mors mortem superávit in ætérnum, allelúja.	**Ant.** Above all the trees of the cedars thou alone art the highest, on whom the life of the world hangs, on whom Christ triumphed, and death overcame death forever, alleluia.

Orátio Deus, qui in præclára salutíferæ Crucis Inventióne, passiónis tuæ mirácula suscitásti: concéde; ut vitális ligni prétio, ætérnæ vitæ suffrágia consequámur: Qui vivis et regnas ...	**Prayer** O God, who in the glorious finding of the life-giving Cross, hast shown us the miracles of Thy Passion: grant; that by the cost of the priceless wood, we may purchase eternal life. He Who liveth and reigneth...
May 4 St. Monica	*Widow*
Orátio Deus, mæréntium consolátor et in te sperántium salus, qui beátæ Mónicæ pias lácrimas in conversióne fílii sui Augustíni misericórditer suscepísti: da nobis utriúsque intervéntu; peccáta nostra deploráre, et grátiæ tuæ indulgéntiam invenire. Per Dóminum nostrum ...	**Prayer** O God, the comforter of the bereaved, and the salvation of those who hope in Thee, who mercifully accepted the tears of the blessed Monica for the conversion of her son Augustine: grant us through the intercession of both to grieve for our sins and to receive the grace of Thy forgiveness. Through our Lord . .
May 5 St. Pius V	*Pope and Confessor*
Orátio Deus, qui, ad conteréndos Ecclésiæ tuæ hostes et ad divínum cultum reparándum, beátum Pium Pontíficem Máximum elígere dignátus es: fac nos ipsíus deféndi præsídiis et ita tuis inhærére obséquiis; ut, ómnium hóstium superátis insídiis, perpétua pace lætémur. Per Dóminum nostrum ...	**Prayer** O God, who hast deigned to choose the blessed Pontiff Pius for the defeat of the enemies of Thy Church, and for the restoration of divine worship: grant that we may be better defended by his protection, and thus adhere to Thy commandments; that having overcome the snares of all our enemies, we may rejoice in perpetual peace. Through our Lord ...
May 7 St. Stanislaus	*Bishop and Martyr*
Orátio Deus, pro cuius honóre gloriósus Póntifex Stanisláus gládiis impiórum occúbuit: præsta, quæsumus; ut omnes, qui eius implórant auxílium, petitiónis suæ salutárem consequántur efféctum. Per Dóminum nostrum ...	**Prayer** O God, for Whose honor the glorious Bishop Stanislaus was slain by the swords of the wicked: grant, we beseech Thee; that all who implore his assistance may obtain the beneficial effect of his prayers. Through our Lord ...
May 9 St. Gregory Nazianzen	*Bishop, Confessor and Doctor*
Orátio Deus, qui pópulo tuo ætérnæ salútis beátum Gregórium minístrum tribuísti: præsta, quæsumus; ut quem Doctórem vitæ habúimus in terris, intercessórem habére mereámur in cælis. Per Dóminum nostrum ...	**Prayer** O God, who gave blessed Gregory, the minister of eternal salvation, to Thy people: grant, we beseech Thee; that through the Teacher of life we had on earth, we will deserve him as an intercessor in heaven. Through our Lord ...

Proper of the Saints Lauds

May 10 St. Antoninus	*Bishop and Confessor*
Orátio Sancti Antoníni, Dómine, Confessóris tui atque Pontíficis méritis adiuvémur: ut, sicut te in illo mirábilem prædicámus, ita in nos misericórdem fuísse gloriémur. Per Dóminum nostrum …	**Prayer** O Lord, may we be assisted by the merits of your Bishop and Confessor, Saint Antoninus, then, as we proclaim Thy wonderful works in him, so may we give glory for Thy mercy shown to us. Through our Lord …
May 11 Sts. Philip and James	*Apostles*
Ant. Ego sum via, véritas, et vita: nemo venit ad Patrem, nisi per me, allelúja.	**Ant.** I am the Way, the Truth, and the Life; no one comes to the Father except through Me, alleluia.
Orátio Deus, qui nos ánnua Apostolórum tuórum Philíppi et Iacóbi solemnitáte lætíficas: præsta, quǽsumus; ut, quorum gaudémus méritis, instruámur exémplis. Per Dóminum nostrum …	**Prayer** O God, who makes us joyful with the annual solemnity of Thine Apostles Philip and James: grant that we may be taught by the example of those in whose merits we rejoice. Through our Lord …
May 12 Sts. Nereus, Achilleus, Domitilla, (Virgin) **Pancratius**	*Martyrs*
Orátio Semper nos, Dómine, Mártyrum tuórum Nérei, Achíllei, Domitíllæ atque Pancrátii fóveat, quǽsumus, beáta solémnitas: et tuo dignos reddat obséquio. Per Dóminum nostrum …	**Prayer** O Lord, on the blessed solemnity of Thy Martyrs Nereus, Achilleus, Domitilla, and Pancratius, we beg Thee to always quicken us and make us worthy of Thy service. Through our Lord …
May 13 St. Robert Bellarmine	*Bishop, Confessor and Doctor*
Orátio Deus, qui ad errórum insídias repelléndas et apostólicæ Sedis iura propugnánda, beátum Robértum Pontíficem tuum atque Doctórem mira eruditióne et virtúte decorásti: eius méritis et intercessióne concéde; ut nos in veritátis amóre crescámus et erróntium corda ad Ecclésiæ tuæ rédeant unitátem. Per Dóminum nostrum …	**Prayer** O God, Who, to repulse the snares of error and to defend the rights of the Apostolic See, hast adorned Thy blessed Bishop and Doctor Robert with magnificent learning and valor: grant by his merits and intercession; that we may grow in the love of the truth, and that the hearts of the wandering may return to the unity of Thy Church. Through our Lord …
May 14 Commemoration of St. Bontiface	*Martyr*
Orátio Da, quǽsumus, omnípotens Deus: ut qui beáti Bonifátii Mártyris tui solémnia cólimus, eius apud te intercessiónibus adiuvémur. Per Dóminum nostrum …	**Prayer** Grant, we beseech Thee, almighty God, that those who celebrate the feast of Thy blessed Martyr Boniface, may be helped by his intercessory prayers to Thee. Through our Lord …

Proper of the Saints Lauds

May 15 St. John Baptist de la Salle	*Confessor*
Orátio Deus, qui, ad christiánam páuperum eruditiónem et ad iuvéntam in via veritátis firmándam, sanctum Ioánnem Baptístam Confessórem excitásti, et novam per eum in Ecclésia famíliam collegísti: concéde propítius; ut eius intercessióne et exémplo, stúdio glóriæ tuæ in animárum salúte ferventes, eius in cælis corónæ partícipes fieri valeámus. Per Dóminum nostrum …	**Prayer** O God, who for the Christian education of the poor and for strengthening the youth in the way of truth, raised up Saint John the Baptist the Confessor, and through him Thou assembled a new family of Religious into the Church: grant, mercifully, that through his intercession and example, fervent in the zeal of Thy glory for the salvation of souls, we may be able to become partakers of his heavenly crown. Through our Lord …
May 16 St. Ubaldus	*Bishop and Confessor*
Orátio Auxílium tuum nobis, Dómine, quǽsumus, placátus impénde: et, intercessióne beáti Ubáldi Confessóris tui atque Pontíficis, contra omnes diáboli nequítias déxteram super nos tuæ propitiatiónis exténde. Per Dóminum nostrum …	**Prayer** We beseech Thee, O Lord, grant us Thy help and mercy, and through the intercession of the blessed Ubaldus, Thy Confessor and Pope, against all the wickedness of the devil, and extend upon us the right hand of Thy compassion. Through our Lord …
May 17 St. Paschal Baylou	*Confessor*
Orátio Deus, qui beátum Paschálem Confessórem tuum mirífica erga Córporis et Sánguinis tui sacra mystéria dilectióne decorásti: concéde propítius; ut, quam ille ex hoc divíno convívio spíritus percépit pinguédinem, eándem et nos percípere mereámur. Qui vivis et regnas …	**Prayer** O God, who adorned Thy Confessor, blessed Paschal, with wondrous love for the sacred mysteries of Thy Body and Blood: grant more mercy; so that as he received the plentitude of the spirit from this divine banquet, we will deserve to experience the same. Who liveth and reigneth …
May 18 St. Venantius	*Martyr*
Capítulum (Wis 5:1) Stabunt iusti in magna constántia advérsus eos qui se angustiavérunt et qui abstulérunt labóres eórum.	**Chapter** (Wis 5:1) Then shall the just stand with great constancy against those that have afflicted them and taken away their labors.
Ant. Fíliæ Ierúsalem, veníte et vidéte Mártyres cum corónis, quibus coronávit eos Dóminus in die solemnitátis et lætítiæ, allelúja, allelúja.	**Ant.** Daughters of Jerusalem, come and see the Martyrs with the crowns with which the Lord crowned them on the day of solemnity and joy, alleluia, alleluia.
Orátio Deus, qui hunc diem beáti Venántii Mártyris tui triúmpho consecrásti: exáudi preces pópuli tui	**Prayer** O God, who consecrated this day with the triumph of Thy blessed Martyr Venantius: hear the

Proper of the Saints Lauds

et præsta: ut, qui eius mérita venerámur, fídei constántiam imitémur. Per Dóminum nostrum …	prayers of Thy people and grant that those who venerate his virtues may imitate his constancy of faith. Through our Lord …
May 19 St. Peter Celestine	*Pope and Confessor*
Orátio Deus, qui beátum Petrum Cælestínum ad summi pontificátus ápicem sublimásti, quique illum humilitáti postpónere docuísti: concéde propítius; ut eius exémplo cuncta mundi despícere, et ad promíssa humílibus præmia pervenire felíciter mereámur. Per Dóminum nostrum	*Prayer* O God, who exalted the blessed Peter Celestine to the summit of the highest Pontificate, and who taught him the virtue of humility: grant, more generously; that by his example we may look down upon all the world, and succeed in attaining the promised reward for the humble of heart. Through our Lord ….
May 20 St. Bernardine of Siena	*Confessor*
Orátio Dómine Iesu, qui beáto Bernardíno Confessóri tuo exímium sancti nóminis tui amórem tribuísti: eius, quæsumus, méritis et intercessióne, spíritum nobis tuæ dilectiónis benígnus infúnde. Qui vivis et regnas …	*Prayer* Lord Jesus, who gave to blessed Bernardine the Confessor an extraordinary love of Thy holy Name: we beseech Thee, by his merits and intercession, to infuse us with the spirit of Thy kind love. Who liveth and reigneth…
May 25 St. Gregory VII	*Pope and Confessor*
Orátio Deus, in te sperántium fortitúdo, qui beátum Gregórium Confessórem tuum atque Pontíficem, pro tuénda Ecclésiæ libertáte, virtúte constántiæ roborásti: da nobis, eius exémplo et intercessióne, ómnia adversántia fórtiter superáre. Per Dóminum nostrum …	*Prayer* O God, with the strength of those who hope in Thee, Who fortified Thy blessed Gregory, Confessor and Pontiff, for the protection of the freedom of the Church with the power of constancy: grant us, by his example and intercession, to overcome all adversities with strength. Through our Lord …
May 26 St. Philip Neri	*Confessor*
Ant. Euge serve bone et fidélis, quia in pauca fuísti fidélis, supra multa te constítuam, intra in gáudium Dómini tui.	**Ant.** Hail, good and faithful servant, because thou hast been faithful in a few things, I will set thee over many things: enter into the joy of thy Lord.
Orátio Deus, qui beátum Philíppum Confessórem tuum Sanctórum tuórum glória sublimásti: concéde propítius; ut, cuius solemnitáte lætámur, eius virtútum proficiámus exémplo. Per Dóminum nostrum …	*Prayer* O God, who exalted Thy blessed Philip the Confessor to the glory of Thy Saints: mercifully grant; that we may rejoice in his solemnity, and follow the example of his virtues. Through our Lord ...

Proper of the Saints Lauds

May 27 St. Bede the Venerable	*Confessor and Doctor*
Orátio Deus, qui Ecclésiam tuam beáti Bedæ Confessóris tui atque Doctóris eruditióne claríficas: concéde propítius fámulis tuis; eius semper illustrári sapiéntia et méritis adiuvári. Per Dóminum nostrum …	*Prayer* O God, who by the learning of the blessed Bede, Thy Confessor and Teacher, glorifies Thy Church: grant that Thy servants may always be enlightened by his wisdom and assisted by his merits. Through our Lord …
May 28 St. Augustine of Canterbury	*Bishop and Confessor*
Orátio Deus, qui Anglórum gentes, prædicatióne et miráculis beáti Augustíni Confessóris tui atque Pontíficis, veræ fídei luce illustráre dignátus es: concéde; ut, ipso interveniénte, erránti um corda ad veritátis tuæ rédeant unitátem, et nos in tua simus voluntáte concórdes. Per Dóminum nostrum …	*Prayer* O God, who hast deigned to enlighten the nations of England with the light of the true faith by the preaching and miracles of the blessed Augustine, Thy confessor and Bishop: grant that, by his intervention, the hearts of the erring may return to the unity of Thy truth, and we may be united in Thy will. Through our Lord…
May 29 St. Mary Magdalen de Pazzi	*Virgin*
Orátio Deus, virginitátis amátor, qui beátam Maríam Magdalénam Vírginem, tuo amóre succénsam, cæléstibus donis decorásti: da; ut, quam festíva celebritáte venerámur, puritáte et caritáte imitémur. Per Dóminum nostrum …	*Prayer* O God, lover of virginity, who hast adorned the blessed virgin, Mary Magdalene, with Thy love and heavenly gifts: we ask that she may be honored with a joyful feast day, and she be imitated in purity and charity. Through our Lord …
May 30 Commemoration of St. Felix	*Pope and Martyr*
Orátio Gregem tuum, Pastor ætérne, placátus inténde: et per beátum Felícem Mártyrem tuum atque Summum Pontíficem perpétua protectióne custódi; quem totíus Ecclésiæ præstitísti esse pastórem. Per Dóminum nostrum …	*Prayer* Look favorably upon Thy flock, O eternal Shepherd, and, through Thy blessed Martyr and Supreme Pontiff Felix, whom Thou hast appointed to be the shepherd of the entire Church and be the guardian with its perpetual protection. Through our Lord …
May 31 Feast of the Blessed Virgin Mary, Queen	*Blessed Virgin Mary*
Capitulum (Ecclus 24:5 & 7) Ego ex ore Altíssimi prodívi, primogénita ante omnem creatúram; ego in altíssimis habitávi, et thronus meus in colúmna nubis.	*Chapter* (Ecclus 24:5 & 7) I came out of the mouth of the most High, the firstborn before all creatures: I dwelt in the highest places, and my throne is in a pillar of a cloud.

Proper of the Saints Lauds

Ant. Regína mundi digníssima, María, Virgo perpétua, intercéde pro nostra pace et salúte, quæ genuísti Christum Dóminum, Salvatórem ómnium, allelúja.	**Ant.** Most worthy Queen of the world, Mary, perpetual Virgin, who gave birth to Christ the Lord, the Savior of all, intercede for our peace and salvation, alleluia.
Orátio Concéde nobis, quǽsumus, Dómine: ut, qui solemnitátem beatæ Maríæ Vírginis Regínæ nostræ celebrámus; eius muníti præsídio, pacem in præsénti et glóriam in futúro cónsequi mereámur. Per Dóminum nostrum ...	*Prayer* Grant us, we beseech Thee, Lord: that we who celebrate the solemnity of the Blessed Virgin Mary, our Queen; under her powerful protection, may we be worthy to achieve peace in the present and glory in the future. Through our Lord ...
June 1 St. Angela Merici	*Virgin*
Orátio Deus, qui novum per beátam Angelam sacrárum Vírginum collégium in Ecclésia tua floréscere voluísti: da nobis, eius intercessióne, angélicis móribus vívere; ut, terrénis ómnibus abdicátis, gáudiis pérfrui mereámur ætérnis. Per Dóminum nostrum ...	*Prayer* O God, who through the blessed Angela established a new society of holy virgins which flourishes in Thy Church: grant us, through her intercession, to live in an angelic way; that having renounced all earthly things, we deserve to enjoy eternal happiness. Through our Lord ...
June 2 Commemoration of Sts. Marcellinus, Peter and Erasmus	*Martyrs*
Orátio Deus, qui nos ánnua beatórum Mártyrum tuórum Marcellíni, Petri atque Erásmi solemnitáte lætíficas: præsta, quǽsumus; ut, quorum gaudémus méritis, accendámur exémplis. Per Dóminum nostrum ...	*Prayer* O God, who makes us joyful with the annual solemnity of Thy blessed Martyrs Marcellinus, Peter, and Erasmus: grant we beseech Thee; that we may be enflamed by the examples of these whose merits we rejoice in. Through our Lord.
June 4 St. Francis Carracciolo	*Confessor*
Orátio Deus, qui beátum Francíscum, novi órdinis institutórem, orándi stúdio et pœniténtiæ amóre decorásti: da fámulis tuis in eius imitatióne ita profícere; ut, semper orántes et corpus in servitútem redigéntes, ad cæléstem glóriam pervenire mereántur. Per Dóminum nostrum ...	*Prayer* O God, who adorned the blessed Francis, founder of the new order, with the zeal of prayer, and with the love of penance: grant that Thy servants may so prosper in his imitation; that by always praying, and reducing the body to servitude, they may deserve to reach heavenly glory. Through our Lord ...

Proper of the Saints Lauds

June 5 St. Boniface	*Bishop and Martyr*
Orátio Deus, qui multitúdinem populórum, beáti Bonifátii Mártyris tui atque Pontíficis zelo, ad agnitiónem tui nóminis vocáre dignátus es: concéde propítius; ut, cuius solémnia cólimus, étiam patrocínia sentiámus. Per Dóminum nostrum …	*Prayer* O God, who hath deigned to call the great multitude of peoples to the knowledge of Thy Name by the zeal of Thy blessed Bishop and Martyr Boniface, mercifully grant that we may also feel the patronage of whose solemnity we honor. Through our Lord …
June 6 St. Norbert	*Bishop and Confessor*
Orátio Deus, qui beátum Norbértum Confessórem tuum atque Pontíficem verbi tui præcónem exímium effecísti, et per eum Ecclésiam tuam nova prole fecundásti: præsta, quǽsumus; ut, eiúsdem suffragántibus méritis, quod ore simul et ópere dócuit, te adiuvánte, exercére valeámus. Per Dóminum nostrum …	*Prayer* O God, who didst make blessed Norbert Thy Confessor and Bishop, an excellent herald of thy word, and through him Thou didst bestow on Thy church a new order: we beseech Thee that we may be able to exercise Thy grace by these virtues which he taught both by word and deed. Through our Lord …
June 9 Commemoration of Sts. Primus and Felician	*Martyrs*
Ant. Vestri capílli cápitis omnes numeráti sunt: nolíte timére: multis passéribus melióres estis vos.	**Ant.** All the hairs of thy head are numbered: fear not thou art of more value than many sparrows.
Orátio Fac nos, quǽsumus, Dómine, sanctórum Mártyrum tuórum Primi et Feliciáni semper festa sectári: quorum suffrágiis protectiónis tuæ dona sentiámus. Per Dóminum nostrum …	*Prayer* Make us, we beseech Thee Lord, always worthily to observe the feast of Thy holy Martyrs Primus and Felician: by whose virtue we may enjoy the reward of Thy protection. Through our Lord …
June 10 St. Margaret	*Queen of Scotland Widow*
Orátio Deus, qui beátam Margarítam regínam exímia in páuperes caritáte mirábilem effecísti: da; ut, eius intercessióne et exémplo, tua in córdibus nostris cáritas iúgiter augeátur. Per Dóminum nostrum …	*Prayer* O God, who made the blessed Queen Margaret extraordinary in her wonderful love for the poor: grant; that, through her intercession and example, Thy love in our hearts may be continually increased. Through our Lord …
June 11 St. Barnabas	*Apostle*
Orátio Deus, qui nos beáti Bárnabæ Apóstoli tui méritis et intercessióne lætíficas: concéde propítius; ut, qui tua per eum benefícia póscimus, dono tuæ grátiæ consequámur.	*Prayer* O God, who made us happy through the intercession of the blessed Barnabas, Thine Apostle: grant more generously; so that those who seek Thy favors

Proper of the Saints Lauds

Per Dóminum nostrum …	through him may obtain the gift of Thy grace. Through our Lord …
June 12 St. John of San Facondo	*Confessor*
Orátio Deus, auctor pacis et amátor caritátis, qui beátum Ioánnem Confessórem tuum mirífica dissidéntes componéndi grátia decorásti: eius méritis et intercessióne concéde; ut, in tua caritáte firmáti, nullis a te tentatiónibus separémur. Per Dóminum nostrum …	**Prayer** O God, author of peace, and lover of charity, who adorned Thy blessed John the Confessor with the wonderful grace of reconciling enemies: so that, firm in Thy love, we may not be separated from Thee by any temptations, grant his merits and intercession. Through our Lord …
June 13 St. Anthony of Padua	*Confessor and Doctor*
Orátio Ecclésiam tuam, Deus, beáti Antónii Confessóris tui atque Doctóris solémnitas votíva lætíficet: ut spirituálibus semper muniátur auxíliis et gáudiis pérfrui mereátur ætérnis. Per Dóminum nostrum …	**Prayer** O God, may Thy church be gladdened by the votive solemnity of the blessed Anthony, Thy Confessor and Teacher: that we may always be fortified with spiritual aids, and may deserve to enjoy eternal happiness. Through our Lord …
June 14 St. Basil the Great	*Bishop, Confessor and Doctor*
Orátio Exáudi, quǽsumus, Dómine, preces nostras, quas in beáti Basílii Confessóris tui atque Pontíficis solemnitáte deférimus: et, qui tibi digne méruit famulári, eius intercedéntibus méritis, ab ómnibus nos absólve peccátis. Per Dóminum nostrum …	**Prayer** Hear, we beseech thee, Lord, our prayers, which we offer on the solemnity of the blessed Basil Thy Confessor and Bishop: who hath merited to serve Thee worthily, by his intercessory merits, absolve us from all our sins. Through our Lord …
June 15 Commemoration of Sts. Vitus, Modestus and Crescentia	*Martyrs*
Orátio Da Ecclésiæ tuæ, quǽsumus, Dómine, sanctis Martýribus tuis Vito, Modésto atque Crescéntia intercedéntibus, supérbe non sápere, sed tibi plácita humilitáte profícere: ut, prava despíciens, quæcúmque recta sunt, líbera exérceat caritáte. Per Dóminum nostrum …	**Prayer** Grant to Thy Church, we beseech Thee, Lord, through the intercession of Thy holy Martyrs Vitus, Modestus, and Crescentia, that we may not be proud-minded, but strive with humility to be pleasing to Thee: so that despising evil, doing whatever is right, we may accomplish all through generous love. Through our Lord …

Proper of the Saints Lauds

June 18 St. Ephrem	*Confessor and Doctor*
Orátio Deus, qui Ecclésiam tuam beáti Ephræm Confessóris tui et Doctóris mira eruditióne et præcláris vitæ méritis illustráre voluísti: te súpplices exorámus; ut, ipso intercedénte, eam advérsus erróris et pravitátis insídias perénni tua virtúte deféndas. Per Dóminum nostrum …	**Prayer** O God, who chose to enlighten Thy Church with the great learning and excellent merits of the blessed Ephrem, Thy Confessor and Teacher: we ask that, by his intercession, Thou mayest defend us by Thy eternal power against the snares of error and wickedness of the enemy. Through our Lord …
June 19 St. Juliana Falconieri	*Virgin*
Orátio Deus, qui beátam Iuliánam Vírginem tuam extrémo morbo laborántem, pretióso Fílii tui Córpore mirabíliter recreáre dignátus es: concéde, quǽsumus; ut, eius intercedéntibus méritis, nos quoque eódem in mortis agóne refécti ac roboráti, ad cæléstem pátriam perducámur. Per eundem Dóminum …	**Prayer** O God, who hast deigned to miraculously revive Thy blessed Virgin Juliana who was suffering from an extreme illness with the precious body of Thy Son: grant, we beseech Thee; that by her intercession, we too, will be refreshed and strengthened at the same agony of death, and may be guided to our heavenly homeland. Through our Lord …
June 20 St. Silverius	*Pope and Martyr*
Orátio Gregem tuum, Pastor ætérne, placátus inténde: et per beátum Silvérium Mártyrem tuum atque Summum Pontíficem perpétua protectióne custódi; quem totíus Ecclésiæ præstitísti esse pastórem. Per Dóminum nostrum …	**Prayer** O Eternal Shepherd, tend Thy flock in peace and, through Thy blessed Silverius, Martyr and Supreme Pontiff, whom Thou hast appointed to be the shepherd of Thy whole Church, keep it under Thy everlasting protection. Through our Lord …
June 21 St. Aloysius Gonzaga	*Confessor*
Orátio Cæléstium donórum distribútor, Deus, qui in angélico iúvene Aloísio miram vitæ innocéntiam pari cum pœniténtia sociásti: eius méritis et précibus concéde; ut, innocéntem non secúti, pœniténtem imitémur. Per Dóminum nostrum …	**Prayer** O God, provider of heavenly gifts, who in the angelic young Aloysius associated the wonderful innocence of life with equal penance: grant through his merits and prayers; that, though we are not innocent as he was, we should imitate him as the penitent. Through our Lord …
June 22 St. Paulinus	*Bishop and Confessor*
Orátio Deus, qui ómnia pro te in hoc sǽculo relinquéntibus, céntuplum in futúro et vitam ætérnam promisísti: concéde propítius; ut, sancti Pontíficis Paulíni	**Prayer** O God, who provided everything for us in this world, Thou hast promised a hundredfold in the future and eternal life: mercifully grant; that following in

Proper of the Saints Lauds

vestígiis inhæréntes, valeámus terréna despícere et sola cæléstia desideráre. Qui vivis et regnas ...	the footsteps of the holy Bishop Paulinus, we should be able to despise earthly things and desire only heavenly things. Thou who livest and reigneth...
June 23 Vigil of St. John the Baptist	*Martyr*
Orátio Præsta, quǽsumus, omnípotens Deus: ut família tua per viam salútis incédat; et beáti Ioánnis Præcursóris hortaménta sectándo, ad eum quem prædíxit, secúra pervéniat, Dóminum nostrum Iesum Christum, Fílium tuum. Qui vivis et regnas ...	*Prayer* Grant, we beseech Thee, almighty God: that Thy family may walk the path of salvation; and by following the exhortations of blessed John the Forerunner, may they come safely to him whom he foretold, our Lord Jesus Christ, Thy Son, Who livest and...
June 24 Nativity of St. John the Baptist	*Martyr*
Capitulum (Isa 49:1) **V.** Audíte, ínsulæ, et atténdite, pópuli de longe: Dóminus ab útero vocávit me, de ventre matris meæ recordátus est nóminis mei. **R.** Deo Grátias.	*Chapter* (Isa 49:1) **V.** Give ear, ye islands, and hearken, ye people from afar. The Lord hath called me from the womb, from the bosom of my mother he hath remembered my name. **R.** Thanks be to God.
Ant. Apértum est os Zacharíæ, et prophetávit dicens: Benedíctus Deus Israël.	*Ant.* The mouth of Zechariah was opened, and he prophesied, saying: Blessed be the God of Israel.
Orátio Deus, qui præséntem diem honorábilem nobis in beáti Ioánnis nativitáte fecísti: da pópulis tuis spirituálium grátiam gaudiórum; et ómnium fidélium mentes dírige in viam salútis ætérnæ. Per Dóminum nostrum ...	*Prayer* O God, who made the present day honored by us in the birth of blessed John: give Thy people the grace of spiritual joys; and direct the minds of all the faithful in the way of eternal salvation. Through our Lord ...
June 28 Vigil of Sts. Peter and Paul	*Apostles*
Orátio Præsta, quǽsumus, omnípotens Deus: ut nullis nos permíttas perturbatiónibus cóncuti; quos in apostólicæ confessiónis petra solidásti. Per Dóminum nostrum Jesum Christum ...	*Prayer* We beseech Thee, almighty God, that Thou may not allow us to be shaken by any disturbances; whom Thou hast solidified in the rock of the apostolic confession. Through our Lord ...
June 29 St. Peter and Paul	*Apostles*
Capitulum (Acts 12:1-3) **V.** Misit Heródes rex manus ut afflígeret quosdam de Ecclésia. Occídit autem Iacóbum fratrem Ioánnis gládio.	*Chapter* (Acts 12:1-3) **V.** King Herod stretched forth his hands to afflict some of the Church. And he killed James the brother of John with the sword. But seeing that it

Videns autem quia placéret Iudǽis, appósuit ut apprehénderet et Petrum. R. Deo grátias.	pleased the Jews, he set out to seize Peter. R. Thanks be to God.
Ant. Quodcúmque ligáveris super terram, erit ligátum et in cælis; et quodcúmque sólveris super terram, erit solútum et in cælis: dicit Dóminus Simóni Petro.	Ant. Whatever thou bindest on earth will be bound in heaven, and whatever thou looseth on earth will be loosed in heaven, said the Lord to Simon Peter.
Orátio Deus, qui hodiérnam diem Apostolórum tuórum Petri et Pauli martýrio consecrásti: da Ecclésiæ tuæ, eórum in ómnibus sequi præcéptum; per quos religiónis sumpsit exórdium. Per Dóminum nostrum ...	*Prayer* O God, who consecrated this day to the martyrdom of Thine apostles Peter and Paul: grant Thy Church to follow their teachings in all things, through whom the Church took its beginning. Through our Lord ...
June 30 Commemoration of St. Paul	*Apostle*
Capitulum (2 Tim 4:7-8) V. Bonum certámen certávi, cursum consummávi, fidem servávi. In réliquo repósita est mihi coróna iustítiæ, quam reddet mihi Dóminus in illa die iustus iudex. R. Deo grátias.	*Chapter* (2 Tim 4:7-8) V. I fought the good fight, I finished the course, I kept the faith. In the rest there is laid up for me the crown of righteousness, which the Lord, the righteous Judge, will give me on that day. R. Thanks be to God.
Orátio Deus, qui multitúdinem géntium beáti Pauli Apóstoli prædicatióne docuísti: da nobis, quǽsumus; ut, cuius natalícia cólimus, eius apud te patrocínia sentiámus. Per Dóminum nostrum......	*Prayer* O God, who taught the multitude of Gentiles by the preaching of the blessed Paul the Apostle: grant us, we beseech Thee; that on whose feast day we honor, we may be blessed by his patronage with Thee. Through our Lord ...
July 1 Most Precious Blood of Our Lord Jesus Christ	
Capitulum (Heb 9:11-12) V. Fratres: Christus assístens Póntifex futurórum bonórum, per ámplius et perféctius tabernáculum non manufáctum, id est, non huius creatiónis: neque per sánguinem hircórum aut vitulórum, sed per próprium sánguinem introívit semel in Sancta, ætérna redemptióne invénta. R. Deo grátias.	*Chapter* (Heb 9:11-12) V. Brethren: Christ, becoming the High Priest of the good things to come, through a greater and more perfect tabernacle not created, that is, not of this creation, nor through the blood of goats or calves, but through His own blood, entered once into the Holy of Holies, found in eternal redemption. R. Thanks be to God.
Ant. Erit sanguis Agni vobis in signum, dicit Dóminus; et vidébo	Ant. The blood of the Lamb will be a sign for you, sayeth the Lord:

sánguinem, et transíbo vos nec erit in vobis plaga dispérdens.	and I will see the blood, and I will pass over you, and there will be no destroying plague among you.
Orátio Omnípotens sempitérne Deus, qui unigénitum Fílium tuum mundi Redemptórem constituísti, ac eius Sánguine placári voluísti: concéde, quǽsumus, salútis nostræ prétium solémni cultu ita venerári, atque a præséntis vitæ malis eius virtúte deféndi in terris; ut fructu perpétuo lætémur in cælis. Per eundem Dóminum nostrum …	**Prayer** Almighty and eternal God, who made Thine only begotten Son the Redeemer of the world, and Thou wished to be appeased by His blood: grant, we beseech Thee, that the price of our salvation should be so venerated with solemn worship, and that we may be protected from the evils of this present life by His power on earth; that we may rejoice forever in the heavens. Through our Lord …
July 2 Visitation of the Blessed Virgin Mary	*Blessed Virgin Mary*
Capítulum (Sir 24:14) V. Ab inítio et ante sǽcula creáta sum, et usque ad futúrum sǽculum non désinam, et in habitatióne sancta coram ipso ministrávi. R. Deo grátias.	**Chapter** (Sir 24:14) V. From the beginning, and before the world, was I created, and unto the world to come I shall not cease to be, and in the holy dwelling place I have ministered before Him. R. Thanks be to God.
Ant. Cum audísset salutatiónem Maríæ Elísabeth, exclamávit voce magna et dixit: Unde hoc mihi, ut véniat Mater Dómini mei ad me? Allelúja.	**Ant.** When Elizabeth heard the greeting of Mary, she cried out with a loud voice and said: Where did this come from for me, that the Mother of my Lord should come to me?
Orátio Fámulis tuis, quǽsumus, Dómine, cæléstis grátiæ munus impertíre: ut, quibus beátæ Vírginis partus éxstitit salútis exórdium; Visitatiónis eius votíva solémnitas, pacis tríbuat increméntum. Per Dóminum nostrum …	**Prayer** Bestow on Thy servants, we beseech thee, Lord, the gift of heavenly grace: that for whom the birth of the blessed Virgin was the beginning of our salvation, the votive solemnity of her visitation, may grant an increase of peace. Through our Lord …
July 3 St. Iraneaus	*Pope and Confessor*
Orátio Deus, qui beáto Irenǽo Mártyri tuo atque Pontífici tribuísti, ut et veritáte doctrínæ expugnáret hǽreses, et pacem Ecclésiæ felíciter confirmáret: da, quǽsumus, plebi tuæ in sancta religióne constántiam; et pacem tuam nostris concéde tempóribus.	**Prayer** O God, who gave the faithful blessed Irenaeus as Thy Martyr and Pontiff, so that he might fight heresies with the truth of doctrine and successfully confirm the peace of the Church: grant, we ask, that Thy people be steadfast in their holy religion; and

Proper of the Saints Lauds

Per Dóminum nostrum …	grant Thy peace to our times. Through our Lord .
July 5 St. Anthony Mary Zaccaria	*Confessor*
Orátio Fac nos, Dómine Deus, supereminéntem Iesu Christi sciéntiam, spíritu Pauli Apóstoli, edíscere: qua beátus Antónius María mirabíliter erudítus, novas in Ecclésia tua clericórum et vírginum famílias congregávit. Per Dóminum nostrum …	*Prayer* Make us, Lord God, in the spirit of St. Paul the Apostle; learn the highest knowledge of Jesus Christ, as was Anthony Mary so wonderfully educated and who gathered together new religious orders of clerics and virgins for Thy Church. Through Our Lord …
July 7 Sts. Cyril and Methodius	*Bishops and Confessors*
Capitulum (Sir 44:16-17) V. Ecce sacérdos magnus, qui in diébus suis plácuit Deo, et invéntus est iustus: et in témpore iracúndiæ factus est reconciliátio. R. Deo grátias.	*Chapter* (Sir 44:16-17) V. Behold a great priest, who pleased God in his days, and was found righteous: and in the time of wrath he was reconciled. R. Thanks be to God.
Ant. In sanctitáte et iustítia serviérunt Dómino ómnibus diébus suis: ídeo stolam glóriæ índuit illos Dóminus, Deus Israël.	*Ant.* In holiness and justice they served the Lord all their days: therefore the Lord God of Israel clothed them with a robe of glory.
Orátio Omnípotens sempitérne Deus, qui Slavóniæ gentes per beátos Confessóres tuos atque Pontífices Cyríllum et Methódium ad agnitiónem tui nóminis veníre tribuísti: præsta; ut, quorum festivitáte gloriámur, eórum consórtio copulémur. Per Dóminum nostrum …	*Prayer* Almighty and eternal God, who through Thy blessed Confessors and Bishops Cyril and Methodius hast given the nations of Slavonia to come to the knowledge of Thy Name: grant; that we may rejoice on their feast day, and we may enjoy their company forever. Through our Lord …
July 8 St. Elizabeth	*Queen of Portugal Widow*
Capitulum (Prov 31:10-11) V. Mulíerem fortem quis invéniet? Procul et de últimis fínibus prétium eius. Confídit in ea cor viri sui, et spóliis non indigébit. R. Deo grátias.	*Chapter* (Prov 31:10-11) V. Who shall find a valiant woman? Far and from the uttermost coasts is the price of her. The heart of her husband trusteth in her, and he shall have no lack of gain. R. Thanks be to God.
Ant. Tu glória Ierúsalem, tu lætítia Israël, tu honorifícentia pópuli tui.	*Ant.* Thou art the glory of Jerusalem, thou art the joy of Israel, thou art the honor of Thy people.
Orátio Clementíssime Deus, qui beátam Elísabeth regínam, inter céteras egrégias dotes, béllici furóris sedándi prærogatíva decorásti: da	*Prayer* Most merciful God, who blessed Queen Elizabeth, among her other excellent gifts, with the gift of extinguishing the fury of

Proper of the Saints Lauds

nobis, eius intercessióne; post mortális vitæ, quam supplíciter pétimus, pacem, ad ætérna gáudia pervenire. Per Dóminum nostrum …	war: grant us, through her intercession, after this mortal life, we imploringly ask for peace and to attain eternal joys. Through our Lord …
July 10 The Seven Holy Brothers and Sts. Rufina and Secunda	*Martyrs, and Virgin Martyrs*
Orátio Præsta, quæsumus, omnípotens Deus: ut, qui gloriósos Mártyres fortes in sua confessióne cognóvimus, pios apud te in nostra intercessióne sentiámus. Per Dóminum nostrum …	*Prayer* We beseech Thee, Almighty God, grant that those who have known the faith of the glorious Martyrs, may enjoy the fruit of their prayers to Thee. Through our Lord. …
July 11 St. Pius I	*Pope and Martyr*
Orátio Gregem tuum, Pastor ætérne, placátus inténde: et per beátum Pium Mártyrem tuum atque Summum Pontíficem perpétua protectióne custódi; quem totíus Ecclésiæ præstitísti esse pastórem. Per Dóminum nostrum …	*Prayer* Preserve Thy flock, Eternal Shepherd, and, through Thy blessed Pius, Martyr and Supreme Pontiff, whom Thou hast appointed to be the shepherd of the entire Church, defend us with everlasting protection. Through our Lord …
July 12 St. John Gualbert	*Abbot*
Orátio Intercéssio nos, quæsumus, Dómine, beáti Ioánnis Abbátis comméndet: ut, quod nostris méritis non valémus, eius patrocínio assequámur. Per Dóminum nostrum …	*Prayer* May the intercession of blessed John the Abbot, we beseech Thee Lord, commend us to that which we are not able to accomplish by our own merits but may obtain by his patronage. Through our Lord …
July 14 St. Bonaventure	*Bishop, Confessor and Doctor*
Orátio Deus, qui pópulo tuo ætérnæ salútis beátum Bonaventúram minístrum tribuísti: præsta, quæsumus; ut quem Doctórem vitæ habúimus in terris, intercessórem habére mereámur in cælis. Per Dóminum nostrum …	*Prayer* O God, who made the blessed Bonaventure a minister of eternal salvation to Thy people: grant, we beseech Thee, that whom we had as a teacher of eternal life, we may deserve as an intercessor in heaven. Through our Lord …
July 15 St. Henry	*Emperor and Confessor*
Orátio Deus, qui hodiérna die beátum Henrícum Confessórem tuum e terréni cúlmine impérii ad regnum ætérnum transtulísti: te súpplices exorámus; ut, sicut illum, grátiæ tuæ ubertáte prævéntum,	*Prayer* O God, who on this day hast raised Thy blessed Henry the Confessor from the throne of an earthly empire to the eternal kingdom: we implore Thee that just as Thou madest him, by the

illécebras sǽculi superáre fecísti, ita nos fácias, eius imitatióne, mundi huius blandiménta vitáre, et ad te puris méntibus perveníre. Per Dóminum nostrum …	freedom of Thy grace, overcome the temptations of the world, so make us in imitation of him to avoid the flattery of this world and come to Thee with pure minds. Through our Lord …
July 16 Our Lady of Mount Carmel	*Blessed Virgin Mary*
Ant. Eréxit nobis Dóminus cornu salútis in domo David púeri sui.	**Ant.** The Lord raised up for us the horn of salvation in the house of His son David.
Orátio Deus, qui beatíssimæ semper Vírginis et Genetrícis tuæ Maríæ singulári título Carméli órdinem decorásti: concéde propítius; ut, cuius hódie Commemoratiónem solémni celebrámus offício, eius muníti præsídiis, ad gáudia sempitérna perveníre mereámur. Qui vivis et regnas ...	*Prayer* O God, who hast honored Thy most Blessed Mother Mary ever Virgin, with the singular title of Mount Carmel, grant mercifully; that today as we celebrate the commemoration of this solemn feast with its defenses, that we will deserve to reach eternal joys. Who liveth and reigneth …
July 17 St. Alexius	*Confessor*
Orátio Deus, qui nos beáti Aléxii Confessóris tui ánnua solemnitáte lætíficas: concéde propítius; ut cuius natalícia cólimus, étiam actiónes imitémur. Per Dóminum nostrum …	*Prayer* O God, who maketh us happy with the annual solemnity of Thy blessed Alexius the Confessor: mercifully grant that we may imitate his deeds whose feast day we celebrate. Through our Lord ….
July 18 St. Camillus De Lellis	*Confessor*
Orátio Deus, qui sanctum Camíllum, ad animárum in extrémo agóne luctántium subsídium, singulári caritátis prærogatíva decorásti: eius, quǽsumus, méritis, spíritum nobis tuæ dilectiónis infúnde; ut in hora éxitus nostri hostem víncere, et ad cæléstem mereámur corónam perveníre. Per Dóminum nostrum …	*Prayer* O God, who hast blessed Saint Camillus for the support of souls struggling in the last earthly trial with the singular gift of charity: we beseech him, fill us with the spirit of Thy love; that in the hour of our death we may conquer the enemy and deserve to reach a heavenly crown. Through our Lord …
July 19 St. Vincent de Paul	*Confessor*
Orátio Deus, qui, ad evangelizándum paupéribus et ecclesiástici órdinis decórem promovéndum, beátum Vincéntium apostólica virtúte roborásti: præsta, quǽsumus; ut, cuius pia mérita	*Prayer* O God, who in order to evangelize the poor and promote the dignity of the clergy, strengthened the blessed Vincent with apostolic power: we praise him and venerate him through his

Proper of the Saints Lauds

venerámur, virtútum quoque instruámur exémplis. Per Dóminum nostrum ...	pious merits, and may we also learn by his virtues. Through our Lord ...
July 20 St. Jerome Emilian	*Confessor*
Orátio Deus, misericordiárum pater, per mérita et intercessiónem beáti Hierónymi, quem órphanis adiutórem et patrem esse voluísti: concéde; ut spíritum adoptiónis, quo filii tui nominámur et sumus, fidéliter custodiámus. Per Dóminum nostrum ...	*Prayer* O God, Father of mercies, through the merits and intercession of the blessed Jerome, whom Thou wished to be the helper and father of orphans: grant that we may faithfully guard the spirit of adoption by which we are called and are Thy children. Through our Lord ...
July 21 St. Lawrence of Brindisi	*Bishop, Confesor and Doctor*
Orátio Deus, qui ad árdua quæque pro nóminis tui glória et animárum salúte beáto Lauréntio, Confessóri tuo atque Doctóri, spíritum sapiéntiæ et fortitúdinis contulísti: da nobis in eódem spíritu et agénda cognóscere; et cógnita, eius intercessióne, perfícere. Per Dóminum nostrum ...	*Prayer* O God, Who, for the glory of Thy Name and the salvation of souls, gave the spirit of wisdom and courage to the blessed Lawrence, Thy Confessor and Teacher, in the same spirit: grant us knowledge of what to do, and having learned, through his intercession, to complete it. Through our Lord ...
July 22 St. Mary Magdalen	*Penitent*
Capitulum (Prov 31:10-11) **V.** Mulíerem fortem quis invéniet? Procul et de últimis fínibus prétium eius. Confídit in ea cor viri sui, et spóliis non indigébit. **R.** Deo grátias.	*Chapter* (Prov 31:10-11) **V.** Who shall find a valiant woman? Far and from the uttermost coasts is the price of her. The heart of her husband trusteth in her, and he shall have no need of spoils. **R.** Thanks be to God.
Ant. María unxit pedes Iesu, et extérsit capíllis suis, et domus impléta est ex odóre unguénti.	**Ant.** Mary anointed the feet of Jesus and wiped them with her hair, and the house was filled with the scent of the perfume.
Orátio Beátæ Maríæ Magdalénæ, quǽsumus, Dómine, suffrágiis adiuvémur: cuius précibus exorátus, quatriduánum fratrem Lázarum vivum ab ínferis resuscitásti. Qui vivis et regnas ...	*Prayer* May Blessed Mary Magdalen, we beseech Thee, Lord, help us with her pleading: as by whose prayers Thou didst raise to life her brother Lazarus from the grave after four days. Who livest and reignest ...
July 23 St. Apollinaris	*Bishop and Martyr*
Orátio Deus, fidélium remunerátor animárum, qui hunc diem beáti Apollináris Sacerdótis tui martýrio	*Prayer* O God, the rewarder of faithful souls, who consecrated this day to the martyrdom of Thy

consecrásti: tríbue nobis, quǽsumus, fámulis tuis; ut, cuius venerándam celebrámus festivitátem, précibus eius indulgéntiam consequámur. Per Dóminum nostrum ...	blessed Bishop Apollinaris, grant, we beseech Thee, that we whose venerable feast day we celebrate, may obtain forgiveness through his prayers. Through our Lord ...
July 24 Commemoration of St. Christina	*Virgin and Martyr*
Orátio Indulgéntiam nobis, quǽsumus, Dómine, beáta Christína Virgo et Martyr implóret: quæ tibi grata semper éxstitit, et mérito castitátis, et tuæ professióne virtútis. Per Dóminum nostrum ...	**Prayer** We beg Thee for mercy, O Lord, and we implore blessed Christina, Virgin and Martyr, through her pure virtue and courage, that she may plead for us for Thy kindness. Through our Lord..
July 25 St. James	*Apostle*
Orátio Esto, Dómine, plebi tuæ sanctificátor et custos: ut, Apóstoli tui Iacóbi muníta præsídiis, et conversatióne tibi pláceat, et secúra mente desérviat. Per Dóminum nostrum ...	**Prayer** Be thou, O Lord, the sanctifier and guardian of Thy people: that we be safeguarded by the protection of Thine Apostle James, may please Thee in prayers, and may serve Thee with a peaceful conscience. Through our Lord ...
July 26 St. Anne, Mother of the Blessed Virgin Mary	*Holy Woman*
Orátio Deus, qui beátæ Annæ grátiam conférre dignátus es, ut Genetrícis unigéniti Fílii tui mater éffici mererétur: concéde propítius; ut, cuius solémnia celebrámus, eius apud te patrocíniis adiuvémur. Per eundem Dóminum nostrum ...	**Prayer** O God, who hast deigned to bestow the grace of blessed Anne, so that she deserved to become the mother of the one to give birth to Thine only-begotten Son: mercifully grant; by whose feast we celebrate, we may be assisted by her patronage with Thee. Through our Lord ...
July 27 Commemoration of St. Pantaleon	*Martyr*
Orátio Præsta, quǽsumus, omnípotens Deus: ut, intercedénte beáto Pantaleóne Mártyre tuo, et a cunctis adversitátibus liberémur in córpore, et a pravis cogitatiónibus mundémur in mente. Per Dóminum nostrum ...	**Prayer** We beseech Thee, almighty God, that through the intercession of the Blessed Pantaleon, Thy Martyr, we may be freed from all adversities in body, and our minds be cleansed from evil thoughts. Through our Lord ...

Proper of the Saints Lauds

July 28 Sts. Nazarius and Celsus, St. Victor I and St. Innocent I	*Martyrs, Pope and Martyr, Pope and Confessor*
Orátio Sanctórum tuórum nos, Dómine, Nazárii, Celsi, Victóris et Innocéntii conféssio beáta commúniat: et fragilitáti nostræ subsídium dignánter exóret. Per Dóminum nostrum ...	**Prayer** May the blessed confession of Thy saints, Nazarius, Celsus, Victor, and Innocent, O Lord, support us that we may be worthy to be raised from our weakness. Through our Lord…
July 29 St. Martha	*Virgin*
Orátio Exáudi nos, Deus, salutáris noster: ut, sicut de beátæ Marthæ Vírginis tuæ festivitáte gaudémus; ita piæ devotiónis erudiámur afféctu. Per Dóminum nostrum …	**Prayer** Hear us, O God, our Savior: that we may rejoice on the feast of Thy blessed Virgin Martha; so we learn the sentiments of loving devotion. Through our Lord …
July 30 Commemoration of Sts. Abdon and Sennen	*Martyrs*
Orátio Deus, qui sanctis tuis Abdon et Sennen ad hanc glóriam veniéndi copiósum munus grátiæ contulísti: da fámulis tuis suórum véniam peccatórum; ut, Sanctórum tuórum intercedéntibus méritis, ab ómnibus mereántur adversitátibus liberári. Per Dóminum nostrum ...	**Prayer** O God, who hast given Thy saints Abdon and Sennen a copious gift of grace to attain this glory: grant us Thy servants the forgiveness of our sins; that through their intercession we may be worthy to be delivered from all adversities. Through our Lord …
July 31 St. Ignatius of Loyola	*Confessor*
Orátio Deus, qui ad maiórem tui nóminis glóriam propagándam, novo per beátum Ignátium subsídio militántem Ecclésiam roborásti: concéde; ut, eius auxílio et imitatióne certántes in terris, coronári cum ipso mereámur in cælis. Per Dóminum nostrum ...	**Prayer** O God, who, for the greater glory of Thy Name, hast strengthened the militant Church with the help of the blessed Ignatius; grant that by his assistance and imitation we may while striving on earth, deserve to be crowned with him in heaven. Through our Lord …
Aug. 1 St. Peter in Chains	*Apostle*
Orátio Deus, qui Beátum Petrum Apóstolum, a vínculis absolútum, illǽsum abíre fecísti: nostrórum, quǽumus, absólve víncula pecatórum; et ómnia mala a nobis propitiátus exclúde. Per Dominum nostrum …	**Prayer** O God, who freed blessed Peter the Apostle from chains and allowed him to escape unharmed: loose our chains of sin and mercifully shut out all evils encompassing us. Through our Lord …

Proper of the Saints Lauds

Aug. 1 Martyrs of the Maccabees	*Martyrs*
Orátio Fratérna nos, Dómine, Mártyrum tuórum coróna lætíficet: quæ et fídei nostræ præbeat increménta virtútum; et multíplici nos suffrágio consolétur. Per Dóminum nostrum …	**Prayer** May the crown of Thy Martyrs, O Lord, make us fraternal: may it also give our faith an increase in virtues, and may we be comforted by our manifold suffrage. Through our Lord …
Aug. 2 St. Alphonus Liguori	*Bishop, Confessor and Doctor*
Orátio Deus, qui per beátum Alfónsum Maríam Confessórem tuum atque Pontíficem, animárum zelo succénsum, Ecclésiam tuam nova prole fecundásti: quæsumus; ut, eius salutáribus mónitis edócti et exémplis roboráti, ad te perveníre felíciter valeámus. Per Dóminum nostrum …	**Prayer** O God, who through blessed Alphonsus Mary, Thy Confessor and Bishop, inflamed with the zeal of saving souls, hast made Thy Church fertile with a new religious order: we ask that, taught by his salutary counsels and strengthened by his example, we may be able to successfully be with Thee in heaven. Through our Lord..
Aug. 4. St. Dominic	*Confessor*
Orátio Deus, qui Ecclésiam tuam beáti Domínici Confessóris tui illumináre dignátus es méritis et doctrínis: concéde; ut eius intercessióne temporálibus non destituátur auxíliis, et spirituálibus semper profíciat increméntis. Per Dóminum nostrum ...	**Prayer** O God, who hast deigned to enlighten Thy Church with the merits and doctrines of Thy blessed Confessor, Dominic: grant that by his intercession we may not lack temporal help, and may always prosper in spiritual growth. Through our Lord …
Aug 6 Transfiguration of Our Lord Jesus Christ	
Capítulum (Phil 3:20-21) V. Salvatórem exspectámus Dóminum nostrum Iesum Christum, qui reformábit corpus humilitátis nostræ configurátum córpori claritátis suæ. **R.** Deo Grátias.	**Chapter** (Phil 3:20-21) V. We await the Savior, our Lord Jesus Christ, Who wills our humble body to be like His glorious body. **R.** Thanks be to God.
Orátio Deus, qui fídei sacraménta in Unigéniti tui gloriósa Transfiguratióne patrum testimónio roborásti, et adoptiónem filiórum perféctam, voce delápsa in nube lúcida, mirabíliter præsignásti: concéde propítius; ut ipsíus Regis glóriæ nos coherédes effícias, et eiúsdem glóriæ tríbuas esse consórtes. Per eundem Dóminum nostrum ...	**Prayer** O God who hast confirmed the mysteries of faith in the glorious Transfiguration of Thy Son by the witness of the fathers, and hast miraculously foretold the perfect adoption of His sons with a voice coming down from a bright cloud: mercifully grant that we may be made co-heirs of the King of Glory Himself, and grant us all to be part of that same glory.

Proper of the Saints Lauds

Aug. 7 St. Cajetan	*Confessor*
Ant. Nolíte sollíciti esse dicéntes: Quid manducábimus, aut quid bibémus? Scit enim Pater vester, quid vobis necésse sit.	**Ant.** Be not anxious, saying what shall we eat, or what shall we drink? For thy Father knows what thou needest.
Orátio Deus, qui beáto Caietáno Confessóri tuo apostólicam vivéndi formam imitári tribuísti: da nobis, eius intercessióne et exémplo, in te semper confidere et sola cæléstia desideráre. Per Dóminum nostrum ...	*Prayer* O God, who bestowed the blessed Confessor Cajetan to imitate the apostolic way of life: grant us, through his intercession and example, to always trust in Thee and to desire only heavenly things. Through our Lord ...
Aug. 8 St. John Mary Vianney	*Confessor*
Orátio Omnípotens et miséricors Deus, qui sanctum Ioánnem Maríam pastoráli stúdio et iugi oratiónis ac pœniténtiæ ardóre mirábilem effecísti: da, quǽsumus; ut, eius exémplo et intercessióne, ánimas fratrum lucrári Christo, et cum eis ætérnam glóriam cónsequi valeámus. Per eundem Dóminum nostrum ...	*Prayer* Almighty and merciful God, who made Saint John Vianney admirable by his pastoral zeal and the fervor for prayer and penance: grant, we beseech Thee; that by his example and intercession, we may be able to win the souls of our brothers to Christ, and with them to obtain eternal glory. Through our same Lord...
Aug. 10 St. Lawrence	*Martyr*
Capitulum (2 Cor 9:6) **V.** Fratres: Qui parce séminat, parce et metet; et qui séminat in benedictiónibus, de benedictiónibus et metet. **R.** Deo grátias.	*Chapter* (2 Cor 9:6) **V.** Brothers: He who soweth sparingly will also reap sparingly: and he who soweth in blessings will also reap in blessings. **R.** Thanks be to God.
Orátio Da nobis, quǽsumus, omnípotens Deus: vitiórum nostrórum flammas exstínguere; qui beáto Lauréntio tribuísti tormentórum suórum incéndia superáre. Per Dóminum nostrum ...	*Prayer* Grant us, we beseech Thee, Almighty God, to extinguish the flames of our vices; who gave the blessed Lawrence strength to overcome his torment by fire. Through our Lord ...
Aug. 11 Commemoration of Sts. Tiburtius and Susanna	*Virgin, Martyrs*
Orátio Sanctórum Mártyrum tuórum Tibúrtii et Susánnæ nos, Dómine, fóveant continuáta præsídia: quia non désinis propítius intuéri; quos tálibus auxíliis concésseris adiuvári. Per Dóminum nostrum ...	*Prayer* May Thy holy Martyrs Tiburtius and Susanna, O Lord, comfort us by Thine unfailing protection: for surely Thou dost not cease to look upon us with mercy, whom Thou hast granted their help. Through our Lord ...
Aug. 12 St. Clare	*Virgin*
Orátio Exáudi nos, Deus, salutáris noster: ut sicut de beátæ Claræ	*Prayer* Hear us, God, our Savior: that, as we rejoice on the feast day

Proper of the Saints Lauds

Vírginis festivitáte gaudémus; ita piæ devotiónis erudiámur afféctu. Per Dóminum nostrum ...	of Thy blessed Virgin Clare, so we may be taught in the love of pious devotions. Through our Lord…
Aug. 13 Commemoration of Sts. Hippolytus and Cassian	*Martyrs*
Orátio Da, quǽsumus, omnípotens Deus: ut beatórum Mártyrum tuórum Hippólyti et Cassiáni veneránda solémnitas, et devotiónem nobis áugeat, et salútem. Per Dóminum nostrum ...	**Prayer** Grant, we beseech Thee, almighty God, that the solemn veneration of Thy blessed Martyrs Hippolytus and Cassian may increase our devotion and lead us to our salvation. Through our Lord …
Aug. 14 St. Eusebius	*Confessor*
Orátio Deus, qui nos beáti Eusébii Confessóris tui ánnua solemnitáte lætíficas: concéde propítius; ut, cujus natalítia cólimus, per ejus ad te exémpla gradiámur. Per Dóminum nostrum ...	**Prayer** O God, who maketh us joyful with the annual solemnity of Thy blessed Confessor Eusebius: grant us mercy; so that, whose feast day we celebrate, we may come to Thee through his example. Through our Lord …
Aug. 15. Assumption of the Blessed Virgin Mary	*Blessed Virgin Mary* Lauds Antiphons Pg. 393
Capitulum (Jdt 13:22-23) **V.** Benedíxit te Dóminus in virtúte sua, quia per te ad níhilum redégit inimícos nostros. Benedícta es tu, fília, a Dómino Deo excélso, præ ómnibus muliéribus super terram. **R.** Deo grátias.	**Chapter** (Jdt 13:22-23) **V.** The Lord hath blessed thee by His power, because by thee He hath brought our enemies to nought. And Ozias the prince of the people of Israel, said to her: Blessed art thou, O daughter, by the Lord the most high God, above all women upon the earth. **R.** Thanks be to God.
Ant. Quæ est ista quæ ascéndit sicut auróra consúrgens, pulchra ut luna, elécta ut sol, terríbilis ut castrórum ácies ordináta?	**Ant.** What is this that riseth like the rising dawn, beautiful as the moon, chosen as the sun, terrible as an army set in array?
Orátio Omnípotens sempitérne Deus, qui Immaculátam Vírginem Maríam, Fílii tui Genetrícem, córpore et ánima ad cæléstem glóriam assumpsísti: concéde, quǽsumus; ut ad supérna semper inténti, ipsíus glóriæ mereámur esse consórtes. Per eundem Dóminum nostrum ...	**Prayer** Almighty and eternal God, who took the Immaculate Virgin Mary, Mother of Thy Son, body and soul to heavenly glory: grant, we beseech Thee; that we who are ever intent on things above, may deserve to be her companions in glory. Through our Lord …
Aug. 16 St. Joachim, Father of the Blessed Virgin Mary	*Confessor*

Proper of the Saints Lauds

Ant. Laudémus virum gloriósum in generatióne sua, quia benedictiónem ómnium géntium dedit illi Dóminus, et testaméntum suum confirmávit super caput eius.	**Ant.** Let us praise the glorious man in his generation, because the Lord gave him the blessing of all nations and confirmed his covenant upon his head.
Orátio Deus, qui præ ómnibus Sanctis tuis beátum Ióachim Genetrícis Fílii tui patrem esse voluísti: concéde, quǽsumus; ut, cuius festa venerámur, eius quoque perpétuo patrocínia sentiámus. Per Dóminum nostrum ...	*Prayer* O God, who, above all Thy Saints, willed the blessed Joachim to be the father of the mother of Thy Son: grant, we beseech Thee, that we who venerate his feast day may also receive his perpetual patronage. Through our Lord ...
Aug. 17 St. Hyacinth	*Confessor*
Orátio Lætétur Ecclésia tua, Deus, beáti Agapíti Mártyris tui confísa suffrágiis: atque, eius précibus gloriósis, et devóta permáneat et secúra consístat. Per Dóminum nostrum ...	*Prayer* O God, who makes us joyful with the annual solemnity of Thy blessed Confessor Hyacinth: grant mercifully, that we may also imitate the actions of whose feast day we celebrate. Through our Lord ...
Aug. 18 Commemoration of St. Agapitus	*Martyr*
Orátio Lætetur Ecclesia tua, Deus, beáti Agapiti Mártyris tui confisa suffragiis: atque ejus precibus gloriosis, et devota permaneat, et secura consistat. Per Dóminum nostrum ...	*Prayer* May Thy Church rejoice, O God, entrusted with the suffering of Thy blessed Martyr Agapite: through his glorious prayers may we continue to be devoted and secure. Through our Lord ...
Aug. 19 St. John Eudes	*Confessor*
Orátio Deus, qui beátum Ioánnem, Confessórem tuum, ad cultum sacrórum Córdium Iesu et Maríæ rite promovéndum, mirabíliter inflammásti, et per eum novas in Ecclésia tua famílias congregáre voluísti: præsta, quǽsumus; ut, cuius pia mérita venerámur, virtútum quoque instruámur exémplis. Per eundem Dóminum nostrum ...	*Prayer* O God, who wonderfully inflamed Thy blessed John the Confessor to properly promote the devotion to the Sacred Hearts of Jesus and Mary, and through him Thou choseth to gather a new community in Thy Church: grant, we beg Thee; so by whose pious deeds we venerate, we may also be taught by the example of his virtues. Through our Lord ...
Aug. 20 St. Bernard	*Abbot and Doctor*
Orátio Deus, qui pópulo tuo ætérnæ salútis beátum Bernárdum minístrum tribuísti: præsta, quǽsumus; ut quem Doctórem vitæ habúimus in terris, intercessórem habére mereámur in cælis.	*Prayer* O God, who gave to Thy people the blessed Bernard, the minister of eternal salvation: we implore Thee; that through the teacher of eternal life that we had on earth, may we deserve to have

Proper of the Saints Lauds

Per Dóminum nostrum ...	him as an intercessor in heaven. Through our Lord .
Aug. 21 St. Jane Frances de Chantal	*Widow*
Orátio Omnípotens et miséricors Deus, qui beátam Ioánnam Francíscam, tuo amóre succénsam, admirábili spíritus fortitúdine per omnes vitæ sémitas in via perfectiónis donásti, quique per illam illustráre Ecclésiam tuam nova prole voluísti: eius méritis et précibus concéde; ut, qui infirmitátis nostræ cónscii de tua virtúte confídimus, cæléstis grátiæ auxílio cuncta nobis adversántia vincámus. Per Dóminum nostrum ...	**Prayer** Omnipotent and merciful God, who gavest the blessed Jane Frances, inflamed with Thy love, admirable strength of spirit along all the paths of life on the way of perfection, and by her longing to enlighten Thy Church, raised up a new spiritual order: grant by her merits and prayers; that we who, aware of our weakness and trust in Thy power, may conquer all that opposes us with the help of Thy heavenly grace. Through our Lord..
Aug. 22 Feast of the Immaculate Heart of the Blessed Virgin Mary	*Blessed Virgin Mary*
Ant. Ant. O beáta Virgo María: tu grátiæ Mater, tu spes mundi, exáudi nos fílios tuos clamántes ad te.	**Ant.** O blessed Virgin Mary: thou Mother of grace, thou hope of the world, hear us thy children crying unto thee.
Orátio Omnípotens sempitérne Deus, qui in Corde beátæ Maríæ Vírginis dignum Spíritus Sancti habitáculum præparásti: concéde propítius; ut eiúsdem immaculáti Cordis festivitátem devóta mente recoléntes, secúndum Cor tuum vívere valeámus. Per Dóminum nostrum ...	**Prayer** Almighty and everlasting God, who hast prepared in the Heart of the Blessed Virgin Mary a dwelling place worthy of the Holy Spirit: grant more mercifully; that we may be able to live according to Thy Heart, recalling with a devout mind the festival of the same Immaculate Heart. Through our Lord ...
Aug. 23 St. Philip Benizi	*Confessor*
Orátio Deus, qui per beátum Philíppum Confessórem tuum, exímium nobis humilitátis exémplum tribuísti: da fámulis tuis próspera mundi ex eius imitatióne despícere, et cæléstia semper inquírere. Per Dóminum nostrum ...	**Prayer** O God, who through Thy blessed Confessor Philip, gave us an excellent example of humility: grant Thy servants to reject the prosperity of the world by his example, and always seek heavenly things. Through our Lord ...
Aug. 24 St. Bartholomew	*Apostle*

Proper of the Saints Lauds

Orátio Omnípotens sempitérne Deus, qui huius diéi venerándam sanctámque lætítiam in beáti Apóstoli tui Bartholomǽi festivitáte tribuísti: da Ecclésiæ tuæ, quǽsumus; et amáre quod crédidit, et prædicáre quod dócuit. Per Dóminum nostrum ...	*Prayer* Almighty and eternal God, who gave the venerable and holy joy of this day in honor of Thy blessed Apostle Bartholomew: grant, to Thy Church we ask Thee; to love what he believed, and to preach what he taught. Through our Lord ...
Aug. 25 St. Louis	*King and Confessor*
Orátio Deus, qui beátum Ludovícum Confessórem tuum de terréno regno ad cæléstis regni glóriam transtulísti: eius, quǽsumus, méritis et intercessióne; Regis regum Iesu Christi, Fílii tui, fácias nos esse consortes. Per Dóminum nostrum ...	*Prayer* O God, who hast raised Thy blessed Louis the Confessor from the earthly kingdom to the glory of the heavenly kingdom: we beseech Thee, by his merits and intercession, make us consorts of the King of Kings, Jesus Christ, Thy Son. Through our Lord ...
Aug. 26 Commemoration of St. Zephyrinus	*Pope and Martyr*
Orátio Gregem tuum, Pastor ætérne, placátus inténde: et per beátum Zephyrínum Mártyrem tuum atque Summum Pontíficem perpétua protectióne custódi; quem totíus Ecclésiæ præstitísti esse pastórem. Per Dóminum nostrum ...	*Prayer* Look mercifully upon Thy flock, O Eternal Shepherd: and, may Thy blessed Zephyrinus, Martyr and Supreme Pontiff, whom Thou hast appointed to be the shepherd of the entire Church, defend us with perpetual protection. Through our Lord ...
Aug. 27 St. Joseph Calasanz	*Confessor*
Orátio Deus, qui per sanctum Ioséphum Confessórem tuum, ad erudiéndam spíritu intellegéntiæ ac pietátis iuventútem, novum Ecclésiæ tuæ subsídium providére dignátus es: præsta, quǽsumus; nos, eius exémplo et intercessióne, ita fácere et docére, ut prǽmia consequámur ætérna. Per Dóminum nostrum ...	O God, who through Thy holy Confessor Joseph, to educate the youth in the spirit of intelligence and holiness hast deigned to provide a fresh help for Thy Church: grant, we beseech Thee, by his example and intercession, that we may obtain eternal salvation. Through our Lord ...
Aug. 28 St. Augustine	*Confessor*
Orátio Adésto supplicatiónibus nostris, omnípotens Deus: et, quibus fidúciam sperándæ pietátis indúlges, intercedénte beáto Augustíno Confessóre tuo atque Pontífice, consuétæ misericórdiæ tríbue benígnus efféctum. Per Dóminum nostrum ...	*Prayer* Attend to our supplications, almighty God: and grant to those who indulge in the hope of Thy mercy, through the intercession of Thy blessed Augustine, Confessor and Bishop, the effect of Thy gracious compassion by his intercession. Through our Lord ...

Aug. 29 Beheading of St. John the Baptist	*Martyr*
Capitulum (Jas 1:12) V. Beátus vir, qui suffert tentatiónem: quóniam cum probátus fúerit, accípiet corónam vitæ, quam repromísit Deus diligéntibus se. R. Deo grátias.	**Chapter** (Jas 1:12) V. Blessed is the man that endureth temptation; for when he hath been proved, he shall receive the crown of life, which God hath promised to them that love him. R. Thanks be to God.
Orátio Sancti Ioánnis Baptístæ Præcursóris et Martýris tui, quǽsumus, Dómine, veneránda festívitas: salutáris auxílii nobis præstet efféctum. Qui vivis et regnas ...	**Prayer** We beseech Thee, O Lord, on the venerable feast of Saint John the Baptist, the Forerunner and Martyr, to grant us the effect of Thy saving help. Who liveth and reigneth...
Aug. 30 St. Rose of Lima	*Virgin*
Orátio Bonórum ómnium largítor, omnípotens Deus, qui beátam Rosam, cæléstis grátiæ rore prævéntam, virginitátis et patiéntiæ decóre Indis floréscere voluísti: da nobis fámulis tuis; ut, in odórem suavitátis eius curréntes, Christi bonus odor éffici mereámur: Qui tecum vivit et regnat ...	**Prayer** Bestower of all good things, almighty God, Who blessed St. Rose with the dew of heavenly grace and the beauty of virginity and patience, and caused her to blossom among the Indians: give us, Thy servants; who running in the fragrance of her sweetness, we too may deserve to become the good fragrance of Christ. Who liveth and reigneth...
Aug. 31 St. Raymund Nonnatus	*Confessor*
Orátio Deus, qui in liberándis fidélibus tuis ab impiórum captivitáte beátum Raymúndum Confessórem tuum mirábilem effecísti: eius nobis intercessióne concéde; ut, a peccatórum vínculis absolúti, quæ tibi sunt plácita, líberis méntibus exsequámur. Per Dóminum nostrum...	**Prayer** O God, who, in delivering Thy faithful from the captivity of the infidels made blessed Raymond Thy wonderful Confessor: grant us his intercession; that, freed from the bonds of sins, we may perform what is pleasing to Thee with free minds. Through our Lord ...
Sep. 1 Commemoration of St. Giles	*Abbot*
Orátio Intercéssio nos, quǽsumus, Dómine, beáti Ægídii Abbátis comméndet: ut, quod nostris méritis non valémus, eius patrocínio assequámur. Per Dóminum nostrum ...	**Prayer** We beseech thee, O Lord, to commend us to the blessed Abbot Giles: so that what we are not able by our own merits to do, we may obtain by his patronage. Through our Lord ...

Proper of the Saints Lauds

Sep. 2 St. Stephen	*King of Hungary, Confessor*
Orátio Concéde, quǽsumus, Ecclésiæ tuæ, omnípotens Deus: ut beátum Stéphanum Confessórem tuum, quem regnántem in terris propagatórem hábuit, propugnatórem habére mereátur gloriósum in cælis. Per Dóminum nostrum ...	*Prayer* Grant, we beseech Thee, almighty God, that Blessed Stephen Thy Confessor, whom Thou hadst as a proponent for Thy Church while reigning on earth, may be our glorious champion in heaven. Through our Lord ...
Sep. 3 St. Pius X	*Pope and Confessor*
Orátio Deus, qui ad tuéndam cathólicam fidem, et univérsa in Christo instauránda sanctum Pium, Summum Pontíficem, cælésti sapiéntia et apostólica fortitúdine replevísti: concéde propítius; ut, eius institúta et exémpla sectántes, prǽmia consequámur ætérna. Per eundem Dóminum nostrum ...	*Prayer* O God, who for the protection of the Catholic faith and for the restoration of all things in Christ, filled Saint Pius, the Supreme Pontiff, with heavenly wisdom and apostolic fortitude: grant Thy mercy; that, by following his instruction and example, we may obtain eternal rewards. Through our Lord ...
Sep. 5 St. Lawrence Justinian	*Bishop and Confessor*
Orátio Da, quǽsumus, omnípotens Deus: ut beáti Lauréntii Confessóris tui atque Pontíficis veneránda solémnitas, et devotiónem nobis áugeat et salútem. Per Dóminum nostrum ...	*Prayer* Grant, we beseech Thee almighty God, that the venerable feast day of the Blessed Lawrence, Thy confessor and Bishop, may increase our devotion and promote our salvation. Through our Lord...
Sep. 8 The Nativity of the Blessed Virgin Mary	*Blessed Virgin Mary*
Capitulum (Sir 24:14) V. Ab inítio et ante sǽcula creáta sum, et usque ad futúrum sǽculum non désinam, et in habitatióne sancta coram ipso ministrávi. R. Deo grátias.	*Chapter* (Sir 24:14) V. I was created from the beginning and before the ages, and I will not cease until the age to come, and I ministered before him in the holy dwellings. R. Thanks be to God.
Ant. Nativitátem hodiérnam perpétuæ Vírginis Genetrícis Dei Maríæ solémniter celebrémus, qua celsitúdo throni procéssit, allelúja.	Ant. Today let us solemnly celebrate the Nativity of Mary, the perpetual Virgin Mother of God, by whom the Most High came to the throne.
Orátio Fámulis tuis, quǽsumus, Dómine, cæléstis grátiæ munus impertíre: ut, quibus beátæ Vírginis partus éxstitit salútis exórdium; Nativitátis eius votíva solémnitas pacis tríbuat creméntum.	*Prayer* To Thy servants, we beseech thee, Lord, impart the gift of heavenly grace: that to whom the birth of the blessed Virgin was the beginning of salvation, the prayerful solemnity of her Nativity

Per Dóminum nostrum ...	may give an increase of peace. Through our Lord ...
Sep. 9 Commemoration of St. Gorgonius	*Martyr*
Orátio Sanctus tuus, Dómine, Gorgónius sua nos intercessióne lætíficet: et pia fáciat solemnitáte gaudére. Per Dóminum nostrum ...	*Prayer* O Lord, may Thy saint, Gorgonius, make us joyful by his intercession: and make us rejoice with pious solemnity. Through our Lord ...
Sep. 10 St. Nicholas of Tolentino	*Confessor*
Orátio Adésto, Dómine, supplicatiónibus nostris, quas in beáti Nicolái Confessóris tui solemnitáte deférimus: ut, qui nostræ iustítiæ fidúciam non habémus, eius qui tibi plácuit, précibus adiuvémur. Per Dóminum nostrum ...	*Prayer* Attend, O Lord, to our supplications, which we offer on the solemnity of the blessed Confessor Nicholas: that we who have no confidence in our own justice may be helped by the prayers of him who pleased Thee. Through our Lord ...
Sept. 11 Commemoration of Sts. Protus and Hyacinth	*Martyrs*
Orátio Beatórum Mártyrum tuórum Proti et Hyacínthi nos, Dómine, fóveat pretiósa conféssio: et pia iúgiter intercéssio tueátur. Per Dóminum nostrum ...	*Prayer* May the precious confession of Thy blessed Martyrs, Protus and Hyacinth, encourage us, O Lord: and may their pious intercession continually protect us. Through our Lord...
Sep. 12 Feast of the Holy Name of Mary	*Blessed Virgin Mary*
Orátio Concéde, quǽsumus, omnípotens Deus: ut fidéles tui, qui sub sanctíssimæ Vírginis Maríæ Nómine et protectióne lætántur; eius pia intercessióne, a cunctis malis liberéntur in terris, et ad gáudia ætérna perveníre mereántur in cælis. Per Dóminum nostrum ...	*Prayer* Grant, we beseech Thee almighty God: that Thy faithful, who may rejoice under the name and protection of the most holy Virgin Mary; by her holy intercession we may be freed from all evils on earth, and may deserve to reach eternal joys in heaven. Through our Lord ...
Sep. 14 The Exaltation of the Holy Cross	
Capitulum (Phil 2:5-7) V. Fratres: Hoc enim sentíte in vobis, quod et in Christo Iesu: qui, cum in forma Dei esset, non rapínam arbitrátus est esse se æquálem Deo: sed semetípsum exinanívit, formam servi accípiens, in similitúdinem	*Chapter* (Phil 2:5-7) V. Brethren: For let this mind be in you, which was also in Christ Jesus: Who being in the form of God, thought it not robbery to be equal with God: But emptied Himself, taking the form of a servant, being made in the likeness

hóminum factus, et hábitu invéntus ut homo. R. Deo grátias.	of men, and in habit found as a man. R. Thanks be to God.
Ant. Super ómnia ligna cedrórum tu sola excélsior, in qua Vita mundi pepéndit, in qua Christus triumphávit, et mors mortem superávit in ætérnum.	**Ant.** Thou alone art higher than all the cedar trees in which the life of the world hangs, in which Christ triumphed, and death overcame death forever.
Orátio Deus, qui nos hodiérna die Exaltatiónis sanctæ Crucis ánnua solemnitáte lætíficas: præsta, quǽsumus; ut, cuius mystérium in terra cognóvimus, eius redemptiónis præmia in cælo mereámur. Per eundem Dóminum nostrum ...	*Prayer* O God, who gives us joy today with the annual solemnity of the Exaltation of the Holy Cross: grant, we beseech Thee; that because Thou hast revealed its mystery on earth, we may deserve the rewards of redemption in heaven. Through our Lord ...
Sep. 15 The Seven Dolors of the Blessed Virgin Mary	*Blessed Virgin Mary*
Capitulum (Lam 2:13) **V.** Cui comparábo te? vel cui assimilábo te, filia Ierúsalem? cui exæquábo te, et consolábor te, virgo fília Sion? Magna est velut mare contrítio tua. **R.** Deo Grátias	*Chapter* (Lam 2:13) **V.** To what shall I compare thee? Or to what shall I liken thee, O daughter of Jerusalem? To what shall I equal thee, that I may comfort thee, O virgin daughter of Zion? For great as the sea is thy destruction: who shall heal thee? **R.** Thanks be to God.
Ant. Veníte, ascendámus ad montem Dómini, et vidéte, si est dolor, sicut dolor meus.	**Ant.** Come, let us go up to the mountain of the Lord, and see if there is sorrow, like my sorrow.
Orátio Deus, in cuius passióne, secúndum Simeónis prophetíam, dulcíssimam ánimam gloriósæ Vírginis et Matris Maríæ dolóris gládius pertransívit: concéde propítius; ut, qui dolóres eius venerándo recólimus, passiónis tuæ efféctum felícem consequámur. Qui vivis et regnas ...	*Prayer* O God, in whose Passion, according to the prophecy of Simeon, the sweetest soul of the glorious Virgin and Mother Mary was pierced by the sword of sorrow: grant, more mercifuly and more abundantly; that we who reverently remember her sorrows, may obtain the happiness earned by Thy Passion. Thou who liveth and reigneth ...
Sep. 16 Sts. Cornelius and Cyprian	*Pope and Bishop, Martyrs*
Orátio Beatórum Mártyrum paritérque Pontíficum Cornélii et Cypriáni nos, quǽsumus, Dómine, festa tueántur: et eórum comméndet orátio veneránda.	*Prayer* Through the feast of the blessed martyrs, Pontiffs Cornelius and Cyprian, we beseech Thee, O Lord, grant us protection and may

Per Dóminum nostrum ...	their venerable prayers commend us to Thee. Through our Lord ...
Sep. 17 The Impression of the Stigmata on The Body of St. Francis	*Confessor*
Orátio Dómine Iesu Christe, qui, frigescénte mundo, ad inflammándum corda nostra tui amóris igne, in carne beatíssimi Francísci passiónis tuæ sacra Stígmata renovásti: concéde propítius; ut eius méritis et précibus crucem iúgiter ferámus, et dignos fructus pæniténtiæ faciámus. Qui vivis et regnas ...	*Prayer* Lord Jesus Christ, who, in a world growing cold, in order to inflame our hearts with the fire of Thy love, renewed in the flesh of the most blessed Francis, the sacred stigmata of Thy Passion: grant more mercifully; that by his merits and prayers we may continually carry the cross and produce worthy fruits of repentance. Who liveth and reigneth...
Sep. 18 St. Joseph of Cupertino	*Confessor*
Orátio Deus, qui ad unigénitum Fílium tuum exaltátum a terra ómnia tráhere disposuísti: pérfice propítius; ut, méritis et exémplo seráphici Confessóris tui Ioséphi, supra terrénas omnes cupiditátes eleváti, ad eum perveníre mereámur. Qui vivis et regnas ...	*Prayer* O God, who hast ordained to draw all things to Thine exalted Son: do it more abundantly, that by the merits and example of Thy seraphic Confessor Joseph, and by being raised above all earthly desires, we may deserve to reach him. Who liveth and reigneth...
Sep. 19 St. Januarius and his Companions	*Martyrs*
Orátio Deus, qui nos ánnua sanctórum Mártyrum tuórum Ianuárii et Sociórum eius solemnitáte lætíficas: concéde propítius; ut quorum gaudémus méritis, accendámur exémplis. Per Dóminum nostrum ...	*Prayer* O God, who makes us happy with the annual solemnity of Thy holy Martyrs, Januarius and his companions: grant more mercifully; that we may be enkindled by the examples of those in whose merits we rejoice. Through our Lord ...
Sep. 21 St. Matthew	*Apostle and Evangelist*
Orátio Beáti Apóstoli et Evangelístæ Matthǽi, Dómine, précibus adiuvémur: ut, quod possibílitas nostra non óbtinet, eius nobis intercessióne donétur. Per Dóminum nostrum ...	*Prayer* Let us be helped, O Lord, by the prayers of the blessed Apostle and Evangelist Matthew: that what our efforts do not obtain, may be granted to us through his intercession. Through our Lord ...

Proper of the Saints Lauds

Sep. 22 St. Thomas of Villanova	*Bishop and Confessor*
Ant. Eleemósynas illius enarrábit omnis ecclésia sanctórum.	**Ant.** All the church of the saints will tell of his alms.
Orátio Deus, qui beátum Thomam Pontíficem insígnis in páuperes misericórdiæ virtúte decorásti: quǽsumus; ut, eius intercessióne, in omnes, qui te deprecántur, divítias misericórdiæ tuæ benígnus effúndas. Per Dóminum nostrum…	***Prayer*** O God, who endowed the blessed Thomas the Pontiff with the power of mercy for the poor: we beseech Thee; that by his intercession Thou may graciously pour out the riches of Thy mercy on all who implore Thee. Through our Lord …
Sep. 23 St. Linus	*Pope and Martyr*
Orátio Gregem tuum, Pastor ætérne, placátus inténde: et per beátum Linum Mártyrem tuum atque Summum Pontíficem perpétua protectióne custódi; quem totíus Ecclésiæ præstitísti esse pastórem. Per Dóminum nostrum …	***Prayer*** Look favorably upon Thy flock, O eternal Shepherd and keep it with perpetual protection through Thy guardian blessed Linus, Thy Martyr and Supreme Pontiff, whom Thou hast appointed to be the shepherd of the whole Church. Through our Lord …
Sep. 24 Our Lady of Ransom	*Blessed Virgin Mary*
Orátio Deus, qui per gloriosíssimam Fílii tui Matrem, ad liberándos Christi fidéles a potestáte paganórum nova Ecclésiam tuam prole amplificáre dignátus es: præsta, quǽsumus; ut, quam pie venerámur tanti operis institutrícem, eius páriter méritis et intercessióne, a peccátis ómnibus et captivitáte dǽmonis liberémur. Per Dóminum nostrum …	***Prayer*** O God, who, through the most glorious Mother of Thy Son, hath deigned to enrich Thy Church with a new spiritual family in order to ransom faithful Christians from the power of the infidels: we are honored to piously venerate the foundress of so great a work and may by her merits and intercession also be freed from all sins and from the captivity of the devil. Through our Lord …
Sep. 26 Commemoration of Sts. Cyprian and Justina	*Virgin, Martyrs*
Orátio Beatórum Mártyrum Cypriáni et Iustínæ nos, Dómine, fóveant continuáta præsídia: quia non désinis propítius intuéri, quos tálibus auxíliis concésseris adiuvári. Per Dóminum nostrum …	***Prayer*** O Lord, may the blessed Martyrs Cyprian and Justina comfort us with perpetual shelter: for Thou dost not cease to look more mercifully on those whom Thou dost grant to be helped by such aids. Through our Lord …

Proper of the Saints Lauds

Sep. 27 Sts. Cosmas and Damian	*Martyrs*
Orátio Præsta, quǽsumus, omnípotens Deus: ut, qui sanctórum Mártyrum tuórum Cosmæ et Damiáni natalícia cólimus, a cunctis malis imminéntibus, eórum intercessiónibus, liberémur. Per Dóminum nostrum ...	**Prayer** Grant, we beseech Thee, Almighty God, that those who celebrate the feast day of Thy holy Martyrs Cosmas and Damian, may be freed by their intercession from all impending evils. Through our Lord ...
Sep. 28 St. Wenceslaus	*Duke and Martyr*
Orátio Deus, qui beátum Wencesláum per martýrii palmam a terréno principátu ad cæléstem glóriam transtulísti: eius précibus nos ab omni adversitáte custódi; et eiúsdem tríbue gaudére consórtio. Per Dóminum nostrum ...	**Prayer** O God, who through the palm of martyrdom transferred the blessed Wenceslaus from earthly dominion to heavenly glory: by his prayers keep us from all adversity, and grant us to rejoice in his company. Through our Lord ...
Sep. 29 The Dedication of St. Michæl, Archangel	*Archangel*
Capitulum (Apoc 1:1-2) **V.** Significávit Deus, quæ opórtet fieri cito, loquens per Angelum suum servo suo Ioánni, qui testimónium perhíbuit verbo Dei, et testimónium Iesu Christi, quæcúmque vidit. **R.** Deo grátias.	**Chapter** (Apoc 1:1-2) **V.** God signified what must be done quickly, speaking through his Angel to his servant John, who bore witness to the word of God and the testimony of Jesus Christ, whatever he saw. **R.** Thanks be to God.
Ant. Factum est siléntium in cælo, dum draco commítteret bellum; et Míchaël pugnávit cum eo, et fecit victóriam, allelúja.	**Ant.** There was silence in heaven, while he was about to make war with the dragon: and Michael fought with him, and was victorious. Alleluia.
Orátio Deus, qui, miro órdine, Angelórum ministéria hominúmque dispénsas: concéde propítius; ut, a quibus tibi ministrántibus in cælo semper assístitur, ab his in terra vita nostra muniátur. Per Dóminum nostrum ...	**Prayer** O God, who established the ministries of men and angels in a wonderful order: grant more mercifully; that he who ministers to Thee in heaven is always assisting our life on earth and protecting us. Through our Lord …
Sept. 30 St. Jerome	*Priest, Confessor and Doctor*
Orátio Deus, qui Ecclésiæ tuæ in exponéndis sacris Scriptúris beátum Hierónymum, Confessórem tuum, Doctórem máximum providére dignátus es: præsta, quǽsumus; ut, eius suffragántibus méritis, quod ore	**Prayer** O God, who hast deigned to provide Thy Church with Blessed Jerome the Confessor, Thy greatest teacher in illuminating the sacred Scriptures: grant, we beg Thee; that by his supporting merits, we may be able to practice what he

Proper of the Saints Lauds

simul et ópere dócuit, te adiuvánte, exercére valeámus. Per Dóminum nostrum ...	taught both by word and by work. Through our Lord ...
Oct. 1 Commemoration of St. Remigius	*Bishop and Confessor*
Orátio Da, quǽsumus, omnípotens Deus: ut beáti Remígii Confessóris tui atque Pontíficis veneránda solémnitas, et devotiónem nobis áugeat et salútem. Per Dóminum nostrum ...	*Prayer* Grant, we beseech Thee, almighty God, that on the venerable solemnity and devotion of Blessed Remigius, Thy Confessor and Bishop, that he may intercede for us and give us peace. Through our Lord...
Oct. 2 The Holy Guardian Angels	
Capitulum (Exod 23:20-21) V. Ecce ego mittam Angelum meum, qui præcédat te, et custódiat in via, et introdúcat in locum, quem parávi. Obsérva eum et audi vocem eius. R. Deo Grátias.	*Chapter* (Exod 23:20-21) V. Behold I will send my angel, who shall go before thee, and keep thee in thy journey, and bring thee into the place that I have prepared. Take notice of him, and hear his voice. R. Thanks be to God.
Ant. Revérsus est Angelus qui loquebátur in me, et suscitávit me; quasi virum qui suscitátur a somno suo.	Ant. The angel who spoke to me returned and raised me up; like a man who is awakened from his sleep.
Orátio Deus, qui ineffábili providéntia sanctos Angelos tuos ad nostram custódiam míttere dignáris: largíre supplícibus tuis; et eórum semper protectióne deféndi, et ætérna societáte gaudére. Per Dóminum nostrum ...	*Prayer* O God, who in Thine ineffable providence hast deigned to send Thy holy angels to watch over us: bestow upon Thy supplicants safety through their perpetual protection and to enjoy their company in eternity. Through our Lord ...
Oct. 3 St. Therese of the Child Jesus	*Virgin*
Orátio Dómine, qui dixísti: Nisi efficiamini sicut parvuli, non intrabitis in regnum cælórum: da nobis, quǽsumus; ita sanctæ Teresiæ Vírginis in humilitate et simplicitate cordis vestigia sectari, ut præmia consequamur ætérna: Qui vivis et regnat. ...	*Prayer* O Lord, who said: Unless ye become like little children, ye will not enter the kingdom of heaven: grant us, we beseech Thee; that we may follow the footsteps of Saint Therese the Virgin in humility and simplicity of heart, so that we may obtain eternal reward. Who liveth and reigneth ...
Oct 4 St. Francis of Assisi	*Confessor*
Orátio Deus, qui Ecclésiam tuam beáti Francísci méritis fœtu novæ prolis amplíficas: tríbue nobis; ex	*Prayer* O God, Who by the merits of the Blessed Francis, built up Thy Church with new spiritual

Proper of the Saints Lauds

eius imitatióne, terréna despícere, et cæléstium donórum semper participatióne gaudére. Per Dóminum nostrum ...	offspring: grant us, by imitating him, to despise the earthly and to always rejoice in sharing Thy heavenly gifts. Through our Lord ...
Oct. 5 Commemoration Sts. Placid and Companions	*Martyrs*
Orátio Deus, qui nos concédis sanctórum Mártyrum tuórum Plácidi et Sociórum eius natalícia cólere, da nobis in ætérna beatitúdine de eórum societáte gaudére. Per Dóminum nostrum ...	**Prayer** O God, who allows us to honor the feast day of Thy holy Martyrs Placid and his Companions: grant us to rejoice in their company in eternal bliss. Through our Lord...
Oct. 6 St. Bruno	*Confessor*
Orátio Sancti Brunónis Confessóris tui, quǽsumus, Dómine, intercessiónibus adiuvémur: ut, qui maiestátem tuam gráviter delinquéndo offéndimus, eius méritis et précibus, nostrórum delictórum véniam consequámur. Per Dóminum nostrum ...	**Prayer** We beseech Thee, Lord, to help us through the intercession of St. Bruno Thy Confessor: that we who have offended Thy majesty by grievously sinning, may obtain pardon of our offenses by his merits and praises Through our Lord ...
Oct. 7 The Most Holy Rosary of the Blessed Virgin Mary	*Blessed Virgin Mary* Lauds Antiphons Pg. 394
Capitulum (Sir 24:25; 39:17) V. In me grátia omnis viæ et veritátis, in me omnis spes vitæ et virtútis. Ego, quasi rosa plantáta super rivos aquárum, fructificávi. R. Deo grátias.	**Chapter** (Sir 24:25; 39:17) V. In me is the grace of all the way and of truth, in me is all the hope of life and virtue: I, like a rose planted above streams of water, have borne fruit. R. Thanks be to God.
Ant. Solemnitátem hodiérnam sacratíssimi Rosárii Genetrícis Dei Maríæ devóte celebrémus, ut ipsa pro nobis intercédat ad Dóminum Iesum Christum.	**Ant.** Let us devoutly celebrate today's solemnity of the most holy Rosary of Mary, the Mother of God, so that she may intercede for us with the Lord Jesus Christ.
Orátio Deus, cuius Unigénitus per vitam, mortem et resurrectiónem suam nobis salútis ætérnæ præmia comparávit: concéde, quǽsumus; ut hæc mystéria sacratíssimo beátæ Maríæ Vírginis Rosário recoléntes, et imitémur quod cóntinent, et quod promíttunt, assequámur Per Dóminum nostrum ...	**Prayer** O God, whose Only Begotten through His life, death and resurrection procured for us the rewards of eternal salvation: grant, we ask, that by reciting these mysteries of the Rosary of the most holy Blessed Virgin Mary, and by imitating what they contain, we may obtain what they promise. Through our Lord...
Oct. 8 St. Bridget	*Widow*
Orátio Sanctórum Mártyrum tuórum nos, Dómine, Sérgii, Bacchi,	**Prayer** O Lord our God, who through Thy only-begotten Son

Marcélli et Apuléii beáta mérita prosequántur: et tuo semper fáciant amóre fervéntes. Per Dóminum nostrum ...	revealed the heavenly secrets to the blessed Bridget: grant us Thy servants, through her pious intercession, to rejoice in the revelation of Thy eternal glory. Through our Lord ...
Oct. 9 St. John Leonard	*Confessor*
Orátio Deus, qui beátum Ioánnem Confessórem tuum ad fidem in géntibus propagándam mirabíliter excitáre dignátus es, ac per eum in erudiéndis fidélibus novam in Ecclésia tua famíliam congregásti: da nobis fámulis tuis; ita eius institútis profícere, ut prǽmia consequámur ætérna. Per Dóminum nostrum ...	*Prayer* O God, who deigned in a wonderful way to raise up Blessed John Thy Confessor for the propagation of faith among the nations, and through him Thou founded a new religious order in Thy Church for the education of the faithful: grant us Thy servants, to prosper in his works that we may obtain eternal rewards. Through our Lord...
Oct. 10 St. Francis Borgia	*Confessor*
Orátio Dómine Iesu Christe, veræ humilitátis et exémplar et prǽmium: quǽsumus; ut, sicut beátum Francíscum in terréni honóris contémptu imitatórem tui gloriósum effecísti, ita nos eiúsdem imitatiónis et glóriæ tríbuas esse consórtes. Qui vivis et regnas ...	*Prayer* O Lord Jesus Christ, model and reward of true humility: we ask; that, as Thou made blessed Francis a glorious imitator of Thee in the contempt of earthly honor, so grant us to be partners in the same imitation and glory. Who liveth and reigneth ...
Oct. 11 Motherhood of the Blessed Virgin Mary	*Blessed Virgin Mary*
Capitulum (Sir 24:12-13) V. Qui creávit me, requiévit in tabernáculo meo, et dixit mihi: in Iacob inhábita, et in eléctis meis mitte radíces. R. Deo grátias.	*Chapter* (Sir 24:12-13) V. He who created me, rested in my tabernacle, and said to me: dwell in Jacob, and put down roots in my chosen ones. R. Thanks be to God.
Ant. Sancta María, succúrre míseris, iuva pusillánimes, réfove flébiles, ora pro pópulo, intérveni pro clero, intercéde pro devóto femíneo sexu: séntiant omnes tuum iuvámen, quicúmque célebrant tuam admirábilem Maternitátem.	*Ant.* Holy Mary, help the poor, help the small-minded, comfort the mourners, pray for the people, intervene for the clergy, intercede for the devoted women: may all experience thy help, whoever celebrates thy wonderful Motherhood.
Orátio Deus, qui de beátæ Maríæ Vírginis útero Verbum tuum, Angelo nuntiánte, carnem suscípere voluísti: præsta supplícibus tuis: ut qui vere eam Genetrícem Dei crédimus, eius	*Prayer* O God, who through the womb of the Blessed Virgin Mary, announcing Thy Word by the Angel, Thou wanted to take on flesh: grant that Thy suppliants;

apud te intercessiónibus adiuvémur. Per Dóminum nostrum ...	who truly believe her to be the Mother of God, may be helped by her intercession. Through our Lord...
Oct. 13 St. Edward	*King and Confessor*
Orátio Deus, qui beátum regem Eduárdum Confessórem tuum æternitátis glória coronásti: fac nos, quǽsumus; ita eum venerári in terris, ut cum eo regnáre possímus in cælis. Per Dóminum nostrum ...	*Prayer* O God, who crowned Blessed King Edward, Thy Confessor, with the glory of eternal life: we implore Thee, that he may be honored on earth so we may reign with him in heaven. Through our Lord ...
Oct. 14 St. Callistus I	*Pope and Martyr*
Orátio Deus, qui nos cónspicis ex nostra infirmitáte defícere: ad amórem tuum nos misericórditer per Sanctórum tuórum exémpla restáura. Per Dóminum nostrum ...	*Prayer* O God, who seeth us fail from our weakness: through the examples of Thy saints, mercifully restore us to Thy love. Through our Lord ...
Oct. 15 St. Teresa	*Virgin*
Capitulum (2 Cor 10:17-18) V. Fratres: Qui gloriátur, in Dómino gloriétur. Non enim qui seípsum comméndat, ille probátus est; sed quem Deus comméndat. R. Deo grátias.	*Chapter* (2 Cor 10:17-18) V. Brethren: He who glorieth, let him glory in the Lord. For it is not he who commendeth himself that is approved: but whom God commendeth. R. Thanks be to God.
Ant. Símile est regnum cælórum hómini negotiatóri quærénti bonas margarítas: invénta una pretiósa, dedit ómnia sua, et comparávit eam.	Ant. The kingdom of heaven is like unto a merchant seeking good pearls: he found one of great price, and gave all he had, and bought it.
Orátio Exáudi nos, Deus, salutáris noster: ut, sicut de beátæ Terésiæ Vírginis tuæ festivitáte gaudémus; ita cæléstis eius doctrínæ pábulo nutriámur, et piæ devotiónis erudiámur afféctu. Per Dóminum nostrum ...	*Prayer* Hear us, O God, our Savior: that as we may celebrate the feast of Blessed Teresa, Virgin; we may be nourished with the food of Thy heavenly doctrine, and trained in the affection of pious devotion. Through our Lord ...
Oct. 16 St. Hedwig	*Widow*
Orátio Deus, qui beátam Hedwígem a sǽculi pompa ad húmilem tuæ crucis sequélam toto corde transíre docuísti: concéde; ut eius méritis et exémplo discámus peritúras mundi calcáre delícias, et in ampléxu tuæ crucis ómnia nobis adversántia superáre. Qui vivis et regnas ...	*Prayer* O God, who taught Blessed Hedwig to pass from the pomp of the world to the humble following of Thy cross with all her heart: grant; that by her merits and example we may learn to tread upon the perishable delights of the world, and in the embrace of Thy cross to overcome all that oppose us. Who liveth and reigneth ...

Oct. 17 St. Margaret Mary Alacoque — *Virgin*

Orátio Dómine Iesu Christe, qui investigábiles divítias Cordis tui beátæ Margarítæ Maríæ Vírgini mirabíliter revelásti; da nobis eius méritis et imitatióne; ut te in ómnibus et super ómnia diligéntes, iugem in eódem Corde tuo mansiónem habére mereámur. Qui vivis et regnas …

Prayer Lord Jesus Christ, who wonderfully revealed the unsearchable riches of Thy Heart to Thy blessed Virgin Margaret Mary: through her merits and imitation; may we care for Thee in all things and above all things, and may we deserve to have a dwelling place in Thy same heart. Who liveth and reigneth…

Oct. 18 St. Luke — *Evangelist, Apostle*

Orátio Intervéniat pro nobis, quǽsumus, Dómine, sanctus tuus Lucas Evangelísta: qui crucis mortificatiónem iúgiter in suo córpore, pro tui nóminis honóre, portávit. Per Dóminum nostrum …

Prayer We beseech thee, O Lord, that Thy holy Evangelist Luke may intercede for us, who on the cross continually bore the mortification in his body for the honor of Thy Name. Through our Lord...

Oct. 19 St. Peter of Alcantara — *Confessor*

Orátio Deus, qui beátum Petrum Confessórem tuum admirábilis pœniténtiæ et altíssimæ contemplatiónis múnere illustráre dignátus es: da nobis, quǽsumus; ut, eius suffragántibus méritis, carne mortificáti, facílius cæléstia capiámus. Per Dóminum nostrum …

Prayer O God, who hast deigned to enlighten Thy blessed Peter the Confessor with the gift of admirable penitence and profound contemplation: grant us, we beseech Thee; that by supporting his merits, mortified in the flesh, we may more easily grasp heavenly things. Through our Lord …

Oct. 20 St. John Cantius — *Confessor*

Ant. Euge, serve bone et fidélis, quia in pauca fuísti fidélis, supra multa te constítuam, intra in gáudium Dómini tui.

Ant. Hail, good and faithful servant, because Thou hast been faithful in a few things, I will set thee over many things, enter into the joy of thy Lord.

Orátio Da, quǽsumus, omnípotens Deus: ut, sancti Ioánnis Confessóris exémplo in sciéntia Sanctórum proficiéntes, atque áliis misericórdiam exhibéntes; eius méritis, indulgéntiam apud te consequámur. Per Dóminum nostrum …

Prayer Grant, we beseech Thee, almighty God, that, following the example of St. John the Confessor, learning from the science of the Saints, and by showing mercy to others, we may obtain pardon from Thee. Through our Lord …

Oct. 21 St. Hilarion — *Abbot*

Orátio Intercéssio nos, quǽsumus, Dómine, beáti Hilariónis Abbátis

Prayer Commend us, O Lord, to the intercession of Blessed Abbot

Proper of the Saints Lauds

comméndit: ut, quod nostris méritis non valémus, ejus patrocínio assequámur. Per Dóminum nostrum ...	Hilarion: that, as we what are not able to accomplish by our own merits, we may obtain by his patronage. Through our Lord ...
Oct. 21 Commemoration of St. Ursula and Companions	*Virgins and Martyrs*
Orátio Da nobis, quǽsumus, Dómine, Deus noster, sanctárum Vírginum et Mártyrum tuárum Ursulæ et Sociárum eius palmas incessábili devotióne venerári: ut, quas digna mente non póssumus celebráre, humílibus saltem frequentémus obséquiis. Per Dóminum nostrum ...	*Prayer* Grant us, we beseech Thee, Lord our God, that the palms of Thy holy Virgins and Martyrs, Ursula and her companions, may be venerated with unceasing devotion; that which we cannot celebrate with a worthy mind, let us at least attend with a humble tribute. Through our Lord ...
Oct. 24 St. Raphæl	*Archangel*
Capitulum (Tob 12:12) V. Quando orábas cum lácrimis, et sepeliébas mórtuos, et derelinquébas prándium tuum, et mórtuos abscondébas per diem in domo tua, et nocte sepeliébas eos, ego óbtuli oratiónem tuam Dómino. R. Deo grátias.	*Chapter* (Tob 12:12) V. When thou prayed with tears, and buried the dead, and left thy meal, and hid the dead all day long in thy house, and buried them at night, I offered thy prayer to the Lord. R. Thanks be to God.
Ant. Ego sum Ráphaël Angelus, qui asto ante Dóminum: vos autem benedícite Deum, et narráte ómnia mirabília eius, allelúja.	Ant. I am Raphael, the Angel, who stands before the Lord: but thou bless God, and tell of all His wonderful works, alleluia.
Orátio Deus, qui beátum Raphaélem Archángelum Tobíæ fámulo tuo cómitem dedísti in via: concéde nobis fámulis tuis; ut eiúsdem semper protegámur custódia et muniámur auxílio. Per Dóminum nostrum ...	*Prayer* O God, who gave Tobias the blessed Archangel Raphael as his companion on the road: grant us Thy servants; that we may always be protected by his guard and fortified with his help. Through our Lord ...
Oct. 25 Commemoration of Sts. Chrysanthus and Daria	*Martyrs*
Orátio Beatórum Mártyrum tuórum, Dómine, Chrysánthi et Daríæ, quǽsumus, adsit nobis orátio: ut, quos venerámur obséquio, eórum pium iúgiter experiámur auxílium. Per Dóminum nostrum ...	*Prayer* O Lord, we beseech Thee, that the prayers of Thy blessed Martyrs, Chrysanthus and Daria may comfort us: that we who venerate them with obedience, may constantly experience their pious help. Through our Lord ...

Proper of the Saints Lauds

Oct. 26 St. Evaristus	*Pope and Martyr*
Orátio Gregem tuum, Pastor ætérne, placátus inténde: et per beátum Evarístum Mártyrem tuum atque Summum Pontíficem perpétua protectióne custódi; quem totíus Ecclésiæ præstitísti esse pastórem. Per Dóminum nostrum …	*Prayer* Eternal Shepherd favorably look upon Thy flock: and, through Blessed Evaristus, Thy Martyr and Supreme Pontiff, whom Thou hast appointed to be the shepherd of the universal Church, safeguard it with the perpetual protection of Thy custody. Through our Lord …
Oct. 28 Sts. Simon and Jude	*Apostles*
Orátio Deus, qui nos per beátos Apóstolos tuos Simónem et Iudam ad agnitiónem tui nóminis veníre tribuísti: da nobis eórum glóriam sempitérnam et proficiéndo celebráre, et celebrándo profícere. Per Dóminum nostrum …	*Prayer* O God, through Thy blessed Apostles, Simon and Jude, who prepared us to come to the recognition of Thy Name: help us share their eternal glory and honor it by rejoicing in this glory, and by celebrating it for our prosperity. Through our Lord …
Nov. 4 St. Charles Borromeo	*Bishop and Confessor*
Orátio Ecclésiam tuam, Dómine, sancti Cároli Confessóris tui atque Pontíficis contínua protectióne custódi: ut, sicut illum pastorális sollicitúdo gloriósum réddidit; ita nos eius intercéssio in tuo semper fáciat amóre fervéntes. Per Dóminum nostrum …	*Prayer* Keep Thy church, O Lord, with the continuous protection of Thy holy Confessor and Bishop, Charles, so that, just as his pastoral care rendered him glorious; so may his intercession always make us fervent in Thy love. Through our Lord …
Nov. 8 Commemoration of the Four Crowned Martyrs	*Martyrs*
Orátio Præsta, quǽsumus, omnípotens Deus: ut, qui gloriósos Mártyres fortes in sua confessióne cognóvimus, pios apud te in nostra intercessióne sentiámus. Per Dóminum nostrum …	*Prayer* Grant, we beseech Thee, Almighty God: that we who have known these glorious Martyrs, strong in their confession, may enjoy their fervent intercession with Thee. Through our Lord …
Nov. 9 St. Theodore	*Martyr*
Orátio Deus, qui nos beáti Theodóri Mártyris tui confessióne gloriósa circúmdas et prótegis: præsta nobis ex eius imitatióne profícere, et oratióne fulcíri. Per Dóminum nostrum …	*Prayer* O God, who surrounds and protects us with the glorious confession of Thy blessed Martyr Theodore: grant that we may advance by his imitation and be supported by his prayer. Through our Lord …

Proper of the Saints Lauds

Nov. 10 St. Andrew Avellino	*Confessor*
Orátio Deus, qui in corde beáti Andréæ Confessóris tui, per árduum cotídie in virtútibus proficiéndi votum, admirábiles ad te ascensiónes disposuísti: concéde nobis, ipsíus méritis et intercessióne, ita eiúsdem grátiæ partícipes fíeri; ut, perfectióra semper exsequéntes, ad glóriæ tuæ fastígium felíciter perducámur. Per Dóminum nostrum ...	*Prayer* O God, who in the heart of Thy blessed Confessor Andrew, and through the arduous vow of daily commitment to virtues, ascended in a wonderful manner to Thee: grant us, through his merits and intercession, to become partakers of the same grace; always striving toward perfection that we may be brought to the pinnacle of Thy glory. Through our Lord ...
Nov. 11 St. Martin of Tours	*Bishop and Confessor*
Capítulum (Sir 44:16-17) V. Ecce sacérdos magnus, qui in diébus suis plácuit Deo, et invéntus est iustus: et in témpore iracúndiæ factus est reconciliátio. R. Deo grátias.	*Chapter* (Sir 44:16-17) V. Behold a great priest, who in his days pleased God, and was found righteous: and in the time of wrath he was reconciled. R. Thanks be to God.
Ant. O beátum virum cujus ánima paradisum possidet: unde exsultant Ángeli, lætantur Archangeli, chorus Sanctórum proclamat, turba Vírginum invitat, Mane nobíscum in ætérnum.	*Ant.* O blessed man whose soul possesses paradise! Whence the Angels exult, the Archangels rejoice, the choir of Saints proclaims, the multitude of Virgins invites, remain with us for ever.
Orátio Deus, qui cónspicis, quia ex nulla nostra virtúte subsístimus: concéde propítius; ut, intercessióne beáti Martíni Confessóris tui atque Pontíficis, contra ómnia advérsa muniámur. Per Dóminum nostrum ...	*Prayer* O God, who seest that we subsist by no strength of our own: grant greater mercy; so that, through the intercession of Thy blessed Martín the Confessor and Pontiff, we are fortified against all adversaries. Through our Lord ...
Nov. 12 St. Martin	*Pope and Martyr*
Orátio Gregem tuum, Pastor ætérne, placátus inténde: et per beátum Martínum Mártyrem tuum atque Summum Pontíficem perpétua protectióne custódi; quem totíus Ecclésiæ præstitísti esse pastórem. Per Dóminum nostrum ...	*Prayer* Look favorably upon Thy flock, eternal Shepherd: and keep it under Thy perpetual protection, through the intercession of Thy blessed Martyr and Supreme Pontiff Martin, whom Thou hast made the shepherd of the universal Church. Through our Lord ...
Nov. 13 St. Didacus	*Confessor*
Orátio Omnípotens sempitérne Deus, qui dispositióne mirábili infirma mundi éligis, ut fórtia quæque confúndas: concéde propítius humilitáti nostræ; ut, piis beáti Dídaci Confessóris tui	*Prayer* Omnipotent and eternal God, who by a wonderful providence chooses the weak of the world and confounds all its strengths: grant mercifully that by the pious prayers of Thy blessed

Proper of the Saints Lauds

précibus, ad perénnem in cælis glóriam sublimári mereámur. Per Dóminum nostrum ...	Confessor Didacus, we may deserve to be exalted to eternal glory in the heavens. Through our Lord ...
Nov. 14 St. Josaphat	*Bishop and Martyr*
Orátio Excita, quǽsumus, Dómine, in Ecclésia tua Spíritum, quo replétus beátus Iósaphat Martyr et Póntifex tuus ánimam suam pro óvibus pósuit: ut, eo intercedénte, nos quoque eódem Spíritu moti ac roboráti, ánimam nostram pro frátribus pónere non vereámur. Per Dóminum nostrum ...	*Prayer* Arouse in Thy Church, we beseech Thee, Lord, the Spirit which filled the blessed Martyr Josaphat, Thy Bishop who laid down his life for the sheep: that, through his intercession, we too, moved and strengthened by the same Spirit, may not be afraid to lay down our lives for our brethren. Through our Lord ...
Nov. 15 St. Albert the Great	*Bishop, Confessor and Doctor*
Orátio Deus, qui beátum Albértum Pontíficem tuum atque Doctórem in humána sapiéntia divínæ fídei subiciénda magnum effecísti: da nobis, quǽsumus; ita eius magistérii inhærére vestígiis, ut luce perfécta fruámur in cælis. Per Dóminum nostrum ...	*Prayer* O God, whose blessed Bishop and Doctor Albert the Great submitted human wisdom to the divine faith: grant us, we ask, that we may follow in the footsteps of his teaching so that we may enjoy perfect light in heaven. Through our Lord ...
Nov. 16 St. Gertrude	*Virgin*
Orátio Deus, qui in corde beátæ Gertrúdis Vírginis iucúndam tibi mansiónem præparásti: ipsíus méritis et intercessióne; cordis nostri máculas cleménter abstérge, et eiúsdem tríbue gaudére consórtio. Per Dóminum nostrum ...	*Prayer* O God, who in the heart of the blessed Virgin, Gertrude, hast prepared for thee a delightful abode: by her merits and intercession, mercifully wipe away the stains of our hearts and let us rejoice in her company. Through our Lord ...
Nov. 17 St. Gregory Thaumaturgus	*Bishop and Confessor*
Orátio Da, quǽsumus, omnípotens Deus: ut beáti Gregórii Confessóris tui atque Pontíficis veneránda solémnitas, et devotiónem nobis áugeat et salútem. Per Dóminum nostrum ...	*Prayer* Grant, we beseech thee almighty God, that the venerable solemnity of Thy blessed Confessor and Bishop Gregory, may increase our devotion and means for salvation. Through our Lord...
Nov. 19 St. Elizabeth	*Widow*
Orátio Da, quǽsumus, omnípotens Deus: ut beáti Gregórii Confessóris tui atque Pontíficis veneránda	*Prayer* May the merciful God enlighten the hearts of Thy faithful: and blessed Elizabeth, with glorious prayers, make us despise

solémnitas, et devotiónem nobis áugeat et salútem. Per Dóminum nostrum ...	the prosperity of the world; and to always enjoy heavenly consolation. Through our Lord ...
Nov. 20 St. Felix of Valios	*Confessor*
Orátio Deus, qui beátum Felícem Confessórem tuum ex erémo ad munus redimiéndi captívos cǽlitus vocáre dignátus es: præsta, quǽsumus; ut per grátiam tuam ex peccatórum nostrórum captivitáte, eius intercessióne, liberáti, ad cæléstem pátriam perducámur. Per Dóminum nostrum ...	*Prayer* O God, who hast deigned to call Thy blessed Confessor Felix from the wilderness to the work of redeeming the captives of heaven: grant, we beseech Thee; that by his intercession we may be delivered from the captivity of our sins to our heavenly fatherland. Through our Lord ...
Nov. 21 Presentation of the Blessed Virgin Mary	*Blessed Virgin Mary*
Orátio Deus, qui beátam Maríam semper Vírginem, Spíritus Sancti habitáculum, hodiérna die in templo præsentári voluísti: præsta, quǽsumus; ut, eius intercessióne, in templo glóriæ tuæ præsentári mereámur. Per Dóminum nostrum ...	*Prayer* Jesus, who wished to present the Blessed Mary ever-Virgin, the abode of the Holy Spirit, today in the temple: grant, we beseech Thee; that by her intercession we may deserve to be presented in the temple of Thy glory. Through our Lord ...
Nov 22 St. Cecilia	*Virgin and Martyr*
Capitulum (2 Cor 10:17-18) V. Fratres: Qui gloriátur, in Dómino gloriétur. Non enim qui seípsum comméndat, ille probátus est; sed quem Deus comméndat. R. Deo grátias.	**Chapter** (2 Cor 10:17-18) V. Brethren: He who glories, let him glory in the Lord. For it is not he who commends himself who is approved, but whom God commends. R. Thanks be to God.
Ant. Dum auróra finem daret, Cæcília exclamávit dicens: Eia, mílites Christi, abícite ópera tenebrárum et induímini arma lucis.	Ant. While the dawn was about to end, Cecilia cried out, saying: Come, soldiers of Christ, cast off the works of darkness, and put on the armor of light.
Orátio Deus, qui nos ánnua beátæ Cæcíliæ Vírginis et Mártyris tuæ solemnitáte lætíficas: da, ut, quam venerámur offício, étiam piæ conversatiónis sequámur exémplo. Per Dóminum nostrum ...	*Prayer* O God, who makes us rejoice in the annual solemnity of Thy blessed Virgin and Martyr Cecilia: grant that, as we venerate her by this devout service, we may also follow the example of her pious conduct. Through our Lord
Nov. 23 St. Clement I	*Pope and Martyr*
Capitulum (Jas 1:12) V. Beátus vir, qui suffert tentatiónem: quóniam cum probátus fúerit, accípiet corónam vitæ, quam repromísit Deus diligéntibus se.	**Chapter** (Jas 1:12) V. Blessed is the man who suffereth temptation, because when he hath been tried, he will receive the crown of life which God hath

Proper of the Saints Lauds

R. Deo grátias.	promised to those who care for Him. R. Thanks be to God.
Ant. Cum iter ad mare cepísset, pópulus voce magna clamábat: Dómine Iesu Christe, salva illum; et Clemens cum lácrimis dicébat: Súscipe, Pater, spíritum meum.	Ant. When he had taken the road to the sea, the people cried out with a loud voice: Lord Jesus Christ, save him: and Clement said with tears: Father receive my spirit.
Orátio Gregem tuum, Pastor ætérne, placátus inténde: et per beátum Cleméntem Mártyrem tuum atque Summum Pontíficem perpétua protectióne custódi; quem totíus Ecclésiæ præstitísti esse pastórem. Per Dóminum nostrum ...	*Prayer* Look favorably upon Thy flock, eternal Shepherd: and keep it under Thy perpetual protection, through the intercession of Thy blessed Martyr and Supreme Pontiff Clement, whom Thou hast made the shepherd of the universal Church. Through our Lord ...
Nov. 24 St. John of the Cross	*Confessor and Doctor*
Orátio Deus, qui sanctum Ioánnem Confessórem tuum atque Doctórem perféctæ sui abnegatiónis et Crucis amatórem exímium effecísti: concéde; ut, eius imitatióni iúgiter inhæréntes, glóriam assequámur ætérnam. Per Dóminum nostrum ...	*Prayer* O God, who made Saint John Thy Confessor and Teacher perfect in self-denial, and an excellent lover of the cross, grant that we may attain eternal glory by constantly following his example. Through our Lord ...
Nov. 25 St. Catherine	*Virgin and Martyr*
Orátio Deus, qui dedísti legem Móysi in summitáte montis Sínai, et in eódem loco per sanctos Angelos tuos corpus beátæ Catharínæ Vírginis et Mártyris tuæ mirabíliter collocásti: præsta, quǽsumus; ut, eius méritis et intercessióne, ad montem, qui Christus est, pervenire valeámus. Qui tecum vivit et regnat ...	*Prayer* O God, who gave the law to Moses on the top of Mount Sinai, and in the same place through Thy holy angels Thou admirably placed the body of the blessed Catherine the Virgin and Martyr, grant, we ask: that by her merits and intercession, we may be able to reach the mountain which is Christ: Who liveth and reigneth ...
Nov. 26 St. Sylvester	*Abbot*
Orátio Clementíssime Deus, qui sanctum Silvéstrum Abbátem, sǽculi huius vanitátem in apérto túmulo pie meditántem, ad erémum vocáre, et præcláris vitæ méritis decoráre dignátus es: te súpplices exorámus; ut, eius exémplo terréna despiciéntes, tui consórtio perfruámur ætérno. Per Dóminum nostrum ...	*Prayer* Most merciful God, Thou deigned to call the holy Abbot Silvester, meditating piously on the vanity of this age in an open tomb, to the desert, and to decorate him with the excellent merits of his life: let us exhort Thy supplicants; that, disdaining earthly things by his example, we may enjoy Thy company eternally. Through our Lord ...

Proper of the Saints (Vespers)

Nov. 30 St. Andrew	*Apostle*
Ant. Cum pervenísset beátus Andréas ad locum, ubi crux paráta erat, exclamávit et dixit: O bona crux, diu desideráta, et iam concupiscénti ánimo præparáta: secúrus et gaudens vénio ad te, ita et tu exsúltans suscípias me discípulum eius, qui pepéndit in te.	Ant. When blessed Andrew had arrived at the place where the cross was prepared, he cried out and said: O good cross, long desired, and already prepared with a lustful heart. I come to thee secure and rejoicing, so may thou also receive me, rejoicing, as His disciple who hangs on thee.
Dec. 4 St. Peter Chrysologus	*Bishop, Confessor and Doctor*
Ant. O Doctor óptime, Ecclésiæ sanctæ lumen, beáte Petre Chrysóloge, divínæ legis amátor, deprecáre pro nobis Fílium Dei.	Ant. O excellent Doctor, light of the Holy Church, blessed Peter Chrysologus, lover of the divine law, intercede for us to the Son of God.
Dec. 8 The Immaculate Conception of the Blessed Virgin Mary	*Blessed Virgin Mary* Lauds Antiphons Pg. 394
Ant. Hódie egréssa est virga de radíce Iesse: hódie sine ulla peccáti labe concépta est María: hódie contrítum est ab ea caput serpéntis antíqui, allelúja.	Ant. Today the rod came forth from the root of Jesse: today Mary was conceived without any blemish of sin: today the head of the ancient serpent was crushed by her, alleluia.
Dec. 13 St. Lucy	*Virgin and Martyr*
Ant. Tanto póndere eam fixit Spíritus Sanctus, ut Virgo Christi immóbilis permanéret.	Ant. The Holy Spirit embued her with such faith that the virgin of Christ remained steadfast.
Jan. 14 St. Hillary	*Bishop, Confessor and Doctor*
Ant. O Doctor óptime, Ecclésiæ sanctæ lumen, beáte Hilári, divínæ legis amátor, deprecáre pro nobis Fílium Dei.	Ant. O excellent Doctor, light of the Holy Church, blessed Hilary, lover of the divine law, intercede for us the Son of God.
Jan. 18 St. Peter's Chair	*Apostle*
Ant. Dum esset summus Póntifex, terréna non métuit, sed ad cæléstia regna gloriósus migrávit.	Ant. While he was high pontiff, he did not fear earthly things, but moved gloriously to the heavenly realms.
Jan. 21 St. Agnes	*Virgin and Martyr*
Ant. Stans beáta Agnes in médio flammæ, expánsis mánibus orábat ad Dóminum: Omnípotens, adoránde,	Ant. Blessed Agnes standing in the midst of the flame with outstretched hands; adoring, worshiping, and trembling; prayed

colénde, treménde, benedíco te, et glorífico nomen tuum in ætérnum.	to the Lord: O Thou Almighty, I bless Thee and glorify Thy Name forever.
Jan. 25 The Conversion of St. Paul	*Apostle*
Ant. Sancte Paule Apostóle, prædicátor veritátis et doctor géntium, intercéde pro nobis ad Deum, qui te elégit.	Ant. Saint Paul the Apostle, preacher of the truth and Doctor of the Gentiles, intercede for us with God who chose thee.
Jan. 29 St. Francis de Sales	*Bishop, Confessor and Doctor*
Ant. O Doctor óptime, Ecclésiæ sanctæ lumen, beáte Francísce, divínæ legis amátor, deprecáre pro nobis Fílium Dei.	Ant. O excellent Doctor, light of the Holy Church, blessed Francis, lover of the divine law, intercede for us to the Son of God.
Feb. 2 Purification of the Blessed Virgin Mary	*Blessed Virgin Mary*
Ant. Hódie beáta Virgo María púerum Iesum præsentávit in templo, et Símeon replétus Spíritu Sancto accépit eum in ulnas suas, et benedíxit Deum in ætérnum.	Ant. Today the Blessed Virgin Mary presented the child Jesus in the temple, and Simeon, filled with the Holy Spirit, took Him in his arms and blessed God forever.
Feb. 9 St. Cyril	*Bishop of Alexandria, Confessor and Doctor*
Ant. O Doctor óptime, Ecclésiæ sanctæ lumen, beáte Cyrílle, divínæ legis amátor, deprecáre pro nobis Fílium Dei.	Ant. O excellent Doctor, light of the Holy Church, blessed Cyril, lover of the divine law, intercede for us to the Son of God.
Feb. 11 Apparition of the Blessed Virgin Mary Immaculate	*Blessed Virgin Mary*
Ant. Hódie gloriósa cæli Regína in terris appáruit; hódie pópulo suo verba salútis et pígnora pacis áttulit; hódie Angelórum et fidélium chori immaculátam Conceptiónem celebrántes gáudio exsúltant.	Ant. Today the glorious Queen of Heaven appeared on earth: today she brought words of salvation and pledges of peace to her people: today the choir of angels and the faithful rejoice celebrating the Immaculate Conception.
Feb. 12 The Seven Holy Founders of the Order of the Servites	*Confessors*
Ant. Nomen eórum pérmanet in ætérnum, pérmanens ad fílios eórum, sanctórum virórum glória.	Ant. Their name endures forever, the glory of holy men remains unto their children.
Mar. 6 Sts. Perpetua and Felicity	*Martyrs*
Ant. Istárum est enim regnum cælórum, qui contempsérunt vitam mundi, et pervenérunt ad præmia regni,	Ant. For such is the kingdom of heaven, they who despised the life of the world and attained to the

Proper of the Saints Vespers

et lavérunt stolas suas in sánguine Agni.	rewards of the kingdom, washed their robes in the blood of the Lamb.
Mar. 12 St. Gregory I	*Pope, Confessor and Doctor*
Ant. O Doctor óptime, Ecclésiæ santæ lumen, beáte Gregóri, divínæ legís amátor, deprecáre pro nobis Fíllium Dei.	Ant. O excellent Doctor, light of the holy Church, blessed Gregory, lover of the divine law, intercede for us, to the Son of God.
Mar. 25 Annunciation of the Blessed Virgin Mary	*Blessed Virgin Mary* Lauds Antiphons Pg. 393
Ant. Gábriel Angelus locútus est Maríæ dicens: Ave grátia plena, Dóminus tecum: benedícta tu in cmuliéribus.	Ant. The angel Gabriel spoke to Mary, saying: Hail, full of grace, the Lord is with thee: blessed art thou among women.
Mar. 27 St. John Damascene	*Confessor and Doctor*
Ant. O Doctor óptime, Ecclésiæ santæ lumen, beáte Joánnes, divínæ legis amátor, deprecáre pro nobis Fílium Dei.	Ant. O Most Excellent Doctor, light of the holy Church, blessed John, lover of the divine law, intercede for us to the Son of God.
Apr. 4 St. Isidore	*Bishop, Confessor and Doctor*
Ant. O Doctor óptime, Ecclésiæ santæ lumen, beáte Isidóre, divínæ legis amátor, deprecáte pro nobis Fílium Dei.	Ant. O Most Excellent Doctor, light of the holy Church, blessed Isidore, lover of the divine law, intercede for us to the Son of God.
Apr. 11 St. Leo I	*Pope, Confessor and Doctor*
Ant. O Doctor óptime, Ecclésiæ santæ lumen, beáte Leo, divínæ legis amátor, deprecáre pro nobis Fílium Dei.	Ant. O excellent Doctor, light of the holy Church, blessed Leo, lover of the divine law, intercede for us to the Son of God.
Apr. 21 St. Anselm	*Bishop, Confessor and Doctor*
Ant. O Doctor óptime, Ecclésiæ santæ lumen, beáteАнсélme, divínæ legis amátor, deprecáre pro nobis Fílium Dei.	Ant. O excellent Doctor, light of the holy Church, blessed Anselm, lover of the divine law, intercede for us to the Son of God.
Apr. 27 St. Peter Canisius	*Confessor and Doctor*
Ant. O Doctor óptime, Ecclésiæ santæ lumen, beáte Petre, divínæ legis amátor, deprecáre pro nobis Fílium Dei.	Ant. O excellent Doctor, light of the holy Church, blessed Peter, lover of the divine law, intercede for us to the Son of God.
May 1 St. Joseph the Worker	*Confessor*
Ant. Et ipse Jesus erat incípiens quasi annórum trigínta, ut putabátur, fílius Joseph, allelúja.	Ant. And Jesus Himself, Who was almost thirty years old, was believed to be the son of Joseph, alleluia.

Proper of the Saints Vespers

May 3 Finding of the Holy Cross	
Ant. O Crux, splendídiot cuntis astris, mundo célebris, homínibus multum amábilis, sánctior univérsis, quæ sola fúlsti dina portáre taléntum mundi, dulce lignum, dúlces clávos, dúlcia ferens póndera; salva præséntem catérvam in tuis hódie láudibus congregátam, allelúija, allelúja.	Ant. O Cross, more splendid than the stars, famous in the world, much loved by the venerable, holier than all, which alone is worthy to bear the weight of the world, sweet wood, sweet nails, bearing sweet weights; save the people assembled to sing Thy praises today, alleluia, alleluia.
May 5 St. Pius V	*Pope and Confessor*
Orátio Deus, qui, ad conteréndos Ecclésiæ tuæ hostes et ad divínum cultum reparándum, beátum Pium Pontíficem Máximum elígere dignátus es: fac nos ipsíus deféndi præsídiis et ita tuis inhærére obséquiis; ut, ómnium hóstium superátis insídiis, perpétua pace lætémur. Per Dominum nostrum …	**Prayer** O God, who, in order to crush the enemies of Thy Church and to restore the divine worship, Thou hast deigned to choose the blessed Pius Maximus Pontiff: grant that he may defend us by his patronage and thus we may adhere to Thy service; that, having overcome all the snares of our enemies, we may rejoice in perpetual peace. Through our Lord …
May 9 St. Gregory Nazianzen	*Bishop, Confessor and Doctor*
Ant. O Doctor óptime, Ecclésiæ sanctæ lumen, beáte Gregóri, divínæ legis amátor, deprecáre pro nobis Fílium Dei, allelúja.	Ant. O excellent Doctor, light of the Holy Church, blessed Gregory, lover of the divine law, intercede for us the Son of God.
May 11 Sts. Philip and James	*Apostles*
Ant. Si manséritis in me, et verba mea in vobis mánserint, quodcúmque petiéritis, fiet vobis, allelúja, allelúja, allelúja.	Ant. If ye abide in Me, and My words abide in you, whatsoever ye shall ask, it shall be done unto you, alleluia, alleluia, alleluia.
May 13 St. Robert Bellarmine	*Bishop, Confessor and Doctor*
Orátio Deus, qui ad errórum insídias repelléndas et apostólicæ Sedis iura propugnánda, beátum Robértum Pontíficem tuum atque Doctórem mira eruditióne et virtúte decorásti: eius méritis et intercessióne concéde; ut nos in veritátis amóre crescámus et errántium corda ad Ecclésiæ tuæ rédeant unitátem. Per Dominum nostrum …	**Prayer** O God, who in order to repulse the snares of error and defend the rights of the Apostolic See, Thou hast adorned Thy blessed Robert Thy Pontiff and Doctor with wonderful learning and virtue: grant us his merits and intercession; that we may grow in the love of the truth, and that the hearts of the erring may return to the unity of Thy Church. Through our Lord …

Proper of the Saints Vespers

May 18 St. Venantius	*Martyr*
Ant. Hic vir despiciens mundum et terréna, triumphans, divitias cælo condidit ore, manu.	Ant. This man, despising the world and the earthly, triumphantly laid up riches in heaven with his speech and hands.
May 19 St. Peter Celestine	*Pope and Confessor*
Ant. Dum esset summus Pontifex terréna non metuit, sed ad cælestia regna gloriósus migravit.	Ant. As long as he was high pontiff he did not fear earthly things, but moved gloriously to the heavenly realms.
May 25 St. Gregory VII	*Pope and Confessor*
Ant. Amavit eum Dóminus, et ornavit eum: stolam glóriæ induit eum, et ad portas paradisi corónavit eum.	Ant. The Lord loved him, and adorned him: he clothed him with a robe of glory, and crowned him at the gates of paradise.
May 27 St. Bede the Venerable	*Confessor and Doctor*
Ant. O Doctor óptime, Ecclésiæ Sanctæ lumen, beáte Beda, divínæ legis amátor, deprecáre pro nobis Fílium Dei.	Ant. O excellent Doctor, light of the Holy Church, blessed Bede, lover of the divine law, intercede for us to the Son of God.
May 31 Feast of the Blessed Virgin Mary, Queen	*Blessed Virgin Mary*
Ant. Beáta Mater et intácta Virgo María, gloriósa Regína mundi, intercéde pro nobis ad Dóminum, allelúja.	Ant. Blessed Mother and Immaculate Virgin Mary, glorious Queen of the world, intercede for us with the Lord.
June 13 St. Anthony of Padua	*Confessor and Doctor*
Ant. O Doctor óptime, Ecclésiæ Sanctæ lumen, beáte Antoni, divínæ legis amátor, deprecáre pro nobis Fílium Dei.	Ant. O excellent Doctor, light of the Holy Church, blessed Antnony, lover of the divine law, intercede for us to the Son of God.
June 14 St. Basil the Great	*Bishop, Confessor and Doctor*
Ant. O Doctor óptime, Ecclésiæ Sanctæ lumen, beáte Basíli, divínæ legis amátor, deprecáre pro nobis Fílium Dei.	Ant. O excellent Doctor, light of the Holy Church, blessed Basil, lover of the divine law, intercede for us to the Son of God.
June 18 St. Ephrem	*Confessor and Doctor*
Ant. O Doctor óptime, Ecclésiæ Sanctæ lumen, beáte Ephræm, divínæ legis amátor, deprecáre pro nobis Fílium Dei.	Ant. O excellent teacher, light of the Holy Church, blessed Ephrem, lover of the divine law, intercede for us the Son of God.

Proper of the Saints Vespers

June 19 St. Juliana Falconieri	*Virgin*
Ant. Veni Sponsa Christi: áccipe corónam, quam tibi Dóminus præparávit in ætérnum.	**Ant.** Come, Bride of Christ: take the crown which the Lord hath prepared for thee forever.
June 24 Nativity of St. John the Baptist	*Martyr*
Capitulum (Isa 49:1) **V.** Audíte, ínsulæ, et atténdite, pópuli de longe: Dóminus ab útero vocávit me, de ventre matris meæ recordátus est nóminis mei. **R.** Deo grátias.	*Chapter* (Isa 49:1) **V.** Hear ye the islands, and pay attention to the people from afar: The Lord called me from the womb, He remembered my name from my mother's womb. **R.** Thanks be to God.
Ant. Puer qui natus est nobis, plus quam prophéta est: hic est enim, de quo Salvátor ait: Inter natos mulíerum non surréxit maior Ioánne Baptísta.	**Ant.** The child who was born to us is more than a prophet: for this is the one of whom the Savior sayeth: Among those born of women there did not arise a greater than John the Baptist.
June 26 Sts. John and Paul	*Martyrs*
Ant. Isti sunt duæ olívæ, et duo candelábra lucéntia ante Dóminum; habent potestátem cláudere cælum núbibus et aperíre portas eius, quia linguæ eórum claves cæli factæ sunt.	**Ant.** These are the two olive trees and the two candlesticks shining before the Lord: they have the power to close heaven with clouds, and to open its gates, because their tongues have become the keys of heaven.
June 29 Sts. Peter and Paul	*Apostles*
Ant. Hódie Simon Petrus ascéndit crucis patíbulum, allelúja: hódie claviculárius regni gaudens migrávit ad Christum: hódie Paulus Apóstolus, lumen orbis terræ, inclináto cápite, pro Christi nómine martýrio coronátus est, allelúja.	**Ant.** Today Simon Peter ascended the gallows of the cross, alleluia: today the clavier of the kingdom went to Christ, rejoicing in the kingdom: today Paul the apostle, the light of the world, bowed his head to the earth, was crowned with martyrdom for the Name of Christ, alleluia.
July 1 The Most Precious Blood of Our Lord Jesus Christ	
Ant. Habébitis autem hunc diem in monuméntum: et celebrábitis eum solémnem Dómino in generatiónibus vestris cultu sempitérno.	**Ant.** And ye shall keep this day as a memorial: and ye shall celebrate it as a solemn feast to the Lord, in Thy generations with everlasting worship.

Proper of the Saints Vespers

Jul 2 Visitation of the Blessed Virgin Mary	*Blessed Virgin Mary*
Ant. Beátam me dicent ómnes generatiónes quia ancíllam húmilem respéxit Deus.	**Ant.** All generations will call me blessed because God looked upon a humble handmaid.
July 7 Sts. Cyril and Methodius	*Bishops and Confessors*
Ant. Isti sunt viri sancti facti amíci Dei, divínæ veritátis præcónio gloriósi: linguæ eórum claves cæli factæ sunt.	**Ant.** These are holy men made friends of God, glorious in the proclamation of divine truth: their tongues have become the keys of heaven.
July 14 St. Bonaventure	*Bishop, Confessor and Doctor*
Ant. O Doctor óptime, Ecclésiæ Sanctæ lumen, beáte Bonaventúra, divínæ legis amátor, deprecáre pro nobis Fílium Dei.	**Ant.** O excellent Doctor, light of the Holy Church, blessed Bonaventure, lover of the divine law, intercede for us to the Son of God.
July 16 Our Lady of Mount Carmel	*Blessed Virgin Mary*
Ant. Glória Líbani data est ei, decor Carméli, et Saron, allelúja.	**Ant.** The glory of Lebanon was given to her, the beauty of Carmel, and Sharon, alleluia.
July 22 St. Mary Magdalen	*Penitent*
Ant. Múlier quæ erat in civitáte peccátrix, áttulit alabástrum unguénti, et stans retro secus pedes Dómini, lácrimis cœpit rigáre pedes eius, et capíllis cápitis sui tergébat.	**Ant.** A woman who was a sinner in the town, brought an alabaster jar of ointment and standing behind Him began to wash the feet of the Lord with tears, and to wipe them with the hair of her head.
Aug. 1 St. Peter in Chains	*Apostle*
Ant. Solve, jubente Deo, terrárum, Petre, caténas, qui facis ut páteant cæléstia regna beátis.	**Ant.** Loose, by the command of God, the worldly chains, O Peter, that thou mayest open the heavenly kingdom for the blessed.
Aug. 2 St. Alphonsus Mary de Liguori	*Bishop, Confessor and Doctor*
Ant. O Doctor óptime, Ecclésiæ Sanctæ lumen, beáte Alphónse María, divínæ legis amátor, deprecáre pro nobis Fílium Dei.	**Ant.** O excellent Doctor, light of the Holy Church, blessed Alphonsus Maria, lover of the divine law, intercede for us to the Son of God.

Aug. 6 Transfiguration of Our Lord Jesus Christ	
Ant. Et audiéntes discípuli cecidérunt in fáciem suam et timuérunt valde: et accéssit Iesus, et tétigit eos dixítque eis: Súrgite et nolíte timére, allelúja.	Ant. And the disciples hearing it fell on their faces and were afraid: and Jesus came and touched them and said to them: Arise and do not be afraid, alleluia.
Aug. 7 St. Cajetan	*Confessor*
Ant. Quǽrite primum regnum Dei et justítiam ejus, et hæc ómnia adjiciéntur vobis.	Ant. Seek ye first the kingdom of God and His righteousness, and all these things shall be added unto you.
Aug. 10 St. Lawrence	*Martyr*
Ant. Beátus Lauréntius, dum in craticula superpósitus urerétur, ad impiíssimum tyránnum dixit: Assátum est iam, versa et mandúca; nam facultátes Ecclésiæ, quas requíris, in cæléstes thesáuros manus páuperum deportavérunt.	Ant. Blessed Lawrence, while he was being burned on the grill, said to the most cruel tyrant: I am already roasted, turn and eat: for the riches of the Church, which thou desirest, have been carried away into heavenly treasures by the hands of the poor.
Aug. 15 Assumption of the Blessed Virgin Mary	*Blessed Virgin Mary* Lauds Antiphons Pg. 393
Ant. Hódie Maria Virgo cælos ascendit: gaudete, quia cum Christo regnat in ætérnum.	Ant. Today the Virgin Mary ascends into the heavens: rejoice, because she reigns with Christ forever.
Aug. 20 St. Bernard	*Abbot and Doctor*
Ant. O Doctor óptime, Ecclésiæ Sanctæ lumen, beáte Bernarde, divínæ legis amátor, deprecáre pro nobis Fílium Dei.	Ant. O excellent Doctor, light of the Holy Church, blessed Bernard, lover of the divine law, intercede for us to the Son of God.
Aug. 22 Feast of the Immaculate Heart of the Blessed Virgin Mary	*Blessed Virgin Mary*
Ant. Exsultávit cor meum in Dómino, et exaltátum est cornu meum in Deo meo, quia lætáta sum in salutári tuo.	Ant. My heart rejoiced in the Lord, and my horn was exalted in my God, because I rejoiced in Thy salvation.
Aug. 28 St. Augustine	*Bishop, Confessor and Doctor*
Ant. O Doctor óptime, Ecclésiæ Sanctæ lumen, beáte Augustine, divínæ legis amátor, deprecáre pro nobis Fílium Dei.	Ant. O excellent Doctor, light of the Holy Church, blessed Augustine, lover of the divine law, intercede for us to the Son of God.

Proper of the Saints Vespers

Aug. 29 The Beheading of St. John the Baptist	*Martyr*
Ant. Misit rex incrédulus minístros detestábiles, et amputári iussit caput Ioánnis Baptístæ.	Ant. The unbelieving king sent vile ministers and ordered the head of John the Baptist to be cut off.
Sept. 3 St. Pius X	*Pope and Confessor*
Ant. Dum esset Summus Póntifex, terréna non métuit, sed ad cæléstia regna gloriósus migrávit.	Ant. As long as he was Supreme Pontiff, he did not fear the world, but went gloriously to the heavenly kingdom.
Sept. 8 Nativity of the Blessed Virgin Mary	*Blessed Virgin Mary*
Ant. Natívitas tua, Dei Génetrix Virgo, gáudium annuntiávit univérso mundo: ex te enim ortus est sol iustítiæ, Christus Deus noster: qui solvens maledictiónem, dedit benedictiónem; et confúndens mortem, donávit nobis vitam sempitérnam.	Ant. Thy birth, Virgin Mother of God, announced joy to the whole world: for from you arose the sun of justice, Christ our God: who, breaking the curse, gave a blessing, and defeating death, gave us eternal life.
Sept. 14 Exautation of the Holy Cross	
Ant. O Crux benedícta, quæ sola fuísti digna portáre Regem cælórum et Dóminum, allelúja.	Ant. O blessed Cross, which alone was worthy to bear the King of heaven and the Lord, alleluia.
Sept. 15 The Seven Sorrows of the Blessed Virgin Mary	*Blessed Virgin Mary*
Ant. Oppréssit me dolor, et fácies mea intúmuit a fletu, et pálpebræ meæ caligavérunt.	Ant. I am overcome with pain and my face is swollen from weeping, and my eyelids have become dim.
Sept. 17 The Impression of the Stigmata on St. Francis	*Confessor*
Ant. Hic vir, despíciens mundum et terréna, triúmphans, divitias cælo cóndidit ore, manu.	Ant. This man, despising the world and the earthly, triumphantly laid up riches in heaven with his voice and hands.
Sept. 18 St. Joeseph of Cupertino	*Confessor*
Ant. Exístimo ómnia detriméntum esse propter eminéntem sciéntiam Iesu Christi Dómini mei.	Ant. I consider all things are a loss except the eminent knowledge of my Lord Jesus Christ.
Sept. 22 St. Thomas of Villanova	*Bishop and Confessor*
Ant. Dispérsit dedit paupéribus: justítia ejus manet in sæculum sæculi.	Ant. He distributed and gave to the poor: his righteousness endures for ever and ever.

Proper of the Saints Vespers

Sept. 29 The Dedication of St. Michael the Archangel	*Archangel*
Ant. Princeps gloriosíssime, Míchael Archángele, esto memor nostri: hic et ubíque semper precáre pro nobis Fílium Dei, allelúja, allelúja.	Ant. Most glorious Archangel Michael, be mindful of us; here and everywhere always pray for us to the Son of God, alleluia.
Sept. 30 St. Jerome	*Priest, Confessor and Doctor*
Ant. O Doctor óptime, Ecclésiæ Sanctæ lumen, beáte Heirónyme, divínæ legis amátor, deprecáre pro nobis Fílium Dei.	Ant. O excellent Doctor, light of the Holy Church, blessed Jerome, lover of the divine law, intercede for us to the Son of God.
Oct. 2 Holy Guardian Angels	*Angels*
Ant. Sancti Ángeli custódes nostri, deféndite nos in prǽlio, ut non pereámus intreméndo judício.	Ant. Our Holy Guardian Angels, defend us in battle, so that we do not perish in that terrible judgment.
Oct. 7 The Most Holy Rosary of the Blessed Virgin Mary	*Blessed Virgin Mary* Lauds Antiphons Pg. 394
Capitulum (Sir 24:25;39:17) V. In me grátia omnis viæ et veritátis, in me omnis spes vitæ et virtútis. Ego, quasi rosa plantáta super rivos aquárum, fructificávi. R. Deo grátias.	*Chapter* (Sir 24:25;39:17) V. In me is the grace of all the way and of truth, in me is all the hope of life and virtue: I, like a rose planted above streams of water, have borne fruit. R. Thanks be to God.
Ant. Beáta Mater et intácta Virgo, gloriósa Regína mundi, séntiant omnes tuum iuvámen, quicúmque célebrant tuam sacratíssimi Rosárii solemnitátem	Ant. Blessed Mother and untouched Virgin, glorious Queen of the world, let all who celebrate the solemnity of thy most holy Rosary experience thy help.
Oct. 11 The Motherhood of the Blessed Virgin Mary	*Blessed Virgin Mary*
Ant. Matérnitas tua, Dei Génetrix Virgo, gáudium annuntiávit univérso mundo: ex te enim ortus est sol iustítiæ, Christus Deus noster.	Ant. Thy motherhood, Virgin Mother of God, announced joy to the whole world: for from thee arose the Sun of Justice, Christ our God.
Oct. 15 St. Theresa	*Virgin*
Ant. Veni Sponsa Christi: áccipe corónam, quam tibi Dóminus præparávit in ætérnum.	Ant. Come, Bride of Christ: take the crown which the Lord hath prepared for thee in eternity.
Oct. 20 St. John Cantius	*Confessor*
Ant. Hic vir despíciens mundum et terréna, triumphans, divítias cælo cóndidit ore, manu.	Ant. This man, despising the world and the earthly,

Proper of the Saints Vespers

	triumphantly laid up riches in heaven with his voice and hands.
Oct. 24 St. Raphæl	*Archangel*
Ant. Princeps gloriosíssime, Ráphaël Archángele, esto memor nostri; hic et ubíque semper precáre pro nobis Fílium Dei.	**Ant.** Most glorious prince, Archangel Raphael, be mindful of us; here and everywhere always pray for us to the Son of God.
Nov. 1 All Saints	
Ant. O quam gloriósum est regnum in quo cum Christo gaudent omnes Sancti, amícti stolis albis sequúntur Agnum quocúmque íerit!	**Ant.** O how glorious is the kingdom in which all the Saints rejoice with Christ, clothed in white robes and follow the Lamb wherever he goes!
Nov. 11 St. Martin	*Bishop and Martyr*
Ant. O beátum Pontíficem, qui totis viscéribus diligébat Christum Regem, et non formidábat impérii principátum! o sanctíssima ánima, quam etsi gládius persecutóris non ábstulit, palmam tamen martýrii non amísit!	**Ant.** O blessed Pontiff, who loved Christ the King with all his strength and did not fear the princes of the empire! O most holy soul, which, though he evaded the sword of the persecutor, yet did not lose the palm of martyrdom!
Nov. 15 St. Albert the Great	*Confessor and Doctor*
Ant. O Doctor óptime, Ecclésiæ Sanctæ lumen, beáte Alberte, divínæ legis amátor, deprecáre pro nobis Fílium Dei.	**Ant.** O excellent Doctor, light of the Holy Church, blessed Albert, lover of the divine law, intercede for us to the Son of God.
Nov. 21 Presentation of the Blessed Virgin Mary	*Blessed Virgin Mary*
Ant. Beáta Dei Génetrix, María, Virgo perpétua, templum Dómini, sacrárium Spíritus Sancti, sola sine exémplo placuísti Dómino nostro Iesu Christo, allelúja.	**Ant.** O Blessed Mary, Mother of God, Virgin for ever, temple of the Lord, sanctuary of the Holy Ghost, thou, without any example before thee, didst make thyself well-pleasing in the sight of our Lord Jesus Christ, alleluia.
Nov. 22 St. Cecilia	*Virgin and Martyr*
Ant. Virgo gloriósa semper Evangélium Christi gerébat in péctore, et non diébus neque nóctibus a collóquiis divínis et oratióne cessábat.	**Ant.** The glorious virgin always carried the gospel of Christ in her breast, and did not cease in the days or nights from divine conversations and prayer.

Proper of the Saints Vespers

Nov. 23 St. Clement I	*Pope and Martyr*
Ant. Dedísti, Dómini, habitáculum Mártyri tuo Cleménti in mari, in modum templi marmórei angélicis mánibus præparátum: iter præbens pópulo terræ, ut enárrent mirabília tua.	**Ant.** Thou gavest, O Lord, the Martyr Clement an abode of the the sea, prepared like unto a marble temple by angelic hands: providing a way for the people of the land to tell of Thy wonders.
Nov. 24 St. John of the Cross	*Confessor and Doctor*
Ant. O Doctor óptime Ecclésiæ Sanctæ lumen, beáte Joánnes, divínæ legis amátor, deprecáre pro nobis Fílium Dei.	**Ant.** O Master, the best light of the Holy Church, blessed John, lover of the divine law, intercede for us to the Son of God.

Proper of the Saints Vespers

Canticles

Cánticum Zachariæ
(Luke 1:68-79)

Benedíctus Dóminus Deus Israël, quia visitávit, et fecit redemptiónem plebis suæ:

⁶⁹et eréxit cornu salútis nobis in domo David púeri sui,

»⁷⁰sicut locútus est per os sanctórum, qui a sǽculo sunt, prophetarum ejus:
⁷¹salútem ex inimícis nostris, et de manu ómnium qui odérunt nos:
»⁷²ad faciendam misericórdiam cum patribus nostris: et memorari testamenti sui sancti:
⁷³jusjurandum, quod juravit ad Abraham patrem nostrum, daturum se nobis
»⁷⁴ut sine timóre, de manu inimicorum nostrórum liberati, serviamus illi
⁷⁵in sanctitate et justítia coram ipso, ómnibus diébus nostris.
»⁷⁶Et tu puer, propheta Altissimi vocaberis: præibis enim ante fáciem Dómini parare vias ejus,

⁷⁷ad dandam scientiam plebi ejus in remissionem peccatórum eórum
»⁷⁸per viscera misericórdiæ Dei nostri, in quibus visitávit nos, oriens ex alto:

⁷⁹Illumináre his, qui in ténebris, et in umbra mortis sedent: ad dirigéndos pedes nostros in viam pacis.

Canticle of Zachariah
(Luke 1:68-79)

Blessed be the Lord God of Israel; because He hath visited and wrought the redemption of His people:
⁶⁹and hath raised up a horn of salvation to us, in the house of David His servant:
»⁷⁰as He spoke by the mouth of His holy prophets, who are from the beginning:
⁷¹salvation from our enemies, and from the hands of all that hate us:
»⁷²To perform mercy to our fathers, and to remember His holy testament,
⁷³the oath, which He swore to Abraham our father, that He would grant to us:
»⁷⁴that being delivered from the hand of our enemies, we may serve Him without fear,
⁷⁵in holiness and justice before Him, all our days.
»⁷⁶And thou, my child, shalt be called the prophet of the Highest: for thou shalt go before the face of the Lord to prepare His way:
⁷⁷To give knowledge of salvation to His people, unto the remission of their sins:
»⁷⁸through the depths of the mercy of our God, in which the dawn from on high hath visited us:
⁷⁹to enlighten them that sit in darkness, and in the shadow of death: to direct their feet into the way of peace.

Canticles

Cánticum Mariæ
(Luke. 1:47-55)

Magníficat ánima mea Dóminum.

⁴⁷Et exsultávit spíritus meus: in Deo, salutári meo.

»⁴⁸Quia respéxit humilitátem ancíllæ suæ: ecce enim ex hoc beátam me dicent ómnes generatiónes.

⁴⁹Quia fecit mihi magna, qui potens est: et sanctum nomen ejus.

»⁵⁰Et misericórdia ejus, a progénie in progénies: timéntibus eum.

⁵¹Fecit poténtiam in bráchio suo: dispérsit supérbos mente cordis sui.

»⁵²Depósuit poténtes de sede: et exaltávit húmiles.

⁵³Esuriéntes implévit bonis: et dívites dimísit ינánes.

»⁵⁴Suscépit Israël púerum suum: recordátus misericórdiæ suæ.

⁵⁵Sicut locútus est ad patres nostros: Ábraham, et sémini ejus in sǽcula.

Magnificat
(Luke. 1:47-55)

My soul doth magnify the Lord.

⁴⁷And my spirit hath rejoiced in God my Savior.

»⁴⁸Because He hath regarded the humility of His handmaid; for behold from henceforth all generations shall call me blessed:

⁴⁹because He that is mighty, hath done great things to me; and holy is His Name.

»⁵⁰And His mercy is from generation unto generations, to them that fear Him.

⁵¹He hath showed might in His arm: He hath scattered the proud in the conceit of their hearts.

»⁵²He hath put down the mighty from their thrones, and hath exalted the humble.

⁵³He hath filled the hungry with good things; and the rich He hath sent away empty.

»⁵⁴He hath received Israel His servant, being mindful of His mercy:

⁵⁵as He spoke to our fathers, to Abraham and to his seed for ever.

Hymns

Hymns

Hymns

Hymn Index

1. Ætérne Rerum Condítor – (Lauds) 7
2. Ætérna Coeli Glória – (Lauds) 385
3. Ætérna Christi Munera – (Apostles) 385
4. Creátor Alme Siderum - (Advent) (Vespers) 136
5. Ales Diei Núntius – (Lauds) 83, 24
6. A Solis Ortus Cardine – (Christmastide) 372
7. Audi Benígne Condítor – (Lent) 372
8. Auróra Cælum Purpurat – (Easter) 384
9. Ave, Maris Stella - (Blessed Virgin Mary) 373
10. Ave Verum Corpus Natum – (Corpus Christi) 374
11. Beáta Nobis Gáudia - (Pentecost) 374
12. Cœli Deus Sanctíssime - (Vespers) 149
13. Cor Arca Legem – (Sacred Heart) 375
14. Deus Tuórum Militum – (Saints/martyrs) 376
15. En Ut Superba - (Sacred Heart) 377
16. Exultet Orbis Gaudis - (Apostles) 377
17. Hominis Superne Conditor - (Vespers) 166
18. Invicte Martyr – (Saints and Martyrs) 382
19. Iste Confessor Dómine – (Confessors) 379
20. Jam Sol Recédit Igneus – (Vespers) 173
21. Jesu, Coróna Vírginum – (Blessed Virgin Mary) 384
22. Jesu, Redémptor Omnium – (Christmastide) 375
23. Lucis Creátor Óptime – (Vespers) 128
24. Lux Ecce Surgit Áuria – (Lauds) 40
25. Magnæ Deus Potentiæ – (Vespers) 158
26. Nox, et Ténebræ, et Núbila – (Lauds) 32
27. O Gloriósa Vírginum – (Blessed Virgin Mary) 56
28. O Sol Salútis - (Lauds) (Lent) 74
29. Paschále Mundo Gáudium – (Ascension) 386
30. Placáre Christe - (Easter) (All Saints) 379
31. Salútis Ætérnæ Dator – (All Saints) 376
32. Salútis Humánæ Sator – (Ascension) 378
33. Splendor Patérnæ Glóriæ - (Lauds) 15
34. Te Lucis Ante Términum – (Compline) 180
35. Te sæculórum Príncipem - (Christ the King) 380
36. Telluris alme Conditor - (Vespers) 387
37. Tu, Trinitatis Unitas - (Holy Trinity) 381
38. Veni Creátor Spíritus - (Pentecost) 381
39. Verbum Supernum Prodiens - (Advent) 383
40. Vexilla Regis - (Palm Sunday) (Lent) 382

Hymns

A Solis Ortus Cárdine
Ad usque terræ límitem,
Christum canámus Príncipem,
Natum María Vírgine.

Beátus auctor sǽculi
Servíle corpus índuit:
Ut carne carnem líberans,
Ne pérderet quos cóndidit.

Castæ Paréntis víscera
Cœléstis intrat grátia:
Venter Puéllæ bájulat
Secréta, quæ non nóverat.

Domus pudici péctoris
Templum repénte fit Dei:
Intácta nésciens virum,
Concépit alvo Fílium.

Enítitur puérpera,
Quem Gábriel prædíxerat,
Quem ventre Matris géstiens,
Baptísta clausum sénserat.

Foeno jacére pértulit:
Præsépe non abhórruit:
Et lacte módico pastus est,
Per quem nec ales ésurit.

Gaudet chorus cæléstium,
Et Ángeli canunt Deo;
Palámque fit pastóribus
Pastor, Creátor ómnium.

Jesus, tibi sit glória,
Qui natus es de Vírgine,
Cum Patre, et almo Spíritu
In sempitérna sǽcula.

Audi Benígne Cónditor
Nostras preces cum flétibus,
In hoc sacro jejúnio
Fusas quadragenária.

Scrutátor alme córdium,
Infírma tu scis vírium;
Ad te revérsis éxhibe
Remissiónis grátiam.

From the Lands that See the Sun Arise
To earth's remotest boundaries,
The Virgin-born to-day we sing,
The Son of Mary, Christ the King.

Blest Author of this earthly frame,
To take a servant's form He came,
That, liberating flesh by flesh,
Whom He had made might live afresh.

In that chaste parent's holy womb
Celestial grace hath found its home;
And she, as earthly bride unknown,
Yet calls that Offspring blest her own.

The mansion of the modest breast
Becomes a shrine where God shall rest:
The pure and undefiled one
Conceived in her womb the Son.

That Son, that Royal Son she bore,
Whom Gabriel's voice had told afore;
Whom, in His mother yet concealed,
The infant Baptist had revealed.

The manger and the straw He bore,
The cradle did He not abhor;
By milk in infant portions fed,
Who gives e'en fowls their daily bread.

The heavenly chorus filled the sky,
The Angels sang to God on high,
What time to shepherds, watching lone,
They made creation's Shepherd known.

All honor, laud, and glory be,
O Jesu, Virgin-born to Thee:
All glory, as is ever meet,
To Father and to Paraclete.

O King Creator, Bow Thine Ear
To mark the cry, to know the tear
Before Thy throne of mercy spent
In this Thy holy fast of Lent.

Our hearts are open, Lord, to Thee:
Thou knowest our infirmity;
Pour out on all who seek Thy face
Abundance of Thy pardoning grace.

Hymns

Multum quidem peccávimus,	Our sins are many, this we know;
Sed parce confiténtibus:	Spare us, good Lord, Thy mercy show;
Ad nóminis laude tui	And for the honor of Thy Name
Confer medélam lánguidis.	Our fainting souls to life reclaim.
Concéde nostrum cónteri	Give us the self-control that springs
Corpus per abstinéntiam;	From discipline of outward things,
Culpæ ut relínquant pábulum	That fasting inward secretly
Jejúna corda críminum.	The soul may purely dwell with Thee.
Præsta beáta Trínitas,	We pray Thee, Holy Trinity,
Concéde simplex Unítas:	One God, unchanging Unity,
Ut fructuósa sint tuis	That we from this our abstinence
Jejuniórum múnera. Amen.	May reap the fruits of penitence.
Ave Maris Stella,	**Ave, Star of Ocean,**
Dei Mater alma,	Child Divine who barest,
Atque semper Virgo,	Mother, Ever-Virgin,
Felix cœli porta.	Heaven's Portal fairest.
Sumens illud Ave	Taking that sweet Ave
Gabriélis ore,	Erst by Gabriel spoken,
Funda nos in pace,	Eva's name reversing,
Mutans Hevæ nomen.	Be of peace the token.
Solve vincla reis,	Break the sinners' fetters,
Profer lumen cæcis,	Light to blind restoring,
Mala nostra pelle,	All our ills dispelling,
Bona cuncta posce.	Every boon imploring.
Monstra te esse matrem,	Show thyself a Mother
Sumat per te preces,	In thy supplication;
Qui pro nobis natus,	He will hear who chose thee
Tulit esse tuus.	At His Incarnation.
Virgo singuláris,	Maid all maids excelling,
Inter ómnes mitis,	Passing meek and lowly,
Nos culpis solútos	Win for sinners pardon,
Mites fac et castos.	Make us chaste and holy.
Vitam præsta puram,	As we onward journey
Iter para tutum,	Aid our weak endeavor,
Ut vidéntes Jesum,	Till we gaze on Jesus
Semper collætémur.	And rejoice forever.
Sit laus Deo Patri,	Father, Son, and Spirit,
Summo Christo decus,	Three in One confessing,
Spíritui sancto,	Give we equal glory
Tribus honor unus.	Equal praise and blessing.

Hymns

Ave Verum Corpus
Natum De Maria Vírgine,
Vere passum, immolátum
In cruce pro hómine,
Cujus latus perforátum
Unda flúxit et sánguine,
Esto nobis prægustátum
Mortis in exámine.
O clemens, O pie,
O dulcis Jesu, Fili Maríæ.

Beáta Nobis Gáudia
Anni redúxit órbita,
Cum Spíritus paráclitus
Illápsus est Apóstolis.

Ignis vibránte lúmine
Linguæ figúram détulit,
Verbis ut essent próflui,
Et caritáte férvidi.

Linguis loquúntur ómnium,
Turbæ pavent Gentílium:
Musto madére députant,
Quos Spíritus replévarat.

Paráta sunt hæc mýstice,
Paschæ perácto témpore,
Sacro diérum círculo,
Quo lege fit remíssio.

Te nunc Deus piíssime
Vultu precámur cérnuo,
Illápsa nobis coélitus
Largíre dona Spíritus.

Dudum sacráta péctora
Tua replésti grátia:
Dimítte nostra crímina,
Et da quiéta témpora.

Deo Patri sit glória,
Et Fílio, qui a mórtuis
Surréxit, ac Paráclito.
In sæculórum sǽcula.

Hail, True Body, Truly Born
Of the Virgin Mary mild,
Truly offered, racked and torn,
On the Cross, for man defiled,
From whose love-pierced, sacred side
Flowed Thy true Blood's saving tide:
Be a foretaste sweet to me
In my death's great agony,
O Thou loving, gentle One,
Sweetest Jesus, Mary's Son.

Round Roll the Weeks
Our Hearts to Greet,
With blissful joy returning;
For lo! The Holy Paraclete
On twelve bright brows sits burning:

With quivering flame He lights on each,
In fashion like a tongue, to teach
That eloquent they are of speech,
Their hearts with true love yearning.

While with all tongues they speak to all,
The nations deem them maddened,
And drunk with wine the Prophets call,
Whom God's good Spirit gladdened;

A marvel this—in mystery done—
The holy Paschaltide outrun,
By numbers told, whose reckoning won
Remission for the saddened.

O God most Holy, Thee we pray,
With reverent brow low bending,
Grant us the Spirit's gifts to-day—
The gifts from heaven descending;

And, since, Thy grace hath deigned to bide
Within our breasts once sanctified,
Deign, Lord, to cast our sins aside,
Henceforth calm seasons sending.

To God the Father, laud and praise,
Praise to the Son be given;
Praise to the Spirit of all grace,
The fount of graces seven.

Cor, Arca Legem Continens

Non servitútis veteris,
Sed grátiæ, sed veniæ,
Sed et misericórdiæ.

Cor, Sanctuárium novi
Intemerátum fœderis,
Templum vetústo sánctius,
Velúmque scisso utílius.

Te vulnerátum cáritas
Ictu paténti vóluit;
Amóris invisibílis
Ut venerémur vúlnera.

Hoc sub amóris sýmbolo
Passus cruénta, et mýstica,
Utrúmque sacríficium
Christus Sacérdos obtúlit.

Quis non amántem rédamet?
Quis non redémptus díligat,
Et Corde in isto séligat
Ætérna tabernácula?

Decus Parénti et Fílio,
Sanctóque sit Spíritui,
Quibus potéstas, glória
Regnúmque in omne est sǽculum.

Jesu, Redémptor Ómnium,

Quem lucis ante originem
Parem patérnæ glóriæ
Pater suprémus edidit.

Tu lumen, et spléndor Patris,
Tu spes perénnis ómnium,
Inténde quas fundunt preces
Tui per órbem servuli.

Memento, rerum Conditor,
Nostri quod olim córporis,
Sacráta ab alvo Vírginis
Nascéndo, formam sumpseris.

Testátur hoc præsens dies,
Currens per anni círculum,
Quod solus e sinu Pátris
Mundi salus advéneris.

Jesus, Behind Thy Temple's Veil,

Hid in an ark of gold,
On stones engraven, lay the Law
Thy finger wrote of old.

But in Thy Body's temple new,
Thy life-blood's throbbing shrine,
Held, upon fleshly tables graved,
The law of Love Divine.

And when that Heart
in death was stilled,
Each temple's veil was riven:
And lo, within Thy Love's red shrine, To
us to look was given.

There make us gaze and see the love
Which drew Thee, for our sake,
O great High-priest, Thyself to God
A sacrifice to make.

Thou, Savior, cause that every soul
Which Thou hast loved so well,
May will within Thine open Heart
In life and death to dwell.

Grant it, O Father, only Son,
And Spirit, God of grace,To whom all
worship shall be done,
In every time and place.

Jesus, the Ransomer of Man,/

Who, ere created light began,/
Didst from the sovereign Father spring,/
His power and glory equalling.

The Father's Light and Splendor Thou,
Their endless Hope to Thee that bow;
Accept the prayers and praise to-day
That through the world Thy servants pay.

Salvation's Author, call to mind
How, taking form of humankind,
Born of a Virgin undefiled,
Thou in man's flesh becam'st a Child.

Thus testifies the present day,
Through every year in long array,
That Thou, salvation's source alone,
Proceededst from the Father's throne.

Hunc astra, tellus, æquora,
Hunc omne quod cælo subest,
Salútis Auctórem novæ
Novo salútat cantico.

Et nos, beata quos sacri
Rigávit unda sánguinis;
Natális ob diem tui
Hýmni tribútum solvimus.

Jesus, tibi sit gloria,
Qui natus es de Vírgine,
Cum Patre, et almo Spiritu
In sempitérna sæcula.

Salútis Ætérnæ Dator,
Jesu, redémptis súbveni:
Virgo parens cleméntiæ
Dona salútem sérvulis.

Vos Angelórum míllia,
Patrúmque cœtus, ágmina
Canóra Vatum: vos reis
Precámini indulgéntiam.

Baptísta Christi prævius,
Summíque cœli Cláviger,
Cum céteris Apóstolis
Nexus resólvant críminum.

Cohors triúmphans Mártyrum,
Almus Sacerdótum chorus,
Et virginális cástitas
Nostros reátus ábluant.

Quicámque in alta síderum
Regnátis aula príncipes,
Favéte votis súpplicum,
Qui dona cœli flágitant.

Virtus, honor, laus, glória
Deo Patri cum Fílio,
Sancto simul Paráclito,
In sæculórum sæcula.

Deus Tuórum Mílitum
Sors, et coróna, præmium,
Laudes canéntes Mártyris
Absólve nexu críminis.

Hic nempe mundi gáudia,
Et blanda fraudum pábula
Imbúta felle députans,
pervénti ad Cælestia.

The heavens above, the rolling main
And all that earth's wide realms contain,
With joyous voice now loudly sing
The glory of their new-born King.

And we who, by Thy precious Blood
From sin redeemed, are marked for God,
On this the day that saw Thy birth,
Sing the new song of ransomed earth.

O Lord, the Virgin-born, to Thee
Eternal praise and glory be,
Whom with the Father we adore
And Holy Ghost forevermore.

Giver of Life, Eternal Lord!
Thy own redeemed defend;
Mother of grace! thy children save,
And help them to the end.

Ye thousand thousand Angel hosts!
Assist us in our need;
Ye Patriarchs! with the Prophet choir!
For our forgiveness plead.

Forerunner blest! and Thou who still
Dost heaven's dread keys retain!
Ye glorious Apostles all!
Unloose our guilty chain.

Army of Martyrs! holy Priests
In beautiful array!
Ye happy troops of Virgins chaste!
Wash all our stains away.

All ye who high above the stars
In heavenly glory reign!
May we through Thy prevailing prayers
Unto Thy joys attain.

Praise, honor, to the Father be,
Praise to His only Son;
Praise, Holy Paraclete, to Thee,
While endless ages run.

O God, of Those that Fought Thy fight,
Portion, and prize, and crown of light,
Break every bond of sin and shame
As now we praise Thy Martyr's name.

He reeked not of the world's allure,
But sin and pomp of sin forswore:
Knew all their gall, and passed them by,
And reached the throne prepared on high.

Hymns

Pœnas cucúrrit fórtiter,
Et sústulit viríliter,
Fundénsque pro te sánguinem,
Ætérna dona póssidet.

Ob hoc precátu súpplici
Te póscimus, piíssime;
In hoc triúmpho Mártyris
Dimítte noxam sérvulis.

Laus et perénnis glória
Patri sit, atque Fílio,
Sancto simul Paráclito,
In sempitérna sǽcula.

Exúltet Orbis Gáudiis:
Cœlum resúltet láudibus:
Apostolórum glóriam
Tellus et astra cóncinunt.

Vos sæculórum júdices,
Et vera mundi lúmina:
Votis precámur córdium,
Audíte voces súpplicum.

Qui templa cæli cláuditis,
Serásque verbo sólvitis,
Nos a reátu nóxios
Solvi jubéte, quǽsumus.

Præcépta quorum prótinus
Languor salúsque séntient:
Sanáte mentes lánguidas;
Augéte nos virtútibus.

Ut, cum redíbit árbiter
In fine Chrístus sǽculi,
Nos sempitérni gaudii
Concédat esse compótes.

Patri, simúlque Fílio,
Tibíque sancta Spíritus,
Sicut fuit, sit júgiter
Sæclum per omne glória.

En ut Supérba Críminum
Et sæva nostrórum cohors
Cor sauciávit innocens
Meréntis haud tale Dei!

Bravely the course of pain he ran,
And bare his torments as a man:
For love of Thee his blood outpoured,
And thus obtained the great reward.

With humble voice and suppliant word
We pray Thee therefore, holy Lord,
While we Thy Martyr's feast-day keep,
Forgive Thy loved and erring sheep.

Glory and praise for aye be done
To God the Father, and the Son,
And Holy Ghost, who reign on high,
One God, to all eternity.

Now Let the Earth with Joy Resound,
And heaven the chant re-echo round;
Nor heaven nor earth too high can raise
The great Apostles' glorious praise.

O ye who, throned in glory dread,
Shall judge the living and the dead,
Lights of the world forevermore!
To Thee the suppliant prayer we pour.

Ye close the sacred gates on high;
At Thy command apart they fly:
Oh! loose for us the guilty chain
We strive to break, and strive in vain.

Sickness and health Thy voice obey;
At Thy command they go or stay:
From sin's disease our souls restore;
In good confirm us more and more.

So when the world is at its end,
And Christ to judgment shall descend,
May we be called those joys to see
Prepared from all eternity.

Praise to the Father, with the Son,
And Holy Spirit, Three in One;
As ever was in ages past,
And so shall be while ages last.

Lo, How the Savage Crew
Of our proud sins hath rent
The Heart of our all-gracious God,
That Heart so innocent.

Vibrántis hastam mílitis Peccáta nostra dírigunt: Ferrúmque diræ cúspidis Mortále crimen ácuit.	The soldier's quivering lance Our guilt it was that drave, Our wicked deeds that to its point Such cruel sharpness gave.
Ex corde scisso Ecclésia Christo jugáta náscitur: Hoc óstium Arcæ in látere est: Genti ad salútem pósitum.	O wounded Heart, whence sprang The Church, the Savior's bride; Thou Door of our Salvation's Ark Set in its mystic side.
Ex hoc perénnis grátia, Ceu septifórmis flúvius; Stolas ut illic sórdidas Lavémus Agni in sánguine.	Thou holy fount, whence flows The sacred sevenfold flood. Where we our filthy roles may cleanse In the Lamb's saving Blood:
Turpe est redíre ad crímina, Quæ Cor beátum lácerent: Sed æmulémur córdibus Flammas amóris índices.	By sorrowful relapse, Thee will we rend no more; But like the flames, those types of love, Strive heavenward to soar.
Hoc, Christe, nobis, hoc, Pater, Hoc sancta, dona, Spíritus, Quibus potéstas, glória Regnúmque in omne est sǽculum	Father and Son supreme And Spirit, hear our cry; Whose is the kingdom, praise and power, Through all eternity.

Salútis Humánæ Sator, Jesu, volúptas córdium, Orbis redémpti Cónditor, Et casta lux amántium:	**Hail, Thou Who Man's Redeemer Art,** Jesu, the joy of every heart; Great Maker of the world's wide frame, And purest love's delight and flame:
Que victus es cleméntia, Ut nostra ferres crímina? Mortem subíres ínnocens, A morte nos ut tólleres?	What nameless mercy Thee o'ercame, To bear our load of sin and shame? For guiltless, Thou Thy life didst give, That sinful erring man might live.
Perrúmpis inférnum chaos; Vinctis caténas détrahis; Victor triúmpho nóbili Ad déxteram Patris sedes.	The realms of woe are forced by Thee, Its captives from their chains set free; And Thou, amid Thy ransomed train, At God's right hand dost victor reign.
Te cogat indulgéntia, Ut damna nostra sárcias Tuíque vultus compotes Dites beáto lúmine.	Let mercy sweet with Thee prevail, To cure the wounds we now bewail; Oh, bless us with Thy holy sight, And fill us with eternal light.

Tu dux ad astra, et sémita,
Sis meta nostris córdibus,
Sis lacrymárum gáudium,
Sis dulce vitæ præmium.

Iste Confessor Dómini Coléntes
Quem pie laudant pópuli per orbem:
Hac die lætus méruit beátas
Scandére sedes.

Qui pius, prudens, húmilis, pudícus,
Sóbriam duxit sine labe vitam,
Donec humános ánimavit auræ
Spíritus artus.

Cujus ob præstans méritum frequénter,
Ægra quæ passim jacuére membra,
Viribus morbi dómitis, salúti
Restituúntur.

Noster hinc illi chorus obsequéntem
Cóncinit laudem, celebrésque palmas;
Ut piis ejus précibus juvémur
Omne per ævum.

Sit salus illi, decus atque virtus,
Qui super cœli sólio corúscans,
Tótius mundi sériem gubérnat
Trinus et unus.

Placáre, Christe, Sérvulis,
Quibus Patris cleméntiam
Tuæ ad tribúnal grátiæ
Patróna Virgo póstulat.

Et vos beáta, per novem
Distíncta gyros ágmina,
Antíqua cum præséntibus,
Futúra damna péllite.

Apóstoli cum Vátibus,
Apud sevérum Júdicem,
Veris reórum flétibus
Expóscite indulgéntiam.

Our guide, our way to heavenly rest,
Be Thou the aim of every breast;
Be Thou the soother of our tears,
Our sweet reward above the spheres.

This the Confessor of the Lord, whose triumph/ Now all the faithful celebrate, with gladness/ Erst on this feast-day merited to enter/ into his glory.

Saintly and prudent, modest in behavior,/ Peaceful and sober, chaste was he, and lowly/ While that life's vigor, coursing through his members,/ Quickened his being.

Sick ones of old time, to his tomb resorting/ Sorely by ailments manifold afflicted,/ Oft-times have welcomed health and strength returning,/ At his petition.

Whence we in chorus gladly do him honor,/ Chanting his praises with devout affection,' That in his merits we may have a portion,/ Now and forever.

His be the glory, power and salvation,/ Who over all things reigneth in the highest,/ Earth's might fabric ruling and directing,/ Onely and Trinal.

O Christ, Thy Guilty People Spare!
Lo, kneeling at Thy gracious throne,
Thy Virgin-Mother pours her prayer,
Imploring pardon for her own.

Ye Angels, happy evermore!
Who in thy circles nine ascend,
As ye have guarded us before,
So still from harm our steps defend.

Ye Prophets and Apostles high!
Behold our penitential tears;
And plead for us when death is nigh,
And our all-searching Judge appears.

Hymns

Vos purpuráti Mártyres,
Vos candidáti præmio
Confessiónis, éxsules
Vocáte nos in pátriam.

Choréa casta vírginum,
Et quos erémus íncolas
Transmísit astris, cǽlitum
Locáte nos in sédibus.

Auférte gentem pérfidam
Credéntium de fínibus,
Ut unus ómnes únicum
Ovíle nos pastor regat.

Deo Patri sit glória,
Natóque Patris único,
Sancto simul Paráclito,
In sempitérna sǽcula.

Te Sæculórum Príncipem,
Te, Christe, Regem géntium,
Te méntium, te córdium
Unum fatémur árbitrum.

Scelésta turba clámitat
Regnáre Christum nólumus;
Te nos ovántes ómnium
Regem suprémum dícimus.

O Christe, Princeps Pácifer,
Mentes rebélles súbice,
Tuóque amóre dévios
Ovíle in unum cóngrega.

Ad hoc cruénta ab árbore
Pendes apértis brácchiis,
Diráque fossum cúspide
Cor igne flagrans éxhibes.

Ad hoc in aris ábderis
Vini dapísque imágine,
Fundens salútem fíliis
Transverberáto péctore.

Te natiónum prǽsides
Honóre tollant público,
Colant magístri, júdices,
Leges et artes éxpriment.

Ye Martyrs all! a purple band,
And Confessors, a white-robed train;
Oh, call us to our native land,
From this our exile, back again.

And ye, O choirs of virgins chaste!
Receive us to thy seats on high;
With Hermits whom the desert waste
Sent up of old into the sky.

Drive from the flock, O Spirit blest!
The false and faithless race away;
That all within one fold may rest,
Secure beneath one Shepherd's sway.

To God the Father glory be,
And to His sole-begotten Son;
And glory, Holy Ghost, to Thee,
While everlasting ages run.

Thou, Prince of all Ages, Thou,
O Christ, the King of the nations,
we acknowledge Thee the one Judge of
all hearts and minds.

The wicked mob screams out.
"We don't want Christ as king,"
While we, with shouts of joy, hail
Thee as the world's supreme King

O Christ, peace-bringing Prince,
subjugate the rebellious minds:
And in Thy love, bring together in one
flock those going astray.

For this, with arms outstretched,
Thou hung, bleeding, on the Cross,
and the cruel spear that pierced Thee,
showed man a Heart burning with love.

For this, Thou art hidden on our altars
under the form of bread and wine,
and pour out on Thy children from Thy
pierced side the grace of salvation.

May the rulers of the world publicly
honor and extol Thee;/ May teachers and
judges reverence Thee;/ May the laws
express Thine order and the arts reflect
Thy beauty.

Hymns

Submíssa regum fúlgeant
Tibi dicáta insígnia:
Mitíque sceptro pátriam
Domósque subde cívium.

May kings find renown in their
submission and dedication to Thee.
Bring under Thy gentle rule our country
and our homes.

Jesu tibi sit glória,
Qui sceptra mundi temperas,
Cum Patre et almo Spíritu,
In sempiterna sǽcula. Amen.

Glory be to Thee, O Jesus, supreme over
all secular authorities;
And glory be to the Father and the loving
Spirit through endless ages.

Tu, Trinitatis Unitas,
Orbem poténter quæ regis,
Atténde laudis cánticum Quod
excubántes psállimus.

O Three in One, and One in Three,/
Who rulest all things mightily:/
Bow down to hear the songs of praise/
Which, freed from bonds of sleep,/
we raise.

Nam léctulo consúrgimus
Noctis quiéto témpore,
Ut flagitémus ómnium
A te medélam vulnerum.

While lingers yet the peace of night,/ We
rouse us from our slumbers light: That
might of instant prayer may win The
healing balm for wounds of sin.

Quo fraude quidquid dǽmonum
In nóctibus delíquimus,
Abstérgat illud coélitus
Tuæ potéstas glóryæ.

If, by the wiles of Satan caught,
This night-time we have sinned in aught,
That sin Thy glorious power to-day,
From heaven descending, cleanse away.

Ne corpus adstit sórdidum,
Nec torpor instet córdium,
Ne críminis contágio
Tepéscat ardor spíritus.

Let naught impure our bodies stain, No
laggard sloth our souls detain, No taint of
sin our spirits know, To chill the fervor
of their glow.

Ob hoc, Redémptor, quǽsumus,
Reple tuo nos lúmine,
Per quod diérum círculis
Nullis ruámus áctibus.

Wherefore, Redeemer, grant that we
Fulfilled with Thine own light may be:
That, in our course, from day to day, By
no misdeed we fall away.

Præsta, Pater piíssime,
Patríque compar Uníce,
Cum Spíritu Paráclito
Regnans per omne sǽculum.

Grant this, O Father ever One With
Christ, Thy sole-begotten Son, And Holy
Ghost, whom all adore, Reigning and
blest forevermore.

Veni Creátor Spíritus,
Mentes tuórum vísita,
Imple superna grátia,
Quæ tu creásti péctora

Creator-Spirit, all-Divine,
Come, visit every soul of Thine,
And fill with Thy celestial flame
The hearts which Thou Thyself didst
frame.

Qui díceris Paráclitus,
Altíssimi donum Dei,
Fons vivus, ignis, caritas,
Et spiritális únctio.

O gift of God, Thine is the sweet
Consoling Name of Paraclete—
And spring of life and fire and love
And unction flowing from above.

Tu septiformis múnere, / Digitus Patérnæ dexteræ, / Tu rite promíssum Patris, / Sermóne ditans gúttura.	The mystic sevenfold gifts are Thine, / Finger of God's right hand divine; / The Father's promise sent to teach / The tongue a rich and heavenly speech.
Accénde lumen sénsibus, / Infúnde amorem córdibus / Infirma nostri córporis / Virtúte firmans pérpeti.	Kindle with fire brought from above / Each sense, and fill our hearts with love; / And grant our flesh, so weak and frail, / The strength of Thee which cannot fail.
Hostem repéllas lóngius, / Pacémque dones prótinus; / Ductóre sic te prǽvio, / Vitémus omne nóxium.	Drive far away our deadly foe, / And grant us Thy true peace to know; / So we, led by Thy guidance still, / May safely pass through every ill.
Per te sciámus da Patrem, / Noscámus atque Fíllium, / Teque utriúsque Spíritum / Credémus omni témpore.	To us, through Thee, the grace be shown / To know the Father and the Son; / And Spirit of Them both, may we / Forever rest our faith in Thee.
Deo Patri sit glória, / Et Fílio, qui a mórtuis / Surréxit, ac Paráclito, / In sæculórum sǽcula.	To Sire and Son be praises meet, / And to the Holy Paraclete; / And may Christ send us from above / That Holy Spirit's gift of love.

Invicte Martyr, únicum
Patris secútus Fílium,
Victis triúmphas hóstibus,
Victor fruens cœléstibus.

Tui precátus múnere
Nostrum reátum dílue,
Arcens mali contágium,
Vitæ repéllens tædium.

Solúta sunt jam víncula
Tui sacráti córporis:
Nos solve vinclis sæculi,
Dono supérni Núminis.

Deo Patri sit glória,
Ejúsque soli Fílio,
Cum Spíritu Paráclito,
Nunc, et per omne sæculum.

Vexílla Regis Pródeunt:
Fulget Crucis mystérium,
Qua vita mortem pértulit,
Et morte vitam prótulit.

Martyr of God, whose strength
was steeled
To follow close God's only Son,
Well didst thou brave thy battlefield,

And well thy heavenly bliss was won!
Now join thy prayers with ours,
who pray
That God may pardon us and bless;
For prayer keeps evil's plague away,

And draws from life its weariness.
Long, long ago, were loosed the chains
That held thy body once in thrall;
For us how many a bond remains!
O love of God release us all.

All praise to God the Father be,
All praise to Thee, Eternal Son;
All praise, O Holy Ghost, to Thee,
While never-ending ages run.

Abroad the Regal Banners fly,
Now shines the Cross's mystery;
Upon it Life did death endure,
And yet by death did life procure.

Quæ vulneráta lánceæ Mucróne diro, críminum Ut nos laváret sórdibus, Manávit unda, et sánguine.	Who, wounded with a direful spear, Did, purposely to wash us clear From stain of sin, pour out a flood Of precious Water mixed with Blood.
Impláta sunt quæ cóncinit David fidéli cármine, Dicéndo natiónibus: Regnávit a ligno Deus.	That which the Prophet-King of old Hath in mysterious verse foretold, Is now accomplished, whilst we see God ruling natiors from a Tree.
Arbor decóra et fúlgida, Ornáta regis púrpura, Elécta digno stípite Tam sancta membra tángere.	O lovely and refulgent Tree, Adorned with purpled majesty; Culled from a worthy stock, to bear Those Limbs which sanctified were.
Beáta, cujus bráchiis Prétium pepéndit sǽculi, Statéra facta córporis, Tulítque prædam tártari.	Blest Tree, whose happy branches bore The wealth that did the world restore; The beam that did that Body weigh Which raised up hell's expected prey.
O Crux ave spes única, Hoc passiónis témpore Piis adáuge grátiam, Reísque dele crímina.	Hail, Cross, of hopes the most sublime! Now in this mournful Passion time, Improve religious souls in grace, The sins of criminals efface.
Te, fons salútis Trínitas, Colláudet omnis spíritus: Quibus Crucis victóriam Largíris, adde prǽmium.	Blest Trinity, salvation's spring, May every soul Thy praises sing; To those Thou grantest conquest by The holy Cross, rewards apply
Verbum Supérnum Pródiens, Nec Patris linquens déxteram, Ad opus suum éxiens, Venit ad vitæ vésperam.	**The Heavenly Word Proceeding Forth,** Yet leaving not the Father's side, And going to His work on earth Had reached at length life's eventide.
In mortem a discípulo Suis tradéndus ǽmulis, Prius in vitæ férculo Se trádidit discípulis.	By false disciple to be given To foemen for His Blood athirst, Himself, the living Bread from Heaven, He gave to His disciples first.
Quibus sub bina spécie Carnem dedit et sánguinem; Ut dúplicis substántiæ Totum cibáret hóminem.	To them He gave, in two-fold kind, His very Flesh, His very Blood: In love's own fulness thus designed Of the whole man to be the food.
Se nascens dedit sócium, Convéscens in edúlium, Se móriens in prétium, Se regnans dat in prǽmium.	By birth, our fellowman was He; Our meat, while sitting at the board; He died, our ransomer to be; He ever reigns, our great reward.

Hymns

O salutáris hóstia,
Quæ cœli pandis óstium,
Bella premunt hostília;
Da robur, fer auxílium.

Uni trinóque Dómino
Sit sempitérna glória:
Qui vitam sine término
Nobis donet in pátria.

Jesu, Coróna Vírginum,
Quem mater illa cóncipit,
Quæ sola Virgo párturit:
Hæc vota clemens áccipe.

Qui pergis inter lilia,
Septus choréis Vírginum,
Sponsus decórus glória,
Sponsísque reddens prǽmia.

Quocúmque tendis, Vírgines
Sequúntur, atque láudibus
Post te canéntes cúrsitant,
Hymnósque dulces pérsonant

Te deprecámur súpplices;
Nostris ut addas sénsibus,
Nescíre prorsus ómnia
Corruptiónis vúlnera.

Virtus, honor, laus, glória
Deo Patri cum Fílio,
Sancto simul Paráclito,
In sæculórum sǽcula.

Auróra Cælum Púrpurat,
Æther resúltat láudibus,
Mundus triúmphans iúbilat,
Horrens avérnus ínfremit
.
Rex ille dum fortíssimus
De mortis inférno specu
Patrum senátum líberum
Edúcit ad vitæ iubar.

Cuius sepúlcrum plúrimo
Custóde signábat lapis
Victor triúmphat, et suo
Mortem sepúlcro fúnerat.

O saving Victim, opening wide
The gate of heaven to man below:
Our foes press on from every side;
Thine aid supply, Thy strength bestow.

To Thy great Name be endless praise,
Immortal Godhead, One in Three!
O grant us endless length of days
In our true native land, with Thee

Jesu, the Virgin's Crown, do Thou
Accept us as in prayer we bow;
Born of that Virgin, whom alone
The Mother and the Maid we own.

Amongst the lilies Thou dost feed,
By Virgin choirs accompanied—
With glory decked, the spotless brides
Whose bridal gifts Thy love provides.

They, wheresoe'er Thy footsteps bend,
With hymns and praises still attend:
In blessed troops they follow Thee,
With dance, and song, and melody.

We pray Thee therefore to bestow
Upon our senses here below
Thy grace, that so we may endure
From taint of all corruption pure.

All laud to God the Father be,
All praise, Eternal Son, to Thee;
All glory as is ever meet,
To God, the holy Paraclete.

The Morn had Spread Her Crimson Rays,/ when rang the skies with shouts of praise;/ Earth joined the joyful hymn to swell,/ that brought despair to vanquished Hell.

He comes victorious from the grave,/
The Lord omnipotent to save,/
and brings with Him to light of day/
the Saints who long imprisoned lay.

Vain is the cavern's three-fold ward,/
the stone, the seal, the armed guard;/
O death, no more thine arm we fear,/
the Victor's tomb is now thy bier.

Sat fúneri, sat lácrimis,
Sat est datum dolóribus:
Surréxit exstínctor necis,
Clamat corúscans Angelus

Ut sis perénne méntibus
Paschále Jesu gáudium,
A morte díra críminum
Vitæ renátos líbera.

Deo Patri sit glória,
Et Fílio, qui a mórtuis
Surréxit, ac Paráclito,
In sempitérna sǽcula.

Ætérna Christi Múnera,
Apostolórum glóriam,
Palmas et hymnos débitos
Lætis canámus méntibus.

Ecclesiárum Príncipes,
Belli triumpháles duces
Cœléstis aulæ mílites,
Et vera mundi lúmina.

Devóta sanctórum fides,
Invícta spes credéntium,
Perfécta Christi cáritas
Mundi tyránnum contérit.

In his Patérna glória,
In his triúmphat Fílius,
In his volúntas Spíritus,
Cœlum replétur gáudio.

Patri, simúlque Filio,
Tibíque sancta Spíritus,
Sicut fuit, sit júgiter
Sæclum per omne glória.

Ætérna Cœli Glória,

Beáta spes mortálium,
Summi Tonántis Unice,
Castǽque proles Vírginis

Da déxteram surgéntibus,
Exsúrgat et mens sóbria,

Let hymns of joy to grief succeed,/
we know that Christ is risen indeed;/
we hear His white-robed Angel's voice,/
and in our risen Lord rejoice.

With Christ we died, with Christ we rose,/
when at the font His Name we chose;/
Oh, let not sin our robes defile,/
and turn to grief the Paschal smile.

To God the Father let us sing,/ To God
the Son, our risen King,/
and equally let us adore/
The Spirit, God forevermore.

The Eternal Gifts of Christ the King,
The Apostles' glory, let us sing;
And all with hearts of gladness raise
Due hymns of thankful love and praise.

For they the Church's Princes are,
Triumphant leaders in the war,
The heavenly King's own warrior band,
True lights to lighten every land.

Theirs was the steadfast faith of Saints,
The hope that never yields nor faints,
The love of Christ in perfect glow,
That lay the prince of this world low.

In them the Father's glory shone,
In them the Spirit's will was done,
The Son Himself exults in them;
Joy fills the new Jerusalem.

Praise to the Father, with the Son,
And Holy Spirit, Three in One;
As ever was in ages past,
And so shall be while ages last.

O Christ, Whose Glory Fills the Heaven,
Our only hope, in mercy given;
Child of a Virgin meek and pure;
Son of the Highest evermore:

Grant us Thine aid Thy praise to sing,
As opening days new duties bring;

Flagrans et in laudem Dei
Grates repéndat débitas

Ortus refúlget lúcifer,
Præítque solem núntius:
Cadunt tenébræ nóctium:
Lux sancta nos illúminet.

Manénsque nostris sénsibus,
Noctem repéllat sǽculi,
Omníque fine témporis
Púrgata servet péctora.

Quæsita jam prímum fides
In corde radíces agat:
Secúnda spes congáudeat,
Qua major exstat cáritas.

Deo Patri sit glória,
Ejúsque soli Fílio,
Cum Spíritu Paráclito,
Nunc, et per omne sǽculum.

Paschále Mundo Gáudium
Sol núntiat formósior,
Cum luce fulgéntem nova
Jesum vident Apóstoli.

In carne Chrísti vúlnera
Micáre tamquam sídera
Mirántur, et quidquid vident
Testes fidéles prǽdicant.

Rex Christe clementíssime,
Tu corda nostra pósside:
Ut lingua grates débitas
Tuo repéndat nómini.

Ut sis perénne méntibus
Paschále Jesu gáudium,
A morte dira críminum
Vitæ renátos libera.

Deo Patri sit glória,
Et Fílio, qui a mórtuis
Surréxit, ac Paráclito,
In sempitérna sǽcula.

That with the light our life may be
Renewed and sanctified by Thee.

The morning star fades from the sky,
The sun breaks forth; night's shadows fly:
O Thou, true Light, upon us shine:
Our darkness turn to light divine.

Within us grant Thy light to dwell;
And from our souls dark sins expel;
Cleanse Thou our minds from stain of ill,
And with Thy peace our bosoms fill.

To us strong faith forever give,
With joyous hope, in Thee to live;
That life's rough way may ever be
Made strong and pure by charity.

All laud to God the Father be,
All praise, Eternal Son, to Thee:
All glory, as is ever meet,
To God the holy Paraclete.

With the Fair Sun of Easter Morn
The world's excelling joy is born,
When, bright with new and greater grace,
The Apostles see the Savior's face.

They in their Lord's fair flesh descry
The wounds that shine as stars on high,
And, wondering, faithful witness bear,
And all that they have seen declare.

O Christ, most loving King, we pray,
Possess our inmost hearts to-day,
While grateful lips with glad acclaim
Sing fervent praises to Thy Name.

Lord Jesu, that Thou mayest be
Our Easter joy eternally,
Our souls from death of sin set free
That they, new born, may live to Thee.

To God the Father, and the Son,
From death arisen, praise be done:
With God the Holy Ghost on high
Henceforth to all eternity.

Hymns

Tellúris alme Cónditor Mundi solum qui séparans, Pulsis aquæ moléstiis, Terram dedísti immóbilem:	**Earth's mighty Maker, Whose Command;** Raised from the sea the solid land; And drove each billowy heap away, And bade the earth stand firm for aye:
Ut germen aptum próferens, Fulvis decóra flóribus, Fœcúnda fructu sísteret, Pastúmque gratum rédderet.	That so, with flowers of golden hue, The seeds of each it might renew; And fruit-trees bearing fruit might yield, And pleasant pasture of the field:
Mentis perústæ vúlnera Munda viróre grátiæ: Ut facta fletu díluat, Motúsque pravos átterat.	Our spirit's rankling wounds efface With dewy freshness of Thy grace: That grief may cleanse each deed of ill, And o'er each lust may triumph still.
Jussis tuis obtémperet: Nullis malis appróximet: Bonis repléri gáudeat, Et mortís ictum nésciat.	Let every soul Thy law obey, And keep from every evil way; Rejoice each promised good to win, And flee from every mortal sin.
Præsta, Pater piíssime, Patríque compar Unice, Cum Spíritu Paráclito Regnans per omne sǽculum.	Hear Thou our prayer, Almighty King! Hear Thou our praises, while we sing, Adoring with the heavenly host, The Father, Son, and Holy Ghost!

Hymns

Index of Psalms

Psalm	Page Nr.	Psalm	Page Nr.
4	178		
5	12, 71	120	134
28	13, 72	121	135
35	37, 96	122	139
42	20, 78	123	139
46	11	124	140
50	59, 69, 77, 85, 93, 103, 113, 276	125	141
62	2, 63, 276	127	145
63	53, 116	129	146
64	28, 87, 275	130	147
66	21, 79	131	147
84	45, 106	132	153
89	36, 95	133	180
90	179	134	23
91	52, 115	134	81
92	1	135	153, 154
95	19	136	156
96	27	137	157
97	35	138	161, 162
98	43	139	163
99	2	140	164
100	29, 88	141	165
109	123	142	44, 105
110	124	143	169, 170
111	125	144	171, 172
112	126	145	31, 90
113	126	146	39, 99
114	132	147	47, 109
115	133	148	6, 64
116	15, 74	149	51
117	60	150	55, 119

Index of Chapters

Verse	Page Nr.	Verse	Page Nr.
1 Chron 29:10-16	14	Acts 12:1-3	318
1 Cor 11:23-24	252-253	Acts 6:8	193, 194
1 Cor 13:1	202	Acts 9:1-2	294
1 Cor 4:1-2	191	Apoc 1:1-2	339
1 Cor 9:24	201	Apoc 14:1	195
1 John 3:13-14	254	Apoc 7:11-12	7
1 John 5:4	233, 234	Apoc 7:12	65
1 Pet 2:11	238	Apoc 7:2-3	271
1 Pet 2:21-22	236	Apoc 1:1-2	339
1 Pet 4:13	298	Apoc 14:1	195
1 Pet 4:7-8	246	Apoc 7:11-12	7
1 Pet 5:6-7	256, 257	Apoc 7:12	65
1 Pet 5:8-9	177	Apoc 7:2-3	271
1 Sam 2:1-10	89	Apoc 1:1-2	339
1 Thess 4:1	208	Col 1:12-13	270
2 Cor 1:3-4	128, 136, 142, 149, 158, 166	Col 3:14-15	308
2 Cor 10:17-18	282, 283, 291, 295, 343, 349, 356	Dan 3:57	64
2 Cor 11:19-20	201	Dan 3:57-88, 56	3
2 Cor 6:1-2	205	Eph 2:19-20	283
2 Cor 9:6	328	Eph 3:8-9	255, 256
2 Tim 4:7-8	319	Eph 5:1-2	212
Acts 1:1-2	244	Exod 15:1-19	97, 117
Acts 2:1-2	247	Exod 23:20-21	340

Reference	Pages	Reference	Pages
Gal 4:22-24	216	Jas 1:12	280, 281, 333, 349
Hab 3:2-19	107	Jas 1:17	240
Heb 1:1-2	193	Jas 1:22-24	242
Heb 9:11-12	220, 319	Jdt 13:22-23	329
Exod 15:1-19	97, 117	Jdt 16:15-22	30
Exod 23:20-21	340	Jer 14:9	181
Gal 4:22-24	216	Jer 31:10-14	38
Hab 3:2-19	107	Lam 2:13	336
Heb 1:1-2	193	Luke 1:47-55	129, 367
Heb 9:11-12	220, 319	Luke 1:68-79	366
Isa 12:1-6	73	Luke 2:51	198
isa 28:10-20	276	Mal 3:1	295
Isa 38:10-22	80	Phil 2:5-7	224, 308, 335
Isa 45:15-26	46	Phil 2:8-10	197
Isa 49:1	318, 356	Phil 3:20-21	327
Isa 60:1	197	Phil 4:4-5	189
Isa 7:14-15	303	Jer 31:10-14	38
Isa 12:1-6	73	Prov 28:20; 27:18	302
Isa 28:10-20	276	Prov 31:10-11	321, 324
Isa 38:10-22	80	Prov 8:22-24	290
Isa 45:15-26	46	Rom 1:1-3	192
Isa 49:1	318, 356	Rom 11:33	173, 251
Isa 60:1	197	Rom 13:11	186
Isa 7:14-15	303	Rom 13:12-14	15, 24, 32, 40, 48, 74, 83, 91, 100, 110, 119
		Rom 15:4	187

Sir 15:1-2	194		Sir 44:16-17	321, 347
Sir 24:12-13	342		Sir 51:1-3	292, 296
Sir 24:14	56, 285, 320, 334		Song 2:13-14	298
Sir 24:25; 39:17	341, 360		Titus 2:11-12	196
Sir 24:5, 7	313		Tob 12:12	345
Sir 31:8-9	281, 282, 344		Tob 13:1-11	21
Sir 36:1-16	54		Wis 5:1	311

Lauds Antiphons for Marian Feasts

Feast of the Annunciation
March 25

Ant 1. Missus est Gábriel Angelus ad Maríam Vírginem desponsátam Ioseph.	**Ant 1.** The Angel Gabriel was sent to the Virgin Mary, betrothed to Joseph
Ant 2. Ave, María, grátia plena; Dóminus tecum: benedícta tu in muliéribus.	**Ant 2.** Hail, Mary, full of grace, the Lord is with thee; blessed art thou among women.
Ant 3. Ne tímeas, María, invenísti grátiam apud Dóminum: ecce concípies et páries fílium.	**Ant 3.** Do not be afraid, Mary, thou hast found favor with the Lord: behold, thou wilt conceive and bear a son.
Ant 4. Dabit ei Dóminus sedem David, patris eius, et regnábit in ætérnum.	**Ant 4.** The Lord wilt give Him the seat of David, His father and He wilt reign forever.
Ant 5. Ecce ancílla Dómini: fiat mihi secúndum verbum tuum.	**Ant 5.** Behold, the handmaid of the Lord: Let it be done to me according to Thy word.

Feast of the Assumption
August 15

Ant 1. Assúmpta est María in cælum: gaudent Angeli, laudántes benedícunt Dóminum.	**Ant 1.** Mary was taken up into heaven: the angels rejoice, praise the Lord.
Ant 2. María Virgo assúmpta est ad æthéreum thálamum, in quo Rex regum stelláto sedet sólio.	**Ant 2.** The Virgin Mary was taken to the heavenly chamber, where the King of kings sits on a throne surrounded by stars.
Ant 3. In odórem unguentórum tuórum cúrrimus: adolescéntulæ dilexérunt te nimis.	**Ant 3.** We ran to the scent of thy perfumes: the young maidens loved thee greatly.
Ant 4. Benedícta fília tu a Dómino: quia per te fructum vitæ communicávimus.	**Ant 4.** Blessed art thou, daughter of the Lord, because through thee we partake in the fruit of life.
Ant 5. Pulchra es et decóra, fília Ierúsalem, terríbilis ut castrórum ácies ordináta.	**Ant 5.** Thou art beautiful and fair, daughter of Jerusalem, terrible as a fortified camp in battle array.

Feast of the Holy Rosary
October 7

Ant 1. Lætáre, Virgo Mater; surréxit Christus de sepúlcro.	**Ant 1.** Rejoice, Virgin Mother; Christ hath risen from the grave.
Ant 2. Ascéndit Deus in iubilatióne, et Dóminus in voce tubæ.	**Ant 2.** God ascendeth with jubilation, and the Lord with the sound of the trumpet.
Ant 3. Spíritus Dómini replévit orbem terrárum.	**Ant 3.** The Spirit of the Lord filled the earth.
Ant 4. Assúmpta est María in cælum: gaudent Angeli, laudántes benedícunt Dóminum, allelúia.	**Ant 4.** Mary is taken up into heaven: the angels rejoice, praising and blessing the Lord, alleluia.
Ant 5. Exaltáta est Virgo María super choros Angelórum, et in cápite eius coróna stellárum duódecim.	**Ant 5.** The Virgin Mary is exalted above the choir of angels, and on her head is a crown of twelve stars.

Feast of the Immaculate Conception
December 8

Ant 1. Tota pulchra es, María, et mácula originális non est in te.	**Ant 1.** Thou art all beautiful, O Mary, and there is no stain of original sin in thee.
Ant 2. Vestiméntum tuum cándidum quasi nix, et fácies tua sicut sol.	**Ant 2.** Thy raiment is as white as snow, and thy face as the sun.
Ant 3. Tu glória Ierúsalem, tu lætítia Israël, tu honorificéntia pópuli nostri.	**Ant 3.** Thou art the glory of Jerusalem, thou art the joy of Israel, thou art the honor of our people.
Ant 4. Benedícta es tu, Virgo María, a Dómino Deo excélso præ ómnibus muliéribus super terram.	**Ant 4.** Blessed art thou, Virgin Mary, by the Lord God, exalted above all women on earth.
Ant 5. Trahe nos, Virgo immaculáta, post te currémus in odórem unguentórum tuórum.	**Ant 5.** Draw us, Immaculate Virgin, we will run after thee in the scent of your perfumes.

OTHER BOOKS PUBLISHED BY THE AUTHOR

English Psalm Tone Propers
Ordinary Time

English Psalm Tone Propers
Seasons and Feasts

Ténebræ, Service of Shadows
Choir and Congregation Editions

Coal Dust in Our Veins
Life in Colorado Coal Country 1940 – 1970

The Book of Proverbs
Wisdom for Living a Good Life

Restoring Soul with Art
The Spiritual and Art in a Technological World

Simple Morning and Evening
Prayer for Families:
An Introduction to the Liturgy of the Hours

The Curse of Pride
The Blessing of Humility:
100 Days of Scripture for Personal Reflection

All available on Amazon

Printed in Great Britain
by Amazon

150ad994-2fdb-4443-9d8a-83687a34a78eR01